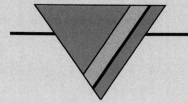

Human Resource
Management

Human Resource Management

Third Edition

Lloyd L. Byars, Ph.D.
Visiting Professor
School of Management
Georgia Institute of Technology

Leslie W. Rue, Ph.D.
Professor
Department of Management
Georgia State University

IRWIN

Homewood, IL 60430
Boston, MA 02116

© RICHARD D. IRWIN, INC., 1984, 1987, and 1991

Sponsoring editor: Craig S. Beytein
Developmental editor: Elizabeth J. Rubenstein
Project editor: Margaret A. Schmidt
Production manager: Carma W. Fazio
Designer: Robyn B. Loughran
Artist: Rolin Graphics, Inc.
Compositor: J.M. Post Graphics, Corp.
Typeface: 10/12 Galliard
Printer: Von Hoffmann Press, Inc.

Library of Congress Cataloging-in-Publication Data

Byars, Lloyd L.
    Human resource management / Lloyd L. Byars, Leslie W. Rue.—3rd ed.
        p.   cm
    ISBN 0-256-08113-1
    1. Personnel management.   I. Rue, Leslie W.   II. Title.
HF5549.B937   1991
658.3—dc20   90–34321
                                                                        CIP

Printed in the United States of America

    2   3   4   5   6   7   8   9   0   VH   7   6   5   4   3   2   1

To Susan, Elizabeth, and Lee Byars
and
Elizabeth, Meggin, and Leslie Rue

▽ *Preface*

Since the publication of the second edition of this text, significant changes have occurred in the human resource management (HRM) field. Changing government and legal requirements, increasing demands for a more skilled and better motivated work force, and intensifying foreign competition are just a few of the factors that have contributed to making HRM more complex and more important to organizations.

This book emphasizes both the theoretical and the practical aspects of HRM. The theoretical material is presented throughout the text and via a new feature—the marginal glossary. To help the student learn the complex HRM terminology, we have created concise definitions of the key terms and placed them in the margins. For lengthier definitions of the same terms, we have retained and expanded our end-of-book glossary.

The practical aspects of HRM are presented in examples and are sprinkled throughout the text of each chapter and the end-of-chapter materials. In addition to review questions, the end-of-chapter materials provide several in-depth discussion questions and two incidents, both of which require that the student apply the concepts presented in the chapter. Also included among the end-of-chapter materials in this edition is an experiential exercise for each chapter. These exercises are designed to illustrate major points made in the chapter and can be done in class. Furthermore, the text portion of each chapter contains several current examples called "HRM in Action," which illustrate how actual organizations have used the concepts presented in the chapter. Additionally, several chapters are followed by a feature called "On the Job," which offers such concrete examples as a resume and a sample job description. All of these features, along with a new, larger trim size, make this the most readable, informative edition to date.

The book's content is arranged in six major sections. Section 1, "Introduction and Equal Employment Opportunity," is designed to provide the student with the foundation necessary to embark on a study of the work of human resource management. This section explores how the legal environment and the implementation of equal employment opportunity influence all areas of human resource management. Section 2, "Staffing the Organization," discusses the topics of job analysis and design, human resource planning, recruitment, and selection. Section 3, "Training and Developing Employees," describes orientation and employee training, management and organizational development, performance appraisal systems, and career planning. Section 4, "Compensating Employees," presents an introductory chapter on organizational reward systems, and chapters on base wage and salary systems, incentive pay systems, and employee benefits. Section 5, "Understanding Unions," explores the development and structure of unions, the collective bargaining process, and discipline and grievance handling. Section 6, "Organizational Maintenance, Communication, and Information Systems," discusses employee safety and health and communication and information systems.

The following individuals provided valuable assistance through their insightful reviews: Peggy Anderson, University of Wisconsin—Whitewater; Mark J. Keppler, California State University—Fresno; Alex Pomnichowski, Ferris State University; Benjamin Wayne Rockmore, Murray State University; Rieann Spence-Gale, Northern Virginia Community College; and Peggy S. Swigart, Western Illinois University.

Finally, we are grateful to Gloria Bivins of Clark Atlanta University and Lucy Hayes of Georgia State University for typing this manuscript.

Lloyd L. Byars
Leslie W. Rue

▽ Contents

▼ **SECTION 1 Introduction and Equal
Employment Opportunity**   **2**

1 Human Resource Management:
Present and Future   4
Human Resource Functions   6
Who Performs the Human Resource Functions   8
    The Human Resource Department   8
The Expanding Role of Human Resource
    Management   10
Human Resource Management Tomorrow   11
Opportunities in Human Resource
    Management   13
    Entering the Field   14
    Advancement Potential   15
    Employment Outlook   15
    Earnings   16
Company Profits and the Human Resource
    Manager   17
Human Resource Management and
    Organizational Performance   17
Summary of Learning Objectives   18
Review Questions   19
Discussion Questions   20
Incident 1–1   20
Incident 1–2   21
Exercise   22
Notes and Additional Readings   22

2 Equal Employment Opportunity:
The Legal Environment   24
Equal Employment Opportunity Laws   26
    Title VII, Civil Rights Act   27
    Age Discrimination in Employment Act   28
    Equal Pay Act   29
    Vocational Rehabilitation Act of 1973,
    as Amended   30
    Vietnam-Era Veterans Readjustment
    Assistance Act   31
    Pregnancy Discrimination Act   31

    Immigration Reform and Control
    Act of 1986   31
Americans with Disabilities Act   32
    Executive Orders 11246, 11375, and 11478   32
    State and Local Government Equal
    Employment Laws   33
Enforcement Agencies   35
    Equal Employment Opportunity
    Commission   35
    Office of Federal Contract Compliance
    Programs   36
Landmark Court Cases   36
    Griggs v. *Duke Power Company*   36
    McDonnell Douglas v. *Green*   37
    Albermarle Paper v. *Moody*   37
    University of California Regents v. *Bakke*   38
    United Steelworkers of America v. *Webster*   39
    Connecticut v. *Teal*   39
    Memphis Firefighters, Local 1784 v. *Stotts*   40
    City of Richmond v. *J. A. Crosan Company*   40
    Wards Cove v. *Atonio*   41
    Martin v. *Wilks*   41
Uniform Guidelines on Employee Selection
    Procedures   42
    Adverse Impact   43
    Where Adverse Impact Exists:
    Basic Options   44
Summary of Learning Objectives   44
Review Questions   46
Discussion Questions   47
Incident 2–1   47
Incident 2–2   48
Exercise   48
Notes and Additional Readings   49

3 Implementing Equal Employment Opportunity   50
EEOC Compliance   52
    Legal Powers of EEOC   52
    EEOC Posting Requirements   52

Records and Reports	54
Compliance Process	57
Preemployment Inquiry Guide	57
Affirmative Action Plans	58
Bona Fide Occupational Qualification (BFOQ)	59
Business Necessity	60
Sexual Harassment	61
Comparable Worth and Equal Pay Issues	61
Other Areas of Employment Discrimination	63
Religion	65
Native Americans (Indians)	66
AIDS	66
Sexual Preference	67
Summary of Learning Objectives	67
Review Questions	68
Discussion Questions	68
Incident 3–1	69
Incident 3–2	69
Exercise 00–0	70
Exercise	70
Notes and Additional Readings	71
On the Job:	
Preemployment Inquiry Guide	72

▼ **SECTION 2 STAFFING THE ORGANIZATION** **78**

4 Job Design and Job Analysis | 80 |
Basic Terminology	83
Job Design	84
Job Content	85
Design Guidelines	87
The Physical Work Environment	87
Sociotechnical Approach to Job Design	89
Job Analysis	89
Uses of Job Analysis	89
Products of Job Analysis	91
Job Analysis Methods	92
Potential Problems with Job Analysis	97
Summary of Learning Objectives	99
Review Questions	100
Discussion Questions	101
Incident 4–1	101
Incident 4–2	102
Exercise	103
Notes and Additional Readings	103
On the Job: Sample Job Description	105
On the Job: Sample Job Analysis	
Questionnaire	107

5 Human Resource Planning | 110 |
How HRP Relates to Organizational Planning	113
Strategy-Linked HRP	113
Steps in the HRP Process	114
Determining Organizational Objectives	115

Determining the Skills and Expertise	
Required (Demand)	117
Determining Additional (Net)	
Human Resource Requirements	119
Developing Action Plans	120
Synthesizing the HRP Process	123
Tools and Techniques of HRP	124
Commitment Manpower Planning	124
Ratio Analysis	124
Time Frame of HRP	126
HRP: An Evolving Process	126
Specific Role of the Human Resource	
Department	127
Common Pitfalls in HRP	128
Summary of Learning Objectives	129
Review Questions	130
Discussion Questions	130
Incident 5–1	130
Incident 5–2	131
Exercise	132
Notes and Additional Readings	132

6 Recruiting Employees | 134 |
Job Analysis, Human Resources Planning, and	
Recruitment	136
Sources of Qualified Personnel	137
Internal Sources	137
External Sources	139
Effectiveness of Recruitment Methods	142
Realistic Job Previews	144
Who Does the Recruiting, and How?	144
Organizational Inducements in Recruitment	145
The Recruitment Interview	146
Equal Employment Opportunity and	
Recruitment	146
Summary of Learning Objectives	147
Review Questions	148
Discussion Questions	148
Incident 6–1	149
Incident 6–2	149
Exercise	150
Notes and Additional Readings	150
On the Job: Writing a Resumé	153

7 Selecting Employees | 166 |
Validation of Selection Procedures	168
Empirical Validity	169
Content and Construct Validity	172
Reliability	172
Guidelines for Validating	
Selection Procedures	173
Selection Process	173
Application Form	174
Preliminary Interview	176
Applicant Testing	176

Diagnostic Interview	179
Reference Checking	182
Physical Examination	182
Making the Final Selection Decision	183
Summary of Learning Objectives	183
Review Questions	184
Discussion Questions	185
Incident 7–1	185
Incident 7–2	187
Exercise	188
Notes and Additional Readings	188
On the Job: Sample Application for Employment and Applicant Flow Record	190

▼ **SECTION 3 TRAINING AND DEVELOPING EMPLOYEES** — **196**

8 Orientation and Employee Training	198
Orientation	200
Shared Responsibility	201
Company Orientation	201
Departmental and Job Orientation	202
Orientation Kit	203
Orientation Length and Timing	205
Follow-Up and Evaluation	205
Training Employees	206
Needs Assessment	206
Establishing Training Objectives	208
Methods of Training	208
On-the-Job Training and Job Rotation	208
Apprenticeship Training	210
Classroom Training	210
Principles of Learning	212
Motivation to Achieve Personal Goals	212
Knowledge of Results	212
Reinforcement	212
Flow of the Training Program	213
Practice and Repetition	213
Spacing of Sessions	213
Whole or Part Training	214
Evaluating Training	214
Reaction	215
Learning	215
Behavior	216
Results	216
Summary of Learning Objectives	216
Review Questions	217
Discussion Questions	217
Incident 8–1	218
Incident 8–2	219
Exercise	219
Notes and Additional Readings	220
9 Management and Organizational Development	222

Management Development Process	224
Determining the Net Management Requirements	224
Organizational Objectives	224
Management Inventory and Succession Plan	225
Changes in the Management Team	226
Needs Assessment	228
Organizational Needs	228
Needs of Individual Managers	228
Establishing Management Development Objectives	228
Methods Used in Management Development	229
Understudy Assignments	230
Coaching	230
Experience	231
Job Rotation	231
Special Projects and Committee Assignments	231
Classroom Testing	232
University and Professional Association Seminars	234
Evaluation of Management Development Activities	234
Assessment Centers	235
Organizational Development	235
Approaches to Management and Organizational Development	236
Summary of Learning Objectives	237
Review Questions	238
Discussion Questions	238
Incident 9–1	239
Incident 9–2	240
Exercise	241
Notes and Additional Readings	241
On the Job: Comparison of Training Methods	240

10 Performance Appraisal Systems	246
Performance Appraisal: Definition and Uses	248
Understanding Performance	250
Determinants of Performance	250
Environmental Factors as Performance Obstacles	250
Selection of a Performance Appraisal Method	251
Performance Appraisal Methods	251
Goal Setting, or Management by Objectives (MBO)	252
Work Standards	253
Essay Appraisal	253
Critical-Incident Appraisal	254
Graphic Rating Scale	254
Checklist	255
Behaviorally Anchored Rating Scales (BARS)	256

Forced-Choice Rating   258
Ranking Methods   258
Potential Errors in Performance Appraisals   260
Overcoming Errors in Performance Appraisals   260
Providing Feedback through the Appraisal
  Interview   261
Performance Appraisal and the Law   261
Summary of Learning Objectives   263
Review Questions   264
Discussion Questions   265
Incident 10–1   265
Incident 10–2   266
Exercise   267
Notes and Additional Readings   268

11 Career Planning   270
Why Is Career Planning Necessary   272
Who Is Responsible for Career Planning   273
Employee's Responsibilities   273
Manager's Responsibilities   274
Organization's Responsibilities   276
Developing a Career Plan   276
Individual Assessment   277
Assessment by the Organization   277
Career Pathing   280
Reviewing Career Progress   280
Career-Related Myths   282
Myths Held by Managers   284
Dealing with Career Plateaus   284
Rehabilitating Ineffective Plateauees   285
Outplacement   286
Summary of Learning Objectives   287
Review Questions   288
Discussion Questions   289
Incident 11–1   289
Incident 11–2   290
Exercise   291
Notes and Additional Readings   291

▼ **SECTION 4 COMPENSATING EMPLOYEES   294**

12 The Organizational Reward System   296
Defining the System   298
Selection Rewards   298
Rating Rewards to Performance   299
Job Satisfaction and Rewards   301
The Satisfaction-Performance Controversy   302
Other Factors in Job Satisfaction   303
Employee Compensation   304
Compensation Policies   304
Pay Secrecy   305
Government and Union Influence   305
The Importance of Fair Pay   307
Pay Equity   308
Pay Satisfaction Model   309

The Role of the Human Resource Manager
  in the Reward System   310
Summary of Learning Objectives   311
Review Questions   312
Discussion Questions   312
Incident 12–1   313
Incident 12–2   313
Exercise   315
Notes and Additional Readings   315

13 Base Wage and Salary Systems   318
Objective of the Base Wage and
  Salary System   320
Job Evaluation   321
Point Method   322
Selection of Key Jobs   323
Selecting Compensable Factors   323
Assigning Weight to Factors   324
Assigning Points to Specific Jobs   326
Factor Comparison Method   326
Job Classification Method   328
Job Ranking Method   329
Comparison of Job Evaluation Methods   330
Pricing the Job   330
Wage and Salary Surveys   330
Wage and Salary Curces   333
Base Wage/Salary Structure   335
Summary of Learning Objectives   336
Review Questions   337
Discussion Questions   337
Incident 13–1   337
Incident 13–2   338
Exercise   339
Notes and Additional Readings   341

14 Incentive Pay Systems   342
Requirements of Incentive Plans   344
Individual Incentives   345
Piece Rate Plans   345
Plans Based on Time Saved   346
Plans Based on Commissions   346
Individual Bonuses   347
Suggestion Systems   347
Bonuses for Managerial Personnel   348
Stock Options for Managerial Personnel   350
Group Incentives   353
Organizationwide Incentives   354
Gain-Sharing or Profit-Sharing Plans   354
Scanlon-Type Plans   354
Employee Stock Ownership Plans (ESOPs)   355
Making Incentive Plans Work   358
Summary of Learning Objectives   358
Review Questions   359
Discussion Questions   360
Incident 14–1   360

Incident 14–2   361
Exercise   362
Notes and Additional Readings   363

15 Employee Benefits   364
What Are Employee Benefits?   366
Growth in Employee Benefits   368
Communicating the Benefit Package   368
Employee Preference among Benefits   371
   Flexible Benefit Plans   372
   Legally Required Benefits   375
Social Security   375
Unemployment Compensation   377
Workers' Compensation   378
   Retirement-Related Benefits   379
Pension Plans   379
Employees Not Covered by Pension Plans   383
Preretirement Planning   383
   Insurance-Related Benefits   383
Health Insurance   384
Health Maintenance Organization (HMOs)   384
Dental Insurance   385
ife Insurance   385
Accident and Disability Insurance   385
   Payment for Time Not Worked   386
Paid Holidays   386
Paid Vacations   386
   Other Benefits   388
   The Benefit Package   388
   Summary of Learning Objectives   388
   Review Questions   390
   Discussion Questions   390
   Incident 15–1   390
   Incident 15–2   391
   Exercise   392
   Notes and Additional Readings   393

▼ **SECTION 5**   **394**

16 Legal Environment and Structure of
Labor Unions   396
Legal Environment of Labor-Management
   Relations   398
   Sherman Anti-Trust Act (1890)   401
   Clayton Act (1914)   401
   Railway Labor Act (1926)   402
   Norris–La Guardia Act (1932)   402
   National Labor Relations
     (Wagner) Act (1935)   402
   Labor-Management Relations
     (Taft-Hartley) Act (1947)   403
   Labor-Management Reporting and
     Disclosure (Landrum-Griffin) Act (1959)   405
   Civil Service Reform Act (1978)   406
Union Structures   407

AFL–CIO   408
   National and International Unions   410
   City and State Federations   410
   Local Unions   410
Current and Future Developments in
   the Labor Movement   411
Summary of Learning Objectives   412
Review Questions   413
Discussion Questions   414
Incident 16–1   414
Incident 16–2   415
Exercise   415
Notes and Additional Readings   416

17 Union Organizing Campaigns and
Collective Bargaining   418
Union Membership Decision   420
   Reasons for Joining   420
   The Opposition View   421
Union Organizing Campaign   421
   Determining the Bargaining Unit   422
   Election Campaigns   423
   Election, Certification, and Decertification   424
Good-Faith Bargaining   426
Participants in Negotiations   427
   Employer's Role   427
   Union's Role   427
   Role of Third Parties   428
Collective Bargaining Agreements   429
Specific Issues in Collective Bargaining
   Agreements   431
   Management Rights   431
   Union Security   432
   Wages and Employee Benefits   432
   Individual Security (Seniority) Rights   433
   Dispute Resolution   434
Impasses in Collective Bargaining   434
Trends in Collective Bargaining   435
Summary of Learning Objectives   435
Review Questions   436
Discussion Questions   437
Incident 17–1   438
Incident 17–2   438
Exercise   438
Notes and Additional Readings   439

18 Discipline and Grievance Handling   440
Discipline Defined   444
Causes of Disciplinary Actions   444
The Discipline Process   445
   Prediscipline Recommendations   446
   Administering Discipline   447
   Legal Restrictions   450
Discipline and Unions   450
Discipline in Nonunionized Organizations   451

The Grievance Procedure 452
    Just Cause 452
    Due Process 455
    Duty of Fair Representation 455
    Time Delays 457
Grievance Arbitration 457
Summary of Learning Objectives 459
Review Questions 460
Discussion Questions 460
Incident 18–1 460
Incident 18–2 461
Exercise 462
Notes and Additional Readings 464

▼ **SECTION 6 ORGANIZATIONAL MAINTENANCE, COMMUNICATION, AND INFORMATION SYSTEMS 466**

19 Employee Safety and Health 468
Occupational Safety and Health Act of 1970
    (OSHA) 470
    OSHA Standards 471
    Penalties 473
    Record-Keeping/Reporting Requirements 473
    Reactions to OSHA 474
The Causes of Accidents 475
    Personal Acts 475
    Physical Environment 475
    Accident Proneness 476
How to Measure Safety 476
Organizational Safety Programs 476
    Promoting Safety 477

Employee Health 478
    Occupational Health Hazards 478
    Stress in the Workplace 479
    Alcoholism and Drug Abuse 482
    AIDS 485
Summary of Learning Objectives 498
Review Questions 490
Discussion Questions 491
Incident 19–1 491
Incident 19–2 492
Exercise 493
Notes and Additional Readings 493

20 Communication and Information Systems 496
Human Resource Communication Systems 498
    Basics of Communication 499
    Pitfalls of Communicating Human
       Resource Programs 501
Human Resource Information Systems (HRIS) 502
    Uses of an HRIS 503
    Necessary Capabilities of an HRIS 505
    Steps in Implementing an HRIS 508
Summary of Learning Objectives 511
Review Questions 512
Discussion Questions 512
Incident 20–1 513
Incident 20–2 513
Exercise 514
Notes and Additional Readings 515

Name Index 537

Subject Index 540

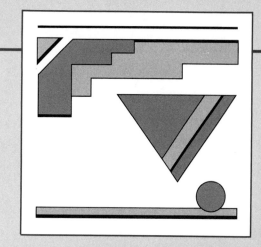

Section 1

Introduction and Equal Employment Opportunity

Chapter 1
Human Resource Management
Present and Future

 Chapter 2
Equal Employment Opportunity .
The Legal Environment

 Chapter 3
**Implementing Equal Employment
Opportunity**

Chapter 1

Human Resource Management

Present and Future

Chapter Outline

Human Resource Functions
Who Performs the Human
 Resource Functions?
 The Human Resource Department
The Expanding Role of Human
 Resource Management
Human Resource Management
 Tomorrow
Opportunities in Human Resource
 Management
 Entering the Field
 Advancement Potential
 Employment Outlook
 Earnings

Company Profits and the Human
 Resource Manager
Human Resource Management and
 Organizational Performance
Summary of Learning Objectives
Review Questions
Discussion Questions
Incident 1–1 Human Resource
 Management and Professionals
Incident 1–2 Choosing a Profession
Exercise: Justifying the Human
 Resources Department
Notes and Additional Readings

● *Learning Objectives*

After studying this chapter, you should be able to:

1. Define human resource management.
2. Describe the functions of human resource management.
3. Summarize the types of assistance provided by the human resource department.
4. Identify several environmental factors that are currently influencing the field of human resource management.
5. Discuss the role of human resource managers in the future.
6. Describe the employment outlook for human resource managers.
7. Explain, in general terms, how human resource managers can affect organizational performance.

"*W*here yesterday's 'personnel administrators' used to be mainly for keeping employees and managers from each others' throats, today's 'human resource managers' bring together employees and employers as a partnership in profitable operation and global competitiveness."

*Martha I. Finney**

Human resource management
Activities designed to provide for and coordinate the human resources of an organization.

Human resource management (HRM) encompasses those activities designed to provide for and coordinate the human resources of an organization. The human resources (HR) of an organization represent one of its largest investments. In fact, government reports show that approximately 73 percent of national income is used to compensate employees.[1] The value of an organization's human resources frequently becomes evident when the organization is sold. Often, the purchase price is greater than the total value of the physical and financial assets. This difference, sometimes called goodwill, partially reflects the value of an organization's human resources. In addition to wages and salaries, organizations often make other sizable investments in their human resources. Recruiting, hiring, and training represent some of the more obvious examples.

Human resource management is a modern term for what has traditionally been referred to as personnel administration or personnel management. However, as the introductory quote indicates, some authors view human resource management as being somewhat different from traditional personnel management. They see personnel management as much narrower and more clerically oriented than human resource management. For the purposes of this book, we will use only the term *human resource management*.

Human Resource Functions

Human resource functions
Tasks and duties that human resource managers perform (e.g., determining the organization's human resource needs; recruiting, selecting, developing, counseling, and rewarding employees; acting as liaison with unions and government organizations; and handling other matters of employee well-being).

Human resource functions refer to those tasks and duties performed in both large and small organizations to provide for and coordinate human resources. Human resource functions are concerned with a variety of activities that significantly influence all areas of an organization and include the following:

1. Ensuring that the organization fulfills all of its equal employment opportunity and other government obligations.
2. Conducting job analyses to establish the specific requirements of individual jobs within an organization.
3. Forecasting the personnel requirements necessary for the organization to achieve its objectives.
4. Developing and implementing a plan to meet these requirements.
5. Recruiting the personnel required by the organization to achieve its objectives.

*Source: Martha I. Finney, "Leading the Way to HR's New Age," *Personnel Administrator*, June 1988, pp. 43–44.

▼ **Figure 1–1   Human resource wheel**

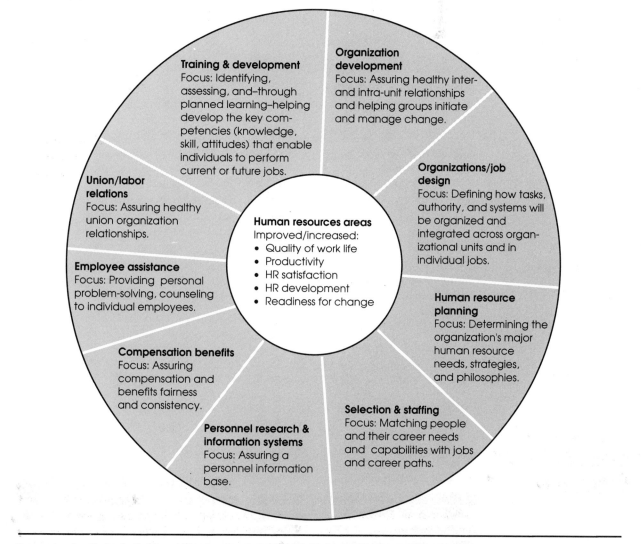

6. Selecting and hiring personnel to fill specific jobs within an organization.
7. Orienting and training employees.
8. Designing and implementing management and organizational development programs.
9. Designing systems for appraising the performance of individual employees.
10. Assisting employees in developing career plans.
11. Designing and implementing compensation systems for all employees.
12. Serving as an intermediary between an organization and its union(s).
13. Designing discipline and grievance handling systems.

14. Designing and implementing programs to ensure employee health and safety and providing assistance to employees with personal problems that influence their work performance.

15. Designing and implementing employee communication systems.

Figure 1–1 presents the Human Resource Wheel developed by the American Society for Training and Development as part of an effort to define the field of human resource management.

In an attempt to cover each of the major areas of human resource management, this book has been organized into six major sections. Section 1 contains one introductory chapter and two chapters on equal employment opportunity. Section 2 explores those human resource functions specifically concerned with staffing the organization: job analysis and design, human resource planning, recruiting, and selecting. Section 3 concentrates on those functions related to training and developing employees. Orientation and employee training, management and organization development, performance appraisal, and career planning are covered here. Section 4 is concerned with all aspects of employee compensation. Motivation theory, base wage and salary systems, incentive pay systems, and employee benefits are discussed. Section 5 deals with unions, the collective bargaining process, and discipline and grievance handling. Section 6 focuses on organizational maintenance and information systems. Employee safety and health and information systems are discussed.

Who Performs the Human Resource Functions?

Operating manager
Person who manages people directly involved with the production of an organization's products or services (e.g., a production manager in a manufacturing plant or a loan manager in a bank).

All managers are periodically involved in some human resource functions. For example, almost all managers, at one time or another, are involved in training, developing, and evaluating their employees. In small organizations, most personnel functions are performed by the owner or **operating managers**. Large organizations usually have a human resource or personnel department responsible for directing the human resource functions. Such a department is normally staffed by one or more **human resource specialists**. These specialists are trained in one or more areas of human resource management.

Human resource specialist
Person specially trained in one or more areas of human resource management (e.g., labor relations specialist, wage and salary specialist).

The Human Resource Department

The primary function of the human resource department is to provide support to operating managers on all human resource matters. Thus, most human resource departments fulfill a traditional staff role and act primarily in an advisory capacity. In addition to advising operating managers, a human resource department customarily organizes and coordinates hiring and training, maintains personnel records, acts as a liaison between management, labor, and government, and coordinates safety programs.

▼ Figure 1–2 Three types of assistance provided by a human resource department

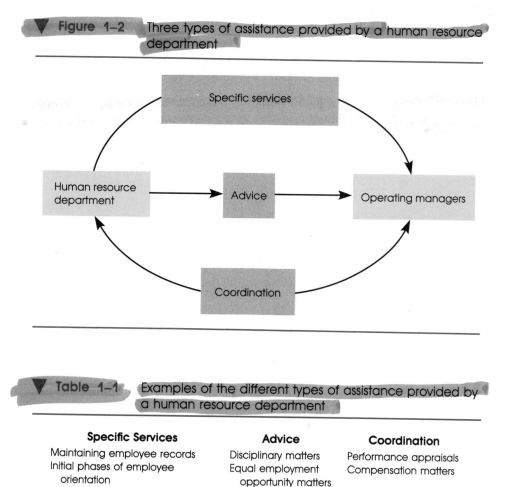

▼ Table 1–1 Examples of the different types of assistance provided by a human resource department

Specific Services	Advice	Coordination
Maintaining employee records	Disciplinary matters	Performance appraisals
Initial phases of employee orientation	Equal employment opportunity matters	Compensation matters

Precisely how all of the functions related to human resources are split between operating managers and the human resource department varies from organization to organization. For example, the human resource department in one company may do all of the hiring below a certain level. In another company, all the hiring decisions may be made by operating managers, with the human resource department acting only in an advisory capacity.

It is helpful to look upon the human resource department as providing three types of assistance: (1) specific services, (2) advice, and (3) coordination. Thus, the human resource department might do the actual hiring in one company; but in another, it might only advise operating managers with regard to hiring matters. Figure 1–2 illustrates the different roles that a human resource department might fill. Table 1–1 presents some typical examples of each of these types of assistance.

As stated earlier, a human resource department normally acts in an advisory capacity and does not have authority over operating managers. As a result, conflict can occur when operating managers appear to ignore the suggestions and recommendations of the human resource department. If the department is to be effective, it must continually cultivate good relations with operating managers.

The Expanding Role of Human Resource Management

Human resource management has expanded and moved beyond mere administration of the traditional activities of employment, labor relations, compensation, and benefits.[2] Today, HRM is much more integrated into both the management and the strategic planning process of the organization.[3]

One reason for this expanded role is that the organizational environment has become much more complex. The deluge of government regulations and laws has placed a tremendous burden on human resource managers. New regulations are regularly issued in the areas of safety and health, equal employment opportunity, pension reform, environment, and quality of work life. For example, at the end of the 1970s, the United States had 100,980 federal government regulators—appointed, not elected. In 1979, these appointees added 7,496 regulations to those that already filled 60,000 pages. Most of these new regulations were aimed at business, with many of them involving jail sentences for noncompliance.[4] There is no reason to believe that this trend has changed in the last decade.

Along with the responsibility for interpreting and implementing the constantly changing government regulations, human resource departments also must deal with a work force that is becoming more demanding with regard to job satisfaction and the quality of work life.[5] In addition, important changes have occurred and are still occurring in the composition of the work force. For example, the percentage of white-collar jobs and the percentage of females in the work force have both increased significantly over the past several decades.

The increasing role of women in the work force has had an impact on human resource managers in numerous ways. For example, child care, spouse relocation assistance programs, and pregnancy leave programs have resulted from this trend.

The aging of the work force is another factor that is having a significant impact on human resource management.[6] Human resource managers are having to come up with ways of better utilizing older employees. Some of the possibilities include job sharing, part-time work, the use of retirees in community relations, and in-house training. HRM in Action 1–1 presents some facts relating to changes in the composition of the work force.

Computerization has also affected the human resources field. In addition to their uses in performing the traditional functions of accounting and payroll calculations, computers are now being used to maintain easily accessible employee data that is valuable in job placement and labor utilization. Computers are also being used in tracking and reporting affirmative action activity, in employee training, in succession planning, and in compensation management. This has naturally increased the responsibilities of the human resource department. A recent survey conducted by *Personnel Journal* found that 63 percent of their respondents characterized their human resource information systems as primarily computerized. Of those respondents still using primarily manual systems, 77 percent planned to convert to computerized systems.[7] The use of computers in human resource management is discussed further in Chapter 20.

▼. HRM in Action 1–1

The Changing Workplace

In recent years, the workplace has changed, and it is expected to change even more in the future. Consider these facts:

- In 1970, 47 percent of the labor force was employed in white-collar jobs, while 53 percent of the labor force was employed in blue-collar jobs. As of 1980, white-collar jobs had increased to 51 percent while blue-collar jobs fell to 49 percent of the total. In June 1989, white-collar jobs had increased to over 55 percent of total jobs.

- In 1972, there were 33.5 million working women. In 1987, there were over 50 million women in the work force. Between 1970 and 1979, the number of female managers and administrators increased over 100 percent. As of 1987, women held over 44 percent of all managerial and professional jobs.

- In 1982, the median age in the United States was 31 years, 20 percent of the population was 55 or older, and 11 percent of the population was 65 or older. By the year 2010, 25 percent of the population will be 55 or older, 12.5 percent will be 65 or older, and the median age will be 37.

Sources: Patricia A. Mathews, "The Changing Work Force: Dual-Career Couples and Relocation," *Personnel Administrator*, April 1984, p. 55; Malcolm H. Morrison, "Retirement and Human Resource Planning for the Aging Work Force," *Personnel Administrator*, June 1984, pp. 151–159; U.S. Department of Commerce, Bureau of the Census, *Statistical Abstract of the United States, 1985* (Washington, D.C.: U.S. Government Printing Office, 1984), p. 400; U.S. Department of Commerce, Bureau of the Census, *Statistical Abstract of the United States, 1989* (Washington, D.C.: U.S. Government Printing Office, 1989), p. 388; and U.S. Department of Labor, *Employment and Earnings* (Washington, D.C.: U.S. Government Printing Office, 1989), p. 30.

Human Resource Management Tomorrow

If the challenges of the future are to be met, tomorrow's human resource departments must be much more sophisticated than their predecessors. With the expanding role that human resource departments must fill, it is essential that human resource managers be integrally involved in an organization's strategic and policymaking activities. Fortunately, there are signs that this is happening in many organizations. For example, in almost every one of the Fortune 500 companies, the head of the human resource department is an officer (usually a vice president) answering to the chief executive officer. In a significant number of companies, the head of the human resource department sits on either the board of directors or the planning committee, or both. A recent survey cosponsored by the American Productivity Center asked 71 corporate CEOs to rank corporate staff functions in order of importance. Human resources came in second only to finance.[8] HRM in Action 1–2 presents several quotes from top-level human resource managers relating to the expanding role of human resource managers.

If tomorrow's human resource managers are to earn the respect of their colleagues and of top management, they must work to overcome certain negative impressions and biases sometimes associated with human resource management. This can be accomplished in several ways. First, human resource managers should become well-rounded businesspeople. One of the requirements of this is to be thoroughly familiar with the business itself. Walter Trosin, Corporate Human Resource Vice President for Merck and Company has offered the following sug-

▽. **HRM in Action 1–2**

The New Human Resource Manager

"Personnel has gone from being an administrative function entirely concerned with hiring and firing to a function very much a part of senior management. The nature of work has changed. We no longer use people for their physical horsepower, we need them for their intellectual horsepower. This has dictated an entirely different approach to management. It has become a strategic function—a management function."

> Walter R. Trosin
> Vice President, Human Resources
> Merck and Co.

"If you compared 1968 with 1988, you would see quite a drastic change. I think the function (human resource management) is playing a much more vital role than ever."

> H. Gordon Smyth
> Senior Vice President, Employee Relations
> E.I. DuPont de Nemours, Inc.

"Human resource management has changed from being administrative to one that is far more strategic and central to the direction of the business."

> Hal Burlingarie
> Senior Vice President, Human Resources
> AT&T

"I can say unquantitatively that HR managers are more professional today than they were even five years ago."

> Ed Schwesinger
> Partner, Coopers & Lybrand Actuarial,
> Benefits and Compensation Group

Sources: Martha I. Finney, "Leading the Way to HR's New Age," *Personnel Administrator,* June 1988, pp. 45–46; and Kirkland Ropp, "HR Management: For All It's Worth," *Personnel Administrator,* September 1987, pp. 36–37.

gestions to help human resource managers become more familiar with their businesses:

- Know the company strategy and business plan
- Know the industry
- Support business needs
- Spend more time with the line people
- Keep your hand on the pulse of the organization[9]

Thoroughly understanding the business will help overcome the common feeling that human resource people do not understand the real problems and issues facing the organization. Second, human resource managers should become fully knowledgeable about present and future trends and issues. This will help them guard against becoming enamored with passing fads or ineffective techniques. Third, human resource managers should promote effective human resource utilization within the organization. Rather than take a moralistic approach when dealing with operating managers, human resource managers should stress the importance of increasing profits through effectively using the organization's human resources. In this light human resource managers should learn to be proactive and seize opportunities to demonstrate how they can positively affect the bottom line.[10]

In addition to performing the traditional human resource functions, human resource managers need to look for fresh and effective approaches to improving organizational performance. For example, it has been suggested that human resource managers should develop or refine their expertise in the following areas: attitude surveys and other upward communication problems, issues related to

▼ Table 1–2   Typical human resource jobs in large organizations

Position	Duties
Employee benefits supervisor	Coordinates and administers benefit programs relating to vacations, insurance, pensions, and other benefit plans.
Employee counselor	Assists employees in understanding and overcoming social and emotional problems; also helps employees appraise their interests, aptitudes, and abilities.
EEO representative	Investigates and resolves equal employment opportunity (EEO) complaints, examines corporate practices for EEO violations, and compiles and submits EEO statistical reports.
Employment interviewer	Interviews job applicants and records and evaluates such information as job experience, education, and training; skills, knowledge, and abilities; physical and personal qualifications; and other pertinent data for classification, selection, and referral.
Job analyst	Collects, analyzes, and develops occupational data concerning jobs, job qualifications, and worker characteristics required to perform jobs.
Labor relations director	Organizes, directs, and coordinates industrial relations functions; these activities include dealing with human resource problems relating to absenteeism, turnover, grievances, strikes, and demands made by labor.
Personnel recruiter	Travels to areas geographically distant from the organization's operations and interviews job applicants.
Test administrator	Administers tests and interprets the results; rates applicants and makes employment recommendations based on the test results.
Training director	Organizes, administers, and conducts training and educational programs for purposes of employee development and improvement of employee performance.
Training representative	Evaluates training needs to develop educational materials for improving employee performance; prepares and conducts training for organization personnel.
Compensation administrator	Establishes and administers the wage and salary system in the organization to ensure that the pay system is equitable and that it conforms to government regulations, organization policy, and agreements with labor unions.

changing working conditions, job humanization, career planning and development, pay and benefits, supplemental uses of the workplace, and flexible work schedules. While this list certainly is not exhaustive, it does point out some possibilities.

Opportunities in Human Resource Management

What are the specific job opportunities in human resource management? In general, the size of the organization determines the number and types of human resource jobs available. Naturally, larger organizations offer more opportunity for specialization. Table 1–2 lists some typical human resource jobs in large organizations.

▼ **Figure 1–3**   Possible advancement paths in the human resource field

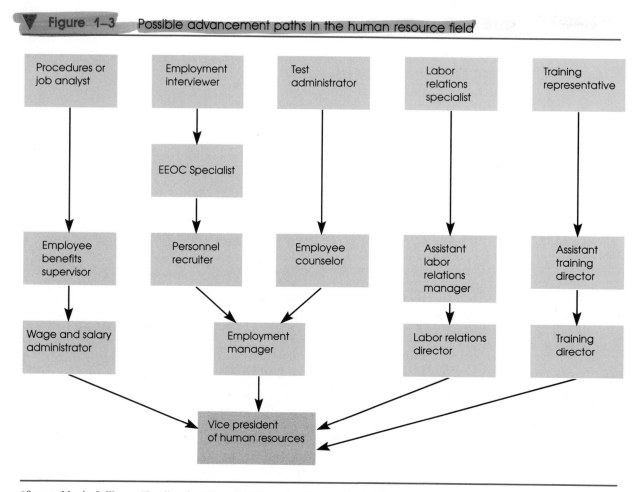

*Source: Martha I. Finney, "Leading the Way to HR's New Age," *Personnel Administrator,* June 1988, pp. 43–44.

Entering the Field

Probably the most desirable path to human resource work is through operating management. By first obtaining experience in an operating capacity, an individual moving into a human resource job can better understand the problems facing operating managers. A human resource manager who does not have this type of experience might be provided with at least occasional operating experience within the organization. This could be done through work on a project, certain committee assignments, or a temporary assignment in another department.

Up until the mid-1970s, many people entered human resource management via promotion from a secretarial or clerical position within the human resource department.[11] However, the expanding role of the human resource department now requires that new entrants have significantly more educational and business experience. Today, for example, firms generally seek college graduates even when filling entry level jobs.[12] The increased professionalization of the field now requires that new entrants carefully plan their career development activities if they want to advance. Unlike those in the past, today's human resource professional is not likely to be someone who could not handle operating management responsibilities, or

▼● HRM in Action 1–3

VP for Individuality

One of the more unusual titles for a human resources manager is that of McDonald's Jim Kuhn, who is VP for Individuality. Jim says that major parts of his job are to maintain the growth of individuals and to keep everyone aware that the success of the company comes from thousands of effective small units all over the world. To support this philosophy, McDonald's goes to great lengths to support individual growth and recognition.

Crew meetings, rap sessions, and a national advisory board made up of people from all levels of the system are used to encourage individuals to express their ideas. Founders Day is a special occasion on which corporate offices are closed and corporate people work in the outlets, side by side with the regular crews.

Source: Phil Farish, "VP for Individuality," *Personnel Administrator,* March 1988, p. 26.

someone who has a liberal arts degree and "likes working with people." A recent college graduate directly entering the human resource area without full-time experience usually will start as a job analyst, employment interviewer, test administrator, or training representative.

Advancement Potential

From an entry position, a person in human resource management has several possible advancement paths. As previously mentioned, more opportunities exist in larger organizations. Figure 1–3 charts some paths that an individual might follow, depending on interests and expertise. The paths shown are by no means the only possibilities, but merely some of the more logical ones that an individual might follow. For example, an employment interviewer might switch paths and become a wage and salary administrator.

The top job in human resource management is given many different titles. Some of these include vice president of human resources, vice president of personnel, personnel manager, or human resources director. HRM in Action 1–3 describes an innovative human resource title used by McDonald's Corporation. Currently, some organizations have people with human resource backgrounds serving as president or chief operating officer of the company. With the expanding role of human resource management, a greater opportunity now exists for human resource employees to advance to these positions.

Employment Outlook

Human resource managers held about 151,000 jobs in the United States as of 1986.[13] Over 85 percent of salaried jobs were in private industry, and the remainder were in federal, state, and local governments. The number of jobs in human resource work has been projected by the U.S. Department of Labor to grow at a pace equal to the average for all occupations through the year 2000 (see Table 1–3). Most of the growth is projected to occur in the private sector, as employers try to provide effective human resource programs for an expanding and aging work force. Furthermore, human resource management has been projected as being one of the hottest careers of the 1990s by several popular magazines.[14]

▼ Table 1–3   Forecasted human resource jobs through 2000*

	1986	2000
Human resource managers	151,000	194,000
Percent change		28.3

*Note: Employment change: average. Annual separation rate: 9.5 percent.
Source: Adapted from U.S. Department of Labor, *Occupational Projections and Training Data,* Bulletin No. 2301, 1988 ed. (Washington, D.C.: U.S. Government Printing Office, 1988), pp. 8, 21.

▼ Table 1–4   Average income by title

	Average Salary
Top human resource management executive	$86,800
Top corporate personnel executive	68,900
Human resource manager	43,000
Labor industrial relations executive	73,100
Division or regional human resource executive	59,800
Top corporate security manager	47,600
Top employee relations executive	54,100
Equal employment opportunity manager	45,700
Employment and recruiting manager	40,900
Recruiter	24,900
Employee training manager	40,200
Management development manager	45,900
Top compensation & benefits executive	59,100
Branch personnel manager	38,900
Personnel assistant	18,900

Source: ASPA/Hansen, 1987 Human Resource Management Compensation Survey, February 1987. Salaries listed are averages only and do not include all available data for these and other job titles. Salaries may vary dependent on individual responsibilities. Reprinted in Kirkland Ropp, "HR Management: For All It's Worth," *Personnel Administrator,* September 1987, p. 36. Reprinted with the permission from the *Personnel Administrator* published by the Society for Human Resource Management, Alexandria, Virginia.

Earnings

Salary is one of great interest to people when selecting a career. Both starting pay and long-term salary potential are important considerations. A 1987 nationwide survey cosponsored by the American Society of Personnel Administrators (ASPA) reported the median incomes for human resource jobs, as shown in Table 1–4. The figures are based on averages and vary with certain demographics such as geographic area, type of employer, size of the organization, educational level, and amount of experience. Specifically, human resource professionals were found to be best compensated in major metropolitan areas. Overall, manufacturing firms provide higher pay than nonmanufacturing companies. A strong positive correlation was found between pay and size of the organization.

These data indicate that the pay in human resource work is competitive. The same survey reported in Table 1–4 found that in 1987, the compensation for top human resource managers increased faster than the average rate of increase in pay for all executives.[15] Thus, if the human resource role continues to expand as forecasted, there is every reason to believe that this expansion will be accompanied by commensurate salary increases.

Company Profits and the Human Resource Manager

There is no doubt that human resource managers spend considerable time working on problems and concerns related to the "human side" of the organization. Because of this, many people perceive human resource managers as being concerned *only* with matters that relate directly to the human side of the organization. Contrary to this view, human resource managers can have a direct impact on company profits.[16] There are a number of specific ways:[17]

1. Reduce unnecessary overtime expenses by increasing productivity during a normal workday.
2. Stay on top of absenteeism and institute programs designed to reduce money spent for time not worked.
3. Eliminate wasted time by employees through sound job design.
4. Minimize employee turnover and unemployment benefit costs by practicing sound human relations and creating a work atmosphere that promotes job satisfaction.
5. Install and monitor effective safety and health programs to reduce lost-time accidents and to keep medical and worker's compensation costs low.
6. Properly train and develop all employees so they can improve their value to the company and do a better job of producing and selling high-quality products and services at the lowest possible cost.
7. Decrease costly material waste by eliminating bad work habits and attitudes and poor working conditions that lead to carelessness and mistakes.
8. Hire the best people available at every level to get more out of them and avoid overstaffing.
9. Maintain competitive pay practices and benefit programs that are important factors in fostering a motivational climate for employees.
10. Encourage employees, who probably know more about the nuts and bolts of their jobs than anyone else, to submit ideas on increasing productivity and reducing costs.

HRM in Action 1–4 illustrates how progressive human resource policies and practices can positively affect profits.

Human Resource Management and Organizational Performance

The primary goal of human resource management in any organization is to facilitate organizational performance. One of the most effective ways of enhancing organizational performance is by increasing productivity. The American Productivity Center defines productivity as the efficiency with which an organization uses its labor, capital, material, and energy resources to produce its output. Human

▽. HRM in Action 1–4

Progressive Human Resource Policies

According to a survey of large companies conducted by consultant Dennis Kravetz, progressive human resource policies pay off. "Progressive" as interpreted by Kravetz refers to policies that encourage open communication, adequate training, employee involvement, and career development. The survey data came from 200 large companies and involved questionnaires, interviews, and focus groups. Those companies that reported higher scores on progressive HR policies also reported significantly higher scores on several measures of profit, including annual profit growth and equity growth.

Source: Phil Farish, "HR Value," *Personnel Administrator*, April 1989, p. 23.

resource managers are somewhat limited as to the impact they can have on the capital, materials, and energy aspects of productivity. However, they can have a great deal of impact on the labor component. Specifically, they can affect the commitment of employees and the management philosophy of the individual managers. Because of this, human resource managers have a unique opportunity to improve productivity.[18]

● *Summary of Learning Objectives*

1. Define human resource management.

    Human resource management encompasses those activities designed to provide for and coordinate the human resources of an organization. Human resource management is also a modern term for what has traditionally been referred to as personnel administration or personnel management.

2. Describe the functions of human resource management.

    Human resource functions refer to those tasks and duties performed in large and small organizations to provide for and coordinate human resources. Human resource functions include the following:

    a. Ensuring that the organization fulfills all of its equal employment opportunity and other government obligations.

    b. Conducting job analyses to establish the specific requirements of individual jobs within an organization.

    c. Forecasting the personnel requirements necessary for the organization to achieve its objectives.

    d. Developing and implementing a plan to meet these requirements.

    e. Recruiting the personnel required by the organization to achieve its objectives.

    f. Selecting and hiring personnel to fill specific jobs within an organization.

    g. Orienting and training employees.

    h. Designing and implementing management and organizational development programs.

    i. Designing systems for appraising the performance of individual employees.

j. Assisting employees in developing career plans.

k. Designing and implementing compensation systems for all employees.

l. Serving as an intermediary between an organization and its union(s).

m. Designing discipline and grievance handling systems.

n. Designing and implementing programs to ensure employee health and safety and providing assistance to employees with personal problems that influence their work performance.

o. Designing and implementing employee communication systems.

3. Summarize the types of assistance provided by the human resource department.

The primary function of the human resource department is to provide support to operating managers on all human resource matters. In general terms the human resource department provides three types of assistance: (1) specific services, (2) advice, and (3) coordination.

4. Identify several environmental factors that are currently influencing the field of human resource management.

Several environmental factors are currently having an effect on the field of human resource management. Some of the more significant include a tremendous increase in government regulations and laws, a changing and more demanding work force, and increasing computerization.

5. Discuss the role of human resource managers in the future.

Human resource managers are predicted to play an increasingly important role in the management of organizations in the future. In fulfilling this role, human resource managers should become thoroughly familiar with the business, be knowledgeable about present and future trends, and learn to emphasize the impact that human resources can have on profit.

6. Describe the employment outlook for human resource managers.

The number of jobs in human resource work has been projected by the U.S. Department of Labor to grow at a pace equal to the average for all occupations through the year 2000. Most of the growth is projected to occur in the private sector.

7. Explain, in general terms, how human resource managers can affect organizational performance.

One of the most effective ways of enhancing organizational performance is by positively influencing the labor component of productivity. Human resource managers can have a significant impact on the commitment of employees and the management philosophy of individual managers.

Review Questions

1. What is human resource management?

2. What functions does a human resource or personnel department normally perform? Why are these functions important in today's organizations?

3. Describe some of the problems characteristic of human resource departments in the past.

4. What are some potential human resource jobs that might be found in a typical large organization?
5. How does the future look for a career in human resource management?
6. Name several specific ways that human resource managers can positively affect an organization's profits.

Discussion Questions

1. Some people believe that human resource management is an area reserved for those "who can't do anything else." Why do you think this belief has emerged, and is there any factual basis for it?
2. Describe some current trends that you feel will have an impact on human resource management in the next 10 years.
3. Many human resource managers claim to love their work because they like to work with people. Do you think that "liking people" is the most important ingredient in becoming a successful human resource manager?
4. As a human resource manager, how might you go about convincing top management that you should be heavily involved in the company's strategic planning process?

▼ INCIDENT 1–1

Human Resource Management and Professionals

You are a senior member of a national law firm in New York City. The managing partner of the firm has asked you to head up the southern branch in Birmingham, Alabama. This branch is one of 10 under the main office. On the whole, the firm has been successful since its establishment in the mid-1920s, but in the last five years, many of the younger staff have elected to leave the organization. The managing partner is convinced that the problem is not salary, because a recent survey indicated that the firm's salary structure is competitive with that of other major firms. However, he requests that you study this matter firsthand in your new assignment.

After getting settled in Birmingham, one of your first projects is to meet with the four senior managers to determine why the branch has had such a high attrition rate among the younger staff. Harding Smith, who is about 45, states that the younger staff lacks dedication and that they fail to appreciate the career opportunities provided by the firm. William Thompson, about 50, says that the younger staff members are always complaining about the lack of meaningful feedback on their performance and that many have mentioned that they would like to have a sponsor in the organization to assist with their development. Thompson further explains that the firm does provide performance ratings to staff and that the previous manager had always maintained an open-door policy. Brian Scott, about 40, says he has received complaints that training is not relevant and is generally dull. He explains that various persons in the firm who worked with training from time to time acted mainly on guidance from New York. Dennis Rutherford, about 38, says he believes the root of the problem is the lack of a human resource department. However, he says that when the idea was mentioned to the managing partner in New York, he rejected it totally.

Questions

1. What do you think about the idea of a human resource department in a professional office?
2. How would you sell the idea of a human resource department to the managing partner?
3. What type of organizational structure would you propose?

▼ INCIDENT 1–2

Choosing a Profession

Tom Russell is a junior majoring in business administration at a large midwestern university. Tom, who is an honor student, hasn't fully decided what his major should be. He has considered majoring in management but just can't get excited about the field. It seems to him that is is too general.

Tom's first course in management did appeal to him; however, this was largely because of the professor. Tom decided to talk to this professor about his dilemma. The following conversation occurred:

Tom: Professor, I would like your advice on selecting a major field of study. Right now I just don't know what to do.

Professor: Tom, just let me say that you are making an important decision and are justified in your concern. How many courses have you taken in the School of Business Administration?

Tom: Only your introductory course in management, a basic course in marketing, and a statistics course. I do know that I don't want to major in statistics!

Professor: How about majoring in human resource management?

Tom: I don't think so. That is basically a staff job that can't really lead anywhere.

Professor: Hold on, Tom, I think I had better tell you a little more about human resource management.

Questions

1. If you were the professor, what would you tell Tom?
2. Describe some jobs in the human resource field that Tom would be qualified for right out of college.

Exercise

Justifying the Human Resources Department

Assume you work in the human resources department for a medium-sized manufacturing company (annual sales of $50 million). The company has been unionized for many years but has never had a strike. The president of the company has just requested that all departments develop a budget for the coming fiscal year and be prepared to justify their budget requests. As part of this justification, your boss, the director of human resources, has just asked you to prepare a list of at least 10 reasons why the human resources department and its performance are important to the success of the entire company. Be prepared to present your list to the class.

Notes and Additional Readings

1. U.S. Department of Commerce, *Statistical Abstract of the United States,* 109th ed. (Washington, D.C.: U.S. Government Printing Office, 1989), p. 425.

2. See Kirkland Ropp, "HR Management: For All It's Worth," *Personnel Administrator,* September 1987, pp. 34–40 and 120–121; and Martha I. Finney, "Leading the Way to HR's New Age," *Personnel Administrator,* June 1988, pp. 42–49.

3. Ibid.

4. F.R. Edney, "The Greening of the Profession," *Personnel Administrator,* July 1980, pp. 27–30.

5. See James Frazer, "Changing Times, Changing Values," *Personnel Administrator,* March 1988, pp. 66–69; Eric G. Flamholz, Yvonne Randle, and Sonja Sackmann, "Personnel Management: The Terror of Today," *Personnel Journal,* June 1987, pp. 68–69; and Jeff Hallett, "New Patterns in Working," *Personnel Administrator,* December 1988, pp. 32–37.

6. Ibid, p. 62.

7. Morton E. Grossman, "The Growing Dependence on HRIS," *Personnel Journal,* September 1988, pp. 53–59.

8. Phil Farish, "CEO's Rank HR High," *Personnel Administrator,* March 1987, p. 21.

9. Phil Farish, "Broader View Needed," *Personnel Administrator,* February 1987, p. 27.

10. William G. Layton and Eric J. Johnson, "Break the Mold: Strategies for Productivity," *Personnel Journal,* May 1987, pp. 74–78.

11. W. E. Hophe (ed), *The Encyclopedia of Careers and Vocational Guidance,* 3rd ed. (Chicago: J. G. Ferguson, 1975), p. 211.

12. U.S. Department of Labor, *Occupation Outlook Handbook,* 1988–89 ed. (Washington, D.C.: U.S. Government Printing Office), 1988, p. 39.

13. Ibid.

14. For example see "25 Hottest Careers," *Working Woman,* July 1989, p. 68.

15. Ropp, "HR Management: For All It's Worth," pp. 37–38.

16. Jack F. Gow, "Human Resources Managers Must Remember the Bottom Line," *Personnel Journal,* April 1985, pp. 30–32.

17. The following list of 10 ways that human resource managers can impact profits are summarized from Gow, "Human Resources Managers," p. 32.

18. E. K. Burton, "Productivity: A Plan for Personnel," *Personnel Administrator,* September 1981, p. 85; and Layton and Johnson, "Break the Mold."

Chapter 2

Equal Employment Opportunity

The Legal Environment

Chapter Outline

Equal Employment Opportunity Laws
Title VII, Civil Rights Act
Age Discrimination in Employment Act
Equal Pay Act
Vocational Rehabilitation Act of 1973, as Amended
Vietnam-Era Veterans Readjustment Assistance Act
Pregnancy Discrimination Act
Immigration Reform and Control Act of 1986
Executive Orders 11246, 11375, and 11478
State and Local Government Equal Employment Laws

Enforcement Agencies
Equal Employment Opportunity Commission
Office of Federal Contract Compliance Programs

Landmark Court Cases
Griggs v. *Duke Power Company*
McDonnell Douglas v. *Green*
Albemarle Paper v. *Moody*

University of California Regents v. *Bakke*
United Steelworkers of America v. *Weber*
Connecticut v. *Teal*
Memphis Firefighters, Local 1784 v. *Stotts*
City of Richmond v. *J. A. Crosan Company*
Wards Cove v. *Atonio*
Martin v. *Wilks*

Uniform Guidelines on Employee Selection Procedures
Adverse Impact
Where Adverse Impact Exists: the Basic Options

Summary of Learning Objectives
Review Questions
Discussion Questions
Incident 2–1 Accept Things as They Are
Incident 2–2 TWA and "Willful" Age Discrimination
Exercise: Legal Issues in Equal Employment Opportunity
Notes and Additional References

● *Learning Objectives*

After studying this chapter, you should be able to:

1. Define equal employment opportunity.
2. Describe the intent of Title VII of the Civil Rights Act of 1964.
3. Define disparate treatment and disparate impact.
4. Discuss the purpose of the Age Discrimination in Employment Act.
5. Describe the intent of the Equal Pay Act.
6. Discuss the purpose of the Vocational Rehabilitation Act.
7. Describe the intent of the Vietnam-Era Veterans Readjustment Assistance Act.
8. Discuss the purpose of the Pregnancy Discrimination Act.
9. Describe the intent of the Immigration Reform and Control Act.
10. Describe the Americans with Disabilities Act.
11. Discuss the purpose of Executive Orders 11246, 11375, and 11478.
12. Describe the significance of the following Supreme Court decisions: *Griggs* v. *Duke Power, McDonnell Douglas* v. *Green, Albemarle Paper* v. *Moody, University of California Regents* v. *Bakke, United Steelworkers of America* v. *Weber, Connecticut* v. *Teal, Memphis Firefighters, Local 1784* v. *Stotts, City of Richmond* v. *J. A. Crosan Company, Wards Cove* v. *Atonio,* and *Martin* v. *Wilks.*
13. Discuss adverse impact.
14. Describe the 4/5ths rule.
15. Discuss the bottom-line concept.

*"F*our score and seven years ago our fathers brought forth on this continent, a new nation, conceived in Liberty, and dedicated to the proposition that all men are created equal."

Abraham Lincoln*

Two of the most important external influences on human resource management are government legislation and regulations and court interpretations of the legislation and regulations. Numerous laws influence recruitment and selection of personnel, compensation, working conditions and hours, discharges, and labor relations. Thus, throughout this text, government legislation and court interpretations of the legislation are described as they relate to the specific area of human resource management being discussed.

However, because equal employment opportunity is so important and covers so many areas of human resource management, two separate chapters are devoted to the topic. The purpose of this chapter is to describe the legal framework of equal employment opportunity. Chapter 3 will describe specific organizational requirements for implementing equal employment opportunity.

Equal Employment Opportunity Laws

Slavery was abolished by the Thirteenth Amendment to the U.S. Constitution in 1865. In addition, Congress passed the Civil Rights Act of 1866, the Fourteenth Amendment to the U.S. Constitution in 1868, and the Civil Rights Act of 1871, and yet Americans continued to live and work in a dual society—one black and one white. Businesses often refused to hire black workers or placed them in low-paying and low-skilled jobs.

Discrimination against women was based on the view that men should work to support their families and women should care for their families at home. Furthermore, it was a rather commonly held belief that women were not equipped to do certain jobs.

Discrimination in society and in the workplace gave impetus to the civil rights movement which, in turn, pressured the U.S. Congress to pass laws designed to eliminate discrimination. As a result, numerous laws have been passed to ensure equal employment opportunity. Unfortunately, a common misconception is that equal employment opportunity means that an employer must give preference to women and minorities in the workplace. However, **equal employment opportunity** refers to the right of all people to work and to advance on the basis of merit, ability and potential.

As is true with most laws, however, ambiguities in the language of the laws leave much room for interpretation by the federal agencies that enforce them. Furthermore, court decisions regarding the laws often raise additional questions

Equal employment opportunity
Refers to the right of all persons to work and to advance on the basis of merit, ability, and potential.

*Source: Opening sentence of Abraham Lincoln's Gettysburg Address.

of interpretation. For these reasons and others, equal employment opportunity is one of the most challenging and complex aspects of human resource management. Nevertheless, a good beginning point for understanding equal employment opportunity is to know the basic legislation covering the area.

Title VII, Civil Rights Act

Title VII of the Civil Rights Act of 1964 is the keystone federal legislation in equal employment opportunity. Several important provisions of Section 703 of the act state:

Sec. 703.
(a) It shall be an unlawful employment practice for an employer—

   (1) to fail or refuse to hire or to discharge any individual, or otherwise to discriminate against any individual with respect to his compensation, terms, conditions, or privileges of employment, because of such individual's race, color, religion, sex, or national origin; or

   (2) to limit, segregate, or classify his employees or applicants for employment in any way which would deprive or tend to deprive any individual, of employment opportunities or otherwise adversely affect his status as an employee, because of such individual's race, color, religion, sex, or national origin.

(b) It shall be an unlawful employment practice for an employment agency to fail or refuse to refer for employment, or otherwise to discriminate against, any individual because of his race, color, religion, sex, or national origin, or to classify or refer for employment any individual on the basis of his race, color, religion, sex or national origin.

(c) It shall be an unlawful employment practice for a labor organization—

   (1) to exclude or to expel from its membership, or otherwise to discriminate against, any individual because of his race, color, religion, sex, or national origin;

   (2) to limit, segregate, or classify its membership or applicants for membership or to classify or fail or refuse to refer for employment any individual, in any way which would deprive or tend to deprive any individual of employment opportunities, or would limit such employment opportunities or otherwise adversely affect his status as an employee or as an applicant for employment, because of such individual's race, color, religion, sex, or national origin; or

   (3) to cause or attempt to cause an employer to discriminate against an individual in violation of this section.

(d) It shall be an unlawful employment practice for any employer, labor organization, or joint labor-management committee controlling apprenticeship or other training or retraining, including on-the-job training programs to discriminate against any individual because of his race, color, religion, sex, or national origin in admission to, or employment in, any program established to provide apprenticeship or other training.

Two basic areas of discrimination are covered under Section 703: disparate treatment and disparate impact. *Disparate treatment* (Section 703(a)1) refers to intentional discrimination and involves treating one class of employees differently from other employees. *Disparate impact* (Section 703(a)2) refers to unintentional discrimination and involves employment practices that appear to be neutral but adversely affect a protected class of people.

Title VII, the name most frequently used to describe the Civil Rights Act, was amended by the Equal Employment Opportunity Act of 1972. Organizations that are presently covered by the provisions of Title VII include the following:

- All private employers of 15 or more people who are employed 20 or more weeks per year
- All public and private educational institutions
- State and local governments
- Public and private employment agencies
- Labor unions that maintain and operate a hiring hall or hiring office or have 15 or more members
- Joint labor-management committees for apprenticeships and training

Title VII also created the Equal Employment Opportunity Commission (EEOC) to administer the act and to prohibit covered organizations from engaging in any unlawful employment practice. The composition and powers of the EEOC are described later in this chapter. HRM in Action 2–1 illustrates a recent settlement made by General Motors concerning a charge of racial discrimination. A new civil rights act is being considered by Congress for passage in 1990.

Age Discrimination in Employment Act

Age Discrimination in Employment Act (ADEA)
Prohibits discrimination against employees over 40 years of age by all companies employing 20 or more people in the private sector.

The **Age Discrimination in Employment Act (ADEA),** passed in 1967, prohibits discrimination in employment against individuals who are at least 40 years of age but less than 70 (i.e., 40 through 69). An amendment to the ADEA that took effect on January 1, 1987, eliminates mandatory retirement at age 70 for employees of companies with 20 or more employees. The prohibited employment practices of ADEA include failure to hire, discharge, denial of employment, and discrimination with respect to terms or conditions of employment because of an individual's age within the protected age group. Organizations covered by the ADEA include:

- Private employers of 20 or more employees for each working day in each of 20 or more calendar weeks in the current or preceding calendar year
- Labor organizations[1]
- Employment agencies
- State and local governments
- Federal government agencies, with certain differences—for example, federal employees cannot be forced to retire at any age

One exception specified in the law is concerned with employees in bona fide executive or high policymaking positions. The act permits mandatory retirement at age 65 for high-level executives whose pensions exceed $44,000 a year.

Section 4f of the ADEA sets forth several conditions under which the act does not apply. The act does not apply where age is a bona fide occupational qualification, reasonably necessary to the normal operation of the particular business. For example, pilots and copilots face mandatory retirement at age 60. In addition, a bus company's refusal to consider applications of individuals between the ages of 40

▼. HRM in Action 2–1

General Motors Settles Racial Discrimination Suit

On February 1, 1989, General Motors settled a class action suit alleging discrimination against salaried black employees. As part of the agreement, GM agreed to set up an unusual computer model to monitor future human resource practices. The system will compare the career advancements of blacks against whites, but will adjust the evaluation for a variety of factors, such as educational background, job experience, and the type of work performed.

The computer model will generate an anticipated percentage of promotions for black employees, taking into account six major factors that determine the qualifications of those covered: length of time spent at the company, time spent on the current job, years of education, degrees obtained, area of study, and when the degrees were obtained.

In addition, GM agreed to pay about $13 million to 3,800 past and present employees for back pay and pay adjustments.

Source: Adopted from Jacob M. Schlesinger, "GM Settles Class Lawsuit Accusing It of Racial Bias," *The Wall Street Journal*, February 1, 1989, p. B1.

and 65 for initial employment as intercity bus drivers was ruled legal.[2] Furthermore, it is not illegal for an employer to discipline or discharge an individual within the protected age group for good cause, such as unsatisfactory job performance. The Supreme Court has also ruled that involuntary retirement prior to age 65 is permissible if the employer has a bona fide retirement plan and if the plan was in existence prior to the passage of the ADEA.[3]

Originally, the secretary of labor was responsible for enforcing the ADEA. However, on July 1, 1979, the EEOC assumed that responsibility. HRM in Action 2–2 presents the results of an age discrimination lawsuit against Hilton Hotels.

Equal Pay Act

The Equal Pay Act of 1963 prohibits sex-based discrimination in rates of pay paid to men and women working on the same or similar jobs. Specifically, the act states:

> No employer having employees subject to [the minimum wage provisions of the Fair Labor Standards Act] shall discriminate, within any establishment . . . , between employees on the basis of sex by paying wages to employees in such establishment at a rate less than the rate at which he pays wages to employees of the opposite sex in such establishment for equal work on jobs the performance of which requires equal skill, effort, and responsibility, and which are performed under similar working conditions.

The act permits differences in wages if the payment is based on seniority, merit, quantity and quality of production, or a differential due to any factor other than sex. The act also prohibits an employer from attaining compliance with the act by reducing the wage rate of any employee.

The Equal Pay Act is actually part of the minimum wage section of the Fair Labor Standards Act (FLSA), described in more detail in Chapter 12. Thus, coverage of the Equal Pay Act is coextensive (covers the same groups) with the coverage of the minimum wage provisions of the FLSA. Generally, employers covered by the act are engaged in commerce or in the production of goods for commerce and

▼. HRM in Action 2–2

Hilton's Hotel-Casino and Age Discrimination

In March 1989, a federal grand jury awarded 36 former casino dealers $38.8 million in a wrongful-termination suit against Hilton Hotels.

The jury found Hilton's Las Vegas Hotel-Casino guilty of age discrimination, breach of contract, bad faith, and inflicting severe emotional distress on the employees. The employees were fired in 1983 following a marked drop in the win level of the casino's blackjack pot, and after Hilton made other attempts to remedy this drop. Hilton stated that the win levels returned to normal after the terminations, but never charged any of the employees with wrongdoing.

Source: Adopted from Pauline Yoshihasho, "Casino Case Jury Awards Judgement of $38.8 Million," *The Wall Street Journal*, March 10, 1989, p. B-6.

have two or more employees. Labor organizations are also covered. Responsibility for enforcing the Equal Pay Act was originally assigned to the secretary of labor but was transferred to the EEOC on July 1, 1979.

Vocational Rehabilitation Act of 1973, as Amended

The Vocational Rehabilitation Act of 1973, as amended, contains the following general provisions:

- Prohibits discrimination against handicapped individuals by employers with federal contracts and subcontracts in excess of $2,500.
- Requires written affirmative action plans from employers of 50 or more employees and federal contracts of $50,000 or more.
- Prohibits discrimination against the handicapped by federal agencies.
- Requires affirmative action by federal agencies to provide employment opportunities for the handicapped.
- Requires federal buildings to be accessible to the handicapped.
- Prohibits discrimination against the handicapped by recipients of federal financial assistance.

Handicapped
Person who has a physical or mental impairment that substantially limits one or more of such person's major life activities, has a record of such impairment, or is regarded as having such an impairment.

Section 7(7)(B) of the Vocational Rehabilitation Act defines a **handicapped** individual as:

any person who:

(i) has a physical or mental impairment which substantially limits one or more of such person's major life activities,

(ii) has a record of such an impairment, or

(iii) is regarded as having such an impairment . . . Such term does not include any individual who is an alcoholic or drug abuser whose current use of alcohol or drugs prevents such individual from performing the duties of the job in question or whose employment, by reason of such current alcohol or drug abuse, would constitute a direct threat to property or the safety of others.

The primary responsibility for enforcing this act lies with the Office of Federal Contract Compliance Programs (OFCCP) of the Department of Labor. OFCCP will be described in more depth later in this chapter.

Vietnam-Era Veterans Readjustment Assistance Act

The Vietnam-Era Veterans Readjustment Assistance Act of 1974 requires that federal government contractors and subcontractors with federal government contracts of $10,000 or more not discriminate in hiring and promoting Vietnam and disabled veterans. Furthermore, employers with 50 or more employees and contracts that exceed $50,000 are required to have written affirmative action programs (AAP) with regard to the people protected by this act. The protected class consists of disabled veterans with a 30 percent or more disability rating or veterans discharged or released for a service-connected disability and veterans on active duty for any part of the time period between August 5, 1964, and May 7, 1975. Covered contractors and subcontractors are also required to list job openings with the state employment service. The act is enforced by the OFCCP.

Pregnancy Discrimination Act

The Supreme Court, in its decision in *General Electric Co.* v. *Gilbert,*[4] made a decision that had a significant impact on the passage of the Pregnancy Discrimination Act. In this case, General Electric provided nonoccupational sickness and accident benefits to all employees under its Weekly Sickness and Accident Insurance Plan in an amount equal to 60 percent of an employee's normal straight-time weekly earnings. Several female employees at GE's Salem, Virginia, plant who were pregnant presented a claim for disability benefits under the plan to cover the period they were absent from work as a result of their pregnancies. These claims were denied by the company on the ground that the plan did not provide disability-benefit payments for such absences. The employees filed suit alleging a violation of Title VII, which prohibits sex discrimination. The Supreme Court ruled that the exclusion of pregnancy-related disabilities from the plan did not constitute sex discrimination.

As a result of this decision, in an effort to protect the rights of pregnant workers, in 1978 Congress passed the Pregnancy Discrimination Act (PDA) as an amendment to the Civil Rights Act. The PDA is formally referenced as Section 701(K) of Title VII and states:

> Women affected by pregnancy, childbirth, or related medical conditions shall be treated the same for all employment-related purposes, including receipt of benefits under fringe benefit programs, as other persons not so affected but similar in their ability or inability to work.

Under the PDA, employers must treat pregnancy just like any other medical condition with regard to fringe benefits and leave policies. The EEOC, responsible for administering the act, has taken the view that an employer may not deny its unmarried employees pregnancy benefits and that if pregnancy benefits are given to female employees, they must also be extended to the spouses of male employees.

Immigration Reform and Control Act of 1986

Recent years have seen an increasing influx of illegal aliens into the United States. These people are often unskilled, and many do not speak English. Unfortunately, their status often leads to abuses in their employment. Thus, the Immigration

Reform and Control Act was passed in 1986 making it illegal for a person or other entity to hire, recruit, or refer for employment in the United States a person knowing that he or she is an unauthorized alien. In order to meet the requirements of the law a company must attest under penalty of perjury that it has verified that the individual is not an unauthorized alien by one of the following:

1. Examining the individual's U.S. passport; certificate of U.S. citizenship; certificate of naturalization; unexpired foreign passport, if the passport has an appropriate, unexpired endorsement of the Attorney General authorizing the individual's employment in the U.S.; or resident alien card.
2. Receiving verification from documents demonstrating employment authorization (social security card, birth certificate, or other documentation that the Attorney General deems acceptable as proof).
3. Receiving documentation establishing identification (e.g., state driver's license with a photograph or other documentation that the Attorney General deems acceptable as proof).

Americans with Disabilities Act

In May 1990 Congress approved the Americans with Disabilities Act (ADA) which gives the disabled sharply increased access to services and jobs. Under this law employers may not:

- Discriminate against persons qualified for a job, in hiring and firing;
- Inquire whether an applicant has a disability, but may ask about ability to perform a job;
- Limit advancement opportunity;
- Use tests or job requirements that tend to screen out the disabled;
- Participate in contractural arrangements that discriminate against the disabled.

Employers must also provide reasonable accommodations to the disabled such as making existing facilities accessible, providing special equipment and training, arranging part-time or modified work schedules, and providing readers for the blind. Employers do not have to provide accommodations that impose an undue hardship on business operations. The bill is designed ultimately to cover all employers with 15 or more employees.

Executive Orders 11246, 11375, and 11478

Executive orders

Orders issued by the president of the United States for managing and operating federal government agencies.

Executive orders are issued by the President of the United States to give direction to governmental agencies. Executive Order 11246, issued in 1965, requires every nonexempt federal contractor and subcontractor not to discriminate against employees and applicants because of race, sex, color, religion, or national origin. The primary exemption from the order is for contracts and subcontracts that do not exceed $10,000. The OFCCP within the Department of Labor is responsible for administering this executive order. The equal opportunity clause specified by Executive Order 11246 requires the contractor or subcontractor to agree to:

1. Comply with the provisions of the executive order.
2. Comply with those rules, regulations, and orders of the secretary of labor that are issued under the order.
3. Permit access to its books and records for purposes of investigation by the secretary of labor.
4. Include the equal employment clause in every subcontract or purchase order so that such provisions will be binding on each subcontractor or vendor.
5. In the event of noncompliance with the executive order, the contract may be canceled, terminated, or suspended.
6. After a hearing on the noncompliance, the contractor may be declared ineligible for future government contracts.

Executive Order 11246 also requires employers with 50 or more employees and contracts and subcontracts that exceed $50,000 to have a written affirmative action program (AAP). The AAP must include an identification and analysis of minority employment problem areas within the employer's work force, and where there are deficiencies, goals and timetables are to be established for the prompt achievement of equal employment opportunity. Part of the AAP is called the **utilization evaluation**, which contains analyses of minority group representation in all job categories; present and past hiring practices; and upgrading, promotions, and transfers. AAP will be described in more detail in Chapter 3.

Utilization evaluation
That part of the affirmative action plan that analyzes minority group representation in all job categories; past and present hiring practices; and upgrades, promotions, and transfers.

Executive Order 11246 also gave the U.S. Office of Personnel Management (OPM) authority to issue regulations dealing with discrimination within federal agencies. In 1966, the OPM (then called the Civil Service Commission) issued regulations that required agencies to correct discriminatory practices and to develop affirmative action programs.

In 1967, Executive Order 11375 amended Executive Order 11246 and prohibited sex-based wage discrimination for government contractors. Finally, Executive Order 11478, which in part superseded Executive Order 11246, was issued in 1969 along with revised regulations by the OPM. The new regulations merely modified a number of the procedures under the previous orders and regulations.

State and Local Government Equal Employment Laws

Many state and local governments have passed equal employment opportunity laws. For example, almost all states have some form of protection against employment discrimination on the basis of handicap. However, at this point it is important to note the Supremacy Clause of the U.S. Constitution,[5] which states:

> The laws of the United States dealing with matters within its jurisdiction are supreme and the judges in every state shall be bound thereby, anything in the Constitution or Laws of any State to the contrary notwithstanding.

As a result of this clause, as would be expected, many state and local laws became invalid after the passage of the Civil Rights Act and other equal employment legislation. For example, the California Supreme Court invalidated a state statute prohibiting females from tending bar.

No federal laws prohibit states from passing laws prohibiting discrimination

▼ **Table 2–1**   Summary of equal opportunity laws and executive orders

Laws	Year	Purpose or Intent	Coverage
Title VII, Civil Rights Act (as amended in 1972)	1964	Prohibits discrimination based on race, sex, color, religion, or national origin.	Private employers with 15 or more employees for 20 or more weeks per year, educational institutions, state and local governments, employment agencies, labor unions, and joint labor-management committees.
Age Discrimination in Employment Act (ADEA)	1967	Prohibits discrimination against individuals who are at least 40 years of age but less than 70. An amendment eliminated mandatory retirement at age 70 for employees at companies with 20 or more employees.	Private employers with 20 or more employees for 20 or more weeks per year, labor organizations, employment agencies, state and local governments, and federal agencies with some exceptions.
Equal Pay Act	1963	Prohibits sex-based discrimination in rates of pay for men and women working in the same or similar jobs.	Private employers engaged in commerce or in the production of goods for commerce and with two or more employees; labor organizations.
Rehabilitation Act, as amended	1973	Prohibits discrimination against the handicapped and requires affirmative action to provide employment opportunity for the handicapped.	Federal contractors and subcontractors with contracts in excess of $2,500, organizations receiving federal financial assistance, and federal agencies.
Vietnam-Era Veterans Readjustment Assistance Act	1974	Prohibits discrimination in hiring disabled veterans with 30 percent or more disability rating, veterans discharged or released for a service-connected disability, and veterans on active duty between August 5, 1964, and May 7, 1975. Also requires written AAPs for certain employers.	Federal contractors and subcontractors with contracts in excess of $10,000; employers with 50 or more employees and contracts in excess of $50,000.
Pregnancy Discrimination Act (PDA)	1978	Requires employers to treat pregnancy just like any other medical condition with regard to fringe benefits and leave policies.	Same as Title VII, Civil Rights Act.
Immigration Reform and Control Act	1986	Prohibits hiring of illegal aliens.	Any individual or company.
Americans with Disabilities Act	1990	Increases access to services and jobs for disabled	Private employers with 15 or more employees

▼ (Table 2–1)   *(concluded)*

Executive Orders	Year	Intent	Coverage
11246	1965	Prohibits discrimination on the basis of race, sex, color, religion, or national origin; requires affirmative action with regard to these factors.	Federal contractors and subcontractors with contracts in excess of $10,000; employers with 50 or more employees and contracts in excess of $50,000.
11375	1967	Prohibits sex-based wage discrimination.	Government contractors and subcontractors.
11478	1967	Superseded Executive Order 11246 and modified some of the procedures under the previous orders and regulations.	

in areas different from the federal law as long as the law does not require or permit an act that is unlawful under federal legislation.

Table 2–1 summarizes the significant points of all of the equal employment opportunity laws discussed in this section.

Enforcement Agencies

Two federal agencies have the primary responsibility for enforcing equal employment opportunity legislation. These agencies are the Equal Employment Opportunity Commission and the Office of Federal Contract Compliance Programs.

Equal Employment Opportunity Commission

The **Equal Employment Opportunity Commission (EEOC)** was created by the Civil Rights Act to administer Title VII of the act. The commission is composed of five members, not more than three of whom may be members of the same political party. Members of the commission are appointed by the President of the United States, by and with the advice and consent of the Senate, for a term of five years. The President designates one member to serve as chairperson of the commission and one member to serve as vice chairperson. The chairperson is responsible on behalf of the commission for its administrative operations.

There is also a general counsel of the commission, appointed by the President with the advice of the Senate for a term of four years. The general counsel is responsible for conducting litigation under the provisions of Title VII.

Originally, the EEOC was responsible for investigating discrimination based on race, color, religion, sex, or national origin. Now, however, it is also responsible for investigating equal pay violations and handicapped and age discrimination.

Equal Employment Opportunity Commission (EEOC)
Federal agency created under the Civil Rights Act of 1964 to administer Title VII of the act and to ensure equal employment opportunity; its powers were expanded in 1979.

EEOC not only has the authority to investigate charges and complaints in these areas but also to intervene through the general counsel in a civil action on the behalf of an aggrieved party. EEOC also develops and issues guidelines to enforce nondiscriminatory practices in all of these areas. Several of these guidelines are discussed in this and the next chapter.

Office of Federal Contract Compliance Programs

Office of Federal Contract Compliance Programs (OFCCP)
Office within the U.S. Department of Labor that is responsible for ensuring equal employment opportunity by federal contractors and subcontractors.

Unlike the EEOC, which is an independent agency within the federal government, the **Office of Federal Contract Compliance Programs (OFCCP)** is within the U.S. Department of Labor. It was established by Executive Order 11246 to ensure that federal contractors and subcontractors follow nondiscriminatory employment practices. Prior to 1978, 11 different government agencies had contract compliance sections responsible for administering and enforcing Executive Order 11246. The OFCCP generally supervised and coordinated their activities. In 1978, Executive Order 12086 consolidated the administration and enforcement functions within the OFCCP.

Landmark Court Cases

Laws passed by Congress usually are broad in nature and are refined when they are applied to specific situations. Furthermore, the general nature of the equal employment laws allowed and caused enforcement agencies such as EEOC to develop guidelines and enforce the acts as they interpreted them. Unfortunately, confusion often resulted among employers about the guidelines and enforcement of equal employment laws by EEOC and OFCCP. This confusion and the anger that resulted have led to many lawsuits concerning the interpretation of equal opportunity laws and guidelines. Again, unfortunately, many court decisions have been not only confusing but, in some instances, apparently conflicting.

Nevertheless, several Supreme Court decisions have provided guidance in the interpretation of equal employment opportunity laws. Some of the more important decisions are described in the following sections.

Griggs v. Duke Power Company[6]

The *Griggs* case was concerned with the promotion and transfer policies of the Duke Power Company at its Dan River Steam Station. Duke permitted incumbent employees who lacked a high school education to transfer from an "outside" job to an "inside" job by passing two tests—the Wonderlic Personnel Test, which purports to measure general verbal facility, and the Bennett Mechanical Aptitude Test. The passing scores approximated the national median for high school graduates.

In a class action suit, black employees argued that these practices violated Title VII, since neither having a high school education nor passing the tests was necessary for successful performance on the jobs in question. The suit also argued that the practices were illegal because a much higher percentage of blacks did not have high school educations. The company argued that the requirements were based on the company's judgment that they generally would improve the overall quality of the work force and that the company had no discriminatory intent in instituting the requirements. The company argued that its lack of discriminatory intent was demonstrated by its efforts to help undereducated employees through company financing of two thirds of the cost of tuition for high school education.

The Supreme Court in 1971 ruled in favor of the black employees. The decision established several significant points concerning equal employment opportunity: (1) The consequences of employment practices, not simply the intent or motivation of the employer, are the thrust of Title VII in that practices that discriminate against one group more than another or continue past patterns of discrimination are illegal regardless of the nondiscriminatory intent of the employer; (2) the **disparate impact doctrine** provides that when the plaintiff shows that an employment practice disproportionately excludes groups protected by Title VII, the burden of proof shifts to the defendent to prove that the standard reasonably relates to job performance; and (3) the EEOC's guidelines that only permitted the use of job-related tests were supported.

Disparate impact doctrine
When the plaintiff shows that an employment practice disproportionately excludes groups protected by Title VII, the burden of proof shifts to the defendant to prove that the standard reasonably relates to job performance.

McDonnell Douglas v. Green[7]

Percy Green, a black man who had been employed by McDonnell Douglas, was laid off as a result of a reduction in McDonnell's work force. After the layoff, Green participated in a protest against alleged racial discrimination by McDonnell in its employment practices. The protest included a "stall-in," whereby Green and others stopped their cars along roads leading to the plant in order to block access during the morning rush hour. At a later date, McDonnell advertised for mechanics. Green applied for reemployment and was rejected by the company on the grounds of his participation in the stall-in, which the company argued was unlawful conduct.

On technical grounds, the Supreme Court remanded the case back to the District Court, but at the same time its ruling set forth standards for the burden of proof in discrimination cases. These standards were as follows:

1. The complainant in a Title VII case carries the initial burden of proof in establishing a *prima facie* case of discrimination. This can be done by showing: (a) that he or she belongs to a racial minority; (b) that he or she applied and was qualified for a job for which the employer was seeking applicants; (c) that, despite his or her qualifications, the applicant was rejected; and (d) that, after the rejection, the position remained open and the employer continued to seek applicants from persons of the complainant's qualifications.

2. If the complainant establishes a *prima facie* case, the burden shifts to the employer to provide some legitimate, nondiscriminatory reason for the employee's rejection.

3. The burden shifts to the employee to prove that the employer's allegedly legitimate reason was pretextual (i.e., that the offered reason was not the true reason for the employer's action).

The court in its ruling stated that Green had established a *prima facie* case and that McDonnell had shown a nondiscriminatory reason for not hiring Green because of his participation in the stall-in.

Albemarle Paper v. Moody[8]

In the *Albemarle Paper* v. *Moody* case, applicants for hire into various skilled lines of progression were required to take the Beta examination, which purportedly measures nonverbal intelligence, and the Wonderlic test, which purportedly measures general verbal facility. The company made no attempt to determine the job relatedness of the tests and simply adopted the national norm score as a cutoff for new job applicants.

The company allowed black workers to transfer to the skilled lines if they could pass the Beta and Wonderlic tests, but few succeeded. Incumbents in the skilled lines, some of whom had been hired before the adoption of the tests, were not required to pass them to retain their jobs or their promotion rights.

Four months before the case went to trial, Albemarle engaged an expert in industrial psychology to validate the relatedness of its testing program. He spent half a day at the plant and devised a study, which was conducted by plant officials without his supervision. This study showed the tests to be job related.

However, in June 1975, the Supreme Court found Albemarle's validation study to be materially defective. The Court's decision was based on the fact that Albemarle's study failed to comply with EEOC's guidelines for validating employment tests. Thus, this decision reaffirmed that tests used in employment decisions must be job related, and it reaffirmed the use of EEOC guidelines in validating tests. The court also held that if an employer establishes that a test is job related, it is the plaintiff's burden to demonstrate the existence of other tests that could comparably serve the employer's legitimate interests with a lesser impact upon a protected group.

University of California Regents v. Bakke[9]

The Medical School of the University of California at Davis opened in 1968 with an entering class of 50 students. No black, Hispanic, or Native American students were in this class. Over the next two years, the faculty developed a special admissions program to increase the participation of minority students. In 1971, the size of the entering class was doubled, and 16 of the 100 positions were to be filled by "disadvantaged" applicants chosen by a special admissions committee. In actual practice, disadvantaged meant a minority applicant.

Allan Bakke, a white male, was denied admission to the medical school in 1973 and 1974. Contending that minority students with lower grade averages and test scores were admitted under the special program, Bakke brought suit. He argued that he had been discriminated against because of his race when he was prevented from competing for the 16 reserved positions, and he alleged that the medical school's special two-track admissions system violated the Civil Rights Act of 1964. Thus, the Bakke case raised the issue of **reverse discrimination**—alleged preferential treatment of one group (minority or female) over another group rather than equal opportunity.

Reverse discrimination
Condition under which there is alleged preferential treatment of one group (minority or women) over another group, rather than equal opportunity.

On June 28, 1978, the Supreme Court ruled in a 5 to 4 decision that Allan Bakke should be admitted to the Medical School of the University of California at Davis and found the school's two-track admissions system to be illegal. However, by another 5 to 4 vote, the Court held that at least some forms of race-conscious admissions procedures are constitutional. The Court stated that race or ethnic background may be deemed a plus in a particular applicant's file, yet it does not insulate the individual from comparison with all other candidates for the available positions. As could be expected, the somewhat nebulous decisions in the Bakke case provided an environment for further court tests of the legal status of reverse discrimination.

United Steelworkers of America v. Weber[10]

In 1974, the Kaiser Aluminum and Chemical Corporation and the United Steelworkers of America signed a collective bargaining agreement that contained an affirmative action plan designed to reduce racial imbalances in Kaiser's then almost exclusively white work force. The plan set hiring goals and established on-the-job training programs to teach craft skills to unskilled workers. Under the plan, 50 percent of the openings in the training programs were reserved for blacks.

At Kaiser's Gramercy, Louisiana, plant, Brian F. Weber, a white male, filed a class action suit against the company because black employees were accepted into the company's in-plant craft-training program before white employees with more seniority. Lower-level courts supported Weber's suit. However, in its 1979 decision on this case, the Supreme Court ruled that the voluntarily agreed-upon plan between Kaiser and the steelworkers was permissible. The court stated that the Title VII prohibition against racial discrimination did not condemn all private, voluntary, race-conscious affirmative action programs. The court ruled that Kaiser's affirmative action plan was permissible because it (1) was designed to break down old patterns of segregation, (2) did not involve the discharge of innocent third parties, (3) did not have any bars to the advancement of white employees, and (4) was a temporary measure to eliminate discrimination. Thus, this decision provided important guidelines for determining the legality of an affirmative action plan.

Connecticut v. Teal[11]

A Connecticut agency promoted several black employees to supervisory positions contingent upon their passing a written examination. When they later failed the exam, the agency refused to consider them as permanent candidates for the positions. These employees alleged that Connecticut violated Title VII by requiring as an absolute condition for consideration for promotion that applicants pass a written test that disproportionately excluded blacks and was not job related. The passing rate on the test for blacks was only 68 percent of the passing rate for whites.

Promotions were made from the eligibility list generated by the written examination. As it turned out, however, the overall result was that 22.9 percent of the black candidates and 13.5 percent of the white candidates were promoted. The District Court ruled that the bottom-line percentages, which were more favorable to blacks than whites, precluded a Title VII violation. The **bottom-line concept** is based on the view that the government should generally not concern itself with

Bottom-line concept
When the overall selection process does not have an adverse impact, the government will usually not examine the individual components of that process for adverse impact or evidence of validity.

individual components of the selection process if the overall effect of that process is nondiscriminatory. However, the Supreme Court, on June 21, 1982, held that the nondiscriminatory bottom-line results of the employer's selection process did not preclude the employees from establishing a *prima facie* case of discrimination and did not provide the employer with a defense in such a case. Thus, it can be concluded from this case that bottom-line percentages are not determinative. Rather, the EEOC or a court will look at each test to determine whether it, by itself, has a disparate impact on a protected group.

Memphis Firefighters, Local 1784 v. *Stotts*[12]

The *Stotts* case was concerned with a conflict between a seniority system and certain affirmative action measures taken by the city of Memphis. In 1980, the Memphis Fire Department entered into a consent decree under which the department would attempt to ensure that 20 percent of the promotions in each job classification would be granted to blacks. The decree was silent on the issues of layoffs, de-motions, or competitive seniority.

In May 1981, budget deficits made layoffs of personnel in the fire department necessary. The layoffs were to be based on seniority. The district court issued an injunction ordering the city to refrain from applying the seniority system because it would decrease the percentage of black employees in certain jobs.

The city then used a modified plan to protect black employees. The modified plan laid off 24 employees, three of whom were black. If the traditional seniority system had been used, six black employees would have been laid off.

The Memphis Firefighters Local 1784 filed a lawsuit objecting to this modified plan. In 1984, the Supreme Court ruled that the district court had exceeded its powers in issuing the injunction requiring white employees to be laid off when the normal seniority system could have required laying off black employees with less seniority. This decision did not ban the use of affirmative action programs but does indicate that a seniority system may limit the use of certain affirmative action measures.[13]

City of Richmond v. *J. A. Crosan Company*[14]

In 1983, the Richmond City Council adopted, in an ordinance, a minority business utilization "set-aside" plan, which required nonminority-owned prime contractors awarded city construction contracts to subcontract at least 30 percent of the dollar amount of the contract to one or more minority business enterprises.

After the adoption of the ordinance, the city issued an invitation to bid on a project for the provision and installation of plumbing fixtures at the city jail. The only bidder, the J. A. Crosan Company, submitted a proposal that did not include minority subcontracting sufficient to satisfy the ordinance. The company asked for a waiver of the set-aside requirement, but the request was denied and the company was informed that the project was to be rebid. The company filed suit claiming that the ordinance was unconstitutional under the equal protection clause of the Fourteenth Amendment to the U.S. Constitution.

In January 1989, the Supreme Court ruled that the city of Richmond's plan was unconstitutional. The Court stated that state and local governments must avoid racial quotas and must take affirmative action steps only to correct well-documented examples of past discrimination. The Court went on to say that the Fourteenth Amendment to the U.S. Constitution, which guarantees equal protection of the laws, requires that government affirmative action programs that put whites at a disadvantage should be viewed with the same legal skepticism that has been applied to many state and local laws discriminating against minorities. The impact that this decision will have on affirmative action plans for private companies is yet to be determined, but its implications may be wide-ranging.

Wards Cove v. Atonio[15]

In June 1989, the Supreme Court, in a close decision (5 to 4), made it easier for employers to rebut claims of racial bias based on statistical evidence. The case developed from discrimination charges against Wards Cove Packing Co., Inc., of Seattle and Castle & Cooke, Inc., of Astoria, Oregon. The companies operate salmon canneries in remote areas of Alaska during the summer salmon run.

Minorities (in this particular case, the minorities were largely Filipinos, Alaska natives, and Asians) alleged that while they held nearly half the jobs at the canneries, the jobs were racially stratified, with whites dominating higher-paying jobs such as machinists, carpenters, and administrators.

The company argued that statistics showing that minorities held most of the lower-paying seasonal jobs and fewer better positions did not prove discrimination by the company.

The Supreme Court's decision said that when minorities allege that statistics show they are victims of discrimination, employers only have the burden of producing evidence that there is a legitimate reason for its business practices. The Court further stated that the plaintiff bears the burden of disproving an employer's assertion that the adverse employment practice is based solely on a legitimate neutral consideration. The Court also limited the statistical evidence that minorities can use to prove discrimination. It ruled that an absence of minorities in skilled jobs is not evidence of discrimination if the absence reflects a dearth of qualified minority applicants for reasons that are not the employer's fault.

Martin v. Wilks[16]

A group of white firefighters sued the city of Birmingham, Alabama, and the Jefferson County Personnel Board, alleging that they were being denied promotions in favor of less-qualified black firefighters. Prior to the filing of the suit, the city had entered into two consent decrees that included goals for hiring and promoting black firefighters. In filing their suit the white firefighters claimed that the city was making promotion decisions on the basis of race in reliance on the consent decrees, and that these decisions constituted racial discrimination in violation of the Constitution and federal statutes. The District Court held that the white firefighters were precluded from challenging employment decisions taken pursuant to the decrees. However, on June 12, 1989, the Supreme Court ruled that the white firefighters could challenge the promotion decisions made pursuant to the consent decrees. Thus, the Court ruled that white firefighters could bring reverse-discrimination claims against court-approved affirmative action plans.

Uniform Guidelines on Employee Selection Procedures

In 1978, the EEOC, the Office of Personnel Management, the Department of Justice, and the Department of Labor adopted and published a document entitled *Uniform Guidelines on Employee Selection Procedures,* more commonly referred to as *Uniform Guidelines.*[17] The *Uniform Guidelines* are designed to provide the framework for determining the proper use of tests and other selection procedures used for any employment decision. Employment decisions include but are not limited to:

Hiring.
Promotion.
Demotion.
Membership (for example, in a labor organization).
Referral.
Retention.
Licensing and certification.
Selection for training.
Transfers.

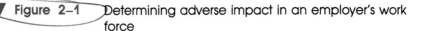

▼ **Figure 2–1**   Determining adverse impact in an employer's work force

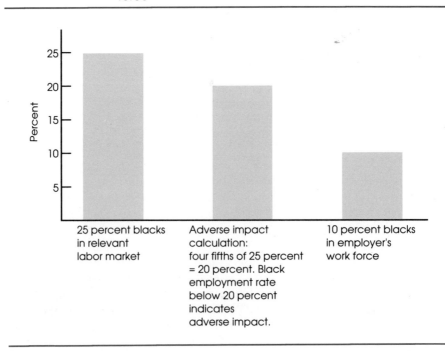

25 percent blacks
in relevant
labor market

Adverse impact
calculation:
four fifths of 25 percent
= 20 percent. Black
employment rate
below 20 percent
indicates
adverse impact.

10 percent blacks
in employer's
work force

Adverse Impact

The fundamental principle underlying the *Uniform Guidelines* is that employment policies and practices that have an **adverse impact** on employment opportunities of any race, sex, or ethnic group are illegal unless justified by business necessity. A selection procedure that has no adverse impact is generally considered to be legal. If adverse impact exists, however, it must be justified on the basis of business necessity. Normally, this means by validation that demonstrates the relationship between the selection procedure and performance on the job.

The *Uniform Guidelines* adopt a "rule of thumb" as a practical means of determining adverse impact. This rule is known as the **4/5ths or 80 percent rule**. This rule is not a legal definition of discrimination, but rather a practical device for determining serious discrepancies in hiring, promoting, or other employment decisions. For example, suppose an employer is doing business in an area where the labor force is 25 percent black. Further, suppose that the employer has 1,000 employees and 100 (10 percent) of the employees are black. Thus, adverse impact exists because 4/5ths of 25 percent equals 20 percent and blacks only make up 10 percent of the employer's work force. (See Figure 2–1.)

Figure 2–2 illustrates how adverse impact can be assessed in an employer's hiring decisions. Suppose 25 men have applied for a job opening and 15 of the

Adverse impact
Condition that occurs when the selection rate for minorities or women is less than 80 percent of the selection rate for the majority group in hiring, promotions, transfers, demotions, or any selection decision.

4/5ths or 80 percent rule
A limit used to determine whether or not there are serious discrepancies in hiring decisions and other employment practices affecting women or minorities.

▼ **Figure 2–2**   Determining adverse impact in an employer's hiring decisions

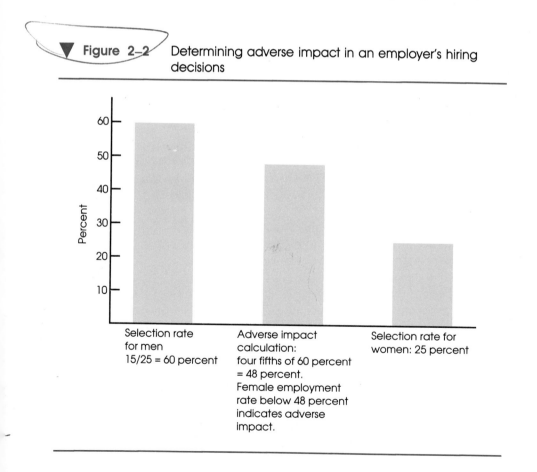

Selection rate for men
15/25 = 60 percent

Adverse impact calculation:
four fifths of 60 percent
= 48 percent.
Female employment rate below 48 percent indicates adverse impact.

Selection rate for women: 25 percent

men were hired. Suppose only 20 women applied and 5 were hired. Adverse impact exists because 4/5ths of 60 percent equals 48 percent, and a selection rate for women below 48 percent indicates adverse impact.

Where Adverse Impact Exists: the Basic Options

After it has been established that adverse impact exists, what steps are required by the *Uniform Guidelines*? First, the employer has the option of modifying or eliminating the procedure that produces the adverse impact. If the employer does not, then it must justify the use of the procedure on the grounds of business necessity. This normally means showing a clear relation between performance on the selection procedure and performance on the job. In the language of industrial psychology, the employer must validate the selection procedure. Validation of selection procedures will be examined in depth in Chapter 7.

● *Summary of Learning Objectives*

1. Define equal employment opportunity.

   Equal employment opportunity refers to the right of all people to work and to advance on the basis of merit, ability, and potential.

2. Describe the intent of Title VII of the Civil Rights Act of 1964.

   Title VII of the Civil Rights Act of 1964 is written to prohibit discrimination based on race, sex, color, religion, or national origin.

3. Define disparate treatment and disparate impact.

   Disparate treatment refers to intentional discrimination and involves treating one class of employees different from other employees. Disparate impact refers to unintentional discrimination and involves employment practices that appear to be neutral but adversely affect a protected class of people.

4. Discuss the purpose of the Age Discrimination in Employment Act.

   This act is written to prohibit discrimination against employees who are over 40 years of age.

5. Describe the intent of the Equal Pay Act.

   This act prohibits sex-based discrimination in rates of pay for men and women working in the same or similar jobs.

6. Discuss the purpose of the Vocational Rehabilitation Act.

   This act prohibits discrimination against and requires affirmative action to provide employment opportunities for the handicapped.

7. Describe the intent of the Vietnam-Era Veterans Readjustment Assistance Act.

   This act prohibits discrimination in hiring disabled veterans with a 30 percent or more disability rating, veterans discharged or released for a service-related disability, and veterans on active duty between August 5, 1964, and May 7, 1975. It also requires that employers with 50 or more employees and contracts in excess of $50,000 must have a written AAP for the people protected under this act.

8. Discuss the purpose of the Pregnancy Discrimination Act.

   This act requires employers to treat pregnancy like any other medical condition with regard to fringe benefits and leave policies.

9. Describe the intent of the Immigration Reform and Control Act.

   This act prohibits the hiring of illegal aliens.

10. Discuss the Americans with Disabilities Act.

    This act increased access to services and jobs for the disabled in private employers with 15 or more employees.

11. Discuss the purpose of Executive Orders of 11246, 11375, and 11478.

    Executive Order 11246 prohibits discrimination by federal contractors and subcontractors with contracts in excess of $10,000 on the basis of race, sex, color, religion, or national origin. Also, it requires contractors and subcontractors with 50 or more employees and contracts in excess of $50,000 to have a written AAP with regard to the protected classes. Executive Order 11375 prohibits sex-biased wage discrimination. Executive Order 11478 superseded Executive Order 11246 and modified some of the procedures under the previous orders and regulations.

12. Describe the significance of the following Supreme Court decisions:

    Griggs v. *Duke Power*—Established that consequences of employment practices, not simply the intent of the employer, are the thrust of Title VII.

    McDonnell Douglas v. *Green*—Set forth standards for the burden of proof in disparate treatment discrimination cases.

    Albemarle Paper v. *Moody*—Affirmed that tests used in employment decisions must be job related and affirmed the use of EEOC guidelines on validating tests.

    University of California Regents v. *Bakke*—Raised the issue of reverse discrimination. Stated that race or ethnic background may be deemed a plus in a particular applicant's file, but it does not insulate the individual from comparison with all other candidates for the available position.

    United Steelworkers of America v. *Weber*—Provided important guidelines for determining the legality of affirmative action programs.

    Connecticut v. *Teal*—Ruled that the bottom line results of an employer's selection process does not preclude employees from establishing a *prima facie* case of discrimination and does not provide the employer with a defense in such a case.

    Memphis Firefighters, Local 1784 v. *Stotts*—Indicated that a seniority system may limit the use of certain affirmative action measures.

    City of Richmond v. *J. A. Crosan Company*—Stated that the Fourteenth Amendment requires government affirmative action programs that put whites at a disadvantage to be viewed with the same legal skepticism as laws that discriminate against minorities.

    Wards Cove v. *Atonio*—Changed the rules in job discrimination suits. Now employees have to prove there was no legitimate business reason for a firm's alleged discriminatory acts.

Martin v. *Wilks*—Ruled that whites may bring reverse-discrimination claims against court-approved affirmative action plans.

13. Discuss adverse impact.

    Employment policies and practices that have an adverse impact on employment opportunities of any race, sex, or ethnic group are illegal unless justified by business necessity.

14. Describe the 4/5ths rule.

    This is a practical device for determining serious discrepancies in hiring, promoting, and other employment decisions.

15. Discuss the bottom-line concept.

    This concept is based on the view that the government should generally not concern itself with individual components of the selection process if the overall effect of that process is nondiscriminatory.

Review Questions

1. What is equal employment opportunity?
2. Outline the intent and coverage of each of the following laws:
   a. Title VII, Civil Rights Act
   b. Age Discrimination in Employment Act
   c. Equal Pay Act
   d. Vocational Rehabilitation Act
   e. Vietnam-Era Veterans Readjustment Assistance Act
   f. Pregnancy Discrimination Act
   g. Immigration Reform and Control Act
   h. Americans with Disabilities Act
   i. Executive Order 11246
   j. Executive Order 11375
   k. Executive Order 11478
3. Define disparate treatment and disparate impact.
4. What two federal agencies have primary responsibility for enforcing equal employment opportunity legislation?
5. Describe the impact of the following Supreme Court decisions:
   a. *Griggs* v. *Duke Power*
   b. *McDonnell Douglas* v. *Green*
   c. *Albemarle Paper* v. *Moody*
   d. *University of California Regents* v. *Bakke*
   e. *United Steelworkers of America* v. *Weber*
   f. *Connecticut* v. *Teal*
   g. *Memphis Firefighters, Local 1784* v. *Stotts*
   h. *City of Richmond* v. *J. A. Crosan Company*
   i. *Wards Cove* v. *Atonio*
   j. *Martin* v. *Wilks*

6. What is adverse impact?
7. Explain the 4/5ths or 80 percent rule.
8. What is the bottom-line concept?

Discussion Questions

1. What area of human resource management is most affected by equal employment opportunity legislation? Discuss.
2. Do you feel that most organizations meet the requirements of equal employment opportunity? Why or why not?
3. What problems do you feel have been caused by equal employment opportunity legislation?
4. Do you feel that there are misconceptions about equal employment opportunity? Discuss.

▼ INCIDENT 2–1

Accept Things as They Are

Jane Harris came to work at the S&J Department Store two years ago. In Jane's initial assignment in the finance department, she proved to be a good and hard worker. It soon became obvious to both Jane and her department head Rich Jackson that she could handle a much more responsible job than the one she presently held. Jane discussed this matter with Rich. It was obvious to him that if a better position could not be found for Jane, S&J would lose a good employee. As there were no higher openings in the finance department, Rich recommended her for a job in the accounting department, which she received.

Jane joined the accounting department as payroll administrator and quickly mastered her position. She became knowledgeable in all aspects of the job and maintained a good rapport with her two employees. A short time later, Jane was promoted to assistant manager of the accounting department. In this job, Jane continued her outstanding performance.

Two months ago, Bob Thomas suddenly appeared as a new employee in the accounting department. Ralph Simpson, vice president of administration for S&J, explained to Jane and Steve Smith, head of the accounting department, that Bob was a trainee. After Bob had learned all areas of the department, he would be used to take some of the load off both Jane and Steve and also undertake special projects for the department. Several days after Bob's arrival, Jane learned that Bob was the son of a politician who was a close friend of the president of S&J. Bob had worked in his father's successful election campaign until shortly before he joined S&J.

Last week, Steve asked Jane to help him prepare the accounting department's budget for next year. While working on the budget, Jane got a big surprise. She found that Bob had been hired at a salary of $3,000 per month. At the time of

Bob's hiring, Jane, as assistant manager of the accounting department, was making only $2,700 per month.

After considering her situation for several days, Jane went to see Ralph Simpson, the division head, about the problem. She told Ralph that she had learned of the difference in salary while assisting Steve with the budget and stated that it was not right to pay a trainee more than a manager. She reminded Ralph of what he had said several times, that Jane's position should pay $40,000 per year considering her responsibility, but that S&J just could not afford to pay her that much. Jane told Ralph that things could not remain as they were at present, and she wanted to give S&J a chance to correct the situation. Ralph told Jane he would get back to her in several days.

About a week later, Ralph gave Jane a reply. He stated that while the situation was wrong and unfair, he did not feel that S&J could do anything about it. He told her that sometimes one has to accept things as they are, even if they are wrong. He further stated that he hoped this could not cause S&J to lose a good employee.

Questions

1. What options does Jane have?
2. What influence, if any, would the federal government have in this case?

▼ INCIDENT 2–2

TWA and "Willful" Age Discrimination

Federal regulations prohibit people from serving as pilots or copilots after they turn 60, but the rules permit pilots to continue working as flight engineers, the third crew member in the cockpit. The Supreme Court ruled in January 1985 that TWA had violated federal age discrimination law by making it difficult for pilots to downgrade their jobs to the status of flight engineer when they reach age 60.

The law permits federal courts to double the amount of damages awarded to employees who win age discrimination lawsuits but only if the employer's discrimination was "willful." The Court's decision defined willful conduct as occurring when an employer "knew or showed reckless disregard for" whether its action was prohibited by federal age discrimination law.

Questions

1. Do you feel that the willful-conduct standard should be applied to all equal employment opportunity legislation?
2. How would one be able to show that requiring pilots and copilots to retire at age 60 is job related?

Exercise

Legal Issues in Equal Employment Opportunity

Break the class into teams of two to three students. Each team should then be given the following assignment:

Go to the library and review the relevant literature on recent legal cases involving equal employment opportunity. Prepare a report for presentation in class concerning the facts, issues, and current status of the case. Each team should make a 5- to 10-minute presentation on its findings.

Notes and Additional Readings

1. The definition of a covered labor union is identical to Title VII's except that where a union is not a referral union, it is not covered by ADEA unless there are 25 or more members as compared to the 15 or more under Title VII.
2. *Usery* v. *Tamiami Trail Tours, Inc.,* 531 F. 2d 224, 12FEP1233 (5th Cir. 1976).
3. *United Air Lines* v. *McMann,* 434 U.S. 192, 16FEP146 (1977).
4. *General Electric Co.* v. *Gilbert,* 429 U.S. 125 (1976).
5. Art. VI, Cl.2.
6. *Griggs* v. *Duke Power Company,* 401 U.S. 424, FEP 175 (1971).
7. *McDonnell Douglas* v. *Green,* 411 U.S. 792 (1973).
8. *Albemarle Paper* v. *Moody,* 422 U.S. 405, 95 S.CT. 2362 (1975).
9. *University of California Regents* v. *Bakke,* 483 U.S. 265 (1978).
10. *United Steelworkers of America* v. *Weber,* 99 S.CT. 2721 (1979).
11. *Connecticut* v. *Teal,* 457 U.S. 440 (1982).
12. *Memphis Firefighters, Local 1784* v. *Stotts,* 104 S.CT. 2576 (1984).
13. Theresa Johnson, "The Future of Affirmative Action: An Analysis of the Stotts Case," *Labor Law Journal,* October 1985, p. 788.
14. *City of Richmond* v. *J. A. Crosan Company,* 102 L Ed. 2d. 854.
15. *Wards Cove* v. *Atonio,* 104 L Ed. 2d. 733.
16. *Martin* v. *Wilks,* 104 L Ed. 2d. 835.
17. "Uniform Guidelines on Employee Selection Procedures," *Federal Register,* August 25, 1978, pp. 38290–315.

Chapter 3

Implementing Equal Employment Opportunity

Chapter Outline

EEOC Compliance
    Legal Powers of EEOC
    EEOC Posting Requirements
    Records and Reports
    Compliance Process
    Preemployment Inquiry Guide
Affirmative Action Plans
Bona Fide Occupational Qualification (BFOQ)
Business Necessity
Sexual Harassment
Comparable Worth and Equal Pay Issues
Other Areas of Employment Discrimination
    Religion
    Native Americans (Indians)
    AIDS
    Sexual Preference
Summary of Learning Objectives
Review Questions
Discussion Questions
Incident 3–1: Affirmative Action
Incident 3–2: Religion and Real Estate
Exercise: Affirmative Action Debate
Exercise: The Layoff
Notes and Additional Readings
On the Job: Preemployment Inquiry Guide

● *Learning Objectives*

After studying this chapter, you should be able to:

1. Explain the role of the Employer Information Report, EEO–1.
2. Define employment parity, occupational parity, systemic discrimination, underutilization, and concentration.
3. Describe an affirmative action plan.
4. Define bona fide occupational qualification (BFOQ).
5. Explain business necessity.
6. Define sexual harassment.
7. Describe the comparable worth theory.

"I have a dream that one day this nation will rise up and live out the true meaning of its creed: 'We hold these truths to be self-evident; that all men are created equal.' "

Martin Luther King, Jr.*

As can be seen from the previous chapter, the legal requirements of equal employment opportunity are quite complex. Regardless of the complexity, however, each organization must develop its own approach to equal employment within the legal guidelines. Thus, the purpose of this chapter is to provide specific information and guidelines for implementing equal employment opportunity.

EEOC Compliance

The Equal Employment Opportunity Commission (EEOC) and the Office of Federal Contract Compliance Programs (OFCCP), both described in the previous chapter, are the two primary enforcement agencies for equal employment opportunity. All organizations with 20 or more employees are required to keep records that can be requested by either the EEOC or the OFCCP.

Legal Powers of EEOC

Section 713 of Title VII, the Age Discrimination in Employment Act, and the Equal Pay Act authorize the EEOC to develop and publish procedural regulations regarding the enforcement of these acts. As a result, the EEOC has issued substantive regulations (or guidelines, as they are more frequently called) interpreting Title VII, the ADEA, and the Equal Pay Act. The "Uniform Guidelines on Employee Selection Procedures" (discussed in the previous chapter) are one example of the guidelines. Since 1972, the EEOC has also had enforcement authority to initiate litigation and to intervene in private litigation.

EEOC Posting Requirements

Title VII requires employers, employment agencies, and labor organizations covered by the act to post EEOC-prepared notices summarizing the requirements of Title VII. The EEOC has prepared such a poster, and a willful failure to display it is punishable by a fine of not more than $100 for each offense. Organizations that are subject to notice requirements by Executive Order 11246 and Title VII can display a poster meeting the requirements of both EEOC and OFCCP. Figure 3–1 shows such a poster.

*Source: Excerpt from speech by Dr. Martin Luther King, on August 28, 1963.

Equal Employment Opportunity is...

Private Employment, State and Local Government, Educational Institutions

Race, Color, Religion, Sex, National Origin
Title VII of the Civil Rights Act of 1964, as amended, prohibits discrimination in hiring, promotion, discharge, pay, fringe benefits, and other aspects of employment, on the basis of race, color, religion, sex or national origin.

Applicants to and employees of most private employers, State and local governments and public or private educational institutions are protected. Employment agencies, labor unions and apprenticeship programs also are covered.

Age
The Age Discrimination in Employment Act of 1967, as amended, prohibits age discrimination and protects applicants and employees aged 40-70 from discrimination in hiring, promotion, discharge, pay, fringe benefits and other aspects of employment. The law covers most private employers, State and local governments, educational institutions, employment agencies and labor organizations.

Sex (wages)
In addition to the sex discrimination prohibited by Title VII of the Civil Rights Act (see above) The Equal Pay Act of 1963, as amended, prohibits sex discrimination in payment of wages to women and men performing substantially equal work in the same establishment. The law covers most private employers, State and local governments and educational institutions. Labor organizations cannot cause employers to violate the law. Many employers not covered by Title VII, because of size, are covered by the Equal Pay Act.

If you believe that you have been discriminated against under any of the above laws, you should immediately contact:

 The U.S. Equal Employment Opportunity Commission 2401 "E" Street, N.W. Washington, D.C. 20506 or an EEOC District Office, listed in most telephone directories under U.S. Government.

Employers holding Federal contracts or subcontracts

Race, Color, Religion, Sex, National Origin
Executive Order 11246, as amended, prohibits job discrimination on the basis of race, color, religion, sex or national origin, and requires affirmative action to ensure equality of opportunity in all aspects of employment.

Handicap
Section 503 of the Rehabilitation Act of 1973, as amended, prohibits job discrimination because of handicap and requires affirmative action to employ and advance in employment qualified handicapped individuals who, with reasonable accommodation, can perform the functions of a job.

Vietnam Era and Disabled Veterans
Section 402 of the Vietnam Era Veterans Readjustment Assistance Act of 1974 prohibits job discrimination and requires affirmative action to employ and advance in employment qualified Vietnam era veterans and qualified disabled veterans.

Applicants to and employees of companies with a Federal government contract or subcontract are protected under the authorities above. Any person who believes a contractor has violated its nondiscrimination or affirmative action obligations under Executive Order 11246, as amended, Section 503 of the Rehabilitation Act or Section 402 of the Vietnam Era Veterans Readjustment Assistance Act should contact immediately:

The Office of Federal Contract Compliance Programs (OFCCP) Employment Standards Administration U.S. Department of Labor 200 Constitution Avenue, N.W. Washington, D.C. 20210 or an OFCCP regional or area office, listed in most telephone directories under U.S. Government, Department of Labor.

Programs or activities receiving Federal financial assistance

Handicap
Section 504 of the Rehabilitation Act of 1973, as amended, prohibits employment discrimination on the basis of handicap in any program or activity which receives Federal financial assistance. Discrimination is prohibited in all aspects of employment against handicapped persons who, with reasonable accommodation, can perform the essential functions of a job.

Race, Color, National Origin
In addition to the protection of Title VII of the Civil Rights Act of 1964, Title VI of the Civil Rights Act prohibits discrimination on the basis of race, color or national origin in programs or activities receiving Federal financial assistance. Employment discrimination is covered by Title VI if the primary objective of the financial assistance is provision of employment, or where employment discrimination causes or may cause discrimination in providing services under such programs.

If you believe you have been discriminated against in a program which receives Federal assistance, you should immediately contact the Federal agency providing such assistance.

Don't Forget...
Equal Employment Opportunity is the Law!

Records and Reports

Employer Information Report (Standard Form 100)

Form that all employers with 100 or more employees are required to file with EEOC; requires a breakdown of the employer's work force in specified job categories by race, sex, and national origin.

Employers with 100 or more employees are required to file annually Standard Form 100, known as the **Employer Information Report, EEO–1**. Figure 3–2 shows the form. The EEO–1 report requires a breakdown of the employer's work force in specified job categories by race, sex, and national origin. Other similar types of forms are required of unions, political jurisdictions, educational institu-

▼ **Figure 3–2**   Standard Form 100

EQUAL EMPLOYMENT OPPORTUNITY

EMPLOYER INFORMATION REPORT EEO-1

Standard Form 100
(Rev. 12/78)
O.M.B. No. 3046-0007
100-210

Joint Reporting Committee

• Equal Employment Opportunity Commission
• Office of Federal Contract Compliance Programs

Section A - TYPE OF REPORT
Refer to instructions for number and types of reports to be filed.

1. Indicate by marking in the appropriate box the type of reporting unit for which this copy of the form is submitted (MARK ONLY ONE BOX).

(1) ☐ Single-establishment Employer Report

Multi-establishment Employer:
(2) ☐ Consolidated Report
(3) ☐ Headquarters Unit Report
(4) ☐ Individual Establishment Report (submit one for each establishment with 25 or more employees)
(5) ☐ Special Report

2. Total number of reports being filed by this Company (Answer on Consolidated Report only) _____

Section B - COMPANY IDENTIFICATION *(To be answered by all employers)*   OFFICE USE ONLY

1. Parent Company

    a. Name of parent company (owns or controls establishment in item 2) omit if same as label   a.

Name of receiving office   Address (Number and street)   b.

City or town | County | State | ZIP code | b. Employer Identification No.

2. Establishment for which this report is filed. (Omit if same as label)

    a. Name of establishment   c.

Address (Number and street) | City or town | County | State | ZIP code   d.

    b. Employer Identification No.   (If same as label, skip.)

3. Parent company affiliation   (Multi-establishment Employers Answer on Consolidated Report only)

    a. Name of parent-affiliated company   b. Employer Identification No.

Address (Number and street) | City or town | County | State | ZIP code

Section C - EMPLOYERS WHO ARE REQUIRED TO FILE *(To be answered by all employers)*

☐ Yes ☐ No   1. Does the entire company have at least 100 employees in the payroll period for which you are reporting?

☐ Yes ☐ No   2. Is your company affiliated through common ownership and/or centralized management with other entities in an enterprise with a total employment of 100 or more?

☐ Yes ☐ No   3. Does the company or any of its establishments (a) have 50 or more employees AND (b) is not exempt as provided by 41 CFR 60-1.5, AND either (1) is a prime government contractor or first-tier subcontractor, and has a contract, subcontract, or purchase order amounting to $50,000 or more, or (2) serves as a depository of Government funds in any amount or is a financial institution which is an issuing and paying agent for U.S. Savings Bonds and Savings Notes?

NOTE: If the answer is yes to ANY of these questions, complete the entire form, otherwise skip to Section G.

tions, school districts, and joint labor-management committees that control apprenticeship programs. Willfully false statements made on EEOC reports are punishable by fine or imprisonment.

In addition to EEO–1, Title VII requires the covered organizations to make and keep certain records that may be used to determine whether unlawful

▼ **Figure 3–2**   (concluded)

Section D - EMPLOYMENT DATA

Employment at this establishment—Report all permanent, temporary, or part-time employees including apprentices and on-the-job trainees unless specifically excluded as set forth in the instructions. Enter the appropriate figures on all lines and in all columns. Blank spaces will be considered as zeros.

JOB CATEGORIES	OVERALL TOTALS (SUM OF COL. B THRU K) A	MALE WHITE (NOT OF HISPANIC ORIGIN) B	BLACK (NOT OF HISPANIC ORIGIN) C	HISPANIC D	ASIAN OR PACIFIC ISLANDER E	AMERICAN INDIAN OR ALASKAN NATIVE F	FEMALE WHITE (NOT OF HISPANIC ORIGIN) G	BLACK (NOT OF HISPANIC ORIGIN) H	HISPANIC I	ASIAN OR PACIFIC ISLANDER J	AMERICAN INDIAN OR ALASKAN NATIVE K
Officials and Managers											
Professionals											
Technicians											
Sales Workers											
Office and Clerical											
Craft Workers (Skilled)											
Operatives (Semi-Skilled)											
Laborers (Unskilled)											
Service Workers											
TOTAL											
Total employment reported in previous EEO-1 report											

(The trainees below should also be included in the figures for the appropriate occupational categories above)

Formal On-the-Job trainees	White collar										
	Production										

1. NOTE: On consolidated report, skip questions 2-5 and Section E
2. How was information as to race or ethnic group in Section D obtained?
   1 ☐ Visual Survey   3 ☐ Other—Specify ....
   2 ☐ Employment Record   ....
3. Dates of payroll period used -

4. Pay period of last report submitted for this establishment

5. Does this establishment employ apprentices?
   This year?   1 ☐ Yes   2 ☐ No
   Last year?   1 ☐ Yes   2 ☐ No

Section E - ESTABLISHMENT INFORMATION

1. Is the location of the establishment the same as that reported last year?
   1 ☐ Yes   2 ☐ No   3. ☐ Did not report last year.   4. ☐ Reported on combined basis.

2. Is the major business activity at this establishment the same as that reported last year?
   1 ☐ Yes   2 ☐ No   3. ☐ No report last year   4. ☐ Reported on combined basis.

OFFICE USE ONLY

3. What is the major activity of this establishment? (Be specific, i.e., manufacturing steel castings, retail grocer, wholesale plumbing supplies, title insurance, etc. Include the specific type of product or type of service provided, as well as the principal business or industrial activity.

e.

Section F - REMARKS

Use this item to give any identification data appearing on last report which differs from that given above, explain major changes in composition or reporting units and other pertinent information.

Section G - CERTIFICATION (See Instructions G)

Check one   1 ☐ All reports are accurate and were prepared in accordance with the instructions (check on consolidated only)
   2 ☐ This report is accurate and was prepared in accordance with the instructions.

Name of Certifying Official	Title	Signature		Date
Name of person to contact regarding this report (Type or print)	Address (Number and street)			
Title	City and State	ZIP code	Telephone Area Code	Number	Extension

All reports and information obtained from individual reports will be kept confidential as required by Section 709 (e) of Title VII.
WILLFULLY FALSE STATEMENTS ON THIS REPORT ARE PUNISHABLE BY LAW, U.S. CODE, TITLE 18, SECTION 1001

▼ **Figure 3–3** Applicant flow chart

NAME OF APPLICANT	DEGREE/ EDUCATION	DATE APPLIED	POSITION APPLIED FOR	EEO JOB CATEGORY (3-4)	E.I. (5)	SEX (6)	AGE (7)	HANDICAP (8)	VETERAN (9)	DISPOSITION

Location _____ QTR. Beginning _____ QTR. Ending _____

Group Code _____ (For EEO office use only) 1·2

CODES:

EEO JOB CATEGORY

01—Officials/Managers
02—Professionals
03—Technicians
04—Sales Workers
05—Office and Clerical
06—Craft Workers
07—Operatives
08—Laborers
09—Service Workers

ETHNIC IDENTIFICATION (E.I.)

W—White
B—Black
H—Hispanic
A—Asian or Pacific Islanders
N—American Indian or Alaskan Native

SEX

M—Male
F—Female

AGE

A—Below 40
B—40-45
C—46-50
D51-55
F—56-60
G—61-65
H—66 & over

HANDICAP

Y—Yes
N—No

VETERAN

Y—Yes
N—No

DISPOSITION

1—Hired
2—Offer Outstanding
3—Offer Rejected
4—Applicant Regjected
5—No offer-No Opening

This Report Should Be Submitted to the Human Resource Department at the End of Every 90-Day Period

*THE NUMBERS ABOVE COLUMNS ARE FOR KEYPUNCH INFORMATION ONLY. SEE BELOW FOR CODE INFORMTION.

Source: Duke Power Company, used with permission

employment practices have been or are being committed. Thus, it is a good practice for covered organizations to maintain records relating to job applicants, payroll records, transfers, recalls, and discharges. The length of time required for the retention of these records varies, but a good time frame for retaining such records is three years.

Since EEOC and OFCCP are interested in the recruitment and selection of protected groups and because the collection of certain data about the protected groups is not permitted on an organization's application form, EEOC allows organizations to use a separate form, often called an applicant flow chart, for collecting certain data. An example of such a form is shown in Figure 3–3. The data (Fig. 3–3) on this form must be maintained separately from all employment information.

Compliance Process

An individual may file a discrimination charge at any EEOC office or with any representative of the EEOC. If the charging party and respondent are in different geographic areas, the office where the charging party resides forwards the charge to the office where the respondent is located. Class action charges or charges requiring extensive investigations are processed in the EEOC's Office of Systemic Programs.

Two methods can be used by EEOC to determine whether discrimination against groups protected by the law has occurred: (1) employment parity and (2) occupational parity. When **employment parity** exists, the proportion of minorities and women employed by an organization equals the proportion in the organization's relevant labor market. **Occupational parity** exists when the proportion of minorities and women employed in various occupations within an organization is equal to their proportion in the organization's relevant labor market. Large differences in either occupational or employment parity are called **systemic discrimination**.

Relevant labor market generally refers to the geographical area in which a company recruits its employees. For example, a small company may only recruit its employees within the standard metropolitan statistical area (SMSA) within which it falls, thus, its relevant labor market would be the SMSA. On the other hand, a large company that recruits nationally may have the whole nation as its relevant labor market. Furthermore, companies can have different relevant labor markets for different occupations. For example, the relevant labor market for a company's clerical employees might be the SMSA, while the relevant labor market for its engineers might be nationwide.

EEOC can also examine the underutilization or concentration of minorities and/or females in certain jobs. **Underutilization** refers to the practice of having fewer minorities or females in a particular job category than would reasonably be expected when compared to their presence in the relevant labor market. **Concentration** refers to the practice of having more minorities or women in a job category than would reasonably be expected when compared to their presence in the relevant labor market.

Table 3–1 summarizes the steps involved in processing a discrimination charge. These are general in nature, and many variations are possible. For example, Section

Employment parity
Situation in which the proportion of minorities and women employed by an organization equals the proportion in the organization's relevant labor market.

Occupational parity
Situation in which the proportion of minorities and women employed in various occupations within an organization is equal to their proportion in the organization's relevant labor market.

Systemic discrimination
Large differences in either occupational or employment parity.

Relevant labor market
The geographical area in which a company recruits its employees.

Underutilization
Practice of having fewer minorities or females in a particular job category than would reasonably be expected when compared to their presence in the relevant labor market.

Concentration
Practice of having more minorities or women in a job category than would reasonably be expected when compared to their presence in the relevant labor market.

▼ **Table 3–1**   Steps in processing a discrimination charge

Step Number	Procedure
1.	Charge is filed with EEOC.
2.	EEOC evaluates charge and determines whether or not to proceed with it.
3.	If it decides to proceed with the charge, EEOC serves respondents with a copy of the actual charge within 10 days.
4.	A face-to-face, fact-finding conference is held between the charging party and the respondent. The conference is conducted by a staff member of EEOC. The charging party is allowed ample time to explain and support each allegation, and the respondent is allowed to present and defend its position.
5.	If the charge is not resolved in Step 4, EEOC conducts an investigation of the charges.
6.	In cases where the EEOC finds reasonable cause that discrimination has occurred, a proposed conciliation agreement is sent to the respondents. The proposal normally includes a suggested remedy to eliminate the unlawful practices and to take appropriate corrective and affirmative action.
7.	If the respondents do not agree to the conciliation agreement, EEOC makes determination on whether the charge is "litigation worthy." As a practical matter, litigation worthy means that the evidence gathered during the investigation will support a lawsuit.
8.	If the charge is deemed litigation worthy, EEOC then files a lawsuit in the appropriate state or federal court. Of course, decisions of these lower courts are often appealed to the Supreme Court.

706 of Title VII requires that before a charge can be filed with the EEOC, it must first be filed for 60 days with the state or local fair employment practices agency, if one exists, where the alleged discrimination occurred. The EEOC gives substantial weight to the final findings and orders of such agencies when its decision is made.

It is also important to note that if EEOC does not decide to file a lawsuit on behalf of the charging party, the individual still has the right to bring suit against the respondent. In this situation, EEOC issues the charging party the statutory notice of a **right-to-sue letter**. The charging party must then file a civil action suit in the appropriate court within 90 days of receipt of the statutory notice of right to sue.

Right-to-sue letter
Statutory notice by EEOC to the charging party if EEOC does not decide to file a lawsuit on behalf of the charging party.

Preemployment Inquiry Guide

The On the Job example at the end of this chapter provides a guide to what can and cannot be asked of a job applicant in order to comply with equal employment opportunity legislation and court interpretations of that legislation. It is illustrative and attempts to answer the questions most frequently asked about equal employment opportunity law.

Affirmative Action Plans

An **affirmative action plan** is a written document outlining specific goals and timetables for remedying past discriminatory actions. All federal contractors and subcontractors with contracts over $50,000 and 50 or more employees are required to develop and implement written affirmative action plans, which are monitored by the OFCCP. While Title VII and EEOC do not require any specific type of written affirmative action plan, court rulings have often required affirmative action when discrimination is found.

A number of basic steps are involved in the development of an effective affirmative action plan. The EEOC has suggested the following eight steps:[1]

1. The chief executive officer of an organization should issue a written statement describing his or her personal commitment to the plan, legal obligations, and the importance of equal employment opportunity as an organizational goal.

2. A top official of the organization should be given the authority and responsibility for directing and implementing the program. In addition, all managers and supervisors within the organization should clearly understand their own responsibilities for carrying out equal employment opportunity.

3. The organization's policy and commitment to that policy should be publicized both internally and externally.

4. Present employment should be surveyed to identify areas of concentration and underutilization and to determine the extent of underutilization.

5. Goals and timetables for achieving the goals should be developed to improve utilization of minorities, males, and females in each area where underutilization has been identified.

6. The entire employment system should be reviewed to identify and eliminate barriers to equal employment. Areas for review include recruitment, selection, promotion systems, training programs, wage and salary structure, benefits and conditions of employment, layoffs, discharges, disciplinary actions, and union contract provisions affecting these areas.

7. An internal audit and reporting system should be established to monitor and evaluate progress in all aspects of the program.

8. Company and community programs supportive of equal opportunity should be developed. Programs might include training of supervisors in their legal responsibilities and the organization's commitment to equal employment, and job and career counseling programs.

Several Supreme Court decisions discussed in Chapter 2 (*Richmond* v. *Crosan, Wards Cove* v. *Atonio,* and *Martin* v. *Wilks*) have removed the pressure for such plans except in cases of specific and probable acts of discrimination. The Court has not ruled out voluntary programs to encourage minority hiring and promotion, but it has opened the door for reverse-discrimination suits by white males who feel harmed by affirmative action programs.

Affirmative action plan
Written document outlining specific goals and timetables for remedying past discriminatory actions.

Bona Fide Occupational Qualification (BFOQ)

Bona fide occupational qualification (BFOQ)
Permits employer to use religion, age, sex, or national origin as a factor in its employment practices when reasonably necessary to the normal operation of that particular business or enterprise.

The **bona fide occupational qualification (BFOQ)** permits employers to use religion, age, sex, or national origin as a factor in their employment practices when it is reasonably necessary to the normal operation of that particular business. Section 703(e) of Title VII provides:

> Notwithstanding any other provision of this [title], (1) it shall not be an unlawful employment practice for an employer to hire and employ employees, for an employment agency to classify or refer for employment any individual, or for an employer, labor organization, or joint labor management committee controlling apprenticeship or other training programs to admit or employ any individual in any such program, on the basis of his religion, sex, or national origin in those certain instances where religion, sex, or national origin is a bona fide occupational qualification reasonably necessary to the normal operation of that particular business or enterprise.

For example, in order for an employer to use sex as a BFOQ in a job that requires lifting 100 pounds, the employer would be required to show that all or substantially all women cannot lift 100 pounds.

In fact, employers most frequently raise the BFOQ exception because of sex. Section 1604.2(a) of the EEOC's *Guidelines on Discrimination because of Sex* states:

> The Commission believes that the bona fide occupational qualification exception as to sex should be interpreted narrowly. Labels—'men's jobs' and 'women's jobs'—tend to deny employment opportunities unnecessarily to one sex or the other.
>
> **(1)** The Commission will find that the following situations do not warrant the application of the bona fide occupational qualification exception:
>
>   **(i)** The refusal to hire a woman because of her sex based on assumptions of the comparative employment characteristics of women in general. For example, the assumption that the turnover rate among women is higher than among men.
>
>   **(ii)** The refusal to hire an individual based on stereotyped characterizations of the sexes. Such stereotypes include, for example, that men are less capable of assembling intricate equipment: that women are less capable of aggressive salesmanship. The principle of non-discrimination requires that individuals be considered on the basis of individual capacities and not on the basis of any characteristics generally attributed to the group.
>
>   **(iii)** The refusal to hire an individual because of the preferences of coworkers, the employer, clients or customers except as covered specifically in subparagraph (2) of this paragraph.
>
> **(2)** Where it is necessary for the purpose of authenticity or genuineness, the Commission will consider sex to be a bona fide occupational qualification, e.g., an actor or actress.

The situations in which employers raise the BFOQ exception normally fall within three general categories:

1. Ability to perform (e.g., physical ability to perform jobs that involve strenuous manual labor).

2.   Same-sex BFOQ that relates to accommodating the personal privacy of clients and customers.

3.   Customer preference BFOQ where the customer states a desire to be served only by person of a given sex.

However, the courts have very narrowly interpreted the sex discrimination defenses based on the BFOQ exception. For example, the courts permitted a same-sex BFOQ in a job that involved a potential invasion of another person's privacy in the *City of Philadelphia* v. *Pennsylvania Human Relations Commission.*[2] The city, in operating youth study centers, restricted the employment of youth supervisors to persons of the same sex as those being supervised. On the other hand, however, in *Ludtke* v. *Kuhn,*[3] the courts ruled that female reporters could not be excluded from a baseball team's postgame locker room since an interview area could be set up providing equal access for all reporters while protecting the privacy interests of the male ballplayers.

In the area of ability to perform the job, the BFOQ defense has generally been rejected. The courts have usually held that each individual job applicant should be permitted an opportunity to demonstrate the ability to perform. Customer preference has also generally been rejected as a BFOQ defense.

Age may be used as a BFOQ in certain limited situations. For example, age may be a BFOQ when public safety is involved, such as with airline pilots or interstate bus drivers.

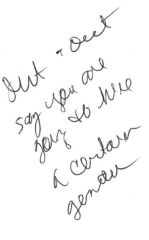

Business Necessity

Business necessity comes into play when an employer has a job specification that is neutral but excludes members of one sex at a higher rate than members of the other. The focus in business necessity is on the validity of various stated job specifications and their relationship to the work performed. For example, in using a business necessity defense, an employer would be required to provide that the ability to lift 100 pounds is necessary in performing a warehouse job.

When a BFOQ is established, an employer can refuse to consider all persons of the protected group. When business necessity is established, an employer can exclude all persons who do not meet specifications regardless of whether the specifications have an adverse impact on a protected group.

Business necessity
Condition that comes into play when an employer has a job criterion that is neutral but excludes members of one sex at a higher rate than members of the opposite sex. The focus in business necessity is on the validity of stated job qualifications and their relationship to the work performed.

Sexual Harassment

One of the more current issues in equal employment opportunity is **sexual harassment**. The EEOC *Guidelines on Discrimination because of Sex* define as unlawful any unwelcome sexual conduct that "has the purpose or effect of unreasonably interfering with an individual's work performance or creating an intimidating, hostile, or offensive work environment." Section 1604.11 of the *Guidelines* is reproduced in Figure 3–4.

Sexual harassment
Unwelcome sexual conduct that has the purpose or effect of unreasonably interfering with an individual's work performance or creating an intimidating, hostile, or offensive work environment.

▼ **Figure 3–4**   EEOC's sex discrimination guidelines

(a) Harassment on the basis of sex is a violation of Sec. 703 of Title VII. Unwelcome sexual advances, requests for sexual favors, and other verbal or physical conduct of a sexual nature constitute sexual harassment when (1) submission to such conduct is made either explicitly or implicitly a term or condition of an individual's employment, (2) submission to or rejection of such conduct by an individual is used as the basis for employment decisions affecting such individual, or (3) such conduct has the purpose or effect of unreasonably interfering with an individual's work performance or creating an intimidating, hostile, or offensive working environment.

(b) In determining whether alleged conduct constitutes sexual harassment, the Commission will look at the record as a whole and at the totality of the circumstances, such as the nature of the sexual advances and the context in which the alleged incidents occurred. The determination of the legality of a particular action will be made from the facts, on a case by case basis.

(c) Applying general Title VII principles, an employer, employment agency, joint apprenticeship committee or labor organization (hereinafter collectively referred to as "employer") is responsible for its acts and those of its agents and supervisory employees with respect to sexual harassment regardless of whether the specific acts complained of were authorized or even forbidden by the employer and regardless of whether the employer knew or should have known of their occurrence. The Commission will examine the circumstances of the particular employment relationship and the job functions performed by the individual in determining whether an individual acts in either a supervisory or agency capacity.

(d) With respect to conduct between fellow employees, an employer is responsible for acts of sexual harassment in the workplace where the employer (or its agents or supervisory employees) knows or should have known of the conduct, unless it can show that it took immediate and appropriate corrective action.

(e) An employer may also be responsible for the acts of non-employees, with respect to sexual harassment of employees in the workplace, where the employer (or its agents or supervisory employees) knows or should have known of the conduct and fails to take immediate and appropriate corrective action. In reviewing these cases the Commission will consider the extent of the employer's control and any other legal responsibility which the employer may have with respect to the conduct of such non-employees.

(f) Prevention is the best tool for the elimination of sexual harassment. An employer should take all steps necessary to prevent sexual harassment from occurring, such as affirmatively raising the subject, expressing strong disapproval, developing appropriate sanctions, informing employees of their right to raise and how to raise the issue of harassment under Title VII, and developing methods to sensitize all concerned.

(g) Other related practices: Where employment opportunities or benefits are granted because of an individual's submission to the employer's sexual advances or requests for sexual favors, the employer may be held liable for unlawful sex discrimination against other persons who were qualified for but denied that employment opportunity or benefit.

The very nature of sexual harassment sometimes makes it difficult to prove. The fact that such conduct is normally done secretly and outside the employer's wishes and can grow out of or be alleged to grow out of consensual relationships makes the investigation of complaints most difficult. However, the courts, when deciding to impose liability on an employer for a supervisor's sexual harassment, have considered an employer's failure to investigate complaints of sexual harassment as significant.[4]

Furthermore, the difficulty that employees face in proving that an adverse decision was due to their sex and their failure to submit to sexual advances has been relaxed somewhat in favor of plaintiffs. In *Bundy* v. *Jackson*,[5] the District of

▼. HRM in Action 3–1

Sexual Harassment at the SEC

The Securities and Exchange Commission (SEC) was ordered in June 1988 to cease and desist creating and condoning a hostile work environment for women. Catherine A. Broderick had brought a lawsuit arguing that sexual relationships were so common at the SEC that they created an offensive work environment. She further argued women in her office were having affairs with supervisors that led to promotions and pay raises for these female employees. The judge agreed with Ms. Broderick.

Under the settlement, Ms. Broderick was promoted two salary grades and received over $100,000 in back pay based on the salary increases to which she would have been entitled. The SEC also agreed to pay for 208 psychiatric counseling sessions for Ms. Broderick over the following two years and for a job-finding service if she decided to leave the SEC.

Source: Adapted from "SEC Harassment Suit Ends," *The New York Times,* June 17, 1988, p. B4.

Columbia Circuit Court established the allocation of the burden of proof in a sexual harassment case:

1. First, the employee must establish a *prima facie* case by providing that he or she was (*a*) subjected to sexual harassment and (*b*) denied a benefit for which he or she was eligible and of which he or she had a reasonable expectation.

2. The burden then shifts to the employer to prove, by clear and convincing evidence, that its decision was based on legitimate, nondiscriminatory grounds.

3. If the employer succeeds in meeting that stringent burden, the employee may then attempt to prove that the employer's stated reasons are pretextual.

Many employers have implemented measures designed to avoid sexual harassment. Developing policies prohibiting sexual harassment and promptly investigating and responding to complaints of sexual harassment are essential to its prohibition. At a minimum, an organization's policy on sexual harassment should (1) define and prohibit sexual harassment and (2) encourage any employee who believes that he or she has been a victim of sexual harassment to come forward to express those complaints to management. HRM in Action 3–1 illustrates sexual harassment problems at the Securities and Exchange Commission.

Comparable Worth and Equal Pay Issues

A controversial issue in equal employment opportunity is the **"comparable worth" theory**. This theory holds that every job by its very nature has a worth to the employer and society that can be measured and assigned a value. Each job should be compensated on the basis of its value and paid the same as other jobs with the same value. Under this theory, market factors such as availability of qualified workers and wage rates paid by other employers would be disregarded.

Comparable worth theory
The idea that every job has a worth to the employer and society that can be measured and assigned a value.

This theory further holds that entire classes of jobs are traditionally undervalued and underpaid because they are held by women and that this inequality amounts to sex discrimination in violation of Title VII of the Civil Rights Act.

Proponents of this theory argue that the Equal Pay Act offers little protection to women workers because the act only applies to those job classifications in which men and women are employed. Further, the most serious form of wage discrimination occurs when women arrive at the workplace with education, training, and ability equivalent to that of men and are assigned lower-paying jobs that are held mainly by females.

In the 1981 case *Country of Washington* v. *Gunther,*[6] the Supreme Court considered a claim of sex-based wage discrimination between prison matrons and prison guards. Prison matrons were being paid approximately 70 percent of what the guards were being paid. In its decision, the court ruled that sex-based wage discrimination violates Title VII of the Civil Rights Act and that the plaintiffs could file suit under the law, even if the jobs were not equal. However, the court's decision specifically stated that it was not ruling on the comparable worth issue.

In early 1985, EEOC issued its first policy statement on comparable worth, stating that unequal pay for work of a similar value wasn't by itself proof of discrimination. The agency stated that it would not pursue "pure" comparable worth cases but would act in cases where it can be shown that employers intentionally paid different wages to women and men in comparable jobs. The exact meaning of this policy statement can, of course, only be determined by the types of cases subsequently pursued by EEOC.

In *AFSCME* v. *State of Washington,*[7] the employer had conducted a job evaluation but had not adjusted the wage rates in the female-dominated jobs to eliminate the wage differential between males and females. A district court had ordered the employer to make the adjustment partially on the basis of the comparable worth theory. However, this decision was overturned by the Ninth Circuit Court of Appeals.[8] The Circuit Court ruled that the value of a particular job to an employer is but one factor influencing the rate of compensation for that job. Other considerations may include the availability of workers willing to do the job and the effectiveness of collective bargaining in a particular industry. The court went further and said that a state could enact a comparable worth plan if it so chooses.

Furthermore, it is important to note that the parties to the *AFSCME* v. *State of Washington* suit reached an agreement in 1986 settling the dispute. Under the agreement, 35,000 employees in female-dominated jobs will reach pay equity with males in 1992. The estimated cost of the settlement to the state will be $482 million.

Regardless of the court and EEOC decisions, however, organizations can take certain preventive steps to guard against pay inequities:

1. Employers should attempt to avoid overconcentrations of men or women (or members of various minority groups) in particular jobs.

2. Employers should evaluate whether there is any direct evidence of bias in setting wage rates, such as discriminatory statements or admission. If so and if there are also overconcentrations of females in particular jobs, the employer should formulate a new compensation plan to correct the disparity in the future. The outline of any plan, of course, will depend on each employer's particular situation.

3. Employers should resist, as much as possible, the temptation to deviate from an internal job evaluation survey or a market survey because of difficulties encountered in hiring or retaining employees at the rates established by such surveys.

4. An employer that utilizes a certain type of job evaluation system companywide and then deviates from it obviously runs a severe risk. Job evaluation, which is a procedure used to determine the relative worth of different jobs, is discussed in depth in Chapter 13.

5. If an employer uses a job evaluation system or systems, it should constantly monitor the system to determine the average wages that are being paid to men and women for comparable jobs. Any disparities should be examined to see if they are defensible. If not, corrections should be made.

Other Areas of Employment Discrimination

Numerous other issues have arisen in the areas of employment discrimination. This section briefly covers some of these additional issues.

Religion

Title VII, as originally enacted, prohibited discrimination based on religion but did not define the term. The 1972 amendments to Title VII added 701(j):

> The term 'religion' includes all aspects of religious observance and practice, as well as belief, unless an employer demonstrates that he is unable to reasonably accommodate an employee's or prospective employee's religious observance or practice without undue hardship on the conduct of the employer's business.

The most frequent accommodation issue under Title VII's religious discrimination provisions arises from the conflict between religious practices and work schedules. The conflict normally occurs for people who observe their Sabbath from sundown on Friday to sundown on Saturday. EEOC's 1980 *Guidelines on Religious Discrimination* proposes:

1. Arranging for voluntary substitutes with similar qualifications; promoting an atmosphere where such swaps are regarded favorably; and providing a central file, bulletin board, or other means of facilitating the matching of voluntary substitutes.

2. Flexible scheduling of arrival and departure times; floating or optional holidays; flexible work breaks; and using lunch time and other time to make up hours lost due to the observation of religious practices.

3. Lateral transfers or changes in job assignments.

One significant case concerning religious discrimination is *TWA* v. *Hardison*.[9] Larry G. Hardison, a TWA employee whose religion required him to observe his

Sabbath on Saturday, was discharged when he refused to work on Saturdays. Hardison had previously held a job with TWA that allowed him to avoid Saturday work because of his seniority. However, he voluntarily transferred to another job in which he was near the bottom of the seniority list. Due to his low seniority, he was required to work on Saturdays. TWA refused to violate the seniority provisions of the union contract, and also refused to allow him to work a four-day workweek. TWA did agree, however, to permit the union to seek a change of work assignments for Hardison, but the union also refused to violate the seniority provisions of the contract.

The Supreme Court upheld the discharge on the grounds that (1) the employer had made reasonable efforts to accommodate the religious needs of the employee, (2) the employer was not required to violate the seniority provisions of the contract, and (3) the alternative plans of allowing the employee to work a four-day workweek would have constituted an undue hardship on the employer.[10]

The Supreme Court's ruling in this case was that an employer must reasonably accommodate religious preferences unless it creates an undue hardship for the employer. Undue hardship was defined as more than a *de minimus* cost; that is, the employer can prove that it has reasonably accommodated a religious preference if it can show that the employee's request would result in more than a small (i.e., *de-minimus*) cost to the employer.

Native Americans (Indians)

Courts have found Native Americans to be protected by Title VII. In addition, Section 703(i) of Title VII benefits Native Americans by exempting them from coverage by the act, in that preferential treatment can be given to Native Americans in certain employment:

> Nothing contained in this title shall apply to any business or enterprise on or near an Indian reservation with respect to any publicly announced employment practice of such business or enterprise under which a preferential treatment is given to any individual because he is an Indian living on or near a reservation.

AIDS

Acquired Immune Deficiency Syndrome (AIDS)
A life-threatening disease that, although not communicable ir most work settings, is causing many work-related debates that have yet to be legally resolved.

In the middle of 1988, the Vocational Rehabilitation Act of 1973 was amended to read that people with contagious diseases are not considered handicapped if their disease neither constitutes a direct threat to the health and safety of other people or makes them unable to perform their job duties. Of course, this change raises several questions relating to **Acquired Immune Deficiency Syndrome (AIDS)** such as: is the employment of an AIDS victim a direct threat to the health and safety of other employees, and aren't people who test positive for AIDS capable of performing most jobs. The issue of AIDS in the workplace will not be resolved in the near future and will likely require additional legislation. HRM in Action 3–2 illustrates Bank America's policy on AIDS and other life-threatening diseases.

▼. **HRM in Action 3–2**

Bank America's Policy on Life-Threatening Illnesses

Bank America's policy statement dealing with employees suffering from life-threatening diseases is as follows:

Bank America recognizes that employees with life-threatening illnesses, including, but not limited to, cancer, heart disease, and AIDS, may wish to continue to engage in as many of their normal pursuits as their condition allows, including work.

As long as these employees are able to meet acceptable performance standards, and medical evidence indicates that their conditions are not a threat to themselves or others, managers should be sensitive to their conditions and ensure that they are treated consistently with other employees.

At the same time, Bank America seeks to provide a safe work environment for all employees and customers. Therefore, precautions should be taken to ensure that an employee's condition does not present a health and/or safety threat to other employees or customers.

Source: Adapted from Michael D. Whitty, "AIDS, Labor Law, and Good Management," *Labor Law Journal*, March 1989, p. 185.

Sexual Preference

The EEOC and the courts have uniformly held that Title VII does not prohibit employment discrimination against effeminate males or against homosexuals.[11] Courts have also held uniformly that adverse action against individuals who undergo or announce an intention to undergo sex-change surgery does not violate Title VII.[12] Therefore, people who fall in those groups are protected only when a local or state statute is enacted to protect them. Furthermore, some court cases have argued that such people are protected by the due process, equal protection, and right-to-privacy provisions of the U.S. Constitution. More court cases, however, must be decided before a clear picture can be gained concerning discrimination against people in these groups.

● *Summary of Learning Objectives*

1. Explain the role of the Employer Information Report, EEO–1.

   This report, also known as *Standard Form 100,* must be completed by employers with 100 or more employees. It requires a breakdown of the employer's work force in specific job categories by race, sex, and national origin.

2. Define employment parity, occupational parity, systemic discrimination, underutilization, and concentration.

   When employment parity exists, the proportion of minorities and women employed by an organization equals the proportion in the organization's relevant labor market. Occupational parity exists when the proportion of minorities and women employed in various occupations within an organization is equal to their proportion in the organization's relevant labor market. Large differences in either occupational or employment parity are called systemic discrimination. Underutilization refers to the practice of having fewer minorities or females in a particular job category than would reasonably be expected when compared to their presence in the relevant labor market. Concentration means having more minorities and women in a job category or department than would reasonably be expected when compared to their presence in the relevant labor market.

3. Describe an affirmative action plan.

    This is a written document outlining specific goals and timetables for remedying past discriminatory actions.

4. Define bona fide occupational qualification (BFOQ).

    BFOQ permits employers to use religion, age, sex, or national origin as a factor in their employment practices when it is reasonably necessary to the normal operation of that particular business.

5. Explain business necessity.

    Business necessity comes into play when an employer has a job requirement that is neutral but which excludes members of one sex at a higher rate than members of the other.

6. Define sexual harassment.

    Sexual harassment is any unwelcome sexual conduct that has the purpose or effect of unreasonably interfering with an individual's work performance or creating an intimidating, hostile, or offensive work environment.

7. Describe the comparable worth theory.

    This theory holds that every job by its very nature has a worth to the employer and society that can be measured and assigned a value.

Review Questions

1. What legal powers does the EEOC have?
2. Explain the purpose of the Employer Information Report, EEO–1.
3. What is an applicant flow record?
4. Outline the steps involved in processing a discrimination charge.
5. What is an affirmative action plan?
6. What is a BFOQ?
7. Define business necessity as it relates to equal employment opportunity.
8. Outline what actions constitute sexual harassment.
9. Explain comparable worth.
10. What steps can be taken to eliminate pay inequities?
11. Explain the amendment to the Vocational Rehabilitation Act that changed the definition of *handicapped*.

Discussion Questions

1. "Affirmative action programs should be eliminated." Discuss your views on this statement.
2. "Comparable worth is an absurd idea." Discuss your views on this statement.

3. "We protect too many classes of people. Why can't we just let employers hire the best person for the job?" Discuss your views on these statements.

4. List several jobs for which you feel age or sex would be a BFOQ. Be prepared to discuss these jobs and your reasons for feeling that age or sex is a BFOQ.

▼ *INCIDENT 3–1*

Affirmative Action

Allen Russell was attending a management development program offered by his company, Southwestern Gas Company. Allen considered this an honor because only a small number of managers are selected for the program each year. The program consists of two sessions, each lasting for one week. The first week consists mostly of classroom training with very little class participation.

At the end of the first week, Southwestern's personnel director Larry Rankin announced that each of the participants would be required to make a 30-minute presentation to the group during the second week of the program. He stated that the subject should be of interest to managers at Southwestern and that each person would be graded on the presentation. Larry asked that each of the participants inform him of their topic within two days.

Allen knew it was important that he do a good job in this presentation if he wanted to move up at Southwestern. After thinking it over, Allen decided to talk about Southwestern's affirmative action program and the manager's role in the program. When Allen called Larry to give him his topic, Larry was delighted. He told Allen, "You know, the affirmative action program is very important, and I don't believe most managers understand their role in it. I'll really be looking forward to hearing your presentation."

Questions

1. Do you think most managers understand their role in affirmative action programs? Why or why not?
2. If you were Allen, what points would you cover in the presentation?

▼ *INCIDENT 3–2*

Religion and Real Estate

Gloria and Robert Sapp, who run a real estate agency, are active Seventh-Day Adventists, as are most of the other employees of the agency.

Ruth Armon, who described herself as a lapsed Lutheran at the time of her employment at the agency, states that she was emotionally upset at being unable to "tune out" statements directed to her about coming catastrophes, devil worship by Christian religions, and the asserted inadequacies of her personal religious observances.

She states that she became a target for statements critical of her beliefs and was told by Gloria Sapp that exposure to such statements was unavoidable in that workplace.

After eight months, Ruth Armon says, she had an argument with Robert Sapp growing out of her complaints about the religious talk and left the job, believing she was fired.

Questions

1. Does Ruth Armon have legitimate grounds for filing a religious discrimination case?
2. Should employees have a right to discuss their religious beliefs on the job?

Exercise

Affirmative Action Debate

Break the class into teams of four to five students. Each team should prepare to debate one of the following statements:

1. The federal government should not require affirmative action programs for private enterprise organizations that are federal contractors or subcontractors.
2. Affirmative action programs have been very helpful to minorities and women. Private enterprise organizations should be required to have affirmative action programs.

After the debate, the instructor should list on the board the points made by each team and discuss the issues involved.

Exercise

The Layoff

Two years ago, your organization experienced a sudden increase in its volume of work. At about the same time, it was threatened with an equal employment opportunity suit that resulted in an affirmative action plan. Under this plan, additional women and minority members have been recruited and hired.

Presently, the top level of management in your organization is anticipating a decrease in volume of work. You have been asked to rank the clerical employees of your section in the event that a layoff is necessary.

Below you will find biographical data for the seven clerical people in your section. Rank the seven people. Rank them according to the order in which they should be laid off, that is, the person ranked first is to be laid off first, etc.

Burt Greene: White male, age 45. Married, four children; five years with the organization. Reputed to be an alcoholic; poor work record.

Nan Nushka: White female, age 26. Married, no children, husband has a steady job; six months with the organization. Hired after the affirmative action plan went into effect; average work record to date. Saving to buy a home.

Johnny Jones: Black male, age 20. Unmarried: one year with organization. High performance ratings. Reputed to be shy—a "loner"; wants to start his own business some day.

Joe Jefferson: White male, age 24. Married, no children but wife is pregnant; three years with organization. Going to college at night; erratic performance attributed to work/study conflicts.

Livonia Long: Black female, age 49. Widow, three grown children; two years with the organization. Steady worker whose performance is average.

Ward Watt: White male, age 30. Recently divorced, one child; three years with the organization. Good worker.

Rosa Sanchez: Hispanic female, age 45. Six children, husband disabled one year ago; trying to help support her family; three months with the organization. No performance appraisal data available.

Questions

1. What criteria did you use for ranking the employees?
2. What implications does your ranking have in the area of affirmative action?

Notes and Additional Readings

1. *Affirmative Action and Equal Employment,* Vol. 1 (Washington, D.C.: U.S. Equal Employment Opportunity Commission, 1974), pp. 10–11.
2. 7 Pa. Commw. Ct. 500, 300 A. 2d 97, 5 FEP 649 (Commw. Ct. 1973).
3. 461 F. Supp. 86, 18 FEP 246 (S.D.N.Y. 1978).
4. *Mumford* v. *James T. Barnes & Co.,* 441 F. Supp. 459, 17 FEP 107 (E.D. Mich. 1977).
5. 641 F. wd 934, 24 FEP 1155 (D.C. Cir. 1981).
6. *County of Washington* v. *Gunther,* 101 Sup. Ct. 2242 (1981).
7. *AFSCME* v. *State of Washington,* 32 FEP (BNA) 1577, Western District of Washington, September 16, 1983.
8. *AFSCME* v. *State of Washington,* CA-9, September 4, 1985.
9. 432 U.S. 63 (1977).
10. See also James G. Frierson, "Religion in the Workplace," *Personnel Journal,* July 1988, pp. 60–67.
11. Barbara L. Schlei and Paul Grossman, *Employment Discrimination Law,* 2nd ed. (Washington, D.C.: Bureau of National Affairs, 1983, p. 436.
12. Ibid.

On the Job

Preemployment Inquiry Guide*

This guide is *not* a complete definition of what can and cannot be asked of applicants. It is illustrative and attempts to answer the questions most frequently asked about equal employment opportunity law. It is hoped that in most cases the given rules, either directly or by analogy, will guide all personnel involved in the preemployment processes of recruiting, interviewing, and selection. This guide pertains only to inquiries, advertisements, etc., directed to all applicants prior to employment. Information required for records such as race, sex, and number of dependents may be requested after the applicant is on the payroll, provided such information is not used for any subsequent discrimination, as in upgrading or layoff.

These laws are not intended to prohibit employers from obtaining sufficient job-related information about applicants, as long as the questions do not elicit information which could be used for discriminatory purposes. Applicants should not be encouraged to volunteer potentially prejudicial information. The laws do not restrict the rights of employers to define qualifications necessary for satisfactory job performance, but require that the same standard of qualifications used for hiring be applied to all persons considered for employment.

It is recognized that the mere routine adherence to these laws will not accomplish the results intended by the courts and Congress. Employment discrimination can be eliminated only if the laws and regulations are followed in the spirit in which they were conceived.

Subject	Permissible Inquiries	Inquiries to be Avoided
1. Name	"Have you worked for this company under a different name? Is any additional information relative to change of name, use of an assumed name or nickname necessary to enable a check on your work and educational record? If yes, explain."	Inquiries about name that would indicate applicant's lineage, ancestry, national origin, or descent. Inquiry into previous name of applicant where it has been changed by court order or otherwise. Inquiries about preferred courtesy title: Miss, Mrs., Ms.

*Source: C. M. Koen, Jr., "The Pre-Employment Inquiry Guide," *Personnel Journal,* October 1980, pp. 826–28. Copyright *Personnel Journal,* reprinted with permission. All rights reserved.

Subject	Permissible Inquiries	Inquiries to be Avoided
2. Marital and family status	Whether applicant can meet specified work schedules or has activities, commitments, or responsibilities that may hinder the meeting of work attendance requirements. Inquiries as to duration of stay on job or anticipated absences that are made to males and females alike.	Any inquiry indicating whether an applicant is married, single, divorced, engaged, etc. Number and age of children. Information on child-care arrangements. Any questions concerning pregnancy. Any such questions which directly or indirectly result in limitation of job opportunities.
3. Age	Requiring proof of age in the form of a work permit or a certificate of age—if a minor. Requiring proof of age by birth certificate after being hired. Inquiry as to whether or not the applicant met the minimum age requirements as set by law, and requirement that upon hire proof of age must be submitted in the form of a birth certificate or other forms of proof of age. If age is a legal requirement, "if hired, can you furnish proof of age?" or statement that hire is subject to verification of age. Inquiry as to whether or not an applicant is younger than the employer's regular retirement age.	Requirement that applicant state age or date of birth. Requirement that applicant produce proof of age in the form of a birth certificate or baptismal record. The Age Discrimination in Employment Act (ADEA) of 1967 forbids discrimination against persons who are 40 years of age but less than 70. An amendment to the ADEA that took effect in 1987 eliminated mandatory retirement at age 70 for employees of companies with 20 or more employees.
4. Handicaps	For employers subject to the provisions of the Rehabilitation Act of 1973, applicants may be "invited" to indicate how and to what extent they are handicapped. The employer must indicate that: (1) compliance with the invitation is voluntary; (2) the information is being sought only to remedy discrimination or provide opportunities for the handicapped; (3) the information will be kept confidential; and (4) refusing to provide the information will not result in adverse treatment. All applicants can be asked if they are able to carry out all necessary job assignments and perform them in a safe manner.	An employer must be prepared to prove that any physical and mental requirements for a job are due to "business necessity" and the safe performance of the job. Except in cases where undue hardship can be proved, employers must make "reasonable accommodations" for the physical and mental limitations of an employee or applicant. "Reasonable accommodation" includes alteration of duties, alteration of work schedule, alteration of physical setting, and provision of aids. The Rehabilitation Act of 1973 forbids employers from asking job applicants general questions about whether they are handicapped or asking them about the nature and severity of their handicaps.

Subject	Permissible Inquiries	Inquiries to be Avoided
5. Sex	Inquiry or restriction of employment is permissible only where a bona fide occupational qualification exists. (This BFOQ exception is interpreted very narrowly by the courts and the EEOC.) The burden of proof rests on the employer to prove that the BFOQ does exist and that *all* members of the affected class are incapable of performing the job. Sex of applicant may be requested (preferably not on the employment application) for affirmative action purposes but may not be used as an employment criterion.	Sex of applicant. Any other inquiry which would indicate sex. Sex is *not* a BFOQ because a job involves physical labor (such as heavy lifting) beyond the capacity of *some* women, and employment cannot be restricted just because the job is traditionally labeled "men's work" or "women's work." Applicant's sex cannot be used as a factor for determining whether or not an applicant will be satisfied in a particular job. Questions about an applicant's height or weight, unless demonstrably necessary as requirements for the job.
6. Race or color	General distinguishing physical characteristics such as scars, etc., to be used for identification purposes. Race may be requested (preferably not on the employment application) for affirmative action purposes but may not be used as an employment criterion.	Applicant's race. Color of applicant's skin, eyes, hair, etc., or other questions directly or indirectly indicating race or color.
7. Address or duration of residence	Applicant's address. Inquiry into length of stay at current and previous addresses. "How long a resident of this state or city?"	Specific inquiry into foreign address which would indicate national origin. Names and relationship of persons with whom applicant resides. Whether applicant owns or rents home.
8. Birthplace	"Can you after employment submit a birth certificate or other proof of U.S. citizenship?"	Birthplace of applicant. Birthplace of applicant's parents, spouse, or other relatives. Requirement that applicant submit a birth certificate before employment. Any other inquiry into national origin.
9. Religion	An applicant may be advised concerning normal hours and days of work required by the job to avoid possible conflict with religious or other personal conviction. However, except in cases where undue hardship can be proven, employers and unions must make "reasonable accommodation" for religious practices of an employee or prospective employee.	Applicant's religious denomination or affiliation, church, parish, pastor, or religious holidays observed. Any inquiry to indicate or identify religious denomination or customs. Applicants may not be told that any particular religious groups are required to work on their religious holidays.

Subject	Permissible Inquiries	Inquiries to be Avoided
	"Reasonable accommodation" may include voluntary substitutes, flexible scheduling, lateral transfer, change of job assignments, or the use of an alternative to payment of union dues.	
10. Military record	Type of education and experience in service as it relates to a particular job.	Type of discharge.
11. Photograph	May be required for identification after hiring.	Requirement that applicant affix a photograph to the application. Request that applicant, at his or her option, submit photograph. Requirement of photograph after interview but before hiring.
12. Citizenship	"Are you a citizen of the United States?" "Do you intend to remain permanently in the U.S.?" "If not a citizen, are you prevented from becoming lawfully employed because of visa or immigration status?" Statement that, if hired, applicant may be required to submit proof of citizenship.	"Of what country are you a citizen?" Whether applicant or parents or spouse are naturalized or native-born U.S. citizens. Date when applicant or parents or spouse acquired U.S. citizenship. Requirement that applicant produce naturalization papers. Whether applicant's parents or spouse are citizens of the United States.
13. Ancestry or national origin	Languages applicant reads, speaks, or writes fluently (if another language is necessary to perform the job).	Inquiries into applicant's lineage, ancestry, national origin, descent, birthplace, or native language.
14. Education	Applicant's academic, vocational, or professional education; school(s) attended. Inquiry into language skills such as reading, speaking, and writing foreign languages.	Any inquiry asking specifically the nationality, racial, or religious affiliation of a school. Inquiry as to how foreign language ability was acquired.
15. Experience	Applicant's work experience, including names and addresses of previous employers, dates of employment, reasons for leaving, salary history. Other countries visited.	
16. Conviction, arrest, and court record	Inquiry into actual *convictions* that relate reasonably to fitness to perform a particular job. (A conviction is a court ruling where the party is found guilty as charged. An arrest is merely the apprehending or detaining of the person to answer the alleged crime.)	Any inquiry relating to arrests. Any inquiry into or request for a person's arrest, court, or conviction record if not *substantially related* to functions and responsibilities of the particular job in question.

Subject	Permissible Inquiries	Inquiries to be Avoided
17. Relatives	Names of applicant's relatives already employed by this company. Names and address of parents or guardian (if applicant is a minor).	Name or address of any relative of adult applicant.
18. Notify in case of emergency	Names and addresses of persons to be notified in case of accident or emergency.	Name and address of *relatives* to be notified in case of accident or emergency.
19. Organizations	Inquiry into any organizations that an applicant is a member of, providing the name or character of the organizations does not reveal the race, religion, color, or ancestry of the membership. "List all professional organizations to which you belong. What offices do you hold?"	"List all organizations, clubs, societies, and lodges to which you belong." The names of organizations to which the applicant belongs, if such information would indicate through character or name the race, religion, color, or ancestry of the membership.
20. References	"By whom were you referred for a position here?" Names of persons willing to provide professional and/or character references for applicant.	Requiring the submission of a religious reference. Requesting reference from applicant's pastor.
21. Credit rating	None.	Any questions concerning credit rating, charge accounts, etc. Ownership of car.
22. Miscellaneous	Notice to applicants that any misstatements or omissions of material facts in the application may be cause for dismissal.	Any inquiry should be avoided that, although not specifically listed among the above, is designed to elicit information concerning race, color, ancestry, age, sex, religion, handicap, or arrest and court record, unless based upon a bona fide occupational qualification.

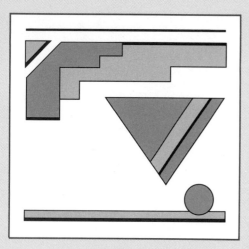

Section 2

Staffing the Organization

Chapter 4
Job Design and Job Analysis

 Chapter 5
Human Resource Planning

 Chapter 6
Recruiting Employees

Chapter 7
Selecting Employees

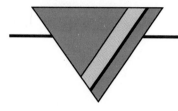

Chapter 4

Job Design and Job Analysis

Chapter Outline

Basic Terminology
Job Design
    Job Content
    Design Guidelines
    The Physical Work Environment
    Sociotechnical Approach to Job Design
Job Analysis
    Uses of Job Analysis
    Products of Job Analysis
    Job Analysis Methods
    Potential Problems with Job Analysis
Summary of Learning Objectives
Review Questions

Discussion Questions
Incident 4–1: The Tax Assessor's Office
Incident 4–2: Turnover Problems
Exercise: Performing a Job Analysis
Notes and Additional Readings
On the Job: A Sample Job Description
On the Job: Sample Job Analysis Questionnaire

● *Learning Objectives*

After studying this chapter, you should be able to:

1. Distinguish among a position, a job, and an occupation.
2. Explain and summarize the job design process.
3. Define job scope and job depth and explain their relationships to job content.
4. Distinguish among job rotation, job enlargement, and job enrichment.
5. Explain the sociotechnical approach to job design.
6. Recount several of the most common uses of a job analysis.
7. Define job description and job specification.
8. List four of the most frequently used methods of job analysis.
9. Interpret the nine-digit code used in the *Dictionary of Occupational Titles*.
10. List several frequently encountered problems associated with job analyses.

"I dare say that you think there is no science in shoveling dirt, that any one can shovel dirt. 'Why,' you say, 'to shovel it you just shovel, that is all there is to it.' Those who have had anything to do with Scientific Management realize, however, that there is a best way in doing everything."

*Frederick W. Taylor**

Organizing
Process that involves the grouping of activities necessary to attain common objectives and the assignment of each grouping to a manager who has the authority necessary to supervise the people performing the activities.

Job design
Defines the specific work activities of an individual or group of individuals.

Micromotion
Simplest unit of work; involves very elementary movements such as reaching, grasping, positioning, or releasing an object.

Element
An aggregation of two or more micromotions; usually thought of as a complete entity, such as picking up or transporting an object.

Organizations provide the means for accomplishing work that could not be completed by individuals working separately. The process of **organizing** is the grouping of activities necessary to attain common objectives and the assignment of each grouping to a manager who has the authority necessary to supervise the people performing the activities.[1] Thus, organizing is basically a process of division of labor accompanied by appropriate delegation of authority. The manner and degree of division of labor define the jobs in an organization.

Labor can be divided either vertically or horizontally. Vertical division of labor is based on the establishment of lines of authority and defines the levels that make up the organizational structure. In addition to establishing the lines of authority, vertical division of labor facilitates the flow of communication within the organization.

Horizontal division of labor is based on specialization of work. The basic assumption underlying this division is that by making each worker's task specialized, more work can be produced with the same effort through increased efficiency and quality. HRM in Action 4–1 discusses a very early example of specialization.

Job design is the process of structuring work to achieve the objectives of the business plan.[2] Structuring the work of an organization is a continuous process of dividing activities, assigning responsibility to groups or individuals, coordinating performance, and specifying the relationships among the jobs created. The structure of an organization is reflected in how groups compete for resources, where responsibilities for profits and other performance measures lie, how information is transmitted, and how decisions are made. In addition to clarifying and defining the organization's strategy through the delegation of authority and responsibility, the structure of the organization can either facilitate or inhibit strategy implementation.

Strategic management literature generally supports the thesis that an organization should be structurally designed to implement its current strategy.[3] This ultimately means that *jobs* should be designed so as to facilitate the implementation of the organization's strategy. Human resource managers often are involved in the job design process because of their knowledge concerning skill requirements and labor availability. Thus, human resource managers can guide and assist top level managers in designing the organization's structure.

Because of its impact on motivation, morale, and productivity, job design is an ever-present concern of human resource managers, even when they are not directly involved in the job design process. Human resource managers should always be aware of the impact that a job's design has on the jobholder.

*Source: F. W. Taylor, "The Principles of Scientific Management," in *Addresses and Discussions at the Conference on Scientific Management* (Hanover, N.H.: Dartmouth College, 1913), p. 36.

▼. HRM in Action 4–1

Adam Smith and the Division of Labor

The division of labor was of concern to managers at least as early as 1776. In *An Inquiry into the Nature and Causes of the Wealth of Nations*, Adam Smith discussed at length the importance of the division of labor and used pin-making as an example of the benefits. According to Smith, the divided labor of pin-making meant that "one man draws out the wire, another straightens it, a third cuts it, a fourth points, a fifth grinds it at the top for receiving the head, and so on. In a factory of ten men, . . . they could, when they exerted themselves, making among them about 12 pounds of pins in a day. There are in a pound upwards of 4,000 pins of middling size." Smith says, "If they had all wrought separately and independently . . . they certainly could not each have made 20, perhaps not 1 pin in a day." Smith concluded that three different circumstances led to the benefits of the division of labor: (1) the increased dexterity of every particular workman, (2) the saving of time lost in moving from one type of work to another, and (3) the invention of machines that enabled one man to do the work of many.

Source: Adam Smith, *An Inquiry into the Nature and Causes of the Wealth of Nations* (Edinburgh, Scotland: Arch. Constable, 1806), pp. 7–8.

Job analysis serves as the cornerstone of all human resource functions. Jobs must be analyzed before many of the other human resource functions can be performed. For example, effective recruitment is not possible unless the recruiter knows and communicates the requirements of the job. Similarly, it is impossible to design basic wage systems without having clearly defined jobs. This chapter examines the methods and techniques used in designing and analyzing jobs.

Task
Consisting of one or more elements, one of the distinct activities that constitute logical and necessary steps in the performance of work by an employee. A task is performed whenever human effort, physical or mental, is exerted for a specific purpose.

Duties
One or more tasks performed in carrying out a job responsibility.

Responsibilities
Obligations to perform certain tasks and assume certain duties.

Position
Collection of tasks and responsibilities constituting the total work assignment of a single employee.

Job
Group of positions that are identical with respect to their major or significant tasks and responsibilities and sufficiently alike to justify their being covered by a single analysis. There may be one or many persons employed in the same job.

Basic Terminology

Today, the word *job* has different meanings depending on how, when, or by whom it is used. It is often used interchangeably with the words *position* and *task*. The Glossary at the end of the book defines the terms frequently encountered in job design and job analysis. Here, we will briefly define some of them, showing how they relate to each other.

The simplest unit of work is the **micromotion**. A micromotion involves a very elementary movement such as reaching, grasping, positioning, or releasing an object. An aggregation of two or more micromotions forms an **element**. An element can be thought of as a complete entity, such as picking up, transporting, and positioning an item. A grouping of work elements makes up a work **task**. Related tasks comprise the **duties** of a job. (Distinguishing between tasks and duties is not always easy. It is sometimes helpful to view tasks as subsets of duties. For example, suppose one duty of a receptionist is to handle all incoming correspondence. One task, as part of this duty, would be to respond to all routine inquiries.) Duties, when combined with **responsibilities** (obligations to be performed), define a **position**. A group of positions that are identical with respect to their major tasks and responsibilities form a **job**. The difference between a position and a job is that a job may be held by more than one person, whereas a position cannot. For example, an organization may have two receptionists performing the same job. However,

▼ **Figure 4–1** Relationships between different job components

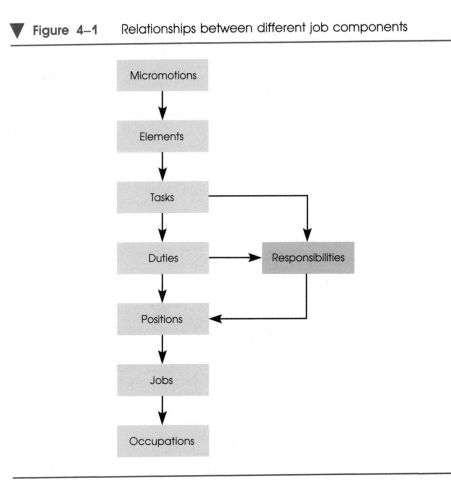

Occupation
A grouping of similar jobs or job classes.

they occupy two separate positions. A group of similar jobs forms an **occupation**. Because the job of receptionist requires similar skill, effort, and responsibility in different organizations, being a receptionist may also be viewed as an occupation. Figure 4–1 graphically shows the relationships between elements, tasks, duties, responsibilities, positions, jobs, and occupations.

Job Design

As mentioned in the introduction, job design is the process of structuring work to achieve the objectives of the business plan. Job design defines the specific work tasks of an individual or group of individuals. It answers the questions of how the job is to be performed, who is to perform it, and where it is to be performed. Figure 4–2 outlines the different components of the job design process. These different components all come together to form the job structure.

The job design process can generally be divided into three phases:

1. The specification of individual tasks. What different tasks must be performed?

▼ **Figure 4-2**   Components of the job design process

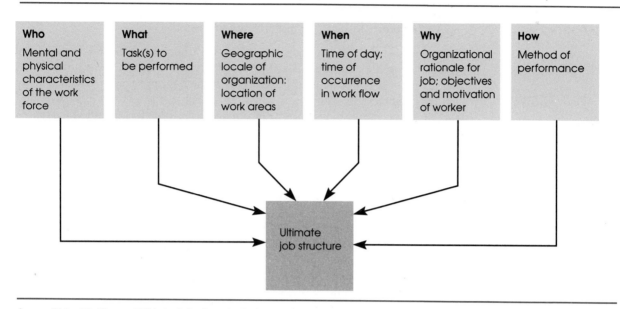

Source: Richard B. Chase and Nicholas J. Aquilano, *Production and Operations Management: A Life-Cycle Approach,* 5th ed. (Homewood, Ill.: Richard D. Irwin, 1989), p. 432.

2. The specification of the method of performing each task. Specifically, how will each task be performed?

3. The combination of individual tasks into specific jobs to be assigned to individuals. How will the different tasks be grouped to form jobs?[4]

Phases 1 and 3 determine the content of the job, while Phase 2 indicates precisely how the job is to be performed.

Job Content

For many years, the prevailing practice in designing the content of jobs was to focus almost totally on the types of tasks performed in the job. This usually meant minimizing short-run costs by minimizing the time it took to produce each unit. The easiest and most convenient way of minimizing the unit production time was usually to make jobs as specialized as possible.

Job Specialization

The basic idea behind specialization is to produce more work with the same effort through increased efficiency. Specifically specialization can result in the following advantages:

1. Fewer skills required per person, which makes it easier to recruit and train employees.

2. Increased proficiency through repetition and practice of the same tasks.

3. More efficient use of skills by primarily utilizing each employee's best skills.

④ Low wages, due to the ease with which labor can be substituted.

⑤ More conformity in the final product or service.

⑥ Different tasks can be performed concurrently.

The major problem with specialization is that it can result in boredom and even degradation of the employee. A vivid example of specialization is the automobile assembly line. It is not hard to imagine the behavioral problems associated with such an assembly line. The key is to specialize but not to overdo it. Several approaches for accomplishing this are discussed later in this chapter. HRM in Action 4–2 describes how Volvo has redesigned its assembly lines to overcome many of the traditional problems.

Obviously, specialization is not more efficient or even desirable in all situations. At least two basic requirements must exist for the successful use of specialization: (1) a relatively large volume of work—enough must be produced to allow for specialization and also to keep each worker busy—and (2) stability in the volume of work, worker attendance, quality of raw materials, product/service design, and production technology.

Job Scope and Job Depth

Job scope
Number and variety of different tasks performed by the jobholder.
HORIZ. JOB LOADING

Job depth
Freedom of jobholders to plan and organize their own work, work at their own pace, and move around and communicate.
VERTICAL JOB LOADING

Job scope and job depth are two important dimensions of job content. **Job scope** refers to the number and variety of different tasks performed by the jobholder. In a job with narrow scope, the jobholder performs a few different tasks and repeats these tasks frequently. The negative efforts of jobs limited in scope vary with the jobholder but can result in more errors and lower quality.

Job depth refers to the freedom of jobholders to plan and organize their own work, to work at their own pace, and to move around and communicate as desired. A lack of job depth can result in job dissatisfaction, which can in turn lead to tardiness, absenteeism, and even sabotage.

A job can be high in job scope and low in job depth, or vice versa. For example, newspaper delivery involves the same few tasks each time, but there is considerable freedom in organizing and pacing the work. Therefore, the job is low in scope but high in depth. Of course, many jobs are low (or high) in both job scope and job depth.

Job Rotation, Job Enlargement, and Job Enrichment

Job rotation
Practice of periodically rotating job assignments. In training, requiring an individual to learn several different jobs in a work unit or department and perform each for a specified time period; also called cross training.

Job enlargement
Involves giving a jobholder more tasks of a similar nature to perform.

Job rotation, job enlargement, and job enrichment are three terms that relate directly to job content and are frequently confused. **Job rotation** is periodically rotating work assignments. For instance, an employee in a retail store might work one month as a salesperson, then one month as a cashier. Banks often use job rotation as a means of familiarizing new management trainees with the different operations of the bank. Under this approach, a new trainee may work one month as a teller, one month as a credit analyst, one month as an assistant to a loan officer, and one month as a service representative.

Job enlargement involves adding more tasks of a nature similar to the job. In other words, enlarging a job means increasing the scope. Under job enlargement, the jobholder is given more things to do but the difficulty and responsibility required by the additional tasks do not change significantly. For example, the job of an assembly-line worker might be enlarged by assigning the jobholder more assembly operations of a similar nature. Thus, the job is enlarged in the sense that the jobholder performs a greater number of operations.

▼. HRM in Action 4–2

Job Redesign at Volvo

Volvo attracted international attention in 1974, when it reorganized its new automobile manufacturing plant at Kalmar, Sweden. Instead of using traditional long assembly lines, the Kalmar plant used work groups consisting of about 20 people each. The time required for each worker to complete his or her work cycle increased from 3 minutes to over 20 minutes. By 1980, Volvo reported numerous benefits from these changes in job design: absenteeism and turnover dropped, the number of faults found in final inspection dropped by 39 percent, and hours of work per car decreased by 40 percent.

Based on the positive experiences at Kalmar, Volvo is taking the concept event further at a new plant being built at Udderolla, Sweden. The Udderolla plant will use work teams of 8 to 10 members who will have responsibility for a much greater part of each car system. Work cycles will be almost twice as long as at the Kalmar plant. Each employee will be trained in all operations so that he or she will be able to shift from job to job in order to reduce monotony.

Source: Phil Farish, "Up from Kalmar," *Personnel Administrator,* August 1988, p. 18.

Job enrichment involves upgrading the job by increasing both job scope and job depth. Thus, in addition to adding more operations, an enriched job is made more challenging, requires additional responsibility, and encourages personal growth. For example, a manager's job might be enriched by giving him or her some additional budgetary responsibilities. Job enrichment is discussed in more depth in Chapter 12.

Job enrichment
Involves upgrading the job by increasing both job scope and job depth.

Design Guidelines

The risk of focusing solely on minimizing the tasks performed by a jobholder have already been outlined. Such an approach often results in jobs that are overly routine and repetitive and, hence, boring. The key to avoiding job boredom is to balance concern for specialization with a concern for human needs. Table 4–1 presents some specific guidelines that can help achieve this balance without sacrificing technical efficiency.

The Physical Work Environment

The physical work environment, which includes factors such as temperature, humidity, ventilation, noise, light, and color, can have an impact on the design of jobs. While there are studies that clearly show that adverse physical conditions do have a negative effect on performance, the degree of influence varies from individual to individual. One study investigated 23 basic office variables such as floor space per employee, temperature, lighting, windows, and work space privacy. The study concluded that companies can increase productivity by up to $1,674 per year for each professional and technical employee through improved office design.[5]

The importance of safety considerations in the design process was magnified by the implementation of the Occupational Safety and Health Act (OSHA) in

▼ **Table 4–1**   Practical guidelines for designing jobs

Elements of Workers' Jobs	Suggested Design Guidelines	Workers' Needs Affected
Workers' job tasks (the work itself—arrangement of machines, workplace layouts, work methods, and sequence of work tasks).	1. Avoid machine pacing of workers. Workers should determine, when possible, rates of output.	Control of one's own job.
	2. When practical, combine inspection tasks into jobs so that workers inspect their own output.	Control of own's own job.
	3. Work areas should be designed to allow open communication and visual contact with other workers in adjacent operations.	Socialization.
	4. When economically feasible and generally desired by workers, combine machine changeovers, new job layouts, setups, and other elements of immediate job planning into workers' jobs.	Self-direction/control of one's own job.
Immediate job setting (the management policies and procedures that directly impinge upon employees' jobs).	1. Rotate workers, where practical, between jobs that are repetitive, monotonous, boring, and short cycled.	Variety and relief from boredom and monotony.
	2. Assign new workers to undesirable jobs for fixed periods of time, then transfer them to more preferred jobs.	Equity.
	3. Provide workers with periodic rest periods away from repetitive jobs to relieve monotony.	Relief of boredom and socialization.
	4. Set higher pay rates for undesirable jobs.	Physiological, security, equity, and achievements.

Table 10.14 from *Production and Operations Management: A Problem Solving and Decision Making Approach* by Norman Gaither, copyright © 1980 by The Dryden Press, a division of Holt, Rinehart and Winston, Inc., reproduced by permission of the publisher.

1970. Designed to reduce the incidence of job-related injuries and illnesses, the act outlines very specific federal safety guidelines that must be followed by all organizations in the United States. OSHA is discussed at length in Chapter 19.

In general, the work environment should allow for normal lighting, temperature, ventilation, and humidity. Baffles, acoustical wall materials, and sound absorbers should be used where necessary to reduce unpleasant noises. If employees must be exposed to less than ideal conditions, it is wise to limit these exposures to short periods of time to minimize the probability that the worker will suffer any permanent physical or psychological damage.[6]

Sociotechnical Approach to Job Design

The thrust of the sociotechnical approach to job design is that both the technical system and the accompanying social system should be considered when designing jobs.[7] According to this concept, jobs should be designed by taking a holistic, or systems, view of the entire job situation, including its physical and social environment. The sociotechnical approach is situational because few jobs involve identical technical requirements and social surroundings. Specifically, the sociotechnical approach requires that the job designer carefully consider the role of the employees in the sociotechnical system, the nature of the tasks performed, and the autonomy of the work group. Ideally, the sociotechnical approach merges the technical needs of an organization with the social needs of the employees involved in decision making. Using the sociotechnical approach, the following guidelines have been developed for designing jobs:[8]

1. A job needs to be reasonably demanding for the individual in terms other than sheer endurance, and yet provide some variety (not necessarily novelty).
2. Employees need to be able to learn on the job and to continue learning.
3. Employees need some minimum area of decision-making that they can call their own.
4. Employees need some minimal degree of social support and recognition in the workplace.
5. Employees need to be able to relate what they do and what they produce to their social life.

The sociotechnical approach to job design has been applied in many countries, often under the heading of "autonomous work groups" or "individual democracy" projects.[9] HRM in Action 4–3 describes an innovative new organization founded on sociotechnical principles.

Job analysis is defined as "the process of determining and reporting pertinent information relating to the nature of a specific job. It is the determination of the tasks which comprise the job and of the skills, knowledge, abilities, and responsibilities required of the holder for successful job performance."[10]

> **Job analysis**
> Process of determining and reporting pertinent information relating to the nature of a specific job.

Uses of Job Analysis

As mentioned earlier, job analysis is the cornerstone of all human resource functions. Specifically, data obtained from job analysis forms the basis for a variety of human resource activities.[11] These include:

Job definition. A job analysis results in a description of the duties and responsibilities of the job. Such a description is useful to the current jobholders and their supervisors as well as to prospective employees.

▼. HRM in Action 4–3

Sociotechnical Systems Managers' Network

A new study and experience-sharing organization has been formed with representatives from companies such as ALCOA, AT&T, Anheuser-Busch, Eastman Kodak, General Electric, General Motors, Johnson and Johnson, Nestlé Foods, Shenandoah Life, and Shell Canada Ltd. The group calls itself Sociotechnical Systems Managers' Network. At its inaugural meeting the group identified organization renewal as the issue of greatest concern.

The network is an offshoot of the Productivity Forum, a unit of the Work in America Institute, Inc. The Work in America Institute, Inc., was set up to study management practices for improving output and the quality of work life.

Source: Phil Farish, "New Work Systems Studied," *Personnel Administrator,* July 1988, pp. 19–20.

Recruitment
Process of seeking and attracting a pool of people from which qualified candidates for job vacancies can be chosen.

Selection
Process of choosing from those available the individuals who are most likely to perform successfully in a job.

Orientation
Introduction of new employees to the organization, work unit, and job.

Training
Learning process that involves the acquisition of skills, concepts, rules, or attitudes to increase employee performance.

Job redesign. A job analysis often indicates when a job needs to be redesigned.

Recruitment. Regardless of whether a job to be filled has been in existence or is newly created, its requirement must be defined as precisely as possible for **recruitment** to be effective. A job analysis not only identifies the job requirements but also outlines the skills needed to perform the job. This information helps determine the type of people to recruit.

Selection and placement. **Selection** is basically a matter of properly matching an individual with a job. To be successful in the process, the job and its requirements must be clearly and precisely known. A job analysis determines the importance of different skills and abilities. Once this has been done, comparisons of various candidates can be made more objectively.

Orientation. Effective job **orientation** cannot be accomplished without a clear understanding of the job requirements. The duties and responsibilities of a job must be clearly defined before a new employee can be taught how to perform a job.

Training. Many aspects of **training** are affected by job analysis. Whether or not a current or potential jobholder needs additional training can be decided only after the specific requirements of the job have been determined through a job analysis. Certainly, the establishment of training objectives is dependent on a job analysis. Another training-related use of job analysis is in helping to determine whether a problem is occurring because of a training need or because of some other reason.

Career counseling. Managers and human resource specialists are in a much better position to counsel employees about their careers when they have a complete understanding of the different jobs in the organization. Similarly, employees can better appreciate their career options when they understand the exact requirements of other jobs.

Employee safety. A thorough job analysis often uncovers unsafe practices and/or environmental conditions associated with a job. By focusing precisely on how a job is done, any unsafe procedures usually become evident.

Performance appraisal. The objective of performance appraisal is to evaluate an individual employee's performance on a job. A prerequisite is a thorough

▽. HRM in Action 4–4

Contents of a Job Description

A job description should be a formal written document usually from one to three pages long. It should include the following:

- Date written
- Job status (full time or part time; salary or wage)
- Position title
- Supervision received (to whom the jobholder reports)
- Supervision exercised, if any (who reports to this employee)
- Job summary (a synopsis of the job responsibilities)

- Detailed list of duties and responsibilities
- Principal contacts (in- and outside the company)
- Competency or position requirements
- Required education and experience
- Career mobility (position[s]) that the jobholder may qualify for next)
- Related meetings to be attended/reports to be filed

Source: Judith A. DeLapa, "Job Descriptions that Work," *Personnel Journal,* June 1989, p. 156.

understanding of exactly what the employee is supposed to do. Then and only then can a fair evaluation be made of how an individual is performing.

Compensation. A proper job analysis helps ensure that employees receive fair compensation for their jobs. Job analysis is the first step in determining the relative worth of a job by identifying its level of difficulty, its duties and responsibilities, and the skills and abilities required to perform the job. Once the worth of a job has been established relative to other jobs, an equitable wage or salary schedule can be established.

As can be seen from the above list, almost all human resource functions are dependent to some extent on a sound job analysis program.

When doing a job analysis, the job and its requirements (as opposed to the characteristics of the person currently holding the job) are studied. The tasks that comprise the job are listed and a determination made concerning the skills, personality characteristics, educational background, and training necessary for successfully performing the job. The initial stage of a job analysis should "report the job as it exists at the time of the analysis, not as it should exist, not as it has existed in the past, and not as it exists in similar establishments."[12]

Products of Job Analysis

Job analysis involves not only analyzing job content but also reporting the results of the analysis. These results are normally presented in the form of a job description and a job specification. A job description concentrates on the job. It explains what the job is and what the duties, responsibilities, and general working conditions are. HRM in Action 4–4 elaborates specifically on what a formal job description should contain. A job specification concentrates on the characteristics needed to perform the job. It describes the qualifications that the incumbent must possess to perform the job. Table 4–2 outlines the general information obtained through a job analysis. Figure 4–3 summarizes the information normally contained in a

Job description
Written synopsis of the nature and requirements of a job.

Job specification
Description of the qualifications that a person holding a job must possess to perform the job successfully.

▼ Table 4–2 Information provided by job analysis

Area of information	Contents
Job title and location	Name of job and where it is located.
Organizational relationship	A brief explanation of the number of persons supervised (if applicable) and the job title(s) of the position(s) supervised. A statement concerning supervision received.
Relation to other jobs	Describes and outlines the coordination required by the job.
Job summary	Condensed explanation of the content of the job.
Information concerning job requirements	The content of this area varies greatly from job to job and from organization to organization. Typically, it includes information on such topics as machines, tools, and materials; mental complexity and attention required; physical demands; and working conditions.

▼ Figure 4–3 The components of job descriptions and job specifications

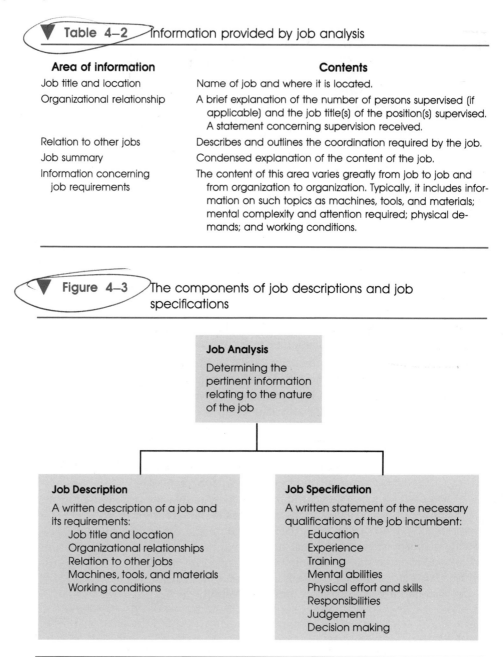

Job Analysis

Determining the pertinent information relating to the nature of the job

Job Description

A written description of a job and its requirements:
  Job title and location
  Organizational relationships
  Relation to other jobs
  Machines, tools, and materials
  Working conditions

Job Specification

A written statement of the necessary qualifications of the job incumbent:
  Education
  Experience
  Training
  Mental abilities
  Physical effort and skills
  Responsibilities
  Judgement
  Decision making

job description and a job specification. On the Job at the end of this chapter contains a sample job description for the human resource manager of a manufacturing plant.

Job Analysis Methods

Several methods are available for conducting a job analysis. Four of the most frequently used methods are discussed below.

Observation

Observation is a method of analyzing jobs that is relatively simple and straight-forward. It can be used independently or in conjunction with other methods of job analysis. With observation, the person making the analysis observes the individual or individuals performing the job and takes pertinent notes describing the work. This information includes such things as what was done, how it was done, how long it took, what the job environment was like, and what equipment was used.

A major drawback is that observation is somewhat limited to jobs involving short and repetitive cycles. Complicated jobs and jobs that do not have repetitive cycles require such a lengthy observation period that direct observation becomes impractical. For example, it would require a tremendous amount of time to observe the work of a traveling salesperson or a lawyer. On the other hand, direct observation can be used to get a feel for a particular job and then be combined with another method for thoroughly analyzing the job. A second drawback is that the observer must be carefully trained to know what to look for and what to record. It is sometimes helpful to use a form with standard categories of information to be filled in as the job is observed. This helps ensure that certain basic information is not omitted.

Interviews

The interview method requires that the person conducting the job analysis meet with and interview the jobholder. Usually, the interview is held at the job site. These interviews can be either structured or unstructured. Unstructured interviews have no definite checklist or preplanned format; the format that is allowed develops as the interview unfolds. In a structured interview, a predesigned format is followed. Structured interviews have the advantage of ensuring that all pertinent aspects of the job are covered. Also, the structured interview makes it easier to compare information obtained from different people holding the same job.

The major drawback to the interview method is that it can be extremely time consuming because of the time required to schedule, get to, and actually conduct the interview. This problem is naturally compounded when several people are interviewed concerning the same job.

Questionnaires

Normally, job analysis questionnaires are three to five pages long and contain both objective and open-ended questions. On the Job at the end of this chapter contains a sample job analysis questionnaire. For existing jobs, the incumbent completes the questionnaire, has it checked by the immediate manager, and returns it to the job analyst. If the job being analyzed is new, the questionnaire normally is sent to the manager who will supervise the employee in the new job. If the job being analyzed is vacant but is duplicated in another part of the organization, the questionnaire is completed by the incumbent in the duplicate job.

The questionnaire method has the advantage of obtaining information from a large number of employees in a relative short time period. Hence, questionnaires are used when a large input is needed and time and cost are limiting factors. A major disadvantage is the possibility of either the respondent or the job analyst misinterpreting the information. Also, questionnaires can be time consuming and expensive to develop.

A popular variation of the questionnaire method is to have the incumbent write an actual description of the job, subject to the approval of the immediate supervisor. A primary advantage of this approach is that the incumbent is often the most knowledgeable about the job. Another benefit is that this method serves as a means of identifying any differences in perceptions held by the incumbent and the manager about the job.[13]

Position Analysis Questionnaire (PAQ).[14]   The Position Analysis Questionnaire involves a highly specialized instrument for analyzing any job in terms of employee activities. Six major categories of employee activities are utilized (see Table 4–3). A total of 194 descriptors, called job elements, describe the six categories in detail. Each descriptor is judged as to the degree that it applies to the job being analyzed.

The primary advantage of the PAQ is that is can be used to analyze almost any type of job. Also, it is relatively easy to use. The major disadvantage is the sheer length of the questionnaire.

Management Position Description Questionnaire (MPDQ).   The MPDQ is a highly structured questionnaire designed specifically for analyzing managerial jobs. It contains 208 items relating to managerial responsibilities, restrictions, demands, and other miscellaneous position characteristics.[15] These 208 items are grouped under the 13 categories shown in Table 4–4. As with the PAQ, the MPDQ requires the analyst to check whether each item is appropriate to the job being analyzed.

Functional Job Analysis

Functional job analysis (FJA) is a job analysis method developed by the United States Training and Employment Service (USTES) of the Department of Labor. FJA uses standardized statements and terminology to describe the content of jobs. The primary premises of FJA include:[16]

1. A fundamental distinction must be made between what gets done and what employees do to get things done. For example, bus drivers do not carry passengers; rather they drive vehicles and collect fares.
2. Jobs are performed in relation to data, people, and things.
3. In relation to things, employees draw on physical resources; in relation to data, employees draw on mental resources; and in relation to people, employees draw on interpersonal resources.
4. All jobs require employees to relate data, people, and things to some degree.
5. Although the behavior of employees and their tasks can be described in numerous ways, there are only a few definitive functions involved. For example, in interacting with machines, employees feed, tend, operate, and/or set up. Although each of these functions occurs over a wide range of difficulty and content, each essentially draws on a relatively narrow and specific range of similar kinds and degrees of employee characteristics and qualifications.
6. The levels of difficulty required in dealing with data, people, and things are hierarchical and can be represented by an ordinal scale.

Table 4–5 defines the levels of difficulty for various jobs with regard to data, people, and things. The lower the number associated with a function, the more

▼ **Table 4–3**) Employee activity categories utilized in the PAQ

Category	Description	Examples
Information input	Where and how does the employee get the information used in performing the job?	Use of written materials. Near-visual differentiation.
Mental processes	What reasoning, decision making, planning, and information-processing activities are involved in performing the job?	Level of reasoning in problem solving. Coding/decoding.
Physical activities	What physical activities does the employee perform, and what tools or devices are used?	Use of keyboard devices. Assembling/disassembling.
Relationships with other people	What relationships with other people are required in performing the job?	Instructing. Contacts with public, customers.
Job context	In what physical or social context is the work performed?	High temperature. Interpersonal conflict situations.
Other job characteristics	What activities, conditions, or characteristics other than those described above are relevant to the job?	Specified work pace. Amount of job structure.

▼ **Table 4–4**) Management position description questionnaire categories

1. Product, marketing, and financial strategy planning.
2. Coordination of other organizational units and personnel.
3. Internal business control.
4. Products and services responsibility.
5. Public and customer relations.
6. Advanced consulting.
7. Autonomy of actions.
8. Approval of financial commitments.
9. Staff service.
10. Supervision.
11. Complexity and stress.
12. Advanced financial responsibility.
13. Broad personnel responsibility.

Source: W. B. Tornov and P. R. Pinto, "The Development of a Managerial Job Taxonomy: A System for Describing, Classifying, and Evaluating Executive Positions," *Journal of Applied Psychology* 61, no. 4 (1976), p. 414.

difficult the function is. For example, synthesizing data (0) is more difficult than compiling data (3). After a job's difficulty has been described using this numerical scheme, the information can be combined with some general information to compare and identify jobs, using the *Dictionary of Occupational Titles* (DOT). Once the closest job in the DOT has been located, the accompanying job description can

▼ Table 4–5   Levels of difficulty for worker functions in FJA

Data	People	Things
0 Synthesizing	0 Mentoring	0 Setting up
1 Coordinating	1 Negotiating	1 Precision working
2 Analyzing	2 Instructing	2 Operating-controlling
3 Compiling	3 Supervising	3 Driving-operating
4 Computing	4 Diverting	4 Manipulating
5 Copying	5 Persuading	5 Tending
6 Comparing	6 Speaking-signaling	6 Feeding-offbearing
	7 Serving	7 Handling
	8 Taking instructions-helping	

Note: The hyphenated factors—speaking-signaling, taking instructions-helping, operating-controlling, driving-operating, and feeding-offbearing—are single functions.

Source: U.S. Department of Labor, *Handbook for Analyzing Jobs* (Washington, D.C.: U.S. Government Printing Office, 1972), p. 73.

▼ Table 4–6   Nine occupational categories used by the DOT

1. Professional, technical, and managerial
2. Clerical and sales
3. Service
4. Agriculture, fishing, forestry, and related
5. Processing
6. Machine trades
7. Bench work
8. Structural work
9. Miscellaneous

then be modified as necessary to fit the specific job being analyzed. At the very least, the DOT job description provides a very good starting point. Functional job analysis has the advantages of being relatively easy to learn and using a standardized format.

Dictionary of Occupational Titles (DOT).   Compiled by the federal government, the DOT classifies and describes approximately 20,000 jobs. A nine-digit code is used to classify each job. The first digit indicates the occupational category, of which there are nine primary categories. (Table 4–6 lists these categories.) The second digit indicates a division within the primary occupational category. For example, occupations in administrative specialization comprise a division within the primary category of professional, technical, and managerial occupations. The third digit indicates the group within the division into which the job is classified. For example, occupations in administrative specialization comprise a division within the primary category of professional, technical, and managerial occupations. The third digit indicates the group within the division into which the job is classified. For example, occupations in personnel administration are a group within the administrative specialization division.

The fourth, fifth, and sixth digits reflect the difficulty on the job with regard

Figure 4–4 Nine-digit code used by the DOT

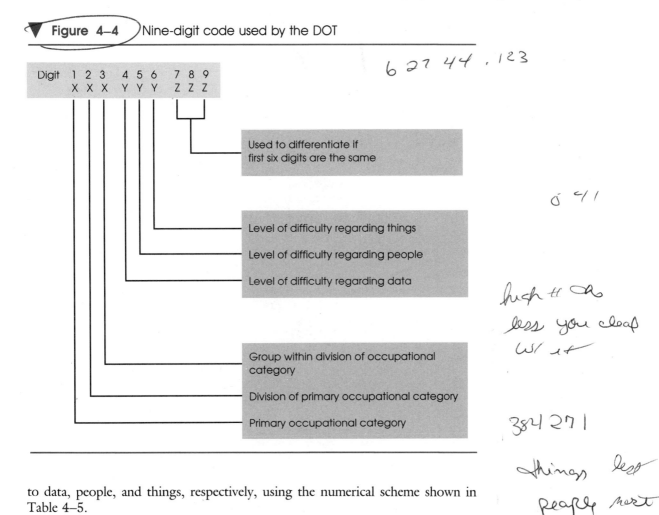

to data, people, and things, respectively, using the numerical scheme shown in Table 4–5.

The last three digits differentiate, in alphabetical order, those jobs that have the same first six digits. Thus, a number of occupations may have the same first six digits, but no two can have the same nine digits. If the first six digits apply to only one occupational title, then the last three digits are always 010. Figure 4–4 summarizes the nine-digit code used to classify jobs. Figure 4–5 shows how a personnel manager is classified by the DOT.

Potential Problems with Job Analysis

In analyzing jobs, certain problems can arise. Some of these result from natural human behavior, others from the nature of the job analysis process. The following section identifies some of the most frequently encountered problems associated with job analyses.[17]

Top management support is missing. Top management should at least make it clear to all employees that their full and honest participation is extremely important to the process. Unfortunately, this message is often not communicated.

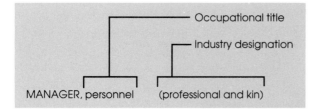

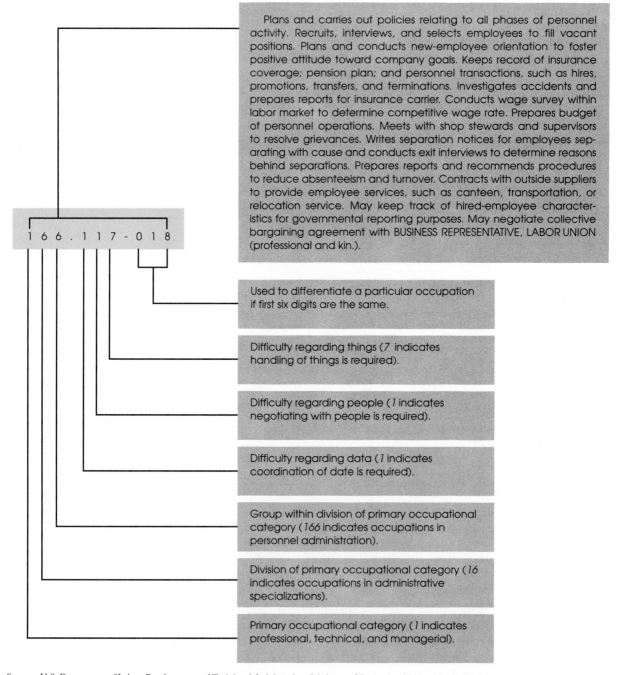

Plans and carries out policies relating to all phases of personnel activity. Recruits, interviews, and selects employees to fill vacant positions. Plans and conducts new-employee orientation to foster positive attitude toward company goals. Keeps record of insurance coverage; pension plan; and personnel transactions, such as hires, promotions, transfers, and terminations. Investigates accidents and prepares reports for insurance carrier. Conducts wage survey within labor market to determine competitive wage rate. Prepares budget of personnel operations. Meets with shop stewards and supervisors to resolve grievances. Writes separation notices for employees separating with cause and conducts exit interviews to determine reasons behind separations. Prepares reports and recommends procedures to reduce absenteeism and turnover. Contracts with outside suppliers to provide employee services, such as canteen, transportation, or relocation service. May keep track of hired-employee characteristics for governmental reporting purposes. May negotiate collective bargaining agreement with BUSINESS REPRESENTATIVE, LABOR UNION (professional and kin.).

Used to differentiate a particular occupation if first six digits are the same.

Difficulty regarding things (7 indicates handling of things is required).

Difficulty regarding people (1 indicates negotiating with people is required).

Difficulty regarding data (1 indicates coordination of date is required).

Group within division of primary occupational category (166 indicates occupations in personnel administration).

Division of primary occupational category (16 indicates occupations in administrative specializations).

Primary occupational category (1 indicates professional, technical, and managerial).

Source: U.S. Department of Labor, Employment and Training Administration, *Dictionary of Occupational Titles*, 4th ed. (Washington, D.C.: U.S. Government Printing Office, 1977).

Only a single means and source are used for gathering data. As discussed previously, there are many proven methods for gathering job data. All too often a job analysis relies on only one of these methods when a combination of methods might provide better data.

The supervisor and job holder do not participate in the design of the job analysis exercise. Too many analyses are planned and implemented by one person who assumes exclusive responsibility for the project. The job holder and his or her supervisor should be involved early in the planning of the project.

No training or motivation for job holders. Job incumbents are potentially a great source of information about the job. Unfortunately, they are seldom trained or prepared to generate quality data for a job analysis. Also, job holders are rarely made aware of the importance of the data and almost never are rewarded for providing good data.

Employees are not allowed sufficient time to complete the analysis. Usually a job analysis is conducted as if it were a crash program and employees are not given sufficient time to do a thorough job analysis.

Activities may be distorted. Without proper training and preparation, employees may submit distorted data—either intentionally or not. For example, employees are likely to speed up if they know they are being watched. Employee involvement from the beginning of the project is a good way to minimize this problem.

There is a failure to critique the job. Many job analyses do not go beyond the initial phase of reporting what the job holder currently does. This data is extremely valuable, but the analysis should not stop here. The job should be critiqued to determine if it is being done correctly or if improvements can be made.

● *Summary of Learning Objectives*

1. Distinguish among a position, a job, and an occupation.

    Job duties, when combined with responsibilities define a position. A group of positions that are identical with respect to their major tasks and responsibilities forms a job. A group of similar jobs forms an occupation.

2. Explain and summarize the job design process.

    Job design defines the specific work tasks of an individual or group of individuals. It answers the questions of how the job is to be performed, who is to perform it, and where it is to be performed. The job design process can generally be divided into three phases: (1) specification of individual tasks, (2) specification of the method of performing each task, and (3) combination of individual tasks into specific jobs to be assigned to individuals.

3. Define job scope and job depth and explain their relationships to job content.

    Job scope refers to the number and variety of different tasks performed by the job holder. Job depth refers to the freedom of job holders to plan and organize their own work, to work at their own pace, and to move around and communicate as desired. Job scope and job depth are both dimensions of job content.

4. Distinguish among job rotation, job enlargement, and job enrichment.

    Job rotation is the process of periodically rotating work assignments. Job enlargement involves adding more tasks of a similar nature to the job. Job enrichment involves upgrading the job by increasing both job scope and job depth.

5. Explain the sociotechnical approach to job design.

    The thrust of the sociotechnical approach to job design is that both the technical system and the accompanying social system should be considered when designing jobs.

6. Recount several of the most common uses of a job analysis.

    Several of the most common uses of job analysis include job definition, job redesign, recruitment, selection and placement, orientation, training, career counseling, employee safety, performance appraisal, and compensation.

7. Define job description and job specification.

    A job description concentrates on the job. It explains what the job is and what the duties, responsibilities, and general working conditions are. A job specification concentrates on the characteristics needed to perform the job. It describes the qualifications that the incumbent must possess to perform the job.

8. List four of the most frequently used methods of job analysis.

    Four of the most frequently used methods of job analysis are observation, interviews, questionnaires, and functional job analysis.

9. Interpret the nine-digit code used in the *Dictionary of Occupational Titles*.

    The first digit indicates the primary occupational category. The second digit indicates a division within the primary occupational category. The third digit indicates the group within the division into which the job is classified. The fourth, fifth, and sixth digits reflect the difficulty of the job with regard to data, people, and things, respectively. The last three digits differentiate, in alphabetical order, those jobs that have the same first six digits.

10. List several frequently encountered problems associated with job analyses.

    Some of the most frequently encountered problems with job analyses include top management support is missing, only a single means and source for gathering data are used, the supervisor and job holder do not participate in the design of the job analysis exercise, no training or motivation is provided, employees are not allowed sufficient time to complete the analysis, job holder activities may be distorted, and there is a failure to critique the job.

Review Questions

1. Describe vertical and horizontal divisions of labor.
2. What are job design and the three phases of the job design process?
3. Explain the difference between job rotation, job enlargement, and job enrichment.
4. Name four different techniques that can be used to design the methods used in performing a job.

5. What is a sociotechnical approach to job design?
6. Define job descriptions and job specifications. How do they relate to the job analysis process?
7. What are the uses of job analysis?
8. Name four of the most frequently used methods for analyzing jobs.
9. What are some potential problems associated with job analysis?

Discussion Questions

1. Discuss the pros and cons of job specialization. In what type of organization would job specialization be most efficient? Most inefficient?
2. Comment on the following statement, which is attributed to Robert Heinlein:

   A human being should be able to change a diaper, plan an invasion, butcher a hog, conn a ship, design a building, write a sonnet, balance accounts, build a wall, set a bone, comfort the dying, take orders, give orders, cooperate, act alone, solve equations, analyze new problems, pitch manure, program a computer, cook a tasty meal, fight efficiently, die gallantly. Specialization is for insects.

3. After completing school, you will probably be entering the work force. What are the implications of job analysis and job design for you?
4. What method of job analysis do you think would be most applicable for jobs in a large grocery store?

▼ INCIDENT 4–1

The Tax Assessor's Office

A workday begins each morning at 8 A.M. in the tax assessor's office. The staff is composed of the director, two secretaries, two clerk-typists, and three file clerks. Until last year, the office operated smoothly with even workloads and well-defined responsibilities.

Over the last year or so, the director has noticed more and more disagreements among the clerk-typists and file clerks. When they approached the director to discuss their disagreements, it was determined that problems have arisen from misunderstandings concerning responsibility for particular duties. There is a strong undercurrent of discontent because the clerk-typists feel the file clerks have too much free time to spend running personal errands and socializing. On the other hand, the secretaries and clerk-typists frequently have to work overtime doing work that they feel could easily be picked up by the file clerks. The file clerks claim they should not have to take on any additional duties, since their paychecks would not reflect the additional responsibilities.

Each person in the office has a general job description that was written several years ago. However, the nature of most positions has changed considerably since then because of the implementation of a computer system. No attempt has been made to put these changes in writing. The director formerly held staff meetings to discuss problems that arose within the office; however, no meetings have been held in several months.

Questions

1. What actions would you recommend to the director?
2. Why do you think that job descriptions are not updated in many organizations?

▼ *INCIDENT 4–2*

Turnover Problems

Ms. Shivers is the manager of a computer division in the federal government. Among her various responsibilities is the central data entry office, with ten GS–4 data entry clerks and one GS–5 supervisor.

The starting salary range for a GS–4 data entry clerk with limited skills is comparable to the starting salary in private industry. However, after about six months of on-the-job experience, most data entry clerks can get a substantial pay increase by taking a job in private industry. It has become common knowledge in industry that Ms. Shivers has a very good training program for data entry clerks and that her division represents a good source of personnel. As a result of this reputation, Ms. Shivers has experienced a heavy turnover during the last several months. In fact, the problem has recently become severe enough to create a tremendous work backlog in her division. In short, she has had to oversee so many trainees that the division's overall productivity has declined.

Within the data entry section are three notable exceptions, who have worked for Ms. Shivers for several years. These three have recently been responsible for most of the work turned out in the division. The GS–5 supervisor has been running the section for five years. Just recently, she informed Ms. Shivers that she has been offered a job with another company with a small pay increase and no supervisory responsibilities.

Ms. Shivers has always felt that the data entry clerks should be upgraded to the GS–5 level and the supervisor's job to GS–6. In fact, on several occasions, Ms. Shivers has mentioned this idea to her boss John Clayton. She believes not only that these jobs should be upgraded but also that this action would go a long way toward solving her turnover problem. Unfortunately, Clayton has never shown much interest in Ms. Shivers' idea.

Questions

1. What do you suggest that Ms. Shivers do to further promote the idea of upgrading the data entry clerk and supervisory positions?
2. Can you think of anything that Ms. Shivers might do from a job design standpoint to help with the turnover problem?

Exercise

Performing a Job Analysis

Use the job analysis questionnaire in On the Job to analyze the most recent job you have held. Your job may have been a summer, part-time, or full-time job. You need not fill in the heading information. After you have completed the questionnaire, answer the following questions:

1. Do you feel that the job analysis questionnaire captured the essence of your job? If not, what was left out?
2. What improvements would you recommend in the job analysis questionnaire?
3. Do you feel that your boss would have answered the questionnaire basically the same way that you did? Why or why not?

Notes and Additional Readings

1. H. Koontz and C. O'Donnell, *Management: A Systems and Contingency Analysis of Managerial Functions,* 6th ed. (New York: McGraw-Hill, 1976), p. 275.
2. Walter L. Polsky and Loretta D. Foxman, "Job Design and Job Evaluation: Surveying New Horizons," *Personnel Journal,* July 1981, p. 36.
3. Leslie W. Rue and Phyllis G. Holland, *Strategic Management: Concepts and Experiences* (New York: McGraw-Hill, 1984), pp. 624–631.
4. L. E. Davis, "Job Design and Productivity: A New Approach," *Personnel,* March 1957, p. 420.
5. "Increasing Worker Productivity and Satisfaction," *Management Review,* April 1983, pp. 5–6.
6. R. A. Johnston, W. T. Newell, and R. C. Vergin, *Production and Operations Management: A Systems Concept* (Boston: Houghton Mifflin, 1974), p. 206.
7. P. B. Vaill, "Industrial Engineering and Socio-Technical Systems," *Journal of Industrial Engineering,* September 1967, p. 535.
8. Louis E. Davis, *Job Satisfaction—A Socio-Technical View,* Report 515-69 (Los Angeles: University of California, 1969), p. 14.
9. Richard B. Chase and Nicholas J. Aquilano, *Production and Operations Management: A Life-Cycle Approach,* 4th ed. (Homewood, Ill.: Richard D. Irwin, 1985), p. 256.
10. War Manpower Commission, Division of Occupational Analysis, *Training and Reference Manual for Job Analysis* (Washington, D.C.: U.S. Government Printing Office, June 1944), p. 7.

11. Partially adapted from J. Markowitz, "Four Methods of Job Analysis," *Training and Development Journal,* September 1981, p. 112.

12. U.S. Department of Labor, *Handbook for Analyzing Jobs* (Washington, D.C.: U.S. Government Printing Office, 1972).

13. N. R. F. Maier, R. Hollman, J. J. Hoover, and W. H. Reed, *Superior-Subordinate Communication in Management* (New York: American Management Association, 1961).

14. The Position Analysis Questionnaire (PAQ) is copyrighted by the Purdue Research Foundation. The PAQ and related materials are available through the University Book Store, 360 West State Street, West Lafayette, IN 47906. Further information regarding the PAQ is available through PAQ Services, Inc., P.O. Box 3337, Logan, UT 84321. Computer processing of PAQ data is available through the PAQ Data Processing Division at this same address in Utah.

15. W. W. Tornov and P. R. Pinto, "The Development of a Managerial Job Taxonomy: A System for Describing, Classifying, and Evaluating Executive Positions," *Journal of Applied Psychology* 61, no. 4 (1976), p. 413.

16. D. Yoder and H. G. Henneman, Jr., eds., *ASPA Handbook of Personnel and Industrial Relations,* vol. 1 (Washington, D.C.: Bureau of National Affairs, 1974), pp. 4–58.

17. Parts of this section are adapted from Philip C. Grant, "What Use Is a Job Description?" *Personnel Journal,* February 1988, pp. 50–55.

On the Job

Sample Job Description

Title of Position: Human Resource Manager, Plant*

Basic Purpose
To develop and maintain an employee relations climate that creates and permits a stable and productive work force. To manage and coordinate all functions of employee relations, including employment, labor relations, compensation and benefit services, work force planning, training and development, affirmative action, and security.

Duties and Responsibilities
1. Selects, trains, develops, and organizes a subordinate staff to perform and meet department responsibilities and objectives effectively.
2. Provides leadership in the establishment and maintenance of employee relations that will assist in attracting and retaining a desirable and productive labor force.
3. Manages the interpretation and application of established corporate and division personnel policies.
4. Directs the preparation and maintenance of reports necessary to carry out functions of the department. Prepares periodic reports for the plant manager; director, employee relations; manager, labor relations; and/or manager, compensation and benefits; as necessary or requested.
5. Directs and maintains various activities designed to achieve and maintain a high level of employee morale.
6. Plans, implements, and maintains a program of orientation for new employees.

*Source: Reprinted by permission of publisher from, *Job Descriptions in Manufacturing Industries*, by John D. Ulery © 1981 AMACOM, a division of American Management Association, New York. All rights reserved.

7. Provides and serves as the necessary liaison between the location employees and the location plant manager.

8. Supervises the labor relations staff in administration of the labor agreements and interpretation of contract language and ensures that the supervisor, labor relations, is well informed to administer the provisions effectively and in accordance with management's philosophy and objectives.

9. Strives to establish an effective working relationship with union representatives to resolve and minimize labor problems more satisfactorily and to avoid inefficient practices and work stoppages.

10. Determines or, in questionable cases, recommends whether grievance cases appealed to the arbitration stage should be settled by concessions or arbitrated. Prepares and presents such cases or supervises subordinates in same.

11. Manages and coordinates planning for plant labor contract negotiations; ensures that labor cost aspects are defined and that major position papers are prepared. Supervises the preparation and publication of contract language and documentation. Serves as chief spokesperson or assists in negotiations at the operating unit level.

12. Establishes operative procedures for ensuring timely compliance with notice, reporting, and similar obligations under agreements with labor organizations.

13. Supervises the compensation and benefits staff in the administration and/or implementation and communication of current and new compensation and benefit programs, policies, and procedures.

14. Directs the development and implementation of approved location affirmative action plans to achieve and maintain compliance in accordance with the letter and intent of equal employment opportunity laws and executive orders.

15. Plans, implements, and maintains supervisory and management development activities.

16. Provides leadership in the establishment and maintenance of a plant security force.

17. Represents the company in the community and promotes the company's goodwill interests in community activities.

Organizational Relationships
This position reports directly to the plant manager and functionally to the director, employee relations. Directly supervises supervisor, labor relations; supervisor, employment; supervisor, compensation benefits; and supervisor, security; and indirectly supervises additional nonexempt employees. Interfaces daily with management and division employee relations.

Position Specifications
Bachelor's degree, preferably in personnel management or equivalent plus six to eight years related experience, including supervisory/managerial experience in a wide range of employee relations activities. Must possess an ability to understand human behavior and be able to lead and motivate people. Must have mature judgment and decision making ability.

On the Job

Sample Job Analysis Questionnaire*

Job Analysis Information Format

Your job title _____ Code _____ Date _____
Class title _____ Department _____
Your name _____ Facility _____
Superior's title _____ Prepared by _____

Superior's name _____ Hours worked _____ AM/PM _____ to _____ AM/PM

1. What is the general purpose of your job?

2. What was your last job? If it was in another organization, please name it.

3. To what job would you normally expect to be promoted?

4. If you regularly supervise others, list them by name and job title.

5. If you supervise others, please check those activities that are part of your supervisory duties:

☐ Hiring   ☐ Coaching   ☐ Promoting
☐ Orienting   ☐ Counseling   ☐ Compensating
☐ Training   ☐ Budgeting   ☐ Disciplining
☐ Scheduling   ☐ Directing   ☐ Terminating
☐ Developing   ☐ Measuring performance ☐ Other _____

6. How would you describe the successful completion and results of your work?

7. *Job duties*—Please briefly describe WHAT you do and, if possible, HOW you do it. Indicate those duties you consider to be most important and/or most difficult.

   (a) *Daily duties:*

   (b) *Periodic duties* (Please indicate whether weekly, monthly, quarterly, etc.):

   (c) *Duties performed at irregular intervals:*

*Source: Richard I. Henderson, *Compensation Management: Rewarding Performance in the Modern Organization,* © 1976, pp. 98–102. Reprinted by permission of Prentice-Hall, Inc., Englewood Cliffs, NJ.

8. *Education*—Please check the blank that indicates the educational *requirements* for the job, not your *own* educational background:

☐ No formal education required   ☐ 4-year college degree
☐ Less than high school diploma   ☐ Education beyond undergraduate
☐ High school diploma or equivalent   degree and/or professional license
☐ 2-year college certificate or equivalent

List advanced degrees or specified professional license or certificate required.

Please indicate the education you had when you were placed on this job:

9. *Experience*—Please check the amount needed to perform your job:

☐ None   ☐ More than 1 year to 3 years
☐ Less than 1 month   ☐ More than 3 years to 5 years
☐ 1 month to less than 6 months   ☐ More than 5 years to 10 years
☐ 6 months to 1 year   ☐ Over 10 years

Please indicate the experience you had when you were placed on this job.

10. *Skills*—Please list any skills required in the performance of your job (for example, amount of accuracy, alertness, precision in working with described tools, methods, systems, etc.).

Please list skills you possessed when you were placed on this job.

11. *Equipment*—Does your work require the use of any equipment?   Yes ___ No ___   If yes, please list the equipment and check whether you use it rarely, occasionally, or frequently:

Equipment	Rarely	Occasionally	Frequently
(1) _____	☐	☐	☐
(2) _____	☐	☐	☐
(3) _____	☐	☐	☐
(4) _____	☐	☐	☐

12. *Physical demands*—Please check all undesirable physical demands required on your job and whether you are required to do so rarely, occasionally, or frequently:

	Rarely	Occasionally	Frequently
☐ Handling heavy material	☐	☐	☐
☐ Awkward or cramped positions	☐	☐	☐
☐ Excessive working speeds	☐	☐	☐
☐ Excessive sensory requirements (seeing, hearing, touching, smelling, speaking)	☐	☐	☐
☐ Vibrating equipment	☐	☐	☐
☐ Others _____	☐	☐	☐

13. *Emotional demands*—Please check all undesirable emotional demands placed on you by your job and whether it is rarely, occasionally, or frequently:

	Rarely	Occasionally	Frequently
☐ Contact with general public	☐	☐	☐
☐ Customer contact	☐	☐	☐
☐ Close supervision	☐	☐	☐
☐ Deadlines under pressure	☐	☐	☐
☐ Irregular activity schedules	☐	☐	☐
☐ Working alone	☐	☐	☐
☐ Excessive traveling	☐	☐	☐
☐ Other _____	☐	☐	☐

14. *Workplace location*—Check type of location of your job and if you consider it to be unsatisfactory or satisfactory:

	Unsatisfactory	Satisfactory
☐ Outdoor	☐	☐
☐ Indoor	☐	☐
☐ Underground	☐	☐
☐ Pit	☐	☐
☐ Scaffold	☐	☐

15. *Physical surroundings*—Please check whether you consider the following physical conditions of your job to be poor, good, or excellent:

	Poor	Good	Excellent
☐ Lighting	☐	☐	☐
☐ Ventilation	☐	☐	☐
☐ Sudden temperature change	☐	☐	☐
☐ Vibration	☐	☐	☐
☐ Comfort of furnishings	☐	☐	☐

16. *Environmental conditions*—Please check the objectionable conditions under which you must perform your job and check whether the condition exists rarely, occasionally, or frequently:

	Rarely	Occasionally	Frequently
☐ Dust	☐	☐	☐
☐ Dirt	☐	☐	☐
☐ Heat	☐	☐	☐
☐ Cold	☐	☐	☐
☐ Fumes	☐	☐	☐
☐ Odors	☐	☐	☐
☐ Noise	☐	☐	☐
☐ Wetness	☐	☐	☐
☐ Humidity	☐	☐	☐
☐ Other _____	☐	☐	☐

17. *Health and safety*—Please check all undesirable health and safety factors under which you must perform your job and whether you are required to do so rarely, occasionally, or frequently:

	Rarely	Occasionally	Frequently
☐ Height of elevated workplace	☐	☐	☐
☐ Radiation	☐	☐	☐
☐ Mechanical hazards	☐	☐	☐
☐ Moving objects	☐	☐	☐
☐ Explosives	☐	☐	☐
☐ Electrical hazards	☐	☐	☐
☐ Fire	☐	☐	☐
☐ Other _____	☐	☐	☐

_____   _____
Signature   Date

SUPERVISORY REVIEW

Do the incumbent's responses to the questionnaire accurately describe the work requirements and the work performed in meeting the responsibilities of the job? Yes ___ No ___ If no, please explain and list any significant omissions or additions.

Chapter 5

Human Resource Planning

Chapter Outline

How HRP Relates to Organizational Planning
Strategy-Linked HRP
Steps in the HRP Process
Determining Organizational Objectives
Determining the Skills and Expertise Required (Demand)
Determining Additional (Net) Human Resource Requirements
Developing Action Plans
Synthesizing the HRP Process
Tools and Techniques of HRP
Commitment Manpower Planning (CMP)
Ratio Analysis

Time Frame of HRP
HRP: An Evolving Process
Specific Role of the Human Resource Department
Common Pitfalls in HRP
Summary of Learning Objectives
Review Questions
Discussion Questions
Incident 5–1: Human Resource Planning—What Is That?
Incident 5–2: A New Boss
Exercise: Avoiding the Pitfalls of Human Resource Planning
Notes and Additional Readings

● *Learning Objectives*

After studying this chapter, you should be able to:
1. Define human resource planning (HRP).
2. Summarize the relationship between HRP and organizational planning.
3. Explain strategy-linked HRP.
4. Name the steps in the HRP process.
5. Discuss the purpose of a skills inventory.
6. Describe succession planning, commitment manpower planning, and ratio analysis.
7. List several common pitfalls in HRP.

*"I*n planning objectives related to profitability and growth, corporate management deals particularly with ideas and problems in terms of the future. Personnel managers must likewise deal more and more in concepts predicated on what lies ahead."

Albert F. Watters*

Human resource planning (HRP)
Process by which the human resource needs of an organization are determined and the organization ensures that it has the right number of qualified people in the right jobs at the right time.

Human resource planning (HRP), sometimes referred to as manpower planning or personnel planning, has been defined as the process of "getting the right number of qualified people into the right job at the right time."[1] Put another way, HRP is "the system of matching the supply of people—internally (existing employees) and externally (those to be hired or searched for)—with the openings the organization expects to have over a given time frame."[2] The first challenge of HRP is to translate the organization's plans and objectives into a timed schedule of employee requirements. Once the employee requirements have been determined, HRP must then devise plans for securing the necessary employees. Basically, all organizations engage in human resource planning either formally or informally. Some organizations do a good job, while others do a poor job.

The long-term success of any organization ultimately depends on having the right people in the right jobs at the right time. Organization objectives and the strategies to achieve these objectives have meaning only when people with the appropriate talent, skill, and desire are available to carry out those strategies.

Poor human resource planning can also cause substantial problems in the short term. For example, consider the following.[3]

- Despite an aggressive search, a vital middle management position in a high-technology organization has gone unfilled for six months. Productivity in the section has plummeted.
- In another company, employees hired just nine months ago have been placed on indefinite layoff because of an unforseen lag in the workload in a specific production area.
- In still another company, thanks to the spectacular efforts of a talented marketing manager, revenues have soared. However, that valued employee has just resigned because he wasn't able to identify career opportunities within the firm.

The necessity for HRP is due to the significant lead time that normally exists between the recognition of the need to fill a job and the securing of a qualified person to fill that need. In other words, it is usually not possible to go out and find an appropriate person overnight. Effective HRP can also help reduce turnover by keeping employees appraised of their career opportunities within the company.

---

*Source: A. F. Watters, "Personnel Management: Future Problems and Opportunities," *Personnel 38,* no. 1 (1961), p. 56.

How HRP Relates to Organizational Planning

HRP involves applying the basic planning process to the human resource needs of an organization. Any human resource plan, if it is to be effective, must be derived from the long-term plans of the organization. In essence, the success of HRP depends largely on how closely the human resource department can integrate effective people planning with the organization's business planning process.[4] Unfortunately, HRP is often not adequately tied in to overall corporate planning. HRM in Action 5–1 discusses the results of a large survey relating to this issue.

Strategic business planning overall seeks to identify various factors that are critical to the success of the organization.[5] It also focuses on how an organization can become better positioned and equipped to compete in its industry. To accomplish this, the planning process should provide:

- A clear statement of the organization's mission
- A commitment from staff members to the mission
- An explicit statement of assumptions
- A plan of action in light of available or acquirable resources, including trained and talented people[6]

Human resource planning contributes significantly to the strategic management process by providing the means to accomplish the desired outcomes from the planning process.

A common error is for human resource planners to focus on the short-term replacement needs and not coordinate their plans with the long-term plans of the organization. Focusing on short-term replacement needs is a natural consequence of not integrating human resource planning with strategic planning. A nonintegrated approach almost always leads to surprises that force human resource planners to concentrate on short-term crises.

Strategy-Linked HRP

All managers, especially line managers, should view human resource planning as one of their most important job responsibilities. Unfortunately, this is often not the case. Far too many managers view HRP as something to do only after everything else has been done. Furthermore, managers often think that HRP should be handled solely by the human resource department. But HRP is not strictly a human resource department function: the role of the human resource department is to assist operating managers in developing their individual plans and integrating these different plans into an overall scheme. The individual managers must, however, provide the basic data on which the plan is built. A joint effort is required by the individual managers and the human resource department. In general, the human resource department provides the structure, the impetus, and assistance. However, individual managers must be actively involved.

One of the best ways to encourage genuine cooperation between human

▼.   ## HRM in Action 5–1

A survey of more than 9,000 managers in 60 companies found that human resource planning is a crucial area requiring significant improvement. Specifically, the responding managers identified several major obstacles to successful strategic planning: a failure to synchronize human resource planning with the business planning cycle, a tendency to plan in response to short-term operating problems, an inadequate data base for planning, a failure to involve key managers in the planning process, and an unwillingness to use the strategic human resource plan to guide day-to-day management actions. In summary, many of the problems reported relate to a lack of coordination between human resource planners and overall strategic planners.

Sources: John A. Hooper, Ralph F. Catalanello, and Patrick L. Murray, "Showing Up the Weakest Link," *Personnel Administrator*, April 1987, p. 50; and John A. Hooper, "A Strategy for Increasing the Human Resource Department's Effectiveness," *Personnel Administrator*, June 1984, pp. 141–148.

resource managers and line managers is to use what is called strategy-linked HRP. Strategy-linked HRP is based on a close working relationship between the human resources department and line managers.[7] Human resource managers serve as consultants to line managers concerning the people-management implications of business objectives and strategies. Line managers, in turn, have a responsibility to respond to the business implications of human resource objectives and strategies. The key in linking human resource planning to the organization's strategy is for both the human resource managers and the line managers to have a sincere appreciation for each other's roles. HRM in Action 5–2 describes how CSX Corporation has combined its human resources and planning and development units into one department.

Steps in the HRP Process

HRP consists of four basic steps:[8]

1. Determining the impact of the organization's objectives on specific organizational units.
2. Defining the skills, expertise, and total number of employees (demand for human resources) required to achieve the organization and departmental objectives.
3. Determining the additional (net) human resource requirements in light of the organization's current human resources.
4. Developing action plans to meet the anticipated human resource needs.

Figure 5–1 illustrates the steps in HRP.

Determining Organizational Objectives

As emphasized earlier, human resource plans must be based on organizational strategic plans. In actual practice, this means that the objectives of the human resource plan must be derived from organizational objectives. Specific human re-

▽• HRM in Action 5–2

Combining Human Resources and Planning

Railroad company CSX Corporation has recently combined its human resource group and its planning and development unit into a single department. According to Alex Mandle, a senior CSX vice president, the move was made to make sure that the "people" side of the equation is taken into account along with other requirements in decisions concerning internal growth and acquisitions. "Eventually rail will be a minor part of our business," he says. "And these transitions require a lot of change—which requires the right people skills. Simultaneous planning of succession, management development, and incentive compensation also encourage strategic vision."

Source: Phil Farish, "Novel Link," *Personnel Administrator*, June 1988, p. 22.

▼ **Figure 5–1**   Steps in the human resource planning process

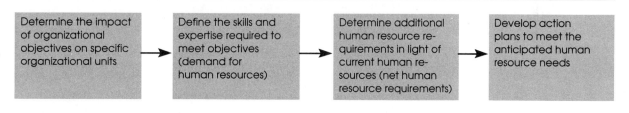

Determine the impact of organizational objectives on specific organizational units → Define the skills and expertise required to meet objectives (demand for human resources) → Determine additional human resource requirements in light of current human resources (net human resource requirements) → Develop action plans to meet the anticipated human resource needs

source requirements in terms of numbers and characteristics of employees should be derived from the objectives of the entire organization.

Organizational objectives give an organization and its members direction and purpose and should be stated in terms of expected results. The objective-setting process begins at the top of the organization with a statement of mission, which defines the organization's current and future business. Long-range objectives and strategies are formulated based on the organization's mission statement. These can then be used to establish short-term performance objectives. Short-term performance objectives generally have a time schedule and are expressed quantitatively. Divisional and departmental objectives are then derived from the organization's short-term performance objectives. Establishing organizational, divisional, and departmental objectives in this manner has been called the **cascade approach** to objective setting. Figure 5–2 illustrates this approach.

The cascade approach is not a form of "top-down" planning, whereby objectives are passed down to lower levels of the organization. The idea is to involve all levels of management in the planning process. Such an approach leads to an upward and downward flow of information during planning. This also ensures that the objectives are communicated and coordinated through all levels of the organization.

The cascade approach, when properly used, involves both operating managers and the human resource department in the overall planning process. During the early stages, the human resource department can influence objective setting by providing information about the organization's human resources. For example, if

Organizational objectives
Statements of expected results that are designed to give an organization and its members direction and purpose.

Cascade approach
Objective-setting process designed to involve all levels of management in the organizational planning process.

▼. HRM in Action 5–3

Linking HRP to the Business Plan

David R. Leigh, manager of corporate management planning and development for Robbins & Myers, Inc., says that "for human resources planning to succeed, it must be tied to strategic business planning." Some of the lessons learned by Robbins & Myers in the area of human resource planning are:

1. *Know the business strategy.* The key human resource planner should be thoroughly familiar with the company's strategic plan and should ensure that any assumptions made when developing the human resource plan are consistent with the business strategy.

2. *The business planning cycle and human resource planning should be linked.* Robbins & Myers found that

linking human resource planning to the existing business planning cycle encouraged line managers to think about human resources while they were thinking about the business plan.

3. *Human resource planning should be a corporate objective.* At Robbins & Myers, the human resource planning system allowed top management to recognize that the company's continued growth might be constrained by lack of human resources and that the problem needed attention at the top levels of the organization.

Source: David R. Leigh, "Business Planning Is People Planning," *Personnel Journal,* May 1984, pp. 44–54.

▼ **Figure 5–2**   Cascade approach to setting objectives

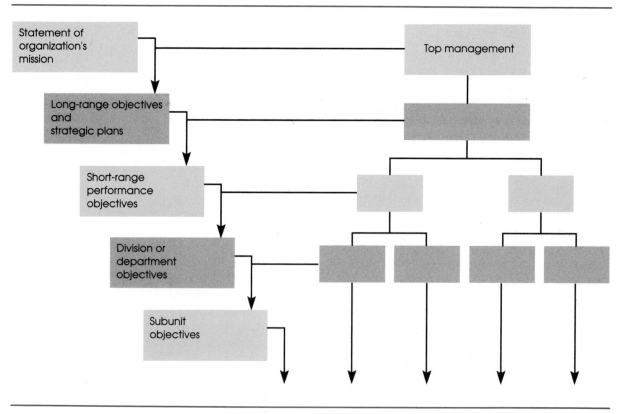

Source: Redrawn from *Managing by Objectives* by Anthony P. Raia. (Scott Foresman and Company, 1974). Reprinted by permission of the author.

▼. **HRM in Action 5–4**

How Human Resource Managers Can Participate in Linking Business and Human Resource Goals

G. Christopher Wood, manager of organizational effectiveness for Coopers & Lybrand, suggests the following steps for human resource executives attempting to participate more directly in their organization's management:

- Ensure that all traditional human resource programs are satisfying the needs of senior and functional management.
- Identify the human resource implications of the company's business plan.

- Identify those human resource issues that may affect business objectives, and notify the appropriate functional managers.
- Convert business objectives into human resource objectives that can provide the foundation of a strategic human resource plan.
- Review the strategic planning process to identify new opportunities for involvement of the human resource department.

Source: G. Christopher Wood, "Planning for People" (Letters to the Editor), *Harvard Business Review*, November–December 1985, p. 230.

the human resource department has identified particular strengths and weaknesses in the organization's personnel, this information could significantly influence the overall direction of the organization. HRM in Actions 5–3 and 5–4 offer specific suggestions for integrating human resource plans into the organization's strategic plans.

Determining the Skills and Expertise Required (Demand)

After organizational, divisional, and departmental objectives have been established, operating managers should determine the skills and expertise required to meet their respective objectives. The key here is not to look at the skills and abilities of present employees but rather to determine the skills and abilities required to meet the objectives. For example, suppose an objective of the production department is to increase total production of a certain item by 10 percent. Once this objective has been established, the production manager must determine precisely how this translates into human resource needs. A good starting point here is to review current job descriptions. Once this has been accomplished, managers are in a better position to determine the skills and expertise necessary to meet their objectives. The final step in this phase is to translate the needed skills and abilities into types and numbers of employees.

Methods of Forecasting Human Resource Needs

Forecasting the organization's human resource needs for the future can be done using a variety of methods, some simple and some complex. Regardless of the method used, forecasts represent approximations and should not be viewed as absolutes.

Methods for forecasting human resource needs can be either judgmentally or mathematically based. Judgmental methods include managerial estimates and the Delphi technique. Under the **managerial estimates** method, managers make estimates of future staffing needs. These estimates can be made by top-level managers

Managerial estimates
Judgmental method of forecasting that calls on managers to make estimates of future staffing needs.

▼ **Table 5–1**   Statistical techniques used to forecast human resource needs

Technique	Description
1. Regression analysis	Past levels of various workload indicators such as sales, production levels, and value added are examined for statistical relationships with staffing levels. Where sufficiently strong relationships are found, a regression (or multiple regression) model is derived. Forecasted levels of the retained indicator(s) are entered into the resulting model and used to calculate the associated level of human resource requirements.
2. Productivity ratios	Historical data are used to examine past levels of a productivity index $$P = \frac{\text{Workload}}{\text{Number of people}}.$$ Where constant, or systematic, relationships are found, human resource requirements can be computed by dividing predicted workloads by P.
3. Personnel ratios	Past personnel data are examined to determine historical relationships among the number of employees in various jobs or job categories. Regression analysis or productivity ratios are then used to project either total or key group human resource requirements, and personnel ratios are used to allocate total requirements to various job categories or to estimate requirements for non-key groups.
4. Time series analysis	Past staffing levels (instead of workload indicators) are used to project future human resource requirements. Past staffing levels are examined to isolate seasonal and cyclical variations, long-term trends, and random movement. Long-term trends are then extrapolated or projected, using a moving average, exponential smoothing, or regression technique.

Source: Lee Dyer, "Human Resource Planning," in *Personnel Management*, ed. Kendrith M. Rowland and Gerald R. Ferris (Boston: Allyn & Bacon, 1982), p. 59.

Delphi technique

Judgmental method of forecasting that uses a panel of experts to make initially independent estimates of future demand. An intermediary then presents each expert's forecast and assumptions to the other members of the panel. Each expert is then allowed to revise his or her forecast as desired. This process continues until some consensus or composite emerges.

and passed down, or by lower-level managers and passed up for further revision, or by some combination of upper- and lower-level managers. Under the **Delphi technique**, each member of a panel of experts makes an independent estimate of what the future demand will be, along with any underlying assumptions. An intermediary then presents each expert's forecast and assumptions to the others and allows the experts to revise their positions if so desired. This process continues until some consensus emerges.

Mathematically based methods for forecasting human resource needs include various statistical as well as modeling methods. Statistical methods use historical data in some manner to project future demand. Table 5–1 summarizes four of the most frequently used statistical methods.

Modeling methods usually provide a simplified view of the human resource demands throughout an organization. By changing the input data, the human resource ramifications for different demand scenarios can be tested.

Historically, judgmental forecasts have been used more frequently than mathematically based forecasts. Judgmental methods are simpler and usually do not require sophisticated analyses. However, with the increasing proliferation of user-friendly computers, mathematically based methods probably will be used more frequently.

▼. **HRM in Action 5–5**

Developing a Microcomputer-Based Skills Inventory File for Less than $1,000

Donald Muller, employee relations manager for Gilbert/Commonwealth, has developed a microcomputer-based skills inventory file for less than $1,000. Muller suggests starting with a commercial database management system. In selecting the system one should consider ease of use, file size, data manipulation capability, the flexibility of the report writer, screen design and control capability, and the ease of making structural file changes. Muller's system converts a large array of descriptive data to single characters, thus making it possible to get a companywide list onto one screen.

Muller's system sets fields 1 and 2 for name and date with each field allowing several characters. The remaining are single-character fields with 3–12 covering education, 35–40 allotted for foreign languages, and 41–127 for skills and expertise. Each single character field can record many different levels of expertise by using the various levels of the alphabet, numbers, or other keyboard characteristics.

Source: Phil Farish, "Low-Cost Skills Bank," *Personnel Administrator*, February 1988, p. 24.

Determining Additional (Net) Human Resource Requirements

Once a manager has determined the types and numbers of employees required, these estimates must be analyzed in light of the current and anticipated human resources of the organization. This process involves a thorough analysis of presently employed personnel and a forecast of expected changes.

Skills Inventory

The purpose of a **skills inventory** is to consolidate information about the organization's human resources. It provides basic information on all employees, including in its simplest form a list of the names, certain characteristics, and skills of employees. Because the information from a skills inventory is used as input into promotion and transfer decisions, it should contain information about each employee's portfolio of skills and not just those relevant to the employee's current job. Thomas H. Patten has outlined seven broad categories of information that should be included in a skills inventory.[9]

Skills inventory
Consolidated list of biographical and other information on all employees in an organization.

1. Personal data: age, sex, marital status
2. Skills: education, job experience, training
3. Special qualifications: membership in professional groups, special achievements
4. Salary and job history: present and past salary, dates of raises, various jobs held
5. Company data: benefit plan data, retirement information, seniority
6. Capacity of individual: test scores on psychological and other tests, health information
7. Special preferences of individual: geographic location, type of job

The popularity of skills inventories has increased rapidly since the proliferation of computers. Although most of the desired information traditionally was available from individual personnel files, compiling it was time consuming before computers became readily available. HRM in Action 5–5 discusses how to develop a computer-based inventory for under $1,000.

The primary advantage of a skills inventory is that it furnishes a means of quickly and accurately evaluating the skills that are available within the organization. In addition to helping determine promotion and transfer decisions, this information is often necessary for making other decisions, such as whether to bid on a new contract or introduce a new product. A skills inventory also aids in planning future employee training and management development programs in recruiting and selecting new employees. Figure 5–3 presents a copy of an actual skills inventory form.

Management Inventory

Because the type of information required about management personnel sometimes differs from that required about nonmanagerial employees, some organizations maintain a separate management inventory. In addition to biographical data, a **management inventory** often contains brief assessments of the manager's past performance, strengths, weaknesses, and potential for advancement.

Management inventory
Specialized, expanded form of skills inventory for an organization's current management team; in addition to basic types of information, it usually includes a brief assessment of past performance and potential for advancement.

Anticipating Changes in Personnel

In addition to appraising present human resources through a skills inventory, managers must also take future changes into account. Certain changes in personnel can be estimated accurately and easily, while other changes are not so easily forecast. However, information is almost always available to help make these forecasts.

Changes such as retirements can be forecast with reasonable accuracy from information in skills inventory. Others, such as transfers and promotions, can be estimated by taking into account such factors as the ages of individuals in specific jobs and the requirements of the organization. Individuals with potential for promotion can and should be identified. Other factors, such as deaths, resignations, and discharges, are much more difficult to predict. However, past experience and historical records often can provide useful information in these areas.

Planned training and development experiences should also be considered when evaluating anticipated changes. By combining the forecast for the human resources needed with the information from the skills inventory and from anticipated changes, managers can make a reasonable prediction of their net human resource requirements for a specified time period.

Developing Action Plans

Once the net human resource requirements have been determined, action plans must be developed for achieving the desired results. If the net requirements indicate a need for additions, plans must be made to recruit, select, orient, and train the specific numbers and types of personnel needed (Chapters 6, 7, and 8 deal with these topics). If a reduction in labor is necessary, plans must be made to realize the necessary adjustments. If time is not of the essence, natural attrition can be used to reduce labor costs. However, if the organization cannot afford the luxury of natural attrition, labor overhead can be cut either by reducing the total number of employees or by making other adjustments that do not result in employees leaving the organization.

Figure 5–3 Skills inventory form used by PPG Industries

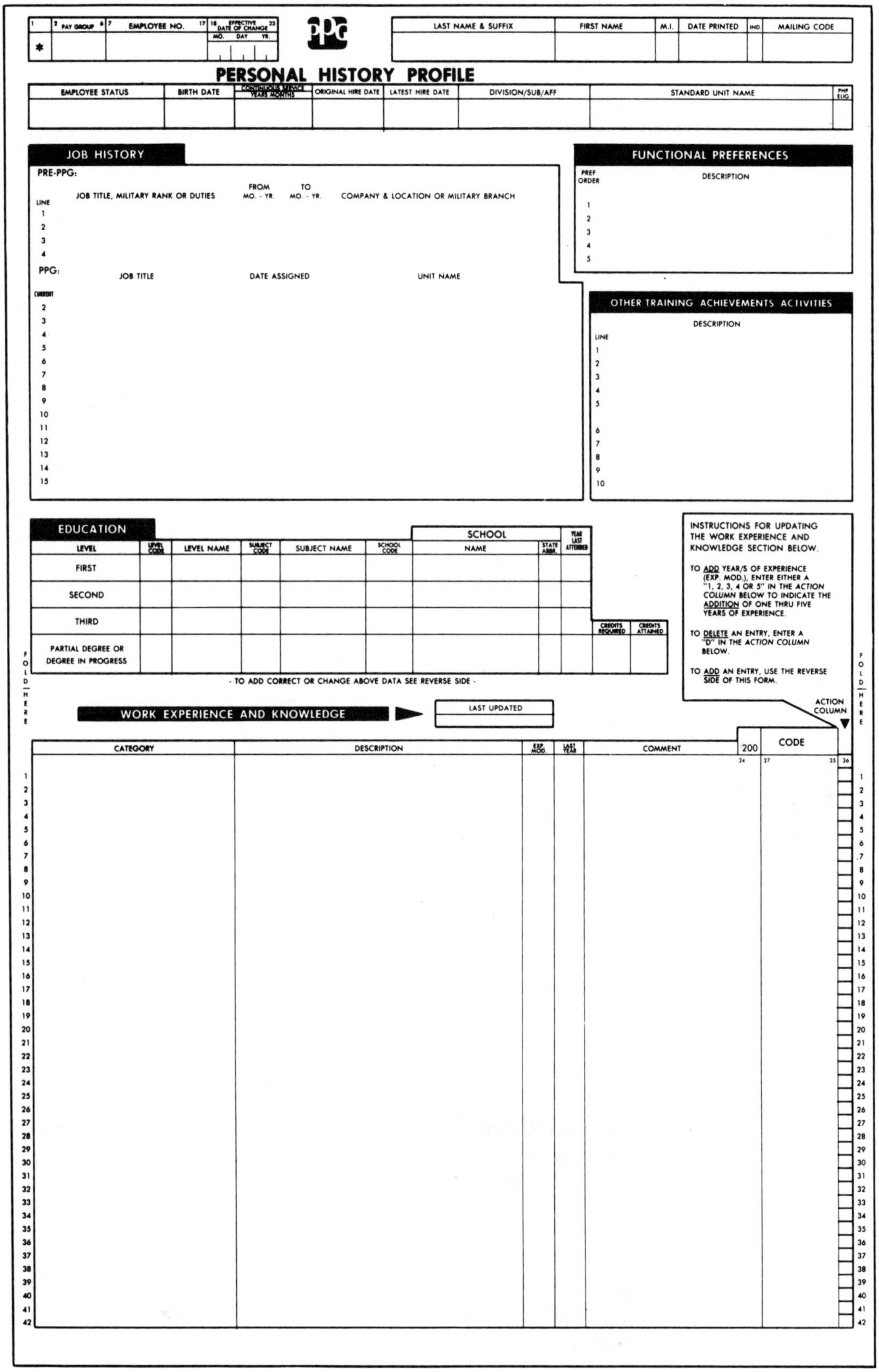

PPG

1 | 2 PAY GROUP 6 | 7 EMPLOYEE NO. 17 | 18 EFFECTIVE DATE OF CHANGE 23 (MO. DAY YR.) | LAST NAME & SUFFIX | FIRST NAME | M.I. | DATE PRINTED | IND | MAILING CODE

*

PERSONAL HISTORY PROFILE

EMPLOYEE STATUS | BIRTH DATE | CONTINUOUS SERVICE YEARS MONTHS | ORIGINAL HIRE DATE | LATEST HIRE DATE | DIVISION/SUB/AFF | STANDARD UNIT NAME | PHP ELIG.

JOB HISTORY

PRE-PPG:

LINE | JOB TITLE, MILITARY RANK OR DUTIES | FROM MO. - YR. | TO MO. - YR. | COMPANY & LOCATION OR MILITARY BRANCH

1
2
3
4

PPG:

| JOB TITLE | DATE ASSIGNED | UNIT NAME

CURRENT
2
3
4
5
6
7
8
9
10
11
12
13
14
15

FUNCTIONAL PREFERENCES

PREF ORDER | DESCRIPTION

1
2
3
4
5

OTHER TRAINING ACHIEVEMENTS ACTIVITIES

LINE | DESCRIPTION

1
2
3
4
5
6
7
8
9
10

EDUCATION

LEVEL	LEVEL CODE	LEVEL NAME	SUBJECT CODE	SUBJECT NAME	SCHOOL CODE	SCHOOL NAME	STATE ABBR.	YEAR LAST ATTENDED	CREDITS REQUIRED	CREDITS ATTAINED
FIRST										
SECOND										
THIRD										
PARTIAL DEGREE OR DEGREE IN PROGRESS										

- TO ADD CORRECT OR CHANGE ABOVE DATA SEE REVERSE SIDE -

INSTRUCTIONS FOR UPDATING THE WORK EXPERIENCE AND KNOWLEDGE SECTION BELOW.

TO ADD YEAR/S OF EXPERIENCE (EXP. MOD.), ENTER EITHER A "1, 2, 3, 4 OR 5" IN THE ACTION COLUMN BELOW TO INDICATE THE ADDITION OF ONE THRU FIVE YEARS OF EXPERIENCE.

TO DELETE AN ENTRY, ENTER A "D" IN THE ACTION COLUMN BELOW.

TO ADD AN ENTRY, USE THE REVERSE SIDE OF THIS FORM.

FOLD HERE

WORK EXPERIENCE AND KNOWLEDGE

LAST UPDATED

ACTION COLUMN

	CATEGORY	DESCRIPTION	EXP. MOD.	LAST YEAR	COMMENT	200 (24)	CODE (27–35)	36	
1									1
2									2
3									3
4									4
5									5
6									6
7									7
8									8
9									9
10									10
11									11
12									12
13									13
14									14
15									15
16									16
17									17
18									18
19									19
20									20
21									21
22									22
23									23
24									24
25									25
26									26
27									27
28									28
29									29
30									30
31									31
32									32
33									33
34									34
35									35
36									36
37									37
38									38
39									39
40									40
41									41
42									42

Source: Used with permission of PPG Industries, Pittsburgh, Pa.

▼ **Figure 5–4** Organizational and human resource planning

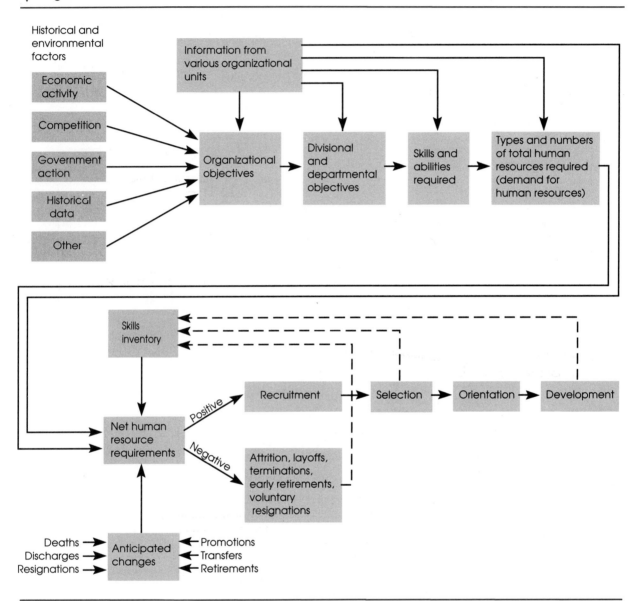

There are four basic ways that the total number of employees can be reduced:
(1) layoffs, (2) terminations, (3) early retirement inducements, and (4) voluntary
resignation inducements.[10] A layoff, as opposed to a termination, assumes that it
is likely that the employee will be recalled at some later date. Most early retirement
and voluntary resignation plans provide some financial inducement to retire early
or to resign.

Approaches that do not result in employees leaving the organization include
(1) reclassification, (2) transfer, and (3) work-sharing. Reclassification involves
either a demotion of an employee, downgrading of job responsibilities, or a com-

▼. HRM in Action 5–6

HRP at Global Insurance Corporation

During 1980–1982, Global Insurance Corporation was caught off-guard by shifts in the economy and consumer preferences. The chief executive officer realized that there were several major human resource problems that needed attention, but the company was unaware of how to proceed.

First, Global initiated a human resource planning audit in order to understand its current situation. The audit involved extensive reviews of existing personnel programs and plans, and interviews with senior management. A key finding of the audit was that the business planning process did not address human resource needs—in effect, there was a total absence of formal human resource planning.

Global identified two immediate human resource needs: (1) a formal process for identifying and selecting candidates for key management positions and (2) a process for designing development plans to ensure that internal candidates were prepared to move into top management.

In order to implement the new human resource planning programs, Global established a task force of six senior managers, who set priorities and developed action steps. To increase the credibility of the effort—and consequently, commitment and the success of implementation—the task force chose to start with programs that addressed highly visible needs. As a result, Global's initial efforts in human resource planning resulted in a list of replacements for upper-level jobs and lists of high-potential managers and their career development needs.

Source: Marten Leshner and Sharon Coleman, "The Case of the Missing HRP," *Personnel Journal,* April 1985, pp. 57–64.

bination of the two. Usually, reclassification is accompanied by a reduction in pay. A transfer involves moving the employee to another part of the organization. Work-sharing seeks to limit layoffs and terminations through the proportional reduction of hours among employees.

Action plans should lay out in a step-by-step sequence exactly how the human resource plans will be implemented.

Synthesizing the HRP Process

Figure 5–4 graphically depicts the relationship between organizational planning and human resource planning. As can be seen, organizational objectives are influenced by many historical and environmental factors. Environmental factors would include variables such as the economy, interest rates, competition, labor availability, and technology. Once the organizational objectives have been established, they are translated into divisional and departmental objectives. Individual managers then determine the human resources necessary to meet their respective objectives. The human resource department assimilates these different requirements and determines the total human resources demand for the organization. Similarly, the additional (net) human resource requirements are determined, based on the information submitted by the different organizational units in light of available resources and anticipated changes. If the net requirements are positive, the organization implements recruitment, selection, training, and development (Chapters 6, 7, 8 and 9 discuss these topics). If the requirements are negative, proper adjustments must be made through attrition, layoffs, terminations, early retirements, or voluntary resignations. As these changes take place, they should be reflected in the skills inventory. Human resource planning is an ongoing process that must be continuously evaluated as conditions change. HRM in Action 5–6 discusses why and how Global Insurance Corporation has implemented a human resource planning program.

Tools and Techniques of HRP

Succession planning
Technique that identifies specific people to fill future openings in key positions throughout the organization.

Organization replacement chart
Chart that shows both incumbents and potential replacements for given positions within an organization.

Many tools are available to assist in the human resource planning process. The skills inventory discussed earlier is one of the most frequently used human resource planning tools. A second useful tool is succession planning. **Succession planning** identifies specific people to fill key positions throughout the organization. Succession planning almost always involves the use of a replacement chart. While there are many variations, a basic **organization replacement chart** shows both incumbents and potential replacements for given positions. Figure 5–5 is an example of a simple replacement chart. Under an optimal succession planning system, individuals are initially identified as candidates to move up after being nominated by management. Then, performance appraisal data is reviewed, potential is assessed, developmental programs are formulated, and career paths are mapped out. Sophisticated succession planning helps ensure that qualified internal candidates are not overlooked. For example, one midwestern company, after installing a more sophisticated succession planning system, discovered a wealth of unexpected talent several levels down in their manufacturing organization.[11]

Commitment Manpower Planning

Commitment manpower planning (CMP)
A new and systematic approach to human resource planning designed to get managers and their subordinates thinking about and involved in human resource planning.

Commitment manpower planning (CMP) is a relatively new approach to human resource planning designed to get managers and their subordinates thinking about and involved in human resource planning. In addition to encouraging managers and subordinates to think about human resource planning, the strength of CMP is that it provides a systematic approach to human resource planning.[12] CMP generates three reports that supply the following information: (1) the supply of employees and the promotability and placement status of each; (2) the organization's demand, arising from new positions and turnover and projected vacancies for each job title; and (3) the balance or status of supply versus demand, including the name, job, and location of all those suitable for promotions.

Ratio Analysis

Ratio analysis
A tool used in human resource planning to measure the organization's human resource vitality as indicated by the presence of promotable personnel and existing backups.

Ratio analysis is another tool that can aid in human resource planning. Two basic premises underlie ratio analysis as it applies to human resource planning.[13] The first is that an organization is "vital" in terms of its human resources to the extent that it has people with high potential who are promotable, either now or in the near future, and backups identified to replace them. The second premise is that an organization is "stagnant" to the extent that employees are not promotable and no backups have been identified to replace the incumbents. The end product of

▼ **Figure 5–5**   Simple organization replacement chart

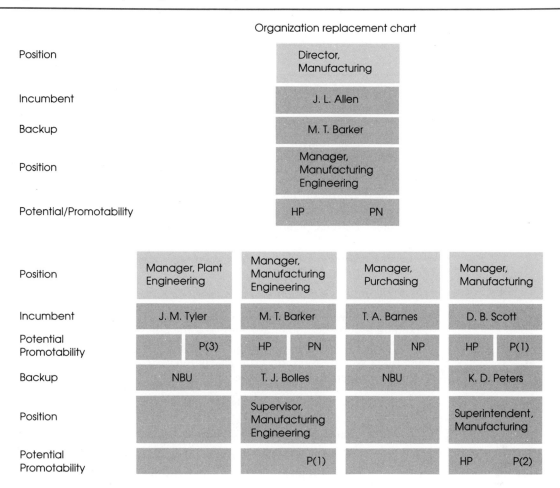

Legend definitions:

HP (high potential) = An above-average or outstanding performer with the potential to advance
at least two levels above current position within five years.

PN (promotable now) = An individual who is promotable now to an identified position one
level above current position.

P (years) = An individual who is promotable in "x" years to an identified position one level above
current position.

NP (not promotable) = An individual who is not promotable above current positions (e.g., individual
desires to remain in current position, has retirement pending, has been promoted to maximum
capabilities, etc.).

NBU (no backup) = No individual identified as a backup for this position.

Source: D. L. Chicci, "Four Steps to an Organization/Human Resource Plan," *Personnel Journal,* June 1979, p. 392.

Organizational vitality index (OVI)

Index that results from ratio analysis; the index reflects the organization's human resource vitality as measured by the presence of promotable personnel and existing backups.

ratio analysis is an overall **organizational vitality index (OVI)**, which can be used as a broad measure of an organization's human resource vitality. The index is calculated based on the number of promotable personnel and the number of existing backups in the organization.[14]

Time Frame of HRP

Because HRP is so closely tied to the organizational planning process, the time frames covered by human resource plans should correspond with those covered by the organizational plans. Organizational plans are frequently classified as short range (0–2 years), intermediate range (2–5 years), or long range (beyond 5 years). Ideally, an organization prepares a plan for each of these horizons. Table 5–2 presents a summary of the major factors affecting long-, intermediate-, and short-range human resource planning.

HRP: An Evolving Process

An organization's human resource planning efforts should not be viewed as an all-or-nothing process but rather as falling at some point along a continuum. At one end of this continuum are those organizations that do no human resource planning; at the other end are those that completely integrate long-range human resource planning into their strategic business plans.

▼ **Table 5–2**   Factors affecting the time frame of HRP

Forecast Factor	Short Range (0–2 Years)	Intermediate Range (2–5 Years)	Long Range (Beyond 5 Years)
Demand	Authorized employment including growth, changes, and turnover.	Operating needs from budgets and plans.	In some organizations, the same as "intermediate"; in others, an increased awareness of changes in environment and technology—essentially judgmental.
Supply	Employee census less expected losses plus expected promotions from subordinate groups.	Human resource vacancies expected from individual promotability data derived from development plans.	Management expectations of changing characteristics of employees and future available human resources.
Net needs	Numbers and kinds of employees needed.	Numbers, kinds, dates, and levels of needs.	Management expectations of future conditions affecting immediate decisions.

Reprinted by permission of *Harvard Business Review*. An exhibit from "Forecasting Manpower Needs" by E. H. Burack and J. W. Walker (Boston: Allyn & Bacon, 1972), p. 94. Copyright © 1990 by the President and Fellows of Harvard College, all rights reserved.

D. Quinn Mills has identified five stages, or benchmarks, along this continuum.[15] Stage 1 companies have no long-term business plans, and they do little or no human resource planning. Companies at Stage 2 have a long-term business plan but tend to be skeptical of HRP. At the same time, such companies do realize to some degree that human resource planning is important. Stage 3 companies do engage in some aspects of human resource planning; but for the most part these efforts are not integrated into the long-range business plan. Stage 4 companies do a good deal of human resource planning, and their top managers are enthusiastic about the process. These companies have at least one human resource component integrated into the long-range plan. Stage 5 companies treat human resource planning as an important and vital part of their long-term business plan. Quite naturally, companies at Stage 5 are highly enthusiastic about HRP. Table 5–3 summarizes the results of a recent survey that investigated the HRP practices of 220 large companies, using this five-stage classification scheme. As reflected in the table, the largest numbers of companies fell into Stages 2 and 3, respectively.

Specific Role of the Human Resource Department

As mentioned earlier, each of the steps in HRP requires a joint effort of the human resources department and the individual managers in the organization. The human resource department's primary roles are to coordinate, monitor, and synthesize the process. The human resource department usually provides the structure and establishes the timetable to be followed by operating managers. This helps ensure a unified effort. As individual managers determine their human resource needs, this information should be channeled through the human resource department to be coordinated and synthesized. By funneling all the information through a central source, maximum efficiency in the process can be attained. For example,

▼ **Table 5–3**   Results of survey investigating HRP practices in large companies

Stage Number	Number of Companies	Percentage of Respondents	Characteristic Activities
Traditional			
1	34	15%	Company picnic
2	81	36	Short-term head-count forecasting
Moderate			
3	60	27	Longer-term head-count forecasting
Advanced			
4	27	14	Skills inventories and succession planning as part of a long-term business plan
5	18	8	Scenarios, trend analysis, management development

Source: D. Quinn Mills, "Planning with People in Mind," *Harvard Business Review*, July–August 1985, p. 101.

interdepartmental transfers and promotions can be used where feasible. Obviously, the information necessary to effect these types of actions would not always be available within the human resource department.

Common Pitfalls in HRP

Unfortunately, HRP is not always successful. While a myriad of things can go wrong, the eight stumbling blocks described below are some of the most frequently encountered.[16]

The identity crisis. Human resource planners work in an environment characterized by ambiguous regulations, company politics, and diverse management styles. Unless human resource planners develop a strong sense of mission (direction), they often spend much of their time looking for something meaningful to do while the organization questions the reason for their existence.

Sponsorship of top management. For HRP to be viable in the long run, it must have the full support of at least one influential senior executive. Such high-ranking support can ensure the necessary resources, visibility, and cooperation necessary for the success of an HRP program.

Size of the initial effort. Many HRP programs fail because of an overcomplicated initial effort. Successful HRP programs start slowly and gradually expand as the program is successful. Developing an accurate skills inventory and a replacement chart are two good places to start.

Coordination with other management and human resource functions. Human resource planning must be coordinated with the other management and human resource functions. Unfortunately, there is a tendency for HRP specialists to become absorbed in their own world and not interact with others.

Integration with organization plans. As emphasized earlier in this chapter, human resource plans must be derived from organization plans. The key here is to develop good communication channels between the organization planners and the human resource planners.

Quantitative versus qualitative approaches. Some people view HRP as a numbers game designed to track the flow of people in, out, up, down, and across the different organizational units. These people take a strictly quantitative approach to HRP. Others take a strictly qualitative approach and focus on individual employee concerns such as individual promotability and career development. As is so often the case, a balanced approach usually yields the best results.

Involvement of operating managers. HRP is not strictly a human resource department function. Successful HRP requires a coordinated effort on the part of operating managers and the human resource department.

The technique trap. As HRP has become more and more popular, new and sophisticated techniques have been developed to assist in HRP. (Several of these were discussed earlier in this chapter.) Many are useful. However, there is sometimes a tendency to adopt one or more of these methods not for what they can do but rather because "everyone is using them." HRP personnel should avoid becoming enamored of a technique merely because it is the "in thing."

● *Summary of Learning Objectives*

1. Define human resource planning (HRP).

   HRP is the process of getting the right number of qualified people into the right job at the right time. Put another way, HRP is the system of matching the supply of people—internally (existing employees) and externally (those to be hired or searched for)—with the openings the organization expects to have over a given time frame.

2. Summarize the relationship between HRP and organizational planning.

   Any human resource plan, if it is to be effective, must be derived from the long-range plans of the organization. In essence the success of HRP depends largely on how closely the human resource department can integrate effective people planning with the organization's business planning process.

3. Explain strategy-linked HRP.

   Strategy-linked HRP is based on a close working relationship between the human resource department and line managers. Human resource managers serve as consultants to line managers concerning the people management implications of business objectives and strategies. Line managers, in turn, have a responsibility to respond to the business implications of human resource objectives and strategies.

4. Name the steps in the HRP process.

   HRP consists of four basic steps: (1) determining the impact of the organization's objectives on specific organizational units, (2) defining the skills, expertise, and total number of employees required to achieve the organization and departmental objectives, (3) determining the additional human resource requirements, and (4) developing action plans to meet the anticipated human resource needs.

5. Discuss the purpose of a skills inventory.

   The purpose of a skills inventory is to consolidate information about the organization's human resources. It provides basic information on all employees including in its simplest form a list of the names, certain characteristics, and skills of employees.

6. Describe succession planning, commitment manpower planning, and ratio analysis.

   Succession planning identifies specific people to fill key positions throughout the organization. Commitment manpower planning is a relatively new approach to human planning designed to get managers and their subordinates thinking about and involved in human resource planning. Ratio analysis produces a broad measure of an organization's human resource vitality (organizational vitality index). The index is calculated based on the number of promotable personnel and the number of existing backups in the organization.

7. List several common pitfalls in HRP.

    Some of the most frequently encountered stumbling blocks to HRP include an identity crisis, a lack of sponsorship by top management, an overcomplicated initial effort, a lack of coordination with other management, a lack of integration with the organizational plan, an organization taking a strictly quantitative approach, operating managers not involved and certain techniques inappropriately used.

Review Questions

1. What is human resource planning (HRP)?
2. How does human resource planning relate to organizational planning?
3. What are the four basic steps in the human resource planning process?
4. Explain the cascade approach to setting objectives.
5. Identify several tools that might be used as aids in the human resource planning process.
6. What is the role of the human resource department in the human resource planning process?
7. List eight common pitfalls in human resource planning.

Discussion Questions

1. Comment on the following statement: "Human resource planning is something to do when you have nothing else to do."
2. Do you think that most human resource planning is undertaken on the basis of organizational objectives or on an "as necessary" basis?
3. How is it possible to accomplish good organizational and, hence, good human resource planning in light of the many changing environmental factors over which the organization has no control?

▼ INCIDENT 5–1

Human Resource Planning—What Is That?

You are a human resource consultant. You have been called by the newly appointed president of a large paper manufacturing firm:

President: I have been in this job for about one month now, and all I seem to do is interview people and listen to personnel problems.

You: Why have you been interviewing people? Don't you have a human resource department?

President: Yes, we do. However, the human resource department doesn't hire top management people. As soon as I took over, I found out that two of my vice presidents were retiring and we had no one to replace them.

You: Have you hired anyone?

President: Yes, I have, and that's part of the problem. I hired a guy from the outside. As soon as the announcement was made, one of my department heads came in and resigned. He said he had wanted that job as vice president for eight years. He was angry because we had hired someone from the outside. How was I supposed to know he wanted the job?

You: What have you done about the other vice president's job?

President: Nothing, because I'm afraid someone else will quit because they weren't considered for the job. But that's not half my problem. I just found out that among our youngest professional employees—engineers and accountants—there has been an 80 percent turnover rate during the past three years. These are the people we promote around here. As you know, that's how I started out in this company. I was a mechanical engineer.

You: Has anyone asked them why they are leaving?

President: Yes, and they all give basically the same answer. They say they don't feel that they have a future here. Maybe I should call them all together an explain how I progressed in this company.

You: Have you ever considered implementing a human resource planning system?

President: Human resource planning? What's that?

Questions

1. How would you answer the president's question?
2. What would be required to establish a human resource planning system in this company?

▼ INCIDENT 5–2

A New Boss

The grants management program of the Environmental Protection Agency (EPA) water division was formed several years ago. The program's main functions are to review grant applications, engineering design reports, and change orders, and to perform operation and maintenance inspections of wastewater treatment facilities.

Paul Wagner, chief of the section, supervised four engineers, one technician, and one secretary. Three of the engineers were relatively new to the agency. The senior engineer, Waymon Burrell, had approximately three years' experience in the grants management program.

Because only Waymon Burrell had experience in grants management, Paul Wagner assigned him the areas with the most complicated projects within the state. The other three engineers were given regions with less complex projects; they were assigned to work closely with Waymon and to learn all they could about the program.

At the beginning of the year, Paul Wagner decided that the new engineers had enough experience to undertake more difficult tasks; therefore, the division's territory could be allotted on a geographical basis. The territory was divided according to river basins, with each engineer assigned two or three areas.

This division according to geography worked fine as the section proceeded to meet all its objectives. However, three months ago, Paul Wagner was offered a job with a consulting engineering company and decided to leave the EPA. He gave two months' notice to top management.

Time passed, but top management did not even advertise for a new section chief. People in the section speculated as to who might be chosen to fill the vacancy; most of them hoped that Waymon Burrell would be, since he knew most about the workings of the section.

On the Monday of Paul's last week, top executives met with him and the section members to announce that they had decided to appoint a temporary section chief until a new one could be hired. The division chief announced that the temporary section chief would be Sam Kutzman, a senior engineer from another EPA division. This came as quite a surprise to Waymon and the others in the grants management program.

Sam Kutzman had no experience in the program. His background was in technical assistance. His previous job had required that he do research in certain treatment processes so that he could provide more technical performance information to other divisions within the EPA.

Questions

1. Do you think Sam Kutzman was a good choice for temporary section chief?

2. How has human resource planning worked in this situation?

Exercise

Avoiding the Pitfalls of Human Resource Planning

Eight potential pitfalls of human resource planning are discussed in the last section of this chapter. Carefully review the list and then rank-order each of them as to which ones you think would cause you the most problems if you were in charge of the human resource planning effort in an actual company. The pitfall ranked Number 1 should be the one that you think would be the hardest to avoid, and the one ranked Number 8 should be the one easiest to avoid. Make any assumptions you deem necessary and be prepared to justify your ranking.

Notes and Additional Readings

1. C. F. Russ, Jr., "Manpower Planning Systems: Part 1," *Personnel Journal,* January 1982, p. 41.

2. Ibid.

3. Excerpted, by permission of the publisher, from "Human Resource Planning: A Four-Phased Approach" by Craig B. Mackey, p. 17, *Management Review,* May 1981 © 1981 by AMACOM, a division of American Management Associations, New York. All rights reserved.

4. John A. Hooper, Ralph F. Catalanello, and Patrick L. Murray, "Shoring Up the Weakest Link," *Personnel Administrator,* April 1987, p. 50.

5. Ernest C. Miller, "Strategic Planning Pays Off," *Personnel Journal,* April 1989, p. 127.

6. Ibid.

7. Much of this section is drawn from Hooper, Catalanello, and Murray, "Shoring Up," pp. 49–55 +.

8. Adapted from D. L. Chicci, "Four Steps to an Organization/Human Resource Plan," *Personnel Journal,* June 1979, pp. 290–92.

9. T. H. Patten, *Manpower Planning and the Development of Human Resources* (New York: John Wiley & Sons, 1971), p. 243.

10. Much of this section is drawn from Richard I. Lehr and David J. Middlebrooks, "Work Force Reduction: Strategies and Options," *Personnel Journal,* October 1984, pp. 50–55.

11. Robert J. Sahl, "Succession Planning—A Blueprint for Your Company's Future," *Personnel Administrator,* September 1987, p. 101.

12. For a more in-depth discussion of CMP, see C. F. Russ, Jr., "Manpower Planning Systems: Part II," *Personnel Journal,* February 1982, pp. 119–23.

13. Chicci, "Four Steps," p. 392.

14. Ibid., pp. 392–94, or a more in-depth discussion of ratio analysis.

15. D. Quinn Mills, "Planning with People in Mind," *Harvard Business Review,* July–August 1985, pp. 97–105.

16. Adapted from Mackey, "Human Resource Planning" pp. 17–20.

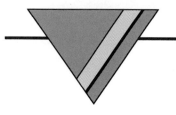

Chapter 6

Recruiting Employees

Chapter Outline

Job Analysis, Human Resource
    Planning, and Recruitment
Sources of Qualified Personnel
    Internal Sources
    External Sources
Effectiveness of Recruitment
    Methods
Realistic Job Previews
Who Does the Recruiting, and
    How?
Organizational Inducements in
    Recruitment
The Recruitment Interview

Equal Employment Opportunity
    and Recruitment
Summary of Learning Objectives
Review Questions
Discussion Questions
Incident 6–1: Inside or Outside
    Recruiting
Incident 6–2: Malpractice Suit
    against a Hospital
Exercise: Want Ads
Notes and Additional Readings
On the Job: Writing a Resume

● *Learning Objectives*

After studying this chapter, you should be able to:

1. Define recruitment.
2. Discuss job analysis, human resource planning, and recruitment.
3. Describe the advantages and disadvantages of using internal methods of recruitment.
4. Discuss job posting and bidding.
5. Describe the advantages and disadvantages of using external methods of recruitment.
6. Define realistic job preview.
7. Define organizational inducements.

*"A*ssembling resources is one of the major divisions of administrative work, along with planning, organizing, directing, and controlling. People to man the positions in the organization, funds to purchase the necessary materials and equipment and to provide working capital, physical facilities with which to work, all must be brought together for the use of the enterprise if it is to function."

*William H. Newman**

Job Analysis, Human Resource Planning, and Recruitment

Recruitment

Process of seeking and attracting a pool of people from which qualified candidates for job vacancies can be chosen.

Recruitment involves seeking and attracting a pool of people from which qualified candidates for job vacancies can be chosen. Most organizations have a recruitment (or, as it is sometimes called, employment) function. This function is managed by the human resource department. In an era when the focus of most organizations has been on efficiently and effectively running the organization, recruiting the right person for the job is a top priority.

The magnitude of an organization's recruiting effort and the methods to be used in that recruiting effort are determined from the personnel planning process and the requirements of the specific jobs to be filled. As brought out in Chapter 5, if the forecast human resource requirements exceed the net human resource requirements, the organization must actively recruit new employees.

On the other hand, recruitment should be concerned with seeking and attracting only qualified job candidates. Successful recruiting is difficult if the jobs to be filled are vaguely defined. Regardless of whether the job to be filled has been in existence or is newly created, its requirements must be defined as precisely as possible for recruiting to be effective. As discussed in Chapter 4, job analysis provides information about the nature and requirements of specific jobs.

Figure 6–1 illustrates the relationships among human resource planning, job analysis, recruitment, and the selection process. Job analysis gives the nature and requirements of specific jobs. Human resource planning determines the specific number of jobs to be filled. Recruitment is concerned with providing a pool of people who are qualified to fill these vacancies. Questions that are addressed in the recruitment process include: What are the sources of qualified personnel? How are these qualified personnel to be recruited? Who is to be involved in the recruiting process? And what inducements does the organization have to attract qualified personnel? The selection process, discussed in detail in the next chapter, is concerned with choosing from the pool of qualified candidates the individual or group of individuals most likely to succeed in a given job.

*Source: W. H. Newman, *Administrative Action* (Englewood Cliffs, N. J.: Prentice-Hall, 1951), p. 317.

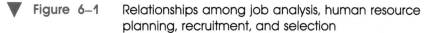

▼ **Figure 6–1** Relationships among job analysis, human resource planning, recruitment, and selection

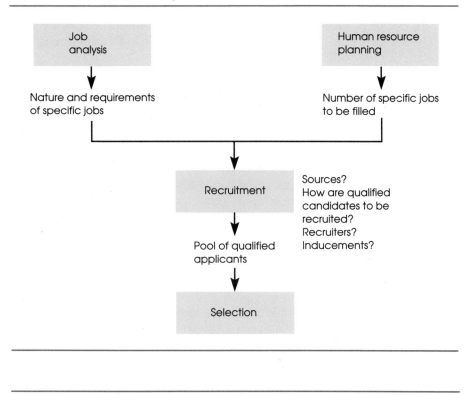

Sources of Qualified Personnel

An organization may fill a particular job either with someone already employed by the organization or with someone from outside. Each of these sources has advantages and disadvantages.

Internal Sources

If an organization has been effective in recruiting and selecting employees in the past, one of the best sources of talent is its own employees. This has several advantages. First, an organization should have a good idea of the strengths and weaknesses of its employees. If an organization maintains a skills inventory, this can be used as a starting point for recruiting from within. In addition, performance evaluations of employees are available. Present and prior managers of the employee being considered can be interviewed to obtain their evaluations of the employee's potential for promotion. In general, more accurate data is available concerning current employees; thus, the chance of making a wrong decision should be reduced.

Not only does the organization know more about its employees, but the employees know more about the organization and how it operates. Therefore, the likelihood of the employee having inaccurate expectations and/or becoming dissatisfied with the organization is reduced when recruiting is done from within.

Another advantage is that recruitment from within can have a significant, positive effect on employee motivation and morale when it creates promotion opportunities or prevents layoffs. When employees know that they will be considered for openings, they have an incentive for good performance. On the other hand, if outsiders usually are given the first opportunity to fill job openings, the effect can be the opposite.

A final advantage relates to the fact that most organizations have a sizeable investment in their work force. Full use of the abilities of an organization's employees improves the organization's return on its investment.

However, there are disadvantages to recruiting from within. One that has been widely publicized is the so-called Peter Principle[1]—that successful people are promoted until they finally reach a level at which they are unable to perform adequately. Another danger associated with promotion from within is that infighting for promotions can become overly intense and have a negative effect on the morale and performance of people who are not promoted.

Another danger involves the inbreeding of ideas. When recruiting is only from internal sources, precautions must be taken to ensure that new ideas and innovations are not stifled by such attitudes as "We've never done it before" or "We do all right without it."

There are two major issues involved if an organization promotes from within. First, the organization needs a strong employee and management development program to ensure that its people can handle larger responsibilities. The second issue concerns the desirability of using seniority as the basis for promotions. Unions generally prefer promotions based on seniority for unionized jobs; many organizations, on the other hand, seem to prefer promotions based on prior performance and potential to do the new job.

Job Posting and Bidding

Job posting and bidding
A method of informing employees of job vacancies by posting a notice in central locations and giving a specified period to apply for the job.

Job posting and bidding is an internal method of recruitment in which notices of available jobs are posted in central locations throughout the organization, and employees are given a specified length of time to apply for the available jobs. Other methods used in publicizing jobs include memos to supervisors and listings in employee publications. Normally, the job notice specifies the job title, rate of pay, and qualifications necessary. The usual procedure is for all applications to be sent to the human resource department for an initial review. The next step is an interview by the prospective manager. Then a decision is made based on qualifications, performance, length of service, and other pertinent criteria.

If a job posting and bidding program is to be successful, specific implementation policies should be developed. Some suggestions include:

- Both promotions and transfers should be posted.
- Openings should be posted for a specified time before external recruitment begins.
- Eligibility rules for the job posting system need to be developed and communicated. For example, one eligibility rule might be that no employee can apply for a posted position unless the employee has been in his or her present position for six months.
- Specific standards for selection should be included in the notice.

- Job bidders should be required to list their qualifications and reasons for requesting a transfer or promotion.
- Unsuccessful bidders should be notified by the human resource department and advised as to why they were not accepted.

Naturally, the actual specifications for a job posting and bidding program must be tailored to the particular organization's needs.

In unionized organizations, job posting and bidding procedures are usually spelled out in the collective bargaining agreement. Because they are concerned about the subjective judgments of managers, unions normally insist that seniority be one of the primary determining factors used in selecting a person to fill available jobs.

External Sources

Organizations have at their disposal a wide range of external sources for recruiting personnel. External recruiting is often needed in organizations that are growing rapidly or have a large demand for technical, skilled, or managerial employees.

One inherent advantage of recruiting from outside is that the pool of talent is much larger than when recruiting is restricted to internal sources. Another advantage is that employees hired from outside can bring new insights and perspectives to the organization. In addition, it is often cheaper and easier to hire technical, skilled, or managerial people from the outside rather than training and developing them internally. This is especially true when the organization has an immediate demand for this type of talent.

One disadvantage to external recruitment is that attracting, contacting, and evaluating the potential employees is more difficult. A second potential disadvantage is that employees hired from the outside need a longer adjustment or orientation period. This can cause problems because even jobs that do not appear unique to the organization require familiarity with the people, procedures, policies, and special characteristics of the organization in which they are performed. A final problem is that recruiting from outside may cause morale problems among those people within the organization who feel qualified to do the job.

Advertising

One of the more widely used common methods of recruitment is **job advertising**. Help-wanted ads are commonly placed in daily newspapers and in trade and professional publications. Other, less frequently used media for advertising include radio, television, and billboards.

Research on the effectiveness of advertising has been limited. However, it generally has suggested that more informal recruiting sources (such as employee referrals) are superior to newspaper advertisements in recruiting long-term or more successful employees.[2] For example, one study found that newspaper advertisements were poorer sources for recruiting than were professional journal/convention advertisements.[3] The same study found that employees recruited through newspaper ads missed almost twice as many days as did those recruited with any other source.[4]

In the past, human resource managers have been encouraged to ensure that

Job advertising
The placement of help-wanted advertisements in daily newspapers, in trade and professional publications, or on radio and television.

their ads accurately describe the job opening and the requirements or qualifications needed to secure the position. However, one study found that the difference was not significant in reader response to a given advertisement that contained a specific description of the candidate qualifications and one containing a nonspecific description.[5] This same study found that corporate image was a more important factor in reader response. In other words, people responded more frequently to advertisements from companies with a positive corporate image than to those companies with a lower corporate image.[6]

In light of such studies, the widespread use of advertising is probably more a matter of convenience than proven effectiveness. If advertising is to be used as a primary source of recruitment by an organization, planning and evaluation of the advertising program should be a primary concern of the human resource department.

Employment Agencies

Both public and private employment agencies can be helpful in recruiting new employees. State employment agencies exist in most U.S. cities with populations of 10,000 or more. Although these agencies are administered by their respective states, they must comply with the policies and guidelines of the Employment and Training Administration of the U.S. Department of Labor to receive federal funds. The Social Security Act requires all eligible individuals to register with the state employment agency before they can receive unemployment compensation. Thus, state employment agencies generally have an up-to-date list of unemployed persons.

Private employment agencies, sometimes called search firms or "headhunters," are found more frequently in larger cities. These agencies usually charge a flat fee for their services or a percentage of the salary earned by the hired employee during the first year. Some organizations pay the fee for the new employee, while others require the new employee to pay the fee. Many private employment agencies concentrate on white-collar and executive recruiting because of the higher fees involved. The fees charged by these agencies are regulated by law in many states. In general, private agencies offer more specialized recruitment services than do state employment agencies.

Temporary help
People working for employment agencies who are subcontracted out to businesses at an hourly rate, for a period of time specified by the businesses.

In fact, one of the fastest-growing areas of recruitment is the use of **temporary help** hired through employment agencies. The salary and benefits of the temporary help are paid by the employment agency; the organization pays the employment agency an agreed-upon figure for the services of the temporary help. The use of temporary help is not dependent on economic conditions. When an organization is expanding, temporary employees are used to augment the current staff, and when an organization is downsizing, temporary employees create a flexible staff that can be laid off easily and recalled when necessary. One of the most obvious disadvantages of using temporary employees, however, is their lack of commitment to the organization.

Employee Referrals and Walk-Ins/Write-Ins

Many organizations involve their employees in the recruiting process. These recruiting systems may be informal and operate by word-of-mouth, or they may be structured with definite guidelines to be followed. Incentives and bonuses are sometimes given to employees who refer subsequently hired persons. One drawback to the use of employee referrals is that cliques may develop within the organization because employees have a tendency to refer only close friends and relatives. HRM

▽. HRM in Action 6–1

Apple Computer and Employee Referrals

Apple Computer implemented an employee referral program focused on travel—a trip for two to Carnival in Rio de Janeiro. The program was structured as follows: with one referral, an employee got one chance to win the trip; on the second referral, the referring employee got an additional two chances; with a third referral, he or she got an additional three chances, equaling six chances to win the trip; and so on. Referrals in selected classifications won even more chances. All employees making referrals also received gift certificates. The program resulted in 85 new hires at $694.11 per hire, which is considerably below the normal cost of recruitment at Apple.

Source: Adapted from Bob Martin, "Recruitment Ad Ventures," *Personnel Journal*, August 1987, p. 58.

▼ **Table 6–1**   Methods of internal and external recruitment

Internal	External
Job posting and bidding	Advertising
	Employment agencies
	Employee referrals and walk-ins/write-ins
	Campus recruiting

in Action 6–1 discusses a program designed by Apple Computer to encourage employee referrals.

Walk-ins/write-ins are also a source of qualified recruits. Corporate image has a significant impact on the number and quality of people applying to an organization in this manner. Compensation policies, working conditions, relationships with labor, and participation in community activities are some of the many factors that can positively or negatively influence an organization's image.

Campus Recruiting

Recruiting on college and university campuses is a common practice of both private and public organizations. **Campus recruiting** activities are usually coordinated by the university or college placement center. Generally, organizations send one or more recruiters to the campus for initial interviews. The most promising recruits are then invited to visit the office or plant before a final employment decision is made.

Campus recruiting
The recruitment activities of employers on college and university campuses.

If campus recruiting is used, steps should be taken by the human resource department to ensure that recruiters are knowledgeable concerning the organization and the jobs to be filled and that they understand and use effective interviewing skills. Recruitment interviewing is discussed later in this chapter.

College recruiters generally review an applicant's resume before conducting the interview. The On the Job episode at the end of this chapter is designed to provide guidance in resume writing.

Another method of tapping the products of colleges, universities, technical/vocational schools, and high schools is through cooperative work programs. In these programs, students may work part time and go to school part time, or they may go to school and work at different times of year. These programs attract people because they offer an opportunity for both a formal education and work experience. As an added incentive to finish their formal education and stay with the organization, employees are often promoted when their formal education is completed.

In summary, many different methods are available to organizations in the recruitment of personnel. Table 6–1 summarizes the methods that have been discussed in this chapter.

Effectiveness of Recruitment Methods

Organizational recruitment programs are designed to bring a pool of talent to the organization. From this pool, the organization hopes to select the person most qualified for the job. An obvious and very important question faced by human resource departments is what method of recruitment supplies the best talent pool.

Many studies have explored this issue. For example, one study concluded that employee referrals were the most effective recruitment source when compared to newspaper advertisements, private employment agencies, and walk-in applicants.[7] This study found that turnover rates for employees hired from employee referrals were lower than for employees hired through the other methods.

Another study examined the relationship between employee performance, absenteeism, work attitudes, and methods of recruitment.[8] This study showed that individuals recruited through a college placement office and, to a lesser extent, those recruited through newspaper advertisements were lower in performance (i.e., quality and dependability) than individuals who made contact with the company on their own initiative or through a professional journal/convention advertisement.

▼ **Table 6–2** Advantages and disadvantages of internal and external recruiting

Source	Advantages	Disadvantages
Internal	Company has a better knowledge of strengths and weaknesses of job candidate.	People might be promoted to the point where they cannot successfully perform the job.
	Job candidate has a better knowledge of company.	Infighting for promotions can negatively affect morale.
	Morale and motivation of employees is enhanced.	Inbreeding can stifle new ideas and innovation.
	The return on investment that an organization has in its present work force is increased.	
External	The pool of talent is much larger.	Attracting, contacting, and evaluating potential employees is more difficult.
	New insights and perspectives can be brought to the organization.	Adjustment or orientation time is longer.
	Frequently, it is cheaper and easier to hire technical, skilled, or managerial employees from outside.	Morale problems can develop among those employees within the organization who feel qualified to do the job.

As mentioned earlier, employees recruited through newspaper ads missed almost twice as many days as did those recruited through any of the other sources. Finally, college recruits showed significantly lower levels of job involvement and satisfaction with their managers than did employees recruited in other ways. This study concluded that campus recruiting and newspaper advertising were poorer sources of employees than were journal/convention advertisements and self-initiated contacts.

Generally, it seems safe to say that research has not identified a single best source of recruitment.[9] Thus, each organization should take steps to identify its most effective recruitment source. For example, a human resource department should monitor the effectiveness of recent hires in terms of turnover, absenteeism, and job performance. It should then contrast the different recruitment sources with respect to employee effectiveness and identify which of the specific recruitment sources produces the best employees. Table 6–2 summarizes the advantages and disadvantages of the internal and external methods of recruitment discussed in this chapter.

▼ **Figure 6–2**   Typical consequences of job preview procedures

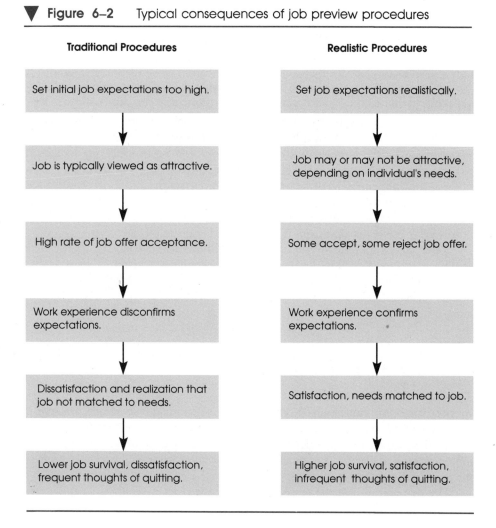

▽
▼.   **HRM IN Action 6–2**

Workshadowing at Touche Ross

Touche Ross, the international accounting firm, has attempted a rather unique approach to giving realistic job previews. Conducted in England in conjunction with Cambridge University, the effort is called *work-shadowing*. In the program, students (who are called *shadows*) follow an employee of Touche Ross (called a *work guide*) wherever they go during a week. The idea is for the shadows to experience a job without having to commit themselves.

The workshadow program is based on the assumption that many students have little work experience. If they come into contact with business, it is often in an artificial context. Putting students into a normal working environment gives them a completely different perspective.

Source: Adapted from Andrew Jack, "Me and My Shadow," *Accountancy*, February 1989, p. 97.

Realistic Job Previews

Realistic job previews
A way of providing complete information, both positive and negative, to the job applicant.

One method proposed for increasing the effectiveness of all recruiting methods is the use of realistic job previews (RJP).[10] **Realistic job previews** provides complete job information, both positive and negative, to the job applicant.

Organizations traditionally have attempted to sell the organization and the job to the prospective employee by making both look good. Normally, this is done to obtain a favorable selection ratio—that is, a large number of applicants in relation to the number of job openings. Then, of course, the company can select the cream of the crop. Unfortunately, these attempts sometimes set the initial job expectations of the new employees too high and can produce dissatisfaction and high turnover among employees recruited in this manner. Figure 6–2 contrasts some of the outcomes that can develop from traditional and realistic job previews.

Research on the effectiveness of RJP indicates that it seems to reduce new employee turnover.[11] However, much more research is needed to ascertain its impact on employee performance on the job. HRM in Action 6–2 discusses a unique realistic job preview at Touche Ross.

Who Does the Recruiting, and How?

In most large- and middle-sized organizations, the human resource department is responsible for recruiting. These organizations normally have an employment office within the human resource department. The employment office has recruiters, interviewers, and clerical personnel who handle the recruitment activities both at the organization's offices and elsewhere.

The role of those in the employment office is crucial. Walk-ins/write-ins, respondents to advertising, and present employees responding to job postings develop an impression of the organization through their contacts with the employment office. If the applicant is treated indifferently or rudely, a lasting negative impression can be developed. On the other hand, if the applicant is pleasantly greeted, provided with pertinent information about job openings, and treated with dignity and respect, then a lasting positive impression is likely to result. Having employees trained in effective communication and interpersonal skills is essential in the employment office.

When recruiting away from the organization's offices, the role of the recruiter is equally critical. Job applicants' impressions about the organization are significantly influenced by the knowledge and expertise of the recruiter.

In small organizations, the recruitment function, in addition to many other responsibilities, is normally handled by one person—frequently, the office manager. It is also not unusual for line managers in small organizations to recruit and interview job applicants.

Organizational Inducements in Recruitment

The objective of recruitment is to attract a number of qualified personnel for each particular job opening. **Organizational inducements** are all the positive features and benefits offered by an organization that serve to attract job applicants to the organization. Three of the more important organizational inducements are organizational compensation systems, career opportunities, and organizational reputation.

Organizational inducements
Positive features and benefits offered by an organization to attract job applicants.

Starting salaries, frequency of pay raises, incentives, and the nature of the organization's fringe benefits can all influence the number of people obtained through the recruitment process. For example, organizations that pay low starting salaries have a much more difficult time finding qualified applicants than do organizations that pay higher starting salaries.

Organizations that have a reputation for providing employees with career opportunities are also more likely to attract a larger pool of qualified candidates through their recruiting activities. Employee and management development opportunities enable present employees to grow personally and professionally; they also attract good people to the organization. Assisting present employees in career planning develops feelings that the company cares. It also acts as an inducement to potential employees.

Finally, the organization's overall reputation, or image, serves as an inducement to potential employees. Factors that affect an organization's reputation include its general treatment of employees, the nature and quality of its products and services, and its participation in worthwhile social endeavors. Unfortunately, some organizations accept a poor image as "part of our industry and business." Regardless of the type of business or industry, organizations should strive for a good image. HRM in Action 6–3 describes an inducement provided by Hardee's.

▼. HRM in Action 6–3

Recruitment Inducements at Hardee's

Hardee's is focusing its recruitment activities on key target groups such as teenagers, working mothers, older workers, people with disabilities, and members of minority groups.

Providing child-care assistance is one way to attract working mothers. A Hardee's restaurant in Minnesota pays the $50 enrollment fee and half the daily or hourly expenses at the local Kinder-Care Learning Center. A similar program is being tested in the Raleigh, North Carolina, area. If the working mother stays for one year, the restaurant will pay 75 percent of the eligible expenses.

Source: Adapted from William H. Wagel, "Hardee's: One Step Ahead in the Race for Employees," *Personnel,* April 1989, p. 21.

The Recruitment Interview

The recruitment interview can be viewed as part of either the recruitment process or the selection process. For example, in campus recruiting, the recruiter's impression of the job applicant plays a role in determining whether the applicant is invited for a visit to the company or, in some cases, whether the job applicant is offered a job. In this case, the recruitment interview serves as part of the recruitment process and as the first step in the selection process.

The content and quality of the recruitment interview influence an applicant's decision to join an organization. Indifferent interviewers can turn applicants away from the organization. However, in spite of the importance of recruitment interviews, many interviewers have little or no training. Chapter 7 describes the interviewing process in much more depth.

Equal Employment Opportunity and Recruitment

The entire subject of recruitment interviewing is made even more complex by equal employment opportunity legislation and court decisions relating to this legislation. For example, if an interviewer asks for certain information such as race, sex, age, marital status, and number of children during the interview, the company risks the chance of an employment discrimination suit. Prior to employment, interviewers should not ask for information that is potentially prejudicial unless the company is prepared to prove (in court, if necessary) that the requested information is job related (see On the Job 3).

Recruitment activities have been significantly influenced by equal employment opportunity legislation. All recruitment procedures for each job category should be analyzed and reviewed to identify and eliminate discriminatory barriers. For example, the Equal Employment Opportunity Commission (EEOC) encourages organizations to avoid recruiting primarily by employee referral and walk-ins because these practices tend to perpetuate the present composition of an organization's work force. If minorities and females are not well represented at all levels of the organization, reliance on such recruitment procedures has been ruled by the courts to be a discriminatory practice.

EEOC also suggests that the content of help-wanted ads should not indicate any race, sex, or age preference for the job unless age or sex is a bona fide occupational qualification (BFOQ). Organizations are also encouraged to advertise in media directed towards minorities and women. Advertising should indicate that the organization is an equal opportunity employer and does not discriminate.[12]

Campus recruiting visits should be scheduled at colleges and universities with large minority and female enrollment. EEOC also recommends that employers develop and maintain contacts with minority, female, and community organizations as sources of recruits.

Employers are encouraged to contact nontraditional recruitment sources, such as women's colleges and organizations that place physically and mentally handicapped persons. It is certain that hiring of both females and minority groups will continue to receive attention, and increased emphasis is likely to be placed on hiring from ethnic groups.

Recruiters will also more than likely have to pay more attention to the spouse, male or female, of the person being recruited. It may become necessary to assist in finding jobs for spouses of recruits. In hiring women, especially for managerial and professional jobs, it may be necessary to consider hiring the husband as well.

● *Summary of Learning Objectives*

1. Define recruitment.

    Recruitment involves seeking and attracting a pool of people from which qualified candidates for job vacancies can be chosen.

2. Discuss job analysis, human resource planning, and recruitment.

    Job analysis gives the nature and requirements of specific jobs. Human resource planning determines the specific number of jobs to be filled. Recruitment provides a pool of qualified people to fill the vacancies.

3. Describe the advantages and disadvantages of using internal methods of recruitment.

    The advantages are that the company has a better knowledge of the strengths and weaknesses of the job candidates; the job candidates have a better knowledge of the company; the employees' motivation and morale are enhanced; and the return on investment that an organization has in its work force is increased.

    The disadvantages are that people can be promoted to the point where they cannot successfully perform the job; infighting for promotions can negatively affect morale; and inbreeding can stifle new ideas and innovation.

4. Discuss job posting and bidding.

    Job posting and bidding is an internal method of recruitment in which notices of available jobs are posted in central locations throughout the organization and employees are given a specified length of time to apply for the available jobs.

5. Describe the advantages and disadvantages of using external methods of recruitment.

    The advantages are that the pool of talent is much larger; new insights and perspectives can be brought to the organization; and it is frequently cheaper and easier to hire technical, skilled, or managerial employees from outside.

    The disadvantages are that attracting, contacting, and evaluating potential employees is more difficult; adjustment or orientation time is longer; and morale problems can develop among those employees within the organization who feel qualified to do the job.

6. Define realistic job previews.

    Realistic job previews provide complete job information, both positive and negative, to the job applicant.

7. Define organizational inducements.

    These are all the positive features and benefits offered by an organization that serve to attract job applicants to the organization.

Review Questions

1. What is recruitment?
2. Describe the relationships among job analysis, personnel planning, recruitment, and selection.
3. Give several advantages of recruiting from internal sources and several external sources.
4. Name and describe at least five methods of recruiting.
5. What are realistic job previews?
6. Define and give examples of organizational inducements.
7. Outline some specific EEOC recommendations for job advertising.

Discussion Questions

1. Discuss the following statement: "An individual who owns a business should be able to recruit and hire whomever he or she pleases."
2. Employees often have negative views on the policy of hiring outsiders rather than promoting from within. Naturally, employees feel that they should always be given preference for promotion before outsiders are hired. Do you think this is in the best interest of the organization?
3. As a potential recruit who will probably be looking for a job upon completion of school, what general approach and method or methods of recruiting do you think would be most effective in attracting you?

▼ INCIDENT 6–1

Inside or Outside Recruiting

Powermat, Inc., has encountered difficulty over the last few years in filling its middle management positions. The company, which manufactures and sells complex machinery, is organized into six semiautonomous manufacturing departments. Top management believes that it is necessary for the managers of these many managerial decisions must be made at that level. Therefore, the company originally recruited strictly from within. However, they soon found that employees elevated to the middle management often lacked the skills necessary to discharge their new duties.

A decision was then made to recruit from outside, particularly from colleges with good industrial management programs. Through the services of a professional recruiter, the company was provided with a pool of well-qualified industrial management graduates. Several were hired and placed in lower management positions as preparation for the middle management jobs. Within two years, all these people had left the company.

Management reverted to its former policy of promoting from within and experienced basically the same results as before. Faced with the imminent retirement of employees in several key middle management positions, the company decided to call in a consultant who could suggest solutions.

Questions

1. Is recruiting the problem in this company?
2. If you were the consultant, what would you recommend?

▼ INCIDENT 6–2

Malpractice Suit against a Hospital

Hospital jumping is a term used by hospital personnel people to describe the movement of incompetent and potentially negligent employees from hospital to hospital. One factor contributing to hospital jumping is the reluctance of hospitals to release information to other hospitals that are checking references.

Ridgeview Hospital was sued for negligence in its screening of employees. The case involved the alleged incorrect administration to an infant of a medication that nearly caused the child's death. The party bringing suit contended that the nurse who administered the drug was negligent, as was the hospital because it had failed to make a thorough investigation of the nurse's work history and background. It was learned that the nurse had been hired by Ridgeview before it had received a letter of reference from her previous employer verifying her employment history. In support of the plaintiff's case, uncontested information was presented about a similar incident of negligence in patient care by the nurse in her previous employment.

Ridgeview Hospital's personnel director John Reeves took the position that reference checks were a waste of time because area hospital personnel directors would not provide information about former employees that they thought might be defamatory. He further stated that in checking reference sources, these same personnel directors would request information that they themselves would not give.

Reeves' lawyer concluded that the hospital would have to choose between two potentially damaging alternatives in adopting a personnel screening policy. It could continue not to verify references, thereby risking malpractice suits such as the one discussed. Alternatively, it could implement a policy of giving out all information on past employees and risk defamation suits. The lawyers recommended the second alternative because they thought that the potential cost would be significantly less if the hospital were convicted of libel or slander than if it were judged guilty of negligence.

Questions

1. What would you recommend to the hospital?
2. What questions could be asked in a recruitment interview to help eliminate the problem?

Exercise

Want Ads

The want ads shown in Exhibit 6–1 appeared in *The Wall Street Journal*. Prepare a report summarizing the strengths and weaknesses of each ad.

Notes and Additional Readings

1. L. J. Peter and R. Hall, *The Peter Principle* (New York: Bantam Books, 1979).

2. David F. Caldwell and W. Austin Spivey, "The Relationship between Recruiting Source and Employee Success: An Analysis by Race," *Personnel Psychology* 36 (1983), p. 71.

3. J. A. Breaugh, "Relationships between Recruiting Sources and Employee Performance, Absenteeism, and Work Attitudes," *Academy of Management Journal*, March 1981, p. 145.

4. Ibid.

5. J. A. Belt and J. G. P. Paolillo, "The Influence of Corporate Image and Specificity of Candidate Qualifications on Response to Recruitment Advertisement," *Journal of Management*, Spring 1982, p. 110.

VICE PRESIDENT MANPOWER PLANNING & SELECTION

Barnett Banks of Florida, Florida's largest and fastest growing bank with over 14,000 employees and 370 offices, is looking for an individual to spearhead new initiatives and manpower. planning & selection.

Reporting to the Executive Vice President of Human Resources, this position will play a key role in establishing Barnett at the leading edge of human resource technology, regardless of the industry.

The ideal candidate should have a minimum of eight years human resource experience with an emphasis on directing the selection and placement activities for a major business unit. This position requires outstanding communication skills and the ability to relate to the needs of our 41 affiliates throughout the State.

"Florida's Bank" offers a compensation and benefits package designed to attract top quality people from any industry. If you are looking for a fast-paced and challenging environment, please send your resume, including salary history, in confidence to: **Paul T. Kerins, EVP, Human Resources, Barnett Banks of Florida, Inc., P.O. Box 40789, Jacksonville, FL 32231.** An equal opportunity employer.

VICE PRESIDENT HU...

Precision Monolithics Inc., a le... high performance, linear integrat... a vice president of Human Resourc... President, the position entails resp... 1,000 employees in multi-plant location... The position requires a broad backgrou... of Human Resources with several years... a high technology environment. The ability to operate successfully in a dyn... environment and initiate innovative approa... Human Resources function is essential.

Send resume to:
President
Precision Monolithics Inc.
1500 Space Park Drive   **P.O. Box 580...**
Santa Clara, CA 95052-8020
PMI is an equal opportunity employer.

LABOR RELATIONS MANAGER

High Visibility Opportunity In Atlanta

We are a Fortune 50 leader in a dynamic, fast-paced industry seeking a seasoned labor relations professional. This position requires 10-12 years experience managing multiple-country labor relations situations for a large, multi-national company. Strong skills in both union and non-union environments are essential.
We offer a competitive salary and excellent benefits. For confidential consideration, please send resume with salary history to:

Dept. NG
P.O. Drawer 1734
Atlanta, GA 30301
An Equal Opportunity Employer

Source: *The Wall Street Journal*, April 22, 1986, pp. 35, 36–41.

6. Ibid.

7. D. P. Schwab, "Organizational Recruiting and the Decision to Participate," in *Personnel Management: New Perspectives,* eds. K. Rowland and G. Ferris (Boston: Allyn & Bacon, 1982).

8. Breaugh, "Relationships between Recruiting Sources," p. 145.

9. For another study, see M. Susan Taylor and Donald W. Schmidt, "A Process-Oriented Investigation of Recruitment Source Effectiveness," *Personnel Psychology* 36 (1983), pp. 343–54.

instance, J. P. Wanous, *Organizational Entry: Recruitment, Se-* *and Socialization of Newcomers* (Reading, Mass.: Addison-Wesley ...shing, 1980).

...aula Popovich and John P. Wanous, "The Realistic Job Preview as a Persuasive Communication," *Academy of Management Review* 7 (1982), p. 572.

12. See John P. Kohl and David B. Stephens, "Wanted: Recruitment Advertising that Doesn't Discriminate," *Personnel*, February 1989, pp. 18–26.

On the Job

Writing a Resume

Bill Osher, Ph.D., and
Sioux Henley Campbell

For employers, the resume is a screening device. Big corporations get hundreds of thousands of them every year. You can pay an employment agency a hundred dollars to come up with a work of art on thirty weight paper, but it's still junk mail to the guy who had to read a hundred of them a day. So you've got ten, maybe twenty seconds to show him that your resume is worth a second look.

It's got to look "mahvelous." Which isn't all that hard to make happen. Use high quality eight and one-half by eleven inch paper—white, off-white, light gray, or beige. Maybe a designer or entertainer could go with something flashier, but most job seekers are best served by a conservative, professional look.

Don't use the typewriter your grandfather used in 1937. Get hold of a good electric that types clean, or hire a professional typist. Better yet, put it on a floppy disk. (This is just one more instance where computer skills come in handy.) If you don't know word processing, any professional secretarial service will be able to do it for you. Don't run it off on a cheap dot-matrix printer. Having it printed looks great; but then you're locked into one generic resume, and that has some real disadvantages. We'll elaborate shortly. All you really need is a good original. You can have any number duplicated on high quality paper at a copy center.

Appearance, as well as content, tells the employer a lot about you. Your resume reflects the kind of work you're capable of producing. It should show that you're well organized, that you can communicate clearly, and that you can make a strong visual presentation. The acid test: Does it look good enough for prospective employers to send out as their own work? If it doesn't, it's not good enough.

Use some of the tricks that commercial artists use. When they design ads, they play up important information in the white space, those areas free from text. In poorly constructed resumes we often see dates in those big chunks of white space

Adapted from *The Blue-Chip Graduate*, Peachtree Publishers, Inc., Atlanta, Georgia, 1987, pp. 155–179.

known as the margin. Dates *are not* selling points. Instead use information that is: job titles, degrees, skills, etc.

Stay away from long paragraphs. Your resume should not look like a page out of your American history text. Ads use a few key words, carefully chosen and strategically placed. You further focus attention by using bold print, larger type, bullets or asterisks. Remember, you've got just ten seconds to get their attention.

The job objective is crucial because it informs the employer if there is a match. The job objective, unlike the rest of the resume, gets close attention on the first pass-through. Therefore, it comes immediately after your name and address at the top of the page. If you're offering what the employer is seeking, he or she will read on.

Taking a Second Look

OK, the employer looked at your resume, and it looked good. Your career objectives matches one of the positions to be filled. Now, the employer's willing to look more closely. And when this happens, there *must not* be any misspelled words, typos, or grammatical errors. So proofread it carefully. Wait a day, and proof it again. Then let a friend take a look at it. Obviously, this means you don't start working on your resume at the last minute. But since you're a blue-chipper, you've got organizational skills. You'll have time to do it right.

Name and Address
You want them to remember your name, so you put it at the top of the page. If possible, use a larger type size then you use on the rest of your resume. If your typewriter or printer doesn't have this capability, there are several other alternatives: rub-on type, lettering templates, or a Kroy lettering machine. Check with your campus bookstore or copy center if you need help. Include your address and a phone number where you can be reached or a message can be left for you during working hours. You might want to consider buying or sharing an answering machine. Or you may be able to have messages left with a friend, neighbor, or relative. In some cases you can have messages taken at the departmental headquarters of your academic major.

Example

MARY Q. STUDENT

Campus Box 007   Atlanta, GA 30332   (494) 894-0000

Job Objective
We've already mentioned that the job objective is the most important piece of information on the page. If employers don't see a potential match, they might not look further, no matter how outstanding your record. Ideally, the job you're looking for is identical to the one they're trying to fill (see the following job objective components chart).

The Job Objective

The following is a component sheet useful in developing a job objective. Pick the ones you feel are applicable to your situation.

- Include the exact job title if you know it. Do not guess! The job objective is used as a screening device. If you apply for a job that does not exist, your resume will probably be eliminated before it is read thoroughly. Don't chance it.
- Make the objective meaningful. Everything else in the resume must support and reflect what is said in the objective.
- Be specific and to the point. Broad objectives are often misinterpreted to be vague and uncertain. Avoid the use of platitudes and cliches. They say nothing and cast doubt on the rest of the resume.
- Include the field you were trained in if this is a selling point. This is especially applicable to those in technical fields.
- Include a subdiscipline if you have specialized in one. This will help to pinpoint where in the company you might be most useful.
- Include the functional area of the company where you want to work. Examples of these company divisions are: research and development, production, technical services, information systems/processing, marketing and sales, and administration and finance.
- Include skills/qualifications that are relevant to the job you are seeking. This will help promote you as a strong job candidate.

   Example: seek a position in civil engineering as a Structural Engineer utilizing my skills in structures, computer programming, and construction.

- Include the type of organization if it is important to you. Keep in mind that this may limit the number of opportunities open to you.
- Note: If you have several different job objectives, you should have several different resumes.

Avoid platitudes and vagueness. All graduates want "A challenging position with opportunities for advancement." If this is your stated career objective, you've told an employer nothing.

Give any information that will tell the employer where you would fit best. For instance, identify where you want to work in the company (sales, finance, etc.); you may also want to indicate the key skills you have to offer (administrative, quantitative, etc.). Companies don't hire generic employees. They hire researchers, accountants, and personnel directors.

We also advise against listing plural job objectives unless they are closely related. You wouldn't, for instance, say you were looking for an "entry-level position in sales or research" because it makes you look as if you have no clear career goals. If you are looking at rather different positions with different companies, we strongly recommend a different resume highlighting the appropriate skills and experience for each position. This is where having a generic resume on a computer, whether it's yours or a professional word processor's, is invaluable. When it comes time to apply for a new job, it is easy to rearrange the material.

Use the actual job titles when you know them—catch the employer's attention right away by showing the possibility of a match. However, don't guess if you're not sure. Personnel may be doing the screening, and they might eliminate you if they don't see what they've been told to look for. If you don't know the exact title, use a standard area such as finance, sales, or research.

Everything else on the resume complements the job objective. The education, experience, and skills all show that you can do the job you're trying to get.

Example

OBJECTIVE:	Seek a position as an **Advertising Sales Representative** using my academic background, proven sales skills, and retail experience

Education

List your educational experience in reverse chronological order. If you went to a prestigious school, highlight the fact by using bold face letters or caps. Be sure to include a high GPA and any honors or awards. List the key courses relevant to the job you are seeking. Omit insignificant schooling such as the summer course you took at the junior college back home. Don't mention your high school unless you went to a truly outstanding one or had an especially distinguished record.

Example

EDUCATION:
St. Anselm's College   GPA: 2.9/4.0
B.A. Communications   6/87

Coursework: Marketing, Advertising, Media Planning, Principles of Persuasion, Managerial Accounting & Control, Consumer Psychology, Communication Ethics & Law, Public Speaking, FORTRAN

Honors and Activities: Dean's List, earned **80%** of college expenses, Young Business Leaders Club

Skills

Employers want to know what skills you have. You can embed them in your work history, but sometimes it's a good idea to have a separate skills section. There you can highlight the main skills required of the position you're seeking. By doing so you increase your changes of creating a match in the employer's mind.

Use the STAR Technique: situation, action, results. Positive results create positive reactions. And if you can quantify your results, you're talking in a language employers understand.

Example

Marketing	• Successfully participated in three-month long computer-based marketing game which simulated the soft drink industry
Organizational Ability	• Actively involved in arranging campus international festival—responsibilities included arranging media events, designing pamphlets, and coordinating the various committees involved

Work Experience

List in reverse chronological order. Play up your work if it's career-related or requires skills you want to emphasize. Whenever possible, use job descriptions that are results-oriented.

Example

WORK HISTORY: MACY'S DEPARTMENT STORE

	Sales Representative	9/83–12/86
Retail Sales	Created furniture displays and performed price markdowns that led to **10% increase in departmental sales** for 1985	
Communication Skills	Reinforced and **interpreted company procedures** and policies to new company employees during training periods	

Some students find it helpful to have two separate work sections—career-related, which is prominently displayed, and other work, which goes toward the bottom of the page. If you have paid for your own education or a good portion of it, say so. It indicates that you're hard working and self-sufficient. Even if work is not directly related to your job objective, you often learn skills that are relevant to it. For example, getting customers for a summer lawn care business demonstrates sales ability.

Additional Information

Every inch of your resume should be used to your advantage. List only information that would be a selling point. Most employers don't really need to know that you enjoy swimming and scuba diving. A marine biologist, however, might find it helpful to include these. An engineer cited her plumbing experience when she applied for a position that required wearing a hard hat. She wanted to show that being a woman didn't mean she was afraid to get her hands dirty. One candidate noted that hunting was one of his hobbies. He was applying for a position in a rural area where hunting was extremely popular. By mentioning his interest in guns, he was able to show that he could be one of the gang even though he'd gone to school in a big city. If you can't find another place to include a selling point, stick it in here. Leave it off if it's not relevant.

References

Choose them carefully. Hopefully, you have many to choose from. Ask them if they are comfortable writing a favorable recommendation for you. Make sure they have copies of your resume. It will help them to discuss you more knowledgeably when they are contacted by employers. Also, when they see the total package they might be able to come up with other job leads for you. We recommend not listing your references on the resume. It's better to use every precious inch of space to promote yourself. Exhibit 6–A shows a sample resume format.

▼ **Exhibit 6–A** Resume format

		NAME		
Address	City	State	Zip	Phone

JOB OBJECTIVE: Most important piece of information on resume; used by employers as screening device or to signal job match; must grab attention and motivate employer to read further (see section on Job Objectives).

EDUCATION: List in reverse chronological order, putting the most promotable facts—school or degree—first.

Mention any outstanding honors or achievements, such as high GPA, Dean's List....

Give examples of relevant coursework and school-related activities if a recent graduate.

SKILLS:
- Choose skills that are most relevant to job objective.
- Give short statements to support skills.
- Make support statements results-oriented.
- Position most marketable skills first.

EMPLOYMENT: Place strongest of the two sections, employment or education, first.

List in reverse chronological order, putting the most promotable facts—employer or job title—first.

Give functional description of job if employment history is strong and supports job objective.

MISCELLANEOUS:
- Call this section anything applicable— INTERESTS, ACTIVITIES, ACCOMPLISHMENTS, or ACHIEVEMENTS.
- Give only information that an employer would be interested in knowing.
- Stay away from personal and chatty information.

REFERENCES: Furnished upon request.

Remember: there are no concrete rules in resume preparation. Modify this guide, when necessary, to make the most favorable impression.

Wording and Phrasing

You control the tone of your resume by the way you write it. There should be no negatives. One student once listed a course in which he made a *D*. That made a memorable resume, but not in a good way.

Your resume should be crisp and have punch. Remember, it's your personal ad. Start sentences with verbs or action words, and you'll create the impression that you're a "doer," not one who sits and waits. Delete pronouns and anything superfluous.

The whole idea is to boil your marketability down to its essence. Recruiters and interviewers, then, will find it easy to remember you. And why they should hire you. Not every recruiter has been trained in personnel. Frequently corporations send new, inexperienced employees to handle screening interviews at college place-ment centers. They don't necessarily know how to compare the credentials of the many different candidates. It is to your advantage to make their job easier. A sharp resume is a first step. Make it clear why you're the one their company is looking for.

Action Words for Resume Construction

A resume will be the first impression an employer has of you. Make it count! Set the tone by using both action and positive words. Starting sentences with verbs can make your message stronger. Be honest, but don't diminish your abilities by using lackluster words.

Exhibit 6–B provides a list of action words to use in constructing your resume. Refer to it often.

Types of Resumes

Chronological
This is the most traditional type—which is its advantage. Employers are familiar with it. The disadvantage of the chronological resume is that it plays up your work history even if it's sketchy or unrelated to your job objective. If you've followed the blue-chip Master Plan, you should have a solid work history. If your professional experience is weak, consider another type of resume. Exhibit 6–C shows a chron-ological resume.

Functional
Since work history is played down, you can emphasize the skills necessary to perform the job you're seeking. And since you're not following any prescribed order, you can position the most relevant skills, experience, for example, higher on the page. Its main disadvantage is that employers see fewer of this type, and that might bother some of them. Of course, it might also catch their eye. Exhibit 6–B shows a functional resume.

Hybrid
We believe there is nothing sacred about resume construction. Your ultimate goal is to create a message that effectively promotes you. We read the resume experts, and we considered the principles of advertising. We did some research of our own—asking recruiters and personnel directors how they appraised resumes. Our guidelines evolved from all these sources. But they're still only guidelines.

Different students may have unique situations that require novel resumes. What about the student who makes a dramatic shift in educational focus? How can you get the most mileage out of a double or a dual degree program? Nontraditional students also present unique problems. How do you highlight your strengths if you're a middle-aged homemaker returning to the work force? (Returning to the *paid* work force would be more accurate). Or suppose you're returning to school after a substantial work history. Some resumes break the rules, but we think they come out stronger for doing so.

actively	chaired	directed	function	managed	primary	reviewed
accelerated	changed	diverted	generated	manufactured	principal	satisfactorily
accomplished	channeled	drafted	graduated	marketed	produced	saved
accurately	chiefly	drew up	guided	maximum	proficient	scheduled
achieved	chosen	earned	helped	measurable	programmed	schematic
adapted	clarified	economically	hired	mediation	progressed	selected
addressed	coached	edited	honored	merchandised	projected	served
adjusted	collaborated	effective	illustrated	merit	promoted	significantly
administered	commended	elected	implemented	methodically	proposed	simplified
adopted	communication	eliminated	improved	minimal	proved	sold
advised	compiled	enhanced	increased	moderated	provided	solved
analyzed	completed	enthusiastic	indexed	modified	publicized	solution
applied	conducted	erected	influenced	most	qualified	specialized
appointed	consistently	established	innovation	motivated	quoted	spoke
appraised	constructed	estimated	inspected	motorized	recommended	stabilized
approved	consulted	evaluated	installed	narrated	recorded	strategy
arbitrated	coordinated	examined	instituted	navigated	reduced (losses)	streamlined
arranged	contracted	executive	instrumental	negotiated	reinforced	structured
assembled	counseled	exhibited	integrated	obtained	renovated	successfully
assessed	created	expanded	interpreted	organized	reorganized	suggested
assisted	credited (with)	expedited	interviewed	orginated	reported	summarized
attentive	debated	experienced	judged	overcame	represented	supervised
audited	decided	explained	knowledgeable	participated	researched	supplemented
authenticated	delegated	expressed	launched	perceptive	resolved	supported
budgeted	delivered	facilitated	lead	performed	responsible	surveyed
built	demonstrated	familiar (with)	lectured	persuaded	responsibilities	systematized
calculated	designed	filed	licensed	pinpointed	restored	taught
capable	determined	finalist	lobbied	planned	revamped	trained
careful	detected	finished	logical	positive	revenue	upgraded
cataloged	developed	forecasted	maintained	prepared	revised	wrote
certified	devised	founded	major	presented		

▼ **Exhibit 6–C**   Chronological resume

ANDREW FOENSTER

Campus Address: P.O. Box 64902, St. Cloud, MN 56301   612/255-9000
Permanent Address: 17 Faribault Place, Omaha, NB 68178   402/448-6413

OBJECTIVE: Position as **Medical Technologist** in clinical laboratory

EDUCATION:

ST. CLOUD STATE UNIVERSITY   12/87
B.S. Medical Technology

LINCOLN COMMUNITY COLLEGE   8/84
A.S. General Sciences

Significant Coursework:

- Hematology
- Immunology
- Clinical Chemistry
- Histology

- Microbiology
- Microscopy
- Immunohematology
- Cell Biology

WORK EXPERIENCE:

HENNEPIN COUNTY MEDICAL CENTER
Intern Technologist   Minneapolis, MN
                                                               1/86–present

Performed **microscopic examinations** of blood and bone marrow. Isolated
and identified **microbiological cultures**. Conducted **renal function tests**
including chemical and microscopic examinations of body fluid analysis.
Performed and correlated **serological testing**.

BHP, INC.   Redland, MN
Operator I/Operator II   10/84–11/85

Manufactured **blood references** for Coulter counters and other specialized
medical uses. Mixed chemical solutions, washed blood, sampled materials,
mixed blood solutions to specified concentrations of various cell types.
Promoted from operator I to operator II in three weeks.

GREATER LINCOLN BLOOD PROGRAM
Interviewed prospective donors   Lincoln, NB
                                                               Summers 1983/84

ACTIVITIES:

Provided **100%** of college expenses; member, **Medical Technology
Association**; member, St. Cloud State Ski Club

REFERENCES AVAILABLE UPON REQUEST

Cover Letters

Cover letters should be strong enough to stand on their own and promote you
even when separated from your other credentials. In other words, no "Dear Mr.
Gronk, I'm interested in working for your organization. Enclosed, please find my
resume. Sincerely. . . ."

▼ **Exhibit 6–D** Functional resume

BENNETT TINDALL

Post Office Box 15933
Atlanta, Georgia 30332
404/892-4400

OBJECTIVE:	Seek position as an **industrial designer** using strong design and project management skills
EDUCATION:	**GEORGIA INSTITUTE OF TECHNOLOGY** 6/87
B.S. Industrial Design	Concentrated in product package, exhibit and graphic design; additional courses included production processes and materials, computer-aided design (CAD), ergonomics, and solid modeler experience
	DUKE UNIVERSITY 6/86–9/86
Studies Abroad Program/France	Studied art history and figure drawing; traveled throughout Europe for two months
QUALIFICATIONS:	
Product Design	Concept model of **mobile parapodium** retained by Atlanta's Henrietta Eggleston Hospital for further development
Computer-Aided Design	Proficient in **solid modeler** and design drafting techniques
Project Management	Served as **President** and **Board Member** for campus organization; responsibilities included revising and implementing annual budget, organizing programs and events, and proposing ideas and strategies for annual goals
WORK HISTORY:	Contributed **60%** of college expenses through work and financial aid as follows:
Delivery Manager	**FUN COMPANY, INC.** Summers 1985–86 Coordinated, scheduled, and produced employee picnics and conventions; **supervised** staffing groups of 20–60
ACTIVITIES:	President and Board Member, Black Student Fellowship—3 years; **Dean's List**; staff artist for student newspaper

**REFERENCES AND PORTFOLIO AVAILABLE
UPON REQUEST**

Use the cover letter to elaborate on any information that is briefly covered in the resume and is a selling point. Use key phrases taken from your resume. Advertising relies on repeated presentations, and you're advertising yourself. "Where's the beef?" is probably still familiar to you several years after the ad stopped running because you heard it so many times.

Format

The opening paragraph needs to serve as a "hook." It should motivate employers to read further. Mentioning something interesting about the company (not just something found in the Yellow pages) shows that you believe their company is worth spending time on. Like the resume, the cover letter needs to show how a

▼ **Exhibit 6–E**   Sample cover letter

February 2, 1990

Museum of Natural Artifacts
    and History
1748 Lincoln Square
New York, NY 10025

Attn: Mr. Carson Donnelly,
        Director of Student Internship Program

Dear Mr. Donnelly:

I am interested in applying for a summer internship offered through the Museum of
Natural Artifacts and History. *American Historian* magazine recently reported that the
MNAH provided the "most extensive training—outside of a dig—to those students
interested in archaeology and anthropology." Although you have 25 summer
internships, it's obvious that you have to be selective in choosing participants. Here's
why I can make a positive contribution.

First, I have prior experience working in a museum. While in high school I was a
volunteer at the Vandernessen Museum of Fine Arts. There I helped the curator set up
exhibits and prepare art objects for shipment. One project that I particularly enjoyed
working on included over 250 Indian artifacts and featured a full-scale replica of a
wigwam.

Second, my academic accomplishments include a GPA of 3.7 after one semester as an
anthropology major at Bates College and membership in the National Honor Society.

Finally, I have strong communication and leadership skills. I have proven experience
in leading groups, being a team member, and working with the public, all assets that
are helpful in a museum environment.

I have enclosed a resume for your convenience. I am eager to discuss internship
opportunities and will contact you in three weeks to arrange an interview.

Sincerely,

Nicholas Bennings

Nicholas Bennings
37-G Addison Hall
Bates College
Lewiston, ME 04240

---

candidate's skills meet the employer's needs. State specifically how you can help
solve the employer's problems. Indicate why you're contacting the employer and
how you found out about the job (magazine article, newspaper ad, professional
contact, etc.).

You'll probably need to do some research in sources such as the *Business
Periodical Index, Reader's Guide, Moody's Index,* and *Dun's Career Guide.* Say specifically why you're interested in the particular organization you're contacting.

Body of Letter

Present your case as a strong candidate. Briefly cite whichever of your academic achievements, skills, accomplishments, and work history is relevant. Give specific examples with details. Repeat some of the key phrases contained in your resume to reinforce your selling points. Tell them "where the beef is." Mention enclosing a resume for their convenience.

Closing Paragraph

Ask for action. Be confident and assertive about doing so. You wouldn't apply for the job if you didn't think you were the right one to do it. State that you will contact them in ten days to two weeks. *And do it.* Exhibit 6–E gives an illustration of a cover letter.

Resume Checklist

You want your resume to be memorable to the employer—but for all the right reasons. An omission or mistake should not be noted as your resume's most outstanding feature. Use this chart to check for any oversights. Have it double-checked by a friend just to ensure you haven't missed anything.

Did You:	Yes	No
1. Prominently display your name?	___	___
2. Put in a complete address and zip code?	___	___
3. List a daytime telephone number and area code?	___	___
4. Specify your job objective?	___	___
5. Position your strongest information first?	___	___
6. Describe your education?	___	___
7. Complete a work experience section?	___	___
8. Detail your relevant skills?	___	___
9. Include information on affiliations?	___	___
10. Use both positive and action words?	___	___
11. Check for accuracy of information—names, dates, etc.?	___	___
12. Verify technical terms and descriptions?	___	___
13. Correct any poor grammar?	___	___
14. Shorten or tighten sentences?	___	___
15. Eliminate repetitiveness?	___	___
16. Leave out anything important?	___	___

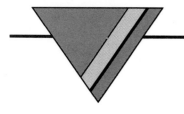

Chapter 7

Selecting Employees

Chapter Outline

Validation of Selection Procedures
  Empirical Validity
  Content and Construct Validity
Reliability
Guidelines for Validating Selection
  Procedures
Selection Process
  Application Form
  Preliminary Interview
  Applicant Testing
  Diagnostic Interview
  Reference Checking
  Physical Examination
  Making the Final Selection Decision

Summary of Learning Objectives
Review Questions
Discussion Questions
Incident 7–1: Promotions at OMG
Incident 7–2: The Pole Climbers
Exercise: Developing a Test
Notes and Additional Readings
On the Job: Sample Application for
  Employment and Applicant Flow
  Record

● *Learning Objectives*

After studying this chapter, you should be able to:

1. Define validity.
2. Explain predictive validity.
3. Explain concurrent validity.
4. Describe content validity.
5. Discuss construct validity.
6. Define reliability.
7. Describe aptitude, psychomotor, job-knowledge, proficiency, interest, and psychological tests.
8. Explain a polygraph test.
9. Describe structured and unstructured interviews.

*"S*elect for farm hands those who are fitted for heavy labor and have some aptitude for agriculture, which can be ascertained by trying them on several tasks and by inquiring as to what they did for their former master. The foreman should have some education, a good disposition, and economical habits, and it is better that he should be older than the hands, for they will be listened to with more respect than if they were boys. The foreman should be very experienced in agricultural works so that workers may appreciate that it is greater knowledge and skill which entitles the foreman to command. The foreman should never be authorized to enforce his discipline with the whips if he can accomplish his result with words. It is wise to choose a foreman who is married because marriage will make him more steady and attach him to the place. The foreman will work more cheerfully if rewards are offered him."

Varro*

Selection
The process of choosing from among available applicants the individuals who are most likely to successfully perform a job.

The objective of the **selection** decision is to choose the individual who can successfully perform the job from the pool of qualified candidates. Job analyses, human resource planning, and recruitment are necessary prerequisites to the selection process. A breakdown in any of these processes can make even the best selection system ineffective.

Validation of Selection Procedures

The selection decision requires the decision maker to know what distinguishes successful performance from unsuccessful performance in the available job and to forecast a person's future performance in that job. Therefore, job analysis is essential in the development of a successful selection system. As discussed in Chapter 4, both job descriptions and job specifications are developed through job analysis. A job description facilitates determining how successful performance of the job is to be measured. These measures are called **criteria of job success**. Possible criteria of job success include performance appraisals, production data (such as quantity of work produced), and personnel data (such as rates of absenteeism and tardiness).

Criteria of job success
Ways of specifying how successful performance of the job is to be measured.

Criterion predictors
Factors such as education, previous work experience, and scores on company-administered tests that are used to predict successful performance of a job.

A job specification facilitates identifying the factors that can be used to predict successful performance of the job. These factors are called **criterion predictors**. Possible criterion predictors include education, previous work experience, scores on company-administered tests, data from application blanks, previous performance appraisals or evaluations, and results of preliminary interviews.

Validity
The effectiveness of a given criterion in predicting job success.

Validity refers to how well a criterion predictor actually predicts the criterion of job success. For example, a job applicant for a typist position who types 120 words per minute should be able to perform well in the job if typing speed is a valid criterion for job success. Any criterion that is used in a selection decision must be valid. Figure 7–1 shows the relationship between job analysis and validity.

*Source: Varro, "Selection of Farm Hands," in *Roman Farm Management* (New York: Macmillan, 1913), p. 277.

▼   **Figure 7–1**   Relationship between job analysis and validity

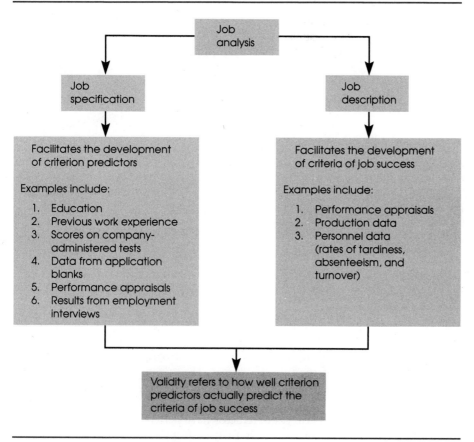

___

It is important to note that some criteria, such as performance appraisals, can be used as both criterion predictors and as criteria of job success. For example, if past performance appraisals are used to forecast that an individual will successfully perform a different job, then the performance appraisals are criterion predictors. Thus, how the criterion is used determines whether it is a criterion predictor or a criterion of job success.

Validity is an extremely important concept in human resource management. Validity in selection decisions can be demonstrated using empirical, content, and construct methods. Each of these is discussed in the following sections.

Empirical Validity

Empirical (also known as criterion-related) validity is established by collecting data and using correlation analysis (a statistical method used to measure the relationship between two sets of data) to determine the relationship between a criterion predictor and the criteria of job success. The degree of validity for a particular criterion predictor is indicated by the magnitude of the coefficient of correlation (r), which can range from $+1$ to -1. Both $+1$ and -1 represent perfect correlation. Zero

▼   Figure 7–2   Predictive validation process

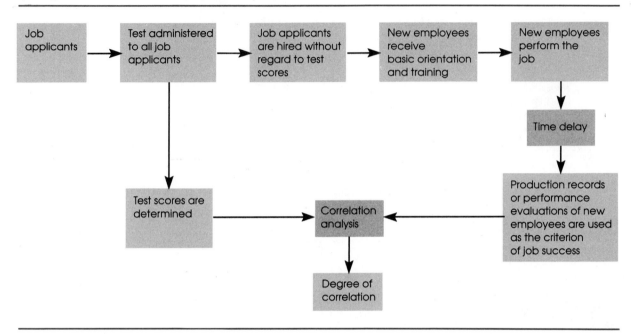

represents total lack of correlation or validity. A positive sign (+) on the coefficient of correlation means that the two sets of data are moving in the same direction, whereas a negative (−) sign means that the two sets of data are moving in opposite directions.

Rarely, if ever, does a criterion predictor have perfect, positive validity (+ 1). Much more commonly, validity is less than perfect. Thus, a significant issue in validity is the degree of correlation required between the criterion predictor and the criteria of job success in order to establish validity. The "Uniform Guidelines on Employee Selection Procedures" (more commonly referred to as "Uniform Guidelines") takes the position that there is no minimum correlation coefficient applicable to all employment situations.[1] The American Psychological Association's Division of Organizational and Industrial Psychology has provided the following guidelines as to the significance of correlation coefficients: Correlations rarely exceed 0.50; a correlation of 0.40 is ordinarily considered very good, and most personnel research workers are usually pleased with a correlation of 0.30.[2] Generally, it is safe to say criterion predictors having a correlation coefficient of under 0.30 would not be accepted as valid.

Two primary methods for establishing empirical validity are predictive validity and concurrent validity.

Predictive Validity

Predictive validity involves identifying a criterion predictor such as a test, administering the test to the entire pool of job applicants, and then hiring people to fill the available jobs without regard to their test scores. At a later date, the test scores are correlated with the criteria of job success to see whether those people with high test scores performed substantially better than those with low test scores.

For example, suppose a company wanted to determine the validity of a test

Predictive validity
Validity established by identifying a criterion predictor, administering it to applicants, hiring people without regard to scores, and later correlating scores with job performance.

▼ **Figure 7–3** Concurrent validation process

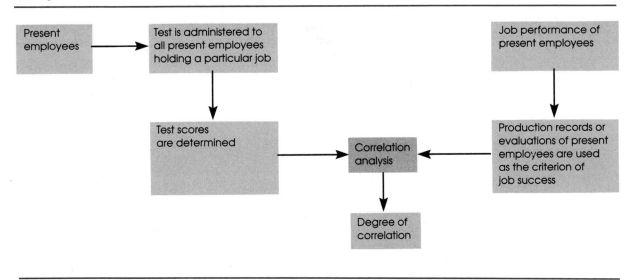

for predicting future performance of production workers. In this example, test scores would be the criterion predictor. Further suppose that the company maintains records on the quantity of output of individual workers and that that quantity of output is to be used as the criterion of job success. In a predictive-validation study, the test would be administered to the entire pool of job applicants, but people would be hired without regard to their test scores. The new employees would be given the same basic orientation and training. Some time later (e.g., one year), the test scores would be correlated to quantity of output. If an acceptable correlation exists, then the test is shown to be valid and can be used for selection of future employees. Figure 7–2 summarizes the steps in performing a predictive-validation study.

Predictive validation is used infrequently because it is costly and slow.[3] To use this method, a large number of new employees must be hired at the same time without regard to their test scores. Potentially, an organization may hire both good and bad employees. Furthermore, for criteria to be predictive, all new employees must have equivalent orientation and training.

Concurrent Validity

Concurrent validity involves identifying a criterion predictor such as a test, administering the test to present employees, and correlating the test scores with the present employees' performance on the job. If an acceptable correlation exists, then the test can be used for selection of future employees. Figure 7–3 summarizes the concurrent-validation process.

One disadvantage to concurrent validation is that in situations in which either racial or sexual discrimination has been practiced in the past, minorities and women will not be adequately represented. Another potential drawback is that among present employees in a particular job, the poorer performers are more likely to have been discharged or quit and the best performers have frequently been promoted. Obviously, a correlation coefficient obtained under these conditions can be misleading.

Concurrent validity
Validity established by identifying a criterion predictor, administering it to an organization's current employees, and correlating the test data with the current employees' job performance.

Empirical-validation procedures (either predictive or concurrent) are preferred by the Equal Employment Opportunity Commission (EEOC) in validation studies. However, because of the cost and difficulties associated with empirical validation, nonempirical methods are frequently used. Nonempirical validation is also accepted by the EEOC.

Content and Construct Validity

Content validity
The extent to which the content of a selection procedure or instrument is representative of important aspects of job performance.

Two nonempirical methods of validation are content and construct validity. **Content validity** refers to whether the content of a selection procedure or selection instrument such as a test is representative of important aspects of performance on the job. Thus, a typing test is content valid for hiring secretaries, although it does not cover all of the skills required to be a good secretary. Content validity is especially useful in those situations where the number of employees is not large enough to justify the use of empirical validation methods. To use content validity, an employer must determine the exact performance requirements of a specific job and develop a selection procedure or selection instrument around an actual sample of the work that is to be performed.

Construct validity
The extent to which a selection criterion measures the degree to which job candidates have identifiable characteristics determined to be important for successful job performance.

Construct validity refers to the extent to which a selection procedure or instrument measures the degree to which job candidates have identifiable characteristics that have been determined to be important for successful job performance. Examples of job-related constructs might include verbal ability, space visualization, and perceptual speed. For example, if a job requires blueprint reading, a test of space visualization might be construct valid for use in employment decisions.

Both of the nonempirical methods of validation are dependent on judgment. However, in many validation situations, they may be the only available options.

Reliability
The reproducibility of results with a criterion predictor.

Reliability

Another important consideration of a selection system is reliability. **Reliability** refers to the reproducibility of results with a criterion predictor. For example, a test is reliable to the extent that the same person working under the same conditions produces approximately the same test results at different time periods. A test is not reliable if a person fails it on one day but in taking it again a week later makes an A.

Test-retest
One method of showing a test's reliability; involves testing a group and giving the same group the same test at a later time.

Three methods can be used to demonstrate the reliability of a criterion predictor. Suppose a given test is used. One method of showing the reliability of the test is **test-retest**. This involves testing a group and later, usually in about two weeks, giving the group the same test. The degree of similarity between the sets of scores determines the test's reliability. Obviously, the results can be influenced by whether the individual studied during the time between tests. A second method of showing reliability, **parallel forms**, involves giving two separate but similar forms of the test at the same time. The degree to which the sets of scores coincide determines reliability. The third method, **split halves**, involves dividing the test into halves to determine whether performance is similar on both halves. Again, the degree of similarity determines reliability.

Parallel forms
A method of showing a test's reliability; involves giving two separate but similar forms of the test at the same time.

Split halves
A method of showing a test's reliability; involves dividing the test into halves to determine whether performance is similar in both sections.

A test or other criterion predictor can be reliable without being valid. However, it cannot be valid if it is not reliable. Consequently, the reliability of a criterion predictor plays an important role in determining its validity.

Guidelines for Validating Selection Procedures

The *Uniform Guidelines on Employee Selection Procedures,* described in Chapter 2, also contain technical standards and documentation requirements for the validation of selection procedures.[4] The guidelines broadly define selection procedures to include not only hiring but also promotion decisions, selection for training programs, and virtually every selection decision made by an organization. The guidelines are intended to be consistent with generally accepted professional standards for evaluating selection procedures such as those described in the *Standards for Educational and Psychological Tests* prepared by a joint committee of the American Psychological Association, the American Educational Research Association, and the National Council of Measurement in Education.[5] These standards are more commonly called the *APA Standards.* Either the Uniform Guidelines or the APA Standards can be used in validation studies. In fact, several court decisions have tended to place more reliance on the professional standards than on the guidelines.

Empirical, content, and construct validity studies are permitted under the Uniform Guidelines. In conducting a validity study, employers are also encouraged to consider available alternatives with less adverse impact, for achieving business purposes.

All validation studies must be thoroughly documented, and the Uniform Guidelines specify in detail the types of records that must be kept in any study. Since job analysis is an essential part of a validation study, specific guidelines are also provided for conducting job analyses.

As was discussed in Chapter 2, the guidelines also define the four-fifths, or 80 percent, rule for determining adverse impact. Furthermore, the relationship between the guidelines and voluntary affirmative action programs is defined. Compliance with the guidelines does not relieve an employer of its affirmative action obligations. In fact, the guidelines encourage employers to implement voluntary affirmative action programs.

Selection Process

A series of steps is normally followed in processing an applicant for a job. Figure 7–4 illustrates the steps in a typical selection process. The size of the organization, the types of jobs to be filled, the number of people to be hired, and outside pressures from EEOC or unions all influence the exact nature of an organization's selection process. Most organizations use a multiple cutoff technique in selection. With this technique, an applicant must be judged satisfactory through a series of screening

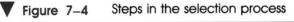

▼ Figure 7–4   Steps in the selection process

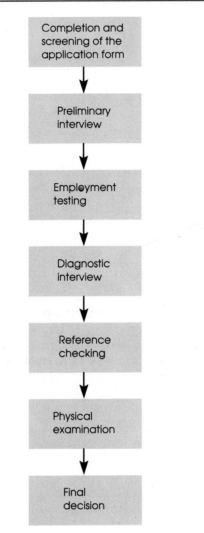

devices, such as application blanks, interviews, and tests. The applicant is eliminated from consideration for the job if any of these is unsatisfactory. All of these screening devices must be valid.

Application Form

Completing an application form is normally the first step in most selection procedures. It provides basic employment information for use in later steps of the selection process and can be used to screen out unqualified applicants. For example, if the job opening requires the ability to type 60 words per minute and the applicant indicates an inability to type, then there is no need to process the application further.

EEOC Requirements

EEOC and the courts have found that many application and interview inquiries disproportionately reject minorities and females and frequently are not job related. Many questions have therefore been explicitly prohibited. Some of the major questions that should be eliminated from preemployment inquiries (both application forms and interviews) or carefully reviewed to ensure their use is job related and nondiscriminatory include:

1. *Race, color, national origin, and religion.* Inquiries about race, color, national origin, or religion are not illegal per se, but asking or recording this information in employment records is carefully examined if discrimination charges are filed against an employer.

2. *Arrest and conviction records.* An individual's arrest record has been ruled by the courts to be an unlawful basis for refusal to employ unless a business necessity for such a policy can be established.[6]

3. *Credit rating.* An applicant's poor credit rating has also been ruled by the courts to be an unlawful basis for refusal to employ unless a business necessity for such a policy can be established.[7] Inquiries about charge accounts and home or car ownership may be unlawful unless required because of business necessity.

The On the Job at the end of Chapter 3 provides a comprehensive listing of permissible questions and questions to be avoided, not only in preemployment interviews but also on application forms. One study of 151 of the largest employers in the United States revealed that all but two employers had at least one inappropriate question on their application forms. Fifty-seven of the employers had 10 or more inappropriate questions, indicating that many employers need to examine and redesign their application forms.[8]

Processing

Normally, the information on the application form is reviewed by a member of the human resource department to determine the applicant's qualifications in relation to the requirements of currently available jobs. Another screening procedure is the use of **weighted application forms**. These assign different weights to different questions. Weights are developed by determining which item responses were given more frequently by applicants who proved to be higher performers but less frequently by applicants who proved to be poorer performers. Weighted application forms are subject to the validity requirements discussed earlier in this chapter. Studies have shown the weighted application form to be useful in the selection of salespeople, clerical workers, production workers, secretaries, and supervisors.[9]

Weighted application forms
Application forms assigning different weights to different questions.

Accuracy of Information

The accuracy of information given on application forms is open to debate. Placing full reliance on information provided on the application form may not be prudent unless some means of verification is employed. Some of the information on the application form can be verified through reference checking, which is described later in this chapter.

Many employers, in an attempt to ensure that accurate information is given, require the applicant to sign a statement similar to the following:

I hereby certify that the answers given by me to the foregoing questions and statements made are true and correct, without reservations of any kind whatsoever and that no attempt has been made by me to conceal pertinent information. Falsification of any information on this application can lead to immediate discharge at the time of disclosure.

Whether this statement actually increases the accuracy of information provided is not known. However, employers view falsification of an application form as a serious offense that, if detected, frequently leads to discharge.

Applicant Flow Record

Applicant flow record
A form completed voluntarily by a job applicant and used by an employer to obtain information that might be viewed as discriminatory.

At the time of completing the application form, the applicant is frequently asked to complete an applicant flow record. An **applicant flow record** is a form used by a company to obtain from a job applicant information that might be viewed as discriminatory. This record is completed voluntarily by the applicant. The On the Job example at the end of this chapter shows a sample combination application form and applicant flow record. Data and information from the applicant flow record can then be used to provide statistical reports to EEOC concerning the employer's recruitment and selection activities involving women and minorities. Information from the voluntarily completed applicant flow record would be recorded on the form illustrated in Figure 3–3 of Chapter 3.

Preliminary Interview

The preliminary interview is used to determine whether the applicant's skills, abilities, and job preferences match any of the available jobs in the organization, to explain to the applicant the available jobs and their requirements, and to answer any questions the applicant has about the available jobs or the employer. A preliminary interview can be conducted either before or after the applicant has completed the application form. It is generally a brief, exploratory interview that is normally conducted by a specialist from the human resource department. Unqualified or uninterested applicants are screened out in this interview. Interview questions must be job related and are subject to questions of validity. The On the Job example provides a summary of permissible inquiries and inquiries to be avoided during the preliminary interview.

Applicant Testing

Applicant testing is one of the most controversial aspects of employee selection procedures. If a test is to be used in the selection process and if the selection process has adverse impact on legally protected groups, EEOC requires the employer to establish validity and reliability, using the procedures outlined in the *Uniform Guidelines on Employee Selection Procedures*.

Many types of tests are available to organizations for use in the selection process.[10] For the purposes of this text, the following five categories of tests are examined: aptitude, psychomotor, job knowledge and proficiency, interests, and psychological. In addition, the use of polygraphs and graphology is examined. HRM in Action 7–1 illustrates the growth in college admissions testing.

▼▼. HRM in Action 7–1

College Admissions Testing—A Growth Business

Standardized college admission tests have often been criticized as inaccurate and biased. But the critics seem to be fighting a losing battle—although the number of high school graduates is declining, the testing business is growing. The Educational Testing Service, which administers the Scholastic Aptitute Test (SAT), brings in about $226 million annually. The American College Testing Program, which administers the ACT, brings in about $50 million annually. In 1988, 134,000 high school seniors took the SAT. The number of students taking the ACT was 842,000.

Source: Adapted from Edward B. Fiske, "College Testing Is a Hard Habit to Break," *The New York Times,* January 15, 1989, p. E28.

Aptitude Tests

Aptitude tests measure a person's capacity or potential ability to learn and perform a job. Some of the more frequently used tests measure verbal ability, numerical ability, perceptual speed, spatial ability, and reasoning ability. Verbal-aptitude tests measure a person's ability to use words in thinking, planning, and communicating. Numerical tests measure ability to add, subtract, multiply, and divide. Perception speed tests measure a person's ability to recognize similarities and differences. Spatial tests measure ability to visualize objects in space and determine their relationships. Reasoning tests measure ability to analyze oral or written facts and make correct judgments concerning these facts on the basis of logical implications.

One of the oldest and, prior to the passage of equal employment opportunity legislation, most frequently used aptitude tests was the general intelligence test. The EEOC views this type of test with disfavor because such tests often contain questions that are not related to successful performance on the job. Thus, employers have largely abandoned the use of intelligence tests in employee selection.

Aptitude tests
Means of measuring a person's capacity or latent ability to learn and perform a job.

Psychomotor Tests

Psychomotor tests are used to measure a person's strength, dexterity, and coordination. Finger dexterity, manual dexterity, wrist-finger speed, and speed of arm movement are some of the psychomotor abilities that can be tested. Abilities such as these might be tested for hiring people to fill assembly-line jobs.

Psychomotor tests
Tests that measure a person's strength, dexterity, and coordination.

Job Knowledge and Proficiency Tests

Job knowledge tests are used to measure the job-related knowledge possessed by a job applicant. These tests can be either written or oral. The applicant must answer questions that differentiate experienced and skilled workers from less experienced and less skilled workers. **Proficiency tests** measure how well the applicant can do a sample of the work that is to be performed. A typing test given to applicants for a secretarial job is an example of a proficiency test.

Job knowledge tests
Tests used to measure the job-related knowledge of an applicant.

Proficiency tests
Tests used to measure how well a job applicant can do a sample of the work to be performed in the job.

Interest Tests

Interest tests are designed to determine how a person's interests compare with the interests of successful people in a specific job. These tests indicate the occupations or areas of work in which the person is most interested. The basic assumption in the use of interest tests is that people are more likely to be successful

Interest tests
Tests designed to determine how a person's interests compare with the interests of successful people in a specific job.

▼. HRM in Action 7–2

Strong-Campbell Interest Inventory

The most commonly administered interest test is the Strong-Campbell Interest Inventory. The test asks the respondent to answer how he or she feels—"Like," "Indifferent," or "Dislike"—about some 325 items, such as repairing clocks or raising money for charity. From the responses, the test determines how the respondent ranks on "theme scales," such as artistic, enterprising, and conventional. It also tells the respondent how his or her pattern of answers compares with those of persons already in particular occupations.

The inventory is not necessarily used to determine one's career path or success in that career. It does, however, predict how long one would remain in that particular job. The inventory's true value is its career planning aid.

Source: Adapted from Walter Kiechel, "The Managerial Mind Probe," *Fortune,* February 7, 1983, p. 114.

in jobs they like. The primary problem with using interest tests for selection purposes is that responses to the questions are not always sincere. HRM in Action 7–2 describes a commonly used interest test.

Psychological Tests

Psychological tests
Tests that attempt to measure personality traits.

Psychological tests attempt to measure personality characteristics. These tests are generally characterized by low validity and reliability and presently have limited use for selection purposes. Two of the better-known psychological tests are the Rorschach inkblot test and the Thematic Apperception Test (TAT). In the Rorschach test, the applicant is shown a series of cards that contain inkblots of varying sizes and shapes. The applicant is asked to tell what the inkblots look like to him or her. With the TAT, the applicant is shown pictures of real-life situations for interpretation. With both of these methods, the individual is encouraged to report whatever immediately comes to mind. Interpretation of these responses requires subjective judgment and the services of a qualified psychologist. Furthermore, responses to psychological tests can also be easily fabricated. It is for these reasons that psychological tests presently have limited application in selection decisions.

Polygraph Tests

Polygraph
A device that records physical changes in a person's body as he or she answers questions (also known as a lie detector).

The **polygraph,** popularly known as the lie detector, is a device that records physical changes in the body as the test subject answers a series of questions. The polygraph records fluctuations in blood pressure, respiration, and perspiration on a moving roll of graph paper. The polygraph operator makes a judgment as to whether the subject's response was truthful or deceptive by studying the physiological measurements recorded on the paper.

The use of a polygraph rests on a series of cause-and-effect assumptions: stress causes certain physiological changes in the body; fear and guilt cause stress; lying causes fear and guilt. The theory behind the use of a polygraph test assumes a direct relationship between the subject's responses to the questions and the physiological responses recorded on the polygraph. However, the polygraph machine itself does not detect lies; it only detects physiological changes. The operator must

▽. HRM in Action 7–3

NCAA Drug Testing Program

The NCAA has been authorized by its member institutions to conduct mandatory drug tests on NCAA athletes during its 73 championship events and 18 post-season football games. The program calls for a testing of each sport's top performers or the participants with the most playing time from each team, in addition to a more random sample of less prominent participants. More than 80 drugs, both performance enhancing and social, are considered banned substances by the NCAA.

Source: NCAA public documents.

interpret the data recorded by the machine. Thus, it is the operator, not the machine, that is the real lie detector.

The Employee Polygraph Protection Act of 1988 became effective on December 27, 1988. This act, with few exceptions, prohibits employers from conducting polygraph examinations of all job applicants and most employees. It also prevents the use of voice stress analyzers and other similar devices that attempt to measure honesty. Paper-and-pencil tests and chemical testing, such as for drugs or AIDS, are not prohibited. HRM in Action 7–3 explains the drug testing policy of the NCAA.

The major exemptions to the law are: (1) all local, state, and federal employees are exempt from coverage, although state laws may be passed to restrict the use of polygraphs; (2) industries with national defense or security contracts are permitted to use polygraphs; (3) businesses with nuclear power-related contracts with the Department of Energy may use polygraphs; and (4) businesses and consultants with access to highly classified information may also use polygraphs.

Private businesses are also allowed to use polygraphs under certain conditions: when hiring private security personnnel, when hiring persons with access to drugs, and during investigations of economic injury or loss by the employer.[11]

Graphology

Graphology (handwriting analysis) involves using a trained analyst to examine the lines, loops, hooks, strokes, curves, and flourishes in a person's handwriting to assess the person's personality, performance, emotional problems, and honesty. As with the polygraph, the use of graphology is dependent on the training and expertise of the person (called a graphologist) doing the analysis.

Graphology has had limited acceptance by organizations in the United States. However, the acceptance of graphology may very well increase, since the passage of the Employee Polygraph Protection Act does not prohibit the use of graphology.[12] HRM in Action 7–4 illustrates the results of graphology.

Graphology
(handwriting analysis)
Use of a trained analyst to
examine a person's
handwriting to assess the
person's personality, emotional
problems, and honesty.

Diagnostic Interview

The diagnostic interview is used by most organizations as an important step in the selection process. Its purpose is to supplement information gained in other steps in the selection process to determine the suitability of an applicant for a specific opening in the organization. It is important to remember that all questions asked

▽. HRM in Action 7–4

What's in a Name?

Graphological Services International analyzes handwriting for over 150 organizations, including departments of Citibank and Bristol-Myers. The company requires a written paragraph in order to develop a personality profile. However, Ruth Brager analyzed signatures in annual reports and offered the following observations on a couple of senior executives: Coca-Cola Chairman Roberto Goizueta is extremely ambitious and has great foresight, and Texaco Chief Executive James Kinnear is described as being thorough and a fast thinker, having high standards, and playing his cards close to his chest.

Source: Adapted from "Watch Out, John Hancock," *Fortune,* January 4, 1988, p. 82.

during an interview must be job related. Equal employment opportunity legislation has placed limitations on the types of questions that can be asked during an interview (see the On the Job in Chapter 3).

Types of Interviews

Structured interview
An interview conducted according to a predetermined outline.

Several different types of interviews are used by organizations. The **structured interview** is conducted using a predetermined outline. Through the use of this outline, the interviewer maintains control of the interview so that all pertinent information on the applicant is covered systematically. Advantages to the use of structured interviews are that it provides the same type of information on all interviewees and allows systematic coverage of all questions deemed necessary by the organization.

Unstructured interview
An interview conducted without a predetermined checklist of questions.

Unstructured interviews are conducted without a predetermined checklist of questions. Opened-ended questions such as "Tell me about your previous job" are used. Interviews of this type pose numerous problems, such as a lack of systematic coverage of information, and are very susceptible to the personal biases of the interviewer. This type of interview, however, does provide a more relaxed atmosphere.

Stress interview
Interview method that puts the applicant under pressure, to determine whether he or she is highly emotional.

Three other types of interviewing techniques have been used to a limited extent by organizations. The **stress interview** is designed to place the interviewee under pressure. In the stress interview, the interviewer assumes a hostile and antagonistic attitude toward the interviewee. The purpose of this type of interview is to detect the highly emotional person. In **board** or **panel interviews**, two or more interviewers conduct a single interview with the applicant. **Group interviews**, in which several job applicants are questioned together in a group discussion, are also sometimes used. Panel interviews and group interviews can involve either a structured or unstructured format.

Board or panel interviews
Interview method in which two or more people conduct a single interview with one applicant.

Group interviews
Interview method in which several applicants are questioned together.

Problems in Conducting Interviews

Although interviews have widespread use in selection procedures, a host of problems exist. The first and certainly one of the most significant problems is that interviews are subject to the same legal requirements of validity and reliability as other steps in the selection process. However, research has indicated that the validity and reliability of most interviews is very questionable.[13] One of the primary reasons seems to be that it is easy for the interviewer to become either favorably or unfavorably impressed with the job applicant for the wrong reasons. First, conclusions about the applicant are often made within the first 10 minutes of the interview. If this occurs, any additional relevant information about the applicant is either overlooked or ignored. Furthermore, interviewers (like all people) have personal biases. These biases play a role in the interviewing process. For example, a qualified male applicant should not be rejected merely because the inteviewer dislikes long hair on males.

Closely related is the problem of the **halo effect** that occurs when the interviewer allows a single prominent characteristic to dominate judgment of all other traits. For instance, it is often easy to overlook other characteristics when a person has a pleasant personality. However, merely having a pleasant personality does not necessarily ensure that the person will be a good employee.

Overgeneralizing is another common problem. An interviewee may not behave exactly the same way on the job as during the interview. For example, the interviewer must remember that the interviewee is under pressure during the interview and that some people just naturally become very nervous during an interview.

Halo effect
Occurs when managers allow a single prominent characteristic of an employee to influence their judgment on each separate item on the performance appraisal.

Conducting Effective Interviews

The problems associated with interviews can be partially overcome through careful planning. The following suggestions are offered to increase the effectiveness of the interviewing process.[14]

1. Careful attention must be given to the selection and training of interviewers. Interviewers should be outgoing and emotionally well-adjusted persons. Interviewing skills can be learned, and the persons responsible for conducting interviews should be thoroughly trained in these skills.

2. The plan for the interview should include an outline specifying the information that is to be obtained and the questions that are to be asked. The plan should also include room arrangements. Privacy and some degree of comfort are important. If a private room is not available, the interview should be conducted in a place where other applicants are not within hearing distance.

3. The interviewer should attempt to put the applicant at ease. He or she should not argue with the applicant or put the applicant on the spot. A brief conversation about a general topic of interest or offering the applicant a cup of coffee can help ease the tension. The applicant should be encouraged to talk. However, the interviewer must maintain control and remember that the primary goal of the interview is to gain information that will aid in the selection decision.

4. The facts obtained in the interview should be recorded in writing immediately after the interview.

5. Finally, the effectiveness of the interviewing process should be evaluated. One way to evaluate effectiveness is to compare the performance appraisals of hired individuals to assessments made during the interview. This cross-check can serve to evaluate the effectiveness of individual interviewers as well as the total interviewing program.

Reference Checking

Reference checking can take place either before or after the diagnostic interview. Many organizations realize the importance of reference checking and provide space on the application form for listing references. Most prospective employers contact individuals from one or more of the three following categories: personal, school, or past employment references. For the most part, personal references have limited value because generally no applicant is going to list someone who will not give a positive recommendation. Contacting individuals who have taught the applicant in a school, college, or university is also of limited value for similar reasons. Previous employers are clearly the most used source and are in a position to supply the most objective information.

Reference checking is most frequently conducted by telephoning previous employers. However, many organizations will not answer questions about a previous employee unless the questions are put in writing. The amount and type of information that a previous employer is willing to divulge varies from organization to organization. The least that normally can be accomplished is to verify the information that has been given on the application form. However, most employers are hesitant to answer questions about previous employees because of the threat of defamation lawsuits.

Government legislation has significantly influenced the process of reference checking. The Privacy Act of 1974 prevents government agencies from making their employment records available to other organizations without the consent of the individual involved. The Fair Credit and Reporting Act (FCRA) of 1971 requires private organizations to give job applicants access to information obtained from a reporting service. It is also mandatory that an applicant be made aware that a check is being made on him or her. Because of these laws, most employment application forms now contain statements that must be signed by the applicant, authorizing the employer to check references and conduct investigations.

Physical Examination

Many organizations require a physical examination before an employee is hired. This is given not only to determine whether he or she is physically capable of performing the job but also to determine the applicant's eligibility for group life, health, and disability insurance. Because of the expense, physical examinations are normally given as one of the last steps in the selection process. The expense of physical examinations has also caused many organizations to have applicants complete a health questionnaire when they fill out their application form. If no serious medical problems are indicated on the medical questionnaire, the applicant is not normally required to have a physical examination.

The Rehabilitation Act of 1973 has also caused many employers to reexamine the physical requirements for many jobs. This act does not prohibit employers from giving medical exams. However, it does encourage employers to make medical inquiries that are directly related to the applicant's ability to perform job-related functions and encourages employers to make reasonable accommodations in helping handicapped people to perform the job.

Making the Final Selection Decision

The final step in the selection process is choosing one individual for the job. The assumption made at this point is that there will be more than one qualified person. If this is true, a value judgment based on all of the information gathered in the previous steps must be made to select the most qualified individual. If the previous steps have been performed properly, the chances of making a successful judgment are improved dramatically.

The responsibility for making the final selection decision is assigned to different levels of management in different organizations. In many organizations, the human resources department handles the completion of application forms; conducts preliminary interviews, testing, and reference checking; and arranges for physical exams. The diagnostic interview and final selection decision are usually left to the manager of the department with the job opening. Such a system relieves the manager of the time-consuming responsibilities of screening out unqualified and uninterested applicants.

In other organizations, the human resources department handles all of the steps up to the final selection decision. Under this system, the human resources department gives the manager with a job opening a list of three to five qualified applicants. The manager then chooses the individual that he or she feels will be the best employee based on all the information provided by the human resource department. Many organizations leave the final choice to the manager with the job opening, subject to the approval of those at higher levels of management.

In some organizations, the human resource department handles all of the steps in the selection process, including the final selection decision. In small organizations, the owner often makes the final choice.

An alternate approach is to involve peers in the final selection decision. Peer involvement has been used primarily with the selection of upper-level managers and professional employees. Peer involvement naturally facilitates the acceptance of the new employee by the work group.

In the selection of managers and supervisors, assessment centers are also sometimes used. An assessment center utilizes a formal procedure involving interviews, tests, and individual and group exercises aimed at evaluating an individual's potential as a manager/supervisor and determining his or her developmental needs. Assessment centers are described at length in Chapter 9.

● *Summary of Learning Objectives*

1. Define validity.

    Validity refers to how well a criterion predictor actually predicts the criterion of job success.

2. Explain predictive validity.

    Predictive validity involves identifying a criterion predictor such as a test, administering the test to the entire pool of job applicants, and then hiring people to fill the available jobs without regard to their test scores. At a later date, the test scores are correlated with the criteria of job success to see whether those people with high test scores performed substantially better than those with low test scores.

3. Explain concurrent validity.

    Concurrent validity involves identifying a criterion predictor such as a test, administering the test to present employees, and correlating the test scores with the present employees' performances on the job.

4. Describe content validity.

    Content validity refers to whether the content of a selection procedure or selection instrument, such as a test, is representative of important aspects of performance on the job.

5. Discuss construct validity.

    Construct validity refers to the extent to which a selection procedure or instrument measures the degree to which job candidates have identifiable characteristics that have been determined to be important for successful job performance. Job-related constructs might include verbal ability, space visualization, and perceptual speed.

6. Define reliability.

    Reliability refers to the reproducibility of results with a criterion predictor.

7. Describe aptitude, psychomotor, job-knowledge, proficiency, interest, and psychological tests.

    Aptitude tests measure a person's capacity or potential ability to learn and perform a job. Psychomotor tests are used to measure a person's strength, dexterity, and coordination. Job-knowledge tests are used to measure the job-related knowledge possessed by a job applicant. Proficiency tests measure how well the applicant can do a sample of the work required in the position. Interest tests are designed to determine how a person's interests compare with the interests of successful people in a specific job. Psychological tests attempt to measure personality characteristics.

8. Explain a polygraph test.

    The polygraph records physical changes in the body as the test subject answers a series of questions. The operator makes a judgment on whether the subject's response was truthful or deceptive by studying the physiological measurements recorded on the paper.

9. Describe structured and unstructured interviews.

    The structured interview is conducted using a predetermined outline. Unstructured interviews are conducted without a predetermined checklist of questions.

Review Questions

1. Define the following terms:
    a. Criterion of job success
    b. Criterion predictor
    c. Validity
    d. Reliability

2. Describe the following methods of validation:
   a. Predictive
   b. Concurrent
   c. Content
   d. Construct
3. Outline the steps in the selection process.
4. Describe some preemployment inquiries that should be eliminated or carefully reviewed to ensure their job relatedness.
5. What is a weighted application form?
6. How is an applicant flow record used?
7. Outline and briefly describe five categories of tests.
8. What is a polygraph test?
9. What is graphology?
10. What is reference checking?
11. Briefly describe some of the methods used by organizations in making the final selection decision.

Discussion Questions

1. "Tests often do not reflect an individual's true ability." What are your views on this statement?
2. "Organizations should be able to hire employees without government interference." Do you agree or disagree? What do you think would happen if organizations could do this?
3. "Reference checking is a waste of time." Do you agree or disagree? Why?
4. How do you feel about the establishment of minimum entrance scores on national tests for acceptance to a college or university?

▼ INCIDENT 7–1

Promotions at OMG

Old Money Group (OMG) is a mutual fund management company based in Seattle. It operates four separate funds, each with a different goal: one each for income growth and income interest production, one for a combination or balance of growth and production, and one for dealing in short-term securities (a money market fund). OMG, which was formed in early 1974 as a financial management firm, started its growth fund in 1977. The balanced fund and the income fund were added in 1979, the money market fund not until 1982. By the end of 1984, OMG had almost $47 million under its management. Over this time period, the company had slightly outperformed the Standard & Poor's 500 average and done slightly better than the stock market as a whole.

In 1962, Congress passed the Keogh Act, which permitted self-employed individuals to set up retirement plans. All contributions to and earnings from the plans are tax exempt until the money is withdrawn by the individual on retirement.

OMG recognized the great potential of using Keogh plans to help market shares in its mutual funds. It launched an aggressive marketing program aimed at persuading those with Keogh plans to buy into the fund. This was very successful. As a result, OMG found it necessary to establish a separate department to handle only Keogh plans. This new department was placed in the corporate account division under division vice president Ralph Simpson. The Keogh department grew rapidly and by the end of 1989 was managing approximately 3,000 separate Keogh plans. The department was responsible for all correspondence, personal contact, and problem solving involved with these accounts.

John Baker, who had graduated from college the previous fall with a degree in history, joined OMG in February. In his interview, John had impressed the human resource department as having managerial potential. The human resource department wanted to place him in an area where he could move into such a position, but at that time, there were none available.

A job that could be used as a stepping stone to more responsible positions came open in the Keogh department. In February, John became assistant to the administrator of the department. He was told that if he handled this position well, he would be considered for a job as plan administrator when an opening occurred. This was communicated to John both by the human resource department and by the head of the Keogh department, Jane Harris.

Over the next six months, it became apparent that John was not working out well. He seemed to show little interest in his work and did only what he had to do to get by; at times, his work was unsatisfactory. He appeared to be unhappy and not suited to the job. John let it be known that he had been looking for another position.

Jane Harris left OMG in June. Her assistant, Roy Johnson, took her place as head of the Keogh department. In August, Roy gave John his six-month review. Knowing that John was looking for another job, Roy decided to take the easy way out. Instead of giving John a bad review and facing the possibility of having to fire him, he gave John a satisfactory peformance review. He hoped that John would find another job so that the problem would go away.

In early October, one of the plan administrators said that she would be leaving OMG in late December. Roy was faced with the task of selecting someone to fill her position. Of those who had expressed an interest in the job, Fran Jenkins appeared the best suited for it. Fran was secretary to the head of the corporate division. She had become familiar with the plan administrators' work because she had helped them during their peak periods for the past three years. The only problem was Fran's lack of a college degree, which was stipulated as a requirement in the job description. Although she was currently taking night courses, she had completed only two and one-half years of college. After Roy discussed the problem with the head of the human resources department, this requirement was waived. Roy then announced that Fran would assume the position of plan administrator in December.

Two weeks later, John Baker informed the head of the human resource department that he had talked to his lawyer. He felt that he had been discriminated against and believed he should have gotten the position of plan administrator.

Questions

1. Do you think that John has a legitimate point?
2. What went wrong in this selection process?

▼ *INCIDENT 7–2*

The Pole Climbers

Ringing Bell Telephone Company has implemented an affirmative action plan in compliance with the Equal Employment Opportunity Commission. Under the current plan, to eliminate discrimination based on sex, women must be placed in jobs traditionally held by men. Therefore, the human resource department has emphasized recruiting and hiring women for such positions. Women who apply for craft positions are encouraged to try for outdoor craft jobs, such as those titled installer-repairer and line worker.

All employees hired as outside technicians must first pass basic installation school, which includes a week of training for pole climbing. During this week, employees are taught to climb 30-foot telephone poles. At the end of the week, they must demonstrate the strength and skills necessary to climb the pole and perform exercises while on it, such as lifting heavy tools and using a pulley to lift a bucket. Only those who pass this first week of training are allowed to advance to the segment dealing with installation.

Records have been maintained on the rates of success or failure for employees who attend the training school. For men, the failure rate has remained fairly constant at 30 percent. However, it has averaged 70 percent for women.

The human resource department has become concerned because hiring and training the employees who must resign at the end of one week is a tremendous expense. In addition, the goal of placing women in outdoor craft positions is not being reached.

As a first step in solving the problem, the human resource department has started interviewing the women who have failed the first week of training. Each employee is asked her reasons for seeking the position and encouraged to discuss probable causes for failure. Interviews over the last two months disclosed that employees were motivated to accept the job because of their wishes to work outdoors, to work without close supervision, to obtain challenging work, to meet the public, to have variety in their jobs, and to obtain a type of job unusual for women. Reasons for failure were physical inability to climb the pole, fear of height while on it, an accident during training such as a fall from the pole, and change of mind about the job after learning that strenuous work was involved.

In many instances, the women who mentioned physical reasons also stated that they were not physically ready to undertake the training; many had no idea it would be so difficult. Even though they still wanted the job, they could not pass the physical strength test at the end of one week.

Some stated that they felt "influenced" by their interviewer from the human resource department to take the job; others said they had accepted it because it was the only job available with the company at the time.

Questions

1. What factors would you keep in mind in designing an effective selection process for the position of outdoor craft technician?
2. What would you recommend to help Ringing Bell reduce the failure rate of women trainees?

Exercise

Developing a Test

You will be given one minute to copy the letter T on a blank sheet of paper as many times as possible. The exercise is timed, and exactly one minute is permitted.

A frequency distribution will then be developed by your instructor (or the class) to show how well the class performed.

1. What is the shape of the distribution?
2. Why is the distribution shaped in this manner?
3. Could this test be used as a selection device for certain jobs? What type of job?
4. How would you demonstrate the validity of this test?

Notes and Additional Readings

1. "Uniform Guidelines on Employee Selection Procedures," *Federal Register*, August 25, 1978, p. 38301.
2. *Amicus Curiae*, Brief of the Executive Committee of the Division of Industrial and Organizational Psychology, American Psychological Association, in *United States* v. *Georgia Power*, 474 F. 2d 906, 5 FEP 587 (5th Cir. 1973).
3. D. Yoder and H. G. Heneman, *ASPA Handbook of Personnel and Industrial Relations* (Washington, D.C.: Bureau of National Affairs, 1979), p. 4–125.
4. See "Uniform Guidelines," pp. 38290–315.
5. The most current version is *Standards for Educational and Psychological Tests* (Washington, D.C.: American Psychological Association, 1985).
6. *Gregory* v. *Litton*, 316 F. Supp. 401 (C.D. California 1970).
7. Commission Decision No. 72–0427, CCH Employment Practice Guide 6312 (August 31, 1971).
8. E. C. Miller, "An EEO Examination of Employment Applications," *Personnel Administrator*, March 1980, pp. 63–69.

9. Yoder and Heneman, *ASPA Handbook*, pp. 4–131.

10. O. K. Buros, *Mental Measurements Yearbook* (Highland Park, N.J.: Gryphon Press, 1981).

11. James G. Frierson, "New Polygraph Test Limits," *Personnel Journal*, December 1988, pp. 84–92.

12. See Dana Bottorff, "While not as Telling as Pinocchio's Nose, Tests that Screen for Honesty Gain Favor," *New England Business*, February 16, 1987, p. 35.

13. Yoder and Heneman, *ASPA Handbook*, pp. 4-146–4-148.

14. Ibid., pp. 4-152–4-154.

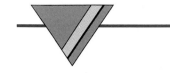

On the Job

Sample Application for Employment and Applicant Flow Record*

This On the Job example is designed to illustrate the types of questions that are normally asked on an application for employment and an applicant flow record. The application form in Exhibit 7–1 provides basic employment information to determine the applicant's qualifications in relation to the requirements of the available jobs and to screen out unqualified applicants. As can be seen, the applicant flow record is a separate document that is voluntarily completed by the applicant. Employers use the flow record to obtain information and data that might be viewed as discriminatory. This data can then be used to provide statistical reports to the EEOC regarding recruitment and selection of women and minorities. Duke Power Company is a public utility that services customers in the western part of North and South Carolina. It is also important to note that this application form was developed after the *Griggs* v. *Duke Power* decision, which was described in detail in Chapter 2.

*Used with permission.

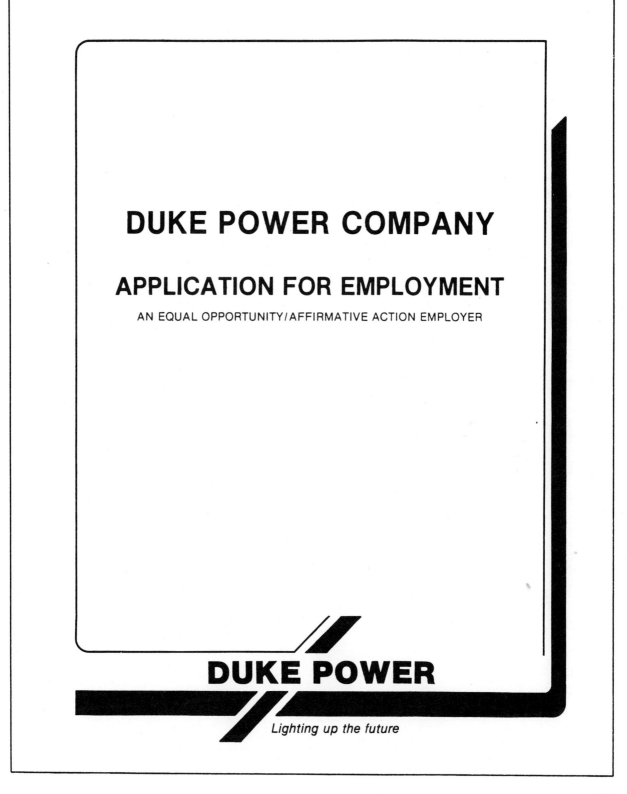

DUKE POWER COMPANY

APPLICATION FOR EMPLOYMENT

AN EQUAL OPPORTUNITY/AFFIRMATIVE ACTION EMPLOYER

DUKE POWER

Lighting up the future

Form 08004   (1-81)

DUKE POWER COMPANY
APPLICATION FOR EMPLOYMENT

Page 1

Please Print In Ink Or Type And Complete All Applicable Sections, Even If Resume is Included

Name _____ Last _____ First _____ Middle

Social Sec. No. _____

Present Mailing Address _____
No. & Street, P.O. Box, Rt. #   City   State   Zip Code   ( ) Telephone No.

Home Mailing Address _____
(If Different From Above)   No. & Street, P.O. Box, Rt. #   City   State   Zip Code   ( ) Telephone No.

Weekday Telephone Number ( ) _____

Position or Type of Work Desired _____

Salary Expected $ _____ Hr., Wk., Mo., Yr.   Will You Consider A Position That Pays Less Than The Expected Amount Listed? ☐ Yes ☐ No

Date Available _____ Do you Have Any Geographical Restrictions? ☐ Yes ☐ No If Yes, Where? _____

Have You Previously Applied For Employment With Duke Power Company? ☐ Yes ☐ No If Yes, When? _____

Where? _____ Have You Previously Been Employed By Duke Power Co.? ☐ Yes ☐ No

If Yes When? _____ Where? _____

In Emergency, Notify: (Name) _____ Telephone No. ( ) _____

Have You Ever Been Convicted Of A Crime? (Include Military Convictions) ☐ Yes ☐ No If Yes, Explain (Use Separate Paper, If Necessary). _____

	Name of School	Dates Attended	Date Graduated Or Expect To Graduate	Certificate/ Diploma/Degree (If Applicable)	Major (If Applicable)
EDUCATION	High School/Equivalent Training				
	Location				
	Technical or Business				
	Location				
	College or University				
	Location				
	College or University				
	Location				
	Graduate School				
	Location				
	Armed Services, Correspondence				
	Location				

MILITARY

Branch of Service _____ Date Inducted And Rank _____

Date Discharged and Rank _____

Type Of Discharge _____ If Other Than "Honorable," Explain _____

Primary Military Occupation _____

Page 2

	Beginning With The Most Recent, List Below The NAMES & ADDRESSES Of All Your Employers, Including Military If Applicable	Dates Employed				Salary At Leaving	Position or Type Of Work Performed	Department/ Supervisor	Reasons For Leaving
		From		To					
		Mo.	Year	Mo.	Year				
EMPLOYMENT	Company								
	Address								
	Company								
	Address								
	Company								
	Address								
	Company								
	Address								
	Company								
	Address								

OTHER TRAINING AND SKILLS

Please Supply The Following Information If It Relates To Position(s) Or Type Of Work For Which Applied:

Typing Speed _____ WPM   Shorthand Speed _____ WPM

Dictating Equipment Skills ☐ Yes ☐ No   Driver's License No. _____ State _____

Please Provide Any Additional Information That May Aid Us In The Consideration Of Your Application Including Special Skills, Training, Qualifications, Membership In Professional Societies, Etc.

_____

_____

_____

I UNDERSTAND THAT the completion of this application does not indicate there are open positions and does not obligate Duke Power Company in any way. If accepted, employment in the position offered will be subject to a determination of physical and mental capability by a physician approved by the Company in accordance with the provisions of the Company's Affirmative Action Plan for the Handicapped.

I FURTHER UNDERSTAND THAT this application will be retained for active consideration for sixty (60) days from date submitted; however, I may reactivate my application for additional 60-day periods upon proper notification to the Company.

I HEREBY CERTIFY THAT my answer to each of the previous questions is true.

I AUTHORIZE the procurement of all available information from past and present employers and other applicable sources and realize that any evidence of falsification of information on this application may be considered adequate cause for discharge.

If the position for which you will be considered requires a security clearance, your offer of employment will be contingent upon receipt of this clearance. Public Law 91-508 requires that we advise you that a routine inquiry may be made which will provide applicable information concerning character, general reputation, personal characteristics and mode of living. Further information on the nature and scope of such report, if made, will be made available to you upon written request.

All information required in this form is necessary to process your application properly and to enable the Company to comply with state and federal laws and regulations.

Applicant's Signature _____   **Date Submitted** _____

INVITATION TO APPLICANTS

I. Handicapped

Duke Power is a government contractor subject to Section 503 of the Rehabilitation Act of 1973. In accordance with this law, it is a company goal to take affirmative action to employ and advance in employment qualified handicapped individuals. A handicapped individual is defined as a person having: (1) a physical or mental impairment which limits one or more life functions, (2) a record or history of such an impairment, or (3) is regarded as having such an impairment. If you have a handicap and would like to be considered under the Affirmative Action Program, please tell us. Submission of this information is voluntary and refusal to provide it will not subject you to discharge or disciplinary treatment. Information obtained concerning individuals shall be kept confidential, except that (i) supervisors and managers may be informed regarding restrictions on the work or duties of handicapped individuals, and regarding necessary accommodations, (ii) first aid and safety personnel may be informed, when and to the extent appropriate, if the condition might require emergency treatment, and (iii) government officials investigating compliance with the Act shall be informed.

If you are handicapped, we would like to include you under the Affirmative Action Program. It would assist us if you tell us about (1) any special methods, skills and procedures which qualify you for positions that you might not otherwise be able to do because of your handicap, so that you will be considered for any positions of that kind, and (2) the accommodations which we could make which would enable you to perform the job properly and safely, including special equipment, changes in the physical layout of the job, elimination of certain duties relating to the job, or other accommodations.

II. Disabled Veterans and Veterans of the Vietnam Era.

Duke Power is also a government contractor subject to Section 402 of the Vietnam Era Veterans Readjustment Assistance Act of 1974 as ammended which requires government contractors to take affirmative action to employ and advance in employment qualified disabled veterans and veterans of the Vietnam Era. A disabled veteran is a person entitled to at least 30 percentum disability compensation under laws administered by the Veterans Administration or whose discharge from active duty was for disability incurred or aggravated in the line of duty. Veteran of the Vietnam Era means a person (1) who (i) served on active duty for a period of more than 180 days, any part of which occurred between August 5, 1964 and May 7, 1975, and was discharged or released therefrom with other than a dishonorable discharge, or (ii) was discharged or released from active duty for a service-connected disability if any part of such active duty was performed between August 5, 1964 and May 7, 1975. If you are a disabled veteran covered by this program and would like to be considered under the Affirmative Action Program please tell us. This information is voluntary and refusal to provide it will not subject you to discharge or disciplinary treatment. Information obtained concerning individuals shall be kept confidential, except that (i) supervisors and managers may be informed regarding restrictions on the work or duties of disabled veterans, and regarding necessary accommodations, and (ii) first aid personnel may be informed, when and to the extent appropriate, if the condition might require emergency treatment. In order to assure proper placement of all employees, we request that you respond to the following statement:

If you have a disability which might affect your performance or create a hazard to yourself or others in connection with the job for which you are applying, please state the following: (1) the skills and procedures you use or intend to use to perform the job notwithstanding the disability and (2) the accommodations we could make which would enable you to perform the job properly and safely, including special equipment, changes in the physical layout of the job, elimination of certain duties relating to the job or other accommodations.

. . . .

NOTE: Please complete page 4 of this form if you wish to be included in the Affirmative Action Program(s) described above.

▼ Exhibit 7–1 (Concluded)

Page 4

NOTE: COMPLETION OF THIS PAGE IS VOLUNTARY; DO NOT COMPLETE UNTIL YOU HAVE READ <u>PAGE 3</u> THOROUGHLY.

I am ☐ handicapped ☐ a disabled veteran ☐ a Vietnam Era Veteran and would like to be included in your Affirmative Action Program.

My Handicap/Disability is: _____

_____

Recommendations for accommodations are indicated below.

_____

_____

_____

_____

_____

AN EQUAL OPPORTUNITY/AFFIRMATIVE ACTION EMPLOYER

(TO BE DETACHED BY AUTHORIZED COMPANY REPRESENTATIVE)

(TO BE DETACHED BY AUTHORIZED COMPANY REPRESENTATIVE) Page 5
DUKE POWER COMPANY

Federal laws and regulations require employers to monitor and report the status of their equal employment opportunity and affirmative action programs on a continuing basis. Therefore, it is requested that you complete the information below. This information will be maintained only for the purpose of monitoring and reporting compliance in accordance with applicable laws and regulations as well as to insure compliance with Company policies and procedures and will not be used for any other purpose.

Name _____ Address _____ Social Security No. _____

☐ Male   ☐ Female   Date of Birth _____ / _____ / _____
                                                      Month   Day   Year

Are you a United States Citizen or Permanent Resident of the United States or otherwise eligible for full-time permanent employment in the United States?
☐ Yes   ☐ No

ETHNIC IDENTIFICATION: ☐ White ☐ Black ☐ Hispanic ☐ Asian or Pacific Islander ☐ American Indian or Alaskan Native

Do you have any relatives currently employed by Duke Power? ☐ Yes   ☐ No

If so, give Name(s) _____ Relationship(s) _____ Department(s) _____

_____ _____ _____

_____ _____ _____

Signature _____ Date _____

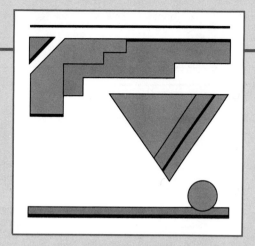

Section 3

Training and Developing Employees

Chapter 8
Orientation and Employee Training

 Chapter 9
**Management and Organizational
Development**

 Chapter 10
Performance Appraisal Systems

 Chapter 11
Career Planning

Chapter 8

Orientation and Employee Training

Chapter Outline

Orientation
Shared Responsibility
Company Orientation
Departmental and Job Orientation
Orientation Kit
Orientation Length and Timing
Follow-Up and Evaluation
Training Employees
Needs Assessment
Establishing Training Objectives
Methods of Training
On-the-Job Training and Job Rotation
Apprenticeship Training
Classroom Training
Principles of Learning
Motivation to Achieve Personal Goals
Knowledge of Results
Reinforcement
Flow of the Training Program

Practice and Repetition
Spacing of Sessions
Whole or Part Training
Evaluating Training
Reaction
Learning
Behavior
Results
Summary of Learning Objectives
Review Questions
Discussion Questions
Incident 8–1: Starting a New Job
Incident 8–2: Implementing On-the-Job Training
Exercise: McDonald's Training Program
Notes and Additional Readings

● *Learning Objectives*

After studying this chapter, you should be able to:
1. Define orientation.
2. Describe an orientation kit.
3. Define training.
4. Describe needs assessment.
5. Outline three categories of training objectives.
6. Describe job rotation.
7. Explain apprenticeship training.
8. Outline the seven principles of learning.
9. List the four areas of training evaluation.

"After we have studied the workman, so that we know his possibilities, we then proceed, as one friend to another, to try to develop every workman in our employ, so as to bring out his best faculties and to train him to do a higher, more interesting and more profitable class of work than he has done in the past."

Frederick W. Taylor*

After employees have been hired, they must be introduced to the organization and to their jobs; they must also be trained to perform their jobs. Furthermore, present employees must periodically have their skills updated and must learn new skills. The orientation and training of new employees and the training of longer-term employees are major responsibilities of the human resource department.

The need for orientation and employee training is directly related to the human resource planning process. Figure 8–1 shows the relationships among orientation, employee training, and other phases of human resource management. The objectives and strategies of the organization, the skills of the organization's present work force as indicated by its skills inventory, and anticipated changes in its work force determine the quantity and quality of personnel required by an organization. If new personnel are required, they must be recruited and go through the selection process. The personnel that are hired must then be oriented and trained in their new jobs. Later, these employees will periodically require training to update their present skills or training in new skills. Even in situations where an organization hires no new personnel, training is still required to update the skills of present employees and/or to train them in new skills.

Orientation

Orientation

The introduction of new employees to the organization, work unit, and job.

Orientation is the introduction of new employees to the organization, work unit, and job. Employees receive orientation from their fellow workers and from the company. The orientation received from fellow workers is usually unplanned and unofficial, and it often provides the new employee with misleading and inaccurate information. This is one of the reasons the official orientation provided by the company is important. An effective orientation program has an immediate and lasting impact on the new employee and can make the difference between a new employee's success or failure.

Job applicants get some orientation to the company even before they are hired. The organization has a reputation as to the type of company that it is and the types of products or services it provides. During the selection process, the new employee usually also learns other general aspects of the organization and what the duties, working conditions, and pay will be.

*Source: F. W. Taylor, "On Scientific Management," *Addresses and Discussions at the Conference on Scientific Management* (Hanover, N.H.: Dartmouth College, 1913), p. 33.

▼ **Figure 8–1**   Relationships among the various phases of human resource management

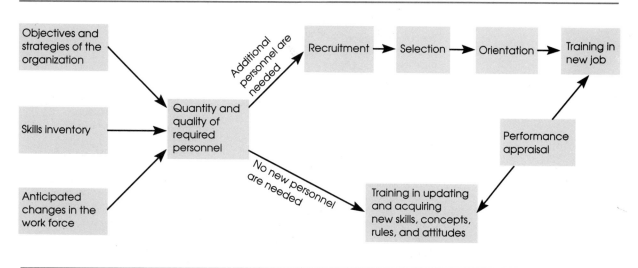

After the employee is hired, the organization's formal orientation program begins. Regardless of the types of company or industry, orientation should usually be conducted at two distinct levels:

1. General company orientation—presents topics of relevance and interest to all employees.
2. Departmental and job orientation—describes topics that are unique to the new employee's specific department and job.

Shared Responsibility

Since there are two distinct levels of orientation, responsibility for it is normally shared between the human resource department and the new employee's immediate manager. The human resource department is responsible for initiating and coordinating both levels of orientation, training line managers in procedures for conducting department and job orientation, conducting general company orientation, and following up the initial orientation with the new employee. The new employee's manager is usually responsible for conducting department and job orientation. Some organizations have instituted a "buddy system" in which the job orientation is conducted by one of the new employee's fellow workers. If a buddy system is to work successfully; the person chosen for this role must be carefully selected and properly trained for such orientation responsibilities.

Company Orientation

The topics presented in the **company orientation** should be based on the needs of both the company and the employee. Generally, the company is interested in making a profit, providing good service to customers and clients, satisfying employee needs and well-being, and being socially responsible. New employees, on

Company orientation
General orientation that presents topics of relevance and interest to all employees.

▼ **Figure 8–2**   Possible topics for a company orientation program

1. Overview of the company
- ☐ Welcoming speech
- ☐ Founding, growth, trends, goals, priorities, and problems
- ☐ Traditions, customs, norms, and standards
- ☐ Current specific functions of the organization
- ☐ Products/services and customers served
- ☐ Steps in getting products/services to customers
- ☐ Scope and diversity of activities
- ☐ Organization, structure, and relationship of company and its branches
- ☐ Facts on key managerial staff
- ☐ Community relations, expectations, and activities

2. Key policies and procedures review

3. Compensation
- ☐ Pay rates and ranges
- ☐ Overtime
- ☐ Holiday pay
- ☐ Shift differential
- ☐ How pay is received
- ☐ Deductions: required and optional, with specific amounts
- ☐ Option to buy damaged products and costs thereof
- ☐ Discounts
- ☐ Advances on pay
- ☐ Loans from credit union
- ☐ Reimbursement for job expenses

- ☐ Tax shelter options

4. Fringe benefits
- ☐ Insurance:
    - ☐ Medical/dental
    - ☐ Life
    - ☐ Disability
    - ☐ Workers' compensation
- ☐ Holidays and vacations (e.g., patriotic, religious, birthday)
- ☐ Leave: personal illness, family illness, bereavement, maternity, military, jury duty, emergency, extended absence
- ☐ Retirement plans and options
- ☐ On-the-job training opportunities
- ☐ Counseling services
- ☐ Cafeteria
- ☐ Recreation and social activities
- ☐ Other company services to employees

5. Safety and accident prevention
- ☐ Completion of emergency data card (if not done as part of employment process)
- ☐ Health and first-aid clinics
- ☐ Exercise and recreation centers
- ☐ Safety precautions
- ☐ Reporting of hazards
- ☐ Fire prevention and control
- ☐ Accident procedures and reporting
- ☐ OSHA requirements (review of key sections)
- ☐ Physical exam requirements
- ☐ Use of alcohol and drugs on the job

the other hand, generally are more interested in pay, benefits, and specific terms and conditions of employment. A good balance between the company's and the new employee's needs is essential if the orientation program is to have positive results. Figure 8–2 provides a listing of suggested topics that might be covered in an organization's orientation program.

Departmental and Job Orientation

Departmental and job orientation
Specific orientation that describes topics unique to the new employee's specific department and job.

The content of **departmental and job orientation** depends on the specific needs of the department and the skills and experience of the new employee. Experienced employees are likely to need less job orientation. However, even experienced personnel usually need some basic orientation. Both experienced and inexperienced employees should receive a thorough orientation concerning departmental matters. Figure 8–3 presents a checklist for the development of departmental and job orientation programs.

▼   **Figure 8-2**   (Concluded)

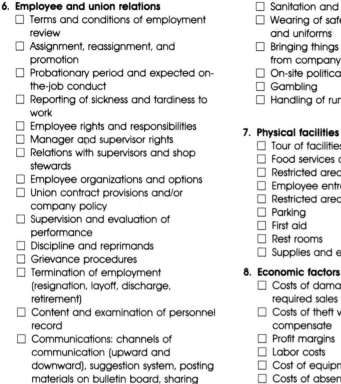

6. Employee and union relations
- ☐ Terms and conditions of employment review
- ☐ Assignment, reassignment, and promotion
- ☐ Probationary period and expected on-the-job conduct
- ☐ Reporting of sickness and tardiness to work
- ☐ Employee rights and responsibilities
- ☐ Manager and supervisor rights
- ☐ Relations with supervisors and shop stewards
- ☐ Employee organizations and options
- ☐ Union contract provisions and/or company policy
- ☐ Supervision and evaluation of performance
- ☐ Discipline and reprimands
- ☐ Grievance procedures
- ☐ Termination of employment (resignation, layoff, discharge, retirement)
- ☐ Content and examination of personnel record
- ☐ Communications: channels of communication (upward and downward), suggestion system, posting materials on bulletin board, sharing new ideas

- ☐ Sanitation and cleanliness
- ☐ Wearing of safety equipment, badges, and uniforms
- ☐ Bringing things on and removing things from company grounds
- ☐ On-site political activity
- ☐ Gambling
- ☐ Handling of rumors

7. Physical facilities
- ☐ Tour of facilities
- ☐ Food services and cafeteria
- ☐ Restricted areas for eating
- ☐ Employee entrances
- ☐ Restricted areas (e.g., from cars)
- ☐ Parking
- ☐ First aid
- ☐ Rest rooms
- ☐ Supplies and equipment

8. Economic factors
- ☐ Costs of damage to select items with required sales to balance
- ☐ Costs of theft with required sales to compensate
- ☐ Profit margins
- ☐ Labor costs
- ☐ Cost of equipment
- ☐ Costs of absenteeism, tardiness, and accidents

Source: W. D. St. John, "The Complete Employee Orientation Program," *Personnel Journal*, May 1980, pp. 376–77. Reprinted with the permission of *Personnel Journal*, Costa Mesa, California; all rights reserved.

Orientation Kit

It is desirable for each new employee to receive an **orientation kit**, or packet of information, to supplement the verbal orientation program. This kit is normally prepared by the human resource department and can provide a wide variety of materials. Care should be taken in the design not only to ensure that essential information is provided but also that too much information is not given. Some materials that might be included in an orientation kit include:

Orientation kit
A packet of written information given to a new employee to supplement the verbal orientation program.

Company organization chart.
Map of the company's facilities.
Copy of policy and procedures handbook.
List of holidays and fringe benefits.
Copies of performance appraisal forms, dates, and procedures.
Copies of other required forms (e.g., expense reimbursement form).
Emergency and accident prevention procedures.
Sample copy of company newsletter or magazine.

Telephone numbers and locations of key company personnel (e.g., security personnel).

Copies of insurance plans.

Many organizations require employees to sign a form indicating that they have received and read the orientation kit. This is commonly required in unionized organizations to protect the company if a grievance arises and the employee alleges that he or she was not aware of certain company policies and procedures. On the

▼ **Figure 8–3** Possible topics for departmental and job orientation programs

1. Department functions
- ☐ Goals and current priorities
- ☐ Organization and structure
- ☐ Operational activities
- ☐ Relationship of functions to other departments
- ☐ Relationships of jobs within the department

2. Job duties and responsibilities
- ☐ Detailed explanation of job based on current job description and expected results
- ☐ Explanation of why the job is important and how the specific job relates to others in the department and company
- ☐ Discussion of common problems and how to avoid and overcome them
- ☐ Performance standards and basis of performance evaluation
- ☐ Number of daily work hours and times
- ☐ Overtime needs and requirements
- ☐ Extra duty assignments (e.g., changing duties to cover for an absent worker)
- ☐ Required records and reports
- ☐ Checkout on equipment to be used
- ☐ Explanation of where and how to get tools, and have equipment maintained and repaired
- ☐ Types of assistance available; when and how to ask for help
- ☐ Relations with state and federal inspectors

3. Policies, procedures, rules, and regulations
- ☐ Rules unique to the job and/or department
- ☐ Handling emergencies
- ☐ Safety precautions and accident prevention

- ☐ Reporting of hazards and accidents
- ☐ Cleanliness standards and sanitation (e.g., cleanup)
- ☐ Security, theft problems, and costs
- ☐ Relations with outside people (e.g., drivers)
- ☐ Eating, smoking, and chewing gum, etc., in department area
- ☐ Removal of things from department
- ☐ Damage control (e.g., smoking restrictions)
- ☐ Time clock and time sheets
- ☐ Breaks/rest periods
- ☐ Lunch duration and time
- ☐ Making and receiving personal telephone calls
- ☐ Requisitioning supplies and equipment
- ☐ Monitoring and evaluating of employee performance
- ☐ Job bidding and requesting reassignment
- ☐ Going to cars during work hours

4. Tour of department
- ☐ Rest rooms and showers
- ☐ Fire-alarm box and fire extinguisher stations
- ☐ Time clocks
- ☐ Lockers
- ☐ Approved entrances and exits
- ☐ Water fountains and eye-wash systems
- ☐ Supervisors' quarters
- ☐ Supply room and maintenance department
- ☐ Sanitation and security offices
- ☐ Smoking areas
- ☐ Locations of services to employees related to department
- ☐ First-aid kit

5. Introduction to department employees

Source: W. D. St. John, "The Complete Employee Orientation Program," *Personnel Journal*, May 1980, p. 377. Reprinted with permission of *Personnel Journal*, Costa Mesa, California; all rights reserved.

other hand, it is equally important that a form be signed in nonunionized organizations, particularly in light of an increase in wrongful discharge litigation. Whether signing a document actually encourages new employees to read the orientation kit is questionable.

Orientation Length and Timing

It is virtually impossible for a new employee to absorb in one long session all of the information in the company orientation program. Brief sessions, not to exceed two hours, spread over several days increase the likelihood that the new employee will understand and retain the information presented. Too many organizations conduct a perfunctory orientation program lasting for a half day or full day. Programs of this nature can result in a negative attitude on the part of new employees.

Unfortunately, many departmental and job orientation programs produce the same results. Frequently, upon arriving in a department, new employees are given a departmental procedures manual and told to read the material and ask any questions they may have. Another frequently used departmental and job orientation method is to give new employees menial tasks to perform. Both of these methods are likely to produce poor results.

Departmental orientations should also be brief and spread over several days. Job orientations should be well planned and conducted using appropriate techniques.

Follow-Up and Evaluation

Formal and systematic follow-up to the initial orientation is essential. The new employee should not be told to drop by if any problems occur. The manager should regularly check on how well the new employee is doing and answer any questions that may have arisen after the initial orientation. The human resource department should have a scheduled follow-up after the employee has been on the job for a month.

The human resources department should also conduct an annual evaluation of the total orientation program. The purpose of this evaluation is to determine whether the current orientation program is meeting the company's and new employees' needs and to ascertain ways of improving the present program.

Feedback from new employees is one method of evaluating the effectiveness of an organization's orientation program. Feedback can be obtained using the following methods:

Unsigned questionnaires completed by all new employees.

In-depth interviews of randomly selected new employees.

Group discussion sessions with new employees who have settled comfortably into their jobs.

Feedback of this type enables an organization to adapt its orientation program to the specific suggestions of actual participants in the program. Finally, organizations should realize that new employees are going to receive an orientation that has an impact on their performance—either from their fellow workers or from the com-

▽. **HRM in Action 8–1**

The College Club at National Semiconductor Corp.

The College Club is a group of previous college hires at National Semiconductor who advise newly relocated graduates about the area, organize social activities for them, and help guide them through the company's College Hire Assimilation Program (CHAP). The College Club convenes frequently to help new employees meet people, sets up monthly trips or outings to acquaint the new hires with the area, and promotes networking. The club even sponsors Thanksgiving and Christmas parties for those who don't go home for the holidays. It also has several events planned throughout the year, including a peak performance workshop; a day of networking and team building, seminars on technology, human resources, and National's business, a seminar dealing with leadership and influence; the assignment of a trained advisor to each college hire; and a picnic in the corporate park.

Source: Adapted from Milan Moravec and Kevin Wheeler, "Speed New Hires into Success," *Personnel Journal*, March 1989, pp. 74–75.

pany. It is certainly in the best interest of the company to have a well-planned, well-executed orientation program.[1] HRM in Action 8–2 summarizes National Semiconductor's approach to orienting new college graduates to the company.

Training Employees

Training
A learning process that involves the acquisition of skills, concepts, rules, or attitudes to increase employee performance.

Training is a learning process that involves the acquisition of skills, concepts, rules, or attitudes to increase the performance of employees. Generally, the new employee's manager has primary responsibility for job training. Sometimes this training is delegated to a senior employee in the department. Regardless, the quality of this initial training can have a significant influence on the employee's productivity and attitude toward the job.

Economic, social, technological, and governmental changes significantly influence the objectives and strategies of all organizations. Changes in these areas can make the skills learned today obsolete in a short time. Also, planned organizational changes and expansions can make it necessary for employees to update their skills or acquire new ones. HRM in Action 8–2 illustrates a massive training program conducted by Federal Express when it decided to introduce a new product.

Needs Assessment

Needs assessment
A systematic analysis of the specific training activities required by an organization to achieve its objectives.

Training must be directed toward the accomplishment of some organizational objective, such as more efficient production methods, improved quality of products/services, or reduced operating costs. This means that an organization should commit its resources only to those training activities that can best help in achieving its objectives. **Needs assessment** is a systematic analysis of the specific training activities required by an organization to achieve its objectives. In general, needs assessment can be determined in three ways: organizational analysis, functional-unit or departmental analysis, and individual employee analysis.

▼. **HRM in Action 8–2**

Zap Mail at the Federal Express Company (FEC)

The core business of Federal Express involves the rapid movement of things from one place to another for a fee. In the beginning, FEC promised next-day service. That evolved into the 10:30 A.M. promise. When even that wasn't fast enough for some customers, Zap Mail, a two-hour electronic mail service, was introduced.

However, before it was introduced, FEC faced a massive training program because Zap Mail was different from FEC's core business. FEC named the training project Gemini.

The training budget for Gemini totaled $6 million. Sixty-four full-time trainers were assigned to the project. The training broke down as follows: 175 senior executives received 1,400 hours of instruction, 1,825 middle managers received 14,600 hours, and 22,000 other employees received 92,000 hours.

Source: Adapted from Ron Zenke, "How Training Put the Zip in Zap Mail," *Training*, March 1986, pp. 59–61.

▼ **Figure 8–4**   Sample of a needs assessment questionnaire (with partial listing of questions)

Instructions: Please read the list of training areas carefully before answering. Circle Yes if you believe you need training in that skill, either for use in your current job or for getting ready for promotion to a better position. Circle the question mark if uncertain. Circle No if you feel no need for training in that area.

1. How to more effectively manage my time	Yes	?	No
2. How to handle stress on the job	Yes	?	No
3. How to improve my written communication skills	Yes	?	No
4. How to improve my oral communication skills	Yes	?	No
5. How to improve my listening skills	Yes	?	No
6. How to improve my personal productivity	Yes	?	No

At the organizational level, records on absenteeism, turnover, tardiness, and accident rates provide objective evidence of problems within the organization. When problems occur, these records should be examined carefully to determine if the problems could be partially resolved through training.

Employee attitude surveys can also be used to uncover training needs at both the organizational and functional-unit levels. Normally, most organizations bring in an independent party to conduct and analyze the survey.

Consumer or customer surveys can also indicate problem areas that may not be obvious to the employees of an organization. Responses to a customer survey may indicate areas of training for the organization as a whole or within functional units of the organization.

A favorite method used in determining training needs at the organizational, departmental, and individual levels is through the administration of a needs assessment questionnaire. Normally, this involves developing a list of skills required to do a particular job effectively and asking employees to check those skills in which they believe they need training. Figure 8–4 shows some typical areas covered by a needs assessment questionnaire.

At the individual level, performance appraisal information is also an excellent source for determining training needs. Regardless of the methods employed, a systematic and accurate needs assessment should be undertaken before any training is conducted.[2]

Establishing Training Objectives

After training needs have been determined, objectives must be established for meeting these needs. Unfortunately, many organizational training programs have no objectives. "Training for training's sake" appears to be the maxim. With this philosophy, it is virtually impossible to evaluate the strengths and weaknesses of a training program.

Effective training objectives should state what the organization, department, or individual is to be like when the training is completed. The outcomes should be in writing. Training objectives can be categorized as:

1. Instructional objectives—
   - What principles, facts, and concepts are to be learned in the training program?
   - Who is to be taught?
   - When are they to be taught?
2. Organizational and departmental objectives—
   - What impact will the training have on organizational and departmental outcomes, such as absenteeism, turnover, reduced costs, and improved productivity?
3. Individual performance and growth objectives—
   - What impact will the training have on the behavioral and attitudinal outcomes of the individual trainee?
   - What impact will the training have on the personal growth of the individual trainee?

When clearly defined objectives are lacking, it is impossible to evaluate a program efficiently. Furthermore, there is no basis for selecting appropriate materials, content, or instructional methods.

Methods of Training

Several methods can be used to satisfy an organization's training needs and accomplish its objectives. Some of the more commonly used methods, however, include on-the-job training, job rotation, apprenticeship training, and classroom training.

On-the-Job Training and Job Rotation

On-the-job training
Training showing the employee how to perform the job and allowing him or her to do it under the trainer's supervision.

On-the-job training (OJT) is normally given by a senior employee or manager. The employee is shown how to perform the job and allowed to do it under the trainer's supervision.

▼ **Figure 8–5**   Steps leading to effective on-the-job training

A. Determining the training objectives and preparing the training area:
   1. Decide what the trainee must be taught in order to do the job efficiently, safely, economically, and intelligently.
   2. Provide the right tools, equipment, supplies, and material.
   3. Have the workplace properly arranged, just as the employee will be expected to keep it.
B. Presenting the instruction:
   Step 1. Preparation of the trainee for learning the job:
      a. Put the trainee at ease.
      b. Find out what the trainee already knows about the job.
      c. Get the trainee interested in and desirous of learning the job.
   Step 2. Breakdown of work into components and identification of key points:
      a. Determine the segments that make up the total job.
      b. Determine the key points or tricks of the trade.
   Step 3. Presentation of the operations and knowledge:
      a. Tell, show, illustrate, and question to put over the new knowledge and operations.
      b. Instruct slowly, clearly, completely, and patiently, one point at a time.
      c. Check, question, and repeat.
      d. Make sure the trainee understands.
   Step 4. Performance tryout:
      a. Test the trainee by having him or her perform the job.
      b. Ask questions beginning with why, how, when, or where.
      c. Observe performance, correct errors, and repeat instructions, if necessary.
      d. Continue until the trainee is competent in the job.
   Step 5. Follow-up:
      a. Put the trainee on his or her own.
      b. Check frequently to be sure the trainee follows instructions.
      c. Taper off extra supervision and close follow-up until the trainee is qualified to work with normal supervision.

One form of on-the-job training is **job rotation**, sometimes called **cross training**. In job rotation, an individual learns several different jobs within a work unit or department and performs each for a specified time period. One of the main advantages of job rotation is that it makes flexibility possible in the department. For example, when one member of a work unit is absent, another can perform that job.

Job rotation or cross training Training that requires an individual to learn several different jobs in a work unit or department and perform each for a specified time period.

The advantages of on-the-job training are that no special facilities are required and the new employee does productive work during the learning process. Its major disadvantage is that the pressures of the workplace can cause instruction of the employee to be haphazard or neglected.

In training an employee on the job, several steps can be taken to ensure that the training is effective. Figure 8–5 summarizes the steps in the training process. Each of these steps is explained more fully below.

Preparation of the Trainee for Learning the Job.   The desire to learn a new job is almost always present in an employee. Showing an interest in the person, explaining the importance of the job, and explaining why it must be done correctly enhance the employee's desire to learn. Determining the employee's previous work experience in similar jobs enables the trainer to use that experience in explaining the present job or to eliminate explanations that are unnecessary.

Breakdown of Work into Components and Identification of Key Points. This breakdown consists of determining the segments that make up the total job. In each segment, something is accomplished to advance the work toward completion. Such a breakdown can be viewed as a detailed road map that guides the employee through the entire work cycle in a rational, easy-to-understand manner, without injury to the person or damage to the equipment.

A key point is any directive or information that helps the employee perform a work component correctly, easily, and safely. Key points are the "tricks of the trade" and are given to the employee to help reduce learning time. Observing and mastering the key points help the employee to acquire needed skills and perform the work more effectively.

Presentation of the Operations and Knowledge. Simply telling an employee how to perform the job is usually not sufficient. An employee not only must be told but also must be shown how to do the job. Each component of the job must be demonstrated. While each is being demonstrated, the key points for that component should be explained. Employees should be encouraged to ask questions about each component.

Performance Tryout. An employee should perform the job under the guidance of the trainer. Generally, an employee should be required to explain what he or she is going to do at each component of the job. If the explanation is correct, the employee is then allowed to perform the component. If the explanation is incorrect, the mistake should be corrected before the employee is allowed to actually perform the component. Praise and encouragement are essential in this phase.

Follow-Up. When the trainer is reasonably sure that an employee can do the job without monitoring, the employee should be encouraged to work at his or her own pace while developing skills in performing the job and should be left alone. The trainer should return periodically to answer any questions and see that all is going well. Employees should not be turned loose and forgotten. They will have questions and will make better progress if the trainer is around to help with problems and answer questions.

Apprenticeship Training

Apprenticeship training dates back to biblical times and is, in simplest terms, training in those occupations requiring a wide and diverse range of skills and knowledge as well as independence of judgment. As practiced by organizations, **apprenticeship training** is a system in which an employee is given instruction and experience, both on and off the job, in all the practical and theoretical aspects of the work required in a skilled occupation, craft, or trade. Most apprenticeship programs range in length from one to five years. Table 8–1 shows the length of some apprenticeship training courses.

Apprenticeship training
Giving instruction, both on and off the job, in the practical and theoretical aspects of the work required in a skilled occupation or trade.

▼ **Table 8–1**   Length of selected apprenticeship courses

Occupation	Length of Course (years)
Airplane mechanic	3–4
Automotive mechanic	3–4
Barber	2
Brewer	2–3
Butcher	2–3
Carpenter	4
Musical-instrument mechanic	3–4
Photographer	3
Radio electrician	4–5
X-ray technician	4

Source: Bureau of Apprenticeship and Training, U.S. Department of Labor.

The U.S. Department of Labor's Bureau of Apprenticeship and Training, which encourages organizations to establish apprenticeship programs and provides assistance to those organizations, has established the following minimum standards for an effective apprenticeship program:

1.   Nondiscrimination in all phases of apprenticeship employment and training.
2.   Organized instruction designed to provide the apprentice with a knowledge in technical subjects related to the trade or skill (a minimum of 144 hours per year is normally considered necessary).
3.   A schedule of work processes in which an apprentice is to receive training and experience on the job.
4.   A progressively increasing schedule of wages.
5.   Proper supervision of on-the-job training, with adequate facilities to train apprentices.
6.   Periodic evaluation of the apprentice's progress, both in job performance and related instruction.
7.   Recognition for successful completions.

Classroom Training

Classroom training is conducted off the job and is probably the most familiar training method. It is an effective means of imparting information quickly to large groups with limited or no knowledge of the subject being presented. It is useful for teaching factual material, concepts, principles, and theories. Portions of orientation programs, some aspects of apprenticeship training, and safety programs are usually presented utilizing some form of classroom instruction. More frequently, however, classroom instruction is used for technical, professional, and managerial employees. Several specific techniques used in classroom training are discussed in Chapter 9.

Classroom training
The most familiar training method; useful for quickly imparting information to large groups with little or no knowledge of the subject.

Principles of Learning

Previous sections of this chapter have discussed not only how training needs are determined but also how they can be met. The use of sound learning principles during the development and implementation of these programs helps to ensure that the programs will succeed. Several principles of learning are presented in the following sections.

Motivation to Achieve Personal Goals

People strive to achieve objectives they have set for themselves. The most frequently identified objectives of employees are job security, financially and intellectually rewarding work, recognition, status, responsibility, and achievement. If a training program helps employees achieve some of these objectives, the learning process is greatly facilitated. For example, unskilled employees who are given the opportunity to learn a skilled trade may be highly motivated because they can see that more money and job security probably will result.

Knowledge of Results

Knowledge of results (feedback) influences the learning process. When employees are informed of their progress as measured against some standard, this helps in setting goals for what remains to be learned. The continuous process of analyzing progress and establishing new objectives greatly enhances learning. However, precautions should be taken to ensure that goals are not so difficult to achieve that the employee becomes discouraged.

Oral explanations and demonstrations by the trainee and written examinations are frequently used tools for providing feedback to both the trainee and the trainer. In addition, the progress of an individual or a group can be plotted on a chart to form what is commonly called a learning curve. The primary purpose of a learning curve is to provide feedback on the trainee's progress. It can also be used to help in deciding when to increase or decrease training or when to change methods. Figure 8–6 illustrates two different learning curves. In the decreasing-returns curve, the trainee initially learns rapidly but later the learning rate slows. In the plateau curve, the trainee initially shows rapid improvement, levels off, and then shows rapid improvement again. Although the decreasing-returns curve is most frequently encountered, many other shapes of learning curves are possible.

Reinforcement

The general idea behind reinforcement is that behavior appearing to lead to a positive consequence tends to be repeated, while behavior appearing to lead to a negative consequence tends not to be repeated. A positive consequence is a reward. Praise and recognition are two typical rewards that can be used in training. For example, a trainee who is praised for good performance is likely to continue to strive to achieve it in the training program.

▼ **Figure 8–6**   Learning curves

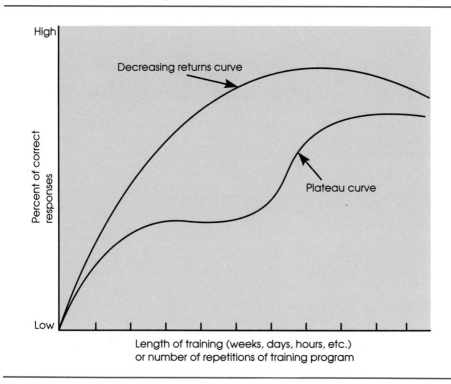

Flow of the Training Program

Each segment of training should be organized so that the individual can see not only its purpose but also how it fits in with other parts of the program. In addition, later segments should build on those presented earlier. Gaps and inconsistencies in material are not conducive to effective learning.

Practice and Repetition

The old adage "practice makes perfect" is applicable in learning. Having trainees perform a particular operation helps them concentrate on the subject. Repeating a task several times develops facility in performing it. Effective learning is almost always enhanced by practice and repetition.

Spacing of Sessions

Organizations frequently want to get an employee out of training and into a productive job as quickly as possible. However, they must decide whether the training should be given on consecutive days or at longer intervals. Generally, spacing out training over a period of time facilitates the learning process. But the interval most conducive to learning depends on the type of training.

▼. HRM in Action 8–3

Clinics at Wells Fargo Bank

Wells Fargo Bank has developed a unique alternative to classroom training—a clinic, which is described as an out-patient alternative to classroom hospitalization. In the clinic, participants work in peer groups to learn and practice new skills. They attend a short, instructional session presented during a staff meeting in their workplace or at a central location. They are taught, coached, and evaluated by a line employee, usually their manager, or a subject-matter expert. (Professional instructors do not present these clinics.) The typical Wells Fargo clinic is between one and one-half and three hours long.

Wells Fargo has found these clinics to be most useful when skill practice is necessary, the need is immediate; the audience has skills or knowledge to expand, build upon, or alter; there are changes in current policies or procedures; and managers are accountable for their employees' learning and results.

Source: Adapted from Carol Haig, "Clinics Fill Training Niche," *Personnel Journal*, September 1987, p. 134.

Whole or Part Training

Should training for a job be completed at once, or should the employee train separately for each different job component? The decision should be based on the content of the specific job, the material being taught, and the needs of those being trained. One method that is often successful is first to give trainees a brief overview of the job as a whole and then divide it into portions for in-depth instruction. HRM in Action 8–3 describes a training approach that incorporates many of the previously discussed principles of learning.

Evaluating Training

When the results of a training program are evaluated, a number of benefits accrue. Less effective programs can be withdrawn to save time and effort. Weaknesses within established programs can be identified and remedied.

Evaluation of training can be broken down into four areas:[3]

1. *Reaction*—How well did the trainees like the program?
2. *Learning*—What principles, facts, and concepts were learned in the training program?
3. *Behavior*—Did the job behavior of the trainees change because of the program?
4. *Results*—What were the results of the program in terms of factors such as reduced costs or reduction in turnover?

Even when great care is taken in designing evaluation procedures, it is difficult to determine the exact effect of training on learning, behavior, and results. Because of this, the evaluation of training is still limited and often superficial.[4]

▼ **Figure 8–7**   Sample reaction evaluation questionnaire

Name of program _____
Instructor _____
Date _____

1. How would you rate the overall program?
   ☐ Excellent   ☐ Very Good   ☐ Good   ☐ Fair   ☐ Poor
   Comments: _____
   _____

2. How were the meeting facilities, luncheon arrangements, etc.?
   ☐ Excellent   ☐ Very Good   ☐ Good   ☐ Fair   ☐ Poor
   Comments: _____
   _____

3. Would you like to attend programs of a similar nature in the future?
   ☐ Yes   ☐ No   ☐ Not sure
   Comments: _____
   _____

4. To what extent was the program relevant to your current job?
   ☐ To a large extent   ☐ To some extent   ☐ Very little
   Comment: _____
   _____

5. How would you rate the abilities and style of the instructor?
   ☐ Excellent   ☐ Very Good   ☐ Good   ☐ Fair   ☐ Poor

6. Other comments and suggestions for future programs: _____
   _____
   _____
   _____

   Signature (optional) _____

Reaction

Reaction evaluation should consider a wide range of topics, including program content, program structure and format, instructional techniques, instructor abilities and style, quality of the learning environment, extent to which training objectives were achieved, and recommendations for improvement. Figure 8–7 illustrates a typical reaction evaluation questionnaire.

Reaction evaluation questionnaires are normally administered immediately following the training, but can be administered several weeks later. The major flaw in using only reaction evaluation is that the enthusiasm of trainees cannot necessarily be taken as evidence of improved ability and performance.

Learning

Learning evaluation is concerned with how well the principles, facts, and skills were understood and absorbed by the trainees. In the teaching of skills, classroom demonstrations by trainees is a fairly objective way to determine how much learning is occurring. Where principles and facts are being taught, paper and pencil tests can be used. Standardized tests can be purchased to measure learning in many areas. In other areas, the trainers must develop their own. In order to obtain an accurate picture of what was learned, trainees should be tested both before and after the program.

Behavior

Behavior evaluation, concerned with the nature of the change in the job behavior of the trainee, is much more difficult than reaction and learning evaluation. The following guidelines are offered for evaluating behavioral change:[5]

1. A systematic appraisal should be made of on-the-job performance on a before-and-after basis.
2. The appraisal of performance should be made by one or more of the following groups (the more the better):
    a. The trainee.
    b. The trainee's superior or superiors.
    c. The trainee's subordinates.
    d. The trainee's peers or other people thoroughly familiar with his or her performance.
3. A statistical analysis should be made to compare performance before and after and to relate changes to the training program.
4. The post-training appraisal should be made several months after the training so that the trainees have an opportunity to put into practice what they have learned.
5. A control group (not receiving the training) should be used.

Results

Results evaluation attempts to measure changes in variables such as reduced turnover, reduced costs, improved efficiency, reduction in grievances, and increases in quantity and quality of production. Pretests, post-tests, and control groups are required, as with behavior evaluation, in performing an accurate results evaluation.

● *Summary of Learning Objectives*

1. Define orientation.
    Orientation is the introduction of new employees to the organization, work unit, and job.
2. Describe an orientation kit.
    An orientation kit is a packet of information given to the new employee to supplement the verbal orientation program.
3. Define training.
    Training is a learning process that involves the acquisition of skills, concepts, rules, or attitudes to increase employee performance.

4.   Describe needs assessment.

Needs assessment is a systematic analysis of the specific training activities required by an organization to achieve its objectives.

5.   Outline three categories of training objectives.

Training objectives can be categorized as instructional objectives, organizational and departmental objectives, and individual performance and growth objectives.

6.   Describe job rotation.

In job rotation, an individual learns several different jobs within a work unit or department and performs each for a specified time period.

7.   Explain apprenticeship training.

Apprenticeship training is a system in which an employee is given instruction and experience, both on and off the job, in all the practical and theoretical aspects of the work required in a skilled occupation, craft, or trade.

8.   Outline the seven principles of learning.

The seven principles of learning are motivation to achieve personal goals, knowledge and results, reinforcement, flow of the training program, practice and repetition, spacing of sessions, and whole or part training.

9.   List the four areas of training evaluation.

Evaluation of training can be broken down into the following areas: reaction, learning, behavior, and results evaluation.

Review Questions

1.   What is orientation? General company orientation? Departmental and job orientation?
2.   Outline several possible topics for a general company orientation.
3.   What is an orientation kit?
4.   What is training?
5.   Define:
     a.   On-the-job training
     b.   Job rotation
6.   Outline five steps that should be followed in training a new employee in how to perform a job.
7.   Define apprenticeship training.
8.   What learning principles should be used in all training programs?
9.   List and explain the four logical areas for evaluating training.

Discussion Questions

1.   Why are most training programs not evaluated?
2.   Which principles of learning are applied in college classrooms? Which ones are most appropriate for use in college classrooms?

3. Why are training programs one of the first areas to be eliminated when an organization's budget must be cut?

4. If you were asked to develop a training program for taxicab drivers, how would you do it? How would you evaluate the program?

▼ INCIDENT 8–1

Starting a New Job

Jack Smythe, branch manager for a large computer manufacturer, had been told by his marketing manager Bob Sprague that Otis Brown had just given two weeks notice. When Jack had interviewed Otis, he had been convinced of his tremendous potential in sales. Otis was bright and personable, an MIT honor graduate in electrical engineering who had the qualifications that the company looked for in computer sales. Now he was leaving after only two months with the company. Jack called Otis into his office for an exit interview.

Jack: Come in, Otis, I really want to talk to you. I hope I can change your mind about leaving.

Otis: I don't think so.

Jack: Well, tell me why you want to go. Has some other company offered you more money?

Otis: No. In fact, I don't have another job; I'm just starting to look.

Jack: You've given us notice without having another job?

Otis: Well, I just don't think this is the place for me!

Jack: What do you mean?

Otis: Let me see if I can explain. On my first day at work, I was told that my formal classroom training in computers would not begin for a month. I was given a sales manual and told to read and study it for the rest of the day.

The next day I was told that the technical library, where all the manuals on computers are kept, was in a mess and needed to be organized. That was to be my responsibility for the next three weeks.

The day before I was to begin computer school, my boss told me that the course had been delayed for another month. He said not to worry, however, because he was going to have James Crane, the branch's leading salesperson, give me some on-the-job training. I was told to accompany James on his calls. I'm supposed to start the school in two weeks, but I've just made up my mind that this place is not for me.

Jack: Hold on a minute, Otis. That's the way it is for everyone in the first couple of months of employment in our industry. Any place you go will be the same. In fact, you had it better than I did. You should have seen what I did in my first couple of months.

Questions

1. What do you think about the philosophy of this company pertaining to a new employee's first few weeks on the job?

2. What suggestions do you have for Jack to help his company avoid similar problems of employee turnover in the future?

▼ INCIDENT 8–2

Implementing On-the-Job Training

The first-year training program for professional staff members of a large national accounting firm consists of classroom seminars and on-the-job training. The objectives of the training are to ensure that new staff members learn fundamental auditing concepts and procedures and develop technical, analytical, and communications skills that, with further experience and training, will help them achieve their maximum potential with the organization.

Classroom training is used to introduce concepts and theories applicable to the work environment. It consists of three two-day and two three-day seminars presented at varying intervals during the staff member's first year. Although new staff members do receive this special training, actual work experience is the principal method for them to develop many skills necessary to become good auditors.

Most of the firm's audits are performed by teams supervised by the senior member. This individual is responsible for conducting the review and producing the required reports. Teams normally are assembled primarily on the basis of member availability. For this reason, a senior auditor may be assigned one or more first-year employees for a team that must undertake a complex assignment. Because senior auditors are measured on productivity, their attention usually is focused on the work being produced. Therefore, they assign routine tasks to new staff employees, with little or no thought to furthering the career development of these employees. Most senior auditors assume that the next supervisor or the individuals themselves will take care of their training and development needs.

Recently, the firm has lost some capable first-year people. The reason most gave for leaving was that they were not learning or advancing in their profession.

Questions

1. What, if anything, do you think the company should do to keep its young employees?
2. Do you think that on-the-job training will work in a situation such as the one described?

Exercise

McDonald's Training Program

Your class has recently been hired by the president of McDonald's to make recommendations for improving the orientation and training programs of employees in their franchise operations. The key job activities in franchise operations are food preparation, order taking and dealing with customers, and routine clean-up operations. The president wants you to make your recommendations based on your observations as customers.

Your assignment is to design a comprehensive orientation and employee training program for each of the key job activities in franchise operations. Be specific by providing an outline, methods of training, and program evaluation procedures for each activity.

1. Break the class into groups of four to five students per team.
2. Each group is responsible for designing the program for one of the key job activities.
3. Have each team prepare a 10- to 15-minute presentation on its recommendations.

Notes and Additional Readings

1. See Jeffrey P. Davidson, "Starting the New Hire on the Right Foot," *Personnel,* August 1986, pp. 67–71.
2. See Steven Lange, "Getting the Most out of Needs Assessments," *Training,* October 1986, pp. 101–04.
3. See D. L. Kirkpatrick, "Evaluation of Training," in *Training and Development Handbook,* ed. R. L. Craig and L. R. Bittel (New York: McGraw-Hill, 1986), p. 18-2.
4. See Nancy M. Dixon, "Meet Training's Goals without Reaction Forms," *Personnel Journal,* August 1987, pp. 108–15.
5. Kirkpatrick, "Evaluation of Training," pp. 18-16–18-17.

Chapter 9

Management and Organizational Development

Chapter Outline

Management Development Process
Determining the Net Management Requirements
Organizational Objectives
Management Inventory and Succession Plan
Changes in the Management Team
Needs Assessment
Organizational Needs
Needs of Individual Managers
Establishing Management Development Objectives
Methods Used in Management Development
Understudy Assignments
Coaching
Experience
Job Rotation
Special Projects and Committee Assignments
Classroom Training

University and Professional Association Seminars
Evaluation of Management Development Activities
Assessment Centers
Organizational Development
Approaches to Management and Organizational Development
Summary of Learning Objectives
Review Questions
Discussion Questions
Incident 9–1: The 30-Year Employee
Incident 9–2: Consolidating Three Organizations
Exercise: Training Methods
Notes and Additional Readings
On the Job: Comparison of Training Methods

Learning Objectives

After studying this chapter, you should be able to:

1. Define management development.
2. Describe a management inventory.
3. Describe a management succession plan.
4. Define the in-basket technique.
5. Explain programmed instruction.
6. Describe a business game.
7. Define an assessment center.
8. Describe organizational development (OD).
9. Discuss behavior modeling.
10. Describe wilderness training.

"*T*here was a time when it was widely believed that management development was an automatic process requiring little attention. It was felt that the normal operation of the industrial organization would permit the cream to rise to the top, where it would become visible and could be skimmed off as needed. . . . Particularly since World War II we have seen an unprecedented growth in management development programs and activities throughout the whole western world. It is rare to find a large or even medium-sized company today which does not have a formal program and a staff to administer it."

Douglas McGregor*

The previous chapter focused on the orientation and training of new employees and the training of longer-term employees. In addition, an organization must be concerned with developing the abilities of its management team, including supervisors, middle-level managers, and executives. The development and implementation of programs to improve management effectiveness is a major responsibility of the human resource department.

Management Development Process

Management development
Process concerned with developing the experience, attitudes, and skills necessary to become or remain an effective manager.

Management development is concerned with developing the experience, attitudes, and skills necessary to become or remain an effective manager. To be successful, it must have the full support of the organization's top executives. Management development should be designed, conducted, and evaluated on the basis of the objectives of the organization, the needs of the individual managers that are to be developed, and anticipated changes in the organization's management team. Figure 9–1 summarizes the total management development process, and the following sections of this chapter discuss each of the elements in depth.

Determining the Net Management Requirements

Organizational Objectives

An organization's objectives play a significant role in determining its requirements for managers. For instance, if an organization is undergoing a rapid expansion program, new managers will be needed at all levels. If, on the other hand, the organization is experiencing limited growth, few new managers may be needed; but possibly, the skills of the present management team should be upgraded.

*Source: D. McGregor, *The Human Side of Enterprise* (New York: McGraw-Hill, 1960), p. 190.

▼ **Figure 9–1**   Management development process

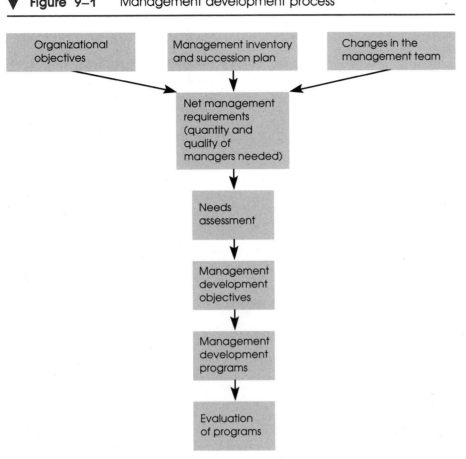

Management Inventory and Succession Plan

A **management inventory**, which is a specialized type of skills inventory, provides certain types of information about an organization's current management team. Management inventories often include information such as present position, length of service, retirement date, education, and past performance evaluations. Figure 9–2 illustrates a simplified management inventory.

A management inventory can be used to fill vacancies that occur unexpectedly— for example, as a result of resignations or deaths. Another use is in planning the development needs of individual managers and in using these to pinpoint development activities for the total organization.

A management inventory can also be used to develop a management succession plan, sometimes called a replacement chart or schedule. A **management succession plan** records potential successors for each manager within an organization. Usually presented in a format similar to an organization chart, this plan may simply be a list of positions and potential replacements. Other information, such as length of

Management inventory
Specialized, expanded form of skills inventory for an organization's current management team; in addition to basic types of information, it usually includes a brief assessment of past performance and potential for advancement.

Management succession plan
Chart or schedule that shows potential successors for each management position within an organization.

▼ **Figure 9–2** Sample of a simplified management inventory

Name	Present Position	Length of Service	Retirement Year	Replacement Positions	Previous Training Received
James W. Burch	Industrial relations manager, Greenville plant	5 years	1997	Corporate industrial relations staff	B.B.A., University of South Carolina; middle-management program, Harvard
George S. Chesser	Engineering trainee	9 months	2017	Plant engineering manager, corporate engineering staff	B.E.E., Purdue
Thomas R. Lackey, Jr.	Supervisor, receiving department, night shift	15 years	1998	Department manager, shipping and receiving	High school diploma, supervisory skills training
Edward C. Sabo	Eastern regional marketing manager	8 years	1999	Vice president, marketing	B.B.A., UCLA; M.B.A., USC; executive development program, Stanford

service, retirement data, past performance evaluations, and salary, might also be shown on the replacement chart. Figure 9–3 is an example of a replacement chart for a company's administrative division.

Management inventories and succession plans are generally kept confidential and can be computerized. They are also maintained by the human resource department for the use of top executives of the organization.

Changes in the Management Team

Certain changes in the management team can be estimated fairly accurately and easily, while other changes are not so easily determined. Changes such as retirements can be predicted from information in the management inventory; changes such as transfers and promotions can be estimated from such factors as the planned retirements of individuals in specific jobs and the objectives of the organization. Deaths, resignations, and discharges are, of course, difficult to forecast. However, when these changes do occur, the management inventory and succession plan can be used to fill these vacancies.

Human resource planning, which was discussed in depth in Chapter 5, is concerned with forecasting changes for both management and operative employees. Analyzing the organization's objectives, studying the management inventory and succession plan, and evaluating changes in the management team can give the human resource department a good picture of both the quantity and quality of managers that will be needed by the organization in the future.

▼ **Figure 9–3**   Replacement plan for administrative division of a typical organization

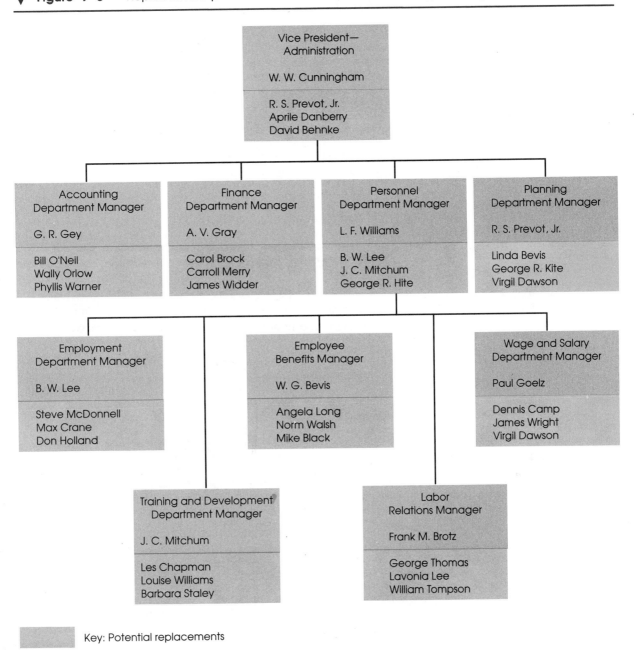

Key: Potential replacements

Needs Assessment

Only after the above analysis has been completed can a needs assessment be performed. Needs assessment is a systematic analysis of the specific management development activities required by an organization to achieve its objectives.

Numerous methods have been proposed for use in assessing such needs. The management development needs of any organization are composed of the aggregate or overall needs of the organization and the development needs of individual managers within the organization. Several of the methods discussed in the previous chapter—consumer surveys and the training needs questionnaire—can be used to determine management development needs.

Organizational Needs

In addition to the analysis described above, the most common source for determining organizational management development needs is an analysis of problem areas within the organization. For example, increases in the number of grievances or in the accident rate within a particular area of the organization often signal the need for management development. High turnover rates and high rates of absenteeism or tardiness might also indicate management development needs.

Projections of management requirements based on the organization's objectives and changes in its management team can also be used to determine an organization's management development needs, as can projected personnel changes, such as promotions.

Needs of Individual Managers

The performance of the individual manager is the primary indicator of individual development needs. Performance evaluations of each manager can be examined to determine areas that need strengthening. The existence of problem situations within a manager's work unit can also signal individual development needs. Planned promotions or reassignments also frequently indicate the need for development.

Establishing Management Development Objectives

After the management development needs of an organization have been determined, objectives for the overall management development program and for individual programs must be established to meet these needs. Both types of objectives should be expressed in writing and should be measurable. As will be recalled from the previous chapter, training objectives can be categorized within three broad areas: instructional, organizational and departmental, and individual performance and growth. This categorization scheme can also be used for management development objectives.

Figure 9–4   Relationship between needs assessment and objectives
in management development

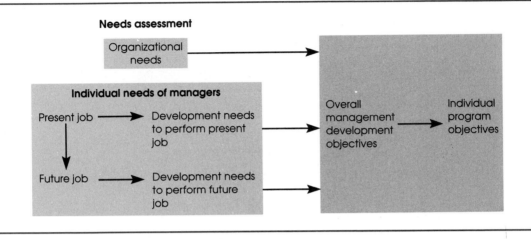

Instructional objectives might incorporate targets relating to the number of trainees that are to be taught, hours of training, cost per trainee, and time required for trainees to reach a standard level of knowledge. Furthermore, objectives are needed for the principles, facts and concepts that are to be learned in the management development program(s).

Organizational and departmental objectives are concerned with the impact that the programs will have on organizational and departmental outcomes, such as absenteeism, turnover, safety, and number of grievances. Individual and personal growth objectives are concerned with the impact on the behavioral and attitudinal outcomes of the individual. They may also be concerned with the impact on the personal growth of the individuals involved in the programs.

After the overall management development objectives have been established, individual program objectives must be identified that specify the skills, concepts, or attitudes that should result. After these objectives are developed, course content and method of instruction can be specified. Figure 9–4 shows the relationship between needs assessment, objectives, identification of overall management development objectives, and identification of objectives for each individual management development program. HRM in Action 9–1 shows a supervisory development program based on needs and objectives.

Methods Used in Management Development

After the company's needs have been assessed and its objectives stated, management development programs must be implemented. This section examines some of the more frequently used methods of management development. At this point, recall the list of conditions for effective learning discussed in the previous chapter. These principles of learning also apply to management development programs.

▽▽. **HRM in Action 9–1**

Supervisory Training at General Cinema

Supervisory training at General Cinema is based on needs and objectives. Before the training was ever launched, General Cinema conducted a year-long needs assessment in an effort to answer two basic questions: First, what were the key generic supervisory skills in need of development? Second, which specific, frequent responsibilities did supervisors find it difficult to handle?

The following objectives were established for the program: (1) it should develop management rather than technical skills, (2) it should center on skills that first-line supervisors actually need, (3) it should minimize learning barriers that people with different levels of ability and experience bring to the program, (4) it should have the commitment of all levels of management, (5) it should use behavior-modeling technology, and (6) its results should be measurable.

Source: Adapted from Edward Jones, "Supervising Training: A New Beginning," *Training,* December 1986, p. 64.

The On the Job example at the end of this chapter defines and summarizes the strengths and weaknesses of training methods used in both management development and employee training courses. As with employee training, management development can be achieved both on the job and off the job. Some of the most popular methods of management development are summarized in Table 9–1 and are discussed below.

Understudy Assignments

Understudy assignments
Method of on-the-job training in which one individual, designated as the heir to a job, learns the job from the present jobholder.

Generally, **understudy assignments** are used to develop an individual's capabilities to fill a specific job. An individual who will eventually be given a particular job works for the incumbent. The title of the heir to the job is usually assistant manager, administrative assistant, or assistant to a particular manager.

The advantage of understudy assignments is that the heir realizes the purpose of the training and can learn in a practical and realistic situation without being directly responsible for operating results. On the negative side, the understudy learns the bad as well as the good practices of the incumbent. In addition, understudy assignments maintained over a long period can become expensive. If an understudy assignment system is used, it should generally be supplemented with one or more of the other management development methods.

Coaching

Coaching
Method of management development conducted on the job, that involves experienced managers advising and guiding trainees in solving managerial problems.

Coaching is carried out by experienced managers and emphasizes the responsibility of all managers for developing subordinates. Under this method of management development, experienced managers advise and guide trainees in solving managerial problems. The idea behind coaching should be to allow the trainees to develop their own approaches to management with the counsel of a more experienced person.

One advantage to coaching is that trainees get practical experience and see the results of their decisions. However, there is a danger that the coach may neglect the training responsibilities or pass on inappropriate management practices. The coach's expertise and experience are of critical importance with this method.

▼ **Table 9–1**   Selected methods used in management development

On the Job	Off the Job
Understudy assignments	Classroom training
Coaching	Lectures
Experience	Case studies
Job rotation	Role playing
Special projects and committee assignments	In-basket techniques
	Programmed instruction
	Business games
	University and professional association seminars

Experience

Development through experience is used in many organizations. Under this method, individuals are promoted into management jobs and allowed to learn on their own, from their daily experiences. The primary advantage in this method is that the individual, in attempting to perform a specific job, may recognize the need for management development and look for a means of satisfying it. However, employees who are allowed to learn management only through experience can create serious problems by making mistakes. Also, it is frustrating to attempt to manage without the necessary background and knowledge. Serious difficulties can be avoided if the experience method is supplemented with other management development techniques.

Job Rotation

Job rotation is designed to give an individual broad experience through exposure to many different areas of the organization. In understudy assignments, coaching, and experience, the trainee generally receives training and development for one particular job. In job rotation, the trainee goes from one job to another within the organization, generally remaining in each from six months to a year. This technique is used frequently by large organizations for training recent college graduates.

One advantage of job rotation is that the trainees can see how management principles can be applied in a cross section of environments. Also, the training is practical and allows the trainee to become familiar with the entire operation of the company. One serious disadvantage of this method is that the trainee is frequently given menial assignments in each job. Another disadvantage is the tendency to leave the trainee in each of the jobs longer than necessary. Both of these disadvantages can produce negative attitudes.

Special Projects and Committee Assignments

Special projects require the subordinate to learn about a particular subject. For example, a trainee may be told to develop a training program on safety. This would require learning about the organization's present safety policies and problems and the safety training procedures used by other companies. The individual must also learn to work with and relate to other employees. However, it is of critical importance that the special assignments provide a developing and learning experience for the subordinate and not just busywork.

Committee assignments, which are similar to special projects, can be used if the organization has regularly constituted or ad hoc committees. In this approach, an individual works with the committee on its regularly assigned duties and responsibilities. Thus, the person exercises skills in working with others and learns through the activities of the committee.

Classroom Training

In this, the most familiar type of training, several methods can be used. Classroom training is used not only in management development programs but also in the orientation and training activities discussed in the previous chapter. Therefore, some of the material in this section is also applicable to those activities. In addition, several of the approaches used in organizational development (discussed later in this chapter) involve classroom training.

Lectures

With lecturing, instructors have control over the situation and can present the material exactly as they desire. Although the lecture is useful for presenting facts, its value in changing attitudes and in teaching skills is somewhat limited.

Case Studies

Case study
Method of classroom training in which the student analyzes real or hypothetical situations and suggests not only what to do but also how to do it.

In this technique, popularized by the Harvard Business School, real and hypothetical situations are presented for the student to analyze. Ideally, the **case study** should force the trainee to think through problems, propose solutions, choose among them, and analyze the consequences of the decision.

One primary advantage of the case method is that it brings a note of realism to the instruction. However, case studies often are simpler than the real situations faced by managers. Another drawback is that when cases are discussed, there is often a lack of emotional involvement on the part of the participants; thus, attitude and behavioral changes are less likely to occur. Also, the success of the case study method depends heavily on the skills of the instructor.

Incident method
Form of case study in which students are initially given the general outline of a situation and receive additional information from the instructor only as they request it.

One variation of case study is the **incident method**. The student is initially only given the general outline of a situation. The instructor then provides additional information as the trainee requests it. Theoretically, the incident method makes students probe the situations and seek additional information, much as they would be required to do in real life.

Role Playing

In this method, participants are assigned different roles and are required to act out these roles in a realistic situation. The idea is for the participants to learn from playing out the assigned roles. The success of this method depends on the ability of participants to assume the roles realistically. Videotaping allows for review and evaluation of the exercise to improve its effectiveness.

▼. HRM in Action 9–2

Computer-Assisted Instruction at IBM

On any given day at IBM, 18,000 of its 390,000 employees take part in some kind of formal education event—in a classroom, through self-study, or via computer-based training. IBM employees around the world complete 5 million student days per year, giving each employee an average of about 12 days. The yearly education budget of $900 million includes the costs of the people, equipment, and facilities needed to deliver the training, but does not include the salaries of the people being trained.

IBM's newest classrooms put technology to work for the instructor and student. A personal computer lets the instructor call on visual material in a myriad of forms. A keypad at each desk lets students answer all the instructor's questions. The instructor's computer tabulates students' responses and displays the pattern of right and wrong answers.

Source: Adapted from Patricia A. Galagan, "IBM Gets Its Arms around Education," *Training and Development Journal*, January 1989, pp. 35–41.

In-Basket Techniques

The **in-basket technique** simulates a realistic situation by requiring each trainee to answer one manager's mail and telephone calls. Important duties are interspersed with routine matters. For instance, one call may come from an important customer who is angry, while a letter from a local civic club may request a donation. The trainees analyze the situations and suggest alternative actions. They are evaluated on the basis of the number and quality of decisions and on the priorities assigned each situation. The in-basket technique has been used not only for management development but also in assessment centers, which are discussed later in this chapter.

In-basket technique
Method of classroom training in which the trainee is required to simulate the handling of a specific manager's mail and telephone calls and to react accordingly.

Programmed and Computer-Assisted Instruction

Programmed instruction requires the trainee to read material on a particular subject and answer questions about the material. Correct answers allow the trainee to move on to more advanced or new material. If the trainee's answers are incorrect, he or she is required to reread the material and answer additional questions. The material in programmed instruction is presented either in text form or on computer video displays. Regardless of the type of presentation, programmed instruction provides active practice, a gradual increase in difficulty over a series of steps, immediate feedback, and an individualized rate of learning. Programmed instruction normally is used to teach factual information. The increased availability and lower cost of small computers may increase the use of programmed instruction, not only in management development but also in employee training and orientation. HRM in Action 9–2 illustrates computer-assisted instruction at IBM.

Programmed instruction
Method of classroom training in which material is presented in text form or on computer video displays; students are required to answer correctly questions about the subject presented, before progressing to more advanced material.

Business Games

Business games generally provide a setting of a company and its environment and require a team of players to make decisions involving company operations. They also normally require the use of computer facilities. In a business game, several different teams act as companies within a type of industry. This method forces individuals not only to work with other group members but also to function in an atmosphere of competition within the industry. Advantages of business games are that they simulate reality, decisions are made in a competitive environment,

Business game
Method of classroom training that simulates an organization and its environment and requires a team of players to make operating decisions based on the situation.

HRM In Action 9–3

Wharton's Business Game

Top Management Experience is a computerized business game developed at the University of Pennsylvania's Wharton School of Business. At the heart of Top Management Experience is an 8,500-equation model. In the game, players are told that they have a certain number of tokens to begin with and are given rules by which they gain or lose what they have. They receive an 80-page manual containing details on their company's business history and how the computer-simulated world works. Each company sells two products in three geographic areas. Each geographic area has its own business cycle. Each team starts out equal, all getting control of companies with identical 18-month histories. Each period, teams make decisions that fall into the following general categories: marketing, personnel, manufacturing, inventory, and finance. The computer simulates the marketplace and gives the teams reports on their stock prices, market share, and returns on sales, assets, and equity.

Source: Adapted from Shlomo Maital and Kim Morgan, "Playing at Management," *Across the Board*, April 1988, pp. 54–62.

feedback is provided concerning decisions, and decisions are made using less-than-complete data. The main disadvantage is that many participants simply attempt to determine the key to winning. When this occurs, the game is not used to its fullest potential as a learning device. HRM in Action 9–3 describes one business game.

University and Professional Association Seminars

Many colleges and universities offer both credit and noncredit courses intended to help meet the management development needs of various organizations. These offerings range from courses in principles of supervision to advanced executive management programs. Professional associations, such as the American Management Association, also offer a wide variety of management development programs. Many of the previously discussed classroom techniques are used in these programs.

Evaluation of Management Development Activities

It is unrealistic to assume that the very difficult job of managing complex organizations can be accomplished by untrained managers. One realistic method of acquiring managerial skills is through effectively planned, conducted, and evaluated management development programs.

In the previous chapter, four areas were described for evaluating employee training: reaction, learning, behavior, and results. All are equally applicable to the evaluation of management development activities. Unfortunately, too many such activities are evaluated solely on the basis of participants' reactions to the training. Objective evaluation of management development is still limited and often superficial.

Assessment Centers

An **assessment center** is a formal method aimed at evaluating an individual's potential as a manager and his or her developmental needs. Assessment centers are used in both the selection and development of managers. Basically, these centers simulate the problems that a person might face in a real-life managerial situation.

In the typical assessment center, 10 to 15 participants of approximately equal organizational rank are brought together for three to five days to work on individual and group exercises similar to ones they would be handling in a typical managerial job. Business games, situational problems, interviews, and cases are normally used to simulate managerial situations. These exercises involve the participants in decision making, leadership, written and oral communication, planning, organizing, and motivation. Assessors observe the participants, evaluate their performance, and then provide feedback to the participants concerning performance and developmental needs.

Assessors can be selected from management ranks above those of the participants. Also, professional psychologists from outside the organization frequently serve as assessors. For a program to be successful, the assessors must be rigorously trained in the assessment process, the mechanics of the exercises that are to be observed, and the techniques of observing and providing feedback.[1]

Assessment center
Formal method used in training and/or selection and aimed at evaluating an individual's potential as a manager by exposing the individual to simulated problems that would be faced in a real-life managerial situation.

Organizational Development

Organizational development (OD) seeks to improve the performance of groups, departments, and the overall organization. Specifically, **organizational development** is an organizationwide, planned effort managed from the top, with a goal of increasing organizational performance through planned interventions and training experiences. In particular, OD looks in depth at the human side of organizations. It seeks to change attitudes, values, organizational structures, and managerial practices in an effort to improve organizational performance. The ultimate goal of OD is to structure the organizational environment so that managers and employees can use their developed skills and abilities to the fullest.

An OD effort has as its initial phase a recognition by management that organizational performance can and should be improved. Following this initial recognition, most OD efforts include the following phases: (1) diagnosis, (2) strategy planning, (3) education, and (4) evaluation.

Diagnosis involves gathering information from employees through the use of questionnaires or attitude surveys. Strategy planning is concerned with developing a plan for organization improvement based on these data. Strategy planning identifies problem areas in the organization and outlines steps to be taken to resolve the problems. Education consists of sharing the information obtained in the diagnosis with the employees who are affected by it and helping them to realize the need for changed behavior. The education phase often involves the use of outside

Organization development
Organizationwide, planned effort managed from the top, with a goal of increasing organizational performance through planned interventions and training experiences.

consultants working with individual employees or employee groups. This phase can also involve the use of the management development programs discussed earlier. Other techniques that might be used in the education phase are examined in the following sections of this chapter. The evaluation phase is very similar to the diagnostic phase. Following diagnosis, strategy planning, and education, additional data are gathered through attitude surveys or questionnaires to determine the effects of the OD effort on the total organization. This information can then, of course, lead to additional planning and educational efforts.

Sensitivity training has been frequently used in OD programs and is designed to make the participants more aware of themselves and their impact on others. Sensitivity training involves a group, normally called an *encounter group*, a training group or T group, which has no agenda or particular focus. The group usually consists of between 10 and 15 people who may or may not know each other. Since the group has no planned structure, the agenda becomes the behavior of individual group members in attempting to deal with the lack of structure. While engaging in group dialogue, members are encouraged to learn about themselves and others in the nonstructured environment. Today, sensitivity training is not widely used in organizational development programs.

Sensitivity training
Method of training normally used in organization development and designed to make the participants more aware of themselves and their impact on others.

Approaches to Management and Organizational Development

One approach used in management and organizational development is **behavior modeling, or interaction management**. Basically, behavior modeling involves identifying interaction problems faced by managers, such as gaining acceptance, overcoming resistance to change, motivating employees, and reducing tardiness. The sequence of learning activities in behavior modeling involves:

Behavior modeling or interaction management
A method of training in which interaction problems faced by managers are identified, practiced, and transferred to specific job situations.

1. A filmed model or demonstration of the skills necessary to solve the problem being studied.
2. Practice in solving the problem through role playing for each trainee.
3. Reinforcement of the correct behaviors in solving the problem during the practice situation.
4. Planning by each trainee of how to transfer the skills back to the specific job situation.

While behavior modeling is a new technique, results have been encouraging.[2]

Wilderness training involves teams of managers taking on a series of structured mental and physical challenges in an outdoor setting. These challenges are designed to approximate management challenges faced by members of the group. The idea is that by solving these physical and mental challenges the group will discover methods that can be used to solve similar challenges in the workplace. Three broad types of physical and mental challenges are provided: group problem-solving challenges, individual challenges requiring team support, and individual challenges requiring personal goal setting and a range of risk-management skills. Examples

Wilderness training
A method of training in which teams of managers perform a series of structured mental and physical outdoor challenges designed to approximate management challenges on the job.

of challenges that a group might be required to perform are climbing a mountain or having each team member walk a swinging balance beam.[3]

● *Summary of Learning Objectives*

1. Define management development.

Management development is concerned with developing the experience, attitudes, and skills necessary to become or remain an effective manager.

2. Describe a management inventory.

A management inventory provides certain types of information about an organization's current management team. Information contained includes present position, length of service, retirement date, education, and past performance evaluations.

3. Describe a management succession plan.

A management succession plan records potential successors for each manager within an organization.

4. Define the in-basket technique.

The in-basket technique simulates a realistic situation by requiring each trainee to answer one manager's mail and telephone calls.

5. Explain programmed instruction.

Programmed instruction requires the trainee to read material on a particular subject and answer questions about the material. Correct answers allow the trainee to move on to more advanced or new material.

6. Describe a business game.

Business games require a team of players to make decisions involving company operations in a setting of a company and its environment, and normally require the use of computer facilities.

7. Define an assessment center.

An assessment center is a formal method aimed at evaluating an individual's potential as a manager and his or her developmental needs.

8. Describe organizational development (OD).

Organizational development (OD) is an organizationwide, planned effort managed from the top, with a goal of increasing organizational performance through planned interventions and training experiences.

9. Discuss behavior modeling.

Behavior modeling involves identifying interaction problems faced by managers and then attempting to solve the problems through the following sequence of learning activities: studying a filmed model or demonstration of the skills necessary to solve the problem, practicing problem solving through role playing, reinforcing the correct behaviors, and developing a plan on how to transfer the skills back to the specific job situation.

10. Describe wilderness training.

Wilderness training involves teams of managers taking on a series of structured mental and physical challenges in an outdoor setting. These challenges are designed to approximate the management challenges faced by members of the group.

Review Questions

1. Define management development.
2. What is a management inventory? A succession plan?
3. Name three classifications for overall management development objectives and give examples of each.
4. Describe the following on-the-job methods of management development:
   a. Understudy assignments
   b. Coaching
   c. Experience
   d. Job rotation
   e. Special projects
   f. Committee assignments
5. Describe the following methods of classroom training:
   a. Lectures
   b. Case studies
   c. Role playing
   d. In-basket technique
   e. Programmed instruction
   f. Business games
6. What is an assessment center?
7. What is organizational development (OD)?
8. Outline the phases of organization development.
9. What is sensitivity training?
10. What is behavior modeling?
11. What is wilderness training?

Discussion Questions

1. Outline a system for evaluating a management development program for supervisors.
2. "It is impossible to evaluate the effectiveness of a supervisory development program." Discuss.
3. "Management games are fun, but you don't really learn anything from them." Discuss.
4. Organizational development generally takes several years to produce any positive results. Describe some of the positive results that might accrue from such a program, thus making the waiting period worthwhile.

▼ *INCIDENT 9–1*

The 30-Year Employee

John Brown, 52 years old, has been at the State Bank for 30 years. For the past 20, he has worked in the bank's Investment Department. During his first 15 years in the department, it was managed by Bill Adams. The department consisted of Bill, John, and two women. Bill made all decisions, while the others performed manual record-keeping functions. When Bill retired five years ago, John held the position of assistant cashier.

Tom Smith took over the Investment Department after Bill Adams retired. Tom, 56, has worked for the State Bank for the past 28 years. Shortly after taking control of the department, Tom recognized that it needed to be modernized and staffed with people capable of giving better service to the bank's customers. As a result, he increased the department work force to 10 people. Of the 10 employees, only John and Tom are older than 33.

When Tom Smith took over the department, John was able to be helpful since he knew all about how the department had been run in the past. Tom considered John to be a capable worker; after about a year, he promoted John to assistant vice president.

After he had headed the department for about a year and a half, Tom purchased a computer package to handle the bond portfolio and its accounting. When the new system was implemented, John said that he did not like computers and would have nothing to do with them. At that time, his attitude created no real problem, since there were still many manual records to be kept. John continued to handle most of the daily record-keeping.

Over the next two years, further changes came about. As the other employees in the department became more experienced, they branched into new areas of investment work. The old ways of doing things were replaced by new, more sophisticated methods. John resisted these changes; he refused to accept or learn new methods and ideas. He slipped more and more into doing only simple but time-consuming drudgery.

Presently, a new computer system is being acquired for the investment section, and another department is being put under Tom's control. John has written Tom a letter stating that he wants no part of the new computer system but would like to be the manager of the new department. In his letter, John said he was tired of being given routine tasks while the young people got all the exciting jobs. John contended that since he had been with the bank longer than anyone else, he should be given first shot at the newly created job.

Questions

1. Who has failed, John or the company?
2. Does the company owe something to a 30-year employee? If so, what?
3. What type of development program would you recommend for John?

▼ *INCIDENT 9–2*

Consolidating Three Organizations

Sitting at his desk, Ray McGreevy considered the situation he faced. His small but prosperous real estate firm had tripled in size because of two simultaneous acquisitions. He now needed to develop a management team that could coordinate the three previously independent companies into one efficient firm. He knew that this would be no easy task, because the two acquired companies had each been operated as independent entities.

In the seven years since Ray had started his real estate brokerage business, he had compiled an enviable record of growth and profits. His staff, originally consisting of himself and a secretary, had grown to more than 25 employees. His organization included himself as president, 2 vice presidents, 16 sales representatives, 4 secretaries, and 2 clerical workers. These employees were distributed equally between the two branches, each supervised by a vice president. The sales representatives reported to the vice president in their particular branch. The two branches covered a large geographic area that was divided into two regions.

About a year ago, Ray had decided to add a branch in a new area. After doing considerable research, he had decided that it might be more feasible to acquire one of the smaller firms already operating in the area. A bank officer whom he had contacted approved his plans and promised to help in locating a company to buy and in financing the acquisition.

Several months went by, and Ray discussed possible mergers with two firms; however, satisfactory terms could not be reached. He was becoming slightly discouraged when the banker called him to set up a meeting with the owner of another real estate firm. This firm had been in business for approximately 30 years, and the owner had only recently decided to retire. The company, which was almost equal in size to Ray's, did not sell in his firm's geographic area. Therefore, it appeared to be a natural choice, and Ray was quite excited about prospects for acquiring it. The owner had agreed to accept payment over several years. Although the price was higher than Ray had originally intended to pay, the deal was too good to refuse.

Then, when the deal seemed ready to be closed, the owners on one of the other firms that he had been interested in buying called and said they wished to renegotiate. Ray was able to make a favorable arrangement with them. After discussing his situation with the banker, he finally decided to purchase both firms. Although this plan far exceeded his original intentions, he knew that opportunities such as these did not happen every day.

Now Ray pondered his next step. He had been so busy in the negotiations that he had not had time to develop a plan for managing his enlarged company. As an entrepreneur, he knew that he needed to develop a professional team to manage the new business properly. He now had three more branches and about 45 additional employees.

There were so many questions to be answered. Would it be better to operate the three as independent divisions? Should he retain the individual identities of the two new firms, or should he rename them after his original one? He needed answers to these and all his other questions.

Questions

1. Does organizational development hold the key to Ray's questions?
2. As a personnel consultant, what recommendations would you make to him?

Exercise

Training Methods

The On the Job at the end of this chapter provides a brief description of many training methods used in management development. Break the class into teams consisting of two students. Assign each team one of the training methods and have the teams prepare 10-minute presentations on the uses, advantages, and disadvantages of the training method.

Notes and Additional Readings

1. Richard Klimoski and Mary Brickner, "Why Do Assessment Centers Work? The Puzzle of Assessment Center Validity," *Personnel Psychology,* Summer 1987, pp. 243–60.
2. Kenneth E. Hultman, "Behavior Modeling for Results," *Training and Development Journal,* December 1986, pp. 60–61.
3. Janet W. Long, "The Wilderness Job Comes of Age," *Training and Development Journal,* March 1987, pp. 30–39.

On the Job

Comparison of Training Methods

Method	Definition	Strengths	Weaknesses
1. Lecture	A speech by the instructor, with very limited discussions.	Clear and direct methods of presentation. Good if there are more than 20 trainees. Materials can be provided to trainees in advance to help in their preparation. Trainer has control over time. Cost effective (cheap).	Since there is no discussion, it is easy to forget. Sometimes it is not effective. Requires a high level of speaking ability. Requires a high level of quick understanding by trainees.
2. Group discussion (conference)	A speech by the instructor, with a lot of participation (questions and comments) from the listeners. Sometimes an instructor not necessary; however, a leader is needed.	Good if the participants are in small groups. Each participant has an opportunity to present own ideas. More ideas can be generated.	Sometimes they get away from the subjects. Some group leaders or instructors do not know how to guide discussions. Sometimes one strong individual can dominate others.
3. Role playing	Creating a realistic situation and having trainees assume parts of specific personalities in the situation. Their actions are based on the roles assigned to them. Emphasis is not on problem solving but rather on skill development.	Good if the situation is similar to the actual work situation. Trainees receive feedback that gives them confidence. Good for interpersonal skills. Teaches individuals how to act in real situations.	Trainees are not actors. Trainees sometimes are not serious. Some situations cannot be implemented in role playing. Uncontrolled role playing may not lead to any sufficient results. If it is very similar to actual life, it may produce adverse reactions.
4. Sensitivity training (laboratory training)	Used for organizational development. Creating situations and examining the participants' reactions and behavior, then having feedback about behavior. Group members exchange thoughts and feelings in unstructured ways.	Helps individuals to find the reasons for their behavior (self-insight). Helps individuals to know the effects of their behavior on others. Creates more group interactions.	People may not like information about their behavior, especially if it is negative. May lead to conflict and anger within the group. May not be related or transferable to jobs.
5. Case study	A written narrative description of a real situation, issue, or incident that a manager faced in a particular organization. Trainees are required to propose a suitable solution or make an appropriate decision.	Cases are usually very interesting. Much group discussion and interaction about many solutions, since there is no absolute solution. Develops trainees' abilities in effective communication and active participation. Develops trainees' ability to figure various factors that influence their decision building. Develops trainees' ability to make proper decisions in real-life situations (transfer of learning).	A slow method of training. Often difficult to select the appropriate case study for specific training situation. Requires high level of skills by both trainees and trainer, as the discussion can become boring. Can create frustration on part of trainees, especially if they fail to arrive at a specific solution.

(continued)

Comparison continued

Method	Definition	Strengths	Weaknesses
6. Management games	Giving the trainees information about the organization and its environment, then dividing into teams. Each team is required to make an operational decision and then evaluate its decision.	Develops practical experience for the trainees. Helps in transferring knowledge and in applying administrative thoughts. Helps to evaluate and correct the trainees' behavior.	Often, it is difficult to study the results of each team's decision. Some teams may not take it seriously. May be a slow process.
7. Simulation exercises	Same as management games, except a digital computer is used to input information and analyze the team decisions. Results of trainees' actions are evaluated and discussed.	Same as management games.	Same as management games. Very costly. Difficult to simulate a very complex system.
8. Wilderness training	Several managers meet out of the workplace and live in cabins or tents for up to seven days. They test their survival skills and learn about their own potentials—for creativity, cooperation, etc.	People learn their limits and capabilities.	Very costly. May not be transferable.
9. In-basket training	Creates the same type of situations trainees face in daily work. Trainees observed on how they arrange the situations and their actions regarding them. Trainees evaluated on the basis of the number and quality of decisions. Used for MD and assessment centers.	Effective for corrective action or reinforcement. Widely used in assessment centers for measuring supervisory potential.	Tendency to be or become overly simplistic.
10. Incident process (problem solving)	Simple variation of the case study method. The basic elements are given to the trainee, who then asks the instructor for the most sufficient information that will help him or her in making a decision. The instructor will only give the requested information.	Has an immediate feedback from the instructor. Develops supervisory skills in fact seeking and decision making.	Requires high degree of instructing skills in forming answers.
11. Vestibule training	Setting up a training area very similar to the work area in equipment, procedures, and environment, but separated from the actual one so trainees can learn without affecting the production schedule. Used for training typists, bank tellers, etc.	Fast way to train employees. Trainees can get the most from this method.	Very expensive.

Comparison concluded

Method	Definition	Strengths	Weaknesses
12. Apprenticeship training	Trainee works under guidance of skilled, licensed instructor and receives lower pay than licensed workers.	Develops special skills like mechanical, electronic, tailoring, etc. Extensive training.	Takes a long time.
13. Internship training	According to agreement, individuals in these programs earn while they learn, but at a lower rate than if they worked full time.	More chance for trainees to apply what they have learned. Trainees get exposure to both the organization and the job.	Takes a long time.
14. Projects	Similar to the group discussion method. Trainees analyze data and reach conclusions together.	Helps trainees to know more about the subject.	Requires instructor's time to ensure the group is going in the right direction.
15. Videotapes and movies	Recording and producing certain events or situations with clear descriptions in order to cover certain subjects. Can be shown many times, then reviewed and discussed to help trainees understand more fully.	Tapes can be played many times to ensure individual's understanding. Many events and discussions can be put on one tape. Because time length is known, presentation and follow-up can be scheduled.	Recording and producing has to be done by professionals to get good quality. Expensive (a typical 20- to 30-minute cassette costs $50, without projector or screen).
16. Multiple management	Lower- and middle-level managers participate formally with top management in planning and administration.	Helps top management to identify top management candidates. Enhances employees participation in the organization.	

Source: Sulaiman M. Al-Malik, unpublished paper, Georgia State University, Winter 1985.

Chapter 10

Performance Appraisal Systems

Chapter Outline

Performance Appraisal: Definition and Uses

Understanding Performance

Determinants of Performance

Environmental Factors as Performance Obstacles

Selection of a Performance Appraisal Method

Performance Appraisal Methods

Goal Setting, or Management by Objectives (MBO)

Work Standards

Essay Appraisal

Critical-Incident Appraisal

Graphic Rating Scale

Checklist

Behaviorally Anchored Rating Scales (BARS)

Forced-Choice Rating

Ranking Methods

Potential Errors in Performance Appraisals

Overcoming Errors in Performance Appraisals

Providing Feedback through the Appraisal Interview

Performance Appraisal and the Law

Summary of Learning Objectives

Review Questions

Discussion Questions

Incident 10–1: The College Admissions Office

Incident 10–2: The Lackadaisical Plant Manager

Exercise: Developing a Performance Appraisal System

Notes and Additional Readings

● *Learning Objectives*

After studying this chapter, you should be able to:

1. Define performance appraisal.
2. Define performance.
3. Explain management by objectives.
4. Describe the work standards approach to performance appraisal.
5. Describe essay appraisal.
6. Explain critical-incident appraisal.
7. Describe the graphic rating scale.
8. Describe the checklist method of performance appraisal.
9. Explain the forced-choice method of performance appraisal.
10. Define leniency, central tendency, recency, and the halo effect.

"*O*n the morning following each day's work, each workman was given a slip of paper informing him in detail just how much work he had done the day before, and the amount he had earned. This enabled him to measure his performance against his earnings while the details were fresh in his mind. Without this there would have been great dissatisfaction among those who failed to climb up to the task asked of them, and many would have gradually fallen off in their performance."

*Frederick W. Taylor**

In modern organizations, performance appraisal systems have undergone major changes from the method described in the above quote. Today's systems require a coordinated effort between the human resources department and the managers of the organization who are responsible for conducting performance appraisals. Generally, the responsibilities of the human resources department are to:

1. Design the formal performance appraisal system and select the methods and forms to be used for appraising employees.
2. Train managers in how to conduct performance appraisals.
3. Maintain a reporting system to ensure that appraisals are conducted on a timely basis.
4. Maintain performance appraisal records for individual employees.

The responsibilities of managers in performance appraisals are to:

1. Evaluate the performance of employees.
2. Complete the forms used in appraising employees and return them to the human resources department.
3. Review appraisals with employees.

The purpose of this chapter is to describe in detail the performance appraisal process.

Performance Appraisal: Definition and Uses

Performance appraisal
Process of determining and communicating to an employee how he or she is performing on the job, and ideally, establishing a plan of improvement.

Performance appraisal is a process that involves determining and communicating to an employee how he or she is performing the job and, ideally, establishing a plan of improvement. When properly conducted, performance appraisals not only let employees know how well they are performing but also influence their future level of effort and task direction. Effort should be enhanced if the employee is properly reinforced. The task perception of the employee should be clarified through the establishment of a plan for improvement.

One of the most common uses of performance appraisals is for making ad-

*Source: F.W. Taylor, *Scientific Management* (New York: Harper & Row, 1911), p. 52.

▼. HRM In Action 10–1

Westinghouse's Performance Appraisal System

Westinghouse found itself needing a new performance appraisal system to complement its new compensation system for nonexempt employees. It decided to use a participative approach in developing the system that involved both the nonexempt employees and the appraising managers. The objective of the performance appraisal system was to link pay to performance. A task force consisting of 25 nonexempt employee volunteers and 20 managers was established to complete the project.

The system that was developed calls for one formal appraisal per calendar year. The task force designed a new appraisal form to guide managers through the formal appraisal session. Unlike the previous form, the new one includes a job description and performance standards for the position.

Source: Adapted from David B. Cowfer and JoAnne Sujansky, "Appraisal Development at Westinghouse," *Training and Development Journal,* July 1987, pp. 40–43.

ministrative decisions relating to promotions, firings, layoffs, and merit pay increases. For example, the present job performance of an employee is often the most significant consideration for determining whether to promote the person. While successful performance in the present job does not necessarily mean that an employee will be an effective performer in a higher-level job, performance appraisals do provide some predictive information. HRM in Action 10–1 illustrates Westinghouse's system of linking pay to performance.

Performance appraisal information can also provide needed input for determining both individual and organizational training and development needs. For example, it can be used to identify individual strengths and weaknesses. These data can then be used to help determine the organization's overall training and development needs. For an individual employee, a completed performance appraisal should include a plan outlining specific training and development needs.

Another important use of performance appraisals is to encourage performance improvement. In this regard, performance appraisals are used as a means of communicating to employees how they are doing and suggesting needed changes in behavior, attitude, skill, or knowledge. This type of feedback clarifies for employees the job expectations held by the manager. Often this feedback must be followed by coaching and training by the manager to guide an employee's work efforts.

Finally, two other important uses of information generated through performance appraisals are (1) input to the validation of selection procedures and (2) input to human resource planning. Both of these topics were described in detail in earlier chapters.

A concern in organizations is how often performance appraisals should be conducted. There seems to be no real consensus on the question of how frequently performance appraisals should be done. The answer seems to be as often as necessary to let the employees know what kind of job they are doing and, if performance is not satisfactory, the measures that must be taken for improvement. For many employees, this cannot be accomplished through one annual performance appraisal. Therefore, it is recommended that informal performance appraisals be conducted two or three times a year, in addition to the annual formal performance appraisals, for most employees.[1]

Understanding Performance

Performance refers to the degree of accomplishment of the tasks that make up an individual's job. It reflects how well an individual is fulfilling the requirements of a job. Often confused with effort, which refers to energy expended, performance is measured in terms of results. For example, a student may exert a great deal of effort in preparing for an examination and still make a poor grade. In such a case, the effort expended was high, yet the performance was low.

Determinants of Performance

Job performance is the net effect of an employee's effort as modified by abilities and role (or task) perceptions. This implies that performance in a given situation can be viewed as resulting from the interrelationships among effort, abilities, and role perceptions.

Effort, which results from being motivated, refers to the amount of energy (physical and/or mental) used by an individual in performing a task. Abilities are personal characteristics used in performing a job. Abilities usually do not fluctuate widely over short periods of time. Role (task) perceptions refer to the direction(s) in which individuals believe they should channel their efforts on their jobs. The activities and behavior that people believe are necessary in the performance of their jobs define their role perceptions.

To attain an acceptable level of performance, a minimum level of proficiency must exist in each of the performance components. Similarly, the level of proficiency in any one of the performance components can place an upper boundary on performance. If employees put forth tremendous effort and have excellent abilities but lack a clear understanding of their roles, performance will probably not be good in the eyes of their managers. Much work will be produced, but it will be misdirected. Likewise, an employee who puts forth a high degree of effort and understands the job but lacks ability probably will rate low on performance. A final possibility is the employee who has good ability and understanding of the role but is lazy and expends little effort. This employee's performance will likely be low. Of course, an employee can compensate up to a point for a weakness in one area by being above average in one or both of the other areas.

Environmental Factors as Performance Obstacles

Other factors beyond the control of the employee can also stifle performance. Although such obstacles are sometimes used merely as excuses, they are often very real and should be recognized.

Some of the more common potential performance obstacles include a lack of or conflicting demands on the subordinate's time, inadequate work facilities and equipment, restrictive policies that affect the job, lack of cooperation from others, type of supervision, temperature, lighting, noise, machine pacing, shifts, and even luck.

Environmental factors should be viewed not as direct determinants of individual performance but as modifying the effects of effort, ability, and direction (see Figure 10–1). For example, poor ventilation or worn-out equipment might

▼ **Figure 10–1**   Environmental factors that modify performance

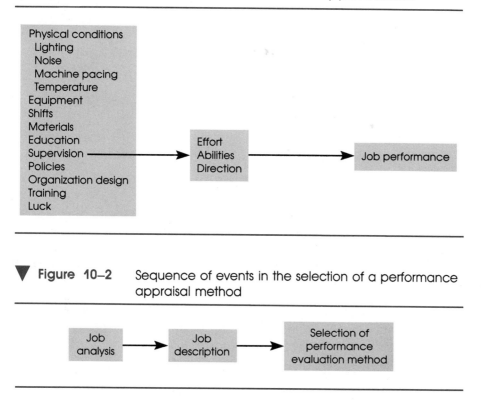

▼ **Figure 10–2**   Sequence of events in the selection of a performance appraisal method

very easily affect the effort exerted by an individual. Unclear policies or poor supervision can also produce misdirected effort. Similarly, a lack of training could result in underutilized abilities. One of management's greatest responsibilities is to provide employees with adequate working conditions and a supportive environment to eliminate or minimize performance obstacles.

Selection of a Performance Appraisal Method

It is important to note at this point that whatever method of performance appraisal an organization uses, it must be job related. Therefore, prior to selecting a performance appraisal method, job analyses must be conducted and job descriptions developed.[2] Figure 10–2 shows the sequences of events.

Performance Appraisal Methods

This section will discuss each of the following performance appraisal methods:

1. Goal setting, or management by objectives (MBO)
2. Work standards approach
3. Essay appraisal
4. Critical-incident appraisal

▼ **Figure 10–3** Sample objectives for MBO

- To answer all customer complaints in writing within three days of receipt of complaint.
- To reduce order-processing time by two days within the next six months.
- To implement the new computerized accounts receivable system by August 1.

5. Graphic rating scale
6. Checklist
7. Behaviorally anchored rating scale (BARS)
8. Forced-choice rating
9. Ranking methods

One study, conducted for the American Management Association (AMA), of 588 organizations belonging to AMA's human resources, finance, marketing, and information systems divisions explored the frequency of use of the various appraisal methods. The method most frequently mentioned was goal setting (used by 85.9 percent). This was followed by written essay statements (81.5 percent), description of critical incidents (79.4 percent), graphic rating scales (64.8 percent), weighted checklists (56.4 percent), and behaviorally anchored rating scales (35 percent). The least used were paired comparisons (16.3 percent), forced choices (22.8 percent), and forced distribution (26.4 percent).[3]

Goal Setting, or Management by Objectives (MBO)

Management by objectives
Management by objectives consists of establishing clear and precisely defined statements of objectives for the work to be done by an employee; establishing an action plan indicating how these objectives are to be achieved; allowing the employee to implement this action plan, measuring objective achievement; taking corrective action, when necessary; and establishing new objectives for the future

The goal-setting approach to performance appraisal, or **management by objectives (MBO)** as it is more frequently called, is more commonly used with professional and managerial employees. Other names for MBO include management by results, performance management, results management, and work-planning and review program.

The MBO process typically consists of:

1. Establishing clear and precisely defined statements of objectives for the work that is to be done by an employee.
2. Developing an action plan indicating how these objectives are to be achieved.
3. Allowing the employee to implement this action plan.
4. Measuring objective achievement.
5. Taking corrective action, when necessary.
6. Establishing new objectives for the future.

If an MBO system is to be successful, several requirements must be met. First, objectives should be quantifiable and measurable; objectives whose attainment cannot be measured or at least verified should be avoided where possible. Objectives should also be challenging and yet achievable, and they should be expressed in writing and in clear, concise, unambiguous language. Figure 10–3 lists some sample objectives that meet these requirements.

MBO also requires that employees participate in the objective-setting process. Active participation by the employee is also essential in developing the action plan.

▽▽. HRM in Action 10–2

The Reprographic Business Group (RBG) at Xerox found that its performance appraisal system, which had been in place for 20 years, was leaving employees discouraged, disgruntled, and, in many cases, totally surprised with their evaluations. As a result, a totally new system was developed with the following features:

- Objectives are set between the manager and employees at the beginning of each year.
- After six months, an interim review takes place.
- A final written review, examined against the objec-

tives, takes place at the end of the year and is discussed with the employee.

- The merit increase discussion takes place one to two months after the appraisal discussion.
- The manager and employee also agree on personal and professional development goals at the beginning of the year.

Source: Adapted from Norman R. Deets and D. Timothy Tyler, "How Xerox Improved Its Performance Appraisals," *Personnel Journal*, April 1986, pp 50–51.

Managers who set an employee's objectives without input and then ask the employee, "You agree to these, don't you?" are unlikely to get high levels of employee commitment.

A final requirement for the successful use of MBO is that the objectives and action plan must serve as a basis for regular discussions between the manager and the employee concerning the employee's performance. These regular discussions provide an opportunity for the manager and employee to discuss progress and to modify objectives when necessary. HRM in Action 10–2 discusses a MBO system of performance appraisal used by Xerox.

Work Standards

The **work standards approach** to performance appraisal is most frequently used for production employees and is basically a form of goal setting for these employees. It involves setting a standard or expected level of output and then comparing each employee's performance to the standard. Generally speaking, work standards should reflect the normal output of a normal person. Work standards attempt to define a fair day's output. Several methods can be used for setting work standards. Some of the more common are summarized in Table 10–1.

An advantage of the work standards approach is that the performance review is based on highly objective factors. Of course, to be effective, the standards must be viewed by the affected employees as being fair. The most serious criticism of work standards is a lack of comparability of standards for different job categories.

Work standards approach
Method of performance appraisal that involves setting a standard or expected level of output and then comparing each employee's level to the standard.

Essay Appraisal

The **essay appraisal** method requires that the evaluation describe an individual's performance in written narrative form. Instructions are often provided as to the topics that should be covered. A typical essay appraisal question may be: "Describe, in your own words, this employee's performance, including quantity and quality of work, job knowledge, and ability to get along with other employees. What are

Essay appraisal
Method of performance appraisal in which the rater prepares a written statement describing an individual's strengths, weaknesses, and past performance.

▼ **Table 10–1** Frequently used methods for setting work standards

Method	Areas of Applicability
Average production of work groups	When tasks performed by all individuals are the same or approximately the same
Performance of specially selected individuals	When tasks performed by all individuals are basically the same and it would be cumbersome and time consuming to use the group average
Time study	Jobs involving repetitive tasks
Work sampling	Noncyclical types of work where many different tasks are performed and there is no set pattern or cycle
Expert opinion	When none of the more direct methods (described above) applies

the employee's strengths and weaknesses?" The primary problem with essay appraisals is that their length and content can vary considerably, depending on the rater. For instance, one rater may write a lengthy statement describing an individual's potential and little about past performance. On the other hand, another rater might concentrate on the individual's past performance. Thus, essay appraisals are difficult to compare. The writing skill of the appraiser can also affect the appraisal. An effective writer can make an average employee look better than the actual performance warrants.

Critical-Incident Appraisal

Critical-incident appraisal
Method of performance appraisal in which the rater keeps a written record of incidents that illustrate both positive and negative behavior of the employee; the rater then uses these incidents as a basis for evaluating the employee's performance.

The **critical-incident appraisal** method requires the evaluator to keep a written record of incidents as they occur, involving job behaviors that illustrate both satisfactory and unsatisfactory performance of the person being rated. The incidents, as they are recorded over time, provide a basis for evaluating performance and providing feedback to the employee.

The main drawback to this approach is that the rater is required to jot down incidents regularly: this can be burdensome and time consuming. Also, the definition of a critical incident is unclear and may be interpreted differently by different people. It is felt that this method can lead to friction between the manager and employee when the employees feel that the manager is keeping a "book" on them.

Graphic Rating Scale

Graphic rating scale
Method of performance appraisal that requires the rater to indicate on a scale where the employee rates on factors such as quantity of work, dependability, job knowledge, and cooperativeness.

With the **graphic rating scale** method, the rater assesses an individual on factors such as quantity of work, dependability, job knowledge, attendance, accuracy of work, and cooperativeness. Graphic rating scales include both numerical ranges and written descriptions. Figure 10–4 gives an example of some of the items that might be included on a graphic rating scale that uses written descriptions.

The graphic rating scale method is subject to some serious weaknesses. One potential weakness is that evaluators are unlikely to interpret written descriptions in the same manner, due to differences in background, experience, and personality.

▼ **Figure 10–4**   Sample items on a graphic rating scale evaluation form

---

Quantity of work—the amount of work an individual does in a workday

( )	( )	( )	( )	( )
Does not meet minimum requirements.	Does just enough to get by.	Volume of work is satisfactory.	Very industrious, does more than is required.	Has a superior work production record.

Dependability—the ability to do required jobs well with a minimum of supervision

( )	( )	( )	( )	( )
Requires close supervision; is unreliable.	Sometimes requires prompting.	Usually completes necessary tasks with reasonable promptness.	Requires little supervision; is reliable.	Requires absolute minimum of supervision.

Job knowledge—information that an individual should have on work duties for satisfactory job performance

( )	( )	( )	( )	( )
Is poorly informed about work duties.	Lacks knowledge of some phases of job.	Is moderately informed; can answer most questions about the job.	Understands all phases of job.	Has complete mastery of all phases of job.

Attendance—faithfulness in coming to work daily and conforming to work hours

( )	( )	( )	( )	( )
Is often absent without good excuse, or frequently reports for work late, or both.	Is lax in attendance or reporting for work on time, or both.	Is usually present and on time.	Is very prompt, regular in attendance.	Is always regular and prompt; volunteers for overtime when needed.

Accuracy—the correctness of work duties performed

( )	( )	( )	( )	( )
Makes frequent errors.	Careless, often makes errors.	Usually accurate, makes only average number of mistakes.	Requires little supervision; is exact and precise most of the time.	Requires absolute minimum of supervision; is almost always accurate.

Another potential problem relates to the choice of rating categories. It is possible to choose categories that have little relationship to job performance or to omit categories that have a significant influence on job performance.

Checklist

In the **checklist** method, the rater makes yes-or-no responses to a series of questions concerning the employee's behavior. Figure 10–5 lists some typical questions. The checklist can also have varying weights assigned to each question.

Normally, the scoring key for the checklist method is kept by the human

▼ **Figure 10–5** Sample checklist questions

	Yes	No
1. Does the individual lose his or her temper in public?	_____	_____
2. Does the individual play favorites?	_____	_____
3. Does the individual praise employees in public when they have done a good job?	_____	_____
4. Does the employee volunteer to do special jobs?	_____	_____

resources department: the evaluator is generally not aware of the weights associated with each question. But because raters can see the positive or negative connotation of each question, bias can be introduced. Additional drawbacks to the checklist method are that it is time consuming to assemble the questions for each job category, a separate listing of questions must be developed for each different job category, and the checklist questions can have different meanings to different raters.

Behaviorally Anchored Rating Scales (BARS)

Behaviorally anchored rating scale (BARS)
Method of performance appraisal that determines an employee's level of performance based on whether or not certain specifically described job behaviors are present.

The **behaviorally anchored rating scale (BARS)** method of performance appraisal is designed to assess behaviors required to successfully perform a job. The focus of BARS and, to some extent, the graphic rating scale and checklist methods, is not on performance outcomes but on functional behaviors demonstrated on the job. The assumption is that these functional behaviors will result in effective job performance.

To understand the use and development of BARS, several key terms must be clearly understood. First, most BARS use the term *job dimension* to mean those broad categories of duties and responsibilities that make up a job. In terms of the definitions given in Chapter 4, a **job dimension** is the same as a **job task**. Each job is likely to have several job dimensions, and separate scales must be developed for each.

Job dimension or job task
Duties and responsibilities that make up a specific job.

Table 10–2 illustrates a BARS written for the job dimension found in many managerial jobs of planning, organizing, and scheduling project assignments and due dates. Scale values appear on the left side of the table and define specific categories of performance. Anchors, which appear on the right side of the table, are specific written statements of actual behaviors that, when they are exhibited on the job, indicate the level of performance on the scale opposite that particular anchor. As the anchor statements appear beside each of the scale values, they are said to "anchor" each of the scale values along the scale.

Rating performance using BARS requires the rater to read the list of anchors on each scale to find the group of anchors that best describes the employee's job behavior during the period being reviewed. The scale value opposite the group of anchors is then checked. This process is followed for all the identified dimensions of the job. A total evaluation is obtained by combining the scale values checked for all the different job dimensions.

BARS are normally developed through a series of meetings attended by both managers and job incumbents. Three steps are usually followed:

▼ **Table 10–2**   Example of a behaviorally anchored rating scale

Scale Values	Anchors
7 [ ] Excellent	Develops a comprehensive project plan, documents it well, obtains required approval, and distributes the plan to all concerned.
6 [ ] Very good	Plans, communicates, and observes milestones; states week by week where the project stands relative to plans. Maintains-up-to-date charts of project accomplishments and backlogs and uses these to optimize any schedule modifications required. Experiences occasional minor operational problems but communicates effectively.
5 [ ] Good	Lays out all the parts of a job and schedules each part; seeks to beat schedule and will allow for slack. Satisfies customers' time constraints; time and cost overruns occur infrequently.
4 [ ] Average	Makes a list of due dates and revises them as the project progresses, usually adding unforeseen events; instigates frequent customer complaints. May have a sound plan, but does not keep track of milestones; does not report slippages in schedule or other problems as they occur.
3 [ ] Below average	Plans are poorly defined, unrealistic time schedules are common. Cannot plan more than a day or two ahead, has no concept of a realistic project due date.
2 [ ] Very poor	Has no plan or schedule of work segments to be performed. Does little or no planning for project assignments.
1 [ ] Unacceptable	Seldom, if ever, completes project, because of lack of planning, and does not seem to care. Fails consistently due to lack of planning and does not inquire about how to improve.

Source: C. E. Schneier and R. W. Beatty, "Developing Behaviorally Anchored Rating Scales (BARS)," *Personnel Administrator*, August 1979, p. 60

1. Managers and job incumbents identify the relevant job dimensions for the job.
2. Managers and job incumbents write behavioral anchors for each of the job dimensions. As many anchors as possible should be written for each dimension.
3. Managers and job incumbents reach a consensus concerning the scale values that are to be used and the grouping of anchor statements for each scale value.

The use of BARS can result in several advantages. First, BARS are developed through the active participation of both managers and job incumbents. This increases the likelihood that the method will be accepted. Second, the anchors are developed from the observations and experiences of employees who actually perform the job. Finally, BARS can be used for providing specific feedback concerning an employee's job performance.

One of the major drawbacks to the use of BARS is that they take considerable time and commitment to develop. Furthermore, separate forms must be developed for different jobs.

Forced-Choice Rating

Many variations of the **forced-choice rating** method exist. However, the most common practice requires the evaluator to rank a set of statements describing how an employee carries out the duties and responsibilities of the job. (Figure 10–6 illustrates a group of forced-choice statements.) The statements are normally weighted, and the weights are not generally known to the rater. After the rater ranks all of the forced-choice statements, the human resource department applies the weights and computes a score.

This method attempts to eliminate evaluator bias by forcing him or her to rank statements that may be seemingly indistinguishable or unrelated. However, it has been reported that the forced-choice method tends to irritate raters, who feel they are not being trusted. Furthermore, the results of the forced-choice appraisal can be difficult to communicate to employees.

Ranking Methods

When it becomes necessary to compare the performance of two or more individuals, **ranking methods** can be used. Three of the more commonly used ranking methods are alternation, paired comparison, and forced distribution.

Alternation Ranking

Using this ranking method, the names of the individuals who are to be rated are listed down the left side of a sheet of paper. The rater is then asked to choose the most valuable employee on the list, cross that name off the left-hand list, and put it at the top of the column on the right side of the paper. The appraiser is then asked to select and cross off the name of the least valuable employee from the left-hand column and move it to the bottom of the right-hand column. The rater then repeats this process for all of the names on the left-hand side of the paper. The resulting list of names in the right-hand column gives a ranking of the employees from most to least valuable.

Paired Comparison Ranking

This method is best illustrated with an example. Suppose a rater is to evaluate six employees. The names of these individuals are listed on the left side of a sheet of paper. The evaluator then compares the first employee with the second employee on a chosen performance criterion, such as quantity of work. If he or she feels that the first employee has produced more work than the second employee, a check mark would be placed by the first employee's name. The first employee would then be compared to the third, fourth, fifth, and sixth employee on the same performance criterion. A check mark would be placed by the name of the employee who had produced the most work in each of these paired comparisons. The process is repeated until each worker is compared to every other worker on all of the chosen performance criteria. The employee with the most check marks is considered to be the best performer. Likewise, the employee with the fewest check marks is the lowest performer. One major problem with the paired comparison method is that is becomes unwieldy when comparing large numbers of employees.

▼ **Figure 10–6**   Sample set of forced-choice statements

Instructions: Rank the following statements according to how they describe the manner in which this employee carries out duties and responsibilities. Rank *1* should be given to the most descriptive, and Rank *5* to the least descriptive. No ties are allowed.

Rank	Description
_____	Is easy to get acquainted with.
_____	Places great emphasis on people.
_____	Refuses to accept criticism.
_____	Thinks generally in terms of money.
_____	Makes decisions quickly.

▼ **Figure 10–7**   Forced distribution curve

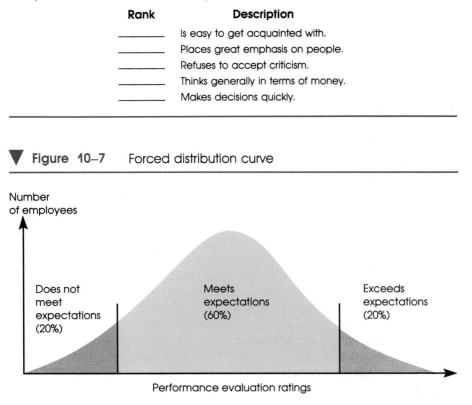

Number of employees

Does not meet expectations (20%)

Meets expectations (60%)

Exceeds expectations (20%)

Performance evaluation ratings

Forced Distribution

This method requires the rater to compare the performance of employees and place a certain percentage of employees at various performance levels. It assumes that the performance level in a group of employees will be distributed according to a bell-shaped, or "normal," curve. Figure 10–7 illustrates how the forced-distribution method works. The rater is required to rate 60 percent of the employees as meeting expectations, 20 percent as exceeding expectations, and 20 percent as not meeting expectations.

One problem with the forced-distribution method is that in small groups of employees, a bell-shaped distribution of performance may not be applicable. Even where the distribution may approximate a normal curve, it is probably not a perfect curve. This means that some employees will probably not be rated accurately. Also, ranking methods are dramatically different from the other methods in that one individual's performance evaluation is a function of the performance of other employees in the job. Furthermore, the Civil Service Reform Act does not permit the use of ranking methods for federal employees.

Potential Errors in Performance Appraisals

Leniency
Occurs in performance appraisals when a manager's ratings are grouped at the positive end instead of being spread throughout the performance scale.

Central tendency
Tendency of a manger to rate all or most employees as having the same basic level of performance

Recency
Tendency of a manager to evaluate employees on work performed most recently—one or two months prior to evaluation.

Several common errors have been identified in performance appraisals. **Leniency** is the grouping of ratings at the positive end instead of spreading them throughout the performance scale. **Central tendency** occurs when appraisal statistics indicate that most employees are appraised as having the same basic level of performance. **Recency** occurs when evaluations are based on work performed most recently— generally work performed one to two months prior to evaluation. Leniency, central tendency, and recency errors make it difficult if not impossible to separate the good performers from the poor performers. In addition, these errors make it difficult to compare ratings from different raters. For example, it is possible for a good performer who is evaluated by a manager committing central tendency errors to receive a lower rating than a poor performer who is rated by a manager committing leniency errors. HRM in Action 10–3 describes Merck's attempt to overcome errors in performance appraisals.

Another common error in performance appraisals is the halo effect.[4] This occurs when a rater allows a single prominent characteristic of an employee to influence his or her judgment on each separate item in the performance appraisal. This often results in the employee receiving approximately the same rating on every item.

Personal preferences, prejudices, and biases can also cause errors in performance appraisals. Managers with biases or prejudices tend to look for employee behaviors that conform to their biases. Appearance, social status, dress, race, and sex have influenced many performance appraisals. Managers have also allowed first impressions to influence later judgments of an employee. First impressions are only a sample of behavior: however, people tend to retain these impressions even when faced with contradictory evidence.

Overcoming Errors in Performance Appraisals

As can be seen from the above discussion, the potential for errors in performance appraisals is great. One approach to overcoming these errors is to make refinements in the design of appraisal methods. For example, it could be argued that the forced-distribution method of performance appraisal attempts to overcome the errors of leniency and central tendency. In addition, behaviorally anchored rating scales are designed to reduce halo, leniency, and central tendency errors, because managers have specific examples of performance against which an employee is to be evaluated. Unfortunately, because refined instruments frequently do not overcome all the obstacles, it does not appear likely that refining appraisal instruments will totally overcome errors in performance appraisals.

A more promising approach to overcoming errors in performance appraisals is to improve the skills of raters. Suggestions on the specific training that should be given to evaluators are often vague, but they normally emphasize that evaluators should be given training to observe behavior more accurately and judge it fairly.

▼. HRM in Action 10–3

Performance Rating Definitions at Merck & Co., Inc.

When Merck & Co., Inc's, performance began to lag behind other leading drug companies, one of the actions it took was to design a new performance evaluation system. Under the company's old system, approximately 97 percent of Merck employees had been grouped within a very narrow band of ratings. As a result, salary increases failed to reflect differences in performance levels.

Merck developed a system to overcome this problem that gave a more precise definition to performance ratings. The performance rating definitions are shown in Exhibit 10–1.

Source: William H. Wagel, "Performance Appraisal with a Difference," *Personnel,* February 1987, pp. 4–6.

More research is needed before a definitive set of topics for rater training can be established. However, at a minimum, appraisers should receive training in the performance appraisal method(s) used by the company, the importance of the appraiser's role in the total appraisal process, the use of performance appraisal information, and the communication skills necessary to provide feedback to the employee.

Providing Feedback through the Appraisal Interview

After one of the previously discussed methods for developing an employee's performance appraisal has been used, the results must be communicated to the employee. Unless this interview is properly conducted, it can and frequently does result in an unpleasant experience for both manager and employee.

Some of the more important factors influencing success or failure of appraisal interviews are:

1. The more employees that participate in the appraisal process, the more satisfied they are with the appraisal interview and with the manager, and the more likely performance improvement objectives are to be accepted and met.

2. The more a manager uses positive motivational techniques (e.g., recognizing and praising good performance), the more satisfied the employee is likely to be with the appraisal interview and with the manager.

3. The mutual setting by the manager and the employee of specific performance improvement objectives results in more improvement in performance than does a general discussion or criticism.

4. Discussing and solving problems that may be hampering the employee's current job performance improve the employee's performance.

5. The amount of thought and preparation that both the manager and the employee devote before the interview increases the benefits of the interview.

6. The more the employee perceives that performance appraisal results are tied to organizational rewards, the more beneficial the interview is.

Exhibit 10-1

Exempt Performance Rating Definitions

Performance Ratings		Performance Definitions		
Rating	*Distri-bution Target*	*Specific Job Measures and Ongoing Duties*	*Planned Objectives*	*Management of People*
EX Exceptional within Merck	5%	Far above Merck peers Capitalized on un-expected events to gain superior results	Made significant breakthroughs or exceptional achievements	Outstanding leader Exceptional develop-ment/recruitment of people Superior commu-nications
WD Merck standard with distinction	15%	Clearly superior to Merck peers in most respects Took advantage of unexpected events to achieve unusually good results	Objectives met and many exceeded	A clear leader among Merck peers Top quality people recruited developed Excellent commu-nications
HS High Merck standard	70%	Comparable to Merck peers Made use of unex-pected events to achieve very good results	Objectives met	A very good leader Hires very good people/develops people as well as peers Very good communications
RI Merck standard with room for improvement	8%	Work is not quite as good as Merck peers Contended with unexpected events	Most objectives met Some shortfalls	Adequate leader Hires good people Satisfactory commu-nications
NA Not adequate for Merck	2%	Work is not up to that of Merck peers Did not fully cope with unexpected events	Missed significant objectives	Poor leader Communications could be better
PR Progressing	Not appli-cable	Typically this employee is new to the company or in a significantly different assignment. Normally this rating would apply only during the first year in the new job.		

Many of the variables that have been identified and associated with positive outcomes from performance appraisal interviews are behaviors and skills that can be taught to managers responsible for conducting the interviews. The human resources department should play a key role in the development and implementation of these training programs.

Performance Appraisal and the Law

Title VII of the Civil Rights Act (discussed in depth in Chapter 2) permits the use of a bona fide performance appraisal system. Performance appraisal systems are not generally considered to be bona fide when they are not job related.

A number of court cases have ruled that performance appraisal systems used by organizations were discriminatory and not job related. In one case involving layoffs, *Brito, et al.* v. *Zia Company*,[5] Spanish-surnamed workers were reinstated with back pay because the company had used a performance appraisal system of unknown validity in an uncontrolled and unstandardized manner. Generally, it can be stated that performance appraisal systems may be illegal if the method of appraisal is not job related, performance standards are not derived through careful job analysis, the number of performance observations is inadequate, ratings are based on evaluation of subjective or vague factors, raters are biased, or rating conditions are uncontrolled or unstandardized.

Some recommendations for ensuring a legally acceptable performance appraisal are:

1. Conduct a job analysis to determine characteristics necessary for successful job performance.
2. Incorporate these characteristics into a rating instrument.
3. Train supervisors to use the rating instrument successfully.
4. Employ formal appeal systems and reviews of ratings by upper-level personnel.
5. Document evaluations.
6. Provide some form of performance counseling or corrective guidance to assist unsatisfactory employees in improving their performance.

● *Summary of Learning Objectives*

1. Define performance appraisal.

   Performance appraisal is a process that involves determining and communicating to an employee how he or she is performing the job and, ideally, establishing a plan of improvement.

2. Define performance.

   Performance refers to the degree of accomplishment of the tasks that make up an individual's job.

3. Explain management by objectives.

   Management by objectives consists of establishing clear and precisely defined statements of objectives for the work to be done by an employee; developing an action plan indicating how these objectives are to be achieved; allowing the employee to implement this action plan, measuring objective achievement; taking corrective action, when necessary; and establishing new objectives for the future.

4. Describe the work standards approach to performance appraisal.

   The work standards approach involves setting a standard or expected level of output and then comparing each employee's performance to the standard.

5. Describe essay appraisal.

   The essay appraisal method requires that the rater describe an individual's performance in written narrative form.

6. Explain critical-incident appraisal.

   This method requires the rater to keep a written record of incidents as they occur, involving job behaviors that illustrate both satisfactory and unsatisfactory performances of the person being rated.

7. Describe the graphic rating scale.

   With this method, the rater assesses an individual on factors such as quantity of work completed, dependability, job knowledge, attendance, accuracy of work, and cooperativeness.

8. Describe the checklist method of performance appraisal.

   In this method, the rater makes yes-or-no responses to a series of questions concerning the employee's behavior.

9. Explain the forced-choice method of performance appraisal.

   Using this method, the rater is required to rank a set of statements describing how an employee carries out the duties and responsibilities of the job.

10. Define leniency, central tendency, recency, and the halo effect.

    Leniency is grouping ratings at the positive end of a curve instead of spreading them throughout the performance scale. Central tendency occurs when appraisal statistics indicate that most employees are appraised as having the same basic level of performance. Recency occurs when evaluations are based only on work performed most recently. The halo effect occurs when a rater allows a single prominent characteristic of an employee to influence his or her judgment on each separate item in the performance appraisal.

Review Questions

1. Define performance appraisal.
2. What is performance? What factors influence an employee's level of performance?
3. Give at least three uses of performance appraisal information.
4. Describe the following methods used in performance appraisal:
   a. Management by objectives
   b. Work standards
   c. Essay
   d. Critical-incident
   e. Graphic rating scale
   f. Checklist
   g. Behaviorally anchored rating scale
   h. Forced-choice rating
   i. Ranking methods
5. Define the following types of performance appraisal errors:
   a. Leniency
   b. Central tendency
   c. Recency
   d. Halo effect
6. Outline some of the conditions associated with the success or failure of appraisal interviews.

7. Describe some of the conditions that might make a performance appraisal system illegal.

8. Outline some recommendations for ensuring a legally acceptable performance appraisal system.

Discussion Questions

1. How often do you think that performance reviews should be conducted?

2. Describe your thoughts about discussing salary raises and promotions during the performance appraisal interview.

3. What technique do you believe would best apply to the evaluation of a college professor?

4. Was your last exam a performance appraisal? Use your last exam to discuss both the reasons for using performance appraisals and the limitations of such appraisals.

▼ INCIDENT 10–1

The College Admissions Office

Bob Luck was hired to replace Alice Carter as administrative assistant in the admissions office of Claymore Community College. Before leaving, Alice had given a month's notice to the director of admissions, hoping that this would allow ample time to locate and train her replacement. Alice's responsibilities included preparing and mailing transcripts at the request of students, mailing information requested by people interested in attending the college, answering the telephone, assisting students or persons interested in enrolling who came to the office, and general supervision of the clerk-typists and student assistants in the office.

After interviewing and testing many people for the position, the director hired Bob, mainly because his credentials were good and he made a good impression. Alice spent many hours during the next 10 days training Bob. He appeared to be quite bright and seemed to quickly pick up the procedures involved in operating a college admissions office. When Alice left, everyone thought that Bob would do an outstanding job.

However, little time had elapsed before it was realized that Bob had not caught on to his job responsibilities. Bob seemed to have personal problems that were severe enough to stand in the way of his work. He asked questions about subjects that Alice had covered explicitly; he would have been able to answer these himself if he had comprehended her instructions.

Bob appeared to have other things on his mind constantly. He seemed to be preoccupied with such problems as his recent divorce, which he blamed entirely on his ex-wife, and the distress of his eight-year-old daughter, who missed her father terribly. His thoughts also dwelled on his search for peace of mind and some reason for all that had happened to him. The director of admissions was aware of Bob's preoccupation with his personal life and his failure to learn the office procedures rapidly.

Questions

1. What would you do at this point if you were the director of admissions?
2. Describe how you might effectively use a performance appraisal in this situation.

▼ INCIDENT 10–2

The Lackadaisical Plant Manager

Plant manager Paul Dorn wondered why his boss Leonard Hech had sent for him. He thought that Leonard had been tough on him lately and he was slightly uneasy at being asked to come to Leonard's office at a time when such meetings were unusual. "Close the door and sit down, Paul," invited Leonard. "I've been wanting to talk to you." After preliminary conversation was completed, Leonard said that because Paul's latest project had been finished, he would receive the raise that he had been promised on its completion.

Leonard went on to say that it was time for Paul's performance appraisal, they might as well do that now. Leonard explained that the performance appraisal was based on four criteria: (1) amount of high-quality merchandise manufactured and shipped on time, (2) quality of relationships with plant employees and peers, (3) progress in maintaining employee safety and health, and (4) reaction to demands of top management. The first criterion had a weight of 40 percent, and the rest had a weight of 20 percent each.

On the first item, Paul received an excellent rating. Shipments were at an all-time high, quality was good, and few shipments had arrived late. On the second item, Paul also was rated excellent. Leonard said that plant employees and peers related well to Paul, that labor relations were excellent, and that there had been no major grievances since Paul had become plant manager.

However, on attention to matters of employee safety and health, the evaluation was below average. Leonard stated that no matter how much he bugged Paul about improving housekeeping in the plant, Paul never seemed to produce results. He also rated Paul below average on meeting demands from top management. He explained that Paul always answered yes to any request and then disregarded it, going about his business as if nothing had happened.

Seemingly surprised at the comments, Paul agreed that perhaps Leonard was right and that he should do a better job on these matters. Smiling as he left, he thanked Leonard for the raise and the frank appraisal.

As weeks went by, Leonard noticed little change in Paul. He reviewed the situation with an associate. "It's frustrating. In this time of rapid growth, we must make constant changes in work methods. Paul agrees but can't seem to make people break their habits and adopt more efficient ones. I find myself riding him very hard these days, but he just calmly takes it. He's well liked by everyone. But somehow, he's got to care about safety and housekeeping in the plant. And when higher management makes demands he can't meet, he's got to say, 'I can't do that and do all the other things you want, too.' Now he has dozens of unfinished jobs because he refuses to say no."

As he talked, Leonard remembered something Paul had told him in confidence once. "I take Valium for a physical condition I have. When I don't take it, I get symptoms similar to a heart attack. But I only take half as much as the doctor prescribed." Now, Leonard thought, I'm really in a spot. If the Valium is what is making him so lackadaisical, I can't endanger his health by asking him to quit taking it. And I certainly can't fire him. Yet, as things stand, he really can't implement all the changes we must have to fulfill the goals we have set for the next two years.

Questions

1. What would you do if you were in Leonard's place?
2. What could have been done differently during the performance appraisal session?

Exercise

Developing a Performance Appraisal System

A large public utility has been having difficulty with its performance evaluation program. The organization has an evaluation program by which all operating employees and clerical employees are evaluated semiannually by their supervisors. The form that they have been using is given in Exhibit 10–A. It has been in use for 10 years. The form is scored as follows: excellent = 5, above average = 4, average = 3, below average = 2, and poor = 1. The scores for each facet are entered in the right-hand column and are totaled for an overall evaluation score.

In the procedure used, each supervisor rates each employee on July 30 and January 30. The supervisor discusses the rating with the employee and then sends the rating to the human resources department. Each rating is placed in the employee's personnel file. If promotions come up, the cumulative ratings are considered at that time. The ratings are also supposed to be used as a check when raises are given.

The system was designed by Joanna Kyle, the human resources manager who retired two years ago. Her replacement was Eugene Meyer. Meyer graduated 15 years go with a degree in commerce from the University of Texas. Since then, he's had a variety of work experience, mostly in utilities. For about five of these years, he did human resources work.

Meyer has been reviewing the evaluation system. Employees have a mixture of indifferent and negative feelings about it. An informal survey has shown that about 60 percent of the supervisors fill the forms out, give about three minutes to each form, and send them to personnel without discussing them with the employees. Another 30 percent do a little better. They spend more time completing the forms but communicate about them only briefly and superficially with their employees. Only about 10 percent of the supervisors seriously try to do what was intended.

▼ **Exhibit 10–A** Performance evaluation form

Performance Evaluation

Supervisors: When you are asked to do so by the personnel department, please complete this form on each of your employees. The supervisor who is responsible for 75 percent or more of an employee's work should complete this form on him or her. Please evaluate each facet of the employee separately.

Facet	Rating					Score
Quality of work	Excellent	Above average	Average	Below average	Poor	
Quantity of work	Poor	Below average	Average	Above average	Excellent	
Dependability at work	Excellent	Above average	Average	Below average	Poor	
Initiative at work	Poor	Below average	Average	Above average	Excellent	
Cooperativeness	Excellent	Above average	Average	Below average	Poor	
Getting along with coworkers	Poor	Below average	Average	Above average	Excellent	

Total _____

Supervisor's signature _____
Employee name _____
Employee number _____

Meyer also found out that the forms were rarely used for promotion or pay raise decisions. Because of this, most supervisors may have felt the evaluation program was a useless ritual. Where he had been previously employed, Meyer had seen performance evaluation as a much more useful experience, which included giving positive feedback to employees, improving future employee performance, developing employee capabilities, and providing data for promotion and compensation.

Meyer has not had much experience with design of performance evaluation system. He feels he should seek advice on the topic.

Write a report summarizing your evaluation of the strengths and weaknesses of the present appraisal system. Recommend some specific improvements or data-gathering exercises to develop a better system for Meyer.

Notes and Additional Readings

1. Craig Eric Schneier, Arthur Geis, and Joseph A. Wert, "Performance Appraisals: No Appointment Needed," *Personnel Journal,* November 1987, pp. 80–87.

2. See James A. Buford, Bettye B. Burkhalter, and Grover T. Jacobs, "Link Job Descriptions to Performance Appraisals," *Personnel Journal,* June 1988, pp. 132–40.

3. Mary Zippo and Marc Miller, "Performance Appraisal: Current Practices and Techniques," *Personnel,* May–June 1984, p. 58.

4. For a more in-depth discussion of the halo effect, see R. Jacobs and S. W. J. Kozlowski, "A Closer Look at Halo Error in Performance Ratings," *Academy of Management Journal,* March 1985, pp. 201–12.

5. *Brito et al.* v. *Zia Company,* 478 F.2d. 1200 (1973).

6. Gerard V. Barrett and Mary C. Kernan, "Performance Appraisal and Terminations: A Review of Court Decisions since *Brito* v. *Zia* with Implications for Personnel Practices," *Personnel Psychology,* Autumn 1987, p. 501.

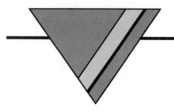

Chapter 11

Career Planning

Chapter Outline

Why Is Career Planning Necessary?

Who Is Responsible for Career Planning?
Employee's Responsibilities
Manager's Responsibilities
Organization's Responsibilities

Developing a Career Plan
Individual Assessment
Assessment by the Organization
Career Pathing

Reviewing Career Progress
Career-Related Myths
Myths Held by Managers

Dealing with Career Plateaus
Rehabilitating Ineffective Plateauees
Outplacement
Summary of Learning Objectives
Review Questions
Discussion Questions
Incident 11–1: The Unhappy Telephone Line Installer
Incident 11–2: "I Didn't Know You Wanted the Job"
Exercise: Becoming an Effective Career Planner
Notes and Additional Readings

● *Learning Objectives*

After studying this chapter, you should be able to:

1. Summarize the benefits of career planning.
2. Explain who should be responsible for career planning.
3. Name the steps involved in career planning.
4. Define career pathing.
5. List several myths held by employees related to career planning and advancement.
6. List several myths held by management related to career planning.
7. Define a career plateau and a plateaued employee.
8. Describe the four principal career states.
9. Define outplacement.

*"T*he emergence and decline of occupations will be so rapid,' says economist Norman Anon, an expert in manpower problems, 'that people will always be uncertain in them.' The profession of airline flight engineer, he notes, emerged and then began to die out within a brief period of 15 years."

*Alvin Toffler**

Not too many years ago, an individual would join an organization and would probably stay with it for his or her entire working career.[1] Gold watches and length-of-service pins were frequently given by organizations.

The concept of organizational loyalty has faded in the decades since World War II. In the 1980s, the average 20-year-old employee was expected to change jobs approximately six or seven times during his or her lifetime. Consequently, instead of thinking in terms of remaining with one organization, many employees now expect to pursue different careers. The accelerated rate of change in today's world has significantly increased employee mobility. Even when an employee desires to remain with the same organization, changes in its environment may make this choice unfeasible (see HRM in Action 11–1). These environmental forces plus changes within the individual make career planning important for today's employees.

Why Is Career Planning Necessary?

An individual who develops a plan to reach career goals is more likely to reach these goals. Realistic career planning forces individuals to look at the available opportunities in relation to their abilities. For example, a person might strongly desire to be a history teacher until discovering that there are two history teachers available for every job.

With a career plan, a person is much more likely to experience satisfaction as progress is made along the career path. A good career plan identifies certain milestones along the way. When these milestones are consciously recognized and reached, the person is much more likely to experience feelings of achievement. Furthermore, these feelings increase the individual's personal satisfaction and motivation.

From the organization's viewpoint, career planning can reduce costs due to employee turnover. HRM in Action 11–2 describes how one bank's career counseling program saved $1.95 million in a year. If a company assists employees in developing career plans, these plans are likely to be closely tied to the organization; therefore, employees are less likely to quit. The fact that an organization shows interest in an employee's career development also has a positive effect on the employee. Under these circumstances, employees feel that they are regarded by the company as part of an overall plan and not just as numbers.

*Source: A. Toffler, *Future Shock* (New York: Random House, 1970), pp. 94–95.

▽. HRM in Action 11–1

The Emerging Workplace?

It has been estimated that between 1983 and 1987 nearly 10,000 companies changed hands and well over 2 million people saw their jobs disappear or deteriorate. A 1986 Harris–*Business Week* pool of managers in the 1,000 largest companies reported that nearly 50 percent expected the company to reduce its salaried work force over the next few years. The same managers saw little relation between how well they did their job and how secure it was. A similar survey of middle managers in 1,600 companies, conducted by The Hay Group, reported a significant drop from 1975 to 1985 in the percentage of employees who had a favorable view of their opportunities for advancement.

Source: Rosabeth Moss Kanter, "The Contingent Job and the Post-Entrepreneurial Career," *Management Review*, April 1989, pp. 22–24.

From the organization's viewpoint, career planning has three major objectives:

- To meet the immediate and future human resource needs of the organization on a timely basis.
- To better inform the organization and the individual about potential career paths within the organization.
- To utilize existing human resource programs to the fullest by integrating the activities that select, assign, develop, and manage individual careers with the organization's plans.[2]

Who Is Responsible for Career Planning?

What are the responsibilities of both the organization and the individual with regard to career planning and development? Which has the primary responsibility? The answer is that successful career planning and development require actions from three sources—the organization, the employee's immediate manager, and the employee.

Employee's Responsibilities

Career planning is not something that one person can do for another; it has to come from the individual.[3] Only the individual knows what he or she really wants out of a career, and certainly these desires vary appreciably from person to person. Therefore, the primary responsibility for career planning rests with the individual employee.

Career planning requires a conscious effort on the part of the employee; it is hard work and it does not automatically happen. Although an individual may be

▽. HRM in Action 11–2

A Cost-Effective Career Planning Program

For years, career planning was viewed by corporate managers as something that an organization did for the employees. Recent experiences of some organizations indicate that career planning is something that should not only be done for the employee but also for the organization. If properly planned and managed, a career planning program can be a cost-effective human resource tool.

A major West Coast bank has implemented a career counseling program that is set up so that all interested employees may participate. Career counseling forms are filled out by the employee, and then the employee and manager jointly prepare development plans. The man-

ager forwards the plans to the staff planning and development department. The plans are used to track the manager's efforts, to help highlight development needs, and to make decisions about promotions and transfers.

The career counseling program is estimated to have saved the bank $1.95 million in one year. Estimates made by an industrial engineer showed 65 percent less turnover, 85 percent performance improvement, 25 percent increased productivity, and 75 percent increased promotability.

Source: Milan Moravic, "A Cost-Effective Career Planning Program Requires a Strategy," *Personnel Administrator,* January 1982, pp. 28–32.

convinced that developing a sound career plan would be in his or her best interest, finding the time to develop such a plan is often another matter. The organization can help by providing trained specialists to encourage and guide the employee. This can best be accomplished by allotting a few hours of company time each quarter to this type of planning.

While the individual is ultimately responsible for career planning and development, experience has shown that when people are not given some encouragement and direction, little progress is made.

Manager's Responsibilities

It has been said that "the critical battleground in career development is inside the mind of the person charged with supervisory responsibility."[4] Although not expected to be a professional counselor, the manager can and should play an important role in facilitating a subordinate's career planning. First and foremost, the manager should serve as a catalyst and sounding board. The manager should show an employee how to go about the process and then help the employee evaluate the conclusions.[5]

Table 11–1 lists several roles that a manager might perform to assist subordinates in career planning. Unfortunately, many managers do not perceive career counseling as part of their managerial duties. It is not that they are opposed to this role but rather that they have never considered it as part of their job.

To help overcome this and other related problems, many organizations have designed training programs to help their managers develop the necessary skills in this area. HRM in Action 11–3 describes what two companies are doing to help their supervisors become better career counselors.

▼ Table 11-1   Potential career planning roles of managers

Communicator
Holds formal and informal discussions with employees.
Listens to and understands an employee's real concerns.
Clearly and effectively interacts with an employee.
Establishes an environment for open interaction.
Structures uninterrupted time to meet with employees.

Counselor
Helps employee identify career-related skills, interests, and values.
Helps employee identify a variety of career options.
Helps employee evaluate appropriateness of various options.
Helps employee design/plan strategy to achieve an agreed-on career goal.

Appraiser
Identifies critical job elements.
Negotiates with employee a set of goals and objectives to evaluate performance.
Assesses employee performance related to goals and objectives.
Communicates performance evaluation and assessment to employee.
Designs a development plan around future job goals and objectives.
Reinforces effective job performance.
Reviews an established development plan on an ongoing basis.

Coach
Teaches specific job-related or technical skills.
Reinforces effective performance.
Suggests specific behaviors for improvement.
Clarifies and communicates goals and objectives of work group and organization.

Mentor
Arranges for employee to participate in a high-visibility activity either inside or outside the organization.
Serves as a role model in employee's career development by demonstrating successful career behaviors.
Supports employee by communicating employee's effectiveness to others in and out of organization.

Advisor
Communicates the informal and formal realities of progression in the organization.
Suggests appropriate training activities that could benefit employee.
Suggests appropriate strategies for career advancement.

Broker
Assists in bringing employees together who might mutually help each other in their careers.
Assists in linking employees with appropriate educational or employment opportunities.
Helps employee identify obstacles to changing present situation.
Helps employee identify resources enabling a career development change.

Referral agent
Identifies employees with problems (e.g., career, personal, health).
Identifies resources appropriate to an employee experiencing a problem.
Bridges and supports employee with referral agents.
Follows up on effectiveness of suggested referrals.

Advocate
Works with employee in designing a plan for redress of a specific issue at higher levels of management.
Works with employee in planning alternative strategies if a redress by management is not successful.
Represents employee's concern to higher-level management for redress of specific issues.

▼. HRM in Action 11–3

Improving Career Counseling by Supervisors

A small group of Sikorsky Aircraft supervisors recently spent two days developing a course on how to handle a career counseling session. The course will eventually be taught to 900 fellow supervisors at Sikorsky. The goal of the course is to help supervisors answer the myriad of questions asked by their subordinates about their career options and what is needed to advance in the company. This supervisory training is one element in a six-part career management program being established. Other elements include job posting, human re-sources planning, external recruiting, setting up better links between pay and performance, and training and development opportunities.

In a similar experiment, B. F. Goodrich's Career Growth System includes a 12-hour training program designed to enhance managers' ability to handle career-related discussions with employees.

Source: Phil Farish, "Career Advice," *Personnel Administrator*, April 1987, pp. 29–30; and Phil Farish, "Career Advice," *Personnel Administrator*, March 1987, p. 26.

Organization's Responsibilities

The organization's responsibilities are to develop and communicate career options within the organization to the employee.[6] The organization should carefully advise an employee concerning possible career paths (series of jobs) to achieve that employee's career goals. The human resource department generally is responsible for ensuring that this information is kept current as new jobs are created and old ones are phased out. Working closely with both employees and their managers, human resource specialists should see that accurate information is conveyed and that interrelationships between different career paths are understood. Thus, rather than bearing the primary responsibility for preparing career plans, the organization should promote the conditions and create the environment that will facilitate employee career development.[7] HRM in Action 11–4 describes the results of a survey that demonstrates the commitment of some companies for providing career planning assistance.

Thus, successful career planning results from a joint effort by the individual, the immediate manager, and the organization; the individual does the planning, the immediate manager provides the guidance and encouragement, and the organization provides the resources and structure.

Developing a Career Plan

Career plan
The analysis of an individual's situation, identification of career objectives, and development of the means for realizing these objectives.

Since human resource managers are primarily interested in employee career paths within the organization, this section deals exclusively with developing a career plan within the context of the present organization. Although many variables are possible, the development of a **career plan** within the current organization involves four basic steps: (1) an assessment by the individual of his/her other abilities, interests, and career goals; (2) an assessment by the organization of the individual's abilities and potential; (3) communication of career options and opportunities within the organization; and (4) career counseling to set realistic goals and plans for their accomplishment.[8]

▼. HRM in Action 11–4

Company Commitment to Career Planning

One of the first things that ambitious employees look for in an organization is the opportunity for advancement. Because of this, companies with obvious or specified career paths are attractive to these employees. Apparently, many companies are doing something positive to help employees plan their careers.

In a survey conducted by *Personnel* magazine, 83 percent of the respondents reported that they have some type of career planning—either formal or informal—in their organizations. Roughly 69 percent of the respondents reported that they have career paths for some employees, and almost half of the respondents have formal or informal mentoring programs.

Many methods were used to help employees plan careers. About 86 percent of the companies reimbursed employees for outside course work. Sixty-nine percent of the respondents reported one-on-one counseling involving the employee and the manager or a member of the human resource staff.

Source: Hermine F. Levine, "Consensus on Career Planning," *Personnel,* March 1985, pp. 67–72. Reprinted by permission of publisher, from *Personnel* (March 1985) © American Management Association, New York. All rights reserved.

Individual Assessment

Many people never stop to analyze their abilities, interests, and career goals. It isn't that most people don't want to analyze these factors, but rather that they simply never take the time. While this is not something an organization can do for the individual, the organization can provide the impetus and structure. A variety of self-assessment materials is available commercially, and some organizations have developed tailor-made forms for the use of their employees.[9] Another option is the use of some form of psychological testing.

An individual's self-assessment should not necessarily be limited by current resources and abilities; career plans normally require that the individual acquire additional training and skills. However, this assessment should be based on reality. For the individual, this involves identifying personal strengths, not only the individual's developed abilities but also the financial resources available.

Assessment by the Organization

Organizations have several potential sources of information that can be used for assessing employees. Traditionally, the most frequently used source has been the performance appraisal process. The assessment center, discussed in Chapter 9, can also be an excellent source of information. Other potential sources include personnel records reflecting information such as education and previous work experience. It is usually a good idea for an organization not to depend on any one source of information but rather to use as many as are readily available. Such an approach provides a natural system of checks and balances.

The organization's assessment of an individual employee should normally be conducted jointly by the human resource department and the individual's immediate manager.

Communicating Career Options

To set realistic career goals, an individual must know the options and opportunities that are available. Several things can be done by the organization to facilitate such awareness. Posting and advertising job vacancies is one activity that helps employees get a feel for their options. Clearly identifying possible paths of advancement within the organization is also helpful. This can be done as part of the performance appraisal process. Another good idea is to share human resource planning forecasts with employees.

Career Counseling

Career counseling is the activity that integrates the different steps in the career planning process. Career counseling may be performed by an employee's immediate manager, a human resource specialist, or a combination of the two. In most cases, it is preferable to have the counseling conducted by the immediate manager with appropriate input from the human resource department. The immediate manager generally has the advantage of practical experience, knows the company, and is in a position to make a realistic appraisal of organizational opportunities.

Some managers are reluctant to attempt counseling for fear that they haven't been trained in the area. However, it is not necessary to be a trained psychologist to be a successful career counselor.[10] In fact, behavioral research and actual experience suggest that the characteristics that make people likable and effective are basically the same qualities that contribute to successful counseling.[11] Of course, the right type of training can be very beneficial to even accomplished career counselors.[12] Figure 11–1 presents a questionnaire that can be used by managers to evaluate their skills in career counseling.

Generally, managers who are good in basic human relations are successful as career counselors. Developing a caring attitude toward employees and their careers is of prime importance. Being receptive to employee concerns and problems is another requirement. In addition, some specific suggestions for helping managers become better career counselors are:[13]

1. *Recognize the limits of career counseling.* Remember the manager and the organization serve as catalysts in the career development process. The primary responsibility for developing a career plan lies with the individual employee.

2. *Respect confidentiality.* Career counseling is very personal and has basic requirements of ethics, confidentiality, and privacy.

3. *Establish a relationship.* Be honest, open, and sincere with the subordinate. Try to be empathetic and see things from the subordinate's point of view.

4. *Listen effectively.* Learn to be a sincere listener. A natural human tendency is to want to do most of the talking. It often takes a conscious effort to be a good listener.

5. *Consider alternatives.* An important goal in career counseling is to help subordinates realize that there are usually a number of available choices. Help the subordinates to expand their thinking and not necessarily be limited by past experience.

6. *Seek and share information.* Be sure the employee and the organization have completed their respective assessments of the employee's abilities, interests, and desires. Make sure that the organization's assessment has been clearly

▼ **Figure 11–1**   Questionnaire: *How do you rate as a career counselor?*

This quiz helps managers to examine their knowledge of the career counseling function and to discover those areas in which some skill building may be necessary. Rate your knowledge, skill, and confidence as a managerial career counselor by scoring yourself on a scale of 0 (low) to 10 (high) on each of the following statements:

_9_ 1. I am aware of how career orientations and life stages can influence a person's perspective and contribute to career planning problems.

_2_ 2. I understand my own career choices and changes and feel good enough about what I have done to be able to provide guidance to others.

_5_ 3. I am aware of my own biases about dual career paths and feel that I can avoid these biases in coaching others to make a decision on which way to go with their careers.

_8_ 4. I am aware of how my own values influence my point of view, and I recognize the importance of helping others to define their values and beliefs so they are congruent with career goals.

_7_ 5. I am aware of the pitfalls of "shooting behind the duck" and try to keep myself well informed about my organization, so I can show others how to "shoot ahead of the duck."

_6_ 6. I know the norms existing within my own department as well as those within other departments and parts of the organization, so I can help others deal with them effectively.

_5_ 7. I understand the organizational reward system (nonmonetary) well enough to help others make informed decisions about career goals, paths, and plans.

____ 8. I have access to a variety of techniques I can use to help others articulate their skills, set goals, and develop action plans to realize their career decisions.

____ 9. I am informed on the competencies required for career success in this organization in both the managerial and technical areas, so I can advise others on the particular skills they need to build on and how to go about developing that expertise.

____10. I feel confident enough about my own skills as a career counselor that I can effectively help my people with their problems and plans and make midcourse corrections when necessary.

Scoring

Add up your score and rate yourself against the following scale:

0–30   It might be a good idea if you found *yourself* a career counselor.

31–60   Some of your people are receiving help from you.... However, do you know how many and which ones are not?

61–80   You're a counselor! You may not be ready for the big league yet, but you are providing help for your people.

81–100 Others have a lot to learn from you. You understand the importance of career counseling, and you know how to provide it.

communicated to the employee and that the employee is aware of potential job openings within the organization.

 7. *Assist with goal definition and planning.* Remember that the employee must make the final decisions. Managers should serve as "sounding boards" and help ensure that the individual's plans are valid.

▼ **Table 11–2** Basic steps of career pathing

1. *Determine or reconfirm the abilities and end behaviors of the target job.* Because jobs tend to change over time, it is important to determine or confirm requirements and review them periodically.
2. *Secure employee background data and review them for accuracy and completeness.* Because interests and career objectives of people tend to shift, these also have to be confirmed. Also, it is often necessary to update the individual's records concerning skills, experience, etc.
3. *Undertake a needs analysis comparison that jointly views the individual and the targeted job.* Determine if the individual and the targeted job tend to match. Surprisingly, many organizations neglect to query individuals when questions arise concerning their backgrounds, potential abilities, and interests.
4. *Reconcile employee career desires, developmental needs, and targeted job requirements with those of organizational career management.* Individuals formalize their career objectives or modify them as circumstances warrant.
5. *Develop individual training work and educational needs using a time-activity orientation.* Identify the individual actions (work education and training experiences) necessary for the individual to progress to the targeted job.
6. *Blueprint career path activities.* This is the process of creating a time-oriented blueprint or chart to guide the individual.

Source: Adapted from E. H. Burack and N. J. Mathys, *Career Management in Organizations: A Practical Human Resource Planning Approach* (Lake Forest, Il.: Brace-Park Press, 1979), pp. 79–80.

Career Pathing

Career pathing
A sequence of developmental activities involving informal and formal education, training, and job experiences that help make an individual capable of holding a more advanced job in the future.

Career pathing is a technique that addresses the specifics of progressing from one job to another in the organization. It can be defined as a sequence of developmental activities involving informal and formal education, training, and job experiences that help make an individual capable of holding more advanced jobs.[14] Career paths exist on an informal basis in almost all organizations. However, career paths are much more useful when formally defined and documented.[15] Such formalization results in specific descriptions of sequential work experiences as well as how the different sequences relate. Table 11–2 outlines the basic steps in career pathing. Career pathing is most useful when used as a part of the overall career planning process. Figure 11–2 summarizes the major variables that affect the career planning process and shows how career pathing fits into the process.

Reviewing Career Progress

Individual careers rarely go exactly according to plan. The environment changes, personal desires change, and other things happen. However, if the individual periodically reviews both the career plan and the situation, adjustments can be made so that career development is not impaired. On the other hand, a career plan that is not kept current rapidly becomes useless. Complacency is the greatest danger once a career plan has been developed. The plan must be changed as the situation and the individual change.

▼ **Figure 11–2**   Major variables affecting career planning

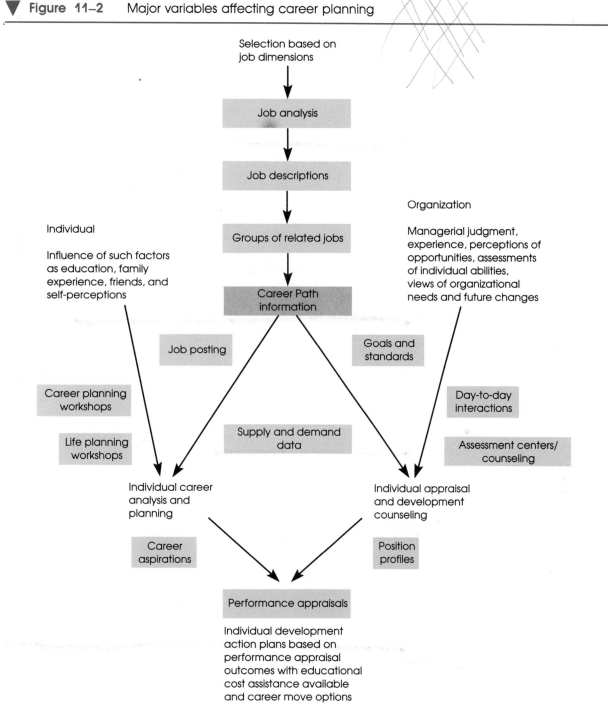

Selection based on
job dimensions

Job analysis

Job descriptions

Individual

Influence of such factors
as education, family
experience, friends, and
self-perceptions

Groups of related jobs

Organization

Managerial judgment,
experience, perceptions of
opportunities, assessments
of individual abilities,
views of organizational
needs and future changes

Career Path
information

Job posting

Goals and
standards

Career planning
workshops

Day-to-day
interactions

Life planning
workshops

Supply and demand
data

Assessment centers/
counseling

Individual career
analysis and
planning

Individual appraisal
and development
counseling

Career
aspirations

Position
profiles

Performance appraisals

Individual development
action plans based on
performance appraisal
outcomes with educational
cost assistance available
and career move options

Source: Kenneth B. McRae, "Career-Management Planning: A Boon to Managers and Employees." Reprinted by permission of publisher, from *Personnel*
(May 1985) © 1985. American Management Association, New York. All rights reserved..

Career-Related Myths

Many myths related to career planning and advancement are held by employees. Frequently, such myths are misleading and can inhibit career planning and growth. The purpose of this section is to explore these myths and provide evidence disproving them.[16]

Myth 1: There is always room for one more person at the top. This myth contradicts the fact that the structures of the overwhelming majority of today's organizations are shaped like a pyramid, with fewer positions available as one ascends the pyramid. Adherence to this myth fosters unrealistic aspirations and generates self-perpetuating frustrations. There is nothing wrong with wanting to become president of the organization; however, an individual must also be aware that the odds of attaining such a position are slim. For example, General Motors Corp. has approximately 748,000 employees and only one president. The major lesson to be learned from Myth 1 is to pick career paths that are realistic and attainable.

Myth 2: The key to success is being in the right place at the right time. Like all the career-related myths, this one has just enough truth to make it believable. One can always find a highly successful person who attributes all his or her success to being in the right place at the right time. People who adhere to this myth are rejecting the basic philosophy of planning: that a person, through careful design, can affect rather than merely accept the future. Adherence to Myth 2 is dangerous, because it can lead to complacency and a defeatist attitude.

Myth 3: Good subordinates make good superiors. This myth is based on the belief that these employees who are the best performers in their current jobs should necessarily be the ones who are promoted. This is not to imply that good performance should not be rewarded, for it should. However, when an individual is being promoted, those making the decision should look carefully at the requirements of the new job in addition to the individual's present job performance. How many times has a star engineer or salesperson been promoted into a managerial role, only to fail miserably? Similarly, outstanding athletes are frequently made head coaches, and everybody seems surprised when the former star fails in this job. Playing a sport and coaching require different talents and abilities. Because someone excels at one job does not mean that he or she will excel at all jobs.

Myth 4: Career planning and development are functions of the human resources department. The ultimate responsibility for career planning and development belongs to the individual and not to the human resource department or the individual's manager. Personnel specialists can assist the individual and answer certain questions, but they cannot develop a career plan for the person. Only the individual can make career-related decisions.

Myth 5: All good things come to those who work long, hard hours. People guided by this myth often spend 10 to 12 hours a day trying to impress their managers and move ahead rapidly in the organization. However, the results of these extra hours on the job often have little or no relationship to what the manager considers important, to the person's effectiveness on the job, and (most important in this context) to the individual's long-range career growth. Unfortunately, many managers reinforce this myth by designing activities "to keep everyone busy."

Myth 6: Rapid advancement along a career path is largely a function of the kind of manager one has. A person's manager can affect an individual's rate of advancement. However, those who adhere to this myth often accept a defensive role and ignore the importance of their own actions. Belief in this myth provides a ready-made excuse for failure. It is easy and convenient to blame failures on one's manager.

Myth 7: The way to get ahead is to determine your weaknesses and then work hard to correct them. Successful salespeople do not emphasize the weak points of their products; rather, they emphasize the strong points. The same should be true in career planning and development. Individuals who achieve their career objectives do so by stressing those things that they do uncommonly well. The secret is to capitalize first on one's strengths and then try to improve deficiencies in other areas.

Myth 8: Always do your best, regardless of the task. This myth stems from the puritan work ethic. The problem is that believers ignore the fact that different tasks have different priorities. Because there is only a limited amount of time, a person should spend that time according to priorities. Those tasks and jobs that rank high in importance in achieving one's career goals should receive the individual's best effort. Those tasks that do not rank high should be done but not necessarily with one's best effort. The idea is to give something less than one's best effort to unimportant tasks in order to have time to give one's best effort to the important tasks.

Myth 9: It is wise to keep home life and work life separated. An individual cannot make wise career decisions without the full knowledge and support of the spouse. Working husbands and wives should share their inner feelings concerning their jobs so that spouses will understand the basic factors that weigh in any career decisions.

A healthy person usually has interests other than a job. Career strategy should be designed to recognize and support, not contradict, these other interests. Career objectives should be a subset of one's life objectives. Too often, however, career objectives conflict with rather than support life objectives.

Myth 10: The grass is always greener on the other side of the fence. Regardless of the career path the individual follows, another one always seems a little more attractive. The fact is, however, that Utopia does not exist. More than likely, the job that John Doe holds involves many of the same problems that every working person might face. As the individual assumes more and more personal responsibilities, the price of taking that "attractive" job becomes higher in terms of possibly relocating, developing a new social life, and learning new duties. This is not to say that job and related changes should not be made—however, one should avoid making such changes hastily.

Myths Held by Managers

In addition to the previously described myths held by employees, management personnel often hold certain myths related to career planning. Some of these are described below.[17]

It will raise expectations. Many managers fear that an emphasis on career planning will raise employee expectations to unrealistically high levels. Career planning should do just the opposite. It should bring employee's aspirations into the open and match their skills, interests, and goals with opportunities that are realistically available.

We will be overwhelmed. This myth is based on the fear that employees will deluge their managers for information about jobs in other parts of the organization and that employees will expect the organization to provide them with a multitude of career opportunities. While this fear is very realistic in the minds of many managers, it is basically unfounded.

Our managers will not be able to cope. Management often becomes concerned that introducing career planning will place their managers in a counseling role for which they are ill prepared. While coaching and counseling should be an important part of any manager's job, the key to career planning is to place the responsibility primarily on the employee.

We do not have the system in place. This myth is based on the belief that before the organization can introduce career planning, it must first put in place a whole series of other human resource planning mechanisms, such as job posting and succession planning. In actuality, many organizations have implemented successful career-planning programs with few formal mechanisms beyond the basic requirement of providing employees good career-planning tools.

Dealing with Career Plateaus

Career plateau
The point in an individual's career where the likelihood of an additional promotion is very low.

A career plateau is defined as "the point in a career where the likelihood of additional hierarchical promotion is very low."[18] Virtually all people reach a plateau in their careers. The difference is that some individuals reach their plateau earlier than others. Plateaued employees are those who "reach their promotional ceiling long before they retire."[19]

Because it is inherently true that fewer positions are available as one moves up the hierarchical ladder, plateauing does not necessarily indicate failure. However, as will be shown in this section, the case of a plateauee may need to be handled differently in some situations from that of an employee still on the rise in the organization.

Figure 11–3 presents a model for classifying managerial careers. The four principal career states are:[20]

Learners
Individuals in an organization who have a high potential for advancement but who are currently performing below standard.

- **Learners.** Individuals with high potential for advancement who are performing below standard (for example, a new trainee).

▼ **Figure 11–3** Classifying managerial careers

Current Performance	Likelihood of Future Promotion	
	Low	High
High	Solid citizens (effective plateauees)	Stars
Low	Deadwood (ineffective plateauees)	Learners (comers)

Source: Adapted from T. P. Ference, J. A. F. Stoner, and E. K. Warren, "Managing the Career Plateau," *Academy of Management Review,* October 1977, p. 603.

- **Stars.** Individuals presently doing outstanding work, with a high potential for continued advancement; these are people on "fast-track" career paths.
- **Solid citizens.** Individuals whose present performance is satisfactory but whose chance for future advancement is small. These people make up the bulk of the employees in most organizations.
- **Deadwood.** Individuals whose present performance has fallen to an unsatisfactory level; they have little potential for advancement.

Naturally, organizations would like to have all stars and solid citizens. The challenge, however, is to transform the learners into stars or solid citizens and to keep the current stars and solid citizens from slipping into the deadwood category. Furthermore, there is a tendency to overlook solid citizens. The learners, stars, and deadwood usually get most of the attention in terms of development programs and stimulating assignments. Neglect of the solid citizens may result in their slipping into the deadwood category.

Three actions can aid in managing the plateauing process: (1) prevent plateauees from becoming ineffective (prevent a problem from occurring); (2) integrate the relevant career-related information systems (improve monitoring so that emerging problems can be detected and treated early); and (3) manage ineffective plateauees and frustrated managers more effectively (cure the problem once it has arisen).[21] The first action basically involves helping plateauees adjust to the solid-citizen category and realize that they have not necessarily failed. Available avenues for personal development and growth should be pointed out. The second suggestion can largely be implemented through a thorough performance appraisal system. Such a system should encourage open communication between the manager and the person being appraised.

Rehabilitating Ineffective Plateauees

Rehabilitating ineffective plateauees is difficult but certainly possible. The first question that the manager might ask is "Why should we try and help ineffective plateauees; don't they often have an overall negative impact on the organization?" Certainly, deadwood can have a negative impact, but there are also several good reasons for trying to salvage these employees:[22]

Stars
Individuals in an organization who are presently doing outstanding work and have a high potential for continued advancement.

Solid citizens
Individuals in an organization whose present performance is satisfactory but whose chance for future advancement is small.

Deadwood
Individuals in an organization whose present performance has fallen to an unsatisfactory level and who have little potential for advancement.

- ~~*Job knowledge.*~~ Plateaued employees usually have been in the job for quite some time and have amassed considerable job knowledge.
- ~~*Organizational knowledge.*~~ Plateaued employees know not only their jobs but also the organization.
- ~~*Loyalty.*~~ Plateaued employees are usually not job-hoppers but often have demonstrated above-average loyalty to the organization.
- ~~*Concern for the well-being of plateauees.*~~ If the organization were to terminate all plateaued employees, this could have a disastrous impact on other employees. Also, the number of plateaued employees could be large.

Given that an organization's management team wants to rehabilitate plateaued employees, what can be done? At least five different possibilities exist.[23]

1. *Provide alternate means of recognition.* If the chances are slim for the employee to receive recognition through a future promotion, look for alternative methods of recognition. Some possibilities include task force or special assignments, participation in brainstorming sessions, representation of the organization to others, and training of new employees.

2. *Develop new ways to make their current jobs more satisfying.* The more employees can be turned on by their current jobs, the less likelihood that they will remain ineffective. Some possibilities here include relating employees' performance to total organizational goals and creating competition in the job.

3. *Effect revitalization through reassignment.* The idea here is to implement systematic job switching to positions at the same level that require many but not necessarily the exact same skills and experiences as the present jobs.

4. *Utilize reality-based self-development programs.* Instead of exposing plateauees to developmental programs designed to help them move into future jobs (which a majority of development programs do), expose them to development programs that can help them do a better job in their present positions.

5. *Change managerial attitudes toward plateaued employees.* It is not unusual for managers and supervisors to give up on and neglect plateaued employees. Such actions are quickly picked up by the affected employees and only compound the problem.

Because plateaued employees often include a significant number of employees who are worth rehabilitating, it would pay for most organizations to address this issue seriously.

Outplacement

Outplacement
Benefit provided by an employer to help an employee leave the organization and get a job someplace else.

Outplacement "refers to a benefit provided by an employer to help an employee terminate and get a job someplace else."[24] Outplacement is a way of terminating employees that is of benefit to both the employee and the organization. The organization gains by terminating the employees before they become deadwood; the employees gain by finding a new job, and at the same time preserving their

▼. HRM in Action 11–5

How Long Will It Take?

Swain and Swain, a firm that specializes in outplacement services, has developed a formula for determining how long it will take for a terminated employee to find another job. The formula utilizes over 50 variables ranging from ease of relocation to likelihood to litigate. The formula also includes an age/salary ratio and assessment of the individual's degree of social sophistication.

Source: Phil Farish, "Work Gap Formula," *Personnel Administrator,* January 1987, pp. 21–22.

dignity. Additionally, an outplacement program can have a very positive effect on employee morale. Sophisticated outplacement programs include assistance in resume preparation, job interviewing, and the generation of job interviews. The best approach to outplacement is to treat it as an alternative within the career planning process. HRM in Action 11–5 describes how sophisticated one firm specializing in outplacement services has become.

● *Summary of Learning Objectives*

1. Summarize the benefits of career planning.

   An individual who develops a plan to reach career goals is more likely to reach them. Realistic career planning forces individuals to look at the opportunities available in relation to their abilities. With a career plan, a person is much more likely to experience satisfaction as progress is made along the career path. From the organization's viewpoint, career planning can reduce costs associated with employee turnover.

2. Explain who should be responsible for career planning.

   Successful career planning requires actions from three sources—the organization, the employee's immediate manager, and the employee. The primary responsibility for career planning rests with the individual employee. Although not expected to be a professional counselor, the manager can and should play an important role in facilitating a subordinate's career planning. The organization's responsibilities are to develop and communicate career options within the organization.

3. Name the steps involved in career planning.

   The development of a career plan involves four basic steps: (1) an assessment by the individual of his or her abilities, interests, and career goals; (2) an assessment by the organization of the individual's abilities and potential; (3) communication of career options and opportunities within the organization; and (4) career counseling to set realistic goals and plans for their accomplishment.

4. Define career pathing.

   Career pathing is a technique that addresses the specifics of progressing from one job to another in the organization.

5. List several myths held by employees related to career planning and advancement.

Many myths related to career planning and advancement are often held by employees: (1) there is always room for one more person at the top; (2) the key to success is being in the right place at the right time; (3) good subordinates make good superiors; (4) career planning and development are functions of the human resource department; (5) all good things come to those who work long, hard hours; (6) rapid advancement along a career path is largely a function of the kind of manager one has; (7) the way to get ahead is to determine your weaknesses and then work hard to correct them; (8) always do your best, regardless of the task; (9) it is wise to keep home life and work life separated; and (10) the grass is always greener on the other side of the fence.

6. List several myths held by management related to career planning.

Management personnel often hold certain myths related to career planning: (1) career planning will raise expectations to unrealistically high levels; (2) management will be overwhelmed with requests; (3) managers will not be able to cope; and (4) management does not have the necessary systems in place.

7. Define a career plateau and a plateaued employee.

A career plateau is the point in a career where the likelihood of additional hierarchical promotion is very low. A plateaued employee is an employee who reaches his or her promotional ceiling long before he or she retires.

8. Describe the four principal career states.

The four principal career states are learners, stars, solid citizens, and deadwood. Learners are individuals with a high potential for advancement who are performing below standard. Stars are individuals presently doing outstanding work, with a high potential for continued advancement. Solid citizens are individuals whose present performance is satisfactory but whose chance for future advancement is small. Deadwood are individuals whose present performance has fallen to an unsatisfactory level and who have little potential for advancement.

9. Define outplacement.

Outplacement refers to a benefit provided by an employer to help an employee terminate employment with the organization and get a job someplace else.

Review Questions

1. Name at least two ways in which career planning might benefit an individual.
2. What are the three major objectives of career planning from the organization's viewpoint?
3. Where does the primary responsibility for career planing belong? Why?
4. What are the four basic steps for the development of a career plan?
5. Give some specific suggestions for helping managers become better career counselors.
6. What are the basic steps involved in career pathing?
7. How often should an individual review and revise his or her career plan?
8. Name several myths often held by employees relating to career planning and advancement.

9. Name several myths often held by management personnel relating to career planning.
10. Define the following categories: learners, stars, solid citizens, and deadwood.
11. Name and briefly describe several methods that might be used to rehabilitate inefficient plateauees in an organization.
12. What is outplacement?

Discussion Questions

1. Do you think that career planning can adversely affect organizational performance in that the process sometimes convinces the involved parties to change jobs?
2. Is the concept of career planning and development realistic in today's rapidly changing environment?
3. Discuss how career-related myths can inhibit career planning and growth.
4. Is it better to tell a person that he or she has reached a plateau in the organization or to allow the person to maintain hope of eventual promotion?

▼ INCIDENT 11–1

The Unhappy Telephone Line Installer

John James had been an installer-repairer for the telephone company for almost six years. Since the work kept him outdoors most of the day, he liked the job; the pay was good, and his fellow employees were congenial. John had gone to work on this job right after high school graduation and had never considered doing anything else. Occasionally, through the years, others in the same job had been promoted into supervisory positions, had taken advantage of company-paid educational benefits, or had received recognition for outstanding service to the company.

John was close friends with Ross Bartlett, his partner on the line. Ross, who had been in his job about two years, was a good worker. About six months ago, Ross began to express dissatisfaction with the routine, monotonous work, saying that there had to be some better way to make a living.

Last week, John learned that the company would pay Ross's way to take college courses in business administration. That same day, John really began to feel some concern about himself and his status with the telephone company. He began having restless, sleepless nights as he thought back over the past years—what he had done with his life, where he was now in his career, and where he was going. His thoughts became so muddled and confused that he realized he was going to need some help.

John had never set any personal goals for himself other than to live reasonably comfortably from day to day and month to month. He had come from a poor family and had received little encouragement or help from his family to develop ambitions when he was young. The one thing that his mother and father had insisted on was that someone in the family was going to be a high school graduate;

luckily, John was that person. He never had any desire to go to college, because graduation from high school had proved to be extremely difficult for him. John could not think of spending four more years in school when he needed and wanted to be out making money for himself and the family.

Now, with people around him moving on in their careers and John's career at a standstill, he felt he was at a dead end. He realized suddenly that he needed to do something, but he was not sure just what.

Questions

1. What advice might you give John?
2. Would a career plan help a person like John?
3. Is John's situation atypical of most employees?

▼ INCIDENT 11–2

"I Didn't Know You Wanted the Job"

Doris Martin had been an employee of the United States Central Bank for eight years. During this time, she had held the position of settlement clerk in the check collection department. Recently, Doris had risen to the position of senior settlement clerk and could not advance any further unless she moved into a supervisory job. Until just a short time ago, her supervisors had no idea that Doris was interested in advancing beyond her present position.

Approximately eight months ago, a clerical position came open in the technical study unit of the check collection department. The position was not an upgrade for Doris; however, every clerk who had held the position had moved up in the department. Doris wanted the job badly.

Kathy Myers, a coworker of Doris's, was selected for the clerical post in the technical study unit. When Doris learned this, she became furious and stormed into the supervisor's office to tell him so. Bill Monk, her supervisor, was stunned.

"Doris, I had no idea that you were interested in the position. Kathy was the only person who applied for an interdepartment transfer, so she was the only one considered."

"Interdepartment transfer?" Doris cried. "What is that? Nobody told me about applications for transfers. How could I have known?"

"Now, Doris, don't get angry," Bill said. "Management has decided to keep those transfers kind of quiet. You know, in the past six months, our department has lost over 15 people to job posting. If we start publicizing interdepartmental transfer opportunities, we won't have any experienced workers. I know what you mean, though. As soon as I get a chance, I'm going to get out of here. I've told my wife we might even have to take a cut in salary, but I don't care. This place is just driving me crazy."

Six months after the incident, Doris was still in her position in the settlement unit. She was, however, selected to attend a personal leadership program, a class run by the training and development unit and aimed at developing the skills of bank employees and their supervisors. A feedback instrument was developed in class by the participants, and if the participants were willing, the form was sent directly to their supervisors. Doris elected to send her form to her supervisor. On the form, Doris asked questions concerning such topics as career development, performance improvement, and skills development.

Bill Monk did not have the answers to Doris's questions, so he forwarded the form on to Sally Cugar, the departmental supervisor. Sally stopped by Doris's desk the next day and said, "Doris, don't pay any attention to what those training people say. I went to that supervisors' course, and all they do is brainwash you. I wouldn't send anybody to that course unless I was forced to. Just forget about those questions on the form. You'll be a lot happier."

Doris was crushed. The questions she had listed on the form were important to her, and she felt put down by Sally's remarks.

Questions

1. What should Doris do?
2. Would a career plan help Doris?

Exercise

Becoming an Effective Career Planner

Look over the nine potential career planning roles of managers listed in Table 11–1. Rank-order them in terms of which roles you think would best fit you (1 being the role you would fit best, 9 being the role you would fit least). After you have completed this ranking, complete the quiz presented in Figure 11–1. How does your score on this quiz correlate with how you ranked the counselor role (i.e., if you scored high on the quiz, did you rank the role of the counselor relatively high, and vice versa)? Make a list of some things you might do to become a better counselor. Be prepared to share your lists with the class.

Notes and Additional Readings

1. A. H. Soverwine, "Why Develop a Career Strategy?" *Management Review,* May 1977, p. 24; and Barbara Moses, "Giving Employees a Future," *Training and Development Journal,* December 1987, p. 25.
2. B. C. Winterscheid, "A Career Development System Coordinates Training Efforts," *Personnel Administrator,* August 1980, pp. 28–32.
3. Frank W. Archer, "Charting a Career Course," *Personnel Journal,* April 1984, p. 62; Norman C. Hill, "Career Counseling: What Employees Should Do—and Expect," *Personnel,* August 1985, p. 43.
4. A. B. Randolph, "Managerial Career Coaching," *Training and Development Journal,* July 1981, pp. 54–55.
5. Archer, "Charting," p. 62.
6. A. W. Hill, "Career Development—Who Is Responsible?" *Training and Development Journal,* May 1976, p. 14.

7. Ibid., p. 15.

8. T. H. Stone, *Understanding Personnel Management* (Hinsdale, Ill.: Dryden Press, 1981), p. 324.

9. Ibid., p. 325.

10. N. T. Meckel, "The Manager as Career Counselor," *Training and Development Journal,* July 1981, pp. 65–69.

11. R. R. Carkhuff, *Helping and Human Relations: A Primer for Lay and Professional Helpers,* vol. 1 and 2 (New York: Holt, Rinehart & Winston, 1969).

12. For a suggested approach, see Z. B. Leibowitz and N. K. Schlossberg, "Training Managers for Their Role in a Career Development System," *Training and Development Journal,* July 1981, pp. 72–79.

13. These suggestions are adapted from Meckel, "The Manager," pp. 67–69.

14. E. H. Burack and N. J. Mathys, *Career Management in Organizations: A Practical Human Resource Planning Approach* (Lake Forest, Ill.: Brace-Park Press, 1979), p. 78.

15. Kenneth B. McRae, "Career-Management Planning: A Boon to Managers and Employees," *Personnel,* May 1985, p. 56.

16. The myths are adapted from E. Staats, "Career Planning and Development Which Way Is Up?" *Public Administration Review,* January–February 1977; and A. H. Soverwine, "A Mythology of Career Growth," *Management Review,* June 1977, pp. 56–60.

17. The myths in this section are drawn from Moses, "Giving Employees," pp. 25–26.

18. T. P. Ference, J. A. F. Stoner, and E. K. Warren, "Managing the Career Plateau," *Management Review,* October 1977, p. 602.

19. Beverly Kaye, "Are Plateaued Performers Productive?" *Personnel Journal,* August 1989, p. 57; and Judith M. Bardwick, *The Plateauing Trap,* New York: The American Management Association, 1986, pp. 1–17.

20. Ference, Stoner, and Warren, "Managing the Career Plateau," pp. 603–04.

21. Ibid., p. 607.

22. The reasons given for salvaging ineffective plateauees are from Richard C. Payne, "Mid-Career Block," *Personnel Journal,* April 1984, p. 42.

23. Ibid., pp. 44–48.

24. T. M. Camden, "Using Outplacement as a Career Development Tool," *Personnel Administrator,* January 1982, p. 35.

Section 4

Compensating Employees

Chapter 12
The Organizational Reward System

 Chapter 13
Base Wage and Salary Systems

Chapter 14
Incentive Pay Systems

Chapter 15
Employee Benefits

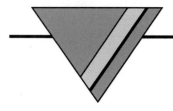

Chapter 12

The Organizational Reward System

Chapter Outline

Defining the System
Selection of Rewards
Relating Rewards to Performance
Job Satisfaction and Rewards
　The Satisfaction-Performance
　　Controversy
　Other Factors in Job Satisfaction
Employee Compensation
　Compensation Policies
　Pay Secrecy
　Government and Union Influence
　The Importance of Fair Pay
　Pay Equity
　Pay Satisfaction Model

**The Role of the Human Resource
　Manager in the Reward System**
Summary of Learning Objectives
Review Questions
Discussion Questions
**Incident 12–1: An Informative
　Coffee Break**
**Incident 12–2: Does Money
　Motivate?**
**Exercise: Relating Rewards to
　Performance**
Notes and Additional Readings

● *Learning Objectives*

After studying this chapter, you should be able to:
1. Define organizational rewards.
2. Distinguish between intrinsic and extrinsic rewards.
3. List several desirable preconditions for implementing a pay-for-performance program.
4. Define job satisfaction and list its five major components.
5. Summarize the satisfaction-performance relationship.
6. Define compensation, pay, incentives, and benefits.
7. List several pieces of government legislation that have had a significant impact on organizational compensation.
8. Explain the equity theory of motivation.
9. Discuss internal, external, individual, and organizational equity.

"*T*he Chairman: Is it not true that a man who is not a good workman and who may not be responsible for the fact that he is not a good workman, has to live as well as the man who is a good workman?

Mr. Taylor: Not as well as the other workman; otherwise, that would imply that all those in the world were entitled to live equally well whether they worked or whether they were idle, and that certainly is not the case. Not as well."*

In most cases, the organizational reward system is one of the most effective motivation tools that managers have at their disposal. The design and use of the organizational reward system is often interpreted by employees as a reflection of management attitudes, intentions, and the entire organizational climate. Also, few things evoke as much emotion as the organization's reward system. The responsibility for coordinating and administering the system usually comes under the purview of the human resource manager.

Defining the System

Organizational reward system
Organizational system concerned with the selection of the types of rewards to be used by the organization.

Organizational rewards
Rewards that result from employment with the organization; includes all types of rewards, both intrinsic and extrinsic.

Intrinsic rewards
Rewards internal to the individual and normally derived from involvement in certain activities or tasks.

Extrinsic rewards
Rewards that are controlled and distributed directly by the organization and are of a tangible nature.

The **organizational reward system** consists of the types of rewards that are to be offered and their distribution. **Organizational rewards** include all types of rewards, both intrinsic and extrinsic, that are received as a result of employment by the organization. **Intrinsic rewards** are rewards that are internal to the individual and are normally derived from involvement in certain activities or tasks. Job satisfaction and feelings of accomplishment are examples of intrinsic rewards. Most **extrinsic rewards** are directly controlled and distributed by the organization and are more tangible than intrinsic rewards. Pay and hospitalization benefits are examples of extrinsic rewards. Table 12–1 provides examples of both types of rewards.

Though intrinsic and extrinsic rewards are different, they are also closely related. Often, the provision of an extrinsic reward provides the recipient with intrinsic rewards. For example, if an employee receives an extrinsic reward in the form of a pay raise, the individual may also experience feelings of accomplishment (an intrinsic reward) by interpreting the pay raise as a sign of a job well done.

Selection of Rewards

Selection of the rewards to be offered is critical if the reward system is to function effectively. As a first step, management must recognize what employees perceive as meaningful rewards. Rewards may include things that are not obvious, such as office location, the allocation of certain pieces of equipment, or informal recognition.

*Source: Hearings before Special Committee of the House of Representatives to investigate the Taylor and other systems of shop management under authority of House Resolution 90 (Washington, D.C.: U.S. Government Printing Office, 1912), pp. 1452–53.

▼ Table 12–1   Intrinsic versus extrinsic rewards

Intrinsic Rewards	Extrinsic Rewards
Achievement	Formal recognition
Feelings of accomplishment	Fringe benefits
Informal recognition	Incentive payments
Job satisfaction	Pay
Personal growth	Promotion
Status	Social relationships
	Work environment

If an organization is going to distribute rewards—and all do—why not get the maximum in return? Such a return can be realized only if the desires of the employees are known. Organizations should learn what the employees perceive (which is not necessarily what management perceives) as meaningful rewards. Traditionally, top managers have assumed that they are fully capable of deciding just what rewards the employees need and want. Unfortunately, this is not always true.

Another closely related and often false assumption is exemplified by the fact that most organizations offer the same mix of rewards to all employees. Studies have shown that many variables, such as age, sex, marital status, number of dependents, and years of service, can influence employee preferences for certain rewards.[1] For example, older employees usually are much more concerned with pension benefits than are younger employees.

Another dimension that should be considered when selecting the types of rewards to be offered is the intrinsic benefits that might accrue as a result of the reward. All too often, managers and employees alike consider only the tangible benefits associated with a reward.[2]

In addition to the internal factors mentioned above, there are always external factors that place limitations on an organization's reward system. These factors include such things as the organization's size, the environmental conditions, the stage in the product life cycle, and the labor market. Since these external factors are usually beyond the control of the organization, this chapter will concentrate primarily on internal factors.

Relating Rewards to Performance

The free enterprise system is based on the premise that rewards should depend on performance. This performance-reward relationship is desirable not only at the organization or corporate level but also at the individual level. The underlying theory is that people will be motivated when they believe that such motivation will lead to desired rewards. Unfortunately, many formal rewards provided by organizations do not lend themselves to being related to performance. Rewards in this category (including paid vacations, insurance plans, and paid holidays) are almost always determined by organizational membership and seniority rather than by performance.

▼. HRM in Action 12–1

Do Companies Relate Pay to Performance?

A survey conducted by the Wyatt Company of more than 5,000 salaried and hourly employees all across the country produced some interesting findings. The survey included manufacturing and service industries as well as union and nonunion organizations. Concerning the issue of pay for performance, 46 percent said that they do not see a link between the two, while 28 percent said that they do. Nearly half of the respondents believe that managers are too tolerant of poor performers. At the same time, 70 percent of the respondents at all levels think their supervisors are technically competent.

Source: Phil Farish, "Job Views Change," *Personnel Administrator*, June 1988, p. 28.

Other rewards, such as promotion, can and should be related to performance. However, opportunities for promotion may occur only rarely. When available, the higher positions may be filled on the basis of seniority or by someone outside the organization.

The primary organizational variable that can be used to reward individuals and reinforce performance is pay. Even though the overwhelming majority of U.S. companies have some type of pay-for-performance program, most do a poor job of relating the two.[3] Surveys repeatedly show that neither top management nor rank-and-file employees have much confidence that a positive relationship exists between performance and pay[4] (see HRM in Action 12–1).

If relating rewards to performance is desirable, then why is it not more widespread? One answer is that it is not easy to do; it is much easier to give everybody the same thing, as evidenced by the ever-popular across-the-board pay increase. Relating rewards to performance requires that performance be accurately measured, and this is often not easily accomplished (Chapter 10 discussed performance appraisal). It also requires discipline to actually match rewards to performance. Another reason is that many union contracts require that certain rewards be based on totally objective variables, such as seniority. While no one successful formula for implementing a pay-for-performance program has yet been developed, a number of desirable preconditions have been identified and generally accepted:[5]

1. *Trust in management.* If employees are skeptical of management, it is difficult to make a pay-for-performance program work.

2. *Absence of performance constraints.* Since pay-for-performance programs are usually based on individual ability and effort, the jobs must be structured such that an individual's performance is not hampered by factors beyond his or her control.

3. *Trained supervisors and managers.* The supervisors and managers must be trained in setting and measuring performance standards.

4. *Good measurement systems.* Performance should be based on criteria that are job specific and focus on results achieved.

5. *Ability to pay.* The merit portion of the salary-increase budget must be large enough to get the attention of the employees.

6. *Clear distinction between cost of living, seniority, and merit.* In the absence of strong evidence to the contrary, employees will naturally assume a pay increase is an economic or longevity increase.

▼. HRM in Action 12–2

Tying Rewards to Performance

Highview Stores specializes in grocery products sold through 14 small retail stores. Each store is run by a store manager and is staffed by one or two clerks. Before 1981, store managers were paid a flat salary with no regular salary review periods or planned salary increases. Salary adjustments were generally based on years of service.

In 1981, Highview decided to revamp its reward system. A compensation plan based on commission plus an annual bonus was installed, with the commission and bonus closely tied to the performance of the store

manager. The managers received a percentage of weekly sales and were responsible for all expenses under their control. They essentially became semiautonomous entrepreneurs and made more money as the stores became more profitable.

The new reward system resulted in an estimated net benefit to the company of $184,599 in the first five months. During this same time period, store managers' mean weekly income rose 8.4 percent.

Source: Stuart C. Freedman, "Performance-Based Pay: A Convenience Store Case Study," *Personnel Journal*, July 1985, pp. 30–34.

---

7. Well-communicated total pay policy. Employees must have a clear understanding of how merit pay fits into the total pay picture.

8. Flexible reward schedule. It is easier to establish a credible pay-for-performance plan if all employees do not receive pay adjustments on the same date.

HRM in Action 12–2 describes how one convenience store chain has reaped the benefits of a performance-based pay system.

Job Satisfaction and Rewards

Job satisfaction is an individual's general attitude about the job. The organizational reward system often has a significant impact on the level of employees' job satisfaction. In addition to their direct impact, the manner in which the extrinsic rewards are dispersed can affect the intrinsic rewards (and satisfaction) of the recipients. For example, if everyone receives an across-the-board pay increase of 7 percent, it is hard to derive any feeling of accomplishment from the reward. However, if pay raises are related directly to performance, an employee receiving a healthy pay increase would more than likely also experience feelings of accomplishment and satisfaction.

The five major components of job satisfaction are (1) attitude toward the work group, (2) general working conditions, (3) attitude toward the company, (4) monetary benefits, and (5) attitude toward supervision.[6] Other components include the individual's state of mind about the work itself and life in general. A person's attitude toward the job may be positive or negative. Health, age, level of aspiration, social status, and political and social activities are factors that can contribute to job satisfaction.

Job satisfaction is not synonymous with **organizational morale**, which is the possession of a feeling of being accepted by and belonging to a group of employees

Job satisfaction
Individual's general attitude about the job.

Organizational morale
Refers to an individual's feeling of being accepted by and belonging to a group of employees through common goals, confidence in the desirability of these goals, and progress toward these goals.

through adherence to common goals and confidence in the desirability of these goals. Morale is the by-product of a group, while job satisfaction is more an individual state of mind. However, the two concepts are interrelated in that job satisfaction can contribute to morale and morale can contribute to job satisfaction.

The Satisfaction-Performance Controversy

For many years, managers generally have believed that a satisfied worker is necessarily a good worker. In other words, if management could keep all the workers happy, good performance would automatically follow. Charles Greene has suggested that many managers subscribe to this belief because it represents "the path of least resistance."[7] Greene's thesis is that if a performance problem exists, increasing an employee's happiness is far more pleasant than discussing with the worker his or her failure to meet standards. Before the satisfaction-performance controversy is discussed further, it might be wise to point out that there are subtle but real differences between being satisfied and being happy. Although happiness eventually results from satisfaction, the latter goes much deeper and is far less tenuous than happiness.

The following incident illustrates two propositions concerning the satisfaction-performance relationship:

> As Ben walked by, smiling on the way to his office, Ben's boss remarked to a friend. "Ben really enjoys his job, and that's why he's the best damn worker I ever had. And that's reason enough for me to keep Ben happy." The friend replied, "No, you're wrong! Ben likes his job because he does it so well. If you want to make Ben happy, you ought to do whatever you can to help him further improve his performance."[8]

The first proposition is the traditional view that satisfaction causes performance. The second is that satisfaction is the effect rather than the cause of performance. In this position, performance leads to rewards that result in a certain level of satisfaction. Thus, rewards constitute a necessary intervening variable in the relationship. Another position considers both satisfaction and performance to be functions of rewards. It postulates that satisfaction is caused by rewards but current performance also affects subsequent performance if rewards are based on current performance.

Research evidence generally rejects the more popular view that satisfaction causes performance. The evidence does, however, provide moderate support for the view that performance causes satisfaction. The evidence also provides strong indications that (1) rewards constitute a more direct cause of satisfaction than does performance and (2) rewards based on current performance cause subsequent performance.[9]

Researchers have also investigated the relationship between intrinsic and extrinsic satisfaction and performance for jobs that were categorized as being either stimulating or nonstimulating.[10] The studies found that the relationship between satisfaction and performance did vary, depending on whether the job was stimulating or nonstimulating to the job holder. These and other studies further emphasize the complexity of the satisfaction-performance relationship. One relationship that has been clearly established is that job satisfaction does have a positive impact on turnover, absenteeism, tardiness, accidents, grievances, and strikes.[11] In addition, satisfied employees are preferred simply because they make the work environment more pleasant. So, even though a satisfied employee is not necessarily a high performer, there are numerous reasons for cultivating employee satisfaction.

Other Factors in Job Satisfaction

As mentioned earlier, a wide range of both internal and external factors affect an individual's level of satisfaction. The left portion of Figure 12–1 summarizes the major factors that determine an individual's level of satisfaction or dissatisfaction. The total impact of these factors causes employees to be either generally satisfied or dissatisfied with their jobs. As indicated by the right side of Figure 12–1, employees who are satisfied with their jobs tend to be committed to the organization—these employees are likely to be very loyal and dependable. Employees who are dissatisfied with their jobs tend to behave in ways that can be detrimental to the organization—these employees are likely to experience higher rates of turnover, absenteeism, tardiness, and more accidents, strikes, and grievances. HRM in Action 12–3 presents some recent information relating to job satisfaction.

Job satisfaction and motivation are not synonymous. Motivation is a drive to perform, while job satisfaction reflects the individual's attitude or happiness with the job situation. The organizational reward system can influence both job satisfaction and employee motivation. The reward system affects job satisfaction by making the employee more or less comfortable as a result of the rewards received. The reward system influences motivation primarily through the perceived value of the rewards and their contingency on performance.

▼ **Figure 12–1**   Determinants of employee satisfaction and dissatisfaction

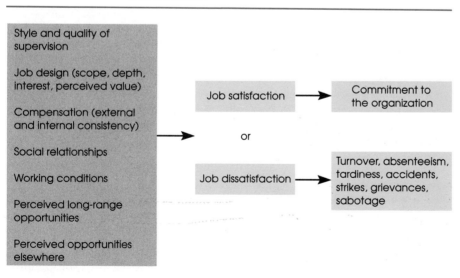

▼● **HRM in Action 12–3**

The Relationship Between Job Satisfaction and Job Performance

The assumption that job satisfaction and job performance are related has much intuitive appeal, and yet reviews of the literature and studies in this area do not support a strong relationship. In a comprehensive review of over 100 published studies involving job satisfaction and job performance, Michelle Iaffaldano and Paul Muchinsky concluded that "the best estimate of the true population correlation between satisfaction and performance is relatively low." Iaffaldano and Muchinsky go on to say that much of the variability in results obtained by different studies has been due to the use of small sample sizes.

Source: Michelle T. Iaffaldano and Paul M. Muchinsky, "Job Satisfaction and Job Performance: A Meta-Analysis," *Psychological Bulletin*, vol. 97, no. 2, 1985, pp. 251–273.

Employee Compensation

Compensation
All the extrinsic rewards that employees receive in exchange for their work; composed of the base wage or salary, any incentives or bonuses, and any benefits.

Pay
Refers only to the actual dollars that employees receive in exchange for their work.

Base wage or salary
The hourly, weekly, or monthly pay that employees receive for their work.

Incentives
Rewards offered in addition to the base wage or salary and usually directly related to performance.

Benefits
Rewards that employees receive as a result of their employment and position with an organization.

Compensation and pay are not synonymous terms. **Compensation** refers to all the extrinsic rewards that employees receive in exchange for their work. **Pay** refers only to the actual dollars that employees receive in exchange for their work. Usually, compensation is composed of the base wage or salary, any incentives or bonuses, and any benefits. The **base wage or salary** is the hourly, weekly, or monthly pay that employees receive for their work. **Incentives** are rewards offered in addition to the base wage or salary and are usually directly related to performance. **Benefits** are rewards that employees receive as a result of their employment and position with an organization. Paid vacations, health insurance, and retirement plans are examples of benefits. Table 12–2 presents some examples of the different types of compensation. The next three chapters in this book are devoted to base wage or salaries, incentives, and benefits, respectively.

Compensation Policies

Certain policies must be formulated before a successful compensation system can be developed and implemented. Naturally, these policies are strongly influenced by an organization's objectives and its environment. Policies must deal with the following issues:[12]

1. What the minimum and maximum levels of pay are (taking into consideration the worth of the job to the organization, its ability to pay, government regulations, union influences, and market pressures).
2. What the general relationships among levels of pay are (between senior management and operating management, operative employees, and supervisors).
3. The division of the total compensation dollar is (i.e., what portion goes into base pay, into incentive programs, and into benefits).

▼ **Table 12–2**   Components of employee compensation

Base Wage or Salary	Incentives	Benefits
Hourly wage	Bonuses	Paid vacation
Weekly, monthly, or annual salary	Commissions	Health insurance
	Profit sharing	Life insurance
Overtime pay	Piece rate plans	Retirement pension

In addition to the above issues, decisions must be made concerning how much money will go into pay increases for the next year, who will recommend them, and, generally, how raises will be determined. Another important decision concerns whether pay information will be kept secret or made public.

Pay Secrecy

Many organizations have a policy of keeping pay-related information secret. This includes information about the pay system as well as individual pay received. The justification for pay secrecy is usually to avoid any discontent that might result from employees knowing what everybody else is being paid. Further justification is that many employees, especially high achievers, feel very strongly that their pay is nobody else's business.[13]

On the other hand, pay secrecy makes it difficult for individuals to determine whether pay is related to performance. Also, pay secrecy does not eliminate pay comparisons, but it may cause employees to overestimate the pay of their peers and underestimate the pay of their supervisors.[14] Both situations can create unnecessary feelings of dissatisfaction. Recent research indicates that pay secrecy versus openness may influence managerial pay allocations.[15]

A good compromise on the issue of pay secrecy is to disclose the pay ranges for various job levels within the organization. This approach clearly communicates the general ranges of pay for different jobs but it does not disclose exactly what any particular individual is making. HRM in Action 12–4 describes how Atlantic Richfield Company is making a point of educating its employees about its salary and pay system.

Government and Union Influence

Government legislation and union contracts are factors that can have a significant impact on organizational compensation. Both of these are discussed in the following sections.

Fair Labor Standards Act (FLSA)

The FLSA, commonly called the Wage and Hour Act, was passed in 1938 and has been amended several times. Its primary requirements are that individuals employed in interstate commerce or in organizations producing goods for interstate commerce must be paid a certain minimum wage and must be paid time and a

▼. HRM in Action 12–4

Educating Employees about Salary Systems at Atlantic Richfield Company

Salary systems are usually a secret in most companies, but not at Atlantic Richfield Company (ARCO). ARCO has initiated a conscientious effort to better inform its employees about its salary and pay system. ARCO began its effort by discussing the subject in its employee magazine. The article began by discussing why competitive salaries are necessary for the company (to attract, retain, and motivate their employees). The article further discussed precisely how salary grades and ranges are established. The article also explained how employees need to be careful when comparing their pay with that of employees in other jobs. The point made is that employees should be sure that they are comparing "apples to apples."

Source: Phil Farish, "Pay Talk," *Personnel Administrator*, August 1987, p. 14.

half for hours over 40 worked in one week. (Table 12–3 shows how the minimum wage has changed over the years.) Section 218 of the FLSA permits states, localities, and collective bargaining agreements to set a higher standard than the federal minimum. In addition, the FLSA places restrictions on the employment of individuals between the ages of 14 and 18. The most complex parts of the law deal with possible exemptions. Amendments to the law have reduced the number of exemptions, but careful study is necessary to determine an organization's obligations.

In discussions of compensation systems, the terms *exempt* and *nonexempt personnel* are often used. Nonexempt employees are covered by the FLSA; they must be paid overtime and are subject to a minimum wage. Among those exempt from coverage under FLSA are executive, administrative, and professional personnel.

Davis-Bacon Act

Passed by Congress on March 3, 1931, the Davis-Bacon Act requires that contractors and subcontractors on federal construction contracts in excess of $2,000 pay the prevailing wage rates for the locality of the project. This prevailing wage rate, which is determined by the secretary of labor, has normally been the same as the prevailing union rate for the area.

Walsh-Healey Public Contracts Act

The Walsh-Healey Public Contracts Act was passed by Congress on June 30, 1936. This act requires that organizations manufacturing for or furnishing to the federal government materials, supplies, articles, or equipment in excess of $10,000 pay at least the minimum wage for the industry, as determined by the secretary of labor.

Federal Wage Garnishment Law

Garnishment
A legal procedure by which an employer is empowered to withhold wages for payment of an employee's debt to a creditor.

Garnishment is a legal procedure by which an employer is empowered to withhold wages for payment of an employee's debt to a creditor. The Federal Wage Garnishment Law, which became effective on July 1, 1970, limits the amount of an employee's disposable earnings that can be garnished in any one week and protects the individual from discharge because of garnishment. However, the law did not substantially alter state laws on this subject. For instance, if the state law prohibits or provides for more limited garnishment than the federal law, the state law is

▼   Table 12-3   History of minimum wage rates

Rate	Rate per Hour
October 24, 1938	$0.25
October 24, 1939	0.30
October 24, 1945	0.40
January 25, 1950	0.75
March 1, 1956	1.00
September 3, 1961	1.15
September 3, 1963	1.25
February 1, 1967	1.40
February 1, 1968	1.60
May 1, 1974	2.00
January 1, 1975	2.10
January 1, 1976	2.30
January 1, 1978	2.65
January 1, 1979	2.90
January 1, 1980	3.10
January 1, 1981	3.35
April 1, 1990	3.80
April 1, 1991	4.25

applied. Thus, a human resource manager must be familiar with applicable state laws relating to garnishment.

Equal Pay Act

Signed into law on June 10, 1963, the federal Equal Pay Act was an amendment to the Fair Labor Standards Act, eliminating pay differentials based solely on sex. The law makes it illegal to pay different wages to men and women on jobs that require equal skill, effort, and responsibility and that are performed under similar conditions.

This law does not prohibit the payment of wage differentials based on seniority systems, merit systems that measure earnings by quantity and quality of production, or systems based on any factor other than sex.

Union Contracts

If an organization is unionized, the wage structure usually is largely determined through the collective bargaining process. Because wages are a primary concern of unions, current union contracts must be considered in formulating compensation policies. Union contracts can even affect nonunionized organizations. For example, the wage rates and increases paid to union employees often influence the wages paid to employees in nonunion organizations.

The Importance of Fair Pay

As discussed earlier in this chapter, employee motivation is closely related to the types of rewards offered and their method of disbursement. While there is considerable debate over the motivational aspect of pay, there is little doubt that inadequate pay can have a very negative impact on an organization. Figure 12-2 presents a simple model that summarizes the reactions of employees when they

▼ **Figure 12–2**   Model of the consequences of pay dissatisfaction

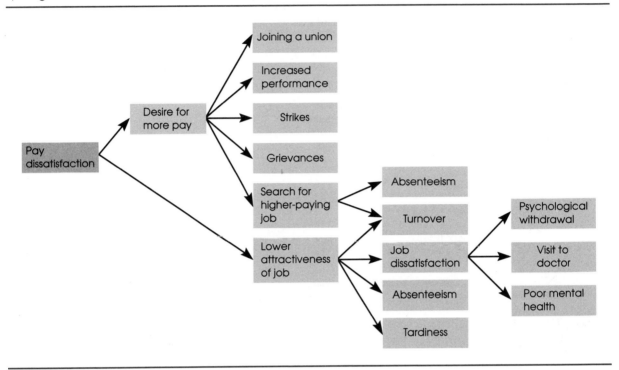

Source: Adapted from Edward E. Lawler III, *Pay and Organizational Effectiveness: A Psychological View* (New York: McGraw-Hill, 1971), p. 233.

are dissatisfied with their pay. According to this model, pay dissatisfaction can influence employees' feelings about their jobs in two ways: (1) it can increase the desire for more money, and (2) it can lower the attractiveness of the job. An individual who has a desire for more money is likely to engage in actions that can increase pay. These actions might include joining a union, looking for another job, performing better, filing a grievance, or going on strike. With the exception of performing better, all of the consequences are generally classified as being undesirable by management. Better performance happens only in those cases where pay is perceived as being directly related to performance. On the other hand, when the job decreases in attractiveness, the individual is more likely to be absent, tardy, quit, or become dissatisfied with the job itself. Thus, while its importance may vary somewhat from situation to situation, pay satisfaction can and usually does have a significant impact on both individual and organizational performance.

Pay Equity

The equity theory of motivation basically holds that employees have a strong need to maintain a balance between what they perceive as their inputs to their jobs and what they receive from their jobs in the form of rewards. Under this theory, employees who perceive inequities will take action to eliminate or reduce them.

For example, if an employee believes he or she is underpaid, that employee will likely reduce expended effort by working slower, taking off early, or being absent. Similarly, if an employee feels he or she is being overpaid, that employee is likely to work harder, or for longer hours.

Pay equity is concerned with whether employees feel that they are being fairly paid. In looking at pay equity there are several dimensions of equity that must be considered. **Internal equity** is concerned with what an employee is being paid for doing a given job compared to what other employees in the same organization are being paid to do their jobs. **External equity** deals with what employees in other organizations are being paid for performing similar jobs. **Individual equity** addresses the issue of rewarding individual contributions and is very closely related to the pay-for-performance question. **Organizational equity** is concerned with how profits are divided up within the organization. In other words, do the employees feel that the organization's profits are fairly distributed? It is important to recognize that employee interpretations of pay equity are based on their perceptions of these dimensions. Because employee feelings about pay equity are based on perceptions, organizations should do whatever they can to make these perceptions as accurate as possible. Also, it is not unusual for an employee to feel good about one or more of the equity dimensions and bad about the others. For example, an employee may feel good about his or her pay in comparison to what friends working in other organizations are making. He or she might also feel that the company profits are fairly distributed within the company. However, this same person may be very unhappy about his or her pay relative to several other people in the same organization.

Internal equity
Addresses the issue of what an employee is being paid for doing a job compared to what other employees in the same organization are being paid to do their jobs.

External equity
Addresses the issue of what employees in an organization are being paid compared to employees in other organizations performing similar jobs.

Individual equity
Addresses the issue of rewarding individual contributions; is very closely related to the pay-for-performance question.

Organizational equity
Addresses the issue of how profits are divided up within the organization.

Pay Satisfaction Model

Figure 12–3 presents Edward Lawler's model of the determinants of pay satisfaction. The model is based on the idea that people will be satisfied with their pay when their perception of what their pay is and of what they think it should be are in agreement. This happens when employees feel good about the internal and external equity of their pay.

Naturally, present pay is a primary factor that influences a person's perception of equity. However, the person's wage history and perception of what others are getting also have an influence. For example, people who have historically received high pay tend to lower their perception of present pay. Similarly, the higher the pay of friends and peers, the lower one's individual pay appears. These factors account for the fact that two people might view the same amount of pay in a very different manner.

The model also shows that a person's perception of what pay should be depends on several other factors, including job inputs, the perceived inputs and outcomes of friends and peers, and nonmonetary outcomes. Job inputs include all the experience, skills, and abilities that an individual brings to the job, in addition to the effort the person puts into the job. The perceived inputs and outcomes refer to the individual's perception of what friends and peers put into their jobs and what kind of pay they get in return. The nonmonetary outcomes received refer to the fact that certain nonmonetary rewards can sometimes substitute for pay, at least up to a point.

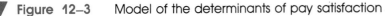

▼ **Figure 12–3** Model of the determinants of pay satisfaction

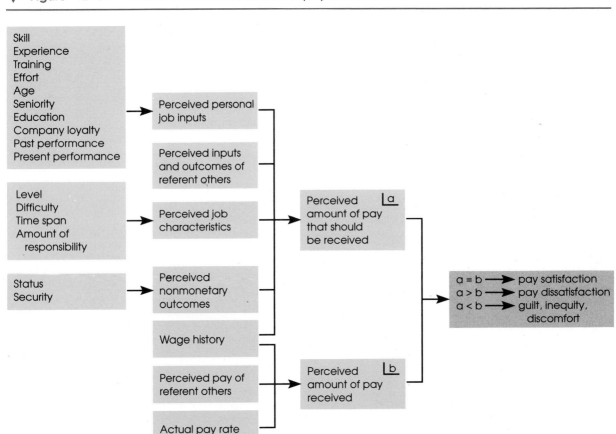

Source: Edward E. Lawler III, *Pay and Organizational Effectiveness: A Psychological View* (New York: McGraw-Hill, 1971), p. 215.

It is also interesting to note that the model makes allowances for people who feel that their pay exceeds what they think it should be. Research has shown that in such cases, people often experience feelings of guilt, inequity, and discomfort.[16]

The Role of the Human Resource Manager in the Reward System

The role of the human resource manager in the overall organizational reward system is to assist in its design and to administer the system. Administering the system inherently carries the responsibility of ensuring that the system is fair to all employees. This places the burden of minimizing real reward inequities and employees' perceptions of reward inequities squarely on the human resource manager. Many tools and techniques are available to assist human resource managers in this endeavor, and many of these are discussed in the following three chapters.

● *Summary of Learning Objectives*

1. Define organizational rewards.

Organizational rewards include all types of rewards, both intrinsic and extrinsic, that are received as a result of employment by the organization.

2. Distinguish between intrinsic and extrinsic rewards.

Intrinsic rewards are rewards internal to the individual and are normally derived from involvement in certain activities or tasks. Extrinsic rewards are directly controlled and distributed by the organization and are more tangible than intrinsic rewards.

3. List several desirable preconditions for implementing a pay-for-performance program.

Several preconditions have been identified for implementing a successful pay-for-performance program. These include: (1) trust in management, (2) absence of performance constraints, (3) trained supervisors and managers, (4) good measurement systems, (5) ability to pay, (6) clear distinction among cost of living, seniority, and merit, (7) well-communicated total pay policy, and (8) flexible reward schedule.

4. Define job satisfaction and list its five major components.

Job satisfaction is an individual's general attitude about the job. The five major components of job satisfaction are (1) attitude toward the work group, (2) general working conditions, (3) attitude toward the company, (4) monetary benefits, and (5) attitude toward supervision.

5. Summarize the satisfaction-performance relationship.

Research evidence generally rejects the popular view that satisfaction causes performance. The evidence does, however, provide moderate support for the view that performance causes satisfaction. The evidence also provides strong indications that rewards constitute a more direct cause of satisfaction than does performance, and rewards based on current performance cause subsequent performance.

6. Define compensation, pay, incentives, and benefits.

Compensation refers to all the extrinsic rewards that employees receive in exchange for their work. Incentives are rewards offered in addition to the base wage or salary and are directly related to performance. Benefits are rewards that employees receive as a result of their employment and position with an organization.

7. List several pieces of government legislation that have had a significant impact on organizational compensation.

Numerous pieces of government legislation have been passed that affect organizational compensation. Some of the most significant include the Fair Labor Standards Act (FLSA), the Davis-Bacon Act, the Walsh-Healey Public Contracts Act, the Federal Wage Garnishment Law, and the Equal Pay Act.

8. Explain the equity theory of motivation.

The equity theory of motivation holds that employees have a strong need to maintain a balance between what they perceive as their inputs to their jobs and what they receive from their jobs in the form of rewards. Under this theory, employees who perceive inequities will take action to eliminate or reduce the inequity.

9. Discuss internal, external, individual, and organizational equity.

Internal equity is concerned with what an employee is being paid for doing a given job compared to what other employees in the same organization are being paid to do their jobs. External equity deals with what employees in other organizations are being paid for performing similar jobs. Individual equity addresses the issue of rewarding individual contributions and is very closely related to the pay-for-performance question. Organizational equity is concerned with how profits are divided up within the organization.

Review Questions

1. What are organizational rewards?
2. Explain the differences between intrinsic and extrinsic rewards.
3. What are some variables that have been found to influence employee preferences for certain rewards?
4. Discuss two reasons why organizations do a poor job of relating rewards to performance.
5. List eight preconditions that have been found to be desirable for establishing a successful pay-for-performance program.
6. What is job satisfaction? What are its major components?
7. Discuss the satisfaction-performance controversy.
8. Define compensation and distinguish it from pay.
9. What is the primary organizational variable that can be used to reward individuals and reinforce performance?
10. Describe some of the consequences of pay dissatisfaction.
11. What are the two general factors relating to the question of fair pay?
12. Describe Lawler's pay satisfaction model. How is pay satisfaction determined by the model?

Discussion Questions

1. The XYZ Company has just decided to take all of its 200 employees to Las Vegas for an expense-paid, three-day weekend to show its appreciation for their high level of performance this past year. What is your reaction to this idea?
2. Comment on the following statement: "Employees are not capable of deciding what rewards they should receive."
3. Recently, a manager was overheard making the following comment: "Most employees are never satisfied with their pay anyway, so why should we even try? I think we should pay as little as possible and just accept the fact that the employees won't like it." If you were this manager's superior, what would you say?
4. Do you think that a very loyal employee is necessarily a good employee? Why?

▼ *INCIDENT 12–1*

An Informative Coffee Break

On Monday morning, April 28, George Smith was given the news that effective May 1 he would receive a raise of 13 percent. This raise came two months before his scheduled performance appraisal. He was informed by his manager Tom Weeks that the basis for the raise was his performance over the past several months and his potential worth to the company. He was told that this was a very considerable increase.

On the next day, Tuesday, a group of fellow workers in George's office were engaging in their normal coffee break. The course of conversation swung to salary increases. One of the group had received a performance review in April, but no indication of an impending salary adjustment had been given. George made a comment concerning the amount of any such increase, specifically questioning the range of increase percentages. A third individual immediately responded, expressing surprise at having received an across-the-board 12 percent increase the previous Friday. A fourth individual had received a similar salary increase. Definitely astounded, George pressed for information, only to learn that several people had received increases of "around" 11 to 13 percent. George broke up the gathering by excusing himself.

That evening, George wrestled with his conscience concerning the foregoing discussion. His first impression of his raise was that it had been given based on performance. His second impression was decidedly sour. Several questions were bothering him:

1. Why did his boss present the raise as a merit increase?
2. Is job performance really a basis for salary increases in his department?
3. Did his superior hide the truth regarding the raise?
4. Can he trust his boss in the future?
5. On what basis will further increases be issued?

Questions

1. What effect do you think that this new information will have on the effort put forth by George Smith?
2. What can Tom Weeks do to regain George Smith's confidence?

▼ *INCIDENT 12–2*

Does Money Motivate?

About four months ago, Greg Holcomb was promoted to supervisor of the claims department for a large eastern insurance company. It is now time for all supervisors to make their annual salary increase recommendations. Greg doesn't feel comfortable in making these recommendations since he has only been in his job for a short time. To further complicate the situation, the former supervisor has left the company and is unavailable for consultation.

There are no formal company restrictions on the kind of raises that can be given, but Greg's boss has said that the total amount of money available to Greg for raises would be 8 percent of Greg's total payroll for the past year. In other words, if the sum total of the salaries for all of Greg's employees was $100,000, then Greg would have $8,000 to allocate for raises. Greg is free to distribute the raises just about any way he wants, within reason.

Summarized below is the best information on his employees that Greg can find from the files of the former supervisor of the claims department. This information is supplemented by feelings Greg has developed during his short time as supervisor.

Sam Jones. Sam has been with Greg's department for only five months. In fact, he was hired just before Greg was promoted into the supervisor's job. Sam is single and seems to be a carefree bachelor. His job performance, so far, has been above average, but Greg has received some negative comments about Sam from his coworkers. Present salary: $26,000.

Sue Davis. Sue has been on the job for three years. Her previous performance appraisals have indicated superior performance. However, Greg does not feel that the previous evaluations are accurate. He feels that Sue's performance is average at best. Sue appears to be well-liked by all of her coworkers. Just last year, she became widowed and is presently the sole supporter of her five-year-old child. Present salary: $28,000.

Evelyn Boyd. Evelyn has been on the job for four years. Her previous performance appraisals were all average. In addition, she has received below-average increases for the past two years. However, Evelyn recently approached Greg and told him that she feels she was discriminated against in the past due to both her age and sex. Greg feels that Evelyn's work so far has been satisfactory but not superior. Most employees don't seem to sympathize with Evelyn's accusations of sex and age discrimination. Present salary: $24,000.

Jane Simond. As far as Greg can tell, Jane is one of his best employees. Her previous performance appraisals also indicate that she is a superior performer. In addition, Greg knows that Jane badly needs a substantial salary increase due to some personal problems. In addition, all of Greg's employees are aware of Jane's problems. She appears to be well-respected by her coworkers. Present salary: $25,000.

Ralph Dubose. Ralph has been performing his present job for eight years. The job is very technical, and he would be difficult to replace. However, as far as Greg can discern Ralph is not a good worker. He is irritable and hard to work with. In spite of this, Ralph has received above-average pay increases for the past two years. Present salary: $30,000.

Questions

1. Indicate the size of the raise that you would give each of these employees.
2. What criteria did you use in determining the size of the raise?
3. What do you think would be the feelings of the other people in the group if they should find out what raises you recommend?

4. Do you feel that the employees would eventually find out what raises others received? Would it matter?

Exercise

Relating Rewards to Performance

Think of the most recent job you have held. This job could have been a summer, part-time, or full-time job. Which of the two situations described below best characterizes this job?

A. Rewards (monetary and nonmonetary) were tied directly to one's level of performance; management did attempt to discriminate between the high and low performers and did reward accordingly.

B. Everyone within very broad, general categories received basically the same rewards; one's level of performance did not substantially affect the rewards received.

Depending on which situation you selected, what effect do you think it had on your level of motivation? If you selected Situation A, explain basically how the system worked. If you selected Situation B, what specific recommendations would you make to improve the performance-reward relationship? Be prepared to discuss your answers with the class.

Notes and Additional Readings

1. J. Brad Chapman and Robert Ottemann, "Employee Preference for Various Compensation Fringe Benefit Options," *Personnel Administrator,* November 1975, p. 34.
2. Many of the basic motivation theories (e.g., Herzberg's dual-factor theory or Maslow's need theory) are based on the assumption that intrinsic rewards greatly influence one's level of motivation.
3. Frederick S. Hills, Robert M. Madigan, K. Dow Scott, and Steven E. Markham, "Tracking the Merit of Merit Pay," *Personnel Administrator,* March 1987, p. 50.
4. E. James Brennan, "The Myth and the Reality of Pay for Performance," *Personnel Journal,* March 1985, p. 73.
5. The following preconditions are drawn from Hills, Madigan, Scott, and Markham, "Tracking the Merit," pp. 56–57.
6. Phillip B. Applewhite, *Organizational Behavior* (Englewood Cliffs, N.J.: Prentice-Hall, 1965), p. 22.
7. Charles N. Greene, "The Satisfaction-Performance Controversy," *Business Horizons,* October 1972, p. 31.
8. Ibid., p. 32.

9. Ibid., p. 40.

10. John M. Ivancevich, "The Performance to Satisfaction Relationship: A Casual Analysis of Stimulating and Nonstimulating Jobs," *Organizational Behavior and Human Performance* 22 (1978), pp. 350–64.

11. Donald P. Schwab and Larry I. Cummings, "Theories of Performance and Satisfactions: A Review," *Industrial Relations,* October 1970, pp. 408–29. For a complete summary of the related research, see E. A. Locke, "The Nature and Causes of Job Satisfaction," in *Handbook of Industrial and Organizational Psychology,* ed. M. D. Dunnette (Skokie, Ill.: Rand McNally, 1976), p. 1343.

12. Richard I. Henderson, *Compensation Management: Rewarding Performance,* 3d ed. (Reston, Va.: Reston Publishing, 1979), pp. 264–65.

13. P. Thompson and J. Pronsky, "Secrecy or Disclosure in Management Compensation," *Business Horizons,* June 1975, pp. 67–74.

14. E. E. Lawler III, "Managers' Perceptions of Their Superiors' Pay and their Supervisors' Pay," *Personnel Psychology,* Winter 1965, p. 413; and E. E. Lawler III, "Should Managers' Compensation Be Kept under Wraps?" *Personnel,* January–February 1965, p. 17.

15. Kathyrn M. Bartol and David C. Martin, "Effects of Dependency, Dependency Threats, and Pay Secrecy on Managerial Pay Allocations," *Journal of Applied Psychology,* vol. 74, no. 2, 1989, p. 112.

16. E. E. Lawler III, *Pay and Organizational Effectiveness: A Psychological View* (New York: McGraw-Hill, 1971), pp. 244–47.

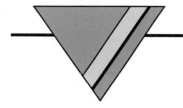

Chapter 13

Base Wage and Salary Systems

Chapter Outline

Objective of the Base Wage and Salary System

Job Evaluation

Point Method
Selection of Key Jobs
Selecting Compensable Factors
Assigning Weights to Factors
Assigning Points to Specific Jobs

Factor Comparison Method

Job Classification Method
Job Ranking Method
Comparison of Job Evaluation Methods

Pricing the Job

Wage and Salary Surveys
Wage and Salary Curves

Base Wage/Salary Structure

Summary of Learning Objectives

Review Questions

Discussion Questions

Incident 13–1: Fair Pay for Pecan Workers

Incident 13–2: A Dead-End Street?

Exercise: Ranking Jobs

Notes and Additional Readings

Learning Objectives

After studying this chapter, you should be able to:

1. Define base wages and salaries and state the objective of any base wage and salary system.
2. Define job evaluation.
3. Name and briefly discuss the four basic methods of job evaluation.
4. Explain the concepts of key jobs and compensable factors.
5. Differentiate between subfactors and degrees.
6. Explain the purpose of wage and salary surveys.
7. Discuss wage and salary curves.
8. Define pay grades and pay ranges.

*"E*mployees who do not have sufficient funds to support their reasonable family needs are distracted from their efforts. Accordingly, the organization should attempt to have salary measure the job itself and provide enough money for reasonable living costs. Incentive compensation is to measure variations in performance."

Robert Townsend*

Base wages and salaries
The hourly, weekly, and monthly pay that employees receive for their work.

Base wages and salaries are the hourly, weekly, or monthly pay that employees receive in exchange for their work. In most situations, base wages or salaries make up the largest portion of an individual's total compensation. In light of the facts that many organizations do not pay incentives and that many employees discount or take for granted the value of benefits, base wages and salaries are the focus of the compensation system in the eyes of employees.

Base wages and salaries form the foundation for most employees' perceptions as to the fairness or equity of the pay system. As discussed in the previous chapter, if employees do not perceive that they are being fairly paid, there are many possible negative effects (tardiness, absenteeism, turnover, strikes, etc.). There is also something to be said for the fact that the base wage and salary system often reflects the tone or atmosphere of the entire organization. If the base wage and salary system is perceived as being fair and equitable, then the organization is usually viewed in the same light. Of course, the reverse of this is also true. Because of its significance to the entire organization, it is critical that an organization develop and maintain a sound base wage and salary system.

Objective of the Base Wage and Salary System

The primary objective of any base wage and salary system is to establish a structure and system for the equitable payment of employees, depending on their job and their level of performance in their job. While this objective is straightforward and clear, successfully attaining it is not an easy matter. Table 13–1 represents some of the basic policy questions that need to be addressed as a first step in establishing a base wage and salary system.

Most base wage and salary systems establish pay ranges for certain jobs, based on the relative worth of the job to the organization. An individual's performance on the job should then determine where that individual's pay falls within the job's range. The key to a sound base wage and salary system is the establishment of different pay ranges for the different jobs within the organization. A pay range for a given job establishes a range of permissible pay, with a minimum and a

*Source: Robert Townsend, *Up the Organization* (New York: Alfred A. Knopf, 1970), p. 76.

▼ **Table 13–1**   Specific policy issues in developing and implementing a base wage and salary structure

1. What is the lowest rate of pay that can be offered for a job that will entice the quality of employees the organization desires to have as its members?
2. What is the rate of pay that must be offered to incumbents to ensure that they remain with the organization?
3. Does the organization desire to recognize seniority and meritorious performance through the base pay schedule?
4. Is it wise or necessary to offer more than one rate of pay to employees performing either identical or similar work?
5. What is considered to be a sufficient difference in base rates of pay among jobs requiring varying levels of knowledge and skills and of responsibilities and duties?
6. Does the organization wish to recognize dangerous and distressing working conditions within the base pay schedule?
7. Should there be a difference in base pay progression opportunities among jobs of varying worth?
8. Do employees have a significant opportunity to higher-level jobs? If so, what should be the relationship between promotion to a higher job and changes in base pay?
9. Will policies and regulations permit incumbents to earn rates of pay higher than established maximums and lower than established minimums? What would be the reasons for allowing such deviations?
10. How will the pay structure accommodate across-the-board, cost-of-living, or other adjustments not related to employee tenure, performance, or responsibility and duty changes?

Source: R. I. Henderson, *Compensation Management: Rewarding Performance*, 3d ed. 1979, pp. 264–65. Reprinted with permission of Reston Publishing Co., a Prentice-Hall Co., 11480 Sunset Hills Road, Reston, VA 22090.

maximum. Establishing pay ranges involves two basic phases: (1) determining the relative worth of the different jobs to the organization (ensuring internal equity) and (2) pricing the different jobs (ensuring external equity). Job evaluation is the primary method used to determine the relative worth of jobs to the organization. Wage surveys represent one of the most commonly used tools for pricing jobs. Both job evaluation and wage surveys are discussed in the following sections. HRM in Action 13–1 describes how base wages differ among the major companies in the pork packing industry.

Job Evaluation

Job evaluation is a systematic determination of the value of each job in relation to other jobs in the organization. This process is used for designing a pay structure, not for appraising the performance of individuals holding the jobs. The general idea of job evaluation is to enumerate the requirements of a job and the job's contribution to the organization and then to classify it according to importance. For instance, a design engineer's job would involve more complex requirements and a potentially greater contribution to an organization than that of an assembler of the designed product. Although both jobs are important, a determination must be made concerning the relative worth of each. While the overriding purpose of

Job evaluation
A systematic determination of the value of each job in relation to other jobs in the organization.

▽. HRM in Action 13–1

Base Wage Variability in the Pork Packing Industry

The United Food & Commercial Workers' Union represents about 31,000 workers in pork packing. The recession of the early 1980s forced many union locals to negotiate agreements that were separate from the national union. As a result, base wages in the pork packing industry have been declining steadily in recent years to about 40 percent below the 1980 wage of $10.69 per hour, and they differ widely from company to company. Since wage costs make up 50 percent of meatpackers' operating costs, differences in wage rates are a key competitive element between companies. Wage rates are also critical since net margins in the industry are expected to remain below an anemic 1 percent.

1985 Figures from the United Food & Commercial Workers' Union showed that the 2,900 workers at Hormel were the highest paid in the industry at $9.00, the 2,500 workers at nonunion Armour were among the lowest paid at $6.00 per hour. Swift & Company workers were in the middle with a base wage of $8.75 per hour.

Source: Patrick Houston and Aaron Bernstein, "The Pork Workers' Beef: Pay Cuts that Persist," *Business Week*, April 15, 1985, pp. 74–76.

job evaluation is to establish the relative worth of jobs, it can serve several other purposes. Table 13–2 presents a list of potential uses of job evaluations.

The first step in a job evaluation program is to gather information on the jobs being evaluated. Normally, information is obtained from current job descriptions. If current job descriptions do not exist, then it is usually necessary to analyze the jobs and create up-to-date descriptions.

The job evaluation process then identifies the factor or factors that are to be used in determining the worth of different jobs to the organization. Some frequently used factors are skill, responsibility, and working conditions.

The job evaluation process also involves developing and implementing a plan that uses the chosen factors for evaluating the relative worth of the different jobs to the organization. Such a plan should consistently place jobs requiring more of the factors at a higher level in the job hierarchy than jobs requiring fewer of the factors. Most job evaluation plans are variations or combinations of four basic methods: point, factor comparison, job classification, and job ranking.

Point Method

Point method

Job evaluation method in which a quantitative point scale is used to evaluate jobs on a factor-by-factor basis.

Surveys have shown that the point method has historically been the most widely used job evaluation plan in the United States (see HRM in Action 13–2). It has the advantages of being relatively simple to use and reasonably objective. When the **point method** is used, a quantitative point scale is developed for the jobs being evaluated. One scale usually cannot be used to evaluate all types of jobs. For example, different scales are normally required for clerical and production jobs. Another scale is usually required to evaluate management and professional jobs. Usually, the human resource department decides which jobs are to be included in a specific evaluation scale.

▼ **Table 13–2**   Potential uses of job evaluations

- To provide a basis for a simpler, more rational wage structure.
- To provide an agreed-on means of classifying new or changed jobs.
- To provide a means of comparing jobs and pay rates with those of other organizations.
- To provide a base for individual performance measurements.
- To reduce pay grievances by reducing their scope and providing an agreed-on means of resolving disputes.
- To provide incentives for employees to strive for higher-level jobs.
- To provide information for wage negotiations.
- To provide data on job relationships for use in internal and external selection, personnel planning, career management, and other personnel functions.

Source: David W. Belcher/Thomas J. Atchison, *Compensation Administration*, 2e, © 1987, p. 151. Reprinted by permission of Prentice Hall, Inc., Englewood Cliffs, New Jersey.

Selection of Key Jobs

After deciding which jobs are to be evaluated on each specific scale, key (benchmark) jobs are selected. Key jobs represent jobs that are common throughout the industry or in the general locale under study. The content of key jobs should be commonly understood. If there is any confusion about the description of a job or what its pay should be, it should probably not be selected as a key job. The general idea is to select a limited number (20 percent is a good measure) of key jobs that are representative of the entire pay structure and the major kinds of work being evaluated.[1] The selection of key jobs should adequately represent the span of responsibilities, duties, and work requirements of the jobs being evaluated. Because key jobs usually represent only a small number of all jobs being evaluated, they may supply only a limited amount of data. However, the commonality and acceptance of key jobs provide a basis for sound understanding and agreement. The goal here is to select enough key jobs to represent each major internal variable in the pay structure for all the jobs being evaluated. A full and detailed job description is necessary for each key job.

Selecting Compensable Factors

Compensable factors are those factors or characteristics of jobs that are deemed important by the organization to the extent that it is willing to pay for them. The degree to which a specific job possesses these compensable factors determines its relative worth.

Early approaches to job evaluation proposed a set of universal factors. The belief was that a given set of factors—usually skill, responsibility, and working conditions—should apply to all jobs. This theory has gradually been replaced by one postulating that each organization must tailor its compensable factors to fit its own special requirements. Thus, complete adoption of any set of universal factors is not recommended.[2] For example, the compensable factors selected for

Compensable factors
Characteristics of jobs that are deemed important by the organization to the extent that it is willing to pay for them.

▼. HRM in Action 13–2

Job Evaluation Systems in Chicago

A survey by the Human Resources Management Association of Chicago of 97 firms in that city reported that the point method was by far the most widely used job evaluation system. Specifically, the point method was used for 45 percent of exempt positions, 42 percent of salaried nonexempt positions, and 24 percent of hourly positions. Thirty-one percent of the responding companies used the point method at the executive level, and 22 percent used it for senior officers.

Nineteen of the firms reported that they did not use

a formal job evaluation system for hourly employees, 15 stated that they did not use a system for executives, and 20 reported that they did not use a system for senior officers. Of the systems currently being used, 50 percent were custom developed. Over one-third of the systems have been in place for more than 10 years. Fewer than 10 percent of the companies indicated a low degree of satisfaction with their present job evaluation programs.

Source: Phil Farish, "Job Rank Study," *Personnel Administrator*, June 1987, p. 18.

---

evaluating production jobs might include skill, effort, and working conditions, whereas the compensable factors selected for evaluating managerial and professional jobs might be knowledge, responsibility, and decision-making requirements. Compensable factors selected for unionized jobs must be acceptable to both management and the union.

Job subfactor
A detailed breakdown of a single compensable factor of a job.

In the point method, **subfactors** are used to describe compensable factors in more detail. For instance, the compensable factor of responsibility might include subfactors for determining organizational policy, responsibility for the work of others, responsibility for the development and maintenance of customer goodwill, or responsibility for organizational assets. **Degree statements**, or profile statements as they are sometimes called, describe the specific requirements of each subfactor. Because each profile is unique, degree statements usually are in the form of written phrases. Table 13–3 presents possible degrees and subfactors for the compensable factor of responsibility. Breaking compensable factors into subfactors and degrees allows for a more precise definition of the job and facilitates the evaluation process.

Degree statements
Written statements used as a part of the point method of job evaluation to further break down job subfactors.

Assigning Weights to Factors

Weights are assigned to each of the factors, subfactors, and degrees to reflect their relative importance. Naturally, the weight assigned varies from job to job. For example, skill might be the most important factor used in evaluating a machinist's job, while responsibility might be more critical to a supervisor's job.

While there are some systematic and helpful approaches for assigning weights, there is no one best method. Regardless of the technique used, both past experience and judgment play major roles in assigning weights. Generally, weights are assigned on the basis of a maximum number of points for any job; this number is often decided arbitrarily. Points are then assigned to the compensable factors, subfactors, and degrees on the basis of their relative importance. Table 13–4 presents a possible point breakdown that totals 1,000 points. In this example, the compensable factor of responsibility was deemed to be the most important factor and was awarded 360 points. The factor of responsibility was divided in four subfactors: responsibility for company policy, responsibility for the work of others, responsibility for

▼ **Table 13–3**   Possible subfactors and degrees for the compensable factor of responsibility

Subfactors	First Degree	Second Degree	Third Degree	Fourth Degree
Determining organizational policy	May make suggestions to superior as to changes, most often minor, in organizational policy.	Often suggests changes in procedures applying mostly to affairs within departments.	May determine minor policies of organization with close control of supervisors; may interpret organizational policy to subordinates.	Determines organizational policy for large group of workers; incorrect execution would result in considerable loss.
Work of others; managerial ability required	Responsible only for own work, including individual work or work of "flow" nature.	Small amount of supervision; performs mechanical operations and may conrol some work.	Supervises many workers or a department, organizing and coordinating with other supervisors.	Responsible for coordination of groups of departments.
Development and maintenance of goodwill with customers and public	Has very little contact with customers or public.	Only contact with customers and public is checked communications or occasional telephone calls.	Tact needed to avoid possible loss of goodwill through close contact with customers through letters or personal interviews.	Considerable contact with customers, other organizations, and public; tact and diplomacy needed.
Organization cash expenditures; judgment needed in expenditures of organization funds	Cash expenditures of not more than $100 monthly.	Cash expenditures of $101 to $300 monthly.	Cash expenditures of $301 to $1,000 monthly.	Cash expenditures of $1,001 to $5,000 monthly.

Source: Adapted from J. L. Otis and R. H. Leukart, *Job Evaluation,* 2d ed. (Englewood Cliffs, N.J.: Prentice-Hall, 1959), pp. 110–11.

▼ **Table 13–4**   Sample point values

Compensable Factor	Maximum Points	Subfactors	Assigned Points per Degree			
			First	Second	Third	Fourth
Skill	260	Job knowledge	35	70	105	140
		Experience	20	40	60	80
		Initiative	10	20	30	40
Effort	240	Physical	20	40	60	80
		Mental	40	80	120	160
Responsibility	360	For company policy	20	40	60	80
		For work of others	40	80	120	160
		For goodwill and public	20	40	60	80
		For company cash	10	20	30	40
Job conditions	140	Working conditions	20	40	60	80
		Hazards	15	30	45	60
Total possible points	1,000					

goodwill and public relations, and responsibility for company cash. Each subfactor was further divided into four degrees. It should be noted that the sum of the points for the highest degree for each of the subfactors totals the maximum number of points for the factor. In Table 13–4, 80 points to company policy plus 160 points for the work of others plus 80 points for goodwill and public relations plus 40 points for company cash equals 360 total points.

Assigning Points to Specific Jobs

After the point scale has been agreed on, point values are derived for key jobs, using the following steps:

1. Examine the job descriptions.
2. Determine the degree statement that best describes each subfactor for each compensable factor.
3. Add the total number of points.

The point totals should bear the same general relationships as the actual pay scales do for the key jobs. That is, a rank ordering of the key jobs according to point totals should be approximately equivalent to a rank ordering of key jobs according to pay. This serves as a check on the appropriateness of the points that have been assigned to the degrees, subfactors, and factors. Non-key jobs can be evaluated in the same manner by determining the appropriate points for each factor from the scale and then totaling the points. Table 13–5 illustrates possible point totals for several banking jobs.

One drawback to the point method is the amount of time required to develop the point scale. However, once a scale has been properly formulated for the key jobs, it does not take long to evaluate the remaining jobs.

Factor Comparison Method

Factor comparison method
Job evaluation technique that uses a monetary scale for evaluating jobs on a factor-by-factor basis.

The factor comparison method of job evaluation was originated by Eugene Benge in 1926 to overcome the inadequacies that he perceived in the point method.[3] The **factor comparison method** is similar to the point method except that it involves a monetary scale instead of a point scale. As with the point method, key jobs are selected. It is absolutely essential that the rates of pay of key jobs are viewed as reasonable and fair to all those making evaluations. Compensable factors are then identified, just as with the point method.

Unlike the point method, however, the factor comparison method does not break down the compensable factors into subfactors and degrees. Another difference between the two techniques involves the ranking of the compensable factors. In the factor comparison method, each compensable factor is ranked according to its importance in each of the key jobs. This is done by assigning a rank to every key job on one factor at a time, rather than ranking one job at a time on all factors. For example, Table 13–6 gives a factor-by-factor ranking of key jobs within a

▼ Table 13–5   Possible point totals for clerical jobs

Job	Points
Head teller	980
L&D (loan) teller	900
Teller	870
Secretary	750
Vault custodian	650
Bookkeeper	540
Courier	500

▼ Table 13–6   Factor-by-factor ranking of key banking jobs

Job	Compensable Factor				
	Mental Requirements	Skill	Physical	Responsibility	Working Conditions
Head teller	1	4	7	1	7
L&D (loan) teller	2	2	4	2	3
Teller	3	3	3	3	2
Secretary	4	5	6	5	5
Vault custodian	5	6	2	4	4
Bookkeeper	6	1	5	6	6
Courier	7	7	1	7	1

bank. Notice in Table 13–6 how each key job is ranked for each compensable factor. Many proponents of the factor comparison method suggest that to validate the rankings, they be done once or twice at later dates without reference to the previous rankings.

After each job has been ranked on a factor-by-factor basis, the next step is to allocate the wage or salary for each job according to the ranking of the factors. It is important to remember that one of the selection criteria of a key job is that its pay rate must be viewed as reasonable and fair by the evaluators. Some proponents of the factor comparison method say that the pay should be allocated without reference to the factor rankings; others believe that the evaluators should refer to the factor rankings when apportioning the pay. Regardless, the money allocation and the factor rankings must ultimately be consistent. If discrepancies occur that cannot be resolved, the job in question should be eliminated from the list of key jobs. Table 13–7 presents a sample pay allocation for the key jobs in Table 13–6. Notice how the figures for each column in Table 13–7 are consistent with the rankings for each column in Table 13–6.

As the final step in the factor comparison method, a monetary scale is prepared for each compensable factor. Each scale not only shows the rank order of the jobs but also establishes their relative differences in pay. Table 13–8 illustrates a monetary scale for the compensable factor of responsibility for banking jobs.

Other jobs are evaluated by studying their respective job descriptions and locating each job on the monetary scale for each compensable factor. The total

▼ **Table 13–7** Sample allocation pay for key banking jobs

| Job | Compensable Factor | | | | | Total |
	Mental Requirements	Skill	Physical	Responsibility	Working Conditions	
Head teller	$120.00	$39.00	$15.00	$75.00	$12.00	*261*
L&D (loan) teller	95.00	46.00	33.00	60.00	19.00	
Teller	90.00	45.00	39.00	51.00	21.00	
Secretary	85.00	44.00	18.00	30.00	15.00	
Vault custodian	58.00	21.00	60.00	36.00	16.00	
Bookkeeper	45.00	65.00	27.00	18.00	13.00	
Courier	40.00	16.00	71.00	9.00	27.00	*163*

▼ **Table 13–8** Monetary scale for responsibility requirements in banking jobs

Monetary Value/Week	Key Job	Monetary Value/Week	Key Job
$ 6.00			
9.00	Courier	$42.00	
12.00		45.00	
15.00		48.00	
18.00	Bookkeeper	51.00	Teller
21.00		54.00	
24.00		57.00	
27.00		60.00	L&D (loan) teller
30.00	Secretary	63.00	
33.00		66.00	
36.00	Vault custodian	69.00	
39.00		72.00	
		75.00	Head teller

worth of a given job is then determined by adding the dollar amounts assigned to each compensable factor.

Job Classification Method

Job classification method
Job evaluation method that determines the relative worth of a job by comparing it to a predetermined scale of classes or grades of jobs.

A third type of job evaluation plan is the **job classification**, or job grading, **method**. Certain classes or grades of jobs are defined on the basis of differences in duties, responsibilities, skills, working conditions, and other job-related factors. The relative worth of a particular job is then determined by comparing its description with the description of each of the classes and assigning the job to the appropriate class. This method has the advantage of simplicity, but it is also less precise because it evaluates the job as a whole. The number of required classes or grades depends on the range of skills, responsibilities, duties and other requirements that exist among the jobs being evaluated. Normally, 5 to 15 classes will suffice. Since 1949, the U.S. government has used the classification method to evaluate all civil service jobs.

▼ **Table 13–9**   Advantages and disadvantages of different job evaluation methods

	Major Advantages	Major Disadvantages
Point method	1. It is detailed and specific—jobs are evaluated on a component basis and compared against a predetermined scale. 2. Employees generally accept this method because of its mathematical nature. 3. The system is easy to keep current as jobs change. 4. Because of its quantitative nature, it is easy to assign monetary values to jobs.	1. It is relatively time consuming and costly to develop. 2. It requires significant interaction and decision making by the different parties involved in conducting the job evaluations.
Factor comparison method	1. It is relatively detailed and specific—jobs are evaluated on a component basis and compared against other jobs. 2. It is usually easier to develop than the point method. 3. It is tied to external market wage rates.	1. It is relatively difficult to explain to employees. 2. It is not easily adapted to changes in the jobs being evaluated.
Job classification method	1. Because it has been used by federal, state, and local governments for years, it is readily accepted by employees. 2. It is readily adaptable to very large organizations with many offices that are geographically dispersed. 3. Because the classifications are broad and not specific, the system can last for years without substantial change.	1. The classification descriptions are so broad that they do not relate to specific jobs; this causes employees to question the grade of their respective jobs. 2. Because of the broad and general classifications, job evaluators may abuse the system.
Job ranking method	1. It is fast and easy to complete. 2. Because it can usually be done in house, it is relatively inexpensive. 3. It is easy to explain.	1. It is limited to smaller organizations where individuals are very familiar with various jobs. 2. This method assumes equal intervals between the rankings, and this is usually not true. 3. The method is highly subjective.

Job Ranking Method

This is the simplest, oldest, and least-used job evaluation technique. In the **job ranking method**, the evaluator ranks whole jobs from the simplest to the most difficult. Often, the evaluator prepares cards with basic information about the jobs and then arranges the cards in the order of importance of the positions. The job ranking method only produces an ordering of jobs and does not indicate the relative degree of difference between them. For example, a job with a ranking number of four is not necessarily twice as difficult as a job with a ranking of two.

Job ranking method
Job evaluation method that ranks jobs in order of their difficulty from simplest to most complex.

Comparison of Job Evaluation Methods

The point and factor comparison methods are commonly referred to as quantitative plans because a number or dollar value ultimately is assigned to each job being evaluated. Numbers or dollars are assigned on the basis of the degree to which the job contains the predetermined compensable factors. The job classification and ranking methods, called qualitative or nonquantitative techniques, compare whole jobs. The point system and the job classification system have a common feature in that they evaluate jobs against a predetermined scale or class, whereas the factor comparison and job ranking methods evaluate jobs only in comparison to the other positions in the organization. Table 13–9 summarizes the advantages and disadvantages of each of the job evaluation methods.

Pricing the Job

The factor comparison method of evaluation is the only technique that relates the worth of jobs to a monetary scale; even then, the results are derived primarily from the wage scale that the organization currently uses. In general, job evaluation cannot be used to set the wage rate; however, it provides the basis for this determination. To ensure that external factors such as labor market conditions, prevailing wage rates and living costs are recognized in the wage scale, information about these factors must be gathered.

Wage and Salary Surveys

Wage and salary survey
Survey of selected organizations within a geographical area or industry designed to provide a comparison of reliable information on policies, practices, and methods of payment.

Wage and salary surveys are used to collect comparative information on the policies, practices, and methods of wage payment from selected organizations in a given geographic location or particular type of industry. Recent data show that more than 90 percent of the large corporations in the United States take part in wage and salary surveys or use them in their compensation systems.[4] In addition to providing knowledge of the market and ensuring external equity, wage surveys can correct employee misconceptions about certain jobs, and they can also have a positive impact on employee motivation.[5]

Data for a wage survey may be gathered from a variety of sources. The Bureau of Labor Statistics of the U.S. Department of Labor regularly publishes wage data broken down by geographic area, industry, and occupation. Industry and employee associations sometimes conduct surveys and publish their results. Trade magazines also may contain wage survey information.

In addition to using these sources, many organizations design and conduct their own surveys. To design a wage survey, the jobs, organizations, and area to be studied must be determined, as must the method for gathering data. If the wage survey is done in conjunction with either the point or factor comparison method of job evaluation, the key jobs selected for these methods are normally the ones that are surveyed. When using the classification or ranking method, the same guidelines followed for selecting jobs with the point and factor comparison methods should be applied in choosing the jobs to be surveyed.

▼. HRM in Action 13–3

Periodic Salary Surveys

Many organizations regularly conduct salary or wage surveys to remain informed. The *Public Relations Journal* (PRJ) periodically polls its readers and reports its findings in a subsequent issue of the journal. PRJ's questionnaire and analysis typically investigate the relationships between salary and numerous other variables such as age, sex, job level, time in job, time with organization, and time in the public relations field. These findings give PRJ's readers, many of whom are managers, some hard data to use for comparative purposes.

Source: John C. Pollock and Michael Winkleman, "Salary Survey," *Public Relations Journal*, June 1987, pp. 15–16.

▼ **Table 13–10**   Possible topics in a wage survey

Length of work day	Vacation practices
Normal work week duration	Holiday practices
Starting wage rates	Cost-of-living clauses
Base wage rates	Where paid
Pay ranges	How often paid
Incentive plans	Policy on wage garnishment
Shift differentials	Description of union contract
Overtime pay	

A geographic area, an industry type, or a combination of the two may be surveyed. The size of the geographic area, the cost-of-living index for the area, and similar factors must be considered when defining the scope of the survey. The organizations to be surveyed are normally competitors or companies that employ similar types of employees. When they are willing to cooperate, it is often desirable to survey the most important and most respected organizations in the area.

The three basic methods of surveying wage data are personal interviews, telephone interviews, and mailed questionnaires. The most reliable and most expensive method is the personal interview. Mailed questionnaires are probably used most frequently. However, questionnaires should only be used to survey jobs that have a uniform meaning throughout the industry. If there is any doubt concerning the definition of a job, the responses to a questionnaire may be unreliable. Another potential problem with mailed questionnaires is that they can be answered by someone who is not thoroughly familiar with the wage structure. The telephone method, which is quick but often yields incomplete information, may be used to clarify responses to mailed questionnaires. Table 13–10 lists some topics that might be covered in a wage survey. HRM in Action 13–3 describes a wage survey conducted regularly by the *Public Relations Journal*.

Pitfalls and Guidelines

Wage and salary surveys can be quite helpful if conducted properly. However, if not done properly, they can yield very distorted and inaccurate information and are often the subject of much criticism centering on the following points.[6]

- Too many surveys are being conducted.
- The quality of the resultant data is often questionable.
- Survey data are often difficult to interpret and use.
- Survey data can have a negative impact on merit pay plans.
- The use of such data can help fuel inflation.

Table 13–11 summarizes the results of a study of the specific problems associated with wage and salary surveys. Regardless of the type of survey used, the following guidelines should be followed to avoid problems:[7]

1. *Make comparisons of the participating companies for comparability.* Not only should factors such as size and type of business be considered, but also other intangibles such as prestige, security, growth opportunity, and location.

2. *Compare more than base wage or salary.* The total compensation package, including incentives and benefits, should be considered. For example, a company might provide few benefits but compensate for this with high base wages and salaries.

3. *Consider variations in job descriptions.* The most widely acknowledged shortcoming of wage and salary surveys is that it is difficult to find jobs that are directly comparable. Usually, more information than a brief job description is needed to properly match jobs in a survey.

4. *Correlate survey data with adjustment periods.* How recently wages and salaries were adjusted before the survey affects the accuracy of the data. Some companies may have just made adjustments, while others may not.

Comparable worth theory, which was discussed in Chapter 3, holds that every job should be compensated on the basis of its value to the employer and society. Under this theory, factors such as availability of qualified employees and wage rates paid by other employers should be disregarded. Under the comparable worth theory, wage surveys would have no value. However, as discussed in Chapter 3,

▼ **Table 13–11**   Problems encountered when using salary survey data

Problem	Percentage of Companies Actually Using Salary Survey Data*
Job categories too broad or imprecise	60%
Industry categories too broad or imprecise	56
Unadjusted for major benefits	51
Salary categories too broad or imprecise	40
Company type/size difficult to relate to own	36
Out-of-date or undated data	30
Samples of firms unrepresentative	27
Samples of firms too small	26
Survey based on unemployed and/or job seekers	19
Survey too broad or imprecise in other ways	16

*Only 57 percent of total survey sample used salary survey data.
Source: "Executive Remuneration and Benefits Survey Report," John Courtis and Partners, 1980; as reported in Joan C. O'Brien and Robert A. Zawacki, "Salary Surveys: Are They Worth the Effort?" *Personnel*, October 1985, p. 73.

the Ninth Circuit Court of Appeals has ruled that the value of a particular job to an employer is only one of many factors that should influence the rate of compensation for that job.

Wage and Salary Curves

Wage and salary curves graphically show the relationship between the relative worth of jobs and their wage or salary rates. In addition, these curves can be used to indicate pay classes and ranges for the jobs. Regardless of the job evaluation method used, a wage curve plots the jobs in ascending order of difficulty along the abscissa (x-axis) and the wage rate along the ordinate (y-axis). If the point method is used for evaluation, the point totals are plotted against their corresponding wage rates as shown in Figure 13–1 to produce a general trend.

> **Wage and salary curves**
> Graphical depiction of the relationships between the relative worth of jobs and their wage rates.

To ensure that the final wage structure is consistent with both the job evaluations and the wage survey data, it is sometimes desirable to construct one wage curve based on present wages and one based on the survey data and to compare the two. Any discrepancies can be quickly detected and corrected. Points on the graph that do not follow the general trend indicate that the wage rate for that job is too low or too high or that the job has been inaccurately evaluated. Underpaid jobs are sometimes called green-circle jobs; when wages are overly high, the positions are known as red-circle jobs. These discrepancies can be remedied by granting either above- or below-average pay increases for the jobs.

Pay Grades and Ranges

To simplify the administration of a wage structure, jobs of similar worth are often grouped into classes, or **pay grades**, for pay purposes. If the point method is used for evaluating jobs, classes are normally defined within a certain point spread. Similarly, a money spread can be used for defining grades if the factor comparison method is used. Table 13–12 illustrates how grades might be defined for the jobs shown in Figure 13–1.

> **Pay grades**
> Classes or grades of jobs that for pay purposes are grouped on the basis of their worth to an organization.

▼ **Figure 13–1**   Wage curve using the point method

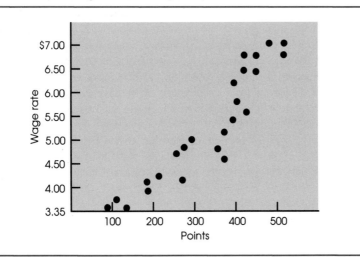

▼ **Table 13–12**   Establishing wage grades

Grade	Point Range
1	0–150
2	151–250
3	251–350
4	351–450
5	451–550

▼ **Figure 13–2**   Establishment of pay grades with ranges

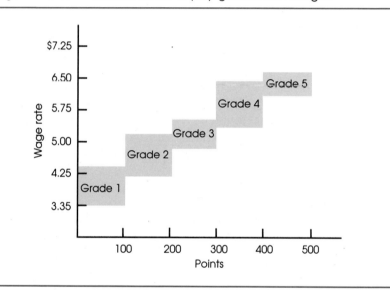

Pay range

A range of permissible pay, with a minimum and a maximum, that is assigned to a given pay grade.

Usually at the same time that pay grades are established, **pay ranges** are determined for each grade. When this is done, each pay grade is assigned a range of permissible pay, with a minimum and a maximum. The maximum of a pay grade's range places a ceiling on the rate that can be paid to any person whose job is classified in that grade. Similarly, the minimum of the pay grade's range places a floor on the rate that can be paid. Two general approaches for establishing pay grades and ranges are to have a relatively large number of grades with identical rates of pay for all jobs within each grade or to have a small number of grades with a relatively wide dollar range for each grade. Most pay structures fall somewhere between these extremes.

Ranges within grades are set up so that distinctions can be made among individuals within grades. Ideally, the placement of individuals within pay grades should be based on performance or merit. In practice, however, the distinction is often based solely on seniority. Figure 13–2 illustrates how pay ranges might be structured for the jobs in Figure 13–1.

On reaching the top of the range for a given grade, an individual can increase his or her pay only by moving to a higher grade. As shown in Figure 13–2, it is not unusual for the ranges of adjacent pay grades to overlap. Under such circum-

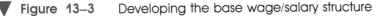

▼   **Figure 13–3**   Developing the base wage/salary structure

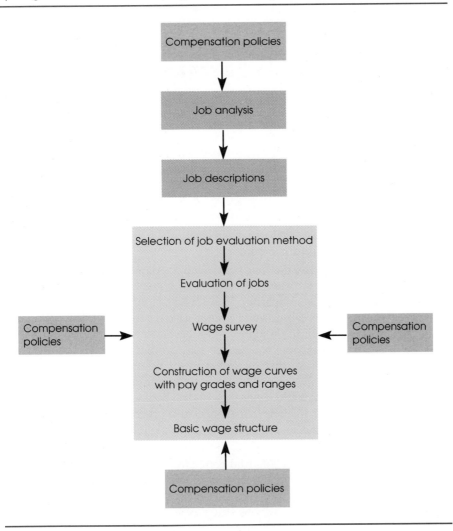

stances, it is possible for an outstanding performer in a lower grade to make a higher salary than a below-average performer in a higher grade.

Base Wage/Salary Structure

Figure 13–3 illustrates how the various segments of the compensation process fit together to establish the base wage or salary structure for an organization. Compensation policies are shown on all sides of the figure to emphasize the fact that each step in the process is influenced by the organization's current compensation policies. Ideally, an organization's compensation system should produce a base wage/salary structure that is both internally and externally equitable. The job evaluation process should ensure internal equity, while wage surveys should ensure external equity. The performance appraisal process, discussed in Chapter 10, is then used to position an individual employee within the established range.

● *Summary of Learning Objectives*

1. Define base wages and salaries and state the objective of any base wage and salary system.

    Base wages and salaries are the hourly, weekly, or monthly pay that employees receive in exchange for their work. The primary objective of any base wage and salary system is to establish a structure and system for the equitable payment of employees, depending on their job and their level of job performance.

2. Define job evaluation.

    Job evaluation is a systematic determination of the value of each job in relation to other jobs in the organization.

3. Name and briefly discuss the four basic methods of job evaluation.

    Most job evaluation plans are variations or combinations of four basic methods: point, factor comparison, job classification, and job ranking. The point method develops a quantitative point scale for the jobs being evaluated. Jobs are broken down into certain recognizable factors and the sum total value of these factors is compared against the scale to determine the job's worth. The factor comparison method is similar to the point method except that it involves a monetary scale instead of a point scale. The job classification method defines certain classes or grades of jobs on the basis of differences in duties, responsibilities, skills, working conditions, and other job-related factors. In the job ranking method, the evaluator ranks whole jobs from the simplest to the most difficult.

4. Explain the concepts of key jobs and compensable factors.

    Key jobs represent jobs that are common throughout the industry or in the general locale under study. The idea is to select a limited number of jobs that will represent the spectrum of jobs being evaluated with regard to responsibilities, duties, and work requirements. Once the key jobs have been evaluated, other jobs can be compared to them. Compensable factors are those factors or characteristics of jobs that are deemed important by the organization to the extent that it is willing to pay for them. The degree to which a specific job possesses compensable factors determines its relative worth.

5. Differentiate between subfactors and degrees.

    Subfactors are used to describe compensable factors in more detail. Degrees are profile statements used to describe the specific requirements of each subfactor.

6. Explain the purpose of wage and salary surveys.

    Wage and salary surveys are used to collect comparative information on the policies, practices, and methods of wage payment from selected organizations in a given geographic location or particular type of industry.

7. Discuss wage and salary curves.

    Wage and salary curves graphically show the relationship between the relative worth of jobs and their wage or salary rates. A wage curve plots the jobs in ascending level of difficulty along the abscissa (x-axis) and the wage rate along the ordinate (y-axis).

8. Define pay grades and pay ranges.

   A pay grade is a grouping of jobs of a similar worth for pay purposes. A pay range is an assigned range of permissible pay, with a minimum and a maximum for each pay grade.

Review Questions

1. Define base wages and salaries.
2. What is the primary objective of any base wage and salary system?
3. What are the two basic phases involved in establishing pay ranges?
4. Define job evaluation.
5. List the four basic methods of job evaluation.
6. What are compensable factors? Subfactors? Degrees?
7. Explain wage surveys and how they might be conducted.
8. What is the purpose of wage curves?
9. What are pay grades and ranges?

Discussion Questions

1. Suppose your organization's recently completed wage survey showed that the pay rates of several jobs were either less or more than they should be. How might you bring these jobs into line?
2. The basic theory behind wage and salary administration is to pay people commensurately with their contributions. What should an organization do if an individual's contributions are not in line with those of others in the same type of job? For example, suppose the company accountant's contributions are deemed to be far in excess of what is usual for someone earning an accountant's pay.
3. The choice of compensable factors is critical to job evaluation. How would you suggest that a job evaluator go about selecting such factors?

▼ INCIDENT 13–1

Fair Pay for Pecan Workers

The Cloverdale Pecan Company is one of the country's largest processors of pecans. Located in a medium-sized southern town, it employs approximately 1,350 people. Although Cloverdale does own a few pecan orchards, the great majority of the nuts it processes are bought on the open market. The processing involves grading the nuts for both size and quality, shelling, packaging, and shipping them to customers. Most buyers are candy manufacturers.

Cloverdale, which was started 19 years ago by the family of company president Jackson Massie, has been continually expanding since its inception. As do most growing companies, Cloverdale has always paid whatever was necessary to fill a vacancy without having a formal wage and salary system. Jackson Massie suspected that some wage inequities had developed over the years. His speculation was supported by complaints about such inequities from several good, long-term employees. Therefore, Jackson hired a group of respected consultants to do a complete wage and salary study of all the nonexempt jobs in the company.

The study, which took five months to complete, confirmed Jackson's suspicion. Wages of several jobs were found to vary from the norm. Furthermore, the situation was complicated by several factors. First, many of the employees earning too much were being paid according to union wage scales. Cloverdale is not unionized, but most of its competitors are. Second, many of those in underpaid jobs were being paid at rates equal to similar positions in other companies in Cloverdale's geographic area. Third, because of a tight labor market, many new employees had been hired at the top of the range for their respective grades. The study also revealed that the nature of many jobs had changed so much that they needed to be completely reclassified.

Questions

1. What should Cloverdale do to correct the existing wage inequities?
2. How could the company have prevented these problems?
3. If it is recommended that some jobs be placed in a lower pay grade, how might Cloverdale implement these adjustments?

▼ INCIDENT 13–2

A Dead-End Street?

Early in December, Roger Tomlin was called in for his annual salary review. Roger was a staff engineer for the Zee Engineering Company, which he had been with for just over 10 years. In the past, Roger had usually received what he considered to be a fair pay raise. During this salary review, his manager Ben Jackson informed Roger that he was recommending a 10 percent raise. Ben went on to extoll the fine job Roger had done in the past year and to explain that Roger should be especially proud of the above-average pay raise he would be getting. Upon reflection, Roger was rather proud; in 10 years, he had been promoted twice, and his annual salary had gone from $23,000 to $38,000.

Things were moving along just fine for Roger until he discovered a few weeks later that a new engineer right out of college had just been hired by Zee at a starting salary of $35,000. It really upset Roger to think that a new, unproven engineer would be starting at a salary almost equal to his.

Roger's first move was to talk to several of his colleagues. Most of Roger's fellow employees were aware of the situation and they didn't like it either. Luke Johnson, who had been an engineer with Zee for over 12 years, asked Roger if he realized that he was probably making less money, in actual dollars, than when he started at Zee. This really floored Roger. Roger realized that inflation had eaten into everyone's paycheck, but he had never even considered the possiblity that he had not kept up with inflation. That evening, on the way home from work, Roger stopped by the local library and looked up the consumer price index (CPI) for the past 10 years. According to Roger's figures, if his pay had kept up exactly with inflation, he would be making $38,500!

After a very restless night, the first thing Roger did upon arriving at work the next day was go straight to personnel manager Joe Dixon's office. After presenting his case about the new employee and about how inflation had eroded his pay, Roger sat back and waited for Dixon's reply.

Joe started out by explaining that he understood just how Roger felt. At the same time, however, Joe stated that Roger had to consider the situation from the company's standpoint. The current supply and demand situation dictated that Zee had to pay $35,000 to get new engineers who were any good at all. Roger explained that he could understand that, but what he couldn't understand was why the company couldn't pay him and other senior engineers more money. Joe again sympathized with Roger but then went on to explain that it was a supply and demand situation. The fact of the matter was that senior engineers just didn't demand that much more pay than engineers just starting!

Questions

1. Do you think Roger is being fairly paid?
2. If you were Roger, how would you react to Joe's explanation?
3. Do you think a wage survey might help in this situation?

Exercise

Ranking Jobs

Based on the seven job descriptions for the air transportation industry given in Exhibit 13–A, evaluate the relative worth of these jobs, using the job ranking method. You may find it helpful to prepare a 3 × 5 card on each job and then

▼ **Exhibit 13–A**   Air transportation industry job descriptions*

AIRPLANE-DISPATCH CLERK (air transportation) flight-operations-dispatch clerk. Compiles flight information to expedite movement of aircraft between and through airports. Compiles aircraft dispatch data, such as scheduled arrival and departure times at checkpoints and scheduled stops, amount of fuel needed for flight, and maximum allowable gross takeoff and landing weight. Submits data to DISPATCHER (air transportation) for approval and flight authorization. Receives messages on progress of flights. Posts flight schedules and weather information on bulletin board. Compiles such information as flight plans, ramp delays, and weather reports, using teletype, computer-printout terminal, and two-way radio, to anticipate off-schedule arrivals or departures, and notifies flight operations of schedule changes. Prepares messages concerning flights for transmittal by radio, telegraph, or telegraphic typewriter to other stations on routes. May operate telegraphic typewriter or two-way radio to send messages. May issue maps to pilot. May duplicate weather maps and telegraph or radio messages [DUPLICATING-MACHINE OPERATOR (clerical) II]. May record flight and weather information on tape recorder for playback to passengers in waiting areas. May verify presence or locate scheduled flight crews, and post changes in flight crew schedule on bulletin board.

(continued)

CARGO AGENT (air transportation) air-freight agent; customer service agent. Routes inbound and outbound air-freight shipments to their destinations: Takes telephone orders from customers and arranges for pickup of freight and delivery to loading platform. Assembles cargo according to destination. Weighs items and determines cost, using rate book. Itemizes charges, prepares freight bills, accepts payments, and issues refunds. Prepares manifest to accompany shipments. Notifies shippers of delays in departure of shipment. Unloads inbound freight, notifies consignees on arrival of shipments, and arranges for delivery to consignees. May force conditioned air into interior of plane for passenger comfort prior to departure, using mobile aircraft air-conditioning unit.

COMMUNICATION CENTER OPERATOR (air transportation). Operates airport authority communication systems and monitors electronic equipment alarms: Operates public address system to page passengers or visitors. Operates telephone switchboard to receive or place calls to and from terminal. Operates two-way internal radio system to communicate with departments. Operates terminal courtesy telephone system to communicate with passengers or visitors. Observes electronic monitoring panel to detect serious malfunction of elevators, escalators, shuttle train, fire alarms, emergency doors, or heating, air-conditioning, and ventilating system.

GATE AGENT (air transportation). Assists passengers and checks flight tickets at entrance gate or station when boarding or disembarking airplane of commercial airline: Examines passenger tickets to ensure that passengers have correct flight or seat, or directs passengers to correct boarding area, using passenger manifest, seating chart, and flight schedules. Verifies names on passenger manifest or separates portions of passenger's ticket and stamps or marks ticket or issues boarding pass to authorize passenger to board airplane. Directs passengers to air-terminal facilities. Opens gate or allows passengers to board airplane. Assists elderly, disabled, or young passengers to board or depart from airplane, such as moving passengers in wheelchairs. May announce flight information, using public address system. May post flight information on flight board.

RESERVATIONS AGENT (air transportation) telephone-sales agent. Makes and confirms reservations for passengers on scheduled airline flights: Arranges reservations and routing for passengers at request of TICKET AGENT (any industry) or customer, using timetables, airline manuals, reference guides, and tariff book. Types requested flight number on keyboard of on-line computer reservation system and scans screen to determine space availability. Telephones customer or TICKET AGENT (any industry) to advise of changes in flight plan or to cancel or confirm reservation. May maintain advance or current inventory of available passenger space on flights. May advise load control personnel and other stations of changes in passenger itinerary to control space and ensure utilization of seating capacity on flights.

SUPERVISOR, TICKET SALES (air transportation) load ticket-sales agent; senior passenger agent; senior ticket-sales agent. Supervises and coordinates activities of personnel engaged in selling tickets for scheduled airline flights in airline ticket office or terminal: Instructs and trains agents. Adjusts disputes between customers and agents. Prepares reports, such as volume of ticket sales and cash received. Maintains records on data, such as weight and location of passengers, cargo, and mail, to ensure compliance with load specifications. Suggests travel itineraries for customers. May reserve space for passengers [RESERVATIONS AGENT (air transportation)] and sell tickets for scheduled flights [TICKET AGENT (any industry)]. Performs other duties as described under SUPERVISOR (clerical).

TICKETING CLERK (air transportation) teleticketing agent; ticket agent. Compiles and records information to assemble airline tickets for transmittal or mailing to passengers: Reads coded data on booking cards to ascertain destination, carrier, flight number, type of accommodation, and stopovers enroute. Selects ticket blank, invoice, and customer account card (if applicable) and compiles, computes, and records identification and fare data, using tariff manuals, rate tables, flight schedules, and pen or ticket imprinter. Separates and files copies of completed tickets. Clips completed tickets and invoices to booking cards and routes to other workers for teletype transmittal or mails tickets to customers. Computes total daily fares, using adding machine, to compile daily revenue report.

---

*These job descriptions are taken from the *Dictionary of Occupational Titles*, 4th ed., U.S. Department of Labor, Employment and Training Administration (Washington, D.C.: U.S. Government Printing Office), 1977.

arrange the cards accordingly. Once you have completed your rankings, go to the library and find any pertinent wage survey data relating to these jobs (a good source of wage survey data is published by the U.S. Department of Labor). After you have gathered sufficient wage survey data, determine whether or not the data supports your rankings. Be prepared to discuss your findings with the class.

Notes and Additional Readings

1. Roger J. Plachy, "Compensation Management: Cases and Applications," *Compensation and Benefits Review,* July 1989, p. 26.

2. Richard I. Henderson, *Compensation Management: Rewarding Performance* 1st ed. (Reston, Va.: Reston Publishing, 1976), p. 123.

3. Richard I. Henderson, *Compensation Management: Rewarding Performance* 4th ed. (Reston, Va.: Reston Publishing, 1985), p. 293.

4. Joan C. O'Brien and Robert A . Zawacki, "Salary Surveys: Are They Worth the Effort?" *Personnel,* October 1985, p. 90.

5. Ibid., p. 72.

6. Ibid., p. 71.

7. The guidelines are summarized from Michael A. Conway, "Salary Surveys: Avoid the Pitfalls," *Personnel Journal,* June 1985, pp. 62–65.

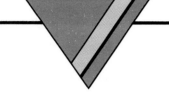

Chapter 14

Incentive Pay Systems

Chapter Outline

Requirements of Incentive Plans

Individual Incentives

Piece Rate Plans
Plans Based on Time Saved
Plans Based on Commissions
Individual Bonuses
Suggestion Systems
Bonuses for Managerial Personnel
Stock Options for Managerial Personnel

Group Incentives

Organizationwide Incentives

Gain-Sharing or Profit-Sharing Plans
Scanlon-Type Plans
Employee Stock Ownership Plans
(ESOPs)

Making Incentive Plans Work

Summary of Learning Objectives

Review Questions

Discussion Questions

**Incident 14–1: Rewarding Good
Performance in a Bank**

**Incident 14–2: Part-Time Pool
Personnel**

**Exercise: Implementing
Incentives**

Notes and Additional Readings

● _Learning Objectives_

After studying this chapter, you should be able to:

1. Name the two basic requirements of an effective incentive plan.
2. Name and briefly discuss two types of individual incentives based on time saved.
3. Distinguish between a bonus and a merit pay increase.
4. Discuss the role that bonuses play in managerial compensation.
5. Differentiate between nonqualified stock options and incentive stock options (ISOs).
6. Explain how group incentives work.
7. Explain what a gain-sharing plan is.
8. Discuss Scanlon-type plans.
9. Explain how an employee stock ownership plan (ESOP) works.

"Your people should be encouraged to earn as much bonus as they can and then spend it on clubs, limousines, other corporate luxuries, or save it, or give it to charity. However, the choice should be theirs. Don't ask your people to subsidize the ego of fat cats at the top."

*Robert Townsend**

Incentive pay plans
Pay plans designed to relate pay directly to performance or productivity, often used in conjunction with a base wage/salary system.

Incentive pay plans attempt to relate pay to performance in an endeavor to reward above-average performance rapidly and directly. Although good performance can be rewarded through the base wage or salary structure either by raising an individual's pay within the range of the job or by promoting the individual into a higher pay grade, these rewards are often subject to delays and other restrictions. Therefore, such rewards often are not viewed by the recipients as being directly related to performance. Incentive pay plans attempt to strengthen the performance-reward relationship and thus motivate the affected employees.

Because of minimum wage laws and labor market competition, most incentive plans include a guaranteed hourly wage or salary. The guaranteed wage or salary is normally determined from the base wage or salary structure. Thus, incentive plans usually function in addition to and not in place of the base wage/salary structure discussed in Chapter 13.

Incentive systems can be categorized on more than one basis. Probably the most popular has to do with whether the plan is applied on an individual, group, or organizational level. Additionally, plans are sometimes classified according to whether they apply to nonmanagement or to professional and management personnel. This chapter classifies incentives as individual, group or organizational and, where appropriate, distinguishes between nonmanagement and management personnel within these categories.

Requirements of Incentive Plans

There are two basic requirements if an incentive plan is to be effective.[1] The first concerns the procedures and methods used to appraise employee performance. If incentives are to be based on performance, then employees must feel that their performance and the performance of others is accurately and fairly evaluated. Naturally, performance is easier to measure in some situations than in others. For example, the performance of a commissioned salesperson is usually easy to measure. On the other hand, the performance of a middle manager is often difficult to evaluate. A key issue in performance measurement is the degree of trust in management. If the employees distrust management, then it is almost impossible to establish a sound performance appraisal system. Performance appraisal was discussed at length in Chapter 10.

The second requirement is that the incentives (rewards) must be based on

*Source: R. Townsend, *Up the Organization* (New York: Alfred A. Knopf, 1970), p. 82.

performance. This may seem like an obvious requirement; yet, it is often violated. Employees must believe that there is a relationship between what they do and what they get. Individual-based incentive plans require that employees perceive a direct relationship between their own performance and their subsequent rewards. Group-based plans require employees to perceive a relationship between the group's performance and the subsequent rewards of the group's members. Furthermore, the group members must believe that their individual performance has an impact on the group's overall performance. Organization-based plans have the same basic requirements as group plans. Employees must perceive a relationship between the organization's performance and their individual rewards; additionally, employees must believe that their individual performance affects the performance of the organization.

Individual Incentives

While there are many types of individual incentive plans, all are tied in some measure to the performance of the individual. At nonmanagerial levels in an organization, individual incentives are usually based on the performance of the individual as opposed to the group or organization. However, at managerial levels, individual incentives are often based on the performance of the manager's work unit.

The primary advantage of individual incentive systems is that the employees can readily see the relationship between what they do and what they get. With group- and organization-based plans, this relationship is often not so clear. It is because of this advantage that individual incentives can also cause problems. Competition among employees can reach the point of producing negative results. For example, salespeople might not share their ideas with one another for fear that their peers might win a prize that is being offered to the top salesperson.

Piece Rate Plans

As early as 1833, many cotton mills in England used individual piece rate incentives.[2] Piece rate plans are the simplest and most common type of incentive plan. Under such a plan, an employee is paid a certain amount for every unit he or she produces. In other words, an individual's wage is figured by multiplying the number of units produced times the rate of pay for each unit. The rate of pay for each unit is usually based on what a fair wage should be for an average employee. For example, if a fair wage for an average machine operator is determined to be $90 per day and it is also determined that the average machine operator should be able to produce 30 units per day, then the unit rate of pay would be $3 per unit.

Several variations of the straight piece rate plan have been developed. In 1895, Frederick W. Taylor proposed his **differential piece rate plan**. Under Taylor's plan, one rate is paid for all acceptable pieces produced up to some standard, or predetermined amount, and then a higher rate for all pieces produced if the output exceeds the standard. Thus, if the standard were 30 units per day, an employee producing 30 or fewer units might receive $2.50 per unit. However, if the employee

Differential piece rate plan
Piece rate plan devised by Frederic W. Taylor that pays one rate for all acceptable pieces produced up to some standard and then a higher rate for all pieces produced if the output exceeds the standard.

produced 31 units, he or she might receive $3 for all 31 units produced for a total of $93. Other plans pay a higher rate only for those units produced above the standard.

Plans Based on Time Saved

Standard hour plans are similar to piece rate plans except that a standard time is set in terms of the time it should take to complete a particular job. Incentive plans based on time saved give an employee a bonus for reaching a given level of production or output in less than standard time. Two common plans of this type are the Halsey premium plan and the Rowan plan. In the **Halsey premium plan**, the employee is paid a guaranteed hourly wage plus a premium for any time saved by producing a given quantity in less than standard time. The standard time required to do a given task is determined from previous experience. For example, an individual who produces an hour's standard output in 45 minutes is paid the regular hourly rate plus a fixed percentage of the value of the 15 minutes saved.

The **Rowan plan** differs from the Halsey premium plan in that the percentage paid for time saved is not fixed but determined by that percentage. It maintains that the wages for the time taken to complete a task will be increased by the same percentage that the standard time for the task has been reduced. For example, an individual who produces standard output in 75 percent of the specified time would receive a 25 percent bonus on wages since 25 percent of the normal time was saved.

Plans Based on Commissions

The previously discussed incentive plans are primarily applicable to blue-collar employees. However, there are incentive plans that apply to other groups of employees. One of the most prevalent types is based on commission. Many salespeople work under some type of **commission plan**. Although a variety of such plans exist, they all reward employees, at least in part, based on sales volume. Some salespeople work on a straight commission basis: their pay is entirely determined by their volume of sales. Others work on a combination of salary plus commission. Under this type of plan, a salesperson is paid a guaranteed base salary plus a commission on sales. Under a third type of commission plan, salespeople are paid a monthly draw that is later subtracted from their commissions. The purpose of the draw is to provide salespeople with enough money on a monthly basis to cover their basic expenses. The difference between a draw plan and the guaranteed salary plus commission plan is that the draw is really an advance against future commissions and must be repaid. The draw plan is especially useful for salespeople whose sales tend to fluctuate dramatically from month to month or season to season.

A commission plan has the advantage of relating rewards directly to performance. Salespeople on a straight commission know that if they do not produce, they will not be paid. A major disadvantage of commission plans is that things beyond the control of the individual can adversely affect sales. For example, a product might be displaced almost overnight by a technological breakthrough. Other environmental factors such as the national economy, the weather, and consumer preferences can also affect a person's sales.

▼▼. HRM in Action 14–1

Substantial Savings from Employee Suggestions

William Arey, administrator of cost reduction for Philip Morris, has described how a routine company practice was turned around by one employee's observations: "For years, we were sending out these 'doctor blades' to get reground. Basically, doctor blades are used to scrape the outside of a rotating drum. When the blades get dull, we need to get them sharpened. An employee began to wonder why they always cost significantly more to ship out than to ship back. He investigated and found the courier was charging us for shipping out *surgical* instruments. . . . Correcting that simple mistake has saved

Philip Morris tens of thousands of dollars over the past year and will save thousands more in years to come."

Edward Anderson, a scientist at Hughes Aircraft Company's Space and Communications Group, saved the company $22 million by coming up with an idea to cut the weight of communications satellites—which ordinarily cost $10,000 to $14,000 per pound to launch into space.

Source: Leslie Stackel, "Employment Relations Programs," *Employment Relations Today*, Summer 1989, pp. 167–68.

Individual Bonuses

A **bonus** is a reward that is offered on a one-time basis for high performance. It should not be confused with a merit increase. A **merit pay increase** is a reward that is based on performance but that is also perpetuated year after year. A bonus may be in cash or in some other form. For example, many sales organizations periodically offer prizes, such as trips, for their top salespeople.

One potential problem with bonuses is that they can become an extension of salary. This occurs when awarding the bonus becomes practically guaranteed because the bonus is not tied to profits or some other measure of performance. In such circumstances, the recipients begin to expect the bonus. They do not view it as resulting from their individual performance or from the profits of the organization. Serious dissatisfaction can result if the expected bonus is not granted because of a decline in profits or for any other legitimate reason.

Bonus
Reward that is offered on a one-time basis for high performance.

Merit pay increase
Reward based on performance but also perpetuated year after year.

Suggestion Systems

The National Association of Suggestion Systems (NASS) estimated that approximately 6,000 formal **suggestion systems** and possibly an equal number of semiformal ones existed in the United States in 1980.[3] However, there is evidence that the popularity of suggestion systems may have waned somewhat in the last several years.[4] This trend is not because suggestion systems don't work, but rather because they are often improperly used. Most suggestion plans offer cash incentives for employee suggestions that positively affect the organization. Examples include suggestions resulting in increased profits, reduced costs, or improved customer relations. In addition to the obvious organizational benefits, suggestion plans can provide a means for making employees feel more a part of the organization and for improved communications between management and employees. The key to having a successful suggestion system is to clearly communicate exactly how the system works. Employees must believe that each and every suggestion will be fairly evaluated. Modern suggestion systems generally involve specific procedures for

Suggestion systems
Systems that usually offer cash incentives for employee suggestions that result in either increased profits or reduced costs.

▼ HRM in Action 14–2

Bonuses at Kentucky Fried Chicken

KFC has introduced a "Quality, Service, and Cleanliness" (QSC) program to ensure clean facilities and a high caliber of service. The program consists of 103 quality control practices and a series of inspectors to determine if KFC units are meeting company standards.

A unit's composite QSC score directly affects the size of the unit manager's quarterly bonus. The bonus, which can be up to 40 percent of a manager's quarterly salary, is based on three criteria: cost of sales, labor costs,

and sales increases over last year. However, no matter how well a manager performs in any of these categories, if the unit does not achieve a composite QSC score of at least 90, the bonus is lost. On the other hand, if a manager's unit scores better than 90, the bonus increases.

Source: Adapted from "Bonus Plan Motivates KFC Managers," *Restaurant Business*, January 20, 1984, p. 111.

▼ Table 14–1   Bonus plans: 1970 compared to 1985 and 1988

Type of Business	Number of Companies Surveyed			Percentage Having Bonus Plans		
	May 1970	May 1985	May 1988	May 1970	May 1985	May 1988
Manufacturing	419	475	254	65%	92%	95%
Retail trade	90	68	33	40	81	88
Commercial banking	248	171	93	19	81	89
Insurance	174	132	91	18	67	89
Energy and utilities	106	97	142	6	36	71

Source: H. Fox, *Top Executive Compensation*, 1981 ed. (New York: Conference Board, 1980), p. 4; H. Fox and C. Peck, *Top Executive Compensation*, 1986 ed. (New York: Conference Board, 1985), p. 2; and E. Arreglado and C. Peck, *Top Executive Compensation*, 1988 ed. (New York: Conference Board, 1988), p. 2.

---

submitting ideas and utilize committees to review and evaluate suggestions. HRM in Action 14–1 provides some examples of the positive effects that employee suggestions can have.

Bonuses for Managerial Personnel

By far the most common type of incentive for managerial personnel is the annual, or cash, bonus. Even though cash bonuses have always been popular among managers, they have become even more popular as a result of the 1986 Tax Reform Act. A 1988 survey of 1,123 companies by Executive Compensation Service, Inc., reported that almost 70 percent of the companies paid bonuses to managerial personnel.[5] A similar 1987 survey of 670 companies conducted by the Conference Board reported that over 88 percent awarded bonuses to their top executives.[6] Most plans provide a year-end bonus based on that year's performance, usually measured in terms of profits, but sometimes measured by other means. HRM in Action 14–2 explains how Kentucky Fried Chicken has tied its managers' annual bonuses to performance. Even though managerial bonuses are usually based on

▼ Table 14–2   Bonuses as a percentage of total compensation and salaries

Industry Category	Number of Companies	Percentage Paying Bonuses	Average Bonus (as a percentage of salaries)	Average Bonus (as a percentage of total compensation)
Durable goods manufacturing	349	78.2%	38.9%	28.0%
Nondurable goods manufacturing	234	81.2	39.9	28.6
Energy	14	71.4	32.2	24.3
Trade	61	78.7	31.2	23.8
Utilities	52	53.9	27.4	21.5
Services	151	67.6	39.2	28.2
Banking & finance	79	74.7	40.2	28.7
Insurance	85	63.5	26.0	20.7
Nonprofits	98	17.4	13.1	11.6
All industry categories combined	1,123	69.6	35.8	26.4

Souce: *Executive Compensation Service Top Management Report,* 39th ed. (Fort Lee, N.J.: Executive Compensation Service, 1988), p. 26.

▼ Table 14–3   Bonuses as a function of managerial level

Position	Average Bonus (percentage of salary)
Chief executive officer	52.7%
Chief operating officer	49.1
Executive vice president	40.1
Administrative vice president	36.2
Top marketing and sales executive	31.6
Top manufacturing executive	31.6
Top financial executive	36.8

Source: *Executive Compensation Service Top Management Report,* 39th ed. (Fort Lee, N.J.: Executive Compensation Service, 1988), p. 25.

organizational or group performance, they are considered individual incentives because of the key roles that managers play in the success of an organization. Typically, a bonus is paid in cash as a lump sum soon after the end of the performance year. It is not unusual for executives to defer receiving some portion of a cash bonus until a later date for income tax purposes.

As can be seen from Table 14–1, the popularity of bonus plans grew substantially from 1970 to 1988. Bonuses often make up a substantial portion of total compensation. The Executive Compensation Service found in its 1988 survey that bonuses composed 35.8 percent of total salary and 26.4 percent of total compensation received by managers (see Table 14–2).[7] Another interesting finding of this survey was that the percentage was even greater for higher-level managers (see Table 14–3).

▼ **Table 14–4** Prevalence of long-term performance plans

Industry Category	Total Companies	May, 1988 Companies with Long-Term Performance Plans		May, 1983 Percentage with Long-Term Performance Plans
		Number	Percentage	
Energy	31	12	39%	*
Diversified service	24	9	38	*
Manufacturing	254	90	35	33%
Communications	17	5	29	*
Commercial banking	93	22	24	15
Insurance	91	22	24	12
Utilities	111	27	24	5
Transportation	16	2	13	*
Trade	33	4	12	12

*Data not available.

Source: Elizabeth R. Arreglado and Charles A. Peck, *Top Executive Compensation,* 1988 ed. (New York: The Conference Board, 1988), p. 3.

Long-Term Performance Plans

In recent years, some companies have adopted managerial incentive plans based on the attainment of certain long-term corporate financial performance goals, as opposed to the more common annual bonus plans. Generally known as **performance share**, or unit **plans**, these usually award top executives a set number of performance units at the beginning of a performance period. The actual value of the units is then determined by the performance of the company over the performance period, usually from three to five years. Table 14–4 indicates how performance share plans have grown in popularity since 1983.

Performance share plans
Incentive plans for top managers that base bonuses on the long-term performance for the organization (usually three to five years).

Stock Options for Managerial Personnel

Stock option plans are generally designed to give managers an option to buy company stock at a predetermined, fixed price. If the price of the stock goes up, the individual exercises the option to buy the stock at the fixed price and realizes a profit. If, on the other hand, the price of the stock goes down, the stock option is said to be "underwater," and the manager does not purchase the stock. The theory behind such plans is providing an incentive for managers to work hard and increase company profits, thus increasing the price of the stock.

Before the passage of the Tax Reform Act of 1976, two major forms of stock options were available: qualified and nonqualified. **Qualified stock options** were those approved by the Internal Revenue Service (IRS) for favorable tax treatment. A qualified option was not taxed until the option was exercised and, in the interim, was treated as a capital asset. Income realized from the eventual sale of the stock usually was taxed as a long-term capital gain. To qualify for tax advantage, the stock option plan and the recipient had to adhere to certain conditions prescribed by the IRS. These conditions centered primarily around the length of time that the executive was required to hold the option before purchasing and selling the stock, and the basis for establishing the price that the executive paid for it. **Non-**

Qualified stock options
Stock options approved by the Internal Revenue Service for favorable tax treatment.

▼ Table 14-5   Comparison of types of stock option plans offered

Industry Category	Total Plans Number	Both ISQ and Nonqualified Number	Both ISQ and Nonqualified Percentage	Only ISO Number	Only ISO Percentage	Only Nonqualified Number	Only Nonqualified Percentage
				Number and Percentage of Plans by Type			
Manufacturing	211	146	69%	16	8%	47	22%
Commerical banking	65	52	80	14	6	7	11
Utilities	39	28	72	3	8	7	18
Insurance: stock	34	24	71	2	6	7	21
Energy	26	17	65	3	12	6	23
Trade	26	16	62	4	15	6	23
Diversified service	19	12	63	—	—	7	37
Communications	16	11	69	3	19	1	6
Transportation	11	9	82	—	—	2	18

Source: E. Arreglado and C. Peck. *Top Executive Compensation*, 1988 ed. (New York: Conference Board, 1988), p. 3.

▼ Table 14-6   Prevalence of stock option plans

Industry Category	May 1983 Percentage with Stock Option Plan	May 1988 Total Companies	May 1988 Companies with Stock Option Plan Number	May 1988 Companies with Stock Option Plan Percentage
Communications	*	17	16	94%
Energy	*	31	26	84
Manufacturing	80%	254	211	83
Diversified service	*	24	19	79
Trade	63	33	26	79
Commercial banking	44	93	65	70
Transportation	*	16	11	69
Insurance: stock	48	68	34	50
Utilities	20	111	39	35

*Data not available.

Source: E. Arreglado and C. Peck, *Top Executive Compensation*, 1988 ed. (New York: Conference Board, 1988), p. 4.

qualified options are similar to qualified options, except that they are not subject to as favorable a tax rate (but neither are they subject to the same restrictions).

As a result of the Tax Reform Act of 1976, no new qualified stock options were created after May 20, 1976 (with a few exceptions). In addition, the act ordered that all qualified options in existence prior to the passage of the act had to be exercised before May 21, 1981. It also affected nonqualified options by increasing the period for which an exercised stock option had to be held to enjoy long-term capital gains tax rates. However, with the adoption of the Economic Recovery Tax Act of 1981, the qualified stock option was resurrected under the new name of **incentive stock option (ISO)**. Under an ISO, a manager does not have to pay any tax until he or she sells the stock. The major drawback to ISOs is that the company granting such options does not get tax reductions, which it

Nonqualified stock options
Similar to qualified options, except that they are not subject to as favorable a tax rate (but neither are they subject to the same restrictions).

Incentive stock option (ISO)
Form of qualified stock option plan made feasible by the Economic Recovery Tax Act of 1981.

▼ **Table 14–7** Salary, bonus, and long-term income of several top-paid executives

Name	Title	Company	1988 Salary and Bonus	Long-Term Compensation	Total Compensation
			Income (in thousands of dollars)		
1. Michael D. Eisner	Chariman	Walt Disney	$ 7,506	$32,588	$40,094
2. Frank G. Wells	President	Walt Disney	3,778	28,357	32,135
3. E. A. Horrigan, Jr.	Former vice-chairman	RJR Nabisco	1,280	20,450	21,730
4. F. Ross Johnson	Former chief executive officer	RJR Nabisco	1,836	19,235	21,071
5. Marvin S. Davis	Chairman	Gulf & Western	3,673	12,577	16,250
6. Richard L. Gelb	Chairman	Bristol-Myers	1,475	12,578	14,053
7. William P. Stiritz	Chairman	Ralston Purina	1,029	11,919	12,948
8. Baine P. Kerr	Chairman, executive committee	Pennzoil	10,706	839	11,545
9. J. Hugh Liedtke	Chairman	Pennzoil	10,872	664	11,536
10. Paul Fireman	Chairman	Reebok International	11,439	—	11,439
11. James D. Robinson III	Chairman	American Express	2,764	8,169	10,933
12. Kenneth H. Olsen	President	Digital Equipment	932	9,052	9,984

Source: Adapted from *Business Week*, May 1, 1989, p. 47.

does with nonqualified options. Because of tax ramifications, ISOs tend to be preferred by the recipients, while nonqualified options tend to be favored by the organizations.

As shown in Table 14–5, most companies with a stock option plan offer both nonqualified options and ISOs; relatively few companies offer only one. Table 14–6 presents the results of a survey of all types of stock options (nonqualified and ISOs) offered in 1983 and in 1988. As Table 14–6 indicates, there has been considerable growth in the use of stock option plans in the last several years.

Stock options often represent the largest portion of an executive's total compensation. For example, Michael D. Eisner, chairman of Disney, received over $40 million in total compensation in 1988. Of this total, $7.5 million was in the form of salary and bonuses; the rest came primarily from stock options. Table 14–7 shows the salary bonuses and long-term income for many of the country's top-paid executives in 1988.

Stock-for-Stock Swaps

A substantial proportion of companies with stock option plans provide for **stock-for-stock swaps**. This procedure allows options to be exercised with shares of previously purchased company stock in lieu of cash. The advantage is that this arrangement postpones the taxation of any gain on stock already owned.

Stock Appreciation Rights (SARs)

Stock appreciation rights (SARs) are often used with stock option plans. Under a SAR, an executive has the right to relinquish a stock option and receive from the company an amount equal to the appreciation in the stock price from the date the option was granted. The gain is taxed as ordinary income at the time it is

Stock-for-stock swap
This procedure allows options to be exercised with shares of previously purchased company stock in lieu of cash; postpones the taxation of any gain on stock already owned.

Stock appreciation rights (SARs)
Type of nonqualified stock option in which an executive has the right to relinquish a stock option and receive from the company an amount equal to the appreciation in the stock price from the date the option was granted. Under a SAR, the option holder does not have to put up any money, as would be required in a normal stock option plan.

received. The advantage of SARs is that the receiver does not have to put up any money to exercise the option, as he or she would with a normal stock option plan. Holders of SARs may have as long as 10 years to exercise their rights.

Phantom Stock Plans

Phantom stock plans can work in several ways. One is for the company to award stock as a part of its normal bonus plan. The receiver then defers this "phantom" stock until retirement. At retirement, the holder receives the accumulated shares of stock or the equivalent value. The second form of phantom stock is very similar to SARs. The receiver is credited with phantom stock. After a stipulated period of time, usually three to five years, the receiver is paid, in cash or equivalent shares, an amount equal to the appreciation in the stock. The major advantage of phantom stock plans is that the receiver does not have to put up any money at any point in the process. Also, if the value of the stock decreases, the holder does not lose any money.

> **Phantom stock plan**
> Special type of stock option plan that protects the holder if the value of the stock being held decreases; does not require the option holder to put up any money.

Restricted Stock Plans

Under a **restricted stock plan**, a company gives shares of stock, subject to certain restrictions, to participating managers. The major restrictions of most plans is that the shares are subject to forfeiture until they are "earned out" over a stipulated period of continued employment. As with SARs and phantom stock plans, the receivers do not put up or risk any of their own money. An advantage from the organization's viewpoint is that restricted stock plans provide an incentive for executives to remain with the organization.

> **Restricted stock plan**
> Plan under which a company gives shares of stock to participating managers, subject to certain restrictions; the major restriction of most plans is that shares are subject to forfeiture until "earned out" over a stipulated period of continued employment.

Group Incentives

Because jobs can be interdependent, it is sometimes difficult to isolate and evaluate individual performance. In these instances, it is often wise to establish incentives based on group performance. For example, an assembly-line operator must work at the speed of the line. Thus, everyone working on the line is dependent on everyone else. With **group incentives**, all group members receive incentive pay based on the performance of the entire group. Many group incentive plans are based on such factors as profits or reduction in costs of operations.

> **Group incentives**
> Incentives based on group rather than individual performance.

Group incentive plans are designed to encourage employees to exert peer pressure on group members to perform. For instance, if a group member is not performing well and thus is lowering the production of the entire group, the group will usually pressure the individual to improve, especially if a group incentive plan is in operation. A disadvantage of group incentives is that the members of the group may not perceive a direct relationship between their individual performance and that of the group. Size and cohesiveness of the group are two factors that affect this relationship. Usually, smaller groups are more cohesive, because more individuals are likely to perceive a relationship between their performance and that of the group. Another potential disadvantage is that different groups can become overly competitive with each other to the detriment of the entire organization.

Organizationwide Incentives

Organizationwide incentives
Incentives that reward all members of the organization, based on the performance of the entire organization.

Organizationwide incentives reward members based on the performance of the entire organization. With such plans, the size of the reward usually depends on the salary of the individual. Most organizationwide incentive plans are based on establishing cooperative relationships among all levels of employees. One of the first and most successful organizationwide incentive plans was the Lincoln Electric plan, developed by James F. Lincoln.[8] In addition to providing many other benefits, this plan calls for a year-end bonus fund for employees, based on the profits of the company. Thus, the plan encourages the employees to unite with management to reduce costs and increase production so that the bonus fund will grow. HRM in Action 14–3 describes the bonuses awarded by Lincoln Electric in 1984.

Some of the most common organizationwide incentive plans include gain-sharing plans, Scanlon-type plans, and employee stock ownership plans (ESOPs). These three types of plans are discussed in the following sections.

Gain-Sharing or Profit-Sharing Plans

Gain sharing
Programs also known as profit sharing, performance sharing, or productivity incentives; generally refer to incentive plans that involve employees in a common effort to achieve a company's productivity objectives. Based on the concept that the resulting incremental economic gains are shared among employees and the company.

Different companies know **gain sharing** by different names, such as profit sharing, performance sharing, or productivity incentives. These programs generally refer to incentive plans that involve employees in a common effort to achieve a company's productivity objectives. Gain sharing is based on the concept that the resulting incremental economic gains are shared among employees and the company.[9] The division of these gains or profits, which are given in addition to normal wages and salaries, usually are based on an employee's base salary or job level. However, many variations are possible, including plans that give all employees the same amount, plans based on seniority, and plans based on individual performance. One recent survey of 223 companies using some type of gain sharing reported that 95 of the responding companies had custom-designed plans.[10] One potential drawback to gain-sharing/profit-sharing plans is that the average employee may not perceive a direct relationship between individual output and the performance of the entire organization. However, it is not unusual for executives and top managers to have a significant amount of their total compensation based on the profits of the company.

Scanlon-Type Plans

Scanlon plan
Organizationwide incentive plan that provides employees with a bonus based on tangible savings in labor costs.

The **Scanlon plan** was developed by Joseph Scanlon in 1927 and introduced at the LaPointe Machine Tool Company in Hudson, Massachusetts.[11] The Scanlon plan provides employees with a bonus based on tangible savings in labor costs and is designed to encourage employees to suggest changes that might increase productivity. Departmental committees composed of management and employee representatives are established to discuss and evaluate proposed labor-saving techniques. Usually, the bonus paid is determined by comparing actual productivity

▼. HRM in Action 14–3

Incentive Pay at Lincoln Electric

Lincoln Electric Company makes arc welding products and industrial motors. For over 50 years, Lincoln Electric has operated an incentive program that pays employees bonuses that average 97 percent of annual employee earnings. The size of the bonus for each employee is determined during the annual performance appraisal.

In 1984, the company's year-end bonuses totalled $41.8 million, or just over 10 percent of the company's net sales of $373.3 million. The bonuses averaged $17,380.78 for each of the company's 2,405 employees. ees. According to the manager of public relations, Richard Sabo, "We do not maintain any reserve funds to make up for the bad years. We pay out the maximum number of dollars available for the bonus with the intent of earning a new bonus fund next year." Lincoln Electric Company has not laid off an employee since the early 1950s and its workers have never belonged to a union.

Source: "Ohio Firm Rewards Workers with $17,380 Holiday Bonus," *Atlanta Journal and Constitution,* December 6, 1984, p. 1.

to a predetermined productivity norm. Actual productivity is measured by comparing the actual payroll to the sales value of production for the time period being measured. Any difference between actual productivity and the norm is placed in a bonus fund. The bonus fund is then shared by the employees and the company. Most Scanlon plans pay 75 percent of the bonus fund to employees and 25 percent to the company. Under the Scanlon plan, any cost savings are paid to all employees, not just to the individual who made the suggestion. Some companies have found that it is beneficial to review and modify their Scanlon plans periodically to take into account changes that might have occurred.[12]

NZ Forest Products Ltd. in New Zealand has introduced an incentive system similar to the Scanlon plan in that incentives are awarded on the basis of a "total productivity index."[13] Total inputs—labor, materials, and capital—and outputs of each production unit are constantly measured against a fixed standard. Employee incentives are then based on any improvements in total productivity. The interesting thing about the NZ plan is that employees are rewarded even when productivity improves solely through the introduction of more-efficient machinery.

Employee Stock Ownership Plans (ESOPs)

An **employee stock ownership plan (ESOP)** is a form of stock option plan in which an organization provides for purchase of its stock by employees at a set price for a set time period based on their length of service and salary and the profits of the organization. An ESOP is established when the company sets up a trust, called an employee stock ownership trust (ESOT), to acquire a specified number of shares of its own stock for the benefit of participating employees. The trust borrows a sum of money to purchase a specified number of shares of the adopting company's stock. Generally, the loan is guaranteed by the adopting company. Then, the company annually pays into the trust an agreed-on sum necessary to amortize and pay the interest on the loan. As the stock

Employee stock ownership plan (ESOP)
Form of stock option plan in which an organization provides for purchase of its stock by employees at a set price for a set time period based on the employee's length of service and salary and the profits of the organization.

▼ **Table 14–8** Major benefits of employee stock ownership plans

To Organization	**To Employees**	**To Stockholders**
Allows use of pretax dollars to finance debt.	Favorable tax treatment of lump-sum distribution, deferment of tax until distribution, and gift and estate tax exemptions.	Provides ready market to sell stock.
Increases cash flow.		Establishes definite worth of shares for estate purposes.
Provides a ready buyer for stock.	Allows employees to share in the success of the company.	Maintains voting control of company.
Provides a protection against unwanted tender offers.	Provides a source of capital-gains income for employees.	Protects the company from having to come up with large sums of money to settle an estate.
Protects the company from estate problems.	Can allow employees some voice in running the company.	Can result in preferential consideration for a government-guaranteed loan.
Can result in substantial tax savings.		
Can motivate employees by giving them a piece of the action.		

is paid for and received by the trust, it is credited to an account established for each employee on the basis of his or her salary, in proportion to the total payroll of the participating employees. When the employee retires or leaves the company, the stock is either given to the employee or purchased by the trust under a buy-back arrangement. As of 1988, over 9,000 companies had enrolled nearly 10 million employees in ESOPs. This was up from fewer than 500,000 covered employees in 1975.[14]

The amount contributed to ESOP plans is limited to 15 percent of the total payroll of covered employees, or up to 25 percent for plans in which stock bonus and other annuity plans are combined. The contribution of individuals is limited to the lesser of $30,000 or 25 percent of their annual compensation. One appealing feature of ESOPs is that they do have specific tax advantage for both the organization and the employees. For example, the organization can use pretax dollars to pay back the loan used to purchase the stock. The dividends a company pays on stock held by its ESOP are treated like interest and are also deductible. An advantage that has recently emerged is using an ESOP to rebuff an unfriendly takeover. The more stock an ESOP holds, the better equipped the company is to fend off an unwanted tender offer. Employees benefit by being able to defer any capital gains until the stock is actually distributed. ESOPs can also give employees some voice in running the company. Table 14–8 summarizes the primary benefits of ESOPs for the organization, the employee, and the stockholders.

One underlying assumption of an ESOP is that having a piece of the action causes employees to take more interest in the success of the company. Several studies have shown that companies combining an ESOP with employee participation in decision making enjoy sharply higher sales and earnings growth.[15] At Brunswick Corporation, for instance, sales per employee have jumped nearly 50 percent since the company set up an ESOP in 1983.[16] On the other hand, ESOPs can have a limited effect as incentives. This is especially true when each employee owns only a miniscule amount of stock. Also, it is possible that the price of the

▼. HRM in Action 14–4

Avis Tries Even Harder

In September 1987, Avis set up an ESOP and bought its car rental company from Wesray Capital Corporation for $1.75 billion. After the buyout, Avis Chairman Joseph V. Vittoria set up an elaborate system that gives Avis employees a significant say in how the company is managed. At the heart of the system are employee participation groups (EPGs), which have representatives from mechanics to rental agents. Employees are encouraged to suggest ways for improving customer service and running the business more efficiently. As of mid-1989, Avis had paid off $90 million of its $395 million buyout debt—$50 million ahead of schedule. Service complaints for the 12 months ended on August 31, 1988, were down 35 percent from the previous year. Furthermore, according to an independent valuation, Avis stock was up to $15.22 at the beginning of 1989, as compared to $5.47 at the time of the buyout.

Source: Harris Collingwood, "With Its ESOP, Avis Tries Even Harder," *Business Week*, May 15, 1989, p. 122.

▼ **Table 14–9**   Summary of most-used incentive plans

Personnel	Type of Plan		
	Individual	**Group**	**Organizational**
Nonmanagers	Piece rate plans Plans based on time saved 　Rowan plan 　Halsey premium plan Commission plans Bonuses based on individual performance Suggestion systems	Bonuses based on group performance	Lincoln Electric plan Gain-sharing/profit-sharing plans Scanlon-type plans Employee stock ownership plans (ESOPs)
Managers	Bonuses based on organizational performance (annual and long-term) Stock option plans 　Stock appreciation rights (SARs) 　Phantom stock plans 　Restricted stock plans Suggestion systems	Bonuses based on group performance	Lincoln Electric plan Gain-sharing/profit-sharing plans Scanlon-type plans Employee stock ownership plans (ESOPs)

stock may go down rather than up. Thus, some people view an employee stock option plan as more of a benefit than an incentive. HRM in Action 14–4 describes the positive impact that an ESOP has had at Avis.

Table 14–9 summarizes and categorizes the different incentive plans that have been discussed.

Making Incentive Plans Work

Incentive plans have been in existence in one form or another for a long time. New plans are periodically developed, often as a result of changes in tax laws. As several examples in this chapter demonstrated, incentive compensation can make up a significant portion of an individual's total compensation. This is especially true with executives. If an incentive plan is to function as intended and generate higher performance among employees, it must be clearly communicated to employees and must be viewed as being fair. It is imperative that a clear explanation of all incentive plans be given to all affected employees. It also follows that the more employees understand an incentive plan, the more confidence and trust they will develop in the organization.

● *Summary of Learning Objectives*

1.   Name the two basic requirements of an effective incentive plan.

If an incentive plan is to be effective, employees must feel that their performance and the performances of others are accurately and fairly evaluated and that the incentives (rewards) are based on performance.

2.   Name and briefly discuss two types of individual incentives based on time saved.

With the Halsey premium plan, employees are paid a guaranteed hourly wage plus a premium for any time saved by producing a given quantity in less than standard time. The Rowan plan differs from the Halsey premium plan in that the percentage paid for time saved is not fixed, but is determined by the percentage of time saved.

3.   Distinguish between a bonus and a merit pay increase.

A bonus is a reward offered on a one-time basis for high performance. A merit pay increase is a reward also based on performance, but perpetuated year after year.

4.   Discuss the role that bonuses play in managerial compensation.

Bonuses are by far the most common type of incentive pay used for managers. The 1986 Tax Reform Act has made bonuses even more popular. Recent surveys have reported that bonuses made up over 35 percent of total salaries and over 25 percent of total compensation received by managers.

5.   Differentiate between nonqualified stock options and incentive stock options (ISOs).

Stock option plans are generally designed to give managers an option to buy company stock at a predetermined, fixed price within a set period of time. Nonqualified stock options do not qualify for favorable tax treatment. Incentive stock options (ISOs) have certain tax advantages. Under an ISO, a recipient does not have to pay any tax until he or she sells the stock.

6.   Explain how group incentives work.

Under a group incentive plan, all members of a specified group receive incentive pay based on the performance of the entire group. Many group incentive plans are based on such factors as profits or reduction in costs of operations.

7. Explain what a gain-sharing plan is.

Gain sharing is also known as profit sharing, performance sharing, or productivity incentives. Gain-sharing plans generally refer to incentive plans that involve employees in a common effort to achieve a company's productivity objective. Gain sharing is based on the concept that the resulting incremental economic gains are shared among employees and the company.

8. Discuss Scanlon-type plans.

Scanlon-type plans provide employees with a bonus based on tangible savings in labor costs and are designed to encourage employees to suggest changes that might increase productivity. Under a Scanlon-type plan, any cost savings are paid to all employees, not just to the individual who made the suggestion.

9. Explain how an employee stock ownership plan (ESOP) works.

An employee stock ownership plan (ESOP) is a form of stock option in which an organization provides for purchase of its stock by employees at a set price for a set time period based on the employee's length of service and salary and the profits of the company. An ESOP is established when the company sets up a trust, called an employee stock ownership trust (ESOT), to acquire a specified number of shares of its own stock for the benefit of participating employees. The trust borrows a sum of money to purchase a specified number of shares of the adopting company's stock. Generally, the loan is guaranteed by the adopting company. Then, the company annually pays into the trust an agreed-on sum necessary to amortize and pay the interest on the loan. As the stock is paid for and received by the trust, it is credited to an account established for each employee on the basis of his or her salary, in proportion to the total payroll of the participating employees. When the employee retires or leaves the company, the stock is either given to the employee or purchased by the trust under a buy-back arrangement.

Review Questions

1. What are two essential requirements for an incentive plan to be effective?
2. Outline the advantages and disadvantages of individual incentive plans.
3. What is a piece rate plan?
4. What is an incentive plan based on time saved? Describe two common plans of this type.
5. Describe an incentive plan based on commission.
6. What is a long-term performance plan?
7. Define a stock option plan.
8. What is a suggestion plan?
9. Name the advantages and disadvantages of a group incentive plan.
10. Describe the most common types of organizationwide incentive plans.
11. What are the benefits of an ESOP to employees? To the organization? To stockholders?

Discussion Questions

1. It has been said that incentive plans only work for a relatively short time. Do you agree or disagree? Why?

2. If you were able to choose the type of incentive pay system your company would offer you, would you choose an individual, group, or organizationwide incentive plan? Why?

3. If you were president of Ford Motor Co. and could design and implement any type of incentive plan, what general type would you recommend for top management? For middle management? For production employees?

4. Do you think that incentive plans are likely to increase or decrease in use over the next several years? Why?

▼ INCIDENT 14–1

Rewarding Good Performance in a Bank

The performance of a bank branch manager often is difficult to measure. Evaluation can include such variables as loan quality, deposit growth, employee turnover, complaint levels, or audit results. However, many other factors that influence performance—such as the rate structure, changes in the market area served by the branch, and loan policy as set by senior management—are beyond the branch manager's control. The appraisal system presently used by the First Trust Bank is based on points. Points are factored in for a manager's potential productivity and for the actual quality and quantity of work. In this system, the vast majority of raises are between 4 and 10 percent of base salary.

Sales growth is a major responsibility of a branch manager. Although many salespeople are paid a salary plus bonuses and commissions, no commissions are paid on business brought in by a branch manager. Therefore, one problem for the bank has been adequately rewarding those branch managers who excel at sales.

In May 1988, the First Trust Bank opened a new branch on Northside Parkway, located in a high-income area. Three competing banks had been in the neighborhood for some 15 years. Jim Bryan, who had grown up in the Northside Parkway area, was selected as branch manager. In addition to Jim, the branch was staffed with five qualified people. Senior executives of the bank had disagreed about the feasibility of opening this branch. However, it was Jim's responsibility to get the bank a share of the market, which consisted at that time of approximately $28 million in deposits.

The results, after one year of operation, was that this branch had the fastest growth of any ever opened by the First Trust Bank. In 12 months, deposits grew to $6 million, commercial loans to $1 million, and installment loans to $.5 million. As measured by federal reserve reports, the new branch captured 50 percent of the market growth in deposits over the 12 months. The customer service provided for previously enrolled and new customers was extremely good, and branch goals for profit were reached ahead of schedule. Aware of the success, Jim looked forward to his next raise.

The raise amounted to 10 percent of his salary. His boss said that he would like to have given Jim more, but the system wouldn't allow it.

Questions

1. Should Jim have been satisfied, since this was the maximum raise he could be given under the system?
2. Do you think the bank is currently offering adequate sales incentives to its branch managers? If not, what would you recommend?

▼ *INCIDENT 14–2*

Part-Time Pool Personnel

The Crystal Clear Pool Company builds and maintains swimming pools in a large midwestern city. Pool maintenance is handled through a contractual arrangement between Crystal Clear and the owners of the pools. Although individualized maintenance plans are available at a premium, the basic contract calls for Crystal Clear to vacuum the pools and adjust their chemical balance once a week. For 80 percent of the maintenance customers, the standard contract covers the months of May through September. The remaining 20 percent, who have either indoor or covered pools, require service year-round.

Because of the seasonal nature of the work, Crystal Clear hires many students during the summer. The maintenance staff is divided into three-person crews, each of which is assigned to service six pools per day. In the summer, one permanent employee and two student workers compose a team, with the permanent staffer responsible for training the students. All maintenance crews are paid on a straight hourly basis.

The present system has been in force for several years, but it has resulted in at least two problems that seem to be getting more serious each year. The first is that the students hired for the summer demand to be paid the same wage rates that apply to the permanent employees. This is because the college students can get other summer jobs at these rates and are simply not willing to work for less. Naturally, the permanent employees resent the idea of their pay being the same as the students. The second major problem involves the assignment of the pools, which vary in size and geographic location. The employees claim that this is unfair because of the travel time required and differences in pool size. Some pools take three or four times as long to clean as others. Thus, some teams must work harder than others to service the six assigned pools.

Questions

1. What suggestions do you have for Crystal Clear to help remedy their compensation problems?
2. Can you think of any way to implement an incentive program at Crystal Clear? Do not ignore the scheduling problems that might be created by such a program.
3. In general, how do you think the problem of having to pay new employees the same rate as old employees could be resolved?

Exercise

Implementing Incentives

Assume you have been hired as a consultant to a medium-sized sales organization to help them structure an incentive system for the three basic categories of employees in the organization. The first category is the sales force, composed of 20 salespeople all working on straight commission. The second category is composed of seven support people (two secretaries, and five packer/shippers). All seven work on a straight hourly wage rate. The third category is made up of the two owner/managers.

The owner/managers like the straight commission system that the salespeople are on, but they suspect that many of the salespeople tend to slack off once they have attained an acceptable level of sales for any given month. The seven support people appear to be steady workers, but management believes their performance could be enhanced with the right incentive program. The owner/managers are satisfied with their current salaries but would like to look for some tax shelter for any additional profits.

Your job is to design an incentive plan that will include parts that will be attractive to each of the three categories of employees. Be prepared to present your plan to the class.

Notes and Additional Readings

1. J. G. Goodale and M. W. Mouser, "Developing and Auditing a Merit Pay System," *Personnel Journal,* May 1981, p. 391.

2. S. Pollard, *The Genesis of Modern Management: A Study of the Industrial Revolution in Great Britain* (Cambridge, Mass.: Harvard University Press, 1965), p. 190.

3. "Suggestion Systems, an Answer to Perennial Problems," *Personnel Journal,* July 1980, p. 553.

4. Donna Brunette and Tim C. Bousum, "Calculate Suggestion Program Savings," *Personnel Journal,* February 1989, p. 33.

5. *Executive Compensation Service Top Management Report,* 39th ed. (Fort Lee, N.J.: Executive Compensation Service, 1988), p. 26.

6. Elizabeth R. Arreglado and Charles A. Peck, *Top Executives Compensation,* 1988 ed. (New York: Conference Board, 1988), p. 2.

7. *Executive Compensation Service Top Management Report,* p. 25.

8. C. W. Brennan, *Age Administration,* rev. ed. (Homewood, Ill.: Richard D. Irwin, 1963), pp. 288–89.

9. Barry W. Thomas and Madeline Hess Olson, "Gain Sharing: The Design Guarantees Success," *Personnel Journal,* May 1988, p. 73.

10. Carla O'Dell and Jerry McAdams, *People, Performance, and Pay* (Houston: The American Productivity Center, 1987), p. 34.

11. Brennan, *Wage Administration,* p. 299.

12. J. Ramquist, "Labor-Management Cooperation—The Scanlon Plan at Work," *Sloan Management Review,* Spring 1982, pp. 49–55.

13. S. Salmons, "Total Productivity Bonus Increases Involvement," *International Management,* September 1978, pp. 35–41.

14. Christopher Farrell and John Hoerr, "ESOPs: Are They Good for You?" *Business Week,* May 15, 1989, p. 118; and John Hoerr and James R. Norman, "ESOPs: Revolution or Ripoff?" *Business Week,* April 15, 1985, p. 94.

15. Christopher Farrell, Tim Smart, and Keith Hammonds, "Suddenly, Blue Chips Are Red-Hot for ESOPs," *Business Week,* March 20, 1989.

16. Christopher Farrell and John Hoerr, "ESOPs: Are They Good For You?," p. 117.

Chapter 15

Employee Benefits

Chapter Outline

What Are Employee Benefits?
Growth in Employee Benefits
Communicating the Benefit Package
Employee Preferences among Benefits
   Flexible Benefit Plans
Legally Required Benefits
   Social Security
   Unemployment Compensation
   Workers' Compensation
Retirement-Related Benefits
   Pension Plans
   Employees Not Covered by Pension Plans
   Preretirement Planning
Insurance-Related Benefits
   Health Insurance
   Health Maintenance Organizations (HMOs)

   Dental Insurance
   Life Insurance
   Accident and Disability Insurance
Payment for Time Not Worked
   Paid Holidays
   Paid Vacations
Other Benefits
The Benefit Package
Summary of Learning Objectives
Review Questions
Discussion Questions
Incident 15–1: Who Is Eligible for Retirement Benefits?
Incident 15–2: Fringe Benefits for Professionals
Exercise: Taking a Raise
Notes and Additional Readings

● *Learning Objectives*

After studying this chapter, you should be able to:

1. Define employee benefits.
2. Describe how employee benefits have grown over the last several years.
3. Explain the concept of a flexible benefit plan.
4. Summarize those benefits that are legally required.
5. Differentiate between a defined benefit pension plan and a defined contribution pension plan.
6. Explain the purposes of the Employee Retirement Income Security Act (ERISA) and the Retirement Equity Act.
7. Distinguish between an IRA and a Keogh plan.
8. Describe a health maintenance organization (HMO) and a preferred provider organization (PPO).
9. Explain the concept of a floating holiday.

"*T*he very expensive but often forgotten stepchild of the total compensation package is that segment frequently called *fringe benefits*. These benefits are primarily the in-kind payments employees receive in addition to the payments they receive in the form of money. At one time, fringe benefits were of marginal importance, but this is no longer true. In many organizations today, they account for at least 35 percent of the total compensation cost for each employee, and possibly in the next decade they will reach 50 percent. (Some organizations have already exceeded this point.) When an element of the compensation package reaches this proportion, it is no longer marginal. The fringe benefits of yesterday have evolved into the employee benefits and services of today."

Richard I. Henderson*

Employee benefits (fringe benefits) Rewards that an organization provides to employees for being members of the organization; usually not related to employee performance.

Employee benefits, sometimes called **fringe benefits**, are those rewards that organizations provide to employees for being members of the organization. Unlike wages, salaries, and incentives, benefits are usually not related to employee performance. Figures compiled by the U.S. Chamber of Commerce show that payments by organizations for employee benefits in 1987 averaged slightly over $10,700 per year per employee.[1] These same figures indicated that benefit payments varied widely among the reporting companies, ranging from under $3,500 to more than $13,000 per year per employee. The average of slightly over $10,700 represents approximately 39 percent of total compensation received by the average employee. A recent survey conducted by Hewitt Associates of benefits directors from 100 major U.S. industrial companies reported that over 50 percent expect benefits to increase in the 1990s as a percentage of total compensation.[2] Only 9 percent of this group expect benefits to decrease as a percentage of total compensation.

The term *fringe benefits* was coined over 40 years ago by the War Labor Board. Reasoning that employer-provided benefits such as paid vacations, holidays, and pensions were "on the fringe of wages," the agency exempted them from pay controls.[3] It has been argued that this action, more than any single event, led to the dramatic expansion of employee benefits that has since occurred. However, because of the significance of benefits to total compensation, the world *fringe* has been dropped by many employers for fear that it has a minimizing effect.[4]

What Are Employee Benefits?

Table 15–1 presents a list of potential employee benefits. In general, these can be grouped into five major categories: (1) legally required, (2) retirement related, (3) insurance related, (4) payment for time not worked, and (5) other. Table 15–2 categorizes many of the most common employee benefits. Table 15–3 shows how total benefit expenditures are allocated among the major categories. Most

*Source: R. I. Henderson, *Compensation Management: Rewarding Performance,* 3d ed. (Reston, VA: Reston Publishing, 1979), p. 308.

▼ Table 15–1   Potential employee benefits

Accidental death, dismemberment insurance	Holidays (extra)	Psychiatric services
Birthdays (vacation)	Home health care	Recreation facilities
Bonus eligibility	Hospital-surgical-medical insurance	Resort facilities
Business and professional memberships	Incentive growth fund	Retirement gratuity
Cash profit sharing	Interest-free loans	Sabbatical leaves
Club memberships	Layoff pay	Salary
Commissions	Legal, estate-planning, and other professional assistance	Salary continuation
Company medical assistance	Loans of company equipment	Savings plan
Company-provided automobile	Long-term disability benefit	Scholarships for dependents
Company-provided housing	Matching educational donations	Severance pay
Company-provided or subsidized travel	Nurseries	Shorter or flexible work week
Day-care centers	Nursing-home care	Sickness and accident insurance
Deferred bonus	Opportunity for travel	Social security
Deferred compensation plan	Outside medical services	Social service sabbaticals
Deferred profit sharing	Paid attendance at business, professional, and other outside meetings	Split-dollar life insurance
Dental and eye care insurance	Parking facilities	State disability plans
Discount on company products	Pension	Stock appreciation rights
Education costs	Personal accident insurance	Stock bonus plan
Educational activities (time off)	Personal counseling	Stock option plans (qualified, nonqualified, tandem)
Employment contract	Personal credit cards	Stock purchase plan
Executive dining room	Personal expense accounts	Survivors' benefits
Free checking account	Physical examinations	Tax assistance
Free or subsidized lunches	Political activities (time off)	Training programs
Group automobile insurance	Price discount plan	Vacations
Group homeowners' insurance	Private office	Wages
Group life insurance	Professional activities	Weekly indemnity insurance
Health maintenance organization fees		

Source: D. J. Thomsen, "Introducing Cafeteria Compensation in Your Company," *Personnel Journal*, March 1977, p. 125. Reprinted with permission of *Personnel Journal*, Costa Mesa, CA. All rights reserved.

▼ Table 15–2   Examples of common benefits, by major category

Legally Required	Retirement Related	Insurance Related	Payment for Time Not Worked	Other
Social security	Pension fund	Medical insurance	Vacation	Company discounts
Unemployment compensation	Annuity plan	Accident insurance	Holidays	Meals furnished by company
Workers' compensation	Early retirement	Life insurance	Sick leave	Moving expenses
State disability insurance	Disability retirement	Disability insurance	Military leave	Severance pay
	Retirement gratuity	Dental insurance	Election day	Tuition refunds
		Survivor benefits	Birthdays	Credit union
			Funerals	Company car
			Paid rest periods	Legal services
			Lunch periods	Financial counseling
			Wash-up time	Recreation facilities
			Travel time	

▼ **Table 15–3**   Benefit expenditures, by major categories

Legally required benefits (employer's share only)	23%
Retirement related	17
Insurance related	22
Payment for time not worked	35
Other	3
Total	100%

Source: Based on figures from U.S. Chamber Survey Research Center, *Employee Benefits,* 1988 ed. (Washington, D.C.: Chamber of Commerce of the United States, 1988), p. 8.

benefits apply to all members of the organization; however, some are reserved solely for executives. Note that some of the examples listed in Table 15–1 are now taken for granted by many employees.

Growth in Employee Benefits

Prior to the passage of the Social Security Act in 1935, employee benefits were not widespread. Not only did the act mandate certain benefits, but its implementation greatly increased the general public's awareness of the area of employee benefits. By this time, unions had grown in strength and had begun to demand more benefits in their contracts. Thus, the 1930s are generally viewed as the birth years for employee benefits.

As productivity continued to increase through and after World War II, more and more employee benefits came into existence. Although the categories used are slightly different from those described earlier, Figure 15–1 shows how employee benefits grew from 1951 to 1987. HRM in Action 5–1 describes how one company put itself into an economic corner by agreeing with its union to provide benefits it couldn't afford.

Communicating the Benefit Package

Although most organizations provide some form of benefits to their employees, the average employee often has little idea of what he or she is receiving. Why are employees often unaware of their benefits? One explanation is that organizations do not make much of an effort to communicate their employee benefits.

Another possible explanation of why employees are not aware of their benefits is that descriptive material on benefits, when available, is often not easily understood by employees. One provision of the Employee Retirement Income Security Act of 1974 (ERISA) requires an employer at specified intervals to communicate certain types of benefit information in a manner employees can understand. Several meth-

Benefits Exceed Book Value of Company

In January 1984, National Steel turned over the assets of its Weirton division to its employees. The purchase was the final step in many months of efforts by owners and employees to save the company from liquidation.

The buyout was the final result of a history of compounding liabilities. In 1959, management and the union negotiated a benefit that permitted workers who began continuous employment at age 18 to retire early at full pension if the plant closed after they reached 49. In 1966, another benefit was negotiated that allowed a worker with 30 years service to retire early for any reason. From 1973 through 1982, the steel industry led all major U.S. industries in wage increases.

When economic conditions forced National Steel to consider closing the Weirton facility, the facts were difficult to accept. If the plant was shut down, 4,100 of the 8,000 workers would be able to retire under one of the plans. Taken together, the present value of the total cash outlays brought about by early-retirement severance pay and health care payments resulting from the plant shutdown would be roughly $450 million. Since the book value of the investment in Weirton was $448 million—an unlikely liquidation figure—management was forced to look for alternatives other than closing the facility. Weirton employees agreed to a 32 percent compensation reduction (still 31 percent higher than the average of workers in all U.S. manufacturing), but only if the company's net assets were turned over to them through a stock ownership plan.

Source: William E. Panham, Jr., "Management, Labor, and the Golden Goose," *Harvard Business Review*, September–October 1985, pp. 131–41.

▼ Figure 15–1   Growth of employee benefits, 1951–1987

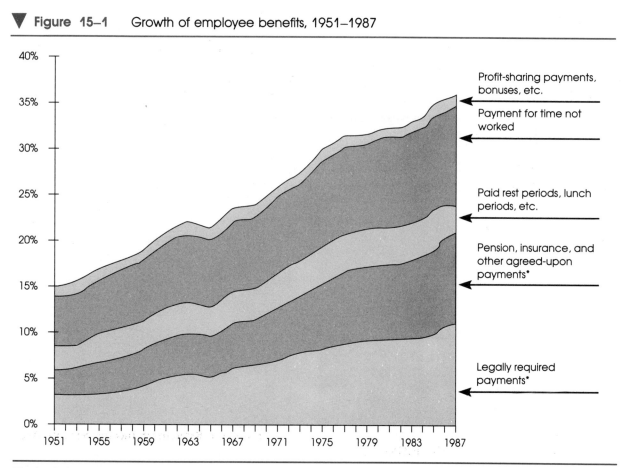

*Employer's share only
Source: Reprinted with the permission of the Chamber of Commerce of the United States from Employee Benefits, copyright © 1988, p. 31.

 **Figure 15–2**   Sample employee earnings and benefits letter

Company Name
Address
Date

Employee's Name
Address

Dear

    Enclosed are your W-2 forms showing the amount of taxable income that you received from _____ during 19____. Listed below in Section A are your gross wages and a cost breakdown of various fringe benefit programs that you enjoy. In addition to the money you received as wages, the company paid benefits for you that are not included in your W-2 statement. These are fringe benefits that are somtimes overlooked. In an easy-to-read form, here's what _____ paid to you in 19____.

Section A—Paid to you in your W-2 earnings:

Cost-of-living allowance   _____
Shift premium   _____
Service award(s)   _____
Vacation pay   _____
Holiday pay   _____
Funeral pay   _____
Jury duty pay   _____
Military pay   _____
Accident & sickness benefits   _____
Regular earnings   _____
Overtime earnings   _____
Allowances   _____
    Gross wages   _____

Section B—Paid for you and not included in your W-2 earnings:

Company contributed to pension plan   _____
Company cost of your hospitalization payments   _____
Company cost of your life & accidental death insurance   _____
Company cost for social security tax on your wages   _____
Company cost of the premium for your workers'
   compensation   _____
Company cost for the tax on your wages for
   unemployment compensation   _____
Company cost for tuition refund   _____
Company cost for safety glasses   _____
    Total cost of benefits not included in W-2 earnings   _____

    Total _____ paid
    for your services in 19____   ====================

    You have earned the amount on the bottom line, but we want to give you a clearer idea of the total cost of your services to the company, and the protection and benefits that are being purchased for you and your family.

                Sincerely,

                Manager of Human Resources

Source: Adapted from J. C. Claypool and J. P. Cargemi, "The Annual Employee Earnings and Benefits Letter," *Personnel Journal*, July 1980, p. 564.

▽. HRM in Action 15–2

MetLife SHOWCASE

Metropolitan Life Insurance Company now offers an interactive benefits communication service called MetLife SHOWCASE.℠ MetLife SHOWCASE resembles an automatic bank teller machine in appearance and operation. The service has the ability to review a plan's general provisions, highlight recent changes, explain how to initiate benefits transactions, and provide personalized benefit information for an employee. The service also has the ability to forecast and answer "What-if" questions in a number of areas, such as changes to savings contributions, benefits coverage changes, take-home pay, and pension size. American Express Travel Related Service Company, Rockwell International Corporation, and Scott Paper Company are some of the organizations now using MetLife SHOWCASE. MetLife SHOWCASE is not limited to providing benefits information; it can also be used for internal job posting, employee surveys, newsletters, and other communications.

Source: Tim Chauran, "Benefits Communication," *Personnel Journal,* January 1989, p. 77.

ods can be used to evaluate the readability of written documents. Generally, in these methods, the number of words per sentence and the percentage of difficult, polysyllabic words in the passage are counted in a readability index that is related to a school-grade reading level.[5] The basic goal is to match the readability index of the benefit description to the educational level of the organization's employees.

The method used in communicating the benefit package is as important as the readability of the document. One successful method of communication is a personalized statement sent periodically to each employee. The employee earnings and benefits letter shown in Figure 15–2 is an example of such a statement. For organizations that use a computerized payroll system, some benefit information can easily be printed on each employee's check stub. Other methods for communicating benefit information include posters and visual presentations, such as movies, slide shows, and flip charts. Meetings and conferences can also be used to explain an organization's benefits. HRM in Action 15–2 describes some new technology that is available to help communicate benefits information.

Employee Preferences among Benefits

If an organization expects to get the maximum return from its fringe benefits package in terms of such factors as motivation, satisfaction, low turnover, and good relations with unions, the benefits should be those most preferred by its employees. Ironically, however, organizations traditionally have done little to ensure that this is the case. Historically, they have offered union benefit packages selected by the human resources department and top management. Only on rare occasions or when demanded by a union contract are employees consulted concerning their benefit preferences.

Organizations that provide benefits without input from employees are assuming that management always knows what is best for the employees and that all employees need and desire the same benefits. Not too long ago a "typical" employee was male, middle-aged, worked full time, supported 2.5 children, and had a wife who stayed home.[6] This so-called typical employee no longer exists. More than 85 percent of today's employees are anything but "typical."[7] Given that the work force is far from homogeneous, it is not surprising that studies have shown that factors such as sex, age, marital status, number of dependents, years of service, and job title appear to influence benefit preferences.[8]

Flexible Benefit Plans

Flexible benefit plan
Same as cafeteria plan of benefits (see below).

Because of the differences in employee preferences, some companies began to offer flexible benefits plans in the mid-1970s. Under a **flexible benefit plan**, individual employees have some choice as to specific benefits that each will actually receive; usually employees select from among several options how they want their direct compensation and benefits to be distributed. The idea is to allow employees to select benefits most appropriate to their individual needs and lifestyles. For example, a middle-aged employee with several children in school might choose to take a set of benefits different from those chosen by a young, single employee.

Cafeteria plans of benefits
Employees have the opportunity to choose, from a wide range of alternatives, how their benefits will be distributed.

Flexible plans are also called **cafeteria plans of benefits** because they provide a "menu," or choice of benefits, from which employees select.[9] The selection possibilities within a flexible benefit plan may vary considerably from plan to plan. Some plans limit the choices to only a few types of coverage, such as life insurance and health insurance. Others allow employees to choose from a wide range of options.

Even though the number of companies offering flexible plans is not huge, it has grown steadily since 1980 (see Figure 15–3). TRW Systems and Energy Group, Educational Testing Service, American Can, Northern States Power, and North

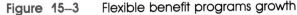

▼ Figure 15–3   Flexible benefit programs growth

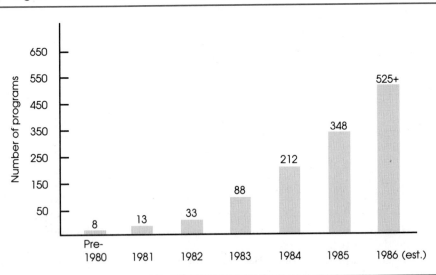

Source: *On Flexible Compensation* (Hewitt Associates, Lincolnshire, Il.), January 1986, p. 1.

American Van Lines (a subsidiary of PepsiCo) were some of the first companies to offer flexible benefits.

Why Are Flexible Plans Attractive?

Flexible plans might be of interest to organizations for several reasons:[10]

1. Employee benefits are an increasing component of overall compensation. Thus, benefits are taking on more and more significance.

2. Flexible benefits can allow employees to limit their contributions without alienating employees, since options give employees some control over the distribution of benefits.

3. Lifestyles have changed in the past several years, causing employees to reevaluate the need for certain traditional benefits. For example, in a family where both spouses work and receive family medical insurance, one coverage is sufficient.

4. Benefits can be useful in recruiting and retaining employees. However, when a mandatory benefits package is largely unresponsive to a prospective employee's needs or to the retention of present employees, the organization is wasting money.

5. The increasing cost of benefits is causing organizations to try to communicate effectively the real cost to the employee. By making specific benefit choices, the employee becomes intimately familiar with the costs associated with each benefit.

6. Because certain benefits are taxable and others are not, different benefit mixes can be attractive to different employees (the tax ramifications of flexible plans are discussed in a later section).

7. A flexible plan can have a positive impact on employee attitudes and behavior.

Problems with Flexible Plans

Unfortunately, flexible plans are not without their difficulties. The major problems are:[11]

1. A flexible plan requires more effort to administer.

2. Unions often oppose flexible plans because they are required to give up control over the program details or face losing some of their previously negotiated benefit improvements.

3. Employees may not choose those benefits that are in their own best interests.

4. Tax laws limit the amount of individual flexibility in certain situations.

Tax Implications of Flexible Plans

Flexible benefits plans that offer employees choices between taxable and nontaxable benefits are subject to special rules under the Internal Revenue Code's Section 125, enacted in 1978. Plans that offer choices only among nontaxable benefits are not subject to Section 125. The Deficit Reduction Act (DEFRA) of 1984 clarified many of the tax questions that had clouded flexible benefits since the inception of Section 125. The following list summarizes many of the requirements resulting from Section 125 and/or DEFRA:

▽. HRM in Action 15–3

Introducing a Flexible Benefits Program

The Rouse Company began looking into flexible benefits in late 1981 as a result of current and projected escalating costs. The first task was to develop the overall benefits design objectives and have them agreed on by senior management. Once the overall objectives were defined, the company established employee focus groups to identify the perceived strengths and weaknesses of the current program and later to test the proposed flexible approach. Four groups of between 15 to 20 people were used. With the overall objectives and inputs from the focus groups, a flexible benefits plan was designed and then sent back to the focus groups for their reactions. After receiving an overwhelmingly positive response from the focus groups, a letter was sent to each employee's home inviting him or her to a luncheon to be held in October 1982, to introduce the new program.

Following the luncheon, group meetings were held over the next month to give employees a more detailed explanation of the program and to distribute the 1983 workbook and election form.

After the program had been in effect for seven months, an opinion survey was conducted to find out how employees viewed the new program. Ninety-nine percent of the respondents felt the new benefits program was a good one, and almost 80 percent reported that the new program was better than the old one. Since first introduced in 1983, changes have been implemented every year (up through 1988) in an attempt to refine and make the program even better.

Source: William D. Boden, "Flexible Benefits: One Company's View," *Compensation and Benefits Review,* pp. 11–16.

- An employer cannot require an employee to complete more than three years of service before becoming eligible under the plan.
- Flexible plans must offer a choice between only taxable and statutory nontaxable benefits. Taxable benefits allowed include cash, group term life insurance in excess of $50,000, and group term life insurance for dependents. Statutory nontaxable benefits include group term life insurance, group legal services, accident and health benefits, dependent care assistance, and certain types of deferred compensation. Vacation days are also treated as nontaxable benefits.
- If more than 25 percent of the total nontaxable benefits in the plan are provided for key employees (as defined by Section 416(i)(1) of the Internal Revenue Code), then the key employees will be taxed on the value of those benefits.
- Employee benefits elections must be irrevocable and made at the beginning of the period of coverage.
- No change in coverage is allowed except in the case of a change in family status.
- No cash-out or carryover of individual balances is allowed if the selected benefits are not fully used. In other words, any monies left in an account at the end of the year must be forfeited.

Although the present laws do place certain restrictions, there is still considerable opportunity to establish effective flexible plans, and the potential gains from them are enough to merit consideration. HRM in Action 15–3 describes how one company successfully implemented a flexible benefits program.

▼ **Table   15–4**   Changes in social security costs*

Year	Percentage Paid by Employee	Maximum Taxable Pay	Maximum Tax
1978	6.05%	$17,700	$1,071
1979	6.13	22,900	1,404
1980	6.13	25,900	1,588
1981	6.65	29,700	1,975
1982	6.70	32,400	2,171
1983	6.70	35,700	2,392
1984	7.00	37,800	2,646
1985	7.05	39,600	2,792
1986	7.15	42,000	3,003
1987	7.15	43,800	3,132
1988	7.51	45,000	3,380
1989	7.51	48,000	3,605
1990	7.65	51,300*	3,924
1991	7.65	54,900*	4,200

*These figures are projected and subject to revision by Congress.

Legally Required Benefits

As discussed earlier, certain benefits have been mandated by law. This section will discuss social security, unemployment, and workers' compensation benefits.

Social Security

Social security is a federally administered insurance system. Under current federal laws, both employer and employee must pay into the system, and a certain percentage of the employee's salary is paid up to a maximum limit. Table 15–4 shows how social security costs have changed over the past several years and how they are forecast to change through 1991.

> **Social security**
> Federally administered insurance system designed to provide funds upon retirement or disability or both and to provide hospital and medical reimbursement to people who have reached retirement age.

With few exceptions, social security is mandatory for employees and employers. The most noteworthy exceptions are state and local government employees. For these employees to become exempt, a majority must vote to do so, and another retirement system must be substituted. Self-employed persons are required to contribute to social security at a rate higher than that paid by a normal employee, but less than the combined percentage paid by both employer and employee. The payments distributed under social security can be grouped into three major categories: retirement benefits, disability benefits, and health insurance.

Retirement Benefits under Social Security

To be eligible for periodic payments through social security, a person must have reached retirement age, must actually be retired, and must be fully insured under the system. The full periodic allotment to which the retiree is entitled may begin at age 65 (this is scheduled to increase to age 67 by the year 2027); those who retire as early as age 62 receive lesser amounts. A person is considered fully retired when he or she is earning from gainful employment less than a prescribed amount of money. (Money earned from gainful employment does not include income from investments, pensions, or other retirement programs.) In 1989, this was $8,880 for people aged 65 and over and $6,480 for people under 65. However, these amounts change almost every year. Persons 70 and older are eligible for full retirement benefits regardless of their level of earned income.

To be fully insured, an employee must have at least as many quarters of coverage as the number of years elapsing after 1950 (or the year that the person reached 21, if later than 1950) and the year that age 62 is reached. However, a person with 40 quarters of coverage is fully insured for life and needs no additional covered employment to quality for retirement benefits. Table 15–5 gives some examples of how to calculate the requirements for being fully insured. In 1989, a person received credit for one quarter of coverage for every $500 earned during a calendar year, up to a maximum of four. Self-employed persons receive one quarter of credit for each $500 of net profit earned in a calendar year.

The size of the retirement benefit varies according to the individual's average earnings under covered employment. However, there are maximum and minimum limits to what eligible individuals and their dependents can receive. Table 15–6 lists dependents who may be eligible for retirement benefits if an eligible employee should die.

▼ **Table 15–5**   Calculating requirements for being fully insured

Date of Birth	Year Becomes 21	Year Becomes 62	Number of Quarters Required to Be Fully Insured
1920	1941	1982	1982 – 1951* = 31
1945	1966	2007	2007 – 1966 = 41**

*Subtract 1951, since it is the number of years *after* 1950.
**A person with 40 quarters of coverage is fully insured for life.

▼ **Table 15–6**   Dependents eligible for retirement benefits in the event of death of a covered employee

1. Widow or widower at age 65, or age 60 if reduced benefits are chosen.
2. Widow or widower at any age, if caring for a child of the deceased. The child must be entitled to social security and be either disabled or under 18.
3. Disabled widow or widower 50 to 59 (at age 60 becomes eligible in above-mentioned widow or widower category).
4. Unmarried children under 18, or 22 if full-time students, and those 18 or over who became disabled before reaching 22.
5. Dependent parents 62 or older.
6. Divorced wife if she is not married and is (1) caring for a child who is under 18 or disabled and who is entitled to social security benefits or (2) age 62 and was married to the deceased for 10 years.

Disability Benefits

Pensions may be granted under social security to eligible employees who have a disability that is expected to last at least 12 months or to result in death. To be eligible, a person must have worked in a job covered by social security for at least 5 out of the 10 years before becoming disabled. These pensions are calculated with basically the same methods used for calculating retirement benefits.

Health Insurance

Health insurance under social security, commonly known as Medicare, provides partial hospital and medical reimbursement for persons over 65. Hospital insurance, which is known as Part A, is financed through the regular social security funds. Most hospital expenses and certain outpatient, posthospital, and home nursing expenses are covered by Part A of Medicare. The medical insurance, known as Part B, helps a participant pay for a number of different medical procedures and supplies that are completely separate from hospital care. For example, normal outpatient visits and checkups would fall under Part B. Participation in the medical insurance program (Part B) of Medicare is voluntary and requires the payment of a monthly fee by those wishing to receive coverage. This fee was $31.90 per month in 1989.

Problems Facing Social Security

Almost everyone is aware of the financial crisis faced by social security, stemming from major demographic changes that have taken place since the system was established. The basic problem is that fewer and fewer people are and will be working to support more and more retirees as the "baby boom" generation reaches retirement age. The sharp increases in payments forecasted to fund social security (see Table 15–4) reflect these demographic changes.

Unemployment Compensation

Unemployment compensation is designed to provide funds to employees who have lost their jobs through no fault of their own and are seeking other jobs. Title IX of the Social Security Act of 1935 requires employers to pay taxes for unemployment compensation. However, the law was written in such a manner as to encourage individual states to establish their own unemployment systems. If a state established its own unemployment compensation system according to prescribed federal standards, the proceeds of the unemployment taxes paid by an employer go to the state. By 1937, all states and the District of Columbia had adopted acceptable unemployment compensation plans.

To receive unemployment compensation, an individual must submit an application through the state employment office and must meet three eligibility requirements: The individual must (1) have been covered by social security for a minimum number of weeks; (2) have been laid off (in some states, discharged employees may qualify); and (3) be willing to accept any suitable employment offered through the state unemployment compensation commission. Many disputes have arisen regarding "suitable employment."

Generally, unemployment compensation is limited to a maximum of 26 weeks. The amount received, which varies from state to state, is calculated on the basis of the individual's wages or salary received in the previous period of employment.

Unemployment compensation is usually funded through taxes paid by

Unemployment compensation Form of insurance designed to provide funds to employees who have lost their jobs and are seeking other jobs.

employers; however, in some states, employees also pay a portion of the tax. The Federal Unemployment Tax Act (FUTA) requires all profit-making employers in business to pay a tax on the first $7,000 of wages paid to each employee. The rate paid varies from employer to employer based on the number of unemployed people an organization has drawing from the state's unemployment fund. Thus, the system is designed to encourage organizations to maintain stable employment.

Workers' Compensation

Workers' compensation
Form of insurance that protects employees from loss of income and extra expenses associated with job-related injuries or illness.

Workers' compensation is meant to protect employees from loss of income and extra expenses associated with job-related injuries or illness. Table 15–7 summarizes the types of injuries and illnesses covered by most workers' compensation laws. Although some form of workers' compensation is available in all 50 states, specific requirements, payments, and procedures vary among states. However, certain features are common to virtually all programs:[12]

1. The laws generally provide for replacement of lost income, medical expense payment, rehabilitation of some sort, death benefits to survivors, and lump-sum disability payments.

2. The worker does not have to sue the employer to get compensation—in fact covered employers are exempt from such lawsuits.

3. The compensation is normally paid through an insurance program financed through premiums paid by employers.

4. Workers' compensation insurance premiums are based on the accident and illness record of the organization. A large number of paid claims results in higher premiums.

5. An element of coinsurance exists in the workers' compensation coverage. Coinsurance is insurance under which the beneficiary of the coverage absorbs part of the loss. In automobile collision coverage, for example, there is often coinsurance in the amount of a $100 deductible for each accident. In workers' compensation coverage, there is coinsurance in that the workers' loss is usually not fully covered by the insurance program.

▼ **Table 15–7**   Job-connected injuries usually covered by workers' compensation

---

Accidents in which the employee does not lose time from work
Accidents in which the employee loses time from work
Temporary partial disability
Permanent partial or total disability
Death
Occupational diseases
Noncrippling physical impairments, such as deafness
Impairments suffered at employer-sanctioned events, such as social events or during travel related to organization business
Injuries or disabilities attributable to an employer's gross negligence

---

Source: Reprinted by permission from *Personnel Administration and the Law*, 2nd ed., by Greenman, Russell L., and Eric J. Schmertz. Copyright © 1979 by The Bureau of National Affairs, Inc., Washington, D.C. 20037, pp. 190–191.

For example, most states provide for a maximum payment of only two-thirds of wages lost due to the accident or illness.

6. Medical expenses, on the other hand, are usually covered in full under workers' compensation laws.

7. It is a no-fault system; all job-related injuries and illnesses are covered regardless of whose negligence caused them.

Workers' compensation coverage is compulsory in all states except South Carolina, New Jersey, and Texas. In these states, it is elective for the employer. When elective, any employers who reject the coverage also give up certain legal protections.

One major criticism of workers' compensation involves the extent of coverage provided by different states. The amounts paid, the ease of collecting, and the likelihood of collecting all vary significantly from state to state.

Retirement-Related Benefits

In addition to the benefits required under social security, many organizations provide additional retirement benefits. These benefits are in the form of private pension and retirement plans.

Pension Plans

Pension and retirement plans, which provide a source of income to people who have retired, represent money paid for past services. **Private pension plans** can be funded entirely by the organization or jointly by the organization and the employee during the time of employment. Plans requiring employee contributions are called contributory plans; those that do not are called noncontributory plans. Funded pension plans are financed by money that has been set aside previously for that specific purpose. Nonfunded plans make payments to recipients out of current contributions to the fund. The most prevalent form of pension plan in U.S. industry is the **defined benefit plan**. Under a defined benefit plan, the employer pledges to provide a benefit determined by a definite formula at the employee's retirement date. The other major type of retirement plan is the **defined contribution plan**, which calls for a fixed or known annual contribution instead of a known benefit.

The 1987 survey reported by the U.S. Chamber of Commerce found that over 85 percent of the participants had pension plans.[13] This can be compared with the fact that less than one-sixth of the nonagricultural work force was covered by private pension plans prior to 1948. Ninety-one percent of the pension plans reported in the 1986 Hay/Huggins Benefits Comparison were defined benefit plans and 8 percent were defined contribution plans.[14]

Private pension plans
Employee benefit that provides a source of income to people who have retired; funded either entirely by the organization or jointly by the organization and employee during employment.

Defined benefit plan
Pension plan under which an employer pledges to provide a benefit determined by a definite formula at the employee's retirement date.

Defined contribution plan
Pension plan that calls for a fixed or known annual contribution instead of a known benefit.

Defined Benefit Plans
As mentioned above, defined benefit plans make up the overwhelming majority of pension plans and have a specified formula for calculating benefits. Although there are numerous such formulas, the most popular approach has been the final-average

pay plan, in which the retirement benefit is based on average earnings in the years, generally two or five, immediately preceding retirement. The actual benefit sum is then computed as a function of the person's calculated average earnings and years of service. In another common approach, the flat-benefit plan, all participants who meet the eligibility requirements receive a fixed benefit regardless of their earnings.

Plans affecting salaried employees usually use the final-average pay plan. Plans limited to hourly paid employees traditionally have used the flat-benefit plan. Where hourly and salaried employees are both affected, a final-average pay formula may be modified to provide a minimum dollar benefit for participants in the lower pay classifications. Many final-average pay plans are now calculated with an offset or deduction for the employee's social security benefits. In these cases, the amount of social security that a person receives is taken into account when determining how much he or she will receive from the pension plan.

Defined Contribution Plans

401(K) plan

Most popular type of defined contribution plan, named after section 401(K) of the Internal Revenue Code. Allows employees to defer a portion of their pay into the plan, thus making contributions tax deductible (up to a limit).

Defined contribution plans are used primarily by companies that do not have a large number of employees. The most popular type of defined contribution plan is the **401(K) plan**. These plans were named after section 401(K) of the Internal Revenue Code, which became effective in 1980. The advantage of 401(K) plan is that contributions are tax deductible up to a limit. Usually a 401(K) plan is set up to allow employees to defer a portion of their pay into the plan. Often employers will match employee contributions to some extent. The 1986 Tax Reform Act limited tax-exempt contributions under a 401(K) plan to a total of $7,000 per year per employee.

Pension Rights

An inherent promise of security in some form exists in every pension plan. However, if the pension benefits are too low or the plan is seriously underfunded, this promise of security is breached, and employees who have spent most of their working lives with companies that have pension plans do not receive an adequate— or any, in some cases—pension.

Vesting

Rights of individuals to receive money paid into a pension or retirement fund on their behalf by their employer, if they should leave the organization prior to retirement.

Another problem involves the vested rights of employees. **Vesting** refers to the rights of individuals to receive, if they should leave the organization prior to retirement, the dollars paid into a pension or retirement fund by their employer. For example, a vested employee can receive, at some later date, the funds invested by the employer. If not vested, the employee cannot receive the fund paid by the employer. A frequent approach is deferred full vesting, in which an employee, on meeting certain age and service requirements, enjoys full vested rights. A similar approach, called deferred graded vesting, gradually gives the employee an increasing percentage of benefits until the age and service requirements for full vesting are met.

Vesting requirements historically have caused problems for both employees and employers. In many old plans, the employee who was terminated or quit before retirement age did not receive any pension benefits regardless of the number of years worked under the pension plan or how close retirement was. Even under plans that did provide vesting rights, the requirements were strict in terms of length of service. Requirements for vesting are often made stringent by employers in an effort to keep employees from leaving the organization, at least until their rights have become fully vested. On the other hand, employers have experienced the problem of employees quitting after they have been vested in the pension plan in order to draw out the funds credited to them. To counteract this, employers have incorporated provisions in their pension plans stating that funds other than those contributed by the employee will not be distributed until the employee reaches a certain age, even if he or she has left the organization.

ERISA and the Retirement Equity Act

In an effort to ensure the fair treatment of employees under pension plans, Congress in 1974 passed the **Employee Retirement Income Security Act (ERISA)**. This law was designed to ensure the solvency of pension plans by restricting the types

Employee Retirement Income Security Act (ERISA)
Federal law passed in 1974, designed to give employees increased security for their retirement and pension plans and to ensure the fair treatment of employees under pension plans.

▼ **Table 15–8**   Major provisions of ERISA

Subject	Provisions
Eligibility	Prohibited plans from establishing eligibility requirements of more than one year of service, or an age greater than 25, whichever is later.
Vesting	Established new minimum standards; employer has three choices: a. 100 percent vesting after 10 years of service. b. 25 percent vesting after 5 years of service, grading up to 100 percent after 15 years. c. 50 percent vesting when age and service (if the employee has at least 5 years of service) equal 45, grading up to 100 percent vesting 5 years later.
Funding	Required the employer to fund annually the full cost for current benefit accruals and amortize past-service benefit liabilities over 30 years for new plans and 40 years for existing plans.
Plan termination insurance	Established a government insurance fund to insure vested pension benefits up to the lesser of $750 a month or 100 percent of the employee's average wages during highest paid five years of employment; the employer pays an annual premium of $1 per participant and is liable for any insurance benefits paid up to 30 percent of the company's net worth.
Fiduciary responsibility	Established the "prudent man" rule as the basic standard of fiduciary responsibility; prohibits various transactions between fiduciaries and parties-in-interest; prohibits investment of more than 10 percent of pension plan assets in the employer's securities.
Portability	Permitted an employee leaving a company to make a tax-free transfer of the assets behind his vested pension benefits (if the employer agrees) or of his vested profit-sharing or savings plan funds to an individual retirement account.
Individual retirement accounts (IRAs)	Provided a vehicle for transfers as noted above and permits employees of private or public employers that do not have qualified retirement plans to deduct 15 percent of compensation, up to $1,500, each year for contributions to a personal retirement fund. Earnings on the fund are not taxable until distributed.
Reporting and disclosure	Required the employer to provide employees with a comprehensive booklet describing plan provisions and to report annually to the Secretary of Labor on various operating and financial details of the plan.
Lump-sum distributions	Changed the tax rules to provide capital gains treatment on pre-1974 amounts and to tax post-1973 amounts as ordinary income, but as the employee's only income and spread over 10 years.
Limits on contributions and benefits	Limited benefits payable from defined-benefit pension plans to the lesser of $75,000 a year or 100 percent of average annual cash compensation during the employee's three highest paid years of service. Limited annual additions to employee profit-sharing accounts to the lesser of $25,000 or 25 percent of the employee's compensation that year.

Source: Adapted from D. G. Carlson, "Responding to the Pension Reform Law," *Harvard Business Review,* November–December 1974, p. 134.

▼ **Table 15–9** Major provisions of the Retirement Equity Act

- Employees must be allowed to participate in a qualified plan no later than age 21 with one year of service (previously, it was age 25 with one year of service).
- Vesting credit must be awarded for years of service beginning at age 18 (previously, service before age 22 could be ignored in most plans).
- For both vesting and participation purposes, as many as 501 hours of service must be awarded to any employee on maternity or paternity leave.
- An election to waive spouse survivor benefits must be made in writing by both the participant *and* spouse and witnessed by a plan representative or notary public.

Source: Stephen P. Kurash and Gene F. Fasoldt, "An Outline of Changes Required by the New Retirement Equity Act," *Personnel Journal*, November 1984, pp. 80–84.

of investments that could be made with the plan's funds and providing general guidelines for fund management. Table 15–8 summarizes the major provisions of ERISA.

The act has been criticized as being too costly. In fact, it has been reported that several companies dropped their pension plans rather than comply with ERISA.[15] Another major complaint has been that it causes an unwieldy amount of paperwork. In 1984, Congress passed the **Retirement Equity Act**. The overall impact of this act was to liberalize the eligibility requirements, vesting provisions, maternity/paternity leaves, and spouse survivor benefits of retirement plans. Table 15–9 summarizes the major provisions of the Retirement Equity Act.

Retirement Equity Act
Act passed in 1984 that liberalized eligibility requirements, vesting provisions, maternity/paternity leaves, and spouse survivor benefits of retirement plans.

Mandatory Retirement

The 1978 amendment to the **Age Discrimination in Employment Act (ADEA)** forbade mandatory retirement before age 70 for companies employing 20 or more people in the private sector (there are certain exceptions, as covered in Chapter 2) and at any age for federal employees. Prior to the effective date of this amendment, January 1, 1979, employers could choose any age for mandatory retirement. An amendment to ADEA that took effect in January 1987 eliminated mandatory retirement at any age for employees of companies with 20 or more employees.

Age Discrimination in Employment Act (ADEA)
Forbids mandatory retirement before age 70 for all companies employing 20 or more people in the private sector and at any age in the federal government.

Early Retirement

As an alternative to mandatory retirement, some organizations offer incentives to encourage early retirement. This method of reducing the work force is often viewed as a humanitarian way of reducing the payroll and rewarding long-tenured employees. The types of incentives offered vary, but usually include a lump-sum payment plus the extension of other benefits, such as medical insurance. A 1986 survey by Hewitt Associates found that among their sample of 529 corporations, one-third had used early retirement incentive within the previous five years.[16]

Most pension plans have special allowances for voluntary early retirement. Usually an employee's pension is reduced by a stated amount for every month that he or she retires before age 65. Popular early retirement ages are 55, 60, and 62. Most plans require that an individual must have worked a minimum number of years with the organization to be eligible for early retirement. Early retirement has grown in popularity, partially because of the pension benefits available. Presently, the earliest that an employee can receive social security retirement benefits (reduced) is at age 62.

Employees Not Covered by Pension Plans

In 1981, legislation was enacted to allow employees to set up individual plans called **individual retirement accounts (IRAs)**. Although the basic purpose of IRAs was to provide an option for employees not covered by private pension plans, anyone who has an earned income can invest in an IRA. With an IRA, an individual could originally make tax-exempt contributions to a maximum of $2,000 per year. In conjunction with a spouse-homemaker, a married person could contribute up to $2,250 per year. The 1986 Tax Reform Act drastically decreased the tax advantages of an IRA. Currently, IRA contributions are totally deductible only if the individual's income is less than $25,000 (singles) or $40,000 (marrieds filing jointly) or if the employee is not covered by a company pension plan. Interest earned on IRA accounts is still deferable. A similar plan, called a Keogh plan, has been effected for self-employed persons. Under a **Keogh plan**, self-employed persons can currently make tax-exempt annual contributions of up to $30,000 or 25 percent of net self-employment income, whichever was less.

Individual retirement accounts (IRAs)
Individual pension plan for employees not covered by private pension plans.

Keogh plan
Pension plan for self-employed persons.

Preretirement Planning

A benefit that has recently evolved is preretirement planning. The purpose of such a planning program is to help employees prepare for retirement, both financially and psychologically. At the most basic level, preretirement planning provides employees with information about the financial benefits they will receive upon retirement. Social security, pensions, employee stock ownership, and health and life insurance coverage are usually discussed. Other programs go beyond financial planning and into such topics as housing, relocation, health, nutrition, sleep, exercise, part-time work, second careers, community service, recreation, and continuing education.

The rapid pace of change in today's world accentuated by volatile inflation rates and uncertainty concerning social security have enhanced the need for some type of preretirement planning. This need is not expected to be diminished in the near future.

Insurance-Related Benefits

Insurance programs of various types represent an important part of any benefit package. For example, the U.S. Chamber of Commerce reported that of 910 companies surveyed in 1987, 99 percent provided some form of medical insurance.[17] Company-sponsored medical insurance programs are designed so that the employer either pays the entire premium or a portion of it, with the employee responsible for the balance.

▼ **Figure 15-4**   Funding of employee and dependent health insurance

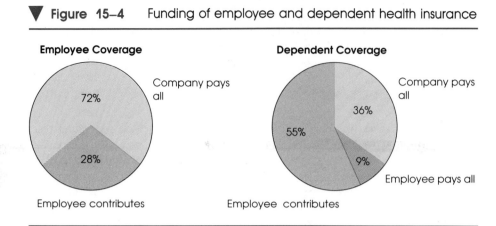

Source: Compiled based on data provided in Bureau of National Affairs, *Health and Life Insurance Benefit Plans,* Personnel Policies Forum Survey no. 137 (Washington, D.C.: BNA, 1984), pp. 19–20.

Health Insurance

In addition to normal hospitalization and outpatient doctor bills, some plans now cover prescription drugs and dental, eye, and medical health care. Many health care plans incorporate a deductible, which requires the employee to pay a certain amount of medical expenses each year (usually $50 or $150 per person) before the insurance becomes effective. The health insurance plan then pays the bulk of the remaining expenses. Some plans pay the entire cost of health insurance for both the employees and dependents, some plans require the employee to pay part of the cost for dependents only, and some plans require the employee to pay part of the cost for both (see Figure 15–4).

Over the years, two distinct plans have evolved in health insurance: the "base plan" and the "major medical expense plan." Base plans cover expenses for specified services within certain limits established for each kind of service. On the other hand, major medical plans define a broad range of covered expenses, including all services that may be required for successful treatment. When used alone, a major medical plan is referred to as a comprehensive plan. Many organizations supplement a base plan with a major medical expense plan. The reason for combining the two is usually to reduce the deductible amount for certain types of treatment. The precise coverage, size of the deductible, and other specifics vary considerably among plans.

Health Maintenance Organizations (HMOs)

Health maintenance organization (HMO)
Health service organization that contracts with companies to provide certain basic medical services around the clock, seven days a week, for a fixed cost.

The Health Maintenance Organization Act of 1973 ushered in a new concept of one-stop, prepaid medical services as an alternative to traditional insurance programs. With this arrangement, organizations contract with an approved **health maintenance organization (HMO)** to provide all the basic medical services needed by the organization's employees for a fixed price. Advantages to HMOs include emphasis on prevention of health problems and costs that are usually cheaper than traditional coverage. The major disadvantage, from the employee's viewpoint, is that they must use physicians employed or approved by the HMO, and these may or may not be the doctors of their choice. HMOs are growing in popularity.

Preferred provider organizations (PPOs) are another alternative that emerged during the 1980s. A PPO is formed by contracting with a group of doctors and hospitals to provide services at a discounted or attractive price. In exchange, these providers are designated as "preferred" providers of care. Unlike HMOs, PPOs do not restrict the provision of care to their own providers. They do, however, offer incentives, such as higher reimbursement levels, when care is received from a PPO member.

Preferred provider organizations (PPOs) Formed by contracting with a group of doctors and hospitals to provide services at a discount or attractive price. Such providers are designated as "preferred" providers of care.

Dental Insurance

Dental insurance has been one of the fastest-growing types of employee benefits in recent years. For example, surveys conducted by the Conference Board show that the number of companies providing dental plans grew from 8 percent in 1973 to 19 percent in 1975 and 41 percent in 1981.[18] The 1987 Chamber of Commerce survey that was referenced earlier found that 54 percent of the companies surveyed provided dental insurance.[19] Some major medical expense plans include dental treatment, but most dental insurance is provided as a separate plan. The majority of dental plans specify a deductible.

Life Insurance

Life insurance is a benefit commonly available from organizations. When provided for all employees, it is called group life insurance. Costs of this type of insurance, based on the characteristics of the entire group covered, typically are the same per dollar of insurance for all employees. Generally, the employer provides a minimum of coverage, usually $10,000 to $20,000. Employees often have the option of purchasing more insurance at their own expense. A physical examination is usually not required for coverage. Presently, employers can provide up to a maximum of $50,000 worth of life insurance for an employee without the cost of the policy being considered as income to the individual.

Accident and Disability Insurance

In addition to health, dental, and life insurance, many organizations provide some form of accident or disability insurance, or both. Most accident insurance is designed to provide funds for a limited period of time, usually up to 16 weeks. The amount of the benefit is often some percentage of the accident victim's weekly salary. **Disability insurance** is designed to protect the employee who experiences a long-term or permanent disability. Normally, a one- to six-month waiting period is required following the disability before the employee becomes eligible for benefits. As with accident insurance, disability insurance benefits are usually calculated as a percentage of wages or salary.

Disability insurance Designed to protect the employee who experiences a long-term or permanent disability.

Payment for Time Not Worked

It is now standard practice for organizations to pay employees for certain times when they do not work. Rest periods, lunch breaks, and wash-up time represent times not worked that are almost always taken for granted as part of the job. Recognized holidays, vacations, and days missed because of sickness, jury duty and funerals represent other compensated times that are not worked.

Paid Holidays

Floating holiday
Holiday that may be observed at the discretion of the employee or the employer.

The number of paid holidays has somewhat stabilized over the last several years. One relatively new concept is the **floating holiday**, which is observed at the discretion of the employee or employer. A 1985 survey conducted by the Bureau of National Affairs (BNA) revealed the following facts:[20]

1. Companies surveyed designate an average of nine specific days as paid holidays each year. The total number of regular and floating holidays averages 10.5 days annually.
2. Christmas Day, New Year's Day, Thanksgiving, Independence Day, Labor Day, and Memorial Day are provided as paid holidays by nearly all companies.
3. Paid floating holidays are used by 65 percent of the companies responding. Thirty-six percent of the companies provide personal floating holidays to be taken at an individual employee's discretion. Thirty-eight percent of the companies provide floating holidays to be taken companywide.
4. In over half of the companies surveyed, employees must work their regularly scheduled days before and after a scheduled holiday to be eligible for holiday pay.
5. The most common method of compensating employees who are required to work on holidays is to pay them regular pay for the holiday, plus time and a half for the hours they work.
6. When a scheduled paid holiday falls on a Sunday, and Sunday is not a regular workday, 88 percent of the responding companies provide a paid day off on the following Monday.

Table 15–10 shows the frequency with which certain holidays are observed by the participants in the BNA survey and how they have changed since 1980.

Paid Vacations

Normally, certain length of service requirements must be met before an employee becomes eligible for a paid vacation. Also, the time allowed in paid vacations generally depends on the employee's length of service. Unlike holiday policies that usually affect everyone in the same manner, vacation policies may differ among

▼ **Table 15–10**   Percentage of companies observing holidays

	All Companies		By Industry			By Size	
	1980	**1985**	**Manufacturing**	**Nonmanufacturing**	**Nonbusiness**	**Large**	**Small**
(Number of companies)	(195)	(216)	(112)	(67)	(37)	(97)	(119)
Christmas Day	100%	100%	100%	100%	100%	100%	100%
New Year's Day	100	99*	99	100	100	100	99
Thanksgiving	100	99*	99	100	100	100	99
Independence Day	100	99	98	100	100	100	98
Labor Day	100	99	98	99	100	99	98
Memorial Day	95	98	96	99	100	97	98
Day after Thanksgiving	54	63	82	49	32	61	66
Washington's Birthday/Presidents Day	42	45	33	58	59	38	51
Good Friday (full or half day)	48	40	54	22	30	41	39
Christmas Eve							
Full day	36	38	55	19	16	38	37
Half day	14	9	6	18	3	9	9
New Year's Eve							
Full day	15	22	31	10	14	23	21
Half day	8	5	3	10	3	6	4
Veteran's Day	25	20	4	37	38	19	22
Columbus Day	23	16	4	25	35	14	18
Employee's birthday	23	16	10	21	24	14	17
Martin Luther King, Jr.'s, Birthday	5	7	0	10	22	6	8
Easter Monday	4	5	9	1	0	3	7
Lincoln's Birthday	3	2	0	6	3	1	3
State/local holiday(s)	12	9	4	13	16	9	9
Other holiday(s)	NA	7	7	1	19	5	9

*Percentage is greater than 99.5.

NA means not applicable.

Source: Bureau of National Affairs, *Paid Holdiays and Vacation Policies,* Personnel Policies Forum Survey no. 142 (Washington, D.C., 1986), p. 3. Used with permission.

categories of employees. The BNA survey reported the following information with regard to paid vacations:[21]

1. The majority of all responding firms grant two weeks of vacation for the first year's service.
2. The median service requirement for a two-week vacation is one year, for a three-week vacation the median service requirement is five years, and for a five-week vacation the median service requirement is 20 years.
3. More than 80 percent of the responding companies allow employees to take vacation by the day or week, but only about half allow employees to take vacation leave in units of less than a day.

Other Benefits

In addition to the previously discussed major benefits, organizations may offer a wide range of additional benefits, including food services, health and first-aid services, financial and legal advice, counseling services, educational and recreational programs, day-care services, and purchase discounts. Employee assistance programs, a type of general service related to employee well being, are discussed in Chapter 19.

The extent and attractiveness of these benefits vary considerably among organizations. For example, purchase discounts would be especially attractive to employees of a major retail store or an airline.

The Benefit Package

Unfortunately, "most benefit packages are thrown together piecemeal, are not well-balanced, and don't show sufficient regard for holes or overlap within the total package."[22] There are many reasons benefit packages are often not well integrated. The major problem is that new benefits are often added or deleted without examining their impact on the total package. Also, benefits are frequently added or deleted for all the wrong reasons, such as a whim of a top manager, union pressures, or a fad. The key to any successful benefit package is to plan the package and to integrate all of the different components. Such an approach ensures that any new benefit additions or deletions will fit in with the other benefits currently being offered.

● *Summary of Learning Objectives*

1. Define employee benefits.

    Employee benefits, sometimes called fringe benefits, are those rewards that organizations provide to employees for being members of the organization. In general, benefits can be grouped into five major categories: (1) legally required, (2) retirement related, (3) insurance related, (4) payment for time not worked, and (5) other.

2. Describe how employee benefits have grown over the last several years.

    Employee benefits have grown steadily over the past several years. Specifically, they have grown from approximately 15 percent of total compensation in 1951 to approximately 39 percent of total compensation in 1987.

3. Explain the concept of a flexible benefit plan.

    Under a flexible benefit plan, individual employees have some choice as to the specific benefits that they will actually receive; usually employees select from among several options how they want their direct compensation and benefits to be distributed. Flexible plans are also known as cafeteria plans of benefits.

4. Summarize those benefits that are legally required.

   The three primary benefits that are mandated by law are social security, unemployment compensation, and workers' compensation benefits. Social security is a federally administered insurance system. Under current federal laws, both employer and employee must pay into the system, and a certain percentage of the employee's salary is paid up to a maximum limit. The payment distributed under social security can be grouped into three major categories: retirement benefits, disability benefits, and health insurance. Unemployment compensation is designed to provide funds to employees who have lost their jobs through no fault of their own and are seeking other jobs. Unemployment compensation is usually funded through taxes paid by employers; however, in some states employees also pay a portion of the tax. Workers' compensation is meant to protect employees from loss of income and extra expenses associated with job-related injuries or illnesses. Workers' compensation coverage varies significantly among different states.

5. Differentiate between a defined benefit pension plan and a defined contribution pension plan.

   Under a defined benefit pension plan, the employer pledges to provide a benefit determined by a definite formula at the employee's retirement date. A defined contribution pension plan calls for a fixed or known annual contribution instead of a known benefit.

6. Explain the purposes of the Employee Retirement Income Security Act (ERISA) and the Retirement Equity Act.

   ERISA was passed by Congress in 1974 as an effort to ensure the fair treatment of employees under pension plans. The law was designed to ensure the solvency of pension plans by restricting the types of investments that can be made with the plan's funds and providing general guidelines for fund managers. The overall impact of the Retirement Equity Act, which was passed in 1984, was to liberalize the eligibility requirements, vesting provisions, maternity/paternity leaves, and spouse survivor benefits of retirement plans.

7. Distinguish between an IRA and a Keogh plan.

   An IRA is a type of individual pension plan that can be used by an individual having earned income. A Keogh is a type of pension plan designed for use by self-employed persons.

8. Describe a health maintenance organization (HMO) and a preferred provider organization (PPO).

   HMOs provide certain basic medical services for an organization's employees for a fixed price. Advantages of HMOs include emphasis on prevention of health problems and generally lower costs. A major drawback is that employees must use physicians employed or approved by the HMO. PPOs are similar to HMOs in many ways. A PPO is formed by contracting with a group of doctors and hospitals to provide services at a discounted or attractive price. Under a PPO, employees are free to go to any doctor or facility on an approved list.

9. Explain the concept of a floating holiday.

   A floating holiday is a holiday observed at the discretion of the employee or the employer.

Review Questions

1. Why are many employees unaware of some of the benefits provided by their organizations?
2. What is the flexible approach to benefits?
3. List the advantages and disadvantages of flexible plans.
4. What is social security? Describe the three major categories of social security.
5. Briefly explain how unemployment compensation works.
6. What types of injuries and illnesses are covered by workers' compensation?
7. Describe the differences between defined benefit pension plans and defined contribution pension plans.
8. State the overriding purpose of the Employee Retirement Income Security Act (ERISA).
9. What are the two alternatives for individuals not covered by private pension plans?
10. Discuss some of the insurance programs offered to employees by organizations.
11. What is a health maintenance organization (HMO)? A preferred provider organization (PPO)?

Discussion Questions

1. If an average production employee is given the option of having an additional $100 per month in salary or the equivalent of $200 per month in voluntary benefits, which do you think the employee would choose? Why? What are the implications of your answer for management?
2. Develop and discuss at least two arguments in support of social security. Compare and contrast your arguments.
3. If your employer offered you an option of joining an HMO, would you be interested? Why or why not?
4. Many people feel that employers use pension vesting requirements solely for the purpose of retaining employees. If this is true or even partially true, do you think that such behavior is ethical? Why?

▼ INCIDENT 15–1

Who Is Eligible for Retirement Benefits?

Preston Jones, 51, had been an hourly worker in the machine shop of the Armon Company for 21 years and 4 months. On a Christmas holiday, he suffered a severe heart attack and was hospitalized for three weeks. At his release, his doctor said he was to rest at home for a couple of months. After his recuperation period, his doctor, along with Armon Company's physicians, were to decide whether or not

Preston should be retired for disability reasons. They never got the opportunity to make this decision—in February, Preston died of a second heart attack.

He left a wife, four sons, two daughters, and two daughters-in-law. Mrs. Jones still had four children at home.

As a part of Preston's estate, his wife received the normal group insurance payments, the balance in his savings plan account, and the other benefits due her. However, she did not receive a pension from Armon as a survivor of an eligible employee.

When Mrs. Jones and the company representatives had discussed the settlement, she had inquired about her husband's pension and about her right to receive it. The personnel department had stated that since contributions to this fund were made only by the company, no survivor's benefits were provided.

Questions

1. What do you think Mrs. Jones should do at this point?
2. Does the Employment Retirement Income Security Act of 1974 have anything to say about this issue?

▼ INCIDENT 15–2

Fringe Benefits for Professionals

LJT, Architect, a small architectural firm organized as a sole proprietorship, serves clients in the New York metropolitan area. Anticipating a good year, Len Elmore, the principal, hopes for a gross of between $300,000 and $400,000.

In an architectural practice, revenue is produced by providing a variety of services that range from creating a design and generating the construction documents used by a contractor in executing the project to visiting the site periodically to verify that construction is progressing according to specifications. Architects are also responsible for coordinating their work with that of the engineers and other consultants associated with projects.

Many small architectural firms such as LJT, Architect, have no permanent employees. Workers are hired for a particular project with the understanding that they might remain after a particular phase of the project is completed but that they might be laid off. Employees are usually needed for the function of design, development, and production of construction documents, which includes approximately 50 to 70 percent of the services provided under a standard architectural agreement.

The personnel needed for these projects are acquired in several ways. They can be hired on a full-time permanent or temporary basis or on a part-time basis to moonlight (that is, as a second job). An employee might also be borrowed from another firm whose contracted work has been completed with no new work foreseen immediately. Len feels that hiring full-time temporary or permanent employees gives him more control over the production aspect of his practice.

At this time, Len does not follow any formal personnel policies. He prefers to "work things out" as issues and problems arise. When hiring, he will agree verbally to certain broad terms of employment, compensation, and benefits common to local professional offices, such as two weeks' vacation per year. He usually insists on a two-week to one-month probationary period during which the salary paid is slightly less than normal. A spot check of some of his colleagues leads him to believe that his salary rates are comparable with those of similar employers. Because the nature of the employment tends to be temporary, Len suggests a contract arrangement with his employees, in which no taxes are withheld and no government-required benefits are provided.

Len's plans for expansion include adding employees until his staff numbers 10. For him, this is the best staff size to provide high-quality professional services. However, the employment situation is easing for workers in architectural firms; more newspaper ads seek applicants and fewer callers contact Len for jobs. Those coming for interviews ask more than "When do I start?" Many ask about vacations, sick leave, paid holidays, medical insurance, and profit-sharing plans. Others want to know about the possibilities of advancement with LJT, Architect, and about such long-range benefits as pensions and education leave.

In view of the situation, Len has decided to look into the possibility of providing his employees with a fringe benefit package. At the same time, however, he fears that his practice may be too small to begin providing these benefits, which may prove to be extremely expensive. He has set aside money from his own earnings to provide these extras for himself and has difficulty in understanding why his employees cannot do the same.

Questions

1. What recommendations would you make to Len?
2. How much do you think your recommendations would cost?

Exercise

Taking a Raise

Assume that you are currently employed as a human resource specialist for a medium-sized company. You have been in your job for a little over two years, and your current salary is $28,000 per year. Two months ago, your company announced that it was going to implement a flexible benefits plan in conjunction with this year's salary raises. Your annual salary review was held last week, and you were informed that your raise would be equivalent to $3,000. For your salary level, the following options are available:

1. Take the entire raise as a monthly salary increase.
2. Take as much of the $3,000 as desired in the form of vacation at the equivalent of $200 per day.
3. Have as much as desired of the $3,000 put into a tax-sheltered retirement plan.
4. Purchase additional term life insurance at the cost of $250 per $100,000 of face value.
5. Purchase dental insurance at the cost of $20 per month for yourself and $10 per month for each dependent.

The company currently provides full health insurance at no cost to employees. How would you elect to take your raise? Be prepared to share your answer with the class.

Notes and Additional Readings

1. U.S. Chamber Survey Research Center, *Employee Benefits,* 1988 ed. (Washington, D.C.: Chamber of Commerce of the United States, 1988), p. 5.

2. Thomas H. Paine, "Benefits in the 1990s," *Personnel Journal,* March 1988, p. 82.

3. R. M. McCaffery, "Employee Benefits: Beyond the Fringe?" *Personnel Administrator,* May 1981, p. 26.

4. Ibid.

5. R. L. Kagerer, "Do Employees Understand Your Benefits Program? *Personnel Administrator,* October 1975, pp. 29–31.

6. John A. Haslinger, "Flexible Compensation: Getting a Return on Benefit Dollars," *Personnel Administrator,* June 1985, p. 39.

7. Ibid.

8. Carolyn A. Baker, "Flex Your Benefits," *Personnel Journal,* May 1988, p. 54.

9. A. Cole, Jr., "Flexible Benefits Are a Key to Better Employee Relations," *Personnel Journal,* January 1983, p. 49.

10. Several of these reasons were adapted from R. B. Cockrum, "Has the Time Come for Employee Cafeteria Plans?" *Personnel Administrator,* July 1982, p. 67.

11. Adapted from J. H. Shea, "Cautions about Cafeteria-Style Benefit Plans," *Personnel Journal,* January 1981, pp. 37–38.

12. S. Ledvinka, *Federal Regulation of Personnel and Human Resource Management* (Boston: Kent Publishing, 1981), p. 144.

13. U.S. Chamber Survey Research Center, *Employee Benefits,* p. 5.

14. Allen Stiteler, "Finally Pension Plans Defined," *Personnel Journal,* February 1987, p. 48.

15. P. S. Greenlaw and W. D. Biggs, *Modern Personnel Management* (Philadelphia: W. B. Saunders, 1979), p. 513.

16. Eugene H. Seibert and Joanne Seibert, "Look into Window Alternatives," *Personnel Journal,* May 1989, p. 80.

17. U.S. Chamber Survey Research Center, *Employee Benefits,* p. 5.

18. *Profile of Employee Benefits* (New York: Conference Board, 1981), p. 6.

19. U.S. Chamber Survey Research Center, *Employee Benefits,* p. 25.

20. Bureau of National Affairs, *Paid Holiday and Vacation Policies,* Personnel Policies Forum Survey no. 142 (Washington, D.C.: BNA, 1986), pp. 1–2.

21. Ibid.

22. R. B. Dunham and R. A. Formisano, "Designing and Evaluating Employee Benefit Systems," *Personnel Administrator,* April 1982, p. 29.

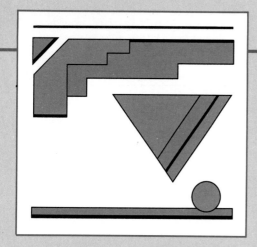

Section 5

Understanding Unions

Chapter 16
Legal Environment and Structure of
Labor Unions

 Chapter 17
Union Organizing Campaigns and
Collective Bargaining

 Chapter 18
Discipline and Grievance Handling

Chapter 16

Legal Environment and Structure of Labor Unions

Chapter Outline

Legal Environment of Labor-Management Relations

Sherman Anti-Trust Act (1890)
Clayton Act (1914)
Railway Labor Act (1926)
Norris-La Guardia Act (1932)
National Labor Relations (Wagner) Act (1935)
Labor-Management Relations (Taft-Hartley) Act (1947)
Labor-Management Reporting and Disclosure (Landrum-Griffin) Act (1959)
Civil Service Reform Act (1978)

Union Structures

AFL–CIO
National and International Unions

City and State Federations
Local Unions

Current and Future Developments in the Labor Movement

Summary of Learning Objectives

Review Questions

Discussion Questions

Incident 16–1: Unions and Management Rights

Incident 16–2: Voluntary Resignations during a Strike

Exercise: Need for Unions

Notes and Additional Readings

● *Learning Objectives*

After studying this chapter, you should be able to:
1. Describe the conspiracy doctrine.
2. Define injunction.
3. Explain a yellow-dog contract.
4. Define the Railway Labor Act.
5. Describe the Norris-La Guardia Act.
6. Define the Wagner Act.
7. Explain the Taft-Hartley Act.
8. Describe right-to-work laws.
9. Describe the Landrum-Griffin Act.
10. Describe the AFL–CIO.
11. Define amalgamation and absorption.

*"T*o the Honorable John S. Phelps, Governor of the State of Missouri, and all Citizens: We request your speedy cooperation in convincing the Legislature, and calling for the immediate passage of the eight-hour law, its stringent enforcement, and a penalty for all violations of the same; the nonemployment of all children under 14 years of age in factories, shops or other uses calculated to injure them."

Executive Committee
*United Working Men of St. Louis**

Prior to the Industrial Revolution in the 19th century, an individual was normally born into a level in society with a predestined standard of living. Custom and tradition kept a person's position relatively stable. After the Industrial Revolution, people were able to contract for employment by offering their skills and services for a wage. However, once people had been hired, they and their work output became the property of the employer.

It was not long before employees resorted to joint action to gain some influence over the terms and conditions of their employment. These attempts, occurring as early as 1741, were initially frowned on by the public and the courts. For the most part, the relationships existing between employees and management were unilateral: employees asking for higher wages approached their employers with a "take it or we'll strike" attitude, and employers usually refused or ignored their requests. Generally, what resulted was a test of economic strength to determine whose wage decisions would prevail. In most instances, employers prevailed. HRM in Action 16–1 illustrates some of the consequences of early strikes.

As time passed, society became more aware of the plight of employees. Legislation was enacted that was much more favorable toward employees and unions. This chapter explores how the legal environment concerning union/management relations has evolved. It also describes the organizational structure of unions and current issues facing unions.

Legal Environment of Labor-Management Relations

The first unions in America appeared between 1790 and 1820. These were local organizations of skilled craftsmen, such as shoemakers in Philadelphia, printers in New York, tailors in Baltimore, and other similar groups. No unions existed among factory employees during this time.

The demands of these unions were similar to those of today. They wanted job security, higher wages, and shorter working hours. When union demands were not agreed to by management, these early unions resorted to strikes, or "turnouts," as they were then called. A strike is the collective refusal of employees to work.

*Source: Samuel Yellen, *American Labor Struggles* (New York: Arno & New York Times, 1969), pp. 31–32.

▽. HRM in Action 16–1

Strike at Colorado Fuel and Iron Company (CFI)

The Colorado Fuel and Iron Company (CFI) owned about 300,000 acres of mineral-rich land in southern Colorado. This geographical insulation helped enable CFI to impose rather primitive conditions over its 30,000 workers. Most of the workers lived in company-owned camps located 10 to 30 miles from any big towns. Within the camps, unsanitary conditions led to 151 persons contracting typhoid in 1912 and 1913. Wages were paid in a currency valid only in company stores.

These conditions sparked union-organizing activity. The United Mine Workers (UMW) demanded an eight-hour day, enforcement of safety regulations, removal of armed guards, and abolition of company currency. The company refused to negotiate on these issues.

Thus, in September 1913, up to 10,000 workers at Colorado Fuel and Iron Company went on strike. After the strike began, tension rose quickly. CFI hired a large number of guards from outside the state, armed them, and paid their salaries.

Violence erupted almost immediately. First, a company detective and a union organizer were killed. A few days later, CFI troops broke up a strikers' mass meeting and killed three workers. Vengeful miners then killed four company men. Governor Ammons called out the National Guard to protect all property and those people who were still working.

On April 20, 1914, a major battle erupted between the strikers and the National Guardsmen. The fire that resulted led to the deaths of two women and 11 children. Several battles occurred over the next several days, and finally, on April 28, 1914, several regiments of federal troops were called in to end the war.

Source: Adapted from Graham Adams, Jr., *Age of Industrial Violence, 1910–1915* (New York: Columbia University Press, 1966), pp. 146–75.

To offset the pressures of these unions, employers formed associations and took legal action against the unions. In the **Philadelphia Cordwainers (shoemakers) case of 1806**, the jury ruled that combinations of workers to raise their wages constituted a conspiracy in restraint of trade. This decision established the **conspiracy doctrine**, which meant that a union could be punished if either the means used or the ends sought were deemed illegal by the courts.

Philadelphia Cordwainers (shoemakers) case of 1806
Case in which the jury ruled that combinations of workers to raise their wages constituted a conspiracy in restraint of trade.

Over the next 35 years, unions ran up against the conspiracy doctrine on numerous occasions. Some courts continued to rule that labor unions were illegal per se. Others ruled that the means used by unions (e.g., strikes) in achieving their demands were illegal or that the ends sought (e.g., closed shops) were illegal. A closed shop prohibits an employer from hiring anyone other than a union member.

Conspiracy doctrine
Notion that courts can punish a union if they deem that the means used or the ends sought by the union are illegal.

In 1842, in the landmark Massachusetts case of *Commonwealth* v. *Hunt,* the Supreme Court of Massachusetts rejected the doctrine that the actions of labor unions were illegal per se. The court noted that the power of a labor union could be used not only for illegal purposes but also for legal purposes. This decision, of course, left open the door for legal actions questioning the means used and ends sought by labor unions. Thus, even after 1842, the legal environment for unions remained vague and uncertain. Some courts held that a closed shop was a lawful objective; thus, strikes for a closed shop were legal. Other courts reached an opposite conclusion. During this time, the legality of union activities depended to a large extent on the court jurisdiction in which the case occurred.

Commonwealth v. Hunt
Landmark court decision in 1842 that declared unions were not illegal per se.

By the 1880s, most courts had moved away from the use of the conspiracy doctrine, and the injection became a favorite technique used by the courts for controlling union activities. An **injunction** is a court order to stop an action that could result in irreparable damage to property when the situation is such that no

Injunction
Court order to stop an action that could result in irreparable damage to property when the situation is such that no other adequate remedy is available to protect the interests of the injunction-seeking party.

other adequate remedy is available to protect the interests of the injunction-seeking party. During this time, the normal procedure used in seeking an injunction in a labor dispute was:

1. The complainant (normally the employer) went to court, filed a complaint stating the nature of the property threat, and requested relief.
2. The judge normally issued a temporary restraining order halting the threatened action until the case could be heard.
3. Shortly thereafter, a preliminary hearing was held so the judge could decide whether to issue a temporary injunction.
4. Finally, after a trial, a decision was made as to whether a permanent injunction should be issued.

Injunctions had three effects. First, failure of the union to abide by the temporary restraining order or the temporary injunction meant risking contempt of court charges. Second, compliance meant a waiting period of many months before the matter came to trial. Often this waiting period was enough to destroy the effectiveness of the union. Third, the courts placed a broad interpretation on the term *property*. Historically, injunctions had been issued to prevent damage to property where an award of money damages would be an inadequate remedy. However, during this time, the courts held that an employer's property included the right to operate the business and make a profit. Thus, the expectation of making a profit became a property right. Any strike, even though it might be peaceful, could be alleged to be injurious to the expectation of making a profit and could be stopped by an injunction.

Injunctions were generally granted by the courts upon request and were frequently used to control union activities until the 1930s. The attitude of the courts over this time seems to have been that management had the right to do business without the interference of unions.

Another device used by employers to control unions during this time was the **yellow-dog contract**. The name was coined by labor unions to describe an agreement between a worker and employer that, as a condition of employment, the worker would not join a labor union. These contracts could be oral or written or both.

In 1917, the Supreme Court upheld the legality of yellow-dog contracts in *Hitchman Coal & Coke Co. v. Mitchell*. This case involved the management of the Hitchman Coal & Coke Company, whose employees had been unionized in 1903, and the United Mine Workers (UMW) in West Virginia. In 1906, a strike was called by the union against the company. However, management defeated the union and resumed operations as a nonunionized company. To ensure that it remained nonunionized, management required all of its employees, as a condition of employment, to sign an agreement saying that they would not join a union as long as they were employed by Hitchman.

Later, the United Mine Workers sent an organizer back into West Virginia. The organizer secretly contacted and signed up the employees of Hitchman Coal. When enough employees signed up, a strike was called and the mine was closed. However, the management of Hitchman brought suit against the union, alleging that the organizer had deliberately induced the employees to break their agreements with the company. The Supreme Court ruled in favor of management and thus upheld the enforceability of the yellow-dog contract. Yellow-dog contracts were

Yellow-Dog contract
Term coined by unions to describe an agreement between a worker and employer stipulating that, as a condition of employment, the worker would not join a labor union. Yellow-dog contracts were made illegal by the Norris-La Guardia Act of 1932.

Hitchman Coal & Coke Co. v. Mitchell
Supreme Court case of 1917 that upheld the legality of yellow-dog contracts.

used until they were declared illegal by the Norris-La Guardia Act of 1932 (discussed later in this chapter).

Sherman Anti-Trust Act (1890)

The Sherman Anti-Trust Act was signed into law in 1890. The law made trusts and conspiracies that restrain interstate commerce illegal and forbade persons from monopolizing or attempting to monopolize interstate trade or commerce. Furthermore, any person who believed that he or she had been injured by violations of the act was given the right to sue for triple the amount of damages sustained and the costs of the suit, including a reasonable attorney's fee.

Generally, it is agreed that the primary intent of Congress in passing the Sherman Anti-Trust Act was to protect the public from the abuses of corporate monopolies. However, in 1908 in the landmark **Danbury Hatters case**, the Supreme Court decided that the Sherman Anti-Trust Act applied to unions. In this case, the United Hatters Union, while attempting to unionize Loewe & Company of Danbury, Connecticut, called a strike and initiated a national boycott against the company's products. The boycott was successful, and Loewe filed a suit against the union alleging violation of the Sherman Anti-Trust Act. The court further held that the individual members of the union were jointly liable for the money damages awarded.

Danbury Hatters case
Landmark case of 1908 in which the Supreme Court decided that the Sherman Anti-Trust Act applied to all unions.

Clayton Act (1914)

Labor unions rejoiced at the passage of the Clayton Act in 1914. In fact, Samuel Gompers, one of the leading spokesmen of the early labor movement, called the Clayton Act the "Industrial Magna Carta."[1] Sections 6 and 20 were of particular importance to labor:

> Section 6: The labor of a human being is not a commodity or article of commerce. Nothing contained in the antitrust laws shall be construed to forbid the existence and operating of labor . . . organizations . . . or to forbid or restrain individual members of such organizations from lawfully carrying out the legitimate objects thereof; nor shall such organizations, or the members thereof be held or construed to be illegal combinations or conspiracies in restraint of trade under the antitrust laws.

> Section 20: No restraining order or injunction shall be granted by any court of the United States . . . in any case between an employer and employees, or between employees, or between persons employed and persons seeking employment, unless necessary to prevent irreparable injury to property, or to a property right, of the party making the application, for which injury there is no adequate remedy at law.

However, the joy of the unions was short-lived. The Supreme Court, in *Duplex Printing Co. v. Deering*,[2] basically gutted the intent of the Clayton Act because of the vague wording of the law. At the time, Duplex was the only nonunionized company manufacturing printing presses. The union attempted to organize the company, requesting that customers not purchase Duplex presses, that a trucking company not transport Duplex presses, and that repair shops not repair Duplex presses. The company asked for an injunction against the union, but was denied

Duplex Printing Co. v. Deering
Case in which the Supreme Court ruled that unions were not exempt from the control of the Sherman Anti-Trust Act.

by both the U.S. district and circuit courts on the basis of Section 20 of the Clayton Act. However, in a split decision, the Supreme Court overruled the lower courts. In this decision, the Court ruled that Section 6 of the Clayton Act did not exempt unions from the control of the Sherman Act. Furthermore, the Court's decision meant that the issuance of injunctions was largely unchanged by the Clayton Act.

Railway Labor Act (1926)

Railway Labor Act
Enacted in 1926, this act set up the administrative machinery for handling labor relations within the railroad industry; was the first important piece of prolabor legislation.

Legislation and its interpretations by the courts were largely antiunion prior to the passage of the **Railway Labor Act** in 1926. This act, which set up the administrative machinery for handling labor relations within the railroad industry, was the first important piece of prolabor legislation in the United States. The act was extended to airlines in 1936.[3]

One provision established the National Mediation Board to administer the act. Another provision eliminated yellow-dog contracts for railroad industry employees. The act also established mechanisms for mediation and arbitration of disputes between employers and unions within the industry. However, it is important to note that the original act applied only to railroad employees and not to those employed in other industries.

Norris-La Guardia Act (1932)

Norris-La Guardia Act of 1932
Prolabor act that eliminated the use of yellow-dog contracts and severely restricted the use of injunctions.

The **Norris-La Guardia Act of 1932** was of significant importance to labor unions because it made yellow-dog contracts unenforceable and severely restricted the use of injunctions. The law prohibited federal courts from issuing injunctions to keep unions from striking, paying strike benefits, picketing (unless the picketing involved fraud or violence), and peacefully assembling.

Other parts of the law further restricted the issuance of injunctions. For example, the employer was required to show that the regular police force was either unwilling or unable to protect the employer's property before an injunction could be issued. Temporary restraining orders could not be issued for more than five days.

The Norris-La Guardia Act also gave employees the right to organize and bargain with employers on the terms and conditions of employment. However, its major weakness was that it established no administrative procedures to ensure implementation of the rights. Employees could gain bargaining rights only if their employer voluntarily agreed to recognize the union or if the employees struck and forced recognition. In other words, the law gave employees the right to organize but did not require management to bargain with their union.

National Labor Relations (Wagner) Act (1935)

National Labor Relations Act (Wagner Act)
Prolabor act of 1935 that gave workers the right to organize, obligated the management of organizations to bargain in good faith with unions, defined illegal management practices relating to unions, and created the National Labor Relations Board (NLRB) to administer the act.

The **National Labor Relations Act**, commonly known as the **Wagner Act** after its principal sponsor, Senator Robert Wagner, Sr., of New York, was passed in 1935. The bill signaled a change in the federal government's role in labor-management relations. As a result of this law, government took a much more active role.

The Wagner Act gave employees the right to organize unions, bargain collectively with employers, and engage in other concerted actions for the purpose of mutual protection. Of course, these rights had already been granted by the Norris-La Guardia Act. However, the Wagner Act went further in that it required employers to recognize unions chosen by workers and to bargain with such unions in good faith. Furthermore, employers were prohibited from engaging in certain unfair labor practices, including:

1. Interference with, restraint of, or coercion of employees in exercising their rights under the act.
2. Domination of, interference with, or financial contributions to a union.
3. Discrimination in regard to hiring, firing, or any term or condition of employment to encourage or discourage membership in a union.
4. Discharge or discrimination against an employee for filing charges or giving testimony under the act.
5. Refusal to bargain in good faith with the legal representative of the employees.

In addition, a three-member National Labor Relations Board (NLRB) was established to administer the Wagner Act (the NLRB is discussed later in this chapter). The act also established procedures for use in union elections. The board was directed to conduct such elections and to investigate unfair practices.

Labor-Management Relations (Taft-Hartley) Act (1947)

After the passage of the Wagner Act, union membership grew from approximately 6 percent of the total work force to approximately 23 percent in 1947. Accompanying this growth was an increase in union militancy. Strikes became much more frequent and widespread. In 1946, a record 4.6 million workers participated in strikes. A nationwide steel strike, an auto strike, two coal strikes, and a railroad strike negatively influenced scores of other industries, causing shortages and layoffs.

It was against this background of events that the **Labor-Management Relations Act** was passed in 1947. Known as the **Taft-Hartley Act**, it was an amendment and extension of the Wagner Act. The Taft-Hartley Act marked another change in the legislative posture toward union-management relations. The act basically placed government in the role of referee to ensure that both unions and management dealt fairly with each other.

Under the Taft-Hartley Act, employees have the right to organize a union, bargain collectively with an employer, and engage in other concerted activities for the purpose of collective bargaining. The act also spelled out unfair labor practices by employers. Most provisions are identical to those of the Wagner Act, but one unfair practice was changed significantly. Under the Wagner Act, employers were prohibited from discriminating in regard to hiring, firing, or any term or condition of employment to encourage or discourage membership in a union. However, closed and preferential shop agreements were permitted. With a closed shop, only union members can be hired, and the preferential shop requires that union members be given preference in filling job vacancies. The Taft-Hartley Act made closed and preferential shops illegal. However, the act permitted agreements in the construction industry, which required union membership within seven days of employment.

Labor Relations Act (Taft-Hartley Act)
Legislation enacted in 1947 that placed the federal government in a watchdog position to ensure that union-management relations are conducted fairly by both parties.

The act also permitted in the construction industry a practice referred to as a union hiring hall, under which unions referred people to employers with existing job openings.

Unlike the Wagner Act, the Taft-Hartley Act also established a number of unfair labor union practices. In general, unions were forbidden to:

1. Coerce employees who do not want to join.
2. Force employers to pressure employees to join a union.
3. Refuse to bargain in good faith with an employer.
4. Force an employer to pay for services not performed (featherbedding).
5. Engage in certain types of secondary boycotts (taking action against an employer that is not directly engaged in a dispute with a union).
6. Charge excessive initiation fees when union membership is required because of a union shop agreement. A union shop agreement requires employees to join the union and remain members as a condition of employment.

The Taft-Hartley Act also contained an important provision, the so-called free-speech clause. This clause stated that management has the right to express its opinion about unions or unionism to its employees, provided that they carry no threat of reprisal or force.

National Labor Relations Board

The Taft-Hartley Act also expanded the size of the **National Labor Relations Board (NLRB)** and created the **Office of the General Counsel**. Presently, the board is a five-member panel appointed by the president of the United States with the advice and consent of the Senate. Each member serves for a five-year term. One of the five is appointed as board chairperson by the president with Senate confirmation. The general counsel, a separate office independent from the board, is appointed by the president and approved by the Senate for a four-year term.

The relationship between the five-member board and the general counsel is similar to the relationship between the judge (or jury) and prosecutor. In unfair labor practice cases, the board sits as the judge and the general counsel acts as the prosecutor. Anyone can file an unfair labor practice complaint with the general counsel. Frequently, people refer to filing an unfair labor practice charge with the board, but it is actually filed with the general counsel. After the charge is filed, the general counsel investigates it and decides the merit of the charge. If the general counsel decides that the act has been violated, a complaint is issued. The case is then tried before the board which decides whether there has been a violation.

The division of authority between the board and the general counsel only applies to unfair labor practice charges. Union election procedures are handled solely by the board. The role of the board in union election campaigns is described in much more depth in Chapter 17.

Much of the work of the board and the Office of the General Counsel is carried out in regional offices established by the board. Each regional office is headed by a regional director appointed by the board. The regional director serves as the local representative of the general counsel in processing unfair labor practice charges and as the local representative of the board in administering union election procedures.

National Labor Relations Board (NLRB)
Five-member panel created by the National Labor Relations Act and appointed by the President of the United States with the advice and consent of the Senate and with the authority to administer the Wagner Act.

Office of the General Counsel
Separate and independent office created by the Taft-Hartley Act to investigate unfair labor practice charges and present those charges with merit to the NLRB.

Right-to-Work States

Section 14(b) of the Taft-Hartley Act is one of the most controversial sections of the law. It states:

> Nothing in this act shall be construed as authorizing the execution or application of agreements requiring membership in a labor organization as a condition of employment in any state or territory in which such execution or application is prohibited by state or territory law.

Thus, section 14(b) permits states and territories to pass laws prohibiting union shops and other arrangements for compulsory union membership. Laws passed by individual states prohibiting compulsory union membership are called **right-to-work laws**, and states that have passed such legislation are right-to-work states. Presently, there are 21 right-to-work states: Alabama, Arizona, Arkansas, Florida, Georgia, Idaho, Iowa, Kansas, Louisiana, Mississippi, Nebraska, Nevada, North Carolina, North Dakota, South Carolina, South Dakota, Tennessee, Texas, Utah, Virginia, and Wyoming. In these states, employees in unionized organizations are represented by the union, but are not required to belong to the union or pay union dues. Unions argue that employees who choose not to belong or pay union dues get a free ride.

The Taft-Hartley Act also created an independent agency known as the Federal Mediation and Conciliation Service within the federal government. This agency assists parties in labor disputes to settle such disputes through conciliation and mediation. Finally, the act also established procedures that can be used by the president of the United States for resolving labor disputes that imperil the national health and safety.

Right-to-work laws
Legislation enacted by individual states under the authority of Section 14(b) of the Taft-Hartley Act that can forbid various types of union security arrangements, including compulsory union membership.

Labor-Management Reporting and Disclosure (Landrum-Griffin) Act (1959)

Even after the passage of the Taft-Hartley Act, complaints continued concerning corruption and heavy-handed activity by a few unions. Thus, Congress created the Senate Select Committee on Improper Activities in the Labor or Management Field, better known as the McClellan Committee. Between 1957 and 1959, the McClellan Committee held hearings on union activities. HRM in Action 16–2 summarizes the findings of the McClellan Committee. As a result of these hearings, in 1959, Congress passed the **Labor-Management Reporting and Disclosure Act (LMRDA)**, usually called the **Landrum-Griffin Act**. This act, which also was an amendment and extension to the Wagner Act, was aimed primarily at regulating internal union affairs and protecting the rights of individual union members.

The main provisions of the act were:

Labor-Management Reporting and Disclosure Act (LMRDA) (Landrum-Griffin Act)
Legislation enacted in 1959, regulating labor unions and requiring disclosure of certain union financial information to the government.

1. Union members are guaranteed the right to vote in union elections.
2. Union members are guaranteed the right to oppose their incumbent leadership both in union meetings and by nominating opposition candidates.
3. A majority affirmative vote of members by a secret ballot is required before union dues can be increased.

▼. HRM in Action 16–2

Findings of the McClellan Committee

In its hearings, the McClellan Committee uncovered the following facts about a few unions:

1. Rank-and-file members have no voice in some unions' affairs, notably in financial matters, and frequently are denied secret ballots.

2. Some international unions have abused their right to place local unions under trusteeship by imposing the trusteeship merely to plunder the local union's treasury or boost the ambitions of candidates for high office.

3. Certain managements have bribed union officials to get sweetheart contracts or other favored treatment.

4. There is frequent misuse of union funds through lack of adequate inspection and auditing procedures.

5. Some unions resort to acts of violence to keep their members in line.

6. Some employers and their agents follow improper practices to influence employees in exercising the rights guaranteed them by NLRA.

7. Organizational picketing is sometimes misused to extort money from employers or to influence employees in their selection of representation.

8. There are cases of infiltration of unions at high levels by criminals.

9. A no man's land sometimes exists, in which employers and unions cannot resort either to the NLRB or state agencies for relief.

Source: Adapted from Benjamin J. Taylor and Fred Witney, *Labor Relations Law* (Englewood Cliffs, N.J.: Prentice-Hall, Inc.), 1971, p. 474.

4. Reports covering most financial aspects of the union must be filed with the U.S. Department of Labor.

5. Officers and employees of unions are required to report any financial dealings with employers that might potentially influence the union members' interests.

6. Each union is required to have a constitution and bylaws filed with the U.S. Department of Labor.

7. Rigid formal requirements are established for conducting both national and local union elections.

8. Union members are allowed to bring suit against union officials for improper management of the union's funds and for conflict-of-interest situations.

9. Trusteeships that allow national or international unions to take over the management of a local union can be established only under provisions specified in the constitution and bylaws of the union and only to combat corruption or financial misconduct.

Civil Service Reform Act (1978)

Executive orders
Orders issued by the President of the United States for managing and operating federal government agencies.

Prior to 1978, labor-management relations within the federal government were administered through **executive orders**. These orders are issued by the president of the United States and relate to the management and operation of federal government agencies. Executive Order 10988, issued by President Kennedy, gave federal employees the right to join unions and required good-faith bargaining by both unions and federal agency management. Executive Order 11491, issued by President Nixon, defined more precisely the rights of federal employees in regard to unionization by establishing unfair labor practices for both unions and federal agency management. It also established procedures to safeguard these rights.

In 1978, the **Civil Service Reform Act** was passed. It basically enacted into law the measures that had previously been adopted under Executive Orders 10988 and 11491. The act gave federal employees the right to organize and establish procedures for handling labor-management relations within the federal government. The main provisions of the act are that it:

1. Established the **Federal Labor Relations Authority (FLRA)** to administer the act. The FLRA is composed of three members, not more than two of whom may be members of the same political party. Members of the authority are appointed by the president with approval of the Senate for a term of five years.
2. Created the Office of the General Counsel within the FLRA to investigate and prosecute unfair labor practices. The general counsel is appointed by the president with approval of the Senate for a term of five years.
3. Created the **Federal Services Impasses Panel (FSIP)** within the FLRA to provide assistance in resolving negotiation impasses between federal agencies and unions. The panel is composed of a chairperson and at least six other members who are appointed by the president for a term of five years.
4. Established unfair labor practices for the management of federal agencies and unions.
5. Established the general areas that are subject to collective bargaining.
6. Required binding arbitration for all grievances that have not been resolved in earlier stages of the grievance procedure.
7. Prohibited strikes in the federal sector.

Civil Service Reform Act
Legislation enacted in 1978, regulating labor-management relations for federal government employees.

Federal Labor Relations Authority (FLRA)
Three-member panel created by the Civil Service Reform Act, whose purpose is to administer the act.

Federal Services Impasses Panel (FSIP)
Entity within the FLRC whose function is to provide assistance in resolving negotiation impasses within the federal sector.

Union Structures

As the previously described legislation was passed and court actions taken, organizational units were developed within the union movement to deal with problems and to take advantage of opportunities. Four main types of such units exist:

• Federations of local, national, and international unions (e.g., AFL–CIO)
• National or international unions
• City and state federations
• Local unions

Some important dates relating to the development of the different union organizational units are shown in Table 16–1.

▼ **Table 16–1**   Important dates in the labor movement

Year	Event
1792	First local union: Philadelphia Shoemaker's Union
1833	First city federation: New York, Philadelphia, Baltimore
1850	First national union: International Typographical Union
1869	First attempt to form a federation of unions: Knights of Labor
1886	Formation of American Federation of Labor (AFL)
1938	Formation of Congress of Industrial Organizations (CIO)
1955	AFL–CIO merger

AFL–CIO

American Federation of Labor–Congress of Industrial Organizations (AFL–CIO)
Combination of national, international, and local unions joined together to promote the interests of unions and workers. The AFL–CIO was formed in 1955 by the amalgamation of the American Federal of Labor (AFL) and the Congress of Industrial Organizations (CIO).

Craft unions
Unions having only skilled workers as members. Most craft unions have members from several related trades (e.g., Bricklayers', Masons', and Plasterers' International Union).

Industrial unions
Unions having as members both skilled and unskilled workers in a particular industry or group of industries.

Structurally speaking, the **American Federation of Labor–Congress of Industrial Organizations (AFL–CIO)** is the largest organizational unit within the union movement. Its primary goal is to promote the interests of unions and workers. The AFL–CIO resulted from the 1955 merger of the American Federation of Labor and the Congress of Industrial Organizations.

Formed in 1886, the AFL was primarily composed of **craft unions**, which only had skilled workers as members. Most such unions had members from several related trades (e.g., the Bricklayers, Masons, and Plasterers International Union). The CIO, formed in 1938, was developed to organize **industrial unions**, which have as members both skilled and unskilled workers in a particular industry or group of industries. The United Automobile Workers is an example of an industrial union.

Technically speaking, the AFL–CIO is not a union itself but is merely an organization composed of affiliated national and international unions, affiliated state and local bodies, local unions affiliated directly with the AFL–CIO, and eight trade and industrial departments. The organizational structure of the AFL–CIO is shown in Figure 16–I. The AFL–CIO is merely a loose, voluntary federation of unions.

The basic policies of the AFL–CIO are set and its executive council elected at a national convention held every two years. The executive council—the president, secretary-treasurer, and 33 vice presidents—carries out the policies established at the convention. Each affiliated national and international union sends delegates to the convention. The number of delegates a particular union sends is determined by the size of its membership.

To deal with specific concerns, the AFL–CIO president appoints and supervises standing committees that work with staff departments to provide services to the union membership. The general board meets at the call of the president or the executive council and acts on matters referred to it by the executive council.

The trade and industrial departments primarily serve to coordinate the activities of unions whose interests overlap, to seek means of resolving jurisdictional disputes between unions, and to promote cooperation in collective bargaining between unions. For example, the Union Label Department promotes the use of union labels on products. The Department of Organization and Field Services assists in union organizing campaigns and contract negotiations.

It is important to note that all national and international unions do not belong

▼ Figure 16–1   Organizational structure of the AFL–CIO

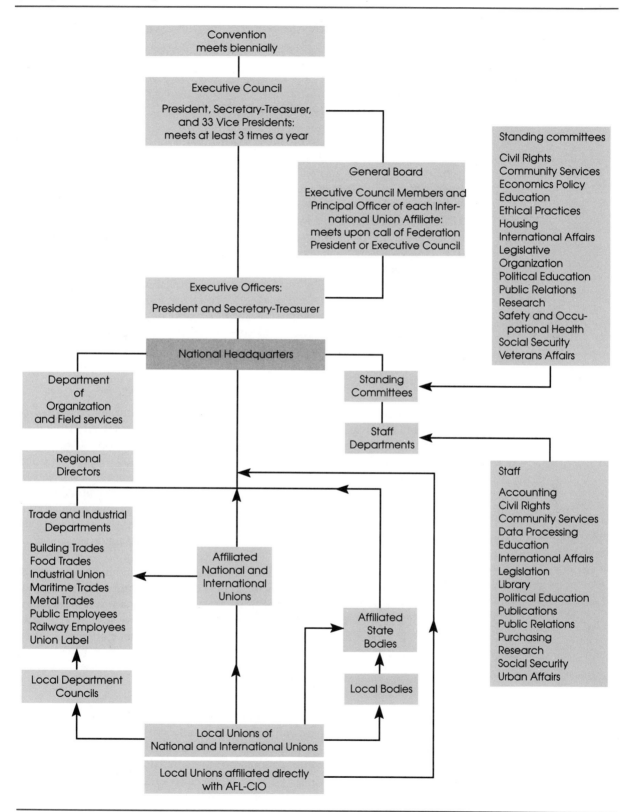

to the AFL–CIO. Presently, for example, the United Automobile Workers and the United Mine Workers do not belong. However, a majority of unions are affiliated with the AFL–CIO.

National and International Unions

The organizational structure of most national and international unions is similar to that of the AFL–CIO. Unions are called international because they often have members in both the United States and Canada. In general, both national and international units operate under a constitution and have a national convention with each local union represented in proportion to its membership. Usually, the convention elects an executive council, which normally consists of a president, secretary-treasurer, and several vice presidents. Normally, the president appoints and manages a staff for handling matters such as organizing activities, research, and legal problems.

The field organization of a national or international union usually has several regional or district offices headed by a regional director. Under the regional director are field representatives who are responsible for conducting union organizing campaigns and assisting local unions in collective bargaining and in handling grievances.

City and State Federations

City federations receive their charter from the AFL–CIO and are composed of local unions within a specified area. Local unions send delegates to city federation meetings, which are generally held on a biweekly or monthly basis.

The primary function of city federations is to coordinate and focus the political efforts of local unions. During elections, city federations usually endorse a slate of candidates. Most city federations maintain an informal lobby at city hall and present labor's issues to legislative committees. City federations do not always focus their efforts only on labor issues. Other issues and activities frequently addressed by city federations include school board policies, community fund-raising drives, and public transportation problems.

State federations are also chartered by the AFL–CIO and are composed of local unions and city federations. The main goal of state federations is to influence political action favorable to unions. Efforts are made to persuade union members to vote for union-endorsed candidates. During state legislative sessions, the state federation actively lobbies for passage of bills endorsed by labor unions.

Local Unions

Most local unions operate under the constitution of their national or international union. However, a number are independent in that they operate without a national affiliation. Furthermore, a local union can be affiliated directly with the AFL–CIO without being connected with a national or international union.

As a rule, the membership of a local union elects officers, who carry out the union activities. In a typical local union, a president, vice president, and secretary-treasurer are elected. Several committees are also normally formed. For example, a bargaining committee is usually appointed to negotiate the contract for the union, and a grievance committee is usually appointed to handle grievances for the membership. The latter committee is generally composed of a chief steward and several departmental stewards. The stewards recruit new employees into the union, listen to worker complaints, handle grievances, and observe management's administration of the union contract. Generally, most local union officials work at a regular job but have some leeway in using working time to conduct union business. In large locals, most officials are full-time, paid employees of the union. The local usually depends heavily on the field representative of its national or international union for assistance in handling contract negotiations, strikes, and arbitration hearings.

In those industries where membership is scattered among several employers, local unions often have a business agent who is a full-time, paid employee of the local union. This agent manages internal union activities, negotiates contracts, meets with company officials to resolve contract interpretation issues, handles grievances, and serves as an active participant in arbitration hearings.

Current and Future Developments in the Labor Movement

Between 1935 (the year the National Labor Relations Act was passed) and the end of World War II, union membership quadrupled. During the post-World War II era through 1970, union membership continued to grow (See Table 16–2). Between 1970 and 1980, union membership grew by slightly more than a million members, but as a percentage of the total work force it dropped significantly. In addition, union membership has dropped in the 1980s by over four million workers, and it has continued to drop as a percentage of the total work force. Although union membership showed a slight increase in 1988, its future growth is uncertain. As a result, it is expected that unions will make several initiatives in an attempt to increase membership. HRM in Action 16–3 describes one such plan, carried out by the AFL–CIO. Several additional initiatives that are likely to occur are described in the following paragraphs.

Historically, labor unions have gained their strength from blue-collar production workers. However, the growth of the work force has occurred and will continue to occur principally in the service sector of the economy. By 1990, service industries will employ almost three-quarters of the labor force. Yet, less than 10 percent of the service sector is currently organized. Unions have been successful in organizing narrow segments of the service sector, such as teachers, pilots, and

▼ Table 16–2   Union membership trends

	1950	1960	1970	1980	1985	1988
Union membership*	14,267	17,049	21,248	22,366	16,996	17,002
Percentage of total work force	31.5	32.1	30.0	24.7	18.0	16.8

*Figures are in millions.
Source: U.S. Department of Labor; Bureau of Labor Statistics.

▼. HRM in Action 16–3

Financial Benefits to Attract Members

In 1987, the AFL–CIO started a campaign of offering a financial benefits package to attract and retain membership. Among the plan's options are: a Master Card with a low finance charge; a legal services plan, which offers free consultations and reduced hourly rates on attorneys' charges; a travel benefits plan, which guarantees the lowest available airfares and discounts on lodging and cars; and reduced premiums on term life insurance. The AFL–CIO is planning an expansion of the benefits. Services to be introduced will run the gamut from car leasing to funeral arrangements. The package will also be made available to nonmembers. Workers will also be allowed to join an AFL–CIO union as associate members.

Source: Adapted from "AFL–CIO Offers Financial Goodies to Attract Members," *American Banker,* December 30, 1987, p. 3.

Amalgamation
Union merger that involves two or more unions, usually of approximately the same size, forming a new union.

Absorption
Union merger that involves the merging of one union into a considerably larger one.

musicians. However, it is expected that a major emphasis of future organizing campaigns will be directed toward convincing unorganized white-collar employees that their personal and professional needs can be satisfied through union representation.

By the late 1990s, investments in private pension plans are expected to reach approximately $3 trillion. Labor unions are likely to attempt to influence how these monies are invested. Specifically, unions will probably request that the funds not be invested in the stock of antiunion companies or companies that engage in antiunion practices.

Another likely development is the continued increase in union mergers. Union mergers take two basic forms. An **amalgamation** involves two or more unions, normally of roughly equal size, forming a new union. An **absorption** involves the merging of one union into a considerably larger one. Roughly 50 of the AFL–CIO affiliates have under 50,000 members, and another 30 have under 100,000 members. Larger unions can, of course, bring much more pressure on management, not only in negotiating collective bargaining agreements but also in union organizing campaigns.

● *Summary of Learning Objectives*

1. Describe the conspiracy doctrine.

    The conspiracy doctrine mandated that a union could be punished if either the means used or ends sought by the union were deemed illegal by the courts.

2. Define injunction.

    An injunction is a court order to stop an action that can result in irreparable damage to property when the situation is such that no adequate remedy is available to protect the interests of the injunction-seeking party.

3. Explain a yellow-dog contract.

    A yellow-dog contract (a term coined by labor unions) is an agreement between a worker and an employer stipulating, as a condition of employment, that the worker will not join a labor union. Yellow-dog contracts are now illegal.

4. Define the Railway Labor Act.

This act set up the administrative machinery for handling labor relations within the railroad and airline industries.

5. Describe the Norris-La Guardia Act.

This act made yellow-dog contracts unenforceable and severely limited the use of injunctions. It also gave employees the right to organize and bargain with employers on the terms and conditions of employment.

6. Define the Wagner Act.

This act gave employees the right to organize unions, bargain collectively with employers, and engage in other concerted actions for the purpose of mutual protection.

7. Explain the Taft-Hartley Act.

This act basically placed government in the role of referee to ensure that both unions and management deal fairly with each other.

8. Describe right-to-work laws.

Laws passed by individual states prohibiting compulsory union membership.

9. Describe the Landrum-Griffin Act.

An act aimed primarily at regulating internal union affairs and protecting the rights of individual union members.

10. Describe the AFL–CIO.

The AFL–CIO is a voluntary federation of unions, whose primary goal is to promote the interests of unions and workers.

11. Define amalgamation and absorption.

An amalgamation involves two or more unions, normally of roughly equal size, forming a new union. An absorption involves the merging of one union into a considerably larger one.

Review Questions

1. Explain the ruling in the Philadelphia Cordwainers case of 1806.
2. What was the decision in the *Commonwealth* v. *Hunt* case of 1842?
3. What is an injunction? How were injunctions used against labor unions?
4. What is a yellow-dog contract?
5. List the major benefits gained by unions with the passage of the Norris-La Guardia Act of 1932.
6. What unfair employer practices were specified by the Wagner Act of 1935?
7. What unfair union practices were specified by the Taft-Hartley Act of 1947?
8. Outline the main areas covered by the Landrum-Griffin Act of 1959.
9. Outline the main areas covered by the Civil Service Reform Act of 1978.
10. Briefly describe the four main types of union organizational units.
11. What trends have occurred in labor union membership from 1935 to the present?

Discussion Questions

1. What reasons can you give to explain why legislation took a prounion turn in the 1930s?
2. Discuss your feelings on the following statement: "Management should always fight hard to keep unions out of their organization."
3. Why do you think white-collar workers should join unions?
4. Do you believe that college professors and nurses are good candidates for unionization? Why or why not?

▼ INCIDENT 16–1

Unions and Management Rights

Example 1

IAM Local 709 voted to end a strike against the Marietta Plant of the Lockheed-Georgia Company. The contract that was agreed on contained a wage increase of about 13 percent and improved retirement, insurance, and other benefits. The company also agreed to pay employees for the seven days over the Christmas and the two days over the Thanksgiving holidays that were missed during the strike.

As far as the Marietta workers were concerned, the main issue was their right to "bump" workers with less seniority from projects during times when there are not enough jobs to go around. Lockheed officials claimed that the bumping procedure, whereby a worker having at least one day's seniority over another could take the junior's job, would hurt production so badly that it could force the company to abandon projects. Lockheed's initial proposal had been that an employee not be allowed to bump without at least three months' seniority over the junior employee. After the union rejected this proposal, the company proposed that employees not be allowed to bump unless they had at least one month's seniority over the junior employee. At that point, negotiations broke down.

The last Lockheed offer, which was accepted, was that the seniority system remain the same for all current Lockheed employees. However, anyone hired after Lockheed's offer was accepted would have to have at least one month's seniority to be able to bump another worker.

Example 2

The Airline Pilots Association (ALPA) rejected the airline industry's proposal that the DC–9–55, also known as the Super 80, be flown with two-person crews. The DC–9–55 is a superstretch version of the popular DC–9 airlines, which was first introduced in 1965. The original DC–9 had a capacity of 70 passengers, while the Super 80 can carry 172. The problem is that a third crew member is used in most larger jets. Even the Boeing 737, smaller in passenger capacity than the Super 80, is flown with three crew members by most airlines.

Since 1970, ALPA has insisted on use of three crew members for all new jets. The management of the airlines contends that the Super 80 is merely an enlargement of an existing design and argues that the third crew member only adds to payroll costs. ALPA's position is that the third crew member is needed for safety.

Questions

1. In light of these two examples, which rights of management do you think a union should not be able to influence?
2. How do you feel about the influence of the union in these two examples? Do you think that the unions are correct?

▼ INCIDENT 16–2

Voluntary Resignations during a Strike*

In July 1985, the Supreme Court ruled in a 5–4 decision that unions can't fine workers who resign their union membership during a strike and return to work in violation of union rules.

The Court, upholding the view of the National Labor Relations Board, said that imposing fines or other restrictions on workers who quit the union during a strike "impairs the policy of voluntary unionism."

The case involved a seven-month strike by the Pattern Makers' League against clothing companies in Illinois and Wisconsin. The union had a rule prohibiting resignations during a strike and enforced it by fining 10 workers the approximate amount they earned after they returned to work during the strike.

Questions

1. Should unions be able to restrict resignations during a strike? Why or why not?
2. What impact will this decision have on union membership?

Exercise

Need for Unions

Break the class into teams of four to five students per team. Each team should then be asked to prepare to debate one of the following statements:

1. Unions served a useful purpose in the past but have outlived their usefulness.

*Source: Adapted from Stephen Wermiel, "Justices Rule Unions Can't Fine Members Who Quit, Resume Work during a Strike," *The Wall Street Journal,* June 28, 1985, p. 5.

2. Unions are as needed today as they have been in the past. Without unions, wages and working conditions of the average employee would deteriorate.

After the debate, the instructor should list on the board some points made by each team and discuss the issues involved.

Notes and Additional Readings

1. Samuel Gompers, "The Charter of Industrial Freedom," *American Federationist,* November 1914, pp. 971–72.
2. 254 U.S. 445 (1921).
3. See Dennis A. Arouca and Henry H. Pettit, Jr., "Transportation Labor Regulation: Is the Railway Labor Act or the National Labor Relations Act the Better Strategy Vehicle?" *Labor Law Journal,* March 1985, pp. 145–72.

Chapter 17

Union Organizing Campaigns and Collective Bargaining

Chapter Outline

Union Membership Decision
    Reasons for Joining
    The Opposition View
Union Organizing Campaign
    Determining the Bargaining Unit
    Election Campaigns
    Election, Certification, and
      Decertification
Good-Faith Bargaining
Participants in Negotiations
    Employer's Role
    Union's Role
    Role of Third Parties
Collective Bargaining Agreements
Specific Issues in Collective
    Bargaining Agreements

    Management Rights
    Union Security
    Wages and Employee Benefits
    Individual Security (Seniority) Rights
    Dispute Resolution
Impasses in Collective Bargaining
Trends in Collective Bargaining
Summary of Learning Objectives
Review Questions
Discussion Questions
Incident 17–1: Florida National
    Guard and NAGE
Incident 17–2: Vote Yes, Vote Yes
Exercise: Contract Negotiations
Notes and Additional Readings

● *Learning Objectives*

After studying this chapter, you should be able to:

1. Define collective bargaining.
2. Explain the captive-audience doctrine.
3. Define bargaining unit.
4. Explain certification, recognition, and contract bars.
5. Describe good-faith bargaining.
6. Discuss boulwarism.
7. Explain mediation.
8. Define checkoff.
9. Explain seniority.
10. Define lockout and strike.

"Good labor relations . . . cannot be brought about by legislation . . . I believe that enlightened labor and enlightened management working together, can accomplish far more by peaceful bargaining than is possible through legislation."

Harry Truman*

Collective bargaining
Process that involves the negotiation, drafting, administration, and interpretation of a written agreement between an employer and a union for a specific period of time.

Collective bargaining is a process that involves the negotiation, drafting, administration, and interpretation of a written agreement between an employer and a union for a specific period of time. The end result of collective bargaining is a contract that sets forth the joint understandings of the parties as to wages, hours, and other terms and conditions of employment. Contracts cover a variety of time periods, the most common being three years.

The basic tenets of the collective bargaining process are:

1. Negotiation of relevant issues in good faith by both management and the union.
2. Incorporation of the parties' understandings into a written contract.
3. Administration of the daily working relationships according to the terms and conditions of employment specified in the contract.
4. Resolution of disputes in the interpretation of the terms of the contract through established procedures.

Normally, the human resource department serves as management's primary representative in all aspects of the collective bargaining process.

Union Membership Decision

Before the collective bargaining process begins, the employees of an organization must decide whether they want to be represented by a union. Thus, an important prerequisite to understanding the collective bargaining process is to develop an appreciation for what attracts employees to unions.

Reasons for Joining

A variety of factors influence an employee's desire to join a union. Employees who are dissatisfied with their wages, job security, fringe benefits, the treatment they receive from management, and their chances for promotion are more likely to vote for union representation. Another important factor in determining employees' interest in union membership is their perception of the ability of the union to change the situation. If employees do not believe that unionization will change

**Source: Harry Truman, Labor Day statement, 1947, as quoted in Kurt Braum, *Labor Disputes and Their Settlement* (Baltimore: The John Hopkins Press, 1955), p. 16.*

the economic and working conditions that dissatisfy them, then they are unlikely to vote for unionization.

While wages, working conditions, and job security are the main issues contributing to the decision to join a union, other factors include employees' desires for:

1. Better communication with management
2. Higher quality of management and supervision
3. Increased democracy in the workplace
4. Opportunity to belong to a group where they can share experiences and fellowship

The Opposition View

Understanding why employees are against unionization is as important as knowing why they favor unionization. The major reason for not joining a union is satisfactory wages, working conditions, and job security. Some employees also have a negative image of labor unions, feeling that unions have too much political influence, require members to go along with decisions made by the union, and have leaders who promote their own self-interests. Other reasons include the belief that unions abuse their power by calling strikes, causing high prices, and misusing union dues and pension funds.

Some employees identify with management and view unions as adversaries. This is especially true of professional employees, such as engineers, nurses, and college professors. However, dissatisfaction with wages, benefits, and working conditions can quickly break down this negative attitude toward unions.

Many organizations have avoided unionization. In most cases, the managements of those organizations have provided satisfactory wages, working conditions, and job security for their employees. Other management practices that decrease the likelihood of unionization include creating a procedure for handling employee complaints, eliminating arbitrary and heavy-handed management and supervisory practices, establishing a meaningful system of two-way communication between management and the work force, eliminating threats to employees' job security, and making the employees feel like they are part of the organization.

Union Organizing Campaign

Most often, union organizing campaigns start with one or more employees requesting that the union begin an organizing campaign. In some instances, national and international unions contact employees in organizations that have been targeted for organizing campaigns. Generally, however, unions will not attempt to organize a facility unless there is a strong body of support among the employees. Typically, interested employees are given cards authorizing the union to represent them in bargaining with their employer. The interested employees and the union organizer then attempt to persuade other employees to sign the authorization cards.

Several restrictions have been placed on where and when support for the union can be solicited.[1] Generally, employees in favor of the union can orally solicit support from other employees in work and nonwork areas but only on nonwork time. In addition, if management allows employees to engage in casual conversation while they are working, the employees can discuss union matters if production is not hindered. Union literature can be distributed only on nonworking time, and management can limit the distribution of literature to nonwork areas.

Exceptions to the general rules for oral solicitation and distribution of union literature are rarely approved by the National Labor Relations Board (NLRB). However, some exceptions have been granted. For example, department stores can establish rules prohibiting oral solicitation on the sales floor, providing that employees are generally prohibited from casual conversations on the sales floor because customers waiting for service may become irritated at seeing employees talking to each other.

The rights to orally solicit union support and distribute union literature on company property apply only to employees. Generally, management can prohibit union organizers from entering company property for these purposes.[2] One exception in this area is that if management allows other solicitors to enter company property, then union organizers cannot be excluded.

Captive-audience doctrine
Management's right to speak against a union on company time to employees and to require employees to attend the meeting.

Under the so-called **captive-audience doctrine**, management has the right to speak against the union on company time to employees and require employees to attend the meeting.[3] On the other hand, the union does not have the right to reply on company time. The primary exception to the captive-audience doctrine is that management is prohibited from giving a speech on company time to a mass employee audience in the 24 hours immediately before an election. However, the 24-hour rule only applies to a speech before a mass group. Managers are permitted to talk against the union to employees individually or in small groups during the last 24 hours.

Determining the Bargaining Unit

When the union obtains signed authorization cards from at least 30 percent of the employees, either the union or the employer can petition the National Labor Relations Board to conduct a representation election. In the event that the union has signed authorization cards from more than 50 percent of the employees, the union can make a direct request to the employer to become the bargaining agent of the employees. When this happens, the employer normally refuses, and the union then petitions the NLRB for an election.

Bargaining unit
Group of employees in a plant, firm, or industry, recognized by the employer, agreed on by the parties to a case, or designated by the NLRB as appropriate for the purposes of collective bargaining.

After a petition is filed, a representative of the NLRB (called an examiner) verifies that the authorization requirement has been fulfilled and then makes a determination as to the appropriate bargaining unit. A **bargaining unit** (or election unit) is defined as a group of employees in a plant, firm, or industry, recognized by the employer, agreed on by the parties to a case, or designated by the NLRB or its regional director as appropriate for the purposes of collective bargaining.

Consent elections
Union elections in which the parties have agreed on the appropriate bargaining unit.

Community of interest
Concept by which the NLRB makes a bargaining unit decision, based on areas of worker commonality.

Although the NLRB is ultimately responsible for establishing an appropriate bargaining unit, the parties usually have a great deal of influence on this decision. Most elections are known as **consent elections**, in which the parties have agreed on the appropriate bargaining unit. When this is not the case, the NLRB must make the bargaining unit decision, guided by a concept called **community of**

▼. HRM in Action 17–1

Bargaining Units in the Health Care Industry

In 1974, Congress extended coverage of the National Labor Relations Act (NLRA) to nonprofit hospitals. In the passage of this amendment, both the Senate and the House cautioned the NLRB that due consideration should be given to preventing proliferation of bargaining units in the health care industry. Congress believed that unwarranted bargaining unit fragmentation would lead to jurisdictional disputes and work stoppages, and felt that this could not be tolerated in the health care industry.

In 1987, the NLRB proposed eight appropriate bargaining units: registered nurses, physicians, other professionals, technicians, skilled maintenance personnel, business office clerical workers, other nonprofessionals, and guards.

Source: Adapted from Rebecca A. Campbell, "Current Developments in Labor-Management Relations," *Employee Relations Law Journal,* Spring 1989, pp. 627–32.

interest. Community-of-interest factors include elements such as similar wages, hours, and working conditions; the employees' physical proximity to each other; common supervision; the amount of interchange of personnel within the proposed unit; and the degree of integration of the employer's production process or operation. HRM in Action 17–1 discusses bargaining units within the health care industry.

Election Campaigns

During the election campaign, certain activities (called unfair labor practices) are illegal. These include (1) physical interference, threats, or violent behavior by the employer toward union organizers; (2) employer interference with employees involved in the organizing drive; (3) discipline or discharge of employees for pro-union activities; and (4) threatening or coercing of employees by union organizers. After filing for an election with the NLRB, a union can picket an employer only if the employer is not presently unionized, the petition has been filed with the NLRB within the past 30 days, and a representation election has not been conducted during the preceding 12 months. Picketing of this type is called **informational picketing**. Individuals patrol at or near the place of employment carrying signs to publicize the fact that the union is requesting an election to become the bargaining agent for the employees.

During the election campaign, management normally initiates a campaign against the union, emphasizing the costs of unionization and the loss of individual freedom that can result from collective representation. Management can legally state its opinion about the possible ramifications of unionization if its statements are based on fact and are not threatening. Management can also explain to employees the positive aspects of their current situation. However, promises to provide or withhold benefits in the future in the event of unionization or nonunionization are prohibited. An employer can conduct polls to verify union strength prior to an election, but it may not, in general, question employees individually about their preferences or otherwise threaten or intimidate them.

During the election campaign, unions emphasize their ability to help employees

Informational picketing
Patrolling at or near an employer's facility by individuals carrying signs to publicize the fact that the union is requesting an election to become the bargaining agent for the employees of the organization.

satisfy their needs and improve their working conditions. The ability of the union to sell these concepts to the employees is a most critical factor in determining the union's success in the election campaign. Employees must believe that the union cares about their problems, can help resolve them, and can assist in improving their wages, benefits, and working conditions. Unions are legally prohibited from coercing or threatening individual employees if they do not join the union.[4]

The actual impact of an election campaign is unclear. However, the campaign tactics of both management and the union are monitored by the NLRB. If the practices of either party are found to be unfair, the election results may be invalidated and a new election conducted. Furthermore, charges of unfair labor practices against management, if serious enough, can result in the NLRB ordering management to bargain with the union. Such situations are called **Gissel bargaining orders**. Gissel bargaining orders are named after a landmark Supreme Court decision, *NLRB* v. *Gissel Packing Company,*[5] which held that bargaining orders by the NLRB are an appropriate remedy for certain types of employer misconduct. Gissel bargaining orders are rarely issued by the NLRB.

Gissel bargaining orders
Situations under which the NLRB orders management to bargain with the union; named after a landmark Supreme Court decision, *NLRB* v. *Gissel Packing Company.*

Election, Certification, and Decertification

If management and the union agree to conduct the election as a consent election, balloting often occurs within a short period of time. However, if management does not agree to a consent election, a long delay may occur. Delays in balloting often increase the likelihood that management will win the election. As a result, management frequently refuses to agree to a consent election

In union elections, the time when an election can be held is an important issue. The so-called **12-month rule** provides that no election can be held in any bargaining unit within which a valid election has been held within the preceding 12-month period. Also, the NLRB will not permit another election in the bargaining unit within 12 months of a union's certification. This is called a **certification bar**. And the NLRB also prohibits an election for up to 12 months after an employer voluntarily recognizes a union. This is called a **recognition bar**. Finally, after a contract is agreed on by both parties, the NLRB does not normally permit an election in the bargaining unit covered by a contract until the contract expires, up to a maximum of three years. This is known as the **contract bar doctrine**.

12-month rule
Provides that no election can be held in any bargaining unit within which a valid election has been held within the preceding 12-month period.

Certification bar
Condition occurring when the NLRB will not permit another election in the bargaining unit within 12 months of a union's certification.

Recognition bar
Condition occurring when the NLRB prohibits an election for up to 12 months after an employer voluntarily recognizes a union.

Contract bar doctrine
Under this, the NLRB does not normally permit an election in the bargaining unit covered by a contract until the contract expires, up to a maximum of three years.

When the exact date for the election is finally established, the NLRB then conducts a secret-ballot election. If the union receives a majority of the ballots cast, it becomes certified as the exclusive bargaining representative of all employees in the unit. Exclusive bargaining representative means that the union represents all employees (both union members and nonmembers) in the bargaining unit in negotiating their wages, hours, and terms and conditions of employment. It is important to note that the union does not have to receive a positive vote from a majority of the employees in the bargaining unit. It only has to receive a majority of the votes cast.

After a union has been certified, it remains by law the exclusive bargaining agent for all employees unless the employees within the unit desire otherwise. In the event that the employees want to oust the union, they can file a petition with the NLRB for a decertification election. If 30 percent of the employees support the petition and a valid election to oust the union has not been held within the

▼ **Figure 17–1**   Steps involved in a union organizing campaign

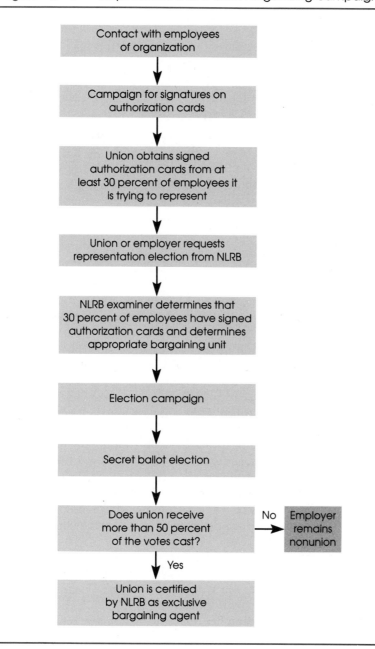

preceding year, a decertification election is conducted. If a majority of the voting employees vote to decertify the union, it no longer legally represents them. Figure 17–1 summarizes the steps involved in an organizing campaign, and HRM in Action 17–2 illustrates a ruling resulting from an organizing campaign held at Harvard.

▽. HRM in Action 17–2

Organizing Clerical Workers at Harvard

In May 1988, the clerical and technical workers of Harvard University voted 1,530 to 1,486 to affiliate with the American Federation of State, County, and Municipal Employees. The union had failed in its organizing attempts at Harvard in 1977 and 1981 and union leaders had considered this recent campaign to be one of the most important in the 1980s. Harvard, which had fought the unionization drive, sought to have the election set aside on the grounds that union officials harassed workers. In October 1988, an administrative law judge upheld the union vote.

Source: Adapted from Allan R. Gold, "Judge Upholds Harvard Employees' Unionization," *The New York Times,* October 25, 1988, p. A16.

Good-Faith Bargaining

Good-faith bargaining
Sincere intention of both parties to negotiate differences and reach a mutually acceptable agreement.

After a union is certified, the employer is required by law to bargain in good faith with the union. Of course, bargaining between an employer and the union also takes place before the expiration of an existing contract. The National Labor Relations Act stipulates the legal requirement of **good-faith bargaining** for private enterprise organizations, whereas the Civil Service Reform Act of 1978 makes the same requirement for federal agencies. Unfortunately, good faith—or the lack of it—is not explicitly defined in either of these laws. Over the years, however, decisions of the NLRB, the Federal Labor Relations Authority (FLRA), and the courts have interpreted good-faith bargaining to be the sincere intention of both parties to negotiate differences and to reach an agreement acceptable to both. Good-faith bargaining does not require the parties to agree; it merely obligates them to make a good-faith attempt to reach an agreement. Thus, the existence of good faith is generally determined by examining the total atmosphere in the collective bargaining process. The essential requirement is that a bona fide attempt is made to reach an agreement.

Boulwarism
Named after a General Electric vice president; occurs when management makes its best offer at the outset of bargaining and firmly adheres to the offer throughout the bargaining sessions. The NLRB has ruled that this is not good-faith bargaining and is, therefore, illegal.

Several bargaining situations have been taken to the NLRB to determine the presence or lack of good-faith bargaining. A key case involved the General Electric company's use of **boulwarism**, which was named after a General Electric vice president and means that management makes its best offer at the outset of bargaining and firmly adheres to the offer throughout the bargaining sessions. The NLRB has ruled that boulwarism is not good-faith bargaining.[6] In its decision, the NLRB held that boulwarism was illegal because the company not only adhered to a rigid position at the bargaining table but, in this case, had also mounted a publicity campaign to convince its employees that the company's offer was best. The company belittled the union in its literature. Since the employer simply ignored the union and went directly to the employees with its proposal, it violated its duty to bargain in good faith with the employee's exclusive bargaining representative (i.e., the union).

Participants in Negotiations

A number of parties may be either directly or indirectly involved in the collective bargaining process. The primary participants are, of course, the employer and union representatives. However, several third parties can play a significant role.

Employer's Role

Participation of the employer in collective bargaining may take one of several different forms. The single-company agreement is most common. Under this approach, representatives of a single company meet with representatives of the union and negotiate a contract. Of course, it is entirely possible for one company to have several different unions, representing different groups of employees within the company. In this situation, representatives of the company would negotiate a different contract with each union. Furthermore, it is entirely possible for one company and union to negotiate different contracts for each of the company's different facilities or plant locations.

In some industries, multiemployer agreements are common. Generally, individual employers in these industries are small and are in a weak position relative to the union. Employers then often pool together in an employer association. A single agreement is negotiated by the association for all involved employers. Multiemployer agreements may be on a local level (e.g., the construction industry within a city), a regional level (e.g., coal and mining), or at the national level (railroad industry). When multiemployer bargaining occurs on a regional or national basis, it is often referred to as industrywide bargaining.

In large organizations such as General Motors, master agreements on wage and benefit issues are negotiated between corporate officials and officials of the national or international union. However, in addition to the master agreement, local supplements are negotiated at the plant level. Local supplements deal with issues that are unique to each plant.

Union's Role

Union participation in negotiations can take several different forms. In single-company agreements, the size of the company determines the nature of union participation. For smaller companies, the local union normally works closely with a field representative of the international or national union in negotiations. In these instances, the international representative gives advice and counsel to the local union and frequently serves as the principal negotiator for the union.

In large companies with multiple plants, negotiations are conducted by the top officials of the national or international union. For example, the president of the United Automobile Workers (UAW) is normally a chief negotiator in negotiations with Ford, General Motors, and Chrysler. Local union officials and a field representative of the national or international union negotiate local supplements to the master agreement for large companies.

In those industries with multiemployer agreements, union participation is normally directed by the president of the national or international union. However, in these types of negotiations, representatives of the local unions to be covered by the multiemployer agreement normally serve on the union's negotiating committee.

It is also possible for several unions to bargain jointly with a single employer. This type of negotiation is called **coordinated bargaining**.

Coordinated bargaining
A form of bargaining where several unions bargain jointly with a single employer.

Role of Third Parties

Several third parties can and frequently do become involved in the collective bargaining process. Normally, the services of third parties are not required unless one or both of the parties feels that the other party is not bargaining in good faith, or the parties reach an impasse in negotiations.

National Labor Relations Board (NLRB)

The National Labor Relations Act (discussed in Chapter 16) requires both unions and management to bargain in good faith. Refusal to bargain by either party can be overridden by an order of the National Labor Relations Board (NLRB). Furthermore, if the board's order has been properly issued, the U.S. Court of Appeals is required to order enforcement under the threat of contempt-of-court penalties.

Besides refusing to bargain, other kinds of behavior can be held to be unfair labor practices. Some of these were described earlier in this chapter. The NLRB has the authority to determine whether a particular behavior is unfair. If either party feels that an unfair labor practice has occurred during negotiations, a charge can be filed with the NLRB. An NLRB representative then investigates the charge and determines whether it is warranted. If so, the parties are given the opportunity to reach an informal settlement before further action is taken by the NLRB. If an informal settlement cannot be reached, the NLRB issues a formal complaint against the accused party, and a formal hearing is then conducted by an NLRB trial examiner. Upon completion of the hearing, the examiner makes recommendations to the NLRB board. Either party may appeal the recommendations of the examiner to the board. If the board decides that the party named in the complaint has engaged in or is engaging in an unfair labor practice, it can order the party to cease from such practice and can take appropriate corrective action. Either party can appeal decisions of the NLRB to the U.S. Circuit Court of Appeals and even to the U.S. Supreme Court.

Federal Labor Relations Authority (FLRA)

The Federal Labor Relations Authority (FLRA) was given its authority by the Civil Service Reform Act of 1978 and serves as the counterpart to the NLRB for federal sector employees, unions, and agencies. Under procedures similar to those of the NLRB, the FLRA investigates unfair labor practice charges, conducts hearings on unfair labor practices, and can issue orders to cease from any such practices.

Federal Services Impasses Panel (FSIP)

If the parties in the federal sector reach an impasse in negotiations, either party may request the Federal Services Impasses Panel (FSIP) to consider the matter. The FSIP is an entity within the FLRC. It has the authority to recommend solutions to resolve an impasse and to take whatever action is necessary to resolve the dispute, as long as the actions are not inconsistent with the Civil Service Reform Act of 1978. In addition to the above, the parties may agree to adopt a procedure for binding arbitration of a negotiation impasse, but only if the procedure is approved by the FSIP. The FSIP is considered to be the legal alternative to a strike in the federal sector.

Federal Mediation and Conciliation Service (FMCS)

Created by the National Labor Relations Act, the **Federal Mediation and Conciliation Service (FMCS)** exists as an independent agency within the executive branch of the federal government. The jurisdiction of the FMCS encompasses employees of private enterprise organizations engaged in interstate commerce, federal government employees, and employees in private, nonprofit hospitals and other allied medical facilities.

One of the responsibilities of the FMCS is to provide mediators to assist in resolving negotiation impasses. **Mediation** (or conciliation, as it is often called) is a process whereby both parties invite a neutral third party (called a mediator) to help resolve contract impasses. Mediators help the parties find common ground for continuing negotiations, develop factual data on issues over which the parties disagree, and set up joint study committees involving members of both parties to examine more difficult issues. In negotiations where the parties have become angry and/or antagonistic toward each other, the mediator often separates them and serves as a buffer carrying proposals and counterproposals between the parties. Mediators cannot impose decisions on the parties. Mediation services are also provided by various state agencies and private individuals such as lawyers, professors, and arbitrators.

Arbitrators

Although **arbitration** is much more frequently used in the resolution of grievances during a contract period, it can be used to resolve impasses during collective bargaining. Arbitration of contract terms is called interest arbitration. Interest arbitration is rarely used in the private sector but is common in the public sector. Such arbitration can take one of two forms: conventional and final-offer. Under **conventional interest arbitration**, the arbitrator listens to arguments from both parties and makes a binding decision, which can be identical to the position of either party or different from the positions of both parties. In **final-offer interest arbitration**, the arbitrator is restricted to selecting the final offer of one of the parties. Furthermore, interest arbitration can be either voluntary or mandatory. Both the Federal Mediation and Conciliation Service and the American Arbitration Association (AAA) provide lists of certified arbitrators.

Collective Bargaining Agreements

The collective bargaining agreement (or union contract) results from the bargaining process and governs the daily relations between employer and employees for a specific period of time. The contract specifies in writing the mutual agreements reached by the parties during the negotiations. Under the Taft-Hartley Act,

Federal Mediation and Conciliation Service (FMCS)
Independent agency within the federal government that, as one of its responsibilities, provides mediators to assist in resolving contract negotiation impasses.

Mediation
Process where both parties invite a neutral third party (called a mediator) to help resolve contract impasses. The mediator, unlike an arbitrator, has no authority to impose a solution on the parties.

Arbitration
Process whereby the parties agree to settle a dispute through the use of an independent third party (called an arbitrator). Arbitration is binding on both parties.

Conventional interest arbitration
Form of arbitration in which the arbitrator listens to arguments from both parties and makes a binding decision, which can be identical to the position of either party or different from the positions of both parties.

Final-offer interest arbitration
Form of arbitration in which the arbitrator is restricted to selecting the final offer of one of the parties.

▼ **Table 17–1**   Prohibited and permitted collective bargaining issues in the federal sector

---

Prohibited Issues

Negotiation of wage rates
Mission, budget, or organization of the agency
Number of employees
Internal security practices of the agency
Hiring, assigning, directing, laying off, and retaining employees in the agency; suspending, removing, reducing grade or pay; or taking other disciplinary action against employees
Assigning work, making determinations with respect to contracting work, and determining the personnel by which agency operations shall be conducted
Filling vacant positions from properly ranked and certified candidates
Taking whatever actions may be necessary to carry out the agency mission during emergencies

Permitted Issues

Numbers, types, and grades of employees or positions assigned to any organizational subdivision, work project, or tour of duty
Technology, means, and methods of performing work
Procedures used by the agency management to exercise its authority in carrying out duties that cannot be negotiated
Arrangements for employees adversely affected by the exercise of management's authority in carrying out duties that cannot be negotiated

---

collective bargaining agreements are legally enforceable contracts. Suits charging violation of a contract between an employer and a union may be brought in any district court of the United States having jurisdiction over the parties.

As discussed earlier in this chapter, the National Labor Relations Act obligates employers and unions to bargain in good faith on wages, hours, and other terms and conditions of employment. These are called mandatory subjects of negotiation. However, as would be expected, controversy has developed over the subjects covered by the phrase "other terms and conditions of employment." Unions attempt to expand the mandatory area by giving a broad interpretation to the phrase. Employers, on the other hand, naturally resist this expansion. Numerous NLRB and court decisions have been rendered concerning this issue. For example, the Supreme Court ruled in one decision that all management decisions representing a departure from prior practice that significantly impair (1) job tenure, (2) employment security, and (3) reasonably anticipated work opportunities must be negotiated as mandatory subjects.[7] The number of mandatory bargaining items has definitely expanded over the years.

An issue on which the parties are not required to bargain is called a nonmandatory, or permissive, issue. During contract negotiations, the parties (if both agree) may bargain about permissive issues, but neither party is legally required to do so. Furthermore, it is an illegal labor practice for one party to insist on bargaining about a permissive issue.[8]

The difficulties of establishing a group of mandatory and permissive issues for all organizations are great. Subjects in one industry or organization that are appropriately handled through collective bargaining may be inappropriate in another industry or organization. Ultimately, however, the courts and the NLRB decide whether an issue is mandatory or permissive.

In addition to mandatory and permissive issues, there is a small group of

▼. **HRM in Action 17–3**

Baseball's Reserve System

Prior to the mid-1970s, when a player signed a professional baseball contract, he became the property of the team. His contract could be renewed by the team year after year, without his consent and at salaries he never agreed to accept. His only options were to play or retire from baseball. Furthermore, he could be traded from team to team, with or without his consent. If he was traded, he was bound to the new team as he had been bound to his former team.

The players argued, unsuccessfully, that this lack of contractural freedom constituted an unlawful restraint of trade. Unable to apply the anti-trust laws, the baseball players sought relief through the process of unionization and collective bargaining.

The result of this collective bargaining, the Uniform Player Contract, contained a renewal clause. Under this clause, if a player and his team could not agree on a new contract, the team could renew the contract for another year. The baseball owners thought this process could continue year after year. However, an arbitrator ruled that the contract gave the team the right to renew the contract for only one year. Thus, the reserve system was broken. Today, through collective bargaining, the owners and the baseball union have created a detailed player restraint system.

Source: Adapted from Robert A. McCormick, "Labor Relations in Professional Sports—Lessons in Collective Bargaining," *Employee Relations Law Journal,* Spring 1989, pp. 501–12.

prohibited issues that cannot be included in a collective bargaining agreement. The leading examples are the closed shop and a hot-cargo clause. A closed shop requires employers to hire only people who are union members. A hot-cargo clause results when an employer agrees with a union not to handle or use the goods of another employer.

For the federal sector, the Civil Service Reform Act of 1978 makes it mandatory to bargain over "conditions of employment." The act defines conditions of employment as personnel policies, practices, and matters affecting working conditions. Table 17–1 summarizes the prohibited and permitted issues for federal government employees.

Specific Issues in Collective Bargaining Agreements

While each contract is different, five issues are included in most contracts: (1) management rights, (2) union security, (3) wages and employee benefits, (4) individual security (seniority) rights, and (5) dispute resolution. HRM in Action 17–3 shows one bargaining issue in baseball.

Management Rights

The question of how many of their prerogatives can be retained in the union-employer relationship is of great concern to most employers. The primary purpose of the management rights clause is retaining for management the right to direct all business activities. Items that are normally regarded as an integral part of management rights include the rights to direct the work force, determine the size of the work force (including the number and class of employees to be hired or laid off), set working hours, and assign work. Generally, in the management rights clause, the union insists on a sentence specifying that management will not discriminate against the union.

Union Security

The issue of union security is the union equivalent of the management rights issue. Union security clauses are concerned with the status of employee membership in the union and attempt to ensure that the union has continuous strength. Nearly all contracts provide some type of union security clause.

Union shop
Provision in a contract that requires all employees in a bargaining unit to join the union and retain membership as a condition of employment; most right-to-work laws outlaw the union shop.

Union security is provided in several forms. A **union shop** requires that all employees in the bargaining unit join the union and retain membership as a condition of employment. A modified union shop requires all employees hired after the effective date of the agreement to acquire and retain union membership as a condition of employment. The inclusion of a "grandfather" clause enables employees who are not members of the union as of the effective date of the contract to remain nonmembers. Under an **agency shop** provision, employees are not required to actually join the union, but they are required to pay a service fee as a condition of employment. A provision for **maintenance of membership** does not require that an employee join the union, but employees who do join are required to remain members for a stipulated period of time as a condition of employment.[9]

Agency shop
Contract provision that does not require employees to join the union but requires them to pay the equivalent of union dues as a condition of employment.

Right-to-work laws, enacted by individual states under the authority of Section 14(b) of the Taft-Hartley Act, restrict the types of union security provisions that can be negotiated. For example, most right-to-work legislation outlaws the union shop. The Taft-Hartley Act also prohibits two additional forms of union security: the closed shop and the preferential shop. In a closed shop, only union members can be hired, whereas the preferential shop requires that union members be given preference in filling job vacancies. However, in certain industries such as construction, exceptions to the act's provisions are permitted.

Maintenance of membership
Contract provision that does not require an employee to join the union, but employees who do join the union are required to remain members for a stipulated time period.

In addition to providing a means for maintaining union membership, union security provisions often include checkoff procedures. A **checkoff** is an arrangement made with the company, under which it agrees to withhold union dues, initiation fees, and assessments from the employees' paychecks and submit this money to the union. Individual union members must sign cards authorizing the withholding before such arrangements can be made.

Checkoff
Arrangement between an employer and a union under which the employer agrees to withhold union dues, initiation fees, and assessments from the employees' paychecks and submit this money to the union.

Wage and Employee Benefits

Traditionally, increased wages have been the primary economic goal of unions. Most contracts contain a provision for general wage increases during the life of the contract. **Cost-of-living adjustments (COLA)** are common in many industries. COLA clauses tie wage increases to rises in the Bureau of Labor Statistics consumer price index (CPI). Most COLA clauses call for hourly increases in wages for each specified rise in the CPI. Adjustments can be made on a quarterly, semi-annual, or annual basis. A recent trend has been an attempt by the management of many organizations to eliminate or restrict the use of COLA clauses.

Cost-of-living adjustments (COLA)
Contract provision that ties wage increases to rises in the Bureau of Labor Statistics consumer price index.

Other wage issues specified in contracts include overtime pay and rates of pay

▼ **Table 17–2**   Definitions of typical supplementary pay items

Item	Definition
Shift differential pay	Bonus paid for working less desirable hours of work
Reporting pay	Pay given to employees who report for work as scheduled but find on arrival that no work is available
Call-in or call-back pay	Pay earned when employees are called in or back to work at some time other than their regularly scheduled hours
Temporary-transfer pay	Pay given when employees are temporarily transferred to another job (If the transfer is to a lower-paying job, normally the employee continues to receive the old rate of pay; if to a higher-paying job, the employee is normally paid the higher rate of pay.)
Hazardous-duty pay	Pay given for performing jobs that, from a safety or health point of view, are considered to be more risky
Job-related expenses	Covers travel expenses, work clothes, or tools required for the job

for work on Saturdays, Sundays, holidays, and sixth or seventh consecutive day of work. Other employee compensation items normally contained in contracts include supplementary pay for shift differentials, reporting and call-in or call-back pay, temporary-transfer pay, hazardous-duty pay, and job-related expenses. Each of these terms is defined in Table 17–2.

The benefits that are normally covered in union contracts include holidays, vacations, insurance, and pensions. Pay is normally required in union contracts for all recognized holidays. Eligibility for holiday pay is of one of two types: a length-of-service requirement or a work requirement. Normally, an employee must have worked a minimum of four weeks with the employer before being eligible for holiday pay. Furthermore, an employee generally must work the day before and the day after a holiday to receive holiday pay.

Vacation provisions are provided in most union contracts. Vacation entitlement is normally tied directly to the employee's length of service. One trend in contracts has been an increase in the amount of vacation time per year and a reduction in the amount of service required for receiving increased vacations.

Most union contracts contain clauses providing health, accident, and life insurance benefits. Major medical insurance, maternity care, accidental death and dismemberment benefits, dental insurance, and coverage for miscellaneous medical expenses such as prescription drugs are also found in many union contracts.

Individual Security (Seniority) Rights

Seniority refers to an employee's relative length of service with an employer. Seniority may be measured on the basis of the employee's length of service in a job classification or a department, or on the individual's length of service with one plant, or with the company as a whole.

Job security for employees is a basic concern for unions. The seniority system is the method most commonly used to achieve job security. In general, union contract provisions specify that seniority is to be used within the bargaining unit

Seniority
Refers to an employee's relative length of service with an employer.

for giving promotions, transfers, layoffs, recalls from layoffs, and choice of work shifts and vacation periods.

Seniority systems are designed to benefit employees with greater length of service. Thus, women and minorities, generally the most recently hired employees, can be adversely affected by a seniority system. Section 703(a) of the 1964 Civil Rights Act prohibits discrimination on the basis of race, color, religion, sex, or national origin. However, Section 703(h) exempts bona fide seniority systems from the mandate of Section 703(a). Section 703(h) suggests that bona fide seniority may have a disproportionate impact on a certain class of people and still be deemed valid. However, such a system may not be the result of an intent to discriminate against a class of individuals.[10] In fact, in the *Stotts* case discussed in Chapter 2, the Supreme Court ruled that an affirmative action plan was illegal that required white employees to be laid off when the otherwise applicable seniority system would have required the layoff of black employees with less seniority. It is important to note that this decision did not ban affirmative action programs. It did indicate, however, that seniority systems may limit the application of certain affirmative action measures.[11]

Dispute Resolution

Inevitably, disputes arise during the life of a contract. Most contracts contain specific clauses describing how disputes are to be resolved.

A "no-strike" clause pledges the union to cooperate in preventing work stoppages. No-strike pledges can either be unconditional or conditional. Unconditional pledges ban any interference with production during the life of the contract. Conditional pledges permit strikes under certain circumstances. The no-strike ban most commonly is lifted after exhaustion of the grievance procedure or after an arbitration award has been violated. In return for a no-strike pledge, the union normally asks for a promise on the part of the company not to engage in lockouts during the term of the contract. A **lockout** is a refusal of the employer to let employees work.

Lockout
Refusal of an employer to let its employees work.

The grievance procedure provision is the most common method for resolving disputes arising during the term of the contract. The final step in the dispute resolution procedure is usually arbitration. Both grievance procedures and arbitration are discussed in Chapter 18.

Impasses in Collective Bargaining

At the end of a contract period, if a new agreement has not been reached, employees can continue working under the terms of the old contract until a new agreement is reached or a strike is called. Normally, union officials will not recommend that the employees continue working unless significant progress is being made in contract negotiations.

Strike
Collective refusal of employees to work.

If no progress is being made and the contract expires, a strike is frequently called. A **strike** occurs when employees collectively refuse to work. Strikes are not permitted for most public employees. To strike, the union must first hold a vote among its members. Unless the vote is heavily in favor of a strike, one will not be called. When a strike does occur, union members picket the employer. In picketing, individual members patrol at or near the place of employment to publicize the existence of the strike and to discourage the public from dealing with the employer. Frequently, members of other unions will refuse to cross the picket line of a striking union. For example, unionized truck drivers often refuse to deliver goods to an employer involved in a strike.

The purpose of a strike is to bring economic hardship to the employer, forcing the employer to agree to union demands. The success of a strike is determined by how well the union is able to interrupt the organization's operations. Employers often attempt to continue operations by using supervisory and management personnel, people not in the striking bargaining unit, people within the bargaining unit who refuse to go on strike, or people hired to replace striking employees. Attempts to continue operations through these methods can increase the difficulty of reaching an agreement and often result in violence.

When the president of the United States feels that a strike may jeopardize the national health and safety, the emergency dispute provisions of the Taft-Hartley Act can be used. Under these provisions, the president is authorized to appoint a special board of inquiry, which makes a preliminary investigation of the impasse prior to issuing an injunction to halt the strike. If the impasse is not resolved during this preliminary investigation, the president can issue an injunction prohibiting the strike action for 80 days. This is called a cooling-off period. The parties then have 60 days to resolve the impasse, after which the NLRB is required to poll the employees to see whether they will accept the employer's last offer. If the employees do not agree to accept the employer's last offer, the injunction is dissolved and the president can refer the impasse to Congress and recommend a course of action.

Trends in Collective Bargaining

Technological change and increased use of automation, changing government regulations, rising foreign competition, the decline in the percentage of blue-collar employees, and high rates of unemployment are just some of the variables that influence the collective bargaining process.[12] These and other variables can change rapidly, making virtually useless a contract provision negotiated two years earlier.

One form of collective bargaining evolving to cope with these rapidly changing variables involves the establishment of joint labor-management committees that meet regularly over the contract period to explore issues of common concern. The essential characteristics of this new form of collective bargaining are:

1. Meetings are held frequently during the life of the contract and are independent of its expiration.
2. Discussions examine external events and potential problem areas rather than internal complaints about current practices.
3. Outside experts such as legal, economic, actuarial, medical, and industry specialists play a major role in making the final decision on some issues.
4. Participants in the meetings are encouraged to take a problem-solving rather than an adversarial approach.

Another likely trend in collective bargaining within U.S. companies is productivity bargaining. Under productivity bargaining, unions and management develop a contract whereby the union agrees to exchange old work procedures and methods for new and more effective ones in return for gains in pay and working conditions. Productivity bargaining involves not only reaching an agreement but also creating an atmosphere of ongoing cooperation in which the changes called for in the agreement can be implemented.

A final trend involves what has been called "take-back bargaining." This form of bargaining involves unions being asked to make concessions on wages and benefits. It has occurred in industries especially hard hit by foreign competition. This trend, however, appears to have peaked during the 1980s.

● *Summary of Learning Objectives*

1. Define collective bargaining.

    Collective bargaining is a process that involves the negotiation, drafting, administration, and interpretation of a written agreement between an employer and a union for a specific period of time.

2. Explain the captive-audience doctrine.

    Under this doctrine, management has the right to speak to employees against the union on company time and require employees to attend the meeting. The union does not have the right to reply on company time. However, management is prohibited from giving a speech on company time to a mass-employee audience in the 24 hours immediately before a union election.

3. Define bargaining unit.

    A bargaining unit is a group of employees in a plant, firm, or industry, recognized by the employer, agreed on by the parties to a case, or designated by the NLRB or its regional director as appropriate for the purposes of collective bargaining.

4. Explain certification, recognition, and contract bars.

    Under a certification bar, the NLRB will not permit another election within 12 months of a union's certification. Under a recognition bar, the NLRB will not permit an election for up to 12 months after an employer voluntarily recognizes a union. Under a contract bar, the NLRB does not normally permit an election on the bargaining unit covered by a contract until the contract expires, up to a maximum of three years.

5. Describe good-faith bargaining.

    Good-faith bargaining is the sincere intention of both parties to negotiate differences and reach an agreement acceptable to both.

6. Discuss boulwarism.

    Boulwarism is a form of collective bargaining under which management makes its best offer at the outset of bargaining and adheres to its position throughout the bargaining sessions. Furthermore, the company bypasses the union in a publicity campaign to convince employees that management's offer is best. Boulwarism is in violation of an employer's obligation to negotiate in good faith and is illegal.

7. Explain mediation.

Mediation is a process whereby both parties invite a neutral third party to help resolve contract impasses.

8. Define checkoff.

Checkoff is an arrangement a union makes with a company, under which the company agrees to withold union dues, initiation fees, and assessments from the employees' paychecks and submit this money to the union.

9. Explain seniority.

Seniority refers to an employee's relative length of service with an employer.

10. Define lockout and strike.

A lockout is a refusal of the employer to let employees work. A strike occurs when employees collectively refuse to work.

Review Questions

1. What is collective bargaining?
2. Describe some of the reasons employees join unions.
3. What is a bargaining unit?
4. Define some unfair labor practices that can occur during a union election campaign.
5. Define good-faith bargaining.
6. What is a multiemployer agreement?
7. Describe the roles of the following third parties in the collective bargaining process:
   a. NLRB
   b. FLRA
   c. FSIP
   d. FMCS
   e. Mediators
   f. Arbitrators
8. Define the following union security clauses:
   a. Union shop
   b. Agency shop
   c. Maintenance of membership
   d. Closed shop
   e. Preferential shop
9. What is the purpose of COLA clauses in a union contract?
10. Define seniority.
11. What is a strike?

Discussion Questions

1. "Seniority provisions in a contract discriminate against women and minorities." What is your opinion of this statement?
2. "Right-to-work laws should be rescinded." Discuss.
3. Identify several management rights that you believe should not be subject to collective bargaining.
4. Why do you think collective bargaining is increasing among white-collar employees?

▼ INCIDENT 17–1

Florida National Guard and NAGE

The Florida National Guard employs full-time civilian technicians to assist in training the guard and to help repair and maintain the guard's equipment and supplies. As a condition of their employment, these technicians are required to maintain membership in the guard. The technicians are represented by the National Association of Government Employees (NAGE).

During negotiations between NAGE and the Florida National Guard, the technicians submitted through their unions a proposal whereby the technicians could opt to wear either their military uniform or agreed-on civilian attire while performing their technician duties. The parties were unable to reach an agreement on this issue. Consequently, NAGE asked the Federal Services Impasses Panel (FSIP) to resolve the matter. FSIP directed the parties to adopt the proposal as part of their collective bargaining agreement. The guard refused.

An unfair labor practice was then filed by NAGE with the Federal Labor Relations Authority (FLRA). The FLRA concluded that the wearing of the uniform was not within the guard's duty to bargain and dismissed the unfair labor practice charge.

Questions

1. What do you feel will be the result of the Guard's refusal to bargain over the issue?
2. If you had been advising the National Guard, would you have recommended that they bargain over this issue? Why or why not?

▼ INCIDENT 17–2

Vote Yes, Vote Yes

A vote on union representation by the employees of the Hudson Oxygen Therapy Sales Company of California was conducted. The union involved in this case was the Teamsters Union. Out of a total of 593 eligible voters, 361 ballots were cast in favor of the union, 173 were cast against the union, and 5 ballots were challenged.

Hudson Oxygen filed several objections to the election with the NLRB. One is described as follows:

> Before the commencement of the afternoon voting period, employees lined up outside the polling place, a lunchroom, waiting to vote. The crowd chanted "Vote yes, vote yes" for a period of two or three minutes, but the chanting ceased several minutes before the opening of the polls.

Hudson Oxygen argued that the chanting violated a NLRB rule against electioneering at the polling place. However, the NLRB ruled that electioneering at the polling place is limited to electioneering that occurs while the polls are open. Therefore, Hudson Oxygen's objection was rejected.

Questions

1. Do you agree or disagree with Hudson Oxygen's objection? Explain.
2. Would you have used this incident as an objection to the election, considering the outcome of the vote?

Exercise

Contract Negotiations*

You will be put on a team of three to four students. Each team in the class will be required to negotiate a contract for a company or a union.

The company's wage scale, $5.80 per hour, compares favorably with most firms in its area but is about 8 percent below those firms that employ workers of equivalent skill. Wages have not increased in proportion to cost-of-living increases over the past three years.

At the last bargaining session, the company and union took the following positions:

1. *Hospital and medical plan*
   Past contract: Company paid one-fourth of cost, employee paid remaining three-fourths.
   Union: Demanded company pay full cost.
   Company: Refused to pay more than one-fourth.

<table>
<tr><td></td><td colspan="4" align="center">Proportion of company payment</td><td></td></tr>
<tr><td>Company</td><td>1/4</td><td>2/4</td><td>3/4</td><td>4/4</td><td>Union</td></tr>
<tr><td></td><td>0</td><td>20,000</td><td>40,000</td><td>60,000</td><td></td></tr>
<tr><td></td><td colspan="4" align="center">Increase in total dollar value per year</td><td></td></tr>
</table>

2. *Wages*
   Past Contract: $5.80 per hour.
   Union: Demanded an increase of 60 cents per hour.
   Company: Refused outright.

---

*Adapted from James A. Vaughan and Samuel D. Deep, "Exercise Negotiations," *Program of Exercises for Management and Organizational Behavior* (Beverly Hills, Calif.: Glencoe Press, 1975), pp. 137–52.

Cents increase per hour

Company	0	10	20	30	40	50	60	Union
	0	31,200	62,400	93,600	124,800	156,000	187,200	

Total dollar value per year

3. *Sliding pay scale to conform to cost of living*
   Past contract: Pay scale is fixed through the term of the contract.
   Union: Demanded pay increases in proportion to increases in the cost of living.
   Company: Rejected outright.

Company	No	Yes	Union
	0	120,000	

Total dollar value per year

4. *Vacation pay*
   Past contract: Two weeks paid vacation for all workers with one year service.
   Union: Wants three weeks paid vacation for workers with 10 years of service
   Company: Rejected.

Company	2 weeks/ 1 year	3 weeks/ 20 years	3 weeks/ 15 years	3 weeks/ 10 years	Union
	0	10,000	20,000	30,000	

Total dollar value per year

Each week on strike (10 minutes of negotiations in the exercise) costs the company $40,000 in lost profits and the workers $40,000 in lost wages.

1. Negotiate the above contract issues with another team (as assigned by your instructor).

2. At the end of negotiations, your instructor will summarize the beginning, ending, and costs for each negotiation.

Notes and Additional Readings

1. See *Norris K. W. Printing Co.,* 231 NLRB No. 156, 97 LRRM 1080 (1977); and *United Parcel Service, Inc.,* 234 LLRB No. 11, 97 LRRM 1212 (1978).

2. See *NLRB* v. *Babcock & Wilcox Co.,* 351 U.S. 105, 38 LRRM 2001 (1956).

3. See *Peerless Plywood Co.,* 107 NLRB No. 106, 33 LRRM 1151 (1953).

4. For a discussion on organizing tactics by unions, see Kenneth Gilberg and Nancy Abrams, "Countering Unions' New Organizing Techniques," *Personnel,* June 1987, pp. 12–16.

5. *NLRB* v. *Gissel Packing Company,* 395 U.S. 575 (1969).

6. *General Electric Company,* 150 NLRB 192 (1964).

7. *Fiberboard Paper Products Corp.* v. *NLRB,* 379 U.S. 203 (1984).

8. *NLRB* v. *Wooster Division of Borg-Warner Corp.,* 356 U.S. 342 (1958).

9. See, for instance, Edward Brantley and Mel E. Schnake, "Exceptions to Compulsory Union Membership," *Personnel Journal,* June 1988, pp. 114–22.

10. Theresa Johnson, "The Future of Affirmative Action: An Analysis of the Stotts Case," *Labor Law Journal,* October 1985, p. 783.

11. Ibid., p. 788.

12. See, for instance, Gary N. Chaison and Mark S. Plovnick, "Is There a New Collective Bargaining?" *California Management Review,* Summer 1986, pp. 54–61.

Chapter 18

Discipline and Grievance Handling

Chapter Outline

Discipline Defined
Causes of Disciplinary Actions
The Discipline Process
 Prediscipline Recommendations
 Administering Discipline
 Legal Restrictions
Discipline and Unions
Discipline in Nonunionized
 Organizations
The Grievance Procedure
 Just Cause
 Due Process

 Duty of Fair Representation
 Time Delays
Grievance Arbitration
Summary of Learning Objectives
Review Questions
Discussion Questions
Incident 18–1: Tardy Tom
Incident 18–2: Keys to the
 Drug Cabinet
Exercise: Mock Arbitration
Notes and Additional Readings

Learning Objectives

After studying this chapter, you should be able to:
1. Define organizational discipline.
2. Explain the hot-stove rule.
3. Describe progressive discipline.
4. Define *prima facie*.
5. Explain employment at will.
6. Define grievance procedures.
7. Define just cause.
8. Explain due process.
9. Describe the duty of fair representation.
10. Define grievance arbitration.

*"I*t is not the duty of the disciplinarian to "take out anybody's grudge" against a man; it is his duty to adjust disagreements. He must remember constantly that his discipline must be of such a nature that the result will be for the permanent best interests of the one disciplined, his co-workers, his associates, and his family."

*Lillian Gilbreth**

When a manager must take action against an employee for violating an organizational work rule or for poor performance, the organization's disciplinary procedure is used to resolve the problem. When an employee has a complaint against the organization or its management, the grievance procedure is normally used to resolve the problem. Some organizations have very formal discipline and grievance procedures, others are less formal, and some organizations have no set procedures at all. The purpose of this chapter is to describe typical discipline and grievance-handling procedures.

Discipline Defined

Discipline
Action taken against an employee when the employee has violated an organizational rule or when the employee's performance has deteriorated to the point where corrective action is needed.

Organizational **discipline** is action taken against an employee when the employee has violated an organizational rule or when the employee's performance has deteriorated to the point where corrective action is needed. Fifty years ago, a manager who objected to an employee's performance or behavior could simply say "You're fired!" and that was it. Justification often played little if any part in the decision. At that time, managers had the final authority to effect discipline at will.

In applying organizational discipline, the primary question should be, "Why are employees disciplined?" Too many managers, when faced with a discipline problem in their organization, immediately think of what and how much: What should the penalty be? And how severely should the employee be punished? The ultimate form of discipline is discharge, or "organizational capital punishment" as it is sometimes called. Organizations should use discharge in the case of repeated offenses or when the act committed is such that discharge is believed to be the only reasonable alternative. HRM in Action 18–1 shows why and how one organization disciplined some of its employees.

Rather than an end in itself, discipline should be viewed as a learning opportunity for the employee and as a tool to improve productivity and human relations.

Causes of Disciplinary Actions

Generally, disciplinary actions are taken against employees for two types of conduct:

1. Poor job performance or conduct that negatively affects an employee's job performance. Absenteeism, insubordination, and negligence are examples of behaviors that can lead to discipline.
2. Actions that indicate poor citizenship. Examples include fighting on the job or theft of company property.

*Source: L. Gilbreth, *The Psychology of Management* (New York: Sturgis & Walton, 1914), p. 72.

▽. HRM In Action 18–1

Sundstrand Takes Disciplinary Action against Management Employees

As a result of its investigation into defense fraud, Sundstrand Corporation fired or otherwise disciplined several employees, who represented several levels of management. The aerospace firm said the disciplinary actions included the resignation or termination of five employees, pay cuts and letters of reprimand to four employees, pay freezes and letters of reprimand to two employees, letters of reprimand and special training for two employees, and special training for four employees.

Source: Adapted from "Sundstrand Takes Action to Discipline Certain Employees," *The Wall Street Journal,* January 6, 1989, p. C15.

▼ **Table 18–1**   Reasons for discipline or discharge of employees

Absenteeism	Disloyalty to employer (includes competing
Tardiness	with employer, conflict of interest)
Loafing	Moonlighting
Absence from work	Negligence
Leaving place of work (includes early	Damage to or loss of machinery or materials
quitting)	Unsatisfactory performance
Sleeping on job	Refusal to accept job assignment
Assault and fighting among employees	Refusal to work overtime
Horseplay	Participation in prohibited strike
Insubordination	Misconduct during strike
Racial slur	Slowdown
Threat to or assault of management	Possession or use of drugs
representative	Possession or use of intoxicants
Abusive language to supervisor	Distribution of drugs
Profane or abusive language	Obscene or immoral conduct
Falsifying company records (including time	Attachment or garnishment of wages
records, production records)	Gambling
Falsifying employment application	Abusing customers
Dishonesty	Sexual harrassment
Theft	

Source: Adapted from F. Elkouri and E. Elkouri, *How Arbitration Works,* 4th ed. (Washington, D.C.: Bureau of National Affairs, 1985), pp. 691–707.

Table 18–1 lists the reasons that often lead to disciplinary actions against or the discharge of employees. HRM in Action 18–2 illustrates conduct that was disciplined by the management of the Veteran's Administration.

The Discipline Process

The first step in the disciplinary process is the establishment of performance requirements and work rules. Performance requirements are normally established through the performance appraisal process discussed in Chapter 10. Work rules should be relevant to successful performance of the job. Because implementation of work rules partially depends on the employee's willingness to accept them,

▽. **HRM in Action 18-2**

Veteran's Administration Disciplines Doctors

The Veteran's Administration (VA) disciplined 33 doctors and other employees for accepting speaking fees, meals, entertainment, and other gratuities from Smith, Kline and French Laboratories. VA officials felt that the employees had violated conflict-of-interest and other federal regulations, including prohibitions against soliciting or accepting money from companies doing business with the VA.

Records showed that three VA employees were suspended, three received reprimands, and 27 received formal admonishments. An undisclosed number of others received counseling, which is not considered disciplinary action.

Source: Adapted from "VA Disciplines Doctors for Accepting Fees from Drug Company," *The New York Times*, February 14, 1987, p. 50.

---

periodic review of their applicability is essential. In addition, it is often desirable to solicit employee input either directly or indirectly in establishing work rules. Work rules are more easily enforced when employees perceive them as being fair and relevant to the job.

The second step in the process is to communicate the performance requirements and work rules to employees. This is normally handled through orientation and performance appraisal. Work rules are communicated in a variety of ways. Generally, an individual who is hired receives a manual that describes the work rules and policies of the organization. The human resource department or the new employee's supervisor explains these work rules and policies to the new employee during orientation. Furthermore, it is not unusual for new employees to be required to sign a document indicating that they have received and read the manual. In unionized organizations, work rules and the corresponding disciplinary action for infractions are frequently part of the labor contract. Bulletin boards, company newsletters, and memos are also commonly used to communicate work rules. In the final analysis, management bears the responsibility for clearly communicating all work rules to employees.

The final step in the disciplinary process is the application of corrective action (discipline) when necessary. Corrective action is needed when an employee's work performance is below expectations or when violations of work rules have occurred.

Prediscipline Recommendations

Before an employee is disciplined, several steps can be taken to ensure that the action will be constructive and will not likely be rescinded by higher levels of management. The importance of maintaining adequate records cannot be overemphasized. Written records often have a significant influence on decisions to overturn or uphold a disciplinary action. Past rule infractions and overall performance should be recorded. Adequate records are of utmost importance in discipline cases.

Another key responsibility of management is the investigation. That which appears obvious on the surface is sometimes completely discredited after investigation. Accusations against an employee must be supported by facts. Many decisions to discipline employees have been overturned due to an improper or less than thorough investigation. Undue haste in taking disciplinary action, taking the action when the manager is angry, and improper and incomplete investigations frequently cause disciplinary actions to be rescinded. An employee's work record should also be considered as part of the investigation. Good performance and a long tenure with the organization are considerations that should influence the severity of a disciplinary action. Naturally, the investigation must take place before any discipline is administered. A manager should not discipline an employee and then look for evidence to support the decision.

A normal step in the investigation of the facts is for management first to discuss the situation with the employee. Providing the employee an opportunity to present his or her side of the situation is essential if a disciplinary system is to be viewed positively by employees.

Employees who are represented by a union are allowed to have a union representative present during any disciplinary interview. This right is protected by the National Labor Relations Board (NLRB).[1] The most significant of the NLRB policies in this area was supported by a Supreme Court decision in 1975. In *NLRB v. Weingarten*,[2] an employee was investigated for allegedly underpaying for food purchased from the employer. The employee requested and was denied union representation at an interview held after the employee was charged with the underpayments. The union filed unfair labor practice charges against the company with the NLRB. The NLRB ruled that the employee had a right to refuse to submit to an interview without union representation but also ruled that this right was available only if the employee requested union representation and applied only when disciplinary actions might reasonably be expected as a result of the interview. However, in a later case, the NLRB ruled that an employee does not have the right to union representation when management meets with the employee simply to inform him or her of discipline that has been previously determined.[3]

NLRB v. *Weingarten*
Supreme Court decision in 1975 holding that an employee has the right to refuse to submit to a disciplinary interview without union representation.

Thus, as the law presently stands, management must be prepared to allow the presence of a union representative in any investigatory meeting. This means that management must not only deal with the employee and the problem but also must do so in the presence of a union representative, who normally acts in the role of an employee advocate.

Besides being involved in the investigation, the union should be kept informed on matters of discipline. Some organizations give unions advance notice of their intention to discipline an employee. Also, copies of warnings are sometimes sent to the union.

Administering Discipline

Administering discipline should be analogous to the burn received when touching a hot stove. Often referred to as the **hot-stove rule**, this approach emphasizes that discipline should be directed against the act rather than the person. Other key points of the hot-stove rule are immediacy, advance warning, and consistency. Figure 18–1 outlines the hot-stove rule.

Hot-stove rule
Set of guidelines used in administering discipline that calls for quick, consistent, and impersonal action preceded by a warning.

Immediacy refers to the length of time between the misconduct and the discipline. For discipline to be most effective, it must be taken as soon as possible but without involving an emotional, irrational decision.

Notation of rules infractions in an employee's record does not constitute advance warning and is not sufficient to support disciplinary action. An employee

▼ **Figure 18–1**   Hot-stove rule for applying discipline

1. The hot stove burns immediately. Disciplinary policies should be administered quickly. There should be no question of cause and effect.
2. The hot stove gives a warning and so should discipline.
3. The hot stove consistently burns everyone that touches it. Discipline should be consistent.
4. The hot stove burns everyone in the same manner regardless of who they are. Discipline must be impartial. People are disciplined for what they have done and not because of who they are.

must be advised of the infraction for it to be considered a warning. Noting that the employee was warned about the infraction and having the employee sign a form acknowledging the warning are both good practices. Failure to warn an employee of the consequences of repeated violations of a rule is one reason often cited for overturning a disciplinary action.

A key element in discipline is consistency. Inconsistency lowers morale, diminishes respect for management, and leads to grievances. Striving for consistency does not mean that past infractions, length of service, work record, and other mitigating factors should not be considered when applying discipline. However, an employee should feel that any other employee under essentially the same circumstances would receive the same penalty. Similarly, management should take steps to ensure that personalities are not a factor when applying discipline. The employee should feel that the disciplinary action is a consequence of what was done and not caused by his or her personality. A manager should avoid arguing with the employee and should administer the discipline with a straightforward, calm manner. Administering discipline without anger or apology and then resuming a pleasant relationship aids in reducing the negative effects of discipline.

Discipline should also be administered in private. The only exception would be in the case of gross insubordination or flagrant and serious rule violations, where a public reprimand would help the manager regain control of the situation. Even in this type of situation, the objective should be to gain control and not to embarrass the employee.

Lower-level managers should be very reluctant to impose disciplinary suspensions and discharges. Usually, discipline of this degree is reserved for higher levels of management. Even a lower-level manager who does not have the power to administer disciplinary suspensions or discharges, however, is nearly always the

▼ **Table 18–2**   Considerations in disciplining or discharging employees

1. Avoid hasty decisions.
2. Document all actions and enter in personnel file.
3. Thoroughly and fully investigate the circumstances and facts of the alleged offense.
   a. Notify the employee of the nature of the offense.
   b. Obtain the employee's version of the circumstances, reasons for the actions, and the names of any witnesses.
   c. If suspension is required until the investigation is completed, inform the employee:
      (1) To return 24 to 72 hours later to receive the decision.
      (2) That there will be reinstatement with pay if the decision is in the employee's favor.
      (3) Of the discipline to be imposed should it not be in the employee's favor.
   d. Interview all witnesses to the alleged misconduct. Obtain signed statements, if necessary.
   e. Check all alternative possible causes (e.g., broken machinery).
   f. Decide whether the employee committed the alleged offense.
4. Determine the appropriate discipline. Consider:
   a. Personnel record: length of service, past performance, past disciplinary record. Has corrective discipline ever been applied?
   b. Nature of the offense.
   c. Past disciplinary action for other employees in similar situations.
   d. Existing rules and disciplinary policies
   e. Provisions in the labor contract, if one exists.
5. Advise the employee of the nature of the offense, the results of the investigation, the discipline to be imposed, and the rationale behind the discipline.

one who must recommend the action to higher management. Since discipline of this nature is more likely to be reviewed, more costly to the organization, and more likely to be reflected in overall morale and productivity, it is very important for the lower-level manager to know when it should be recommended. Observing the hot-stove rules is essential for administering suspensions and discharges.

Management is expected to use **corrective** or **progressive discipline** whenever possible. Progressive or corrective discipline means that the normal sequence of actions taken by management in disciplining an employee would be oral warning, written warning, suspension, and discharge. There are, however, some offenses that may justify discharge, such as stealing, striking a coworker or member of management, and gross insubordination. Management must be able to show, generally through the preponderance of evidence, that the offense was committed. Attention to the points covered regarding prediscipline recommendations is especially important in supporting a decision to discharge an employee.

As in any lesser discipline but even more essential in suspension and discharge, the employee has the right to a careful and impartial investigation. This involves allowing the employee to state his or her side of the case, gather evidence to support that side, and usually to question the accuser. In the case of very serious offenses, the employee may be suspended pending a full investigation. This may be necessary when an employee has been accused of a serious crime that could affect the safety of others.

The suggestions outlined in the preceding paragraphs are designed to assist managers in applying discipline in a positive manner and with minimal application of the harsher forms of discipline. In the disciplinary procedure, observance of these suggestions should reduce the chance of a grievance or, if a grievance is filed, the chance of having the disciplinary action overruled. Table 18–2 provides a checklist of rules to observe when applying discipline.

Corrective (progressive) discipline
The normal sequence of actions taken by management in disciplining an employee: oral warning, written warning, suspension, and then discharge.

Legal Restrictions

The Civil Rights Act of 1964 and the Age Discrimination in Employment Act of 1967 as amended in 1978 changed an employer's authority in making decisions and taking actions involving employment conditions. Specifically, Title VII of the Civil Rights Act prohibits the use of race, color, religion, sex, or national origin as the basis of any employment condition. The Age Discrimination in Employment Act makes similar prohibitions involving persons over 40 years of age. Discipline is, of course, a condition of employment and is subject to these laws. Under these laws, employees have the right to appeal to the Equal Employment Opportunity Commission (EEOC) and to the courts any disciplinary action they consider discriminatory.

Alexander v. Gardner-Denver
Supreme Court decision in 1974 that ruled that using the final and binding grievance procedure in an organization does not preclude an aggrieved employee from seeking redress through court action.

The landmark case guaranteeing employees this right was decided in 1974 by the Supreme Court in the ***Alexander v. Gardner-Denver*** case. In this case, the Supreme Court ruled that using the grievance procedure in an organization did not preclude the aggrieved employee from seeking redress through court action.[4] Basically, the Court decided that the Civil Rights Act guaranteed individuals the right to pursue remedies of illegal discrimination regardless of prior rejections in another forum.

Prima facie
Legal term that describes evidence sufficient in law to raise a presumption of fact or establish the fact in question unless rebutted.

The courts have developed a concept of the shifting burden of proof in disciplinary cases where alleged discrimination has occurred. Initially, the burden of proof rests on the employee to establish that a *prime facie* case of discrimination exists. ***Prima facie*** is a legal term that describes evidence sufficient in law to raise a presumption of fact or establish the fact in question unless rebutted. In discipline cases, *prima facie* evidence can be established by producing evidence that the aggrieved employee's discipline was different from that applied to a similarly situated employee outside of the protected group. If a *prima facie* case is established, the employer must then prove that the discipline was applied in a non-discriminatory manner. If the employer successfully shows that this was so, then the employee has the right to show that the reasons given by the employer are not legitimate.[5]

Discipline and Unions

Management's authority to administer discipline has been greatly affected by unions. Central to the goals of unionism is the desire to protect employees from arbitrary and unfair treatment. The philosophy of unions has been that employees are economically dependent on the employer and, as a result, are helpless against the whims of management. Therefore, disciplinary policy is viewed as being an integral part of the collective bargaining process. Union contracts contain provisions specifying how management can deal with employees accused of rule violations or misconduct. Table 18–3 gives some sample rules for discipline from a typical union contract.

While management usually reserves the right to make reasonable rules for employee performance and conduct, the union often can question management's application and the reasonableness of these rules through the grievance procedure.

▼ **Table 18–3**   Discipline rules in typical labor contracts

Offense	Discipline
Minor	
Absence without notification as per existing absentee and lateness policy	1st offense—written warning
	2nd offense—one-day suspension
Horseplay	3rd offense—two-day suspension
Major	
Possession of, drinking, smoking, or being under the influence of intoxicants or narcotics on company property	1st offense—written warning that may result in suspension of up to three days without pay
Sleeping on the job	2nd offense—treated as an intolerable offense
Gambling on company property	
Intolerable	
Stealing company or personal property	1st offense—subject to discharge
Fighting on company property	

Source: Adapted from the labor agreement between Babcock and Wilcox Company and the Laborers International Union of North America.

Furthermore, when new work rules are established, the union must frequently be notified before the rules can be implemented.

Discipline in Nonunionized Organizations

Until recently, management decisions on discipline or discharge in nonunionized organizations have been relatively free of judicial review. Courts intervened only in those cases violating legislation concerning equal employment opportunity. Generally, the concept of **employment at will** has applied. Employment at will means that when an employer in the private sector hires employees to work for an indefinite period of time and the employees do not have a contract limiting the circumstances under which they can be discharged, the employer can terminate the employees at any time for any reason or for no reason at all.

This situation has been gradually changing as the courts have begun to hear discharge cases involving allegations of capricious or unfair treatment in nonunionized organizations. In some cases, the courts have ruled in favor of the discharged employees when the employee had been guaranteed due process under company procedures. Basically, the courts seem to be moving toward requiring nonunionized organizations to use a wrongful discharge standard, which is somewhere between the employment at will and just cause positions.

In light of these developments, many organizations have established appeal procedures for disciplinary actions taken by management. The most common type of nonunion appeal procedures is an open-door policy that allows employees to bring appeals to successively higher levels of management. An open-door policy gives an employee the right to appeal a disciplinary action taken against him or her to the manager's superior.

Employment at will
Term used to describe the situation in which an employer hires employees to work for an indefinite period of time and the employees do not have a contract limiting the circumstances under which they can be discharged. Under these conditions, the employer can terminate the employee at any time for any reason or for no reason at all.

The Grievance Procedure

Nonunionized as well as unionized organizations have grievance procedures. However, the main emphasis of this section is grievance procedures in unionized organizations. In this context, **grievance procedures** are a systematic means of resolving disagreements over the collective bargaining agreement and providing assurance that the terms and conditions agreed to in negotiations are properly implemented. Grievance procedures outline the steps to be taken by employees in appealing any management action that they feel violates the union contract. Grievance procedures are used not only to appeal disciplinary actions, but also to resolve matters concerning contract interpretation.

In general, the grievance process is initiated by an employee who has a complaint regarding some action perceived to be inconsistent with the terms of the union contract. While it is highly unlikely that the organization would initiate a grievance, it can do so. Initially, the grievant (aggrieved employee) contacts the union representative (usually called a union steward), and they discuss the events causing the grievance. The grievant and the union steward then meet with the grievant's supervisor. If a mutually agreeable settlement cannot be reached at this meeting, the grievance is then put into writing. Generally, in the next step, the union steward discusses the grievance with the department manager or another appropriate management representative. Management's reaction is then presented, usually in writing. If the grievance is not resolved at this point, the next step generally involves the human resource or labor relations manager and higher officials of the union, such as the business agent or international representative. After fully investigating and discussing the grievance, the human resource department usually issues the final company decision. In the event that the grievance is still unresolved, the party initiating the grievance can request arbitration. Grievance arbitration (discussed later in this chapter) is a process whereby the employer and union agree to settle a dispute through an independent third party. Because of the expense to both the union and management, every attempt should be made to resolve grievances in the stages before arbitration. Figure 18–2 illustrates the steps involved in the grievance procedure. Figure 18–3 shows the grievance procedure outlined in an actual union contract.

Just Cause

All union contracts recognize the right of management to discipline or discharge employees for just cause. In fact, in most discipline or discharge cases, the basic issue is whether or not management acted with just cause. In general, **just cause** is concerned with the burden and degree of proof of wrongdoing and with the severity of punishment.

It is generally agreed that the burden of proof in matters of discipline and discharge lies with the company. However, once the case has been established by the company, the burden of proof shifts to the union to disprove or discredit the company's contention.

Once an organization proves that an employee was guilty of wrongdoing, the

▼ **Figure 18–2**   General process followed in a union grievance procedure

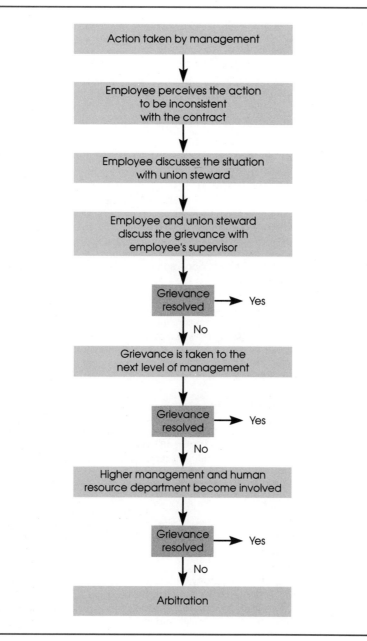

second area of concern in determining just cause relates to the severity of the punishment. Just cause results when the severity of the punishment coincides with the seriousness of the wrongdoing. The following general guidelines are frequently used by arbitrators for determining just cause as it relates to the severity of punishment.

▼ **Figure 18–3**   Typical union grievance procedure

Purpose

(53) The procedure under this article is available to the union for the presentation and settlement of grievances arising under the interpretation or application of the terms of this agreement as they relate to wages, hours of work, and working conditions and all other conditions of employment, including discharge cases.

Foreman and superintendent's step

(54) *a.* An employee or group of employees, having a question, dispute, or alleged grievance arising under the terms of this agreement, shall present the matter verbally to his or her supervisor in person or in company with his or her departmental steward. The supervisor and the steward shall use their best efforts to resolve the matter.

 b. If deemed necessary by the supervisor or the departmental steward, the departmental head and a grievance committee may be requested to participate in reaching a satisfactory settlement.

 c. If the grievance cannot be settled satisfactorily in the foregoing step within three working days, it may be reduced to writing on forms provided by the company. The grievance shall be signed by the aggrieved employee or employees, and the departmental steward. The departmental supervisor shall have two working days thereafter to submit a decision in writing. The grievance shall be considered abandoned or settled if it is not appealed to the next step within five working days.

Industrial relations manager's step

(55) If the disposition in the foregoing step has not satisfactorily settled the grievance, it may be appealed to the industrial relations manager's step, not later than five working days from the time of receiving the foreman's disposition. The industrial relations manager shall review and investigate the grievance, conferring with a member of the grievance committee and such other persons essential to resolving the issue. The company's disposition shall be given to the union within three working days following such conference. The grievance shall be considered abandoned or settled if it is not appealed to the next step within 10 working days.

President and general manager's step

(56) If the industrial relations manager's disposition has not satisfactorily settled the employee grievance, it may then be appealed by the union grievance committee to the general manager (or designated representative) within 10 working days, in a further effort to adjust the grievance. An international union staff representative shall participate in all general manager appeal step meetings. Any grievance not appealed within the time limit shall be automatically closed on the basis of the previous decision and shall not be subject to further appeal. The general manager shall issue the company's final disposition of the grievance within five working days after the appeal meeting is held. Any grievance not appealed to arbitration in writing as hereinafter provided within 21 working days after the issuance of the general manager's decision shall automatically be closed on the basis of such decision and shall not be subject to further appeal.

Arbitration

(57) If a grievance shall not be satisfactorily disposed of under the preceding steps, it may be submitted to arbitration upon proper notification by the union. Notice of appeal of a grievance by the union to arbitration shall be given in writing to the company not later than 21 working days following the date of the written decision of the general manager. This time limit may be extended by mutual agreement.

Source: Agreement between Powermatic Houdaille, Inc., and United Steelworkers of America. Used with permission.

1. The past performance of the employee should be considered.
2. Previous disciplinary actions taken against other employees in similar situations should be considered.
3. Any unusual circumstances surrounding the alleged offense should be considered.

Due Process

Due process refers to the employee's right to be dealt with fairly and justly during the investigation of the alleged offense and the administration of discipline. Due process typically guarantees that the employee will be notified of the allegations and have them explained, an impartial investigation will be held prior to the imposition of discipline, and the employee can present his or her version of the incident. As was discussed earlier, unionized employees have the right to union representation in the disciplinary review if they request it and if disciplinary actions might reasonably be expected to result.

A breach of due process during the grievance procedure can result in either a modification or a complete reversal of a disciplinary action. Procedural requirements are often spelled out in the grievance procedures of the contract. Failure to follow such provisions may constitute a breach of due process. In general, to ensue that an employee is afforded due process, all contract terms should be followed, adequate warning should be given prior to the discipline, explicit statements should be made to the employee and the union about possible disciplinary action being taken if the employee's actions do not change, and a full and fair investigation should be conducted immediately after the offense.

Due process
Right of an employee to be dealt with fairly and justly during the investigation of an alleged offense and the administration of any subsequent disciplinary action.

Duty of Fair Representation

Under the National Labor Relations Act of 1935, the union has a statutory duty to fairly represent all employees in the bargaining unit, whether or not they are union members. This duty has been termed the **duty of fair representation**.

The rationale underlying the duty of fair representation is that the union is the exclusive representative of all employees in the bargaining unit. The extent of the union's duty to fairly represent its members and other employees was defined in a landmark case, *Vaca v. Sipes*, in 1967.[6] In this case, an employee who had a history of high blood pressure returned to work after six months of sick leave. Although his personal physician and another doctor had certified his fitness to resume work, the company doctor concluded that his blood pressure was too high to permit his reinstatement, and as a result, he was permanently discharged. The employee filed a grievance, and the union took the grievance through the steps leading up to arbitration. The employee was then sent to a new doctor at the union's expense. When this examination did not support the employee's contention that he could safely return to work, the union decided not to take the grievance to arbitration, even though the employee demanded it. The employee sued the officers and representatives of the union for breach of their duty of fair representation. The case ultimately went to the Supreme Court, which held that (1) an individual does not have the absolute right to have a grievance taken to arbitration; (2) a union must make decisions as to the merits of particular grievances in good

Duty of fair representation
Under the National Labor Relations Act of 1935, the statutory duty of a union to fairly represent all employees in the bargaining unit, whether or not they are union members.

Vaca v. Sipes
Supreme Court decision in 1967 that held a union is not obligated to take all grievances to arbitration but rather has the authority to decide whether or not the grievance has merit. If such a decision is made fairly and nonarbitrarily, the union has not breached its duty of fair representation.

▽. **HRM in Action 18–3**

Fair Representation: United Glass and Ceramic Workers of North America

Earl Carpenter was employed by the predecessor of West Virginia Flat Glass in August 1977 to work on the production line. In June 1978, he injured his back while cleaning behind his machine and missed three weeks of work. In January 1979, he reinjured his back and was unable to work for several months. While he was out, the company halted production and sold the plant. When the plant reopened in October 1979, Carpenter attempted to return to work. After another reinjury, he claimed he was unable to do the heavy renovation work that was then available at the plant. His doctor, Dr. Martin, gave him a "light duty" slip, but the company had no light work available. Carpenter then obtained a "no duty" slip.

West Virginia Flat Glass asked Dr. Wilson, the company doctor, to examine Carpenter. Dr. Wilson did not explicitly state whether Carpenter could or could not work. He reported on November 13, 1979, that Carpenter had a 5 percent permanent partial disability and that maximum improvement had been achieved. Based on these findings and Carpenter's claim that he was unable to perform heavy labor without pain, the company discharged him on November 19, 1979.

The local union filed a timely grievance, taking the position that Carpenter was able to work and that his position was supported by his treating physician, Dr. Martin. The company took the position, based on Dr. Wilson's report, that Carpenter was unable to work and therefore was properly discharged. The local union processed the grievance through the first three stages of the grievance process without success.

At the fourth stage, under the terms of the collective bargaining agreement, the international union became involved. A representative from the international union met with company officials in April 1980, and the parties agreed to obtain a third opinion as to whether Carpenter could work, from a doctor chosen by Dr. Martin and Dr. Wilson. The parties agreed to be bound by that opinion. The agreement also provided that Carpenter should relinquish his claim for back pay. Carpenter approved the agreement.

Carpenter was examined by the third doctor, Dr. Mills, who reported on April 25, 1980, that Carpenter had a 5 percent permanent partial disability and that maximum improvement had been reached. He did not state specifically whether he thought Carpenter was able to work in the plant. The company interpreted the report to be consistent with Dr. Wilson's diagnosis of November 1979, the union agreed, and the company affirmed the discharge on May 7, 1980.

On September 29, 1980, Carpenter filed suit under §301 of the National Labor Relations Act, 29 U.S.C. §185(b), against the company for wrongful discharge and against the local union for breaching its duty to represent him fairly in the grievance process. In July 1981, he amended his complaint to include the international union. He subsequently settled his claims against the local union and his employer.

Carpenter's principal complaint against the international union was its failure to contact Dr. Mills about his April 1980 report, which omitted to answer the parties' inquiry about whether Carpenter could work. The international union contended that it was justified in not pursuing the matter because Dr. Mills' report was consistent with Dr. Wilson's report.

In his testimony at the trial, Dr. Mills acknowledged that although he had been asked to determine Carpenter's ability to work, he had not reported on this question. Neither the company nor the international union called this omission to his attention. He testified that in his opinion at the time of his examination, Carpenter was physically able to work.

The plant manager testified that if Dr. Mills' report had stated that Carpenter could return to work, he would have abided by this decision and reemployed Carpenter.

The Circuit Court of Appeals ruled that the international union did not fairly represent Earl Carpenter.

Source: Adapted from *Carpenter* v. *West Virginia Flat Glass*, 119LRRM 2846 (1985).

faith and nonarbitrarily; and (3) if a union decides in good faith and in a nonarbitrary manner that a grievance is not meritorious, a breach of fair representation does not exist, even if it is proved that the grievance was, in fact, meritorious.

An exception to this court ruling is included in a provision of the Taft-Hartley Act, which states that an individual employee may present a grievance to the employer without the aid of the union. However, this is contingent on the fact that any resulting adjustments must be consistent with the terms of the contract and must be conveyed to the union. This has been interpreted as meaning that the employer is under no obligation to consider such grievances. However, if a grievance is presented to the employer by the union, the employer is obligated to consider it and to resolve it through arbitration (if this is provided for in the contract) when the grievance has not been resolved in the earlier stages of the grievance process.

In addition, individuals cannot take the case into their own hands if they think that it is not being effectively handled. Courts have held that the employee must thoroughly exhaust the grievance procedure before taking individual action, and such action is then contingent upon proof of a breach of the duty of fair representation.

A Supreme Court decision, **Bowen v. United States Postal Service**[7] in 1983, established that an employee may be entitled to recover damages from both the union and the employer in cases where the employer has violated the labor agreement and the union has breached its duty of fair representation. HRM in Action 18–3 details a case in which the union was ruled to have violated its duty of fair representation.

Bowen v. United States Postal Service (1983) Supreme Court decision that established that an employee may be entitled to recover damages from both the union and the employer in cases where the employer has violated the labor agreement and the union has breached its duty of fair representation.

Time Delays

Perhaps the greatest criticism of the grievance procedure is that a great deal of time may be necessary to resolve a grievance that goes through the entire process. Often, the internal stages of appeal may take several months to complete. If the case goes to arbitration, the parties usually request a list of potential arbitrators from an arbitration service. The parties must contact the arbitrator and must agree on an acceptable date for the hearing—one that coincides with the schedules of the union representatives, the company representatives, and the arbitrator. Furthermore, after the hearing has taken place, the parties may desire to submit briefs, which can take several additional weeks. When the hearing is closed upon receipt of all briefs, the arbitrator normally renders a decision within 30 to 90 days. Thus, many months and sometimes a year or more may elapse before a final decision is reached. An argument could be made that this time delay in itself denies the grievant due process.

Grievance Arbitration

Grievance arbitration is the process whereby the parties voluntarily agree to settle a dispute through the use of an independent third party. In the United States, arbitration evolves from the voluntary agreement by two parties to submit their unresolved disputes to a privately selected neutral third party (an arbitrator). Both parties agree in advance to abide by the arbitrator's decision. The arbitrator, who

▽. HRM in Action 18–4

Discharge at American Motors

The grievant had been employed as a shipping and receiving clerk at American Motors for 10 years. On November 30, the grievant asked a purchasing clerk to look up the purchasing information (part number, location, and price) on several parts, including a jeep door. The grievant testified that his intention was to buy the door for a sheriff friend who was going to fix a DUI ticket for him. The grievant obtained the door and stored it on a shelf near his workplace until he completed his shift. At quitting time, the grievant left his workplace, carrying the door, and proceeded to the parking lot.

The grievant was seen putting the door in his van by a member of management. Later that evening, another employee contacted the grievant and informed him that a member of management had seen him carrying the door to his van. On December 1, the grievant brought in a check to cover the price of the door. The company refused to accept the check and fired the employee for misappropriation of company property.

Union witnesses testified to many instances where employees removed parts from the company without the prior knowledge or approval of management and paid for them at a later date. Much evidence was also presented that procedures for removing and paying for parts were haphazardly observed and not in writing.

The arbitrator overruled the discharge because of management's failure to establish, communicate, and properly administer a procedure for removing parts.

Source: Labor arbitration award by Lloyd L. Byars. Case involved the American Motors Corporation and the United Automobile Workers.

functions in a quasi-judicial role, must work within the framework that the parties have negotiated in their collective bargaining agreement. Arbitrators have no legal power to subpoena witnesses or records and are not required to conform to legal rules of hearing procedures, other than that of giving all parties the opportunity to present evidence. HRM in Action 18–4 describes a discipline situation that was overturned by an arbitrator.

Grievance arbitration

Arbitration that attempts to settle unresolved disputes arising during the term of the collective bargaining agreement that involve questions of its interpretation or application.

Grievance arbitration attempts to settle unresolved disputes arising during the term of the collective bargaining agreement that involve questions of its interpretation or application. Provision for grievance arbitration is not, in general, mandated by law. However, most labor contracts provide an arbitration clause as the final step in the grievance process. This is considered to be the *quid pro quo* (even exchange) for the union's agreement to a no-strike clause.

An arbitrator may serve on either a temporary (ad hoc) or permanent basis. In ad hoc arbitration, an arbitrator is selected by the parties to hear a single case. Permanent arbitrators settle all grievance disputes arising between the parties for a period of time.

Arbitrators charge for their services. Normally, arbitrators' charges are paid on a 50–50 basis by the company and the union. Both the Federal Mediation and Conciliation Service (FMCS) and the American Arbitration Association (AAA) provide lists of qualified arbitrators to the parties upon request. FMCS's services are available to both the private and public sector. AAA is a private, nonprofit organization that also provides lists of arbitrators to both the private and public sectors.

Enterprise Wheel

Supreme Court ruling in 1960 that as long as an arbitrator's decision involves the interpretation of a contract, the courts should not overrule the arbitrator merely because their interpretation of the contract was different from that of the arbitrator.

Generally, court reviews of arbitration awards have been extremely narrow in scope. The attitude of the U.S. Supreme Court was expressed in the **Enterprise Wheel** case: "It is the arbitrator's interpretation which was bargained for, and so far as the arbitrator's decision concerns interpretation of the contract, the courts have no business overruling him because their interpretation of the contract is different from his."[8] In spite of this opinion, some arbitration awards in discharge cases have been overturned by the courts. However, the tendency, for the most part, has been to defer to the arbitrator's decision.

● *Summary of Learning Objectives*

1. Define organizational discipline.

    Organizational discipline is action taken against an employee when the employee has violated an organizational rule or when the employee's performance has deteriorated to the point where corrective action is needed.

2. Explain the hot-stove rule.

    This is an approach to discipline that emphasizes that discipline should be directed against the act rather than the person. Key points of the hot-stove rule are immediacy, advance warning and consistency.

3. Describe progressive discipline.

    Progressive discipline means that the normal sequence of actions taken by management on disciplining an employee would be oral warning, written warning, suspension, and discharge.

4. Define *prima facie*.

    Prima facie is a legal term that describes evidence sufficient in law to raise a presumption of fact or establish the fact in question unless rebutted.

5. Explain employment at will.

    Employment at will means that when an employer in the private sector hires employees to work for an indefinite period of time and the employees do not have a contract limiting the circumstances under which they can be discharged, the employer can terminate the employees at any time for any reason or for no reason at all.

6. Define grievance procedures.

    Grievance procedures are a systematic means of resolving disagreements over the collective bargaining agreement and providing assurance that the terms and conditions agreed to in negotiations are properly implemented.

7. Define just cause.

    Just cause is concerned with the burden and degree of proof of wrongdoing and with the severity of punishment.

8. Explain due process.

    Due process refers to the employee's right to be dealt with fairly and justly during the investigation of the alleged offense and the administration of discipline.

9. Describe the duty of fair representation.

    The duty of fair representation refers to the union's statutory duty to fairly represent all employees in the bargaining unit, whether or not they are union members.

10. Define grievance arbitration.

    Grievance arbitration attempts to settle unresolved disputes arising during the term of the collective bargaining agreement that involve questions of its interpretation or application. Under greivance arbitration, the parties voluntarily agree to settle a dispute through the use of an independent third party.

Review Questions

1. Define organizational discipline.
2. What are the three types of conduct that normally result in the disciplining of an employee?
3. Outline the steps in the disciplinary process.
4. What was the significance of the decision in the *NLRB* v. *Weingarten* case?
5. List the key points of the hot-stove rule.
6. What was the significance of the decision in the *Alexander* v. *Gardner-Denver* case?
7. What are grievance procedures?
8. Define just cause, due process, and duty of fair representation.
9. What is arbitration?

Discussion Questions

1. "You simply can't discipline employees the same way you could 20 years ago." Do you agree or disagree? Discuss.
2. Two employees violate the same work rule. One is above average in performance and has been with your company for eight years. The other employee is an average performer who has been with your company for a little over a year. Should these employees receive the same discipline? Why?
3. Under the doctrine of fair representation, unions are required to represent both members and nonmembers in the bargaining unit. Do you think that unions should be required to represent nonmembers? Explain.
4. If you were starting your own company, what type of grievance procedure would you establish for your employees?

▼ INCIDENT 18–1

Tardy Tom

On September 30, 1988, Tom Holland was hired as a mechanic for a large national automobile-leasing firm in Columbus, Ohio. Tom, the only mechanic employed by the firm in Columbus, was to do routine preventive maintenance on the cars. When he first began his job, he was scheduled to punch in on the time clock at 7 A.M. On October 30, 1988, Tom's supervisor Russ Brown called him to his office and said, "Tom, I've noticed during October that you've been late for work seven times. What can I do to help you get here on time?"

Tom replied, "It would be awfully nice if I could start work at 8 A.M. instead of 7 A.M."

Russ then stated, "Tom I'm very pleased with your overall work performance, so it's OK with me if your workday begins at 8 A.M."

During the month of November 1988, Tom was late eight times. Another conversation occurred similar to the one at the end of October. As a result of it, Tom's starting time was changed to 9 A.M.

On January 11, 1989, Russ Brown posted the following notice on the bulletin board:

> Any employee late for work more than two times in any one particular pay period is subject to termination.

On January 20, 1989, Russ called Tom into his office and gave him a letter that read, "During this pay period, you have been late for work more than two times. If this behavior continues, you are subject to termination." Tom signed the letter to acknowledge that he had received it.

During February 1989, Tom was late eight times and between March 1 and March 11, five times. On March 11, 1989, Russ notified Tom that he had been fired for his tardiness.

On March 12, 1989, Tom came in with his union representative and demanded that he get his job back. Tom alleged that there was another employee in the company, a woman, who had been late as many times as he had, or more. Tom further charged that Russ was punching the time clock for this woman because Russ was having an affair with her. The union representative stated that three other people in the company had agreed to testify, under oath, to these facts. The union representative then said, "Russ, rules are for everyone. You can't let one person break a rule and penalize someone else for breaking the same rule. Therefore, Tom should have his job back."

Questions

1. What is your position to this case?
2. What would you do if you were an arbitrator in the dispute?

▼ INCIDENT 18–2

Keys to the Drug Cabinet

John Brown, a 22-year-old black, had been employed for only two and a half weeks as a licensed practical nurse in the section under security at a local hospital's alcohol and drug treatment center. John worked the 11 P.M. to 7 A.M. shift. His responsibilities included having charge of the keys to the drug cabinet.

One morning at 1 A.M., he became ill. He requested and received permission from the night supervisor, Margaret Handley, to go home. A short time later, the supervisor realized that John had failed to leave the keys when he signed out. She immediately tried to reach him by telephoning his home.

More than a dozen attempts to call John proved futile; each time Margaret got a busy signal. Finally, at 3 A.M., a man answered but refused to call John to the phone, saying that he was too ill to talk. She became frantic and decided to call the police to retrieve the keys.

The police arrived at John's home at 6:30 A.M. They found him preparing to leave to return the keys to the hospital. The police took the keys and returned them.

Later that day, John reported to work on his assigned shift, apologized for not returning the keys, and questioned the necessity of calling the police.

Two days later, the unit director Marcus Webb informed John that he had been terminated. The reason cited for the discharge was that he had failed to leave the drug cabinet keys before leaving the hospital and that the keys had been in his possession from 1 A.M. until 7 A.M. the following day. John learned that Margaret Handley had been verbally reprimanded for her handling of the case.

John filed an appeal regarding his dismissal with the human resource director of the hospital. However, the unit director's recommendation was upheld.

Following this decision, John immediately filed charges with the EEOC that he had been discriminated against because of his race. Both the night supervisor and the unit director were white. He requested full reinstatement with back pay. He also requested that his personnel file be purged of any damaging records that alluded to the incident.

Questions

1. What would your decision be if you were asked to decide this case?
2. Should a supervisor and an employee be disciplined equally?

Exercise

Mock Arbitration

Summarized below is a situation in which you are to conduct a mock arbitration. The class will be divided into teams, five to six students per team. Each team will then be assigned to represent either the union or the company. Your team must decide on the witnesses that you want at the hearing. Your opposing team must be given the names and job titles of your witnesses. During class time, two teams will conduct the mock arbitration.

Situation

Background

General Telephone Company of the Southeast (Georgia), hereinafter referred to as the company, provides local telephone service within certain areas of the state of Georgia. Its employees, as defined by Article I and Appendix A of the Agreement, are represented by the Communication Workers of America, hereinafter referred to as the union. The parties are operating under an agreement that became effective June 28, 1988.

The grievant Cassandra Horne was hired by the company as a service representative. On August 30, 1987, she was promoted to installer-repairer and was responsible for installing and repairing residential and single-line business customers. The grievant's record is free of any disciplinary entries, and she is considered by her supervisor Fred Carter to be a satisfactory employee.

On May 19, 1988, the grievant suffered an on-the-job injury to her knee while attempting to disconnect a trailer from a company van. At some time after the injury, the grievant went on disability for approximately eight weeks. She then returned to work with a statement from the company physician, allowing her to perform her normal work. After approximately three weeks, the grievant was still experiencing pain in her knee and was diagnosed by a different physician as having a tear in the cartilage below her kneecap. She went back on disability and had surgery performed on October 19, 1988, to repair cartilage and ligament damage to her knee.

During the grievant's absence, her disability benefits expired, and she agreed to take a six-month leave of absence beginning November 10, 1988. When the grievant's leave expired on May 11, 1989, she was terminated from her employment with the company.

The company argued that the company physician had stated the grievant could not perform installer-repairer work and that no other jobs were open that could be performed by the grievant. The union argued that the grievant had been cleared by her personal physician and that she felt she could do the work of installer-repairer. A grievance was filed at Step I on May 12, 1989, and was denied by division personnel manager Jerry L. Leynes. The grievance was submitted to arbitration and is now properly before the arbitrator for decision and award.

The company states that the issue before the arbitrator is as follows: Did the company violate the contract by separating the grievant from her position as an installer-repairer; and if so, what should be the remedy? The union states that the issue before the arbitrator is as follows: Is the discharge of the grievant for just or proper cause; and if not, what should the remedy be?

Pertinent Provisions of the Agreement

Article I, Recognition: The company recognizes the union as the whole and exclusive collective bargaining agency with respect to rates of pay, hours of employment, and other conditions of employment for all employees within the exchanges coming under the operating jurisdiction of the above-named company. All supervisory and professional employees and those performing confidential labor relations duties are excluded from the bargaining unit.

Article 4, Work Jurisdiction:

1. The company recognizes the right of its employees to perform its work and will make every reasonable effort to plan its work and forces to accomplish this end.
2. The company agrees that in its employment of contract labor to assist in the carrying out of its programs of construction, installation, removal, maintenance, and/or repair of telephone plant, it will not lay off or reduce part-time status, nor continue on layoff or part-time status, any regular employee performing the same work as that which is being performed by contract labor.

Article 11, Absences from Duty:

1. Leave of absence, without pay, not to exceed six (6) months will be granted by the company for good and compelling reason upon receipt of written

request for such leave. Each such request will be approved or disproved dependent on the merit of the request. Such leaves may be extended for an additional period of not to exceed three (3) months.

1.1 Working for another employer during leave shall constitute grounds for termination of employment.

1.2 Applying for unemployment compensation during leave may constitute grounds for termination of employment, except this shall not be applicable where the employee has requested reinstatement in accordance with the provisions of this article and no work is available.

1.3 A leave of absence shall not carry a guarantee of reemployment, but the employee concerned, desiring to return from leave, shall be given opportunity for reemployment before any new employees are hired, provided the returning employee is qualified to perform the work.

Article 12, Paid Absences:

4. In cases of physical disability resulting from compensable accidental injury while on the job, the company will pay the difference, if any, between the amount paid to the employee under workers' compensation and the employee's basic rate in accordance with the schedule set forth below. No waiting period will be required.

4.1 Up to five (5) years accredited service, full pay not to exceed thirteen (13) weeks.

Article 23, Discharges, Suspensions and Demotions:

1. Requirements and limitations

1.1 Any discharge, suspension, or demotion shall be only for proper cause and by proper action.

1.2 Any employee who is discharged, suspended, or demoted shall, at the time of discharge, suspension, or demotion, be given a written statement setting forth the complete reasons for such action.

Notes and Additional Readings

1. See Chapter 16 for a description of the NLRB.
2. *NLRB* v. *Weingarten,* 202 NLRB 446 (19750.
3. *Baton Route Water Works,* 246 NLRB 161 (1980).
4. *Alexander* v. *Gardner-Denver,* 415 U.S. 36, 7 FEP 81 (1974).
5. *McDonnell Douglas Corporation* v. *Green,* 5 FEP 965 (1973).
6. *Vaca* v. *Sipes,* 386 U.S. 171, 87 Sup. CT, 903, 17 L. Ed 2d 843 (1967).
7. *Bowen* v. *United States Postal Service,* 81 U.S. (1983).
8. *United Steelworkers of America* v. *Enterprise Wheel and Car Corporation,* 46 LRRM 2423 S. CT. (1960).

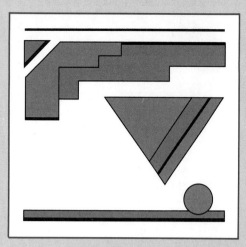

Section 6

Organizational Maintenance, Communication, and Information Systems

Chapter 19
Employee Safety and Health

 Chapter 20
Communication and Information
Systems

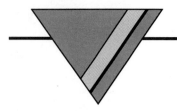

Chapter 19

Employee Safety and Health

Chapter Outline

Occupational Safety and Health Act of 1970 (OSHA)
OSHA Standards
Penalties
Record-Keeping/Reporting
  Requirements
Reactions to OSHA
The Causes of Accidents
Personal Acts
Physical Environment
Accident Proneness
How to Measure Safety
Organizational Safety Programs
Promoting Safety

Employee Health
Occupational Health Hazards
Stress in the Workplace
Alcoholism and Drug Abuse
AIDS
Employee Assistance Programs (EAPs)
Summary of Learning Objectives
Review Questions
Discussion Questions
**Incident 19–1: Safety Problems at
  Blakely**
Incident 19–2: Credibility at OSHA
Exercise: Filing OSHA Reports
Notes and Additional Readings

● *Learning Objectives*

After studying this chapter, you should be able to:

1. State the purpose of the Occupational Safety and Health Act (OSHA) and discuss its major provisions.
2. List the three major causes of accidents in the workplace.
3. Define frequency rate and severity rate.
4. Offer several suggestions for promoting safety in the workplace.
5. Explain the requirements of the Toxic Substance Control Act of 1976.
6. Discuss the Hazard Communication rule.
7. Differentiate between stress and burnout.
8. Name several work-related consequences of alcohol and drug abuse.
9. Offer several guidelines for implementing a drug-testing program.
10. Discuss the legal requirements for terminating an employee with AIDS.
11. Explain the three basic types of employee assistance programs (EAPs).

*"I*f you are in conformity with OSHA regulations and any of its state counterparts, if you are actively promoting a safe workplace, and if you respond when unsafe conditions are called to your attention, then you are unlikely to open yourself up—as a corporation or as an individual—to a criminal liability. But if you believe that ignorance is bliss, then criminal culpability is one more reason to change your ways."

*James O. Castagnera**

Employee safety and health are important concerns in today's organization. For example, the National Safety Council estimates that 11,100 deaths and 1.8 million disabling injuries resulted from occupational accidents in 1987;[1] the associated total work-accident cost was estimated to be over $42 billion.[2]

As early as 1970, new cases of occupational diseases were estimated to exceed 300,000 each year.[3] As reflected by these figures, the costs associated with workplace injuries or illnesses are high. Other indirect costs include employers' costs for health insurance and workers' compensation (both discussed in Chapter 15). For example, employee health care costs represented 9.7 percent of total payroll costs in 1987.[4] These costs vividly illustrate an incentive for organizations to reduce work-related injuries and illnesses and to improve overall employee health.

While health costs have escalated dramatically in the last decade, occupational injuries and illnesses have been around for a long time. For example, 35,000 occupational deaths occurred in 1936.[5] In spite of the known injuries and associated costs, for years many organizations did very little to reduce the problem. Because of this, a bipartisan U.S. Congress passed the Occupational Safety and Health Act in 1970.

Occupational Safety and Health Act of 1970 (OSHA)[6]

Occupational Safety and Health Act (OSHA)
Federal law passed in 1970 to ensure safe and healthful working conditions for every working person.

General-duty clause
Clause in the Occupational Safety and Health Act covering those situations not addressed by specific standards; in essence, it requires employers to comply with the intent of the act.

The **Occupational Safety and Health Act (OSHA)** became effective on April 28, 1971. The act established federal regulations relating to employee safety and health. OSHA applies to all businesses with one or more employees. (There are certain exceptions, such as self-employed persons.) Its stated purpose is "to assure so far as possible every working man and woman in the nation safe and healthful working conditions and to preserve our human resources."[7] The act contains a **general-duty clause** to cover those situations not addressed by specific standards. This clause states that each employer "shall furnish . . . a place of employment which is free from recognized hazards that are causing or are likely to cause death or serious physical harm to . . . employees." In essence, the general-duty clause requires employers to comply with the intent of the act.

*Source: J.O. Castagnera, "Corporate Culpability in Work-Place Fatalities—A Growing Trend?" *Personnel*, September 1985, p. 12.

The Occupational Safety and Health Administration of the U.S. Department of Labor enforces the act and is authorized to:

1. Encourage employers and employees to reduce workplace hazards and to implement new or improve existing safety and health programs.
2. Provide for research in occupational safety and health and develop innovative ways of dealing with occupational safety and health problems.
3. Establish "separate but dependent responsibilities and rights" for employers and employees for the achievement of better safety and health conditions.
4. Maintain a reporting and record-keeping system to monitor job-related injuries and illnesses.
5. Establish training programs to increase the number and competence of occupational safety and health personnel.
6. Develop mandatory job safety and health standards and enforce them effectively.
7. Provide for the development, analysis, evaluation, and approval of state occupational safety and health programs.[8]

OSHA Standards

OSHA establishes legally enforceable standards relating to employee health and safety. Usually, the human resource department is responsible for being familiar with these standards and ensuring that the organization is complying with them.

Currently, OSHA publishes six different volumes of standards (see Table 19–1) covering four major categories: general industry, maritime, construction, and agriculture. The **Federal Register**, available in many public and college libraries, also regularly publishes all OSHA standards and amendments. Annual subscriptions can be purchased from the Superintendent of Documents, U.S. Government Printing Office, Washington, D.C. 20402. OSHA also offers a subscription service through the Superintendent of Documents. In addition to providing all standards, interpretations, and regulations, the OSHA subscription service periodically sends out notices of changes and additions.

Federal Register
Periodical found in many public and college libraries that regularly publishes all OSHA standards and amendments.

▼ **Table 19–1**   Standards manuals published by OSHA

Volume	Title
I	General Industry Standards and Interpretations (includes agriculture)
II	Maritime Standards and Interpretations
III	Construction Standards and Interpretations
IV	Other Regulations and Procedures
V	Field Operations Manual
VI	Industrial Hygiene Field Operations Manual

Establishment of Standards

OSHA can initiate standards on its own or on petitions from other parties, including the U.S. Secretary of Health and Human Services (HHS), the National Institute for Occupational Safety and Health (NIOSH), state and local governments, any nationally recognized standards-producing organization, employers, labor organizations, or any other interested party. NIOSH, which was established by the act as an agency under HHS, conducts research on various safety and health problems. NIOSH recommends most of the standards that are adopted by OSHA.

Workplace Inspections

Marshall v. Barlow's, Inc.
1978 Supreme Court decision that ruled that employers are not required to admit OSHA inspectors onto their premises without a search warrant; also ruled that probable cause needed to obtain the search warrant would be much less than that required in a criminal matter.

OSHA compliance officers (inspectors) are authorized under the act to conduct workplace inspections. Originally, employers were not given advance notice of inspections and could not refuse to admit OSHA inspectors. However, a 1978 Supreme Court decision, *Marshall* v. *Barlow's, Inc.*,[9] ruled that employers are not required to admit OSHA inspectors onto their premises without a search warrant. At the same time, however, the court ruled that the probable cause needed to obtain a search warrant would be much less than what would be required in a criminal matter. HRM in Action 19–1 summarizes the *Marshall* v. *Barlow's, Inc.* case.

Inspection Priorities

Because OSHA does not have the resources to inspect all workplaces covered by the act, a system of inspection priorities has been established:

Those situations involving imminent danger

Investigation of fatalities and catastrophes resulting in the hospitalization of five or more employees

Employee complaints of alleged violation of standards or of unsafe or unhealthful working conditions

Programs of inspection aimed at specific high-hazard industries, occupations, or health substances

Reinspection of organizations previously cited for alleged serious violations

Inspection Procedures

Upon the OSHA inspector's arrival, the representatives of the employer should first ask to see the inspector's OSHA credentials. Normally, the inspector then conducts a preliminary meeting with the top management of the organization. The manager of the human resource department is usually present at this meeting. At this time, the inspector explains the purpose of the visit, the scope of the inspection, and the standards that apply. The inspector then normally requests an employer representative (often someone from the human resource department), an employee representative, and a union representative (where applicable) to join in an inspection tour of the facility. The inspector then proceeds with the inspection tour, which may cover part or all of the facilities. Afterward, the inspector meets again with the employer or the employer's representatives. During this meeting, the inspector discusses what has been found and indicates all apparent violations for which a citation may be issued or recommended.

▼. **HRM in Action 19–1**

Marshall v. Barlow's, Inc.

Barlow's, Inc., is an electrical and plumbing installation business in Pocatello, Idaho. In September 1975, an OSHA inspector asked Mr. Barlow if he could search the business for safety violations. When Mr. Barlow asked the inspector whether complaints had been filed against the business, the inspector said no, that Barlow's had turned up as part of a routine selection procedure. Mr. Barlow refused to allow the inspection.

Three months later, Secretary of Labor Ray Marshall petitioned the U.S. District for the state of Idaho to issue an order forcing Barlow to admit the inspector. Barlow again refused and sought an injunction to prevent what he considered to be a warrantless search. On December 30, 1976, a three-judge court ruled in Barlow's favor, and Marshall appealed. On May 23, 1978, the U.S. Supreme Court ruled that OSHA's searches of work areas for safety hazards and violations were unconstitutional without a warrant.

Source: *"Marshall v. Barlow's, Inc.," Supreme Court Reporter,* vol. 98A (St. Paul, Minn.: West Publishing, 1980), pp. 1816–34.

Citations

In some cases, the inspector has authority to issue citations at the work site immediately following the closing conference. This occurs only in cases where immediate protection is necessary. Normally, citations are issued by the OSHA area director and sent by certified mail. Once the citation is received, the employer is required to post a copy of the citation at or near the place where the violation occurred for three days or until the violation is corrected, whichever is longer.

Penalties

Table 19–2 summarizes the five major types of violations that may be cited and the respective penalties that may be proposed. Under certain conditions, some of the proposed penalties can be adjusted downward. Additional penalties may be imposed for such things as falsifying records and assaulting an inspector.

Record-Keeping/Reporting Requirements

Employers of 11 or more persons must maintain records of occupational injuries and illnesses as they occur. This includes all occupational illnesses, regardless of severity, and all occupational injuries resulting in death, one or more lost workdays, restriction of work or motion, loss of consciousness, transfer to another job, or medical treatment other than first aid.

Many OSHA standards have special record-keeping and reporting requirements, but all employers covered by the act must maintain two forms. **OSHA Form 200 (Log and Summary of Occupational Injuries and Illnesses)** requires that each occupational injury and illness be recorded within six working days from the time the employer learns of the accident or illness. **OSHA Form 101 (Supplementary Record of Occupational Injuries and Illnesses)** requires much more detail about each injury or illness. It also must be completed within six working days from the time the employer learns of the work-related injury or illness. Both

OSHA Form 200 (Log and Summary of Occupational Injuries and Illnesses)
Form for recording all occupational injuries and illnesses. Each occurrence must be recorded on this form within six working days from the time the employer learns of the accident or illness.

OSHA Form 101 (Supplementary Record of Occupational Injuries and Illnesses)
Form that requires detailed information about each occupational injury or illness. Form 101 must be completed within six working days from the time the employer learns of an occupational injury or illness.

Form 200 and Form 101 are maintained on a calendar-year basis. These forms must be retained for five years by the organization and must be available for inspection.

Reactions to OSHA

Few laws have evoked as much negative reaction as OSHA. While not many people would question the intent of OSHA, many have criticized the manner in which the act has been implemented. The sheer volume of regulations is immense. A second criticism concerns the costs of complying with and keeping OSHA-related records. Another frequent criticism is the vague wording of many OSHA regulations. OSHA has also been criticized for issuing standards that seem trite and petty. For example, one standard states: "Where working clothes are provided by the employer and become wet or are washed between shifts, provision shall be made to ensure that such clothing is dry before reuse." In fairness to OSHA, many of the original regulations have been simplified, rewritten, or even dropped.

In spite of the criticisms it has attracted, progress has been made in reducing death, injury, and illness at work sites, since the passage of OSHA.[10]

▼ **Table 19–2**   Types of OSHA violations

Violation	Definition	Proposed Penalty
Other than serious	Violation that has a direct relationship to job safety and health but probably would not cause death or serious physical harm	Up to $1,000 for each violation (discretionary)
Serious	Violation where there is substantial probability that death or serious physical harm could result and that the employer knew or should have known of the hazard	Up to $1,000 for each violation (mandatory)
Willful	Violation that the employer intentionally and knowingly commits, either knowing act constitutes a violation or aware that a hazardous condition exists and has made no reasonable effort to eliminate it	Up to $10,000 for each willful violation (mandatory); violation resulting in death of an employee punishable by court-imposed fine of not more than $10,000 or by up to six months imprisonment, or both; second conviction doubles these maximum penalties
Repeated	Violation of any standard, regulation, rule, or order where, on reinspection, another violation of the same section is found	Up to $10,00 for each such violation
Failure to correct prior violation	Failure to correct previous violation cited by OSHA	Civil penalty of up to $1,000 for each day the violation continues beyond the prescribed abatement date

Source: *All about OSHA*, rev. ed. (Washington, D.C.: U.S. Department of Labor, 1985), pp. 27–29.

The Causes of Accidents

Accidents are caused by a combination of circumstances and events, usually resulting from unsafe work acts, an unsafe work environment, or both.

Personal Acts

It has been estimated that unsafe personal acts cause as much as 80 percent of organizational accidents.[11] Unsafe personal acts include such things as taking unnecessary risks, horseplay, failing to wear protective equipment, using improper tools and equipment, and taking unsafe shortcuts.

It is difficult to determine why employees commit unsafe personal acts. Fatigue, haste, boredom, stress, poor eyesight, and daydreaming are all potential reasons. However, these reasons do not totally explain why employees intentionally neglect to wear prescribed equipment or don't follow procedures. Most employees think of accidents as always happening to someone else. Such an attitude can easily lead to carelessness or a lack of respect for what can happen. It is also true that some people get a kick out of taking chances and showing off.

Research studies have also shown that employees with positive attitudes have fewer accidents than employees with negative attitudes.[12] This is not surprising, when one considers that negative attitudes are likely to be related to employee carelessness.

Physical Environment

Accidents can and do happen in all types of environments, such as offices, parking lots, and factories. There are, however, certain work conditions that seem to result in more accidents. Table 19–3 presents a list of commonly encountered unsafe work conditions.

▼ **Table 19–3**   Unsafe conditions in the work environment

Unguarded or improperly guarded machines (such as an unguarded belt)

Poor housekeeping (such as congested aisles, dirty or wet floors, loose carpeting, and improper stacking of materials)

Defective equipment and tools

Poor lighting

Poor or improper ventilation

Improper dress (such as wearing clothes with loose and floppy sleeves when working on a machine that has rotating parts)

Sharp edges

Accident Proneness

A third reason often given for accidents is that certain people are accident prone. Some employees, due to their physical and mental makeup, are more susceptible to accidents. This condition may result from inborn traits, but it often develops as a result of an individual's environment. However, this tendency should not be used to justify an accident. Given the right set of circumstances, anyone can have an accident. For example, an employee who was up all night with a sick child might very well be accident prone the next day.

How to Measure Safety

Frequency rate
Ratio that indicates the frequency with which disabling injuries occur.

Disabling injuries
Work-related injuries that cause an employee to miss one or more days of work.

Severity rate
Ratio that indicates the length of time that injured employees are out of work.

Accident frequency and accident severity are the two most widely accepted methods for measuring an organization's safety record. A **frequency rate** is used to indicate how often disabling injuries occur. **Disabling injuries** cause an employee to miss one or more days of work following an accident. Disabling injuries are also known as lost-time injuries. A **severity rate** indicates how severe the accidents were by calculating the length of time injured employees were out of work. Only disabling injuries are used in determining frequency and severity rates. Figure 19–1 gives the formulas for calculating an organization's frequency and severity rates.

Neither the frequency rate nor the severity rate mean much until they are compared with similar figures for other departments or divisions within the organization, for the previous year, or for other organizations. It is through these comparisons that an organization's safety record can be objectively evaluated.

Organizational Safety Programs

The heart of any organizational safety program is accident prevention. It is obviously much better to prevent accidents than to react to them. A major objective of any safety program is to get the employees to "think safety." Therefore, most programs are designed to keep safety and accident prevention on employees' minds. Many different and varied approaches are used to make employees more aware of safety. However, four basic elements are present in most successful safety programs. First, it must have the genuine, not casual support of top and middle management. If upper management takes an unenthusiastic approach to safety, employees are quick to pick up on this. Second, it must be clearly established that safety is a responsibility of operating managers. All operating managers should consider safety to be an integral part of their job. Third, a positive attitude toward safety must exist and be maintained. The employees must believe that the safety program is worthwhile and that it produces results. Finally, one person or department should

▼ **Figure 19-1** Formulas for computing accident frequency rate and severity rate

$$\text{Frequency rate} = \frac{\text{Number of disabling injuries} \times 1 \text{ million}}{\text{Total number of labor-hours worked each year}}$$

$$\text{Severity rate} = \frac{\text{Days lost* due to injury} \times 1 \text{ million}}{\text{Total number of labor-hours worked each year}}$$

*The American National Standards Institute has developed tables for determining the number of lost days for different types of accidents. To illustrate, an accident resulting in death or permanent total disability is charged with 6,000 days (approximately 25 working years).

be in charge of the safety program and responsible for its operation. Often the human resource manager or a member of that staff has primary responsibility for the safety program.

Promoting Safety

Many things can be done to promote safety. Some suggestions include:

1. Make the work interesting. Uninteresting work often leads to boredom, fatigue, and stress, which all can cause accidents. Often, simple changes can be made to make the work more meaningful. Attempts to make the job more interesting are usually successful if they add responsibility, challenge, and other similar factors that increase the employee's satisfaction with the job.

2. Establish a safety committee composed of operative employees and representatives of management. The safety committee provides a means of getting employees directly involved in the operation of the safety program. A rotating membership is desirable. The size should usually range from 5 to 12 members. Normal duties for the safety committee include inspecting, observing work practices, investigating accidents, and making recommendations. Committee meetings should be held at least once a month, and attendance should be mandatory.

3. Feature employee safety contests. Give prizes to the work group or worker having the best safety record for a given time period. Contests can also be held to test safety knowledge. Prizes can be awarded periodically to employees who submit good accident prevention ideas.

4. Publicize safety statistics. Monthly accident reports should be posted. Ideas should be solicited as to how these accidents can be avoided.

5. Periodically hold safety meetings. Have employees participate in these meetings as role players or instructors. Use themes such as "Get the (electric) shock out of your life." Audiovisual aids such as movies and slides might also be used.

6. Use bulletin boards throughout the organization. Pictures, sketches, and cartoons can be effective if properly presented. One thing to remember when using bulletin boards is to change them frequently.

Employee Health

Until relatively recent times, safety and accident prevention received far more attention than did employee health. However, this has changed. Statistics show that occupational diseases may cost industry as much or more than occupational accidents.[13] In addition, there are many diseases and health-related problems that are not necessarily job related, but may affect job performance. Many organizations now not only attempt to remove health hazards from the workplace, but also have investigated programs to improve health.

Occupational Health Hazards

"A coal miner in West Virginia can't breathe. A pesticide plant worker in Texas can't walk. A hospital anesthesiologist in Chicago suffers a miscarriage."[14] These people, along with hundreds of thousands of other employees, are victims of occupational diseases. An occupational illness can be defined as any abnormal condition or disorder (other than that resulting from an occupational injury) caused by exposure to environmental factors associated with employment. Approximately 190,000 new cases of occupational illnesses were reported among U.S. employees in private industry during 1987.[15] The U.S. Department of Labor uses seven major categories to classify occupational illnesses: (1) occupational skin diseases or disorders, (2) dust diseases of the lungs, (3) respiratory conditions due to toxic agents, (4) poisoning (systemic effects of toxic materials), (5) disorders due to physical agents (other than toxic materials), (6) disorders associated with repeated trauma, and (7) all other occupational illnesses. In 1987, the overall incidence rate of occupational illnesses was 26.1 per 10,000 full-time employees.[16] Of the total number of occupational illnesses, disorders with repeated trauma were the most common, followed by skin diseases and disorders.

Increased awareness of occupational disease was one factor that contributed to the passage of the Occupational Safety and Health Act. In addition, the **Toxic Substance Control Act** of 1976 requires the pretesting of the approximately 700 new chemicals marketed each year. A 1980 rule issued by OSHA requires organizations to measure for safety and to record employee exposure to certain potentially harmful substances. These medical records must be made available to employees, their designated representatives, and OSHA. Furthermore, these records must be maintained for 30 years, even if the employee leaves the job. Additional rules have been issued related to specific hazards.

Toxic Substance Control Act
Federal law passed in 1976 requiring the pretesting for safety of new chemicals marketed.

Cancer and the Workplace

Society has been aware of certain occupational diseases, such as black lung disease, for years. However, it has only been in recent years that the potential extent of occupational diseases has been realized. Table 19–4 lists 10 of the major substances that have been linked to occupational diseases. Note that 7 of the 10 can produce some form of cancer. One government study estimates that between 20 and 38 percent of all cancer in this country is occupationally related.[17] In October 1977, OSHA issued a policy aimed at regulating carcinogens (substances that have been

▼ **Table 19–4**   Ten suspected hazards in the workplace

Potential Dangers	Diseases That May Result
Arsenic	Lung cancer, lymphoma
Asbestos	White lung disease (asbestosis), cancer of lungs and lining of lungs, cancer of other organs
Benzene	Leukemia, aplastic anemia
Bichloromethylether (BCME)	Lung cancer
Coal dust	Black lung disease
Coke oven emissions	Cancer of lungs and kidneys
Cotton dust	Brown lung disease (byssinosis), chronic bronchitis, emphysema
Lead	Kidney disease, anemia, central nervous system damage, sterility, birth defects
Radiation	Cancer of thyroid, lungs, and bone; leukemia; reproductive effects (spontaneous abortion, genetic damage)
Vinyl chloride	Cancer of liver and brain

Source: "Is Your Job Dangerous to Your Health?" *U.S. News & World Report,* February 5, 1979, p. 42. Copyright, February 5, 1979, U.S. News & World Report.

identified as causing cancer) in the workplace. In January 1980, OSHA issued additional rules designed to clarify precisely how to identify and classify such carcinogens. However, because of problems in applying and interpreting these rules, they were subsequently placed on hold and are not currently being enforced.

Hazard Communications

Because of the threats posed by chemicals in the workplace, OSHA issued its Hazard Communication rule in the early 1980s. This rule is also known as the right to know rule. The basic purpose of the rule is to ensure that employers and employees know what chemical hazards exist in their workplace and how to protect themselves against those hazards. The goal of the rule is to reduce the incidence of illness and injuries caused by chemicals.

The **Hazard Communication Standard** establishes uniform requirements to ensure that the hazards of all chemicals imported into, produced, or used in the workplace are evaluated and that the results of these evaluations are transmitted to affected employers and exposed employees. OSHA has developed a variety of materials to help employers and employees implement effective hazard communication programs.

Hazard Communication Standard
Standard issued by OSHA in the early 1980s that established uniform requirements to ensure that the hazards of all chemicals imported into, produced, or used in the workplace are evaluated and that the results of these evaluations are transmitted to affected employers and exposed employees.

Stress in the Workplace

Stress is the mental and physical condition that results from a perceived threat of danger (physical or emotional) and the pressure to remove it.[18] The potential for stress exists when an environmental situation presents a demand threatening to exceed a person's capabilities and resources for meeting it, under conditions in which the person expects a substantial difference in rewards and costs resulting

▼ **Table 19–5** Common sources of suggested causes of job-related stress

Sources	Suggested Causes
Job mismatch	Job demands skills or abilities that the employee does not possess (job incompetence).
	Job does not provide opportunity for the employee to fully utilize skills or abilities (underutilization).
Conflicting expectations	Formal organization's concept of expected behavior contradicts the employee's concept of expected behavior.
	Informal group's concept of expected behavior contradicts the employee's concept.
	Individual employee is affected by two (or more) strong influences.
Role ambiguity	Employee is uncertain or unclear about how to perform on the job.
	Employee is uncertain or unclear about what is expected in the job.
	Employee is unclear or uncertain about the relationship between job performance and expected consequences (rewards, penalties, and so forth).
Role overload	Employee is incompetent at job.
	Employee is asked to do more than time permits (time pressure).
Fear/responsibility	Employee is afraid of performing poorly or failing.
	Employee feels pressure for high achievement.
	Employee has responsibility for other people.
Working conditions	Job environment is unpleasant; for example, there is inadequate lighting or improper regulation of temperature and noise.
	Requirements of the job may unnecessarily produce pacing problems, social isolation, and so forth.
	Machine design and maintenance procedures create pressure.
	Job involves long or erratic work hours.
Working relationships	Individual employees have problems relating to and/or working with superiors, peers, and/or subordinates.
	Employees have problems working in groups.
Alienation	There is limited social interaction.
	Employees do not participate in decision making.

Source: Adapted from Charles R. Stoner and Fred L. Fry, "Developing a Corporate Policy for Managing Stress," *Personnel*, May–June 1983, p. 70. Reprinted by permission of publisher, from *Personnel*, May–June © 1983. American Management Association, New York. All rights reserved.

from meeting the demand versus not meeting it.[19] Stress manifests itself among employees in several ways: increased absenteeism, job turnover, lower productivity, and mistakes on the job. In addition, excessive stress can result in both physical and emotional problems. Some common stress-related disorders include tension and migraine headaches; coronary heart disease; high blood pressure; muscle tightness in the chest, neck, and lower back; gastritis, indigestion; ulcers; diarrhea; constipation; bronchial asthma; rheumatoid arthritis; and some menstrual and sexual dysfunctions.[20] From a psychological perspective, inordinate or prolonged stress can adversely affect personal factors such as concentration, memory, sleep, appetite, motivation, mood, and the ability to relate to others.[21] Table 19–5 lists some of the more common sources and suggested causes of job-related stress.

▼. HRM In Action 19–2

Reducing Stress from Trauma

In an effort to reduce employee stress following a serious job-related accident to a fellow employee, the Los Angeles Department of Water and Power has established a Trauma Response Program. The department first became aware of the problem when an electrical worker sought help from the company's Employee Assistance Program after witnessing a serious accident. Now, after an accident, the Employee Assistance Program sends two staff members as quickly as possible to talk to other members of the crew. These staff members help the crew members express their feelings and also discuss the lingering effects that sometimes appear. A third staff person is sent to the hospital or the injured employee's home to offer support.

A second type of help is the Trauma Response Training Program, which was developed to assist managers in understanding and responding to the emotional needs of employees and their families after a serious accident.

Source: Phil Farish, "Reducing Stress," *Personnel Administrator*, August 1987, p. 18.

The cost of stress to organizations in the form of absenteeism, medical expenses, and lost productivity has been estimated at $50 to $75 billion per year, or $750 per employee.[22] In an effort to combat this, many organizations have conducted training programs designed to help reduce employee stress. Most of these programs attempt to teach employees self-help techniques for individually reducing their own stress. HRM in Action 19–2 describes one way that the Los Angeles Department of Water and Power is attempting to reduce stress among its employees.

Burnout

Burnout occurs when work is no longer meaningful to a person. Burnout can result from stress or a variety of other work-related or personal factors. Figure 19–2 illustrates the sequence of events that often leads to professional burnout. As burnout has become more recognized, certain related myths have surfaced:[23]

Burnout
Occurs when work is no longer meaningful to a person; can result from stress or a variety of other work-related or personal factors.

Myth 1. Burnout is just a new-fangled notion that gives lazy people an excuse not to work. Although burnout is a relatively new term, the behavior has been around for centuries. History is full of examples of workers, such as writers, artists, and scientists, who gradually or suddenly stopped producing.

Myth 2. As long as people really enjoy their work, they can work as long and hard as they want and never experience burnout. Any work that inherently includes significant and continuing frustration, conflict, and pressure can lead to burnout.

Myth 3. Individuals know when they are burning out and, when they do, all they need to do is take off for a few days or weeks, and then they'll be as good as new. Unfortunately, most people do not realize that burnout is occurring until it reaches its later stages.

Myth 4. Individuals who are physically and psychologically strong are unlikely to experience burnout. Physically and psychologically strong individuals may indeed be able to work harder than less strong people. However, without proper stress skills, the inordinate amount of work can cause serious damage.

Myth 5. Job burnout is always job related. Burnout usually results from a combination of work, family, social, and personal factors.

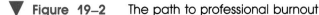

▼ **Figure 19–2**   The path to professional burnout

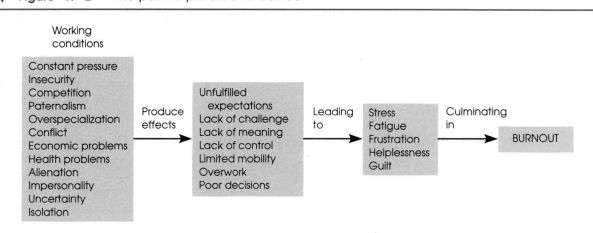

Source: Reprinted by permission from *Business* Magazine, "Helping Employees Cope with Burnout," by Donald P. Rogers, October–December 1984. Copyright © 1984 by the College of Business Administration, Georgia State University, Atlanta.

▼ **Table 19–6**   Ten jobs likely to produce burnout

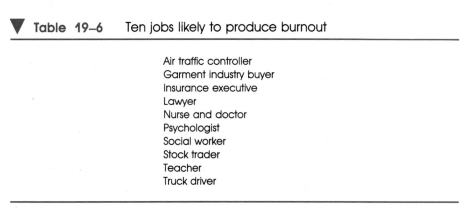

Air traffic controller
Garment industry buyer
Insurance executive
Lawyer
Nurse and doctor
Psychologist
Social worker
Stock trader
Teacher
Truck driver

Source: Adapted from Julie Batten, "10 Jobs that Cause Burnout," *Careers,* December 1985, p. 43.

From the organization's viewpoint, the first step in reducing burnout is to identify those jobs with the highest potential for burnout. Certain jobs are more likely to lead to burnout than others (Table 19–6 lists 10 jobs whose workers are highly susceptible to burnout). Once those jobs have been identified, several actions are possible. Some of the possibilities include redesigning the jobs, clarifying expectations, improving physical working conditions, and training the jobholders.

Alcoholism and Drug Abuse

It has been estimated that between 10 and 30 percent of the work force use drugs, and approximately 10 million employees use drugs while working.[24] Even more disturbing is the apparent growth rate in employee drug use. A 1988 survey of mayors, governors, and CEOs of *Fortune* 1,000 companies reported that 57 percent of the respondents perceived substance abuse as a significant problem in their organization.[25] A similar survey five years earlier reported only 46 percent consid-

▼ **Table 19–7** Statistics related to alcoholics

- 50 percent of alcoholics are women.
- 25 percent are white-collar workers, such as secretaries, bookkeepers, and other office workers.
- 30 percent are blue-collar workers, normally in the more skilled crafts such as machinists and electricians.
- 45 percent are professional managerial personnel.
- 13 percent have completed less than a grammer school education.
- 37 percent are high school graduates, and 50 percent have completed or attended college.
- 66 percent are members of households, whereas only 3 percent are of the so-called skid-row category.

Source: Gopal C. Pati and John I. Adkins, Jr., "The Employer's Role in Alcoholism Assistance," *Personnel Journal*, July 1983, p. 568.

ered the problem significant.[26] The work-related consequences of alcohol and drug abuse include absenteeism, tardiness, reduced productivity, poor decision making, equipment damage, safety violations, lower morale, and even outright theft to pay for drug habits.

Alcoholism

For years, people viewed alcoholics as people lacking in self-control and morals. Today, alcoholism is recognized as a disease with no single cause. Alcoholism does not strike any particular group—it can strike employees from the janitor to the chief executive officer. Table 19–7 provides some general statistics concerning alcoholics.

The National Council on Alcoholism estimates that the economic loss to the employer of an alcoholic employee amounts to 25 percent of the employee's wage.[27] Compared with nonalcoholic employees, alcoholics incur twice the rate of absenteeism caused by illness. Alcoholics are also two to three times more likely to be involved in a work-related accident.[28] Some people estimate that as many as 50 percent of all problem employees in industry are actually alcoholics.[29]

In spite of the well-documented costs associated with alcoholism, organizations have only recently undertaken widespread efforts to reduce employee alcoholism. A 1973 survey reported that only 400 major U.S. companies had any type of program designed to help overcome employee alcoholism.[30] Similar surveys subsequently reported that the number had grown to over 5,000 by 1982 and over 9,000 by 1987.[31]

A 1986 *Time* magazine story reported that about 30 percent of the *Fortune* 500 largest industrial organizations had established in-house alcoholic-treatment programs.[32] Most of the available information indicates that in-house alcoholic-treatment programs achieve a high rate of success, based on both recovery rates and cost-effectiveness measures.[33] For example, the New York City Police Department reports a 75 percent recovery rate; Du Pont, 66 percent; Consolidated Edison, 60 percent; Illinois Bell, 57 percent; Eastman Kodak, 75 percent; General Motors, 80 percent; and Inland Steel, 82 percent.[34] Programs for combating alcoholism are normally administered as part of an employee assistance program (EAP). EAPs are discussed at length later in this chapter.

Other Drugs

The use of drugs other than alcohol is a relatively new phenomenon. Other drug usage usually falls into one of three categories: marijuana abuse, prescription-drug abuse, and hard-drug abuse. Studies have found that drug-using employees are far less productive than their coworkers, miss 10 or more times as many work days, are three times as likely to injure themselves or someone else, and are much more likely to steal from the company.[35] Although most employees who use drugs are young, they are not all blue-collar employees. Employees on drugs are often much more difficult to detect than are drinking employees—alcohol can usually be smelled, whereas drugs cannot. Also, it is relatively easy to pop a pill at lunch or on a break undetected.

Drug Testing

As a result of the increased use of drugs in the workplace, more and more companies have begun to use some form of drug testing for both job applicants and existing employees. For example, the percentage of *Fortune* 500 companies routinely using urinalysis on job applicants and/or existing employees to detect drug use grew from 5 percent to almost 33 percent from 1983 to 1987.[36] However, there are certain legal risks involved in drug testing and, therefore, extreme caution should be exercised. An employer can be exposed to substantial liability for defamation if there is a false accusation of drug or alcohol use (juries have made awards as high as $450,000 for such defamation[37]). The following guidelines are suggested for implementing a drug-testing program:[38]

- Establish a routine, uniform, systemwide policy of substance abuse and adhere to it in a consistent and nondiscriminatory manner.
- Assume employees are drug free until proven otherwise.
- Make negative test scores a bona fide occupational qualification whenever possible.
- Include testing in uniform preemployment agreements and have them signed by new employees. For existing employees, establish drug tests as a prerequisite to recalls, promotions and transfers.
- Train supervisors to detect and refer problem employees for testing.
- Use a high-quality type of urinalysis, not just the cheapest method.
- Use monitored laboratories that employ blind testing to ensure the integrity of the testing procedures.
- Use appropriate supervision and custody arrangements to ensure that the samples tested are valid.
- Require tested employees to list all legal, over-the-counter drugs that they are taking at the time of testing.
- Develop and maintain profiles of well-employee urinalysis results that can later be used for comparative purposes.
- Keep all results confidential.

One criticism of drug-testing programs in general is that they tend to focus on off-duty conduct. Many employees view this as an invasion of privacy, which has led to morale problems and numerous lawsuits.[39] As a result of this and other objections to drug testing, a new form of testing, called performance testing, has emerged.[40] Instead of testing for byproducts that may or may not cause impairment,

▽. HRM In Action 19–3

Substance Abuse Policy at WMATA

The Washington Metropolitan Area Transit Authority (WMATA) recently confronted the growing problem of drug and alcohol abuse with a substance abuse policy and an employee assistance program. The goals were to make sure that transportation safety would be maintained, and to assist in the rehabilitation of employees who develop substance abuse problems. Basically, the substance abuse policy establishes procedures for dealing with two categories of employees: those who voluntarily seek rehabilitation and those who test positive as a result of a medical examination following an on-the-job incident, such as a bus collision. To encourage abusers to voluntarily seek rehabilitation, employees in the first category are given access to jobs that are not safety sensitive, can use the employee assistance program as often as needed, and are not subject to random drug testing after they have successfully completed rehabilitation. Employees in the second category lose their pay status and benefits and, after returning to work, are subject to random, unannounced drug tests for six months.

The cost of rehabilitation is paid for by the employee's health insurance. The rehabilitation time depends on the substance being abused. The union representing WMATA operating personnel adopted and signed the substance abuse policy, although there were challenges to WMATA's unilateral establishment of the programs and to the dismissal of certain employees.

Source: William H. Wagel, "A Drug-Screening Policy that Safeguards Employees' Rights," *Personnel*, February 1988, p. 10.

performance testing measures physical variables such as coordination and response time to certain tasks. For example, a test might consist of watching a CRT screen and manipulating a joystick or keyboard. The person's score can then be compared to a standard or to a previous score. Commercial performance tests are just now coming on the market in most areas of the country. HRM in Action 19–3 describes the substance abuse policy recently adopted by the Washington Metropolitan Area Transit Authority.

AIDS

As defined by the U.S. Centers for Disease Control (CDC), AIDS is "a reliably diagnosed disease that is at least moderately indicative of an underlying cellular immunodeficiency in a person who has had no known underlying cause of cellular immunodeficiency nor any other cause of reduced resistance reported to be associated with that disease."[41] CDC has predicted that the cumulative number of AIDS patients will exceed 250,000 by 1991.[42]

The Vocational Rehabilitation Act of 1973 and numerous state laws offer certain protection to employees infected with AIDS. Under these laws, AIDS-infected employees may file discrimination suits if employment opportunities are denied solely on the basis of their having AIDS. The **Vocational Rehabilitation Act** of 1973 prohibited discrimination against otherwise qualified handicapped individuals solely on the basis of their disability. It should be noted, however, that the Vocational Rehabilitation Act only applies to federal contractors who hold a contract of $2,500 or more, subcontractors to such an employer, recipients of federal financial aid, and federal agencies. Companies that do not meet the previously stated requirements of the Vocational Rehabilitation Act are subject only to applicable state and local statutes, which may vary considerably from state to state.

Vocational Rehabilitation Act
Legislation enacted in 1973 that prohibited discrimination against otherwise qualified handicapped individuals solely on the basis of their disability; applies only in certain situations involving federal contracts, recipients of federal assistance, or federal agencies.

If an individual with AIDS is covered by the Vocational Rehabilitation Act, certain other issues must be addressed. These issues include determining if the individual meets the definition of a handicapped individual, if the handicapped individual is otherwise qualified to do the job, and if the employee's contagiousness poses a threat to others. If the infected employee does not meet the provision for being handicapped, is not otherwise qualified, or does pose a threat to others, he or she is not protected by the Vocational Rehabilitation Act.

It should be noted, however, that the Vocational Rehabilitation Act does not prevent employers from terminating an employee who can no longer perform the duties of his or her job, provided that reasonable accommodations were made by the company. Reasonable accommodations are defined as those that do not pose undue financial nor administrative burdens on an employer. As more and more is learned about AIDS, it is expected that additional laws and interpretations will be enacted to provide further guidance to employers.

Employee Assistance Programs (EAPs)

Many large organizations and a growing number of smaller ones are attempting to help employees with personal problems. These problems include not only alcohol and drug abuse but depression, anxiety, domestic trauma, financial problems, and other psychiatric/medical problems. This help is not purely altruistic—it is largely based on cost savings. The help is generally offered in the form of **employee assistance programs (EAPs)**.

Employee assistance programs (EAPs)
Company-sponsored programs designed to help employees with personal problems such as alcohol and drug abuse, depression, anxiety, domestic trauma, financial problems, and other psychiatric/medical problems.

Cost of Personal Problems

A primary result of personal problems brought to the workplace is reduced productivity. Absenteeism and tardiness also tend to increase. Increased costs of insurance programs, including sickness and accident benefits, are a direct result of personal problems brought to the workplace. Lower morale, more friction among employees, more friction between supervisors and employees, and more grievances also result from troubled employees. Permanent loss of trained employees due to disability, retirement, and death is also associated with troubled employees. Difficult to measure, but a very real cost associated with troubled employees, is the loss of business and damaged public image.

Organization Involvement

Until recently, organizations attempted to avoid employees' problems that were not job-related. Although aware of the existence of these problems, organizations did not believe that they should interfere with employees' personal lives. In the past, organizations tended to get rid of troubled employees. In recent years, however, cost considerations, unions, and government legislation have altered this approach. The accepted viewpoint now is that employees' personal problems are private until they begin affecting their job performance. When and if that happens, personal problems become a matter of concern for the organization.

Studies have shown that absenteeism can be significantly reduced by employee assistance programs. It has also been found that EAPs help to reduce on-the-job accidents and grievances. Workers' compensation premiums, sickness and accident benefits, and trips to the infirmary also tend to decrease with an EAP. For example, Kennecott Copper Corporation reported a 52 percent improvement in attendance, a 75 percent decrease in nonindustrial health and accident insurance, and a 55 percent reduction in hospital medical and surgical costs for the 150 employees who participated in their EAP.[43] It has been estimated that between 9,000 and 20,000 EAPs were in existence in the United States as of late 1987.[44]

Types of EAPs

There are several types of employee assistance programs. In one type which is rarely used, diagnosis and treatment of the problem are provided directly by the organization. In a second type of program, the organization hires a qualified person to diagnose the employee's problem; then, the employee is referred to the proper agency or clinic for treatment. The third and most common type of program employs a coordinator who evaluates the employee's problem only sufficiently to make a proper referral to the proper agency or clinic for diagnosis. Sometimes, the coordinator serves only as a consultant to the organization and is not a full-time employee. This type of program is especially popular with smaller employers and branch operations of large employers.

Features of a Successful EAP

For an EAP to be successful, it must first be accepted by the employees; they must not be afraid to use it. Experience has shown that certain elements are critical to the success of an EAP. Table 19–8 summarizes several of the most important characteristics of an EAP.

Dr. William Mayer, administrator of the Federal Alcohol, Drug Abuse, and

▼ **Table 19–8**   Ten critical elements of an EAP

Element	Significance
Management backing	Without this at the highest level, key ingredients and overall effect are seriously limited.
Labor support	The EAP cannot be meaningful if it is not backed by the employees' labor unit.
Confidentiality	Anonymity and trust are crucial if employees are to use an EAP.
Easy access	For maximum use and benefit.
Supervisor training	Crucial to employees needing understanding and support during receipt of assistance.
Union steward training	A critical variable is employees' contact with the union—the steward.
Insurance involvement	Occasionally, assistance alternatives are costly, and insurance support is a must.
Breadth of service components	Availability of assistance for a wide variety of problems (e.g., alcohol, family, personal, financial, grief, medical, etc.).
Professional leadership	A skilled professional with expertise in helping, who must have credibility in the eyes of the employee.
Follow-up and evaluation	To measure program effectiveness and overall improvement.

Source: Adapted from F. Dickman and W. G. Emener, "Employee Assistance Programs: Basic Concepts, Attributes, and An Evaluation," *Personnel Administrator,* August 1982, p. 56. Reprinted with the permission from the *Personnel Administrator* published by the Society for Human Resource Management, Alexandria, VA.

▽. HRM In Action 19–4

Employee Fitness Programs

Kimberly Clark operates its Health Services Center with the objective of reducing potential health problems of employees. The staff of nearly 40 people performs blood tests, vision and hearing tests, body-fat percentage tests, and treadmill tests for heart irregularities. The staff then prepares for the employee a health prescription that may involve exercise, nutrition, or an employee assistance program.

Tenneco operates a 21,000-square-foot facility for employees. Tenneco has conducted studies to determine the benefits of the exercise program and has estimated a savings in health care claims of up to $300,000 a year. Tenneco's studies show that health care claims are nearly double for those who do not exercise regularly. The company results also show a definite relationship between regular exercise and an improvement in performance ratings.

Source: Homer S. Klock II, "The Benefit That's Growing by Leaps and Bounds," *Personnel*, July 1985, pp. 13–16.

Mental Health Administration, has estimated that EAPs return $8 for every $1 invested.[45] Others have estimated the return to be as high as $10 for every $1 invested.[46] Because of the obvious benefits to both employees and employers, it is estimated that EAPs will continue to grow in popularity.

Wellness Programs

In addition to the EAPs discussed in the previous section, many companies have installed programs designed to prevent illness and enhance employee wellness. These programs are referred to as **wellness programs** and include such things as periodic medical exams, stop-smoking clinics, improved dietary practices, hypertension detection and control, weight control, exercise and fitness, stress management, accident-risk reduction, immunizations, and cardiopulmonary resuscitation training (CPR). Current estimates are that most companies get an approximate return of $3 for every $1 invested.[47] Experts in the wellness field report that even small companies can offer wellness programs and that they do not have to be expensive. Some of the documented results of wellness programs include fewer sick days, reduced coronary heart disease, and lower major medical costs. In light of the continual rise in health care costs, it is predicted that company-sponsored wellness programs will grow rapidly in the future. HRM in Action 19–4 describes physical fitness programs at Kimberly Clark and Tenneco.

Wellness programs
Company-implemented programs designed to prevent illness and enhance employee wellness.

● Summary of Learning Objectives

1. State the purpose of the Occupational Safety and Health Act (OSHA) and discuss its major provisions.

   The stated purpose of OSHA is "to assure so far as possible every working man and woman in the nation safe and healthful working conditions." The act established the Occupational Health and Safety Administration to set up standards and to conduct workplace inspections. Many OSHA standards have special record-keeping and reporting requirements that must be adhered to by companies.

2. List the three major causes of accidents in the workplace.

    The three major causes of work-related accidents are unsafe personal acts, an unsafe physical environment, and accident proneness.

3. Define frequency rate and severity rate.

    A frequency rate is used to indicate how often disabling injuries occur. A severity rate indicates how severe accidents were by calculating the average length of time injured employees were unable to work.

4. Offer several suggestions for promoting safety in the workplace.

    Many things can be done to promote safety in the workplace. Some suggestions include: (1) make the work interesting, (2) establish a safety committee, (3) feature employee safety contests, (4) publicize safety statistics, (5) hold periodic safety meetings, and (6) post safety-related pictures, cartoons, and sketches on bulletin boards.

5. Explain the requirements of the Toxic Substance Control Act of 1976.

    The Toxic Substance Control Act of 1976 requires the pretesting of the approximately 700 new chemicals marketed each year.

6. Discuss the Hazard Communication rule.

    The Hazard Communication rule is also known as the right-to-know rule. Its basic purpose is to ensure that employers and employees know what chemical hazards exist in the workplace and how to protect themselves against these hazards. The rule requires that certain chemicals be evaluated for danger and that the results be communicated to affected employers and exposed employees.

7. Differentiate between stress and burnout.

    Stress is the mental and physical conditions that results from a perceived threat of danger (physical or emotional) and the pressure to remove it. Burnout occurs when work is no longer meaningful to a person. Burnout can result from stress or from a variety of other work-related or personal factors.

8. Name several work-related consequences of alcohol and drug abuse.

    Possible work-related consequences of alcohol and drug abuse include absenteeism, tardiness, reduced productivity, poor decision making, equipment damage, safety violations, lower morale, and even outright theft to pay for drug habits.

9. Offer several guidelines for implementing a drug-testing program.

    Suggested guidelines for implementing a drug-testing program include: (1) establish a routine, uniform, systemwide policy of substance abuse and adhere to it in a consistent manner, (2) assume employees are drug free until proven otherwise, (3) make negative drug testing scores a bona fide occupational qualification whenever possible, (4) include drug testing as a part of a preemployment agreement, (5) train supervisors to detect and refer problem employees for testing, (6) use a high-quality type of test, (7) use monitored laboratories to process and interpret the test results, (8) use appropriate supervision and custody arrangements to ensure that the samples tested are valid, (9) require tested employees to list all legal drugs that they are taking, (10) develop and maintain profiles of well-employee urinalysis results that can later be used for comparative purposes, and (11) keep all results confidential.

10. Discuss the legal requirements for terminating an employee with AIDS.

First it must be determined if the employee is covered by the Vocational Rehabilitation Act of 1973. If the employee is not covered by this act, then the company is subject only to applicable state and local statutes, which vary considerably from state to state. If the individual is covered by the Vocational Rehabilitation Act, then it must be determined if he or she meets the provisions of a handicapped individual, is otherwise qualified, and whether his or her contagiousness poses a threat to others. If the infected employee does not meet the provisions for being handicapped, is not otherwise qualified, or poses a threat to others, he or she is not protected by the act. The act does not prevent employers from terminating employees who can no longer perform their job duties, provided that reasonable accommodations were made by the company.

11. Explain the three basic types of employee assistance programs (EAPs).

In one type of EAP, diagnosis and treatment of the problem are provided directly by the organization. In a second type, the organization hires a qualified person to diagnose the employee's problem and then refers the employee to a proper agency or clinic for treatment. The third and most common type employs a coordinator who evaluates the employee's problem only sufficiently to make a proper referral to the proper agency or clinic for diagnosis.

Review Questions

1. What is the Occupational Safety and Health Administration (OSHA) authorized to do?
2. What is the general-duty clause, as related to OSHA?
3. List the inspection priorities established by OSHA.
4. What is the usual inspection procedure followed by OSHA?
5. Name and discuss the three primary causes of accidents.
6. How do organizations measure their safety records?
7. What four basic elements are present in most successful safety programs?
8. What can be done to promote safety in organizations?
9. What does the Toxic Substance Control Act of 1976 require?
10. Distinguish between stress and burnout.
11. List several guidelines that should be followed when implementing a drug-testing program.
12. Define performance testing and describe how it differs from normal drug testing.
13. How does the Vocational Rehabilitation Act of 1973 affect the dismissal of employees with AIDS?
14. Describe the three general types of employee assistance programs (EAPs).

Discussion Questions

1. Express your personal philosophy regarding the responsibilities of management, especially human resource managers, for the well-being of employees.

2. On July 1, 1985, the president, plant manager, and foreman of Film Recovery Systems, Inc., were sentenced to 25 years in the Illinois State Prison and fined $10,000 each after being found guilty of murder in the 1983 death of an employee exposed to cyanide in a silver-recovery process.* The court found that the three executives were "totally knowledgeable of the hazards of cyanide" and failed to communicate those hazards to employees, who were mostly undocumented Polish and Mexican immigrants. What is your reaction to what are believed to be the first work-related homicide convictions in the United States?

3. Do you think that an organization has any responsibility to help employees with health problems totally unrelated to their work environment?

▼ INCIDENT 19–1

Safety Problems at Blakely

Several severe accidents have recently occurred in the 12-employee assembly department of Blakely Company, which has a total work force of 65 employees. The supervisor of this department, Joe Benson, is quite perturbed and, in response to questions by the general manager and part owner of the company, claimed that the employees do not listen to him. He has warned them about not taking safety precautions, he explained, but he can't police their every move. The general manager countered with, "Accidents cost us money for repairs, lost time, medical expenses, human suffering, and what not. It's important that you stop it. Your department has a bad safety record—the worst in the company. You are going to have to correct it."

Joe felt he had taken the necessary precautions but that he was not getting satisfactory results. He also believed there were more possibilities of accidents occurring in his department than in any other department of the company. He decided to talk it over with the human resource manager, Fay Thomas. From Fay, he got the idea of scheduling a 10-minute safety talk by a different employee each week. The first subject would be "using machine guards." Joe felt that "good housekeeping and safety" and "no smoking" would also be good subsequent subjects.

Fay suggested that Joe schedule part of his time to review his department periodically. Furthermore, she suggested that any unsafe act he discovered should result in an immediate two-day suspension for the offender. "You have to get tough when it comes to safety. Your people are taking safety much too lightly. Of course,

---

*This information is from Betty S. Murphy, Wayne E. Barlow, and D. Diane Hatch, "Murder in the Workplace," *Personnel Journal*, October 1985, p. 27.

you start by making an announcement of what you are going to do. Put a notice to that effect on the bulletin board. Then enforce it to the letter."

Joe believed that simply talking personally to each of his employees and urging them to work safely might get better results. However, he really felt that some type of incentive was needed. As a result, he devised a plan in which the employee with the fewest safety violations over the next three months would be given a day off with pay. Joe's plan was approved by his boss.

Questions

1. What is Joe's problem?
2. In your opinion, how did this problem develop? What were its main causes? Discuss.
3. What actions do you recommend Joe take? Why?

▼ INCIDENT 19–2

Credibility at OSHA

Time magazine reported the following two situations involving OSHA.*

> OSHA inspectors have turned up in the most unlikely places with some very implausible demands. Michael Armstrong, manager of In-Line, Inc., a North Carolina construction firm, recalls the investigator who insisted that he provide a portable toilet for his crew while they were digging a tunnel under a highway. Armstrong argued in vain that his men never complained about using the bathroom at a filling station 50 yards away. OSHA was even determined to give cowboys a new kind of home on the range, complete with a portable flush toilet within five-minutes walking distance. Ranch hands, who felt that nature provided ample resources for their needs, hooted the proposal down. "Can you imagine a cowboy carrying his own rest room on the back of his horse?" scoffed Doug Huddleston, president of the Colorado Cattlemen's Association.

> The contradictions can be incredible and infuriating, as shown by just two conflicts between OSHA and the Department of Agriculture. OSHA demands grated floors in butcher shops to reduce the risk of employees' slipping. The Department of Agriculture declares that the same floors must be smooth because grates increase the hazards of contamination. Last year, OSHA also directed that the Made-Rite Sausage company of Sacramento, California, place protective guards on its meat-grinding machine to keep employees' hands out of it, even though the machine is too high for workers to reach. But such a guard would have violated Agriculture Department regulations, because it would have made the machine too difficult to clean. The company did the only sensible thing: nothing.

*"Rage over Rising Regulation," *Time*, January 2, 1978, p. 49.

Questions

1. With situations like the above occurring, can OSHA ever hope to be accepted by the business community as something other than a "bad guy"?

2. As human resource manager of a large organization, what are some actions you might take to encourage employees to pay attention to and abide by OSHA rules?

Exercise

Filing OSHA Reports

Assume you are the director of human resources for your company and that one of your responsibilities is to handle all contact with OSHA. Three days ago, on Monday, two injuries occurred in the plant. In the first case, a machine operator got careless and smashed his thumb. The operator received first aid on the floor, went home early, and was back on the job the next morning. In the second case, an office worker slipped going down some steps and broke her arm. She is expected to report back to work at the start of the next week.

1. What OSHA forms should be filed in each of these cases? When should the forms be filed?

2. Go to your library or a local OSHA office and get copies of the OSHA forms needed for each of the cases described above. Complete the forms. Make any reasonable assumptions that you deem necessary about the accidents.

Notes and Additional Readings

1. *Accident Facts,* 1988 ed. (Chicago: National Safety Council, 1988), p. 2.
2. Ibid., p. 3.
3. *All about OSHA,* rev. ed. (Washington, D.C.: U.S. Department of Labor, 1985).
4. Douglas C. Harper, "Control Health Care Costs," *Personnel Journal,* October 1988, p. 65.
5. David S. Thelan, Donna Ledgerwood, and Charles F. Walters, "Health and Safety in the Workplace: A New Challenge for Business Schools," *Personnel Administrator,* October 1985, p. 37.
6. Much of this section is drawn from *All about OSHA.*
7. Ibid., p. 1.
8. Ibid., p. 2.
9. *Marshall* v. *Barlow's, Inc.,* 76-1143 (1978).
10. Thelan, Ledgerwood, and Walters, "Health and Safety," p. 37.

11. G. R. Terry and L. W. Rue, *A Guide to Supervision* (Homewood, Ill.: Learning Systems, 1982), p. 131.

12. John D. Jordan and Rabbi D. Simons, "It's No Accident: What You Think Is What You Do," *Personnel Journal,* April 1984, pp. 16–20.

13. Craig S. Weaver, "Understanding Occupational Disease," *Personnel Journal,* June 1989, pp. 86–94.

14. "Is Your Job Dangerous to Your Health?" *U.S. News & World Report,* February 5, 1979, p. 41.

15. *Occupational Injuries and Illnesses in the United States by Industry, 1987,* Bulletin 2 (Washington, D.C.: U.S. Department of Labor, Bureau of Labor Statistics, 1988), p. 1.

16. Ibid.

17. M. C. Anderson, R. N. Isom, K. Williams, and L. J. Zimmerman, eds., *Proceedings of a Conference for Workers on Job-Related Cancer,* Houston, Texas, March 30, 1981, p. 29.

18. Genevieva La Greca, "The Stress You Make," *Personnel Journal,* September 1985, p. 43.

19. J. E. McGarth, "Stress and Behavior in Organizations," in *Handbook of Industrial and Organizational Psychology,* ed. M. D. Dunnette (Skokie, Ill.: Rand McNally, 1976), p. 1352.

20. Michael E. Cavanagh, "What You Don't Know about Stress," *Personnel Journal,* July 1988, p. 55.

21. Ibid.

22. La Greca, "The Stress You Make," p. 43.

23. These myths are adapted from Cavanagh, "What You," pp. 56–57.

24. Joseph H. Lodge, "Drugs: Abuse Is an Economic Issue," *Credit,* November–December 1987, p. 28.

25. Seven H. Appelbaum and Barbara T. Shapiro, "The ABCs of EAPs," *Personnel,* July 1989, p. 40.

26. Ibid.

27. Ibid.

28. Ibid.

29. Gopal C. Pati and John I. Adkins, Jr., "The Employer's Role in Alcoholism Assistance," *Personnel Journal,* July 1983, p. 569.

30. "Battling Employee Alcoholism," *Dun's Business Monthly,* June 1982, p. 48.

31. Ibid.; and Leslie Stackel, "EAPs in the Work Place," *Employee Relations Today,* Autumn 1987, p. 289.

32. Janice Castro, "Battling the Enemy Within," *Time,* March 17, 1986, p. 57.

33. Pati and Adkins, "The Employer's Role," p. 569.

34. Ibid.

35. Castro, "Battling the Enemy," p. 53.

36. Ian A. Miners, Nick Nykadyn, and Diane Traband, "Put Drug Detection to the Test," *Personnel Journal,* August 1987, p. 96.

37. James R. Redeker and Jonathan A. Segel, "Profits Low? Your Employees May Be High!" *Personnel,* June 1989, p. 75.

38. These guidelines are adapted from Miners, Nykadyn, and Traband, "Put Drug," p. 97.

39. Redeker and Segel, "Profits Low," p. 77.

40. Ibid.

41. David L. Wing, "AIDS: The Legal Debate," *Personnel Journal,* August 1986, p. 114.

42. Geralyn McClure Franklin and Robert K. Robinson, "Aids and the Law," *Personnel Administrator,* April 1988, p. 118.

43. E. Norris, "Alcohol: Companies Are Learning It Pays to Help Workers Beat the Bottle," *Business Insurance,* November 16, 1981, p. 53.

44. Stackel, "EAPs" p. 289; and *Savings Institutions,* January 1988, p. 70.

45. M. Tuthill, "Joining the War on Drug Abuse," *Nation's Business,* June 1982, p. 64.

46. Miners, Nykadyn, and Traband, "Put Drug," p. 97.

47. James S. Howard, "Employee Wellness: It's Good Business," *D&B Reports,* May–June 1987, pp. 34–37.

Chapter 20

Communication and Information Systems

Chapter Outline

Human Resource Communication Systems
Basics of Communication
Pitfalls of Communicating Human Resource Programs
Human Resource Information Systems (HRIS)
Use of a HRIS
Necessary Capabilities of a HRIS
Steps in Implementing a HRIS
A Word of Caution

Summary of Learning Objectives
Review Questions
Discussion Questions
Incident 20–1: Promoting a New Training Program
Incident 20–2: Amori Manufacturing Company
Exercise: Communicating a Job
Notes and Additional Readings

● *Learning Objectives*

After studying this chapter, you should be able to:

1. Explain the importance of clearly communicating human resource programs.
2. Describe the two basic forms of communication within an organization.
3. Recount several communication-related pitfalls associated with implementing human resource programs.
4. Define a human resource information system (HRIS).
5. List numerous potential applications or uses of an HRIS.
6. Explain which human resource functions are most commonly computerized.
7. Name the three major functional components of an HRIS.
8. Reiterate the specific procedures involved in developing and implementing an HRIS.

"*T*he human resources information system's (HRIS') greatest value to an organization lies in its potential for offering support to management information analysis and presentation."

*Kirk J. Anderson**

Communicating human resource programs has been compared to the marketing of a new product.[1] Consider the fact that approximately 90 percent of all new consumer products fail. In some cases, the failure is due to a poor product that does not fill a current need. In other cases, however, the product fails because of a breakdown in the marketing system. The product may have been inadequately researched, the salespeople may not have been properly trained, the distribution system may have been poor, or the overall marketing strategy may have been misguided. Unfortunately, many well-designed human resource programs also fail because they are not properly "marketed." In the case of human resource programs, the customers are the employees, and the price is often employee commitment, motivation, and cooperation.

In today's organizations, the computer has become almost as familiar as the typewriter was 30 years ago. One major use (if not *the* major use) of computers is to communicate information. Increased human resource requirements, government regulations, and expanded microcomputer capabilities have all helped justify the need and feasibility of an information system within the human resource department. These information systems are referred to as human resource information systems (HRIS). This chapter discusses the roles of communication and information systems in human resource management.

Human Resource Communication Systems

Communication
Transfer of information that is meaningful to those involved.

Communication is much more than talking, speaking, and reading. True communication takes place when an understanding has been transferred from one party or source to another. Therefore, **communication** can be defined as the transfer of information that is meaningful to those involved.

In this light, each and every one of the human resource functions discussed in this book requires some degree of effective communication if it is to be successful. For example, think of the importance that communication plays in career planning, recruiting, and performance appraisal. In all too many instances, human resource managers spend tremendous amounts of time developing very good programs, only to subsequently do a poor job of communicating them. The end result is often "great" programs that go largely unused.

A human resource manager's first step in becoming an effective communicator is to develop an appreciation for the importance of communication. It is not that human resource managers have a tendency to belittle the importance of communication but rather that they often fail to think consciously about it. As suggested by the opening paragraph of this chapter, one helpful approach is for human

*Source: Kirk J. Anderson, "Putting the 'I' in HRIS," *Personnel*, September 1988, p. 12.

resource managers to get in the habit of thinking in marketing terms. Think of the employees as the customers and the human resource programs as the products.

Basics of Communication

Communication in organizations can be viewed in one of two perspectives: interpersonal (between individuals) and organizational (within the formal organization structure). These two basic forms of communication are interdependent in that interpersonal communication is almost always a part of organizational communication.

Interpersonal Communication

Effective communication between individuals is critical to most human resource programs. **Interpersonal communication** occurs between individuals. It is an interactive process that involves a person's effort to attain understanding and to respond to it. It involves sending and receiving verbal and nonverbal messages. These come not only from other people but also from the physical and cultural settings of both the sender and the receiver.[2]

> **Interpersonal communication**
> Communication between individuals.

The basic purpose of interpersonal communication is to transmit ideas, thoughts, or information so that the sender of the message both is understood and understands the receiver. Figure 20–1 depicts the basic interpersonal communication process.

Organizational Communication

Organizational communication occurs within the formal organization structure. In general, organizational communication systems are downward, upward, or horizontal (lateral). Overlapping these three formal systems is the informal communication system called the grapevine.

> **Organizational communication**
> Communication occurring within the formal organizational structure.

▼ **Figure 20–1**   Interpersonal communication process

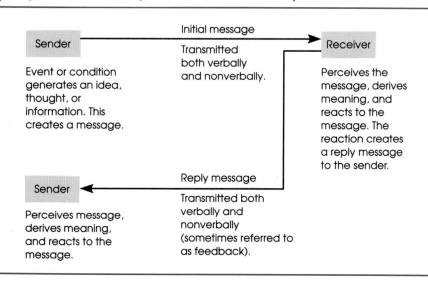

Sender	Initial message
Event or condition generates an idea, thought, or information. This creates a message.	Transmitted both verbally and nonverbally.

Receiver
Perceives the message, derives meaning, and reacts to the message. The reaction creates a reply message to the sender.

Sender	Reply message
Perceives message, derives meaning, and reacts to the message.	Transmitted both verbally and nonverbally (sometimes referred to as feedback).

▼ Table 20–1   Examples of upward communication

Informal inquiries or discussion with employees
Exit interviews
Discussion with first-line supervisors
Grievance or complaint procedures
Grapevine
Union representatives
Counseling
Formal meetings with employees
Suggestion systems
Formal attitude surveys
Question- and-answer column in employee publication
Gripe boxes
Hot-line system

Downward communication
Transmitting of information from higher to lower levels of the organization.

Upward communication
Communication originating at the lower levels of an organization and flowing toward the top.

Horizontal (lateral) communication
Communication across organizational units that are at the same approximate level in the organizational hierarchy.

Organizational grapevine
Informal channels of communication resulting from casual contacts between friends or acquaintances in various organizational units.

Traditional views of the communication processes in organizations have been dominated by **downward communication** systems. Such systems transmit information from higher to lower levels of the organization. The chain of command determines the flow of downward information. Policy manuals, bulletins, organizational magazines, job descriptions, orders, and directives are all examples of downward communication.

Upward communication starts at the lower levels of the organization and flows toward the top. An upward communication system should help management to judge the effectiveness of its downward communications and to learn about organizational problems. Four major areas of information should normally be communicated from below: (1) the activities of subordinates in terms of their achievements, progress, and future plans; (2) unresolved work problems in which subordinates may need help currently or in the future; (3) the feelings of subordinates about their jobs, associates, and the organization; and (4) suggestions or ideas for improvements within work groups or the organization as a whole. Table 20–1 lists forms of upward communication. As can be seen, human resource management is directly responsible for many of these systems.

Communication across the lines of the formal chain of command is called **horizontal, or lateral, communication**. Specialized departments (such as human resources, engineering, marketing, research, and quality control) perform functions such as gathering data, issuing reports, preparing directives, coordinating activities, and advising higher levels of management. Such specialized departments are generally quite active in horizontal communication because their activities influence several chains of command rather than just one. Departments that depend on one another for achieving their respective goals also need horizontal communication. This is true of the human resource department, which often engages in horizontal communication. Interdepartmental committee meetings and distribution of written reports are two of the more commonly used methods of horizontal communication.

The **organizational grapevine** is composed of informal networks that carry information on routes not prescribed by the organization. Organizational grapevines often result from the organization's informal work groups. Although generally not formally sanctioned, the grapevine always exists and does not follow the organizational hierarchy. It may go from secretary to vice president or from engineer

▽● **HRM in Action 20–1**

A Team Approach to Suggestion Systems

Harleyville Insurance Company recently devised an employee suggestion system called Discovery. The original purpose of Discovery was to increase employee involvement. Not only did Discovery result in increased enthusiasm and involvement among employees, it also produced cost savings of $3.5 million. In addition to this, 253 new ideas were approved to improve employees' jobs and make the company a better place in which to work.

The Discovery program utilized a team approach marketed by the Maritz Motivation Company of St. Louis. Discovery differed from the firm's previous suggestion system in that teams, rather than individuals, were used to produce new ideas, and the rewards were superior.

In addition to the tangible benefits of the program, there were significant intangible benefits. Employees gained experience not only in developing new ideas but in casting them out and determining if they would work. Other intangible benefits included giving many employees leadership experience, having employees communicate across departmental lines, and letting employees examine company records to see how much everything costs. Out of 1,500 employees, 1,225 volunteered for the program.

Source: Rick L. Lansing, "The Power of Teams," *Supervisory Management,* February 1989, pp. 39–41.

to clerk. The grapevine is not limited to nonmanagement employees; it also operates among managers and professional personnel.

As discussed in Chapter 14, suggestion systems are frequently used as a type of incentive. But even then, their major purpose is to improve upward communication. Most suggestion systems have progressed far beyond the early-1950s complaint box on the wall. Modern suggestion systems generally involve specific procedures for submitting ideas and utilize committees to review and evaluate the suggestions. HRM in Action 20–1 describes how one company used a suggestion system to get employees involved in communicating new ideas.

Pitfalls of Communicating Human Resource Programs

As discussed earlier, it is helpful for human resource managers to develop a marketing approach when implementing their programs. Even when this is successfully done, there are numerous other communication-related pitfalls to avoid. Some of these are discussed in the following paragraphs.[3]

Avoid communicating in peer group or "privileged class" language. The level of the communication should be determined by the receiving audience and not by the instigator of the communication. Take, for example, the common procedure for developing employee benefit information. What often happens is that a highly educated writer makes a first draft and gives it to the department head. The department head, being a specialist, then adds a few "clarifying" remarks. The company lawyer and perhaps an actuary or an insurance person then add more explanations to guard against liability and to be legally correct. Thus, the final document may be accurate and legal, but also not easily understood by the employees for whom it is intended! The key is to consciously remember for whom the communication is intended.

Don't ignore the cultural aspects of communication. Be careful with words, symbols, and expressions. Today's work force is much more culturally sensitive than it was one or two decades ago. Expressions like "They wear the black hats" or "You act like an old lady" can easily be taken out of meaning and offend someone in the audience.

Back up communications with management action. The old saying "People watch what you do and not what you say" is certainly true with regard to employee communications. Promises made either orally or in writing must be backed up by actions if they are to be successful.

Periodically reinforce employee communications. Most communications tend to be forgotten unless they are periodically reinforced. This is especially true with many personnel-related communications. It is a good idea, for example, to periodically remind employees of the value of the benefits they receive.

Data
Raw material from which information is developed; composed of facts that describe people, places, things, or events and that have not been interpreted.

Transmit information and not just data. **Data** has been defined as "the raw material from which information is developed; it is composed of facts that describe people, places, things, or events and that have not been interpreted."[4] Data that has been interpreted and that meets a need of one or more managers is **information**. Employees receive piles of data from numerous sources; but until the data has been interpreted, it is not of much value. Human resource managers need to guard against transmitting numbers, statistics, and other data that have little meaning without an accompanying interpretation.

Information
Data that has been interpreted and that meets a need of one or more managers.

Don't ignore the perceptual and behavioral aspects of communication. Try to anticipate employee reactions to communications and act accordingly. For example, it might be a good strategy to informally separate older employees from younger employees when introducing a new pension program through employee meetings. It would only be natural for these different groups to have different questions and levels of interest.

The above suggestions, to a large extent, involve good common sense and practicality. It is not that human resource managers are not practical, but rather that they often do not take the time to think through a communication. One good approach is to ask the question "How could this message be misinterpreted?" The answer to this question should then be taken into account when structuring the communication.

Human Resource Information Systems (HRIS)

The proliferation of computers, especially personal and minicomputers, has greatly altered the manner in which human resource managers gather and disperse information. The first computerized human resource application in business took place at General Electric in the early 1950s.[5] A 1984 survey of 1,000 *Personnel Journal* subscribers, which yielded 434 usable returns, revealed that 99.7 percent of the respondents used computers in one capacity or another in the personnel function.[6]

A similar survey conducted in 1988 found that 99.8 percent of the respondents have automated one or more personnel functions.[7] This is quite an evolution to have taken place in just a few decades.

Originally human resource departments began using computers by sharing hardware and files with other departments. As the needs of the human resource departments grew, the sharing of files with other departments became increasingly cumbersome. It was at this point that companies began to develop information systems devoted exclusively to human resource applications. These systems became known as **human resource information systems (HRIS)**. Increased emphasis on human resources, more government requirements, and the development of micro-computers all have contributed to the proliferation of human resource information systems.

Human resource information system (HRIS)
Refers to prepackaged computerized human resource systems or to internally developed comprehensive human resource management information systems.

Uses of an HRIS

A major advantage of an HRIS is its potential for producing more accurate and more timely information for operating, controlling, and planning purposes than manual or payroll-based systems can produce. Computers simply do not make arithmatic errors, and they can do calculations many times faster than humans. Many of the reports generated by an HRIS take only minutes to produce electronically, but would take many hours to do manually.

The major disadvantage of an HRIS is that it can be expensive in terms of the financial outlay and labor requirements necessary to implement the system. Furthermore, an HRIS can be threatening and intimidating to certain employees who have a basic fear of computers. The following areas represent some specific potential applications for an HRIS.[8] When evaluating the feasibility an HRIS, it should always be remembered that the overriding purpose of any HRIS should be to assist human resource managers and other top managers in making sound decisions.

1. *Clerical applications.* Automating certain routine clerical tasks will avoid the use of additional staff, overtime, and temporary help.
2. *Applicant search expenditures.* An HRIS can easily store a summary of applicant qualifications and subsequently perform searches for candidates for certain positions. This can help the company avoid using an employment agency.
3. *Risk management.* Today it is critical, in many industries, that people in certain jobs have licenses, safety training, and even physical examinations. An HRIS can be used to monitor these requirements and report any discrepancies by jobholders.
4. *Training management.* An HRIS can be used to compare job training requirements with the actual training experiences of individual jobholders. This system can then be used to determine both individual and organizational training needs.
5. *Financial planning.* By using an HRIS, human resource managers can simulate the financial impact of salary and benefit changes. It is then possible for the human resource department to recommend an increase strategy that stays within an overall budget goal.

Figure 20–2   Frequency of HRIS applications

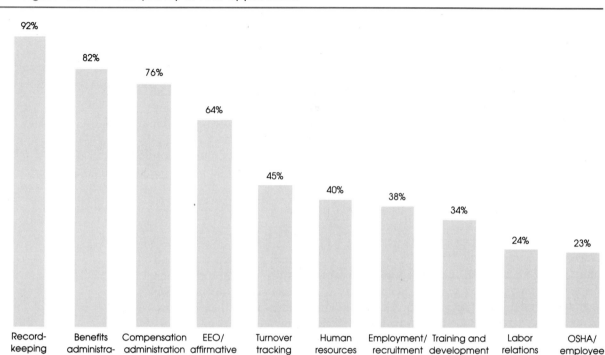

Source: Morton E. Grossman and Margaret Magnus, "The Growing Dependence on HRIS," *Personnel Journal,* September 1988, pp. 55–56.

6. *Turnover analysis.* Turnover can be closely monitored with an HRIS. Turnover characteristics can be identified and analyzed for probable causes.

7. *Succession planning.* A logical progression path and the steps required for advancement can be identified by an HRIS. Individual progress can then be monitored.

8. *Flexible benefits administration.* An HRIS can be used to administer a flexible benefits program. Without an HRIS, such programs can be expensive to implement and administer.

9. *Compliance with government regulations.* An HRIS can be used to keep up with current EEO and other related government-required regulations. An HRIS can also help keep companies in compliance by better scanning job applicants who meet specific requirements and keeping management informed of the situation.

10. *Attendance reporting and analysis.* The documentation of sick days, vacation time, personal time, and tardiness can be a significant expense if done manually. An HRIS can easily track this information.

11. *Human resource planning.* Human resource planning can be greatly assisted by an information system that is capable of making projections based on the current work force.

▼. **HRM in Action 20–2**

Computerized Training

Computers are frequently used in industry for training new and experienced employees. The use of a computer to keep records and administer tests frees instructors for other tasks and provides quick results.

In the petroleum industry, computers are used to train operators in troubleshooting techniques. Many different, dangerous situations can be simulated graphically. Operators can then learn how to control or prevent the situations, without costly or dangerous practice sessions.

Airline companies are frequent users of computers for training purposes. Airline pilots receive their early flight training using computer terminals with touch-sensitive screens. The pilots are able to learn the instrumentation and controls at the simulator before moving on to the cockpit.

In manufacturing industries, engineers and technicians are trained in electronics and computer technology on computers. The training programs allow workers to become familiar with the technology of microprocessor-based production tools and equipment and to learn how to perform maintenance.

Source: William H. Hultgren, "An Introduction to Computerized Training," *Personnel Journal*, October 1984, pp. 22–23.

---

12. *Accident reporting and prevention.* An HRIS can be used to record accident details and subsequently provide analyses that can help prevent future accidents.

The 1988 *Personnel Journal* survey cited earlier found that recordkeeping and administration, benefits administration, compensation administration, and EEO/affirmative action tracking are by far the most frequent uses of an HRIS.[9] Figure 20–2 summarizes these findings. As indicated by Figure 20–2, most HRIS applications to date have involved storage and retrieval of basic information. However, the trend is moving more toward specialized functions.[10] HRM in Action 20–2 describes how several industries use an HRIS for training purposes.

Necessary Capabilities of an HRIS[11]

What should be the minimum capabilities of an HRIS? When answering this question, one should always keep in mind that the critical requirement of any HRIS system is the data; if you have the data necessary to support the various human resource functions, you can easily put that data on a computer. Any HRIS system has three major functional components: inputs, data maintenance, and outputs. Each of these is discussed below as to its role in the overall system.

Input Function

The **input function** provides the capabilities needed to get human resource information into the HRIS. Figure 20–3 illustrates the components of a typical HRIS input function.

Some of the first things that must be established are the procedures and processes required to gather the necessary data. In other words, where, when, and how will the data be collected? Once collected, it must be entered into the system. Some information may require coding before entering (for example, raw salary information may be converted to a coded salary grade).

Input function
Provides the capabilities needed to get human resource information into the HRIS.

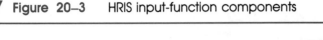

▼ **Figure 20–3** HRIS input-function components

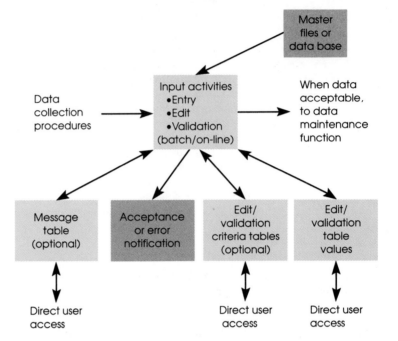

Source: Sidney H. Simon, "The HRIS: What Capabilities Must It Have?" Reprinted, by permission of publisher, from *Personnel*, September–October © 1983. American Management Association. All rights reserved.

Once the data has been input, it must be validated to ensure that it is correct. Edit/validation tables can be used to determine if the data is acceptable. They contain approved values that the data is automatically checked against. The system should have the capability of easily updating and changing the validation tables.

Data Maintenance Function

The data maintenance function is responsible for the actual updating of the data stored in the various storage devices. Figure 20–4 illustrates a typical data maintenance function. As changes (such as a pay increase) occur in human resource information, this information should be incorporated into the system. As new data are brought into the system, it is often desirable to maintain the old data in the form of historical information.

Output Function

The output function of an HRIS is the most visible and familiar. This is because the majority of HRIS users are not involved or concerned with collating, editing/validating, and updating human resource data; rather, they are concerned with the information and reports produced by the system. Figure 20–5 illustrates a typical HRIS output function.

Most human resource reporting consists of:[12]

1. Selecting a segment of the total population for further evaluation; the selection is usually based on the values of such items as exempt/nonexempt,

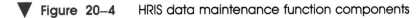

▼ **Figure 20–4** HRIS data maintenance function components

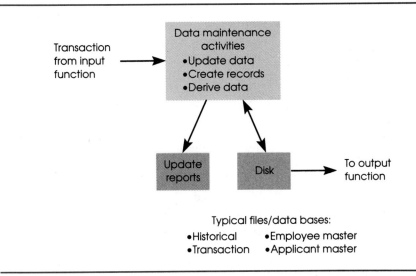

Source: Sidney H. Simon, "The HRIS: What Capabilities Must It Have?" Reprinted, by permission of publisher, from *Personnel,* September–October © 1983. American Management Association. All rights reserved.

▼ **Figure 20–5** HRIS output-function components

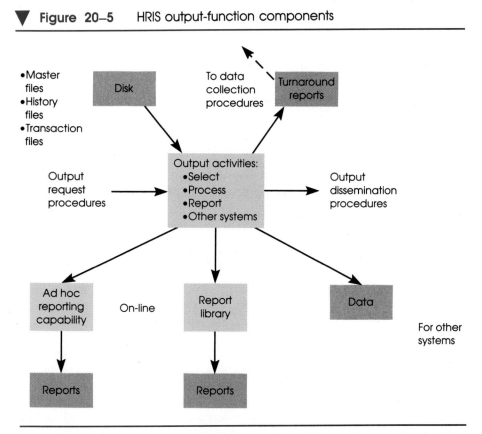

Source: Sidney H. Simon, "The HRIS: What Capabilities Must It Have?" Reprinted, by permission of publisher, from *Personnel,* September–October © 1983. American Management Association. All rights reserved.

salary grades/classifications, age, sex, departments, continuous service, and so on.

2. Performing some type of calculations using the population previously selected in item 1, such as calculating average salaries, average merit increases, and so forth.

3. Providing a report containing specific information regarding the selected population and/or the calculation results.

The demands of the output function are the major factors that influence the particular type of software to be used.

In addition to being able to produce a specific report on request, the output function should have the capability of providing and updating a reports library. A **reports library** basically stores the program and historical data necessary to generate reports that are periodically requested. This feature saves substantial time by automatically updating the data needed to produce the reports in the library.

Another desirable capability is the ability to generate turnaround documents. **Turnaround documents** basically are simple reports that show the current data values and provide a place to indicate any changes. They are used to help solicit updates to the data.

Naturally, the specific inputs, frequency of updates, and reports required for an organization's HRIS will differ somewhat with each situation. However, the basic components and capabilities discussed above should apply in almost all situations, regardless of size and complexity.

Reports library
A type of computer software program that stores the program and historical data necessary to generate reports that are periodically requested.

Turnaround documents
Simple reports that show the current data values of an HRIS and provide a place to indicate any changes.

Steps in Implementing an HRIS

The steps outlined below describe the specific procedures involved in developing and implementing an HRIS:[13]

Step 1: Inception of idea. The idea for having an HRIS must originate somewhere. The originator of the idea should prepare a preliminary report showing the need for an HRIS and what it can do for the organization. This preliminary report should be designed to get management's attention. The most critical part of this step is to clearly illustrate how an HRIS can assist management in making certain decisions.

Step 2: Feasibility study. The feasibility study evaluates the present system and details the benefits of an HRIS. It evaluates the cost/benefit of an HRIS by showing the labor and material savings as compared to the cost of the system. It also evaluates the intangible savings, such as increased accuracy and fewer errors. Of course, it is possible that the feasibility study would recommend against an HRIS.

Step 3: Selecting a project team. Once the feasibility study has been accepted and the resources allocated, a project team should be selected. The project team should consist of a human resource representative, knowledgeable about the organization's human resource functions and activities, and about the organization itself, and representatives from both management information systems and payroll. As the project progresses, additional clerical people from the human resource department will need to be added.

Step 4: Defining the requirements. A statement of requirements specifies in detail exactly what the HRIS will do. A large part of the statement of requirements normally deals with the details of the reports that will be produced. Naturally, any other specific requirements are also described. The key here is to make sure that the mission of the HRIS truly matches management's needs for an HRIS.[14]

Step 5: Vendor analysis. The purpose of this step is to determine what hardware and software are available that will best meet the organization's needs for the least price. This is a difficult task. The best approach is usually not to ask vendors *if* a particular package can meet the organization's requirements, but rather *how* it will meet the organization's requirements. The results of this analysis will determine whether to purchase an "off-the-shelf" package or to develop the system internally.

Step 6: Package contract negotiation. After a vendor has been selected, the contract must be negotiated. The contract stipulates the vendor's responsibilities with regard to software, installation service, maintenance, training, and documentation.

Step 7: Training. Training usually begins as soon as possible after the contract has been signed. First, the members of the project team are trained to use the HRIS. Toward the end of the implementation, the human resource representative will train managers from other departments in how to submit information to the HRIS and how to request information from it.

Step 8: Tailoring the system. This step involves making changes to the system to best fit the needs of the organization. A general rule of thumb is not to modify the vendor's package, because modifications frequently cause problems. An alternate approach is to develop programs that augment the vendor's program rather than altering it.

Step 9: Collecting the data. Prior to start-up of the system, data must be collected and entered into the system.

Step 10: Testing the system. Once the system has been tailored to the organization's needs and the data entered, a period of testing follows. The purpose of the testing phase is to verify the output of the HRIS and to make sure that it is doing what it is supposed to do. All reports should be critically analyzed for accuracy.

Step 11: Starting up. Start-up begins when all data and current actions are put into the system and reports are produced. It is wise to attempt start-up during a lull period so that as much time as possible can be devoted to the HRIS. Even though the system has been tested, some additional errors often surface during start-up.

Step 12: Running in parallel. Even after the new HRIS has been tested, it is desirable to run the new system in parallel with the old system for a period of time. This allows for the outputs of both systems to be compared and examined for any inaccuracies.

▼. HRM in Action 20–3

HRIS Implementation at Chase Manhattan Bank

Chase Manhattan Bank successfully installed a new HRIS by encouraging a high level of user involvement. A key to the success was a strong commitment by top management to the idea that the human resource users should be key participants in the design and implementation of the HRIS. The new system was created to meet needs including the simplified maintenance of employee data and on-line access to historical information. The new HRIS is somewhat unique in that it retains many parts of the previous system, which was meeting many needs. The approach was to incorporate the best aspects of the old system and at the same time avoid the worst effects of a totally new HRIS. User involvement included the creation of a user group with representatives who had commitment and functional knowledge. This group received extensive training and helped to develop the system documentation. The project proved to Chase Manhattan that the benefits of user involvement can be substantial.

Source: Douglas Harders and Joanne Wisniewski, "Chase Manhattan Manages HRIS Implementation," *Personnel Journal*, January 1989, pp. 120–24.

Step 13: Maintenance. It normally takes several weeks or even months for the human resource people to feel comfortable with the new system. During this stabilization period, any remaining errors and adjustments should be handled.

Step 14: Audit. After the HRIS has been in place for at least one year, the project team should perform an audit. The audit should determine whether or not the HRIS has performed up to its expectations. If it has not, corrective actions should be taken. A written summary of the audit should be presented to top management.

Following the above steps when implementing an HRIS will not guarantee success, but it will increase the probability. HRM in Action 20–3 describes how Chase Manhattan Bank recently implemented a new HRIS.

A Word of Caution

As emphasized earlier in this chapter, the overriding purpose of any HRIS is to assist human resource managers and other top managers in making sound decisions. If this is to be accomplished, the HRIS must produce information that is useful to the organization. Unfortunately, many human resource information systems are disappointments to managers simply because they do not produce the types of information that management values. The problem is often that the managers designing the HRIS do not have a thorough understanding of what constitutes quality information to the users of the information.

If the information provided by an HRIS is to be valued by its users, it must meet five critical standards: (1) accuracy, (2) significance and relevance, (3) comprehensiveness, (4) readability and visual impact, and (5) consistency of format.[15] Accuracy should be defined by the user and does not necessarily have to be 100 percent error free. However, it should meet the expectations of the user. For example, if the user is primarily interested in a "big picture" view, there should be more tolerance for data inaccuracy than when the user is primarily interested in specific values and details. Significance and relevance is concerned with making sure that the users get the information they need and don't get information they don't need. Comprehensiveness means that the information answers not only the immediate question but also probable follow-up questions. Information that is comprehensive provides insight that may not be obvious strictly from the data. Readability and visual impact should ensure that the information can be easily interpreted by the user. Graphs and tables should be used where appropriate and information should be presented in a manner easy to read. Consistency of format simply means that once the right format has been developed and used it should not be changed without good reason.

Producing information that is of quality to the user obviously requires an investment in time, effort, and communication on the part of HRIS managers. However, this investment can result in an information system that wins the respect of top management and one that they come to depend on.

● *Summary of Learning Objectives*

1. Explain the importance of clearly communicating human resource programs.

   In all too many instances, human resource managers spend tremendous amounts of time developing very good programs only to subsequently do a poor job of communicating the programs. The end result is often "great" programs that go largely unused.

2. Describe the two basic forms of communication within an organization.

   Communication in organizations can be viewed in one of two ways: interpersonal and organizational. Interpersonal communication occurs between individuals. Organizational communication occurs within the formal organization structure.

3. Recount several communication-related pitfalls associated with implementing human resource programs.

   Communication-related pitfalls to avoid when implementing human resource programs include communicating in "privileged class" language, ignoring the cultural aspects of communication, not backing up communication with management action, omitting to periodically reinforce employee communications, transmitting only data and not information, and ignoring the perceptual and behavioral aspects of communication.

4. Define a human resource information system (HRIS).

   Information systems developed and used exclusively for human resource applications are referred to as human resource information systems (HRIS).

5. List numerous potential applications or uses of an HRIS.

   Potential uses of an HRIS include clerical applications, applicant searches, risk management, training management, financial planning, turnover analysis, succession planning, flexible benefits administration, compliance with government regulations, attendance reporting and analysis, human resource planning, and accident reporting and prevention.

6. Explain which human resource functions are most commonly computerized.

   Currently the human resource functions that are most widely computerized are recordkeeping and administration, benefits administration, compensation administration, and EEO/affirmative action tracking.

7. Name the three major functional components of an HRIS.

   The three major functional components of an HRIS are inputs, data maintenance, and outputs. The input function of an HRIS should provide the capability to edit and validate data after input. The data maintenance function should provide the capability for updating the data stored on the various storage devices. The output function is the most visible function of an HRIS, responsible for producing reports.

8. Reiterate the specific procedures involved in developing and implementing an HRIS.

   Fourteen steps are involved in successfully developing and implementing an HRIS. These include: (1) developing the idea, (2) conducting a feasibility study, (3) selecting a project team, (4) defining the requirements of the system, (5) conducting a vendor analysis, (6) negotiating a package contract, (7) training people how to use the system, (8) tailoring the system to the needs of the users, (9) collecting the data, (10) testing the system, (11) starting up the system, (12) running the new HRIS and the old system in parallel, (13) maintaining the system, and (14) auditing the system.

Review Questions

1. Define communication.
2. Name and briefly describe the two basic types of communication.
3. Distinguish among downward, upward, and horizontal communication. Give several examples of each type.
4. Briefly describe at least five communication-related potential pitfalls faced by human resource managers.
5. Briefly describe how human resource information systems have evolved.
6. Summarize the major advantages and disadvantages of an HRIS.
7. Name at least 10 potential applications or uses of an HRIS.
8. What are the four most frequently computerized human resource functions?
9. What is the purpose of a reports library?
10. Name the steps involved in planning and developing an HRIS.
11. What are the five critical standards that must be met if information provided by an HRIS is to be viewed by the users as quality information?

Discussion Questions

1. Do you believe that human resource managers should take a marketing approach when implementing their programs, or do you think such an approach might "cheapen" or throw a negative light on the human resource function? Support your answer.

2. Respond to the following statement: "Learning about human resource information systems should be reserved for computer specialists."

3. Why do you think that many human resource managers are reluctant to use an HRIS?

▼ INCIDENT 20–1

Promoting a New Training Program

Fred Jackson, the human resource manager at Velcan, Inc., had worked for several months arranging for a series of in-house management training sessions for his company. The five training sessions were to be conducted by consultants and were specifically designed for new managers and employees with high management potential. Each training session would last two hours and address a particular management function such as planning, organization, or controlling. The training sessions were to be offered on the first Friday of each month from October through January. In order to participate, employees would have to be recommended by their immediate supervisor or manager.

Fred Jackson was enthusiastic about the training plan and felt the programs would be very beneficial to new and upcoming managers. In July, Fred enclosed a paragraph in the management newsletter announcing that the training program would be available in October. The paragraph included a statement that managers should reserve a place for their employees by the September 1st deadline.

On September 1st, Fred was very disappointed because he had received only one reservation. It was hardly worth bringing in outside consultants with only one participant! He had expected at least 20 participants and had hoped for as many as 30.

Fred knew that Sandra Vochek had two employees she felt had management potential. When Fred asked Sandra why neither of her high-performing employees was signed up for the training sessions, Sandra answered, "When I read about it in July, I thought it sounded like a good idea. I remember thinking I'd like more information. I'm sorry, Fred, July was two months ago—I completely forgot about it."

Questions

1. Why was there so little interest in the program?
2. What could Fred have done to generate interest in the program?

▼ INCIDENT 20–2

Amori Manufacturing Company

Amori Manufacturing Company, a producer of specialty industrial chemicals, employs 750 people at three locations. The company has experienced very rapid growth in the last few years and is expected to continue to grow very rapidly for at least the next three years. The number of employees is expected to increase by 20 percent within the next 18 months.

In order to meet the increased requirements for employees and managers, the company is actively involved in recruiting new employees and training existing employees. The company feels it is in a strong position to recruit well-qualified new employees because of its elaborate stock bonus plan, which is available to all employees with three years' tenure with the company.

All company records are maintained manually. Recently, a new director of human resource management was hired. The first thing she suggested was that the company invest in a computerized human resource information system.

Questions

1. In what ways might Amori Manufacturing Company use a computerized HRIS?

2. Discuss the steps the company should take in planning and developing an HRIS. Include in your answer a discussion of who should be involved during each step and what information would be needed.

Exercise

Communicating a Job

Carefully read the job description below and try to identify the job being discussed.* After you have correctly identified the job (or your instructor has told you what the job is), rewrite the job description using clearer terminology.

Description of Duties and Responsibilities:

Without direct or intermediate supervision and with a broad latitude for independent judgment and discretion, the incumbent directs, controls, and regulates the movement of interstate commerce, representing a cross section of the wealth of the American economy.

On the basis of personal judgment founded on past experience, conditioned by erudication, and disciplined by mental intransigence, the incumbent integrates the variable factors in an evolving situation and on the basis of simultaneous cogitation formulates a binding decision relative to the priority flow of interstate and intrastate commerce, both animate and inanimate. These decisions are irreversible and are not subject to appellate review by a higher authority, nor can they be reversed by legal determination of any echelon of our judicial complex.

The decisions of the incumbent are important, since they affect with great finality movement of agricultural products, forest products, finished goods, semifinished products, small business, large business, public utilities, and governmental agencies.

In effective implementation of these responsibilities, the incumbent must exercise initiative, ingenuity, imagination, intelligence, industry, and/or discerning versatility. The incumbent must be able to deal effectively with all types of personalities and all levels of education from college president and industrial tycoon to truck drivers. Above all, the incumbent must possess decisiveness and the ability

---

*The source of this job description is unknown.

to implement motivation on the part of others consistent with the decision the incumbent has indicated. An erroneous judgment or a failure to properly appraise the nuances of an unfolding development could create a complex obfuscation of personnel and equipment generating an untold loss of mental equilibrium on the part of innumerable members of American industry.

Notes and Additional Readings

1. Joseph A. Banik, "The Marketing Approach to Communicating with Employees," *Personnel Journal,* October 1985; and Joe Pasqueletto, "An HRIS Marketing Strategy," *Personnel Journal,* June 1989, pp. 62–71.

2. Lyman W. Porter and Karlene W. Roberts, "Communication," in *Handbook of Industrial and Organizational Psychology,* ed. Marvin D. Dunnette (Skokie, Ill.: Rand McNally, 1976), p. 1558.

3. Much of this section is drawn from Banik, "The Marketing Approach," pp. 62–68.

4. David Lynch, "MIS: Conceptual Framework, Criticisms, and Major Requirements for Success," *Journal of Business Communication,* Winter 1984, p. 20.

5. Albert L. Lederer, "Information Technology: 1. Planning and Developing a Human Resource Information System," *Personnel,* May–June 1984, pp. 14–15.

6. Margaret Magnus and Morton E. Grossman, "Computers and the Personnel Department," *Personnel Journal,* April 1985, p. 42.

7. Morton E. Grossman and Margaret Magnus, "The Growing Dependence on HRIS," *Personnel Journal,* September 1988, p. 55.

8. Much of this section is drawn from William I. Travis, "How to Justify a Human Resources Information System," *Personnel Journal,* February 1988, pp. 83–86.

9. Grossman and Magnus, "The Growing Dependence," p. 56.

10. Ibid.

11. Much of this section is adapted from Sidney H. Simon, "The HRIS: What Capabilities Must It Have?" *Personnel,* September–October 1983, pp. 36–49.

12. Ibid., p. 46.

13. These steps are adapted from Lederer, "Information Technology," pp. 19–26.

14. Joe Pasqualetto, "Evaluating the Future of HRIS," *Personnel Journal,* August 1988, p. 82.

Glossary of Terms

12-month rule Provides that no election can be held in any bargaining unit within which a valid election has been held within the preceding 12-month period. (p. 424)

4/5ths or 80 percent rule A limit used to determine whether or not there are serious discrepancies in hiring decisions and other employment practices affecting women or minorities. (p. 42)

401(K) plan Most popular type of defined contribution plan, named after section 401(K) of the Internal Revenue Code. Allows employees to defer a portion of their pay into the plan, thus making contributions tax deductible (up to a limit). (p. 380)

Absorption Union merger that involves the merging of one union into a considerably larger one. (p. 412)

Acquired Immune Deficiency Syndrome (AIDS) A life-threatening disease that, although not communicable in most work settings, is causing many work-related debates that have yet to be legally resolved. (p. 66)

Adverse impact Condition that occurs when the selection rate for minorities or women is less than 80 percent of the selection rate for the majority group in hiring, promotions, transfers, demotions, or any selection decision. (p. 42)

Affirmative action plan Written document outlining specific goals and timetables for remedying past discriminatory actions. (p. 59)

Age Discrimination in Employment Act (ADEA) Prohibits discrimination against employees over 40 years of age by all companies employing 20 or more people in the private sector. (pp. 28, 382)

Agency shop Contract provision that does not require employees to join the union but requires them to pay the equivalent of union dues as a condition of employment. (p. 432)

Alexander v. Gardner-Denver Supreme Court decision in 1974 that ruled that using the final and binding grievance procedure in an organization does not preclude an aggrieved employee from seeking redress through court action. (p. 450)

Amalgamation Union merger that involves two or more unions, usually of approximately the same size, forming a new union. (p. 412)

American Federation of Labor–Congress of Industrial Organizations (AFL–CIO) Combination of national, international, and local unions joined together to promote the interests of unions and workers. The AFL–CIO was formed in 1955 by the amalgamation of the American Federation of Labor (AFL) and the Congress of Industrial Organizations (CIO). (p. 408)

Applicant flow record A form completed voluntarily by a job applicant and used by an employer to obtain information that might be viewed as discriminatory. (p. 176)

Apprenticeship training Giving instruction, both on and off the job, in the practical and theoretical aspects of the work required in a skilled occupation or trade. (p. 210)

Aptitude tests Means of measuring a person's capacity or latent ability to learn and perform a job. (p. 177)

Arbitration Process whereby the parties agree to settle a dispute through the use of an independent third party (called an arbitrator). Arbitration is binding on both parties. (p. 429)

Assessment center Formal method used in training and/or selection and aimed at evaluating an individual's potential as a manager by exposing the individual to simulated problems that would be faced in a real-life managerial situation. (p. 235)

Bargaining unit Group of employees in a plant, firm, or industry, recognized by the employer, agreed on by the parties to a case, or designated by the NLRB as appropriate for the purposes of collective bargaining. (p. 422)

Base wage or salary The hourly, weekly, or monthly pay that employees receive for their work. (pp. 304, 320)

Behavior modeling or interaction management A method of training in which interaction problems faced by managers are identified, practiced, and transferred to specific job situations. (p. 236)

Behaviorally anchored rating scale (BARS) Method of performance appraisal that determines an employee's level of performance based on whether or not certain specifically described job behaviors are present. (p. 256)

Benefits Rewards that employees receive as a result of their employment and position with an organization. (p. 304)

Board or panel interviews Interview method in which two or more people conduct a single interview with one applicant. (p. 180)

Bona fide occupational qualification (BFOQ) Permits employer to use religion, age, sex, or national origin as a factor in its employment practices when reasonably necessary to the normal operation of that particular business or enterprise. (p. 60)

Bonus Reward that is offered on a one-time basis for high performance. (p. 347)

Bottom-line concept When the overall selection process does not have an adverse impact, the government will usually not examine the individual components of that process for adverse impact or evidence of validity. (p. 39)

Boulwarism   Named after a General Electric vice president; occurs when management makes its best offer at the outset of bargaining and firmly adheres to the offer throughout the bargaining sessions. The NLRB has ruled that this is not good-faith bargaining and is, therefore, illegal. (p. 426)

Bowen v. United States Postal Service (1983)   Supreme Court decision that established that an employee may be entitled to recover damages from both the union and the employer in cases where the employer has violated the labor agreement and the union has breached its duty of fair representation. (p. 457)

Burnout   Occurs when work is no longer meaningful to a person; can result from stress or a variety of other work-related or personal factors. (p. 481)

Business game   Method of classroom training that simulates an organization and its environment and requires participants to make operating decisions based on the situation. (p. 233)

Business necessity   Condition that comes into play when an employer has a job criterion that is neutral but excludes members of the sex at a higher rate than members of the opposite sex. The focus in business necessity is on the validity of stated job qualifications and their relationship to the work performed. (p. 61)

Cafeteria plans of benefits   Employees have the opportunity to choose, from among a wide range of alternatives, how their benefits will be distributed. (p. 372)

Campus recruiting   The recruitment activities of employees on college and university campuses. (p. 141)

Captive-audience doctrine   Management's right to speak against a union on company time to employees and to require employees to attend the meeting. (p. 422)

Career pathing   A sequence of developmental activities involving informal and formal education, training, and job experiences that help make an individual capable of holding a more advanced job in the future. (p. 280)

Career plan   The analysis of an individual's situation, identification of career objectives, and development of the means for realizing these objectives. (p. 276)

Career plateau   The point in an individual's career where the likelihood of an additional promotion is very low. (p. 284)

Cascade approach   Objective-setting process designed to involve all levels of management in the organizational planning process. (p. 115)

Case study   Method of classroom training in which the student analyzes real or hypothetical situations and suggests not only what to do but also how to do it. (p. 232)

Central tendency   Tendency of a manager to rate all or most employees as having the same basic level of performance. (p. 260)

Certification bar   Condition occurring when the NLRB will not permit another election in the bargaining unit within 12 months of a union's certification. (p. 424)

Checklist   Method of performance appraisal in which the rater answers with a yes or no a series of questions about the behavior of the individual being rated. (p. 255)

Checkoff   Arrangement between an employer and a union under which the employer agrees to withhold union dues, initiation fees, and assessments from the employees' paychecks and submit this money to the union. (p. 432)

Civil Service Reform Act of 1978   Legislation enacted in 1978, regulating labor-management relations for federal government employees. (pp. 259, 407)

Classroom training   The most familiar training method; useful for quickly imparting information to large groups with little or no knowledge of the subject. (p. 211)

Coaching   Method of management development conducted on the job, that involves experienced managers advising and guiding trainees in solving managerial problems. (p. 230)

Collective bargaining   Process that involves the negotiation, drafting, administration, and interpretation of a written agreement between an employer and a union for a specific period of time. (p. 420)

Commission plan   Incentive plan that rewards employees, at least in part, based on their sales volume. (p. 346)

Commitment manpower planning (CMP)   A new and systematic approach to human resource planning designed to get managers and their subordinates thinking about and involved in human resource planning. (p. 124)

Commonwealth v. Hunt   Landmark court decision in 1842 that declared unions were not illegal per se. (p. 399)

Communication   Transfer of information that is meaningful to those involved. (p. 498)

Community of interest   Concept by which the NLRB makes a bargaining unit decision, based on areas of worker commonality. (p. 422)

Company orientation   General orientation that presents topics of relevance and interest to all employees. (p. 201)

Comparable worth theory   The idea that every job has a worth to the employer and society that can be measured and assigned a value. (p. 63)

Compensable factors   Characteristics of jobs that are deemed so important by the organization to the extent that it is willing to pay for them. (p. 323)

Compensation   All the extrinsic rewards that employees receive in exchange for their work; composed of the base wage or salary, any incentives or bonuses, and any benefits. (p. 304)

Concentration   Practice of having more minorities or women in a job category than would reasonably be expected when compared to their presence in the relevant labor market. (p. 57)

Concurrent validity   Validity established by identifying a criterion predictor, administering it to an organization's current employees, and correlating the test data with the current employees' performance. (p. 170)

Consent elections   Union elections in which the parties have agreed on the appropriate bargaining unit. (p. 422)

Conspiracy doctrine   Notion that courts can punish a union if they deem that the means used or the ends sought by the union are illegal. (p. 399)

Construct validity   The extent to which a selection criterion measures the degree to which job candidates have identifiable characteristics determined to be relevant to successful job performance. (p. 172)

Content validity   The extent to which the content of a selection procedure or instrument is representative of important aspects of job performance. (p. 172)

Contract bar doctrine   Under this, the NLRB does not normally permit an election in the bargaining unit covered by a contract until the contract expires, up to a maximum of three years. (p. 424)

Conventional interest arbitration   Form of arbitration in which the arbitrator listens to argument from both parties and makes a binding decision, which can be identical to the position of either party or different from the positions of both parties. (p. 429)

Coordinated bargaining   A form of bargaining where several unions bargain jointly with a single employer. (p. 428)

Corrective (progressive) discipline   The normal sequence of actions taken by management in disciplining an employee: oral warning, written warning, suspension, and then discharge. (p. 449)

Cost-of-living adjustments (COLA)   Contract provision that ties wage increases to rises in the Bureau of Labor Statistics consumer price index. (p. 432)

Craft unions   Unions having only skilled workers as members. Most craft unions have members from several related trades (e.g., Bricklayers', Masons', and Plasterers' International Union). (p. 408)

Criteria of job success   Ways of specifying how successful performance of the job is to be measured. (p. 168)

Criterion predictors   Factors such as education, previous work experience, and scores on company-administered tests that are used to predict successful performance of a job. (p. 168)

Critical-incident appraisal   Method of performance appraisal in which the rater keeps a written record of incidents that illustrate both positive and negative behavior of the employee; the rater then uses these incidents as a basis for evaluating the employee's performance. (p. 254)

Cross training   *See* Job rotation.

Danbury Hatters case   Landmark case of 1908 in which the Supreme Court decided that the Sherman Anti-Trust Act applied to all unions. (p. 401)

Data   Raw material from which information is developed; composed of facts that describe people, places, things, or events and that have not been interpreted. (p. 502)

Deadwood   Individuals in an organization whose present performance has fallen to an unsatisfactory level and who have little potential for advancement. (p. 285)

Defined benefit plan   Pension plan under which an employer pledges to provide a benefit determined by a definite formula at the employee's retirement date. (p. 379)

Defined contribution plan   Pension plan that calls for a fixed or known annual contribution instead of a known benefit. (p. 379)

Degree statements   Written statements used as a part of the point method of job evaluation to further break down job subfactors. (p. 324)

Delphi technique Judgmental method of forecasting that uses a panel of experts to make initially independent estimates of future demand. An intermediary then presents each expert's forecast and assumptions to the other members of the panel. Each expert is then allowed to revise his or her forecast as desired. This process continues until some consensus or composite emerges. (p. 118)

Departmental and job orientation Specific orientation that describes topics unique to the new employee's specific department and job. (p. 202)

Differential piece rate plan Piece rate plan devised by Frederic W. Taylor that pays one rate for all acceptable pieces produced up to some standard and then a higher rate for all pieces produced if the output exceeds the standard. (p. 345)

Disability insurance Designed to protect the employee who experiences a long-term or permanent disability. (p. 385)

Disabling injuries Work-related injuries that cause an employee to miss one or more days of work. (p. 476)

Discipline Action taken against an employee when the employee has violated an organizational rule or when the employee's performance has deteriorated to the point where corrective action is needed. (p. 444)

Disparate impact doctrine When the plaintiff shows that an employment practice disproportionately excludes groups protected by Title VII, the burden of proof shifts to the defendant to prove that the standard reasonably relates to job performance. (p. 36)

Downward communication Transmitting of information from higher to lower levels of the organization. (p. 500)

Due process Right of an employee to be dealt with fairly and justly during the investigation of an alleged offense and the administration of any subsequent disciplinary action. (p. 455)

Duplex Printing Co.* v. *Deering Case in which the Supreme Court ruled that unions were not exempt from the control of the Sherman Anti-Trust Act. (p. 401)

Duties One or more tasks performed in carrying out a job responsibility. (p. 83)

Duty of fair representation Under the National Labor Relations Act of 1935, the statutory duty of a union to fairly represent all employees in the bargaining unit, whether or not they are union members. (p. 455)

Element An aggregation of two or more micromotions; usually thought of as a complete entity, such as picking up or transporting an object. (p. 82)

Employee assistance programs (EAPs) Company-sponsored programs designed to help employees with personal problems such as alcohol and drug abuse, depression, anxiety, domestic trauma, financial problems, and other psychiatric/medical problems. (p. 486)

Employee benefits (fringe benefits) Rewards that an organization provides to employees for being members of the organization; usually not related to employee performance. (p. 366)

Employee Retirement Income Security Act (ERISA) Federal law passed in 1974, designed to give employees increased security for their retirement and pension plans and to ensure the fair treatment of employees under pension plans. (p. 381)

Employee stock ownership plan (ESOP)   Form of stock option plan in which an organization provides for purchase of its stock by employees at a set price for a set time period based on the employee's length of service and salary and the profits of the organization. (p. 355)

Employer Information Report (Standard Form 100)   Form that all employers with 100 or more employees are required to file with EEOC; requires a breakdown of the employer's work force in specified job categories by race, sex, and national origin. (p. 54)

Employment at will   Term used to describe the situation in which an employer hires employees to work for an indefinite period of time and the employees do not have a contract limiting the circumstances under which they can be discharged. Under these conditions, the employer can terminate the employee at any time for any reason or for no reason at all. (p. 451)

Employment parity   Situation in which the proportion of minorities and women employed by an organization equals the proportion in the organization's relevant labor market. (p. 57)

Enterprise Wheel   Supreme Court ruling in 1960 that as long as an arbitrator's decision involves the interpretation of a contract, the courts should not overrule the arbitrator merely because their interpretation of the contract was different from that of the arbitrator. (p. 458)

Equal employment opportunity   Refers to the right of all persons to work and to advance on the basis of merit, ability, and potential. (p. 26)

Equal Employment Opportunity Commission (EEOC)   Federal agency created under the Civil Rights Act of 1964 to administer Title VII of the act and to ensure equal employment opportunity; its powers were expanded in 1979. (p. 35)

ERISA   *See* Employment Retirement Income Security Act

ESOP   *See* Employee stock option plan

Essay appraisal   Method of performance appraisal in which the rater prepares a written statement describing an individual's strengths, weaknesses, and past performance. (p. 253)

Executive orders   Orders issued by the President of the United States for managing and operating federal government agencies. (pp. 32, 406)

External equity   Addresses the issue of what employees in an organization are being paid compared to employees in other organizations performing similar jobs. (p. 309)

Extrinsic rewards   Rewards that are controlled and distributed directly by the organization and are of a tangible nature. (p. 298)

Factor comparison method   Job evaluation technique that uses a monetary scale for evaluating jobs on a factor-by-factor basis. (p. 326)

Federal Labor Relations Authority (FLRA)   Three-member panel created by the Civil Service Reform Act whose purpose is to administer the act. (p. 407)

Federal Mediation and Conciliation Service (FMCS)   Independent agency within the federal government that, as one of its responsibilities, provides mediators to assist in resolving contract negotiation impasses. (p. 429)

Federal Register   Periodical found in many public and college libraries that regularly publishes all OSHA standards and amendments. (p. 471)

Federal Services Impasses Panel (FSIP)   Entity within the FLRC whose function is to provide assistance in resolving negotiation impasses within the federal sector. (p. 407)

Final-offer interest arbitration   Form of arbitration in which the arbitrator is restricted to selecting the final offer of one of the parties. (p. 429)

Flexible benefit plan   Same as cafeteria plan of benefits. (p. 372)

Floating holiday   Holiday that may be observed at the discretion of the employee or the employer. (p. 386)

Forced-choice rating   Method of performance appraisal that requires the rater to rank a set of statements describing how an employee carries out the duties and responsibilities of the job. (p. 258)

Frequency rate   Ratio that indicates the frequency with which disabling injuries occur. (p. 476)

Gain sharing   Programs also known as profit sharing, performance sharing, or productivity incentives; generally refer to incentive plans that involve employees in a common effort to achieve a company's productivity objectives. Based on the concept that the resulting incremental economic gains are shared among employees and the company. (p. 354)

Garnishment   A legal procedure by which an employer is empowered to withhold wages for payment of an employee's debt to a creditor. (p. 306)

General-duty clause   Clause in the Occupational Safety and Health Act covering those situations not addressed by specific standards; in essence, it requires employers to comply with the intent of the act. (p. 470)

Gissel bargaining orders   Situations under which the NLRB orders management to bargain with the union; named after a landmark Supreme Court decision, *NLRB* v. *Gissel Packing Company*. (p. 424)

Good-faith bargaining   Sincere intention of both parties to negotiate differences and reach a mutually acceptable agreement. (p. 426)

Graphic rating scale   Method of performance appraisal that requires the rater to indicate on a scale where the employee rates on factors such as quantity of work, dependability, job knowledge, and cooperativeness. (p. 254)

Graphology (handwriting analysis)   Use of a trained analyst to examine a person's handwriting to assess the person's personality, emotional problems, and honesty. (p. 179)

Grievance arbitration   Arbitration that attempts to settle unresolved disputes arising during the term of the collective bargaining agreement that involve questions of its interpretation or application. (p. 458)

Grievance procedures   Systematic means of resolving disagreements over the collective bargaining agreement and providing assurance that the terms and conditions agreed to in negotiations are properly implemented. (p. 452)

Group incentives   Incentives based on group rather than individual performance. (p. 353)

Group interviews   Interview method in which several applicants are questioned together. (p. 180)

Halo effect   Occurs when managers allow a single prominent characteristic of an employee to influence their judgment on several items of a performance appraisal. (pp. 181, 260)

Halsey premium plan   Incentive plan under which the employee is paid a guaranteed hourly wage plus a premium for any time saved by producing a given quantity in less than standard time. (p. 346)

Handicapped   Person who has a physical or mental impairment that substantially limits one or more of such person's major life activities, has a record of such impairments, or is regarded as having such an impairment.

Hazard Communication Standard   Standard issued by OSHA in the early 1980s that established uniform requirements to ensure that the hazards of all chemicals imported into, produced, or used in the workplace are evaluated and that the results of these evaluations are transmitted to affected employers and exposed employees. (p. 479)

Health maintenance organization (HMO)   Health service organization that contracts with companies to provide certain basic medical services around the clock, seven days a week, for a fixed cost. (p. 384)

Hitchman Coal & Coke Co.* v. *Mitchell   Supreme Court case of 1917 that upheld the legality of yellow-dog contracts. (p. 400)

Horizontal (lateral) communication   Communication across organizational units that are at the same approximate level in the organizational hierarchy. (p. 500)

Hot-stove rule   Set of guidelines used in administering discipline that calls for quick, consistent, and impersonal action preceded by a warning. (p. 447)

HRIS   *See* Human resource information system

Human resource functions   Tasks and duties that human resource managers perform (e.g., determining the organization's human resource needs; recruiting, selecting, developing, counseling, and rewarding employees; acting as liaison with unions and government organizations; and handling other matters of employee well-being). (p. 6)

Human resource information system (HRIS)   Refers to prepackaged computerized human resource systems or to internally developed comprehensive human resource management information systems. (p. 503)

Human resource management   Activities designed to provide for and coordinate the human resources of an organization. (p. 6)

Human resource planning (HRP)   Process by which the human resource needs of an organization are determined and the organization ensures that it has the right number of qualified people in the right jobs at the right time. (p. 112)

Human resource specialist   Person specially trained in one or more areas of human resource management (e.g., labor relations specialist, wage and salary specialist). (p. 8)

Immigration Reform and Control Act   1986 act making it illegal for a person or other entity to hire, recruit, or refer for U.S. employment anyone known to be an unauthorized alien. (p. 32)

In-basket technique   Method of classroom training in which the trainee is required to simulate the handling of a specific manager's mail and telephone calls and to react accordingly. (p. 233)

Incentive pay plans   Pay plans designed to relate pay directly to performance or productivity, often used in conjunction with a base wage/salary system. (p. 344)

Incentive stock option (ISO)   Form of qualified stock option plan made feasible by the Economic Recovery Tax Act of 1981. (p. 351)

Incentives   Rewards offered in addition to the base wage or salary and usually directly related to performance. (p. 304)

Incident method   Form of case study in which students are initially given the general outline of a situation and receive additional information from the instructor only as they request it. (p. 232)

Individual equity   Addresses the issue of rewarding individual contributions; is very closely related to the pay-for-performance question. (p. 309)

Individual retirement accounts (IRAs)   Individual pension plan for employees not covered by private pension plans. (p. 383)

Industrial unions   Unions having as members both skilled and unskilled workers in a particular industry or group of industries. (p. 408)

Information   Data that has been interpreted and that meets a need of one or more managers. (p. 502)

Informational picketing   Patrolling at or near an employer's facility by individuals carrying signs to publicize the fact that the union is requesting an election to become the bargaining agent for the employees of the organization. (p. 423)

Injunction   Court order to stop an action that could result in irreparable damage to property when the situation is such that no other adequate remedy is available to protect the interests of the injunction-seeking party. (p. 399)

Input function   Provides the capabilities needed to get human resource information into the HRIS. (p. 505)

Interaction management   *See* Behavior modeling

Interest tests   Tests designed to determine how a person's interests compare with the interests of successful people in a specific job.

Internal equity   Addresses the issue of what an employee is being paid for doing a job compared to what other employees in the same organization are being paid to do their jobs. (p. 309)

Interpersonal communication   Communication between individuals. (p. 499)

Intrinsic rewards   Rewards internal to the individual and normally derived from involvement in certain activities or tasks. (p. 298)

Job   Group of positions that are identical with respect to their major or significant tasks and responsibilities and sufficiently alike to justify their being covered by a single analysis. There may be one or many persons employed in the same job. (p. 83)

Job advertising   The placement of help-wanted advertisements in daily newspapers, in trade and professional publications, or on radio and television. (p. 139)

Job analysis   Process of determining and reporting pertinent information relating to the nature of a specific job. (p. 89)

Job bidding   Requirement that employees bid for a job based on seniority, experience, or other specific qualifications. *See also* Job posting.

Job classification method   Job evaluation method that determines the relative worth of a job by comparing it to a predetermined scale of classes or grades of jobs. (p. 328)

Job depth   Freedom of jobholders to plan and organize their own work, work at their own pace, and move around and communicate. (p. 86)

Job description   Written synopsis of the nature and requirements of a job. (p. 91)

Job design   Defines the specific work activities of an individual or group of individuals. (p. 82)

Job dimension or job task   Duties and responsibilities that make up a specific job. (p. 256)

Job task   *See* Job dimension

Job enlargement   Involves giving a jobholder more tasks of a similar nature to perform. (p. 86)

Job enrichment   Involves upgrading the job by increasing both job scope and job depth. (p. 87)

Job evaluation   A systematic determination of the value of each job in relation to other jobs in the organization. (p. 321)

Job knowledge tests   Tests used to measure the job-related knowledge of an applicant. (p. 177)

Job posting   Method of making employees aware of job vacancies by posting a notice in central locations throughout an organization and giving a specified period to apply for the job.

Job ranking method   Job evaluation method that ranks jobs in order of their difficulty from simplest to most complex. (p. 329)

Job rotation or cross training   Training that requires an individual to learn several different jobs in a work unit or department and perform each for a specified time period. (p. 209)

Job satisfaction   Individual's general attitude about the job. (p. 301)

Job scope   Number and variety of different tasks performed by the jobholder.

Job specification   Description of the qualifications that a person holding a job must possess to perform the job successfully.

Job task   *See* Job dimension

Just cause   Requires that management initially bear the burden of proof of wrongdoing in discipline cases and that the severity of the punishment must coincide with the seriousness of the offense. (p. 452)

Keogh plan   Pension plan for self-employed persons. (p. 383)

Labor Relations Act (Taft-Harley Act)   Legislation enacted in 1947 that placed the federal government in a watchdog position to ensure that union-management relations are conducted fairly by both parties. (p. 403)

Labor-Management Reporting and Disclosure Act (LMRDA) (Landrum-Griffin Act)   Legislation enacted in 1959, regulating labor unions and requiring disclosure of certain union financial information to the government. (p. 405)

Landrum-Griffin Act of 1959   Labor-Management Reporting and Disclosure Act, regulating labor unions and requiring disclosure of union financial information to the government.

Learners   Individuals in an organization who have a high potential for advancement but who are currently performing below standard. (p. 284)

Leniency   Occurs in performance appraisals when a manager's ratings are grouped at the positive end instead of being spread throughout the performance scale. (p. 260)

Lockout   Refusal of an employer to let its employees work. (p. 434)

Maintenance of membership   Contract provision that does not require an employee to join the union, but employees who do join the union are required to remain members for a stipulated time period. (p. 432)

Management by objectives   Management by objectives consists of establishing clear and precisely defined statements of objectives for the work to be done by an employee; establishing an action plan indicating how these objectives are to be achieved; allowing the employee to implement this action plan, measuring objective achievement; taking corrective action when necessary; and establishing new objectives for the future. (p. 252)

Management development process   Process concerned with developing the experience, attitudes, and skills necessary to become or remain an effective manager. (p. 224)

Management inventory   Specialized, expanded form of skills inventory for an organization's current management team; in addition to basic types of information, it usually includes a brief assessment of past performance and potential for advancement. (p. 225)

Management succession plan   Chart or schedule that shows potential successors for each management position within an organization. (p. 225)

Managerial estimates   Judgmental method of forecasting that calls on managers to make estimates of future staffing needs.

Marshall v. Barlow's, Inc.   1978 Supreme Court decision that ruled that employers are not required to admit OSHA inspectors onto their premises without a search warrant; also ruled that probable cause needed to obtain the search warrant would be much less than that required in a criminal matter. (p. 472)

Mediation   Process where both parties invite a neutral third party (called a mediator) to help resolve contract impasses. The mediator, unlike an arbitrator, has no authority to impose a solution on the parties. (p. 429)

Merit pay increase   Reward based on performance but also perpetuated year after year. (p. 347)

Micromotion   Simplest unit of work; involves very elementary movements such as reaching, grasping, positioning, or releasing an object.

National Labor Relations Act/Wagner Act   Prolabor act of 1935 that gave workers the right to organize, obligated the management of organizations to bargain in good faith with unions, defined illegal management practices relating to unions, and created the National Labor Relations Board (NLRB) to administer the act. (p. 402)

National Labor Relations Board (NLRB)   Five-member panel created by the National Labor Relations Act and appointed by the President of the United States with the advice and consent of the Senate and with the authority to administer the Wagner Act. (p. 404)

Needs assessment   A systematic analysis of the specific training activities required by an organization to achieve its objectives. (p. 206)

Needs assessment   A systematic analysis of the specific management development activities required by an organization to achieve its objectives. (p. 228)

NLRB* v. *Weingarten   Supreme Court decision in 1975 holding that an employee has the right to refuse to submit to a disciplinary interview without union representation. (p. 447)

Nonqualified stock options   Similar to qualified options, except that they are not subject to as favorable a tax rate (but neither are they subject to the same restrictions). (p. 351)

Norris-La Guardia Act of 1932   Prolabor act that eliminated the use of yellow-dog contracts and severely restricted the use of injunctions. (p. 402)

Occupation   Grouping of jobs or job classes that involve similar skill, effort, and responsibility within a number of different organizations.

Occupational parity   Situation in which the proportion of minorities and women employed in various occupations within an organization is equal to their proportion in the organization's relevant labor market.

Occupational Safety and Health Act (OSHA)   Federal law passed in 1970 to ensure safe and healthful working conditions for every working person. (p. 470)

Office of Federal Contract Compliance Programs (OFCCP)   Office within the U.S. Department of Labor that is responsible for ensuring equal employment opportunity by federal contractors and subcontractors.

Office of the General Counsel   Separate and independent office created by the Taft-Hartley Act to investigate unfair labor practice charges and present those charges with merit to the NLRB. (p. 404)

On-the-job training   Training showing the employee how to perform the job and allowing him or her to do it under the trainer's supervision. (p. 208)

Operating manager   Person who manages people directly involved with the production of an organization's products or services (e.g., a production manager in a manufacturing plant or a loan manager in a bank).

Organizational communication   Communication occurring within the formal organizational structure. (p. 499)

Organizational development   Organizationwide, planned effort managed from the top, with a goal of increasing organizational performance through planned interventions and training experiences. (p. 235)

Organizational equity   Addresses the issue of how profits are divided up within the organization. (p. 309)

Organizational grapevine   Informal channels of communication resulting from casual contacts between friends or acquaintances in various organizational units. (p. 500)

Organizational inducements   Positive features and benefits offered by an organization to attract job applicants.

Organizational morale   Refers to an individual's feeling of being accepted by and belonging to a group of employees through common goals, confidence in the desirability of these goals, and progress toward these goals. (p. 301)

Organizational objectives   Statements of expected results that are designed to give an organization and its members direction and purpose.

Organizational replacement chart   Chart that shows both incumbents and potential replacements for given positions within an organization.

Organizational reward system   Organizational system concerned with the selection of the types of rewards to be used by the organization. (p. 298)

Organizational rewards   Rewards that result from employment with the organization; all types of rewards, both intrinsic and extrinsic. (p. 298)

Organizational vitality index (OVI)   Index that results from ratio analysis; the index reflects the organization's human resource vitality as measured by the presence of promotable personnel and existing backups.

Organizationwide incentives   Incentives that reward all members of the organization, based on the performance of the entire organization. (p. 354)

Organizing   Process that involves the grouping of activities necessary to attain common objectives and the assignment of each grouping to a manager who has the authority necessary to supervise the people performing the activities.

Orientation   The introduction of new employees to the organization, work unit, and job. (p. 200)

Orientation kit   A packet of written information given to a new employee to supplement the verbal orientation program. (p. 203)

OSHA Form 101 (Supplementary Record of Occupational Injuries and Illness)   Form that requires detailed information about each occupational injury or illness. Form 101 must be completed within six working days from the time the employer learns of an occupational injury or illness. (p. 473)

OSHA Form 200 (Log and Summary of Occupational Injuries and Illness)   Form for recording all occupational injuries and illnesses. Each occurrence must be recorded on this form within six working days from the time the employer learns of the accident or illness. (p. 473)

Outplacement   Benefit provided by an employer to help an employee leave the organization and get a job someplace else. (p. 286)

Parallel forms   A method of showing a test's reliability; involves giving two separate but similar forms of the test at the same time.

Pay   Refers only to the actual dollars that employees receive in exchange for their work. (p. 304)

Pay grades   Classes or grades of jobs that for pay purposes are grouped on the basis of their worth to an organization. (p. 333)

Pay range   A range of permissible pay, with a minimum and a maximum, that is assigned to a given pay grade. (p. 334)

Performance   Degree of accomplishment of the tasks that make up an individual's job. (p. 250)

Performance appraisal   Process of determining and communicating to an employee how he or she is performing on the job, and ideally, establishing a plan of improvement. (p. 248)

Performance share plans   Incentive plans for top managers that base bonuses on the long-term performance for the organization (usually three to five years). (p. 350)

Phantom stock plan   Special type of stock option plan that protects the holder if the value of the stock being held decreases; does not require the option holder to put up any money. (p. 353)

***Philadelphia Cordwainers* (shoemakers) case of 1806**   Case in which the jury ruled that combinations of workers to raise their wages constituted a conspiracy in restraint of trade. (p. 399)

Point method   Job evaluation method in which a quantitative point scale is used to evaluate jobs on a factor-by-factor basis. (p. 322)

Polygraph   Commonly known as a lie detector. A machine that records fluctuations in a person's blood pressure, respiration, and perspiration on a moving roll of graph paper in response to questions asked of the person.

Position   Collection of tasks and responsibilities constituting the total work assignment of a single employee. There are as many positions as there are employees in the organization.

Predictive validity   Validity that is established by identifying a criterion predictor such as a test, administering the test to all job applicants, hiring people without regard to their test scores, and at a later date correlating the test scores with the performance of these people on the job.

Preferred provider organizations (PPOs)   Formed by contracting with a group of doctors and hospitals to provide services at a discount or attractive price. Such providers are designated as "preferred" providers of care. (p. 385)

Prima facie.   Legal term that describes evidence sufficient in law to raise a presumption of fact or establish the fact in question unless rebutted. (p. 450)

Private pension plans   Employee benefit that provides a source of income to people who have retired; funded either entirely by the organization or jointly by the organization and employee during employment. (p. 379)

Proficiency tests   Tests that measure how well a job applicant can do a sample of the work that is to be performed.

Profit-sharing plans   *See* Gain sharing

Programmed instruction   Method of classroom training in which material is presented in text form or on computer video displays; students are required to answer correctly questions about the subject presented, before progressing to more advanced material. (p. 233)

Psychological tests   Tests that attempt to measure personality characteristics.

Psychomotor tests   Tests that measure a person's strength, dexterity, and coordination.

Qualified stock options   Stock options approved by the Internal Revenue Service for favorable tax treatment. (p. 350)

Railway Labor Act   Enacted in 1926, this act set up the administrative machinery for handling labor relations within the railroad industry; was the first important piece of prolabor legislation. (p. 402)

Ranking methods   Methods of performance appraisal in which the performance of an individual is ranked relative to the performance of others. (p. 258)

Ratio analysis   Tool used in human resource planning to measure the organization's human resource vitality as indicated by the presence of promotable personnel and existing backups.

Realistic job previews   Provide complete job information, both positive and negative, to the job applicant.

Recency   Tendency of a manager to evaluate employees on work performed most recently—one or two months prior to evaluation (p. 260)

Recognition bar   Condition occurring when the NLRB prohibits an election for up to 12 months after an employer voluntarily recognizes a union. (p. 424)

Recruitment   Process of seeking and attracting a pool of people from which qualified candidates for job vacancies can be chosen. (pp. 90, 136)

Relevant labor market   Generally refers to the geographical area in which a company recruits its employees.

Reliability   Refers to the reproducibility of results with a criterion predictor.

Reports library   A type of computer software program that stores the program and historical data necessary to generate reports that are periodically requested. (p. 508)

Responsibilities   Obligations to perform certain tasks and assume certain duties.

Restricted stock plan   Plan under which a company gives shares of stock to participating managers, subject to certain restrictions; major restriction of most plans is that shares are subject to forfeiture until "earned out" over a stipulated period of continued employment. (p. 353)

Retirement Equity Act   Act passed in 1984 that liberalized eligibility requirements, vesting provisions, maternity/paternity leaves, and spouse survivor benefits of retirement plans. (p. 382)

Reverse discrimination   Condition under which there is alleged preferential treatment of one group (minority or women) over another group, rather than equal opportunity.

Right-to-sue letter   Statutory notice by EEOC to the charging party if EEOC does not decide to file a lawsuit on behalf of the charging party.

Right-to-work laws   Legislation enacted by individual states under the authority of Section 14(b) of the Taft-Hartley Act that can forbid various types of union security arrangements, including compulsory union membership. (p. 405)

Rowan plan   Incentive plan under which an employee is paid a guaranteed hourly wage plus a premium based directly on any time saved. (p. 346)

Scanlon plan   Organizationwide incentive plan that provides employees with a bonus based on tangible savings in labor costs. (p. 354)

Selection   Process of choosing from those available the individuals who are most likely to perform successfully in a job.

Seniority   Refers to an employee's relative length of service with an employer. (p. 433)

Sensitivity training   Method of training normally used in organization development and designed to make the participants more aware of themselves and their impact on others. (p. 236)

Severity rate   Ratio that indicates the length of time that injured employees are out of work. (p. 476)

Sexual harassment   Unwelcome sexual conduct that has the purpose or effect of unreasonably interfering with an individual's work performance or creating an intimidating, hostile, or offensive work environment.

Skills inventory   Consolidated list of biographical and other information on all employees in an organization.

Social security   Federally administered insurance system designed to provide funds upon retirement or disability or both and to provide hospital and medical reimbursement to people who have reached retirement age. (p. 375)

Solid citizens   Individuals in an organization whose present performance is satisfactory but whose chance for future advancement is small. (p. 285)

Split halves   A method of showing a test's reliability; involves dividing the test into halves to determine whether performance is similar in both sections.

Stars   Individuals in an organization who are presently doing outstanding work and have a high potential for continued advancement. (p. 285)

Stock appreciation rights (SARs)   Type of nonqualified stock option in which an executive has the right to relinquish a stock option and receive from the company an amount equal to the appreciation in the stock price from the date the option was granted. Under a SAR, the option holder does not have to put up any money, as would be required in a normal stock option plan. (p. 352)

Stock-for-stock swap   This procedure allows options to be exercised with shares of previously purchased company stock in lieu of cash; postpones the taxation of any gain on stock already owned. (p. 352)

Stress interview   Interview method that puts the applicant under pressure, to determine whether he or she is highly emotional.

Strike   Collective refusal of employees to work. (p. 434)

Structured interview   An interview conducted using a predetermined outline.

Subfactor   A detailed breakdown of a single compensable factor of a job. (p. 324)

Succession planning   Technique that identifies specific people to fill future openings in key positions throughout the organization.

Suggestion systems   Systems that usually offer cash incentives for employee suggestions that result in either increased profits or reduced costs. (p. 347)

Systemic discrimination   Large differences in either occupational or employment parity.

Taft-Hartley Act of 1947   Labor-Management Relations Act, which placed the federal government in a watchdog position to ensure that union-management relations are conducted fairly by both parties.

Task Consisting of one or more elements, one of the distinct activities that constitute logical and necessary steps in the performance of work by an employee. A task is performed whenever human effort, physical or mental, is exerted for a specific purpose.

Temporary help People working for employment agencies who are subcontracted out to businesses at an hourly rate, for a period of time specified by the businesses.

Test-retest One method of showing a test's reliability; involves testing a group and giving the same group the same test at a later time.

Toxic Substance Control Act Federal law passed in 1976 requiring the pretesting for safety of new chemicals marketed. (p. 478)

Training A learning process that involves the acquisition of skills, concepts, rules, or attitudes to increase employee performance. (p. 206)

Turnaround documents Simple reports that show the current data values of an HRIS and provide a place to indicate any changes. (p. 508)

Understudy assignments Method of on-the-job training in which one individual, designated as the heir to a job, learns the job from the present jobholder. (p. 230)

Underutilization The practice of having fewer minorities or women in a particular job category than their corresponding numbers in the relevant labor market.

Unemployment compensation Form of insurance designed to provide funds to employees who have lost their jobs and are seeking other jobs. (p. 377)

Union shop Provision in a contract that requires all employees in a bargaining unit to join the union and retain membership as a condition of employment; most right-to-work laws outlaw the union shop. (p. 432)

Unstructured interview An interview conducted without a predetermined checklist of questions.

Upward communication Communication originating at the lower levels of an organization and flowing toward the top. (p. 500)

Utilization evaluation Part of the affirmative action plan that analyzes minority group representation in all job categories; past and present hiring practices; and upgrades, promotions, and transfers.

Vaca* v. *Sipes Supreme Court decision in 1967 that held that a union is not obligated to take all grievances to arbitration but rather has the authority to decide whether or not the grievance has merit. If such a decision is made fairly and nonarbitrarily, the union has not breached its duty of fair representation. (p. 455)

Validity How well a given criterion actually predicts successful performance on the job.

Vesting Rights of individuals to receive the money paid into a pension or retirement fund on their behalf by their employer, if they should leave the organization prior to retirement. (p. 380)

Vocational Rehabilitation Act Legislation enacted in 1973 that prohibited discrimination against otherwise qualified handicapped individuals solely on the basis of their disability; applies only in certain situations involving federal contracts, recipients of federal assistance, or federal agencies. (p. 485)

Wage and salary curves   Graphical depiction of the relationships between the relative worth of jobs and their wage rates. (p. 333)

Wage and salary survey   Survey of selected organizations within a geographical area or industry designed to provide a comparison of reliable information on policies, practices, and methods of payment. (p. 330)

Wagner Act of 1935   National Labor Relations Act; prolabor act that gave workers the right to organize, obligated the management of organizations to bargain in good faith with unions, defined illegal management practices relating to unions, and created the National Labor Relations Board (NLRB) to administer the act.

Weighted application form   Assigns different weights or values to different questions on an application form.

Wellness programs   Company-implemented programs designed to prevent illness and enhance employee wellness. (p. 488)

Wilderness training   A method of training in which teams of managers perform a series of structured mental and physical challenges designed to approximate management challenges on the job. (p. 236)

Work standards approach   Method of performance appraisal that involves setting a standard or expected level of output and then comparing each employee's level to the standard. (p. 253)

Workers' compensation   Form of insurance that protects employees from loss of income and extra expenses associated with job-related injuries or illness. (p. 378)

Yellow-dog contract   Term coined by unions to describe an agreement between a worker and employer stipulating that, as a condition of employment, the worker would not join a labor union. Yellow-dog contracts were made illegal by the Norris-La Guardia Act of 1932. (p. 400)

▽ Name Index

A

Abrams, Nancy, 440
Adams, Graham, Jr., 399
Adkins, John I., Jr., 483, 494
Al-Malik, Sulaiman M., 244
Anderson, Kirk J., 498
Anderson, M. C., 494
Applebaum, Seven H., 494
Applewhite, Phillip B., 315
Aquilano, Nicholas J., 85, 103
Archer, Frank W., 291
Arey, William, 347
Arouca, Dennis A., 416
Arreglado, E., 348, 350, 351, 362
Atchison, Thomas J., 323

B

Baker, Carolyn A., 393
Bakke, Allan, 38–39
Banik, Joseph A., 515
Barlow, Wayne E., 491
Barrett, Gerard V., 269
Bartol, Kathryn M., 316
Batten, Julie, 482
Beatty, R. W., 257
Belcher, D. W., 323
Benge, Eugene, 326
Bernstein, Aaron, 322
Biggs, W. D., 393
Bittel, L. R., 220
Boden, William D., 374
Bousum, Tim C., 362
Brantley, Edward, 441
Braum, Kurt, 420
Brennan, C. W., 362, 363
Brennan, E. James, 315
Brickner, Mary, 241
Brunette, Donna, 362
Buford, James A., 269
Burack, E. H., 280, 292
Burkhalter, Bettye B., 269
Burlingarie, Hal, 12
Byars, Lloyd, L., 458

C

Camden, T. M., 292
Campbell, Rebecca A., 423
Cargemi, J. P., 370
Carkhuff, R. R., 292
Carlson, D. G., 381
Carpenter, Earl, 456
Castagnera, James O., 470
Castro, Janice, 494
Catalanello, Ralph F., 114, 133
Cavanagh, Michael E., 494
Chaison, Gary N., 441
Chapman, J. Brad, 315
Chase, Richard B., 85, 103
Chauran, Tom, 371
Chicci, D. L., 125, 133
Claypool, J. C., 370
Cockrum, R. B., 393
Cole, A., Jr., 393
Coleman, Sharon, 123
Collingwood, Harris, 357
Conway, Michael A., 341
Craig, R. L., 220
Cummings, Larry I., 316

D

Davidson, Jeffrey P., 220
Davis, L. E., 103
Deep, Samuel D., 439
Deets, Norman R., 253
DeLapa, Judith A., 91
Dickman, F., 487
Dixon, Nancy M., 220
Dunham, R. B., 393
Dunnette, M. D., 316, 494

E

Edney, F. R., 22
Eisner, Michael D., 352
Elkouri, E., 445
Elkouri, F., 445
Emener, W. G., 487

F

Farish, Phil, 18, 90, 119, 276, 287, 300, 306, 324, 481
Farrell, Christopher, 363
Fasoldt, Gene F., 382
Ference, T. P., 285, 292
Formisano, R. A., 393
Fox, H., 348
Foxman, Loretta D., 103
Franklin, Geralyn McClure, 495
Frazer, James, 22
Freedman, Stuart C., 301
Frierson, James G., 71
Fry, Fred L., 480

G

Gaither, Norman, 88
Galagan, Patricia A., 233
Geis, Arthur, 268
Gilberg, Kenneth, 440
Gilbreth, Lillian, 444
Gold, Allan R., 426
Gompers, Samuel, 416
Goodale, J. G., 362
Gow, Jack F., 23
Grant, Philip G., 104
Green, Percy, 37
Greene, Charles N., 315
Greenlaw, P. S., 393
Greenman, Russell L., 378
Grossman, Paul, 71
Grossman, Morton E., 22, 504, 515

H

Haig, Carol, 214
Hallett, Jeff, 22
Hammonds, Keith, 363
Hardison, Larry G., 65
Harper, Douglas C., 493
Haslinger, John A., 393
Hatch, Diane, 491

Henderson, Richard I., 316, 321, 341, 366
Henneman, H. G., Jr., 104
Hill, A. W., 291
Hills, Frederick S., 315
Hoerr, John, 363
Holland, Phyllis G., 103
Hollman, R., 104
Hooper, John A., 114, 133
Hoover, J. J., 104
Hophe, W. E., 22
Houston, Patrick, 322
Howard, James S., 495
Hultgren, William H., 505
Hultman, Kenneth E., 241

I

Iaffaldano, Michelle T., 304
Isom, R. N., 494
Ivancevich, John M., 316

J

Jacobs, Grover T., 269
Johnson, Eric J., 22, 23
Johnson, Theresa, 49, 441
Johnston, R. A., 103
Jones, Edward, 230
Jones, P. R., 279
Jordan, John D., 494

K

Kagerer, R. L., 393
Kanter, Rosabeth Moss, 273
Kaye, B., 279, 292
Kernan, Mary C., 269
King, Martin Luther, Jr., 52
Kirkpatrick, D. L., 220
Klimoski, Richard, 241
Klock, Homer S., II, 488
Koen, C. M., Jr., 72
Koontz, H., 103
Kozlowski, S. W. J., 269
Kravetz, Dennis, 18
Kurash, Stephen P., 382

L

La Greca, Genivieva, 494
Lange, Steven, 220
Lansing, Rick L., 501
Lawler, Edward E., III, 308, 309, 310, 316
Layton, William G., 22, 23
Lederer, Albert L., 515
Ledgerwood, Donna, 493
Ledvinka, S., 393
Lehr, Richard I., 133

Leibowitz, Z. B., 275, 292
Leigh, David R., 116
Leukart, R. H., 325
Leshner, Martin, 123
Levine, Hermine F., 277
Lincoln, Abraham, 26
Locke, E. A., 316
Lodge, Joseph H., 494
Long, Janet W., 241
Lynch, David, 515

M

Mackey, Craig B., 132, 133
Madigan, Robert M., 315
Magnus, Margaret, 504, 515
Maier, N. R. F., 104
Maital, Shlomo, 234
Markham, Steven E., 315
Markowitz, J., 104
Marshall, Ray, 4
Martin, David C., 316
Mathews, Patricia A., 11
Mathys, N. J., 280, 292
Mayer, William, 487
McAdams, Jerry, 362
McCaffery, R. M., 393
McCormick, Robert A., 431
McGarth, J. E., 494
McGregor, Douglas, 224
McRae, Kenneth B., 281, 292
Meckel, N. T., 292
Middlebrooks, David J., 133
Miller, Ernest C., 133
Miller, Marc, 269
Mils, D. Quinn, 127, 133
Miners, Ian A., 494, 495
Moravec, Milan, 206, 274
Morgan, Kim, 234
Morrison, Malcolm H., 11
Mouser, M. W., 362
Muchinsky, Paul M., 304
Murphy, Betty S., 491
Murray, Patrick L., 114, 133

N

Newell, W. T., 103
Norman, James R., 363
Norris, E., 495
Nykadyn, Nick, 494, 495

O

O'Brien, Joan C., 332, 341
O'Dell, Carla, 362
O'Donnell, C., 103
Olson, Madeline Hess, 362
Otis, J. L., 325
Ottermann, Robert, 315

P

Paine, Thomas H., 393
Panham, William E., Jr., 369
Pasqualetto, Joe, 515
Pati, Gopal C., 484, 494
Patten, Thomas H., 119, 133
Payne, Richard C., 292
Peck, C., 348, 350, 351, 362
Pettit, Henry H., Jr., 416
Pinto, P. R., 95, 104
Plachy, Roger J., 341
Plovnick, Mark S., 441
Pollard, S., 362
Pollock, John C., 331
Polsky, Walter L., 103
Porter, Lyman W., 515
Pronsky, J., 316

R

Raia, Anthony P., 116
Ramquist, J., 363
Randolph, A. B., 291
Reed, W. H., 104
Redeker, James R., 495
Roberts, Karlene W., 515
Robinson, Robert K., 495
Rogers, Donald P., 482
Ropp, Kirkland, 12, 22, 23
Rue, Leslie W., 103, 494
Russ, C. F., Jr., 132

S

Sahl, Robert J., 133
St. John, W. D., 203, 204
Salmons, S., 363
Scanlon, Joseph, 354
Schlei, Barbara L., 71
Schlesinger, Jacob M., 29
Schlossberg, N. K., 275, 292
Schmertz, Eric J., 378
Schnake, Mel E., 441
Schneier, C. E., 257, 268
Schwab, Donald P., 316
Schwesinger, Ed, 12
Scott, K. Dow, 315
Segel, Jonathan A., 495
Seibert, Eugene H., 393
Seibert, Joanne, 393
Shapiro, Barbara T., 494
Shea, J. H., 393
Simon, Sidney H., 506, 507, 515
Simons, Rabbi D., 494
Smart, Tim, 363
Smith, Adam, 83
Smith, H. Gordon, 12
Soverwine, A. H., 291, 292
Staats, E., 292
Stackel, Leslie, 347, 494, 495

Stiteler, Allen, 393
Stone, T. H., 292
Stoner, Charles R., 480
Stoner, J. A. F., 285, 292
Sujansky, JoAnne, 249

T

Taylor, Benjamin J., 406
Taylor, Frederick W., 82, 200, 248, 345
Taylor, H. R., 279
Terry, G. R., 494
Thelan, David S., 493
Thomas, Barry W., 362
Thompson, P., 316
Toffler, Alvin, 272
Tornov, W. B., 95, 104
Townsend, Robert, 320, 344
Traband, Diane, 494, 495
Travis, William I., 515

Trosin, Walter, 11, 12
Truman, Harry, 420
Tuthill, M., 495
Tyler, D. Timothy, 253

U–V

Ulery, John D., 105
Vaill, P. B., 103
Vaughan, James A., 439
Vergin, R. C., 103
Vittoria, Joseph V., 357

W

Wagel, William H., 261, 485
Walters, Charles F., 493
Warren, E. K., 285, 292
Watters, Albert F., 112
Weaver, Craig S., 494

Weber, Brian F., 39
Wermiel, Stephen, 415
Wheeler, Kevin, 206
Whitty, Michael D., 67
Williams, K., 494
Wing, David L., 495
Winkleman, Michael, 331
Winterscheid, B. C., 291
Witney, Fred, 406
Wood, G. Christopher, 117

Y–Z

Yellen, Samuel, 398
Yoder, D., 104
Yoshihasho, Pauline, 30
Zawacki, Robert A., 332, 341
Zenke, Ron, 207
Zimmerman, L. J., 494
Zippo, Mary, 269

▽ Subject Index

A

Absorption merger of unions, 412
Accident insurance, 385
Acquired Immune Deficiency Syndrome
(AIDS), 66–67
Adverse impact, 43–44
Affirmative action programs (AAPs), 32–
33, 59
AFSCME v. *State of Washington,* 64
Age Discrimination in Employment Act
(ADEA), 28–29, 52, 382
Agency shop, 432
AIDS (Acquired Immune Deficiency
Syndrome), 66–67, 485–86
Albermarle Paper v. *Moody,* 37
Alcoholism, 482–83
Alexander v. *Gardner-Denver,* 450
Alternative ranking, 258
Amalgamation merger of unions, 412
American Arbitration Association, 429,
459
American Federation of Labor (AFL),
408
American Federation of Labor–Congress
of Industrial Organizations
(AFL-CIO), 408–12
American Management Association
(AMA), 252
American Motors, 458
American Productivity Center, 17
American Society for Training and
Development, 8
Americans with Disabilities Act, 32,
34
Applicant flow chart, 57
Apprenticeship training, 210–11,
244
Arbitration, 429, 434
grievance, 457–59
Assessment center, 235
Atlantic Richfield Company (ARCO),
306
Avis, 357

B

Bargaining unit, 422
Base wage and salary system, 304,
320–36
base wage/salary structure, 335–36
job evaluation, 321–30
objective of system, 320–21
wage and salary curves, 333–35
wage and salary surveys, 330–33
Behaviorally-anchored rating scale
(BARS), 256–57
Behavior modeling, 236
Benefits; *see* Employee benefits
Bona fide occupational qualification
(BFOQ), 60–61
Bonus
individual, 347
managerial personnel, 348–49
Bottom-line concept, 39–40
Boulwarism, 426
Bowen v. *United States Postal Service,* 457
Brito et al v. *Zia Company,* 263
Bundy v. *Jackson,* 62
Bureau of Labor Statistics, 330
Burnout, 481–82
Business games, 233–34, 243

C

Cafeteria plans of benefits, 372
Career counseling, 90, 274, 276, 278–80
Career pathing, 280, 281
Career planning, 272–87
assessment by organization, 277–80
counseling, 90, 274, 276, 278–80
dealing with career plateaus, 284–86
definition, 276
employee's responsibilities, 273–74
individual assessment, 277
manager's responsibilities, 274–75
myths related to careers, 282–84
necessity for, 272–73
organizational responsibilities, 276

Career planning—*Cont.*
outplacement, 287
reviewing career progress, 280
Career plateau, 284
Carpenter v. *West Virginia Flat Glass,*
456
Cascade approach to objective setting,
115, 116
Case study as management development
method, 232, 243
Central tendency, 260
Certification bar, 424
Checklist method of performance
appraisal, 255–56
Checkoff, 432
City federation of labor, 410
City of Philadelphia v. *Pennsylvania
Human Relations Commission,* 61
City of Richmond, v. *J. A. Crosan
Company,* 40–41, 59
Civil Rights Act of 1866, 26
Civil Rights Act of 1871, 26
Civil Rights Act of 1964, title VII, 27–
28
discipline, 450
discrimination in hiring, 434
equal opportunity laws, 33–34, 52
homosexuals, 67
native Americans, 66
performance appraisal, 262
sex discrimination, 65
Civil Service Reform Act (1978)
labor unions, 406–7, 426, 429, 431
performance appraisal, 259
Classroom training
employees, 211
management development, 232
business games, 233, 243
case studies, 232, 242
in-basket techniques, 233, 243
lectures, 232
programmed instruction, 233
role playing, 232, 242
seminars, 234

Clayton Act (1914), 401
Closed shop, 399, 431
Coaching, 230
Collective bargaining
  bargaining unit, 422–23
  campaign and elections, 423–26
  definition, 420
  dispute resolution, 434
  employer's role, 427
  good faith bargaining, 426
  impasses in, 434–35
  labor-management committees, 435
  management rights, 431–32
  multiemployer agreements, 427–28
  productivity bargaining, 436
  prohibited and permitted issues, 430
  seniority rights, 433–34
  take-back bargaining, 436
  third party role, 428–29
  union security, 432
  union's role, 427–28
  wage and employee benefits, 432–33
Colorado Fuel and Iron Company, 399
Commissions, 346
Commitment manpower planning
  (CMP), 124
Commonwealth v. *Hunt*, 399
Communication
  basics, 499–501
  human resource programs, 501–2
Community of interests in union
  bargaining units, 422–23
Company orientation, 201–3
Comparable worth, 63–65
Compensable factors, 323–24
  assigning weights to, 324–28
Compensation, 91, 304–10
  definition, 304
  government laws affecting, 305–7
  job analysis, 90
  pay equity, 308–9
  pay satisfaction model, 309–10
  policies, 304–5
  union contracts, 307
Computer-assisted instruction, 233
Computerization of human resources
  management, 10
  information systems, 502–3, 505–8
Concentration, 57
Conciliation, 429
Congress of Industrial Organizations
  (CIO), 408
Connecticut v. *Teal*, 39
Consent elections, 422, 424
Conspiracy doctrine, 399
Consumer price index (CPI), 432
Contract bar doctrine, 424
Conventional interest arbitration, 429
Coordinated bargaining, 428
Corrective (progressive) discipline, 449

Cost-of-living adjustments (COLA), 432
County of Washington v. *Gunther*, 64
Cowfer, David B., 249
Craft unions, 408
Critical-incident appraisal method, 254
J. A. Crosan Company, 40
Cross training, 209

D

Danbury Hatters case, 401
Data, 502
  human resource information, 506–7
Davis-Bacon Act (1931), 306
Deadwood, 285
Deficit Reduction Act (DEFRA) of
  1984, 373–74
Defined benefit plans, 379–80
Defined contribution plans, 380
Degree statements, 324
Delphi technique, 118
Dental insurance, 385
Departmental and job orientation, 203,
  204
Dictionary of Occupational Titles
  (DOT), 95–98
Differential price rate plan, 345
Disability insurance, 385
Discipline, 444–57
  administering, 447–49
  causes of, 444–45
  corrective or progressive, 449
  defined, 444
  nonunionized organizations, 451
  prediscipline recommendations,
    446–47
  process, 445–46
  unions, 450–51
Disparate impact, 27, 37
Disparate treatment, 27
Division of labor, 82, 83
Downward communication, 500
Drugs, 484–85
  testing, 485–86
Due process, 455
Duplex Printing Co. v. *Deering*, 401
Duties of a job, 83–84

E

Economic Recovery Tax Act of 1981,
  351
80 percent rule (4/5ths rule), 42
Element as unit of work, 82–83
Employee assistance programs (EAPs),
  483, 486–88
Employee benefits, 304, 366–88
  communicating, 368–71
  definition, 366

Employee benefits—*Cont.*
  employee preferences, 371–72
  examples of, 367
  flexible plans, 372–74
  growth of, 368, 369
  insurance-related benefits, 383–85
  legally required, 375–79
  paid holidays and vacations, 386–87
  private pension plans, 379–83
  retirement-related benefits, 379–83
  social security, 375–77
  unemployment compensation,
    377–78
  worker's compensation, 378–79
Employee participation groups (EPGs),
  357
Employee Retirement Income Security
  Act of 1974 (ERISA), 368, 381–82
Employee safety and health, 90
  causes of accidents, 475
  measuring safety, 476
  occupational health hazards, 478–88
    AIDS, 485
    alcoholism and drug abuse, 482–85
    burnout, 481–82
    cancer and the workplace, 478–79
    communications, 479
    employee assistance programs,
      486–88
    stress, 479–81
  Occupational Safety and Health Act,
    87–88, 470–74
  organizational programs, 476–77
  promoting safety, 477
  wellness programs, 488
  worker's compensation, 378–79
Employee stock ownership plans
  (ESOPs), 355
Employee stock ownership trust (ESOT),
  355
Employer Information Report, EEO-1
  (Standard Form 100), 54–55
Employment at will, 451
Employment parity, 57
Encounter group, 236
Enterprise Wheel case, 458
Equal employment opportunity
  definition, 26
  implementing, 52–67
Equal Employment Opportunity Act of
  1972, 28
Equal Employment Opportunity
  Commission (EEOC), 28, 35–36
  AIDS, 66–67
  bona fide occupational qualification,
    60–61
  business necessity, 61
  comparable worth, 63–65
  compliance process, 57–58
  discipline policies, 450

Equal Employment Opportunity
  Commission (EEOC)—*Cont.*
  guidelines on sex discrimination, 60–
    64
  homosexuals, 67
  legal powers, 52
  native Americans, 66
  posting requirements, 52–53
  preemployment inquiry guide, 58, 72–
    76
  records and reports, 54–57
  religion discrimination guidelines, 65–
    66
  sexual harassment, 61–63
Equal employment opportunity laws,
  26–36
  court cases, 36–41
  enforcement agencies, 35–36
  state and local government, 33–35
Equal Pay Act (1963), 29–30, 34, 64,
  307
Equity theory of motivation, 308–9
Essay appraisal method of performance
  evaluation, 253–54
Exclusive bargaining representative, 424
Executive Compensation Service, Inc.,
  348–49
Executive orders
  definition, 32, 406
  10988, 406–7
  11491, 407
  11246, 33, 34, 52
  11375, 33, 34, 52
Exempt and nonexempt personnel, 306
Experience as management development
  method, 231
External equity, 309
Extrinsic rewards, 298–99

F

Factor comparison method of job
  evaluation, 326–28, 329–30
Fair Labor Standards Act (FLSA)
  (1938), 29, 305–6
  Equal Pay Act amendment, 307
Fair representation, duty of, 455–57
Federal Alcohol, Drug Abuse and Mental
  Health Administration, 488
Federal Express Company (FEC), 207
Federal Labor Relations Authority
  (FLRA), 407, 426, 428
Federal Mediation and Conciliation
  Service (FMCS), 405, 429, 458
Federal Register, 471
Federal Services Impasses Panel (FSIP),
  407, 428–29
Federal Wage Garnishment Law, 306
Feedback
  orientation evaluation, 205

Feedback—*Cont.*
  performance appraisal, 261–62
  training of employees, 212
Final-offer interest arbitration, 429
Flexible benefit plans, 372–74
  problems with, 373
  tax implications, 373–74
Floating holiday, 386
Forced-choice rating, 258, 259
Forced-distribution method of
  performance rating, 259
4/5ths (80 percent) rule, 43
401 (K) plan, 380
Fourteenth Amendment to the U.S.
  Constitution, 26
Functional job analysis (FJA), 94

G

Gain-sharing plan, 354
Garnishment, 306–7
General Cinema, 230
General-duty clause, 470
General Electric Company, 426, 502
General Motors Company
  labor relations, 427
  racial discrimination suit, 29
Gissel bargaining orders, 424
Good faith bargaining, 426
Goodwill, 6
Grapevine, 500–501
Graphic rating scale, 254–55
Grievance procedure, 452–59
  arbitration, 457–59
  due process, 455
  duty of fair representation, 455–57
  just cause, 452–57
Griggs v. *Duke Power Company,* 36
Group discussion, 242
Group incentive pay systems, 353, 357

H

Halo effect, 260
Halsey premium plan, 346
Handicapped persons, employment
  opportunity laws, 30
Hazard Communication Standard, 479
Health and safety; *see* Employee safety
  and health
Health insurance, 384–85
Health maintenance organizations
  (HMOs), 384–85
Health Maintenance Organization Act of
  1973, 384
Hilton's Hotel-Casino, 30
Hitchman Coal & Coke Co. v. *Mitchell,*
  400
Homosexuals, discrimination in
  employment, 67

Horizontal communication, 500
Hot-cargo clause, 431
Hot-stove rule, 447–48
Hughes Aircraft Company, 347
Human resource department, 8–10,
  127–28, 420
Human resource functions, 6–9
Human resource information systems
  (HRIS), 498, 502–11
  computerization, 502–3, 505–8
  critical standards, 510
  data maintenance function, 506–7
  disadvantages, 503
  input function, 505–6
  necessary capabilities, 505
  output function, 506–8
  steps in implementing, 508–10
  uses of, 503–5
Human resource management (HRM)
  definition, 6
  expansion of role in organizations, 10–
    11
  future of, 11–13
  government legislation and regulation,
    26–44
  job opportunities, 13–16
  organizational performance
    enhancement, 17–18
  profits of organization, 17
Human resource planning (HRP), 112
  action plans, 120–23
  common pitfalls in, 127–29
  definition, 112
  determination of skills and expertise
    required, 117
  methods of forecasting needs, 117–20
  organizational objectives
    determination, 115–16
  relation to organizational planning,
    113, 122, 123
  role of human resource department,
    127–28
  steps in planning process, 114–23
  strategy-linked, 113–15
  time frame, 126
  tools and techniques, 124–26
Human resources (HR), value of, 6
Human Resources Management
  Association of Chicago, 324
Human resource specialist, 8
Human resource wheel, 7–8

I

IBM, 233
Immigration Reform and Control Act of
  1986, 31–32, 34
In-basket technique, 233, 243
Incentive pay plans, 344–58
  group incentives, 353–57

Incentive pay plans—*Cont.*
  individual, 345–53, 357
  organizationwide, 354–57
  requirements of, 344–45
Incentive stock option (ISO), 351–52
Incentives, definition, 304
Incident process (problem solving), 244
Individual equity, 309
Individual pay incentives, 345–53, 357
Individual retirement accounts (IRAs),
  383
Industrial unions, 405
Information
  definition, 502
  human resource system, 498, 502–11
Informational picketing, 423
Injunction, 399–400
Insurance-related benefits, 383–85
  disability, 385
  health, 384–85
  life, 385
Interaction management, 236
Internal equity, 309
Internal Revenue Code, Section 125,
  373–74
Internship training, 244
Interpersonal communication, 499
Interviews, 93
Intrinsic rewards, 298–99

J

Job
  definition, 83
  duties and responsibilities, 83–84
  work environment, 87–88
Job analysis, 89–99
  functional, 94
  methods, 92–97
  potential problems, 97–99
  products of, 91–92
Job classification method of job
  evaluation, 328–29, 330
Job depth, 86
Job description, 89, 91–92
  samples, 106–7
Job design, 84–89
  content, 85
  definition, 82
  guidelines, 87–88
  redesign, 90
  sociotechnical approach to, 89
  specialization, 85–86
Job dimensions, 256
Job enlargement, 86
Job enrichment, 86
Job evaluation
  factor comparison method, 326–28,
    329–30
  job classification method, 328–29, 330

Job evaluation—*Cont.*
  job ranking method, 329, 330
  key jobs, 323, 326, 327
  point method, 322–26, 329–30
Job ranking method, 329, 330
Job redesign, 90
Job rotation, 86, 209, 231
Job satisfaction, 301–4
  related to performance, 302–4
  related to rewards, 301
Job scope, 86
Job security, 433–34
Job specification, 91–92
Job subfactors, 324
Job task, 256
Just cause, 452–53
Justice Department, U.S., 41

K

Kaiser Aluminum and Chemical
  Corporation, 39
Kentucky Fried Chicken, 348
Keogh plan, 383
Key jobs, 323, 326, 327
Kimberly Clark, 488

L

Labor, Department of, 42
Labor-management committees, 436
Labor-management relations
  current and future developments,
    411–12
  history, 398
  legal environment, 398–407
  union structure, 407–11
Labor-Management Relations Act (Taft-
  Hartley Act) (1947), 403–4,
  405
Labor-Management Reporting and
  Disclosure Act (LMRDA)
  (Landrum-Griffin Act) (1958), 405–
  6
LaPointe Machine Tool Company, 354
Lateral communication, 500
Layoffs, 122
Learners, 284
Learning principles, 212
Lectures as management training
  method, 232, 242
Leniency, 260
Life insurance, 385
Lincoln Electric Company, 355
Local unions, 410–11
Lockout, 434
Los Angeles Department of Water and
  Power, Trauma Response Program,
  481
Ludtke v. *Kuhn,* 61

M

Maintenance of membership provisions
  in union contracts, 432
Management by objectives (MBO),
  251–53
Management development, 224–37
  behavior modeling, 236
  evaluation of activities, 234–35
  interaction management, 236
  methods used in training, 229–34
    comparison of, 242–44
  needs assessment, 228–29
  objectives, 224, 228–29
  sensitivity training, 236, 243
  team changes, 226
  wilderness training, 236–37, 243
Management inventory, 120, 225–26
Management Position Description
  Questionnaire (MPDQ), 94, 95
Management succession plan, 225–26
Managerial estimates method, 117–18
Mandatory retirement, 382
Mandatory subjects of collective
  bargaining, 430–31
Manpower planning, 112
Maritz Motivation Company, 501
Marshall v. *Barlow's, Inc.,* 472–73
Martkin v. *Wilks,* 41, 59
McDonnell Douglas v. *Green,* 37–38
Mediation, 429
Memphis Firefighters, Local 1784 v. *Stotts,*
  40
Merck & Co., Inc., 260, 261
Merit pay increase, 347
Micromotion, 83
Motivation, 303, 307
  equity theory of, 308–9
Multiple management, 244

N

National Association of Suggestion
  Systems (NASS), 347
National Council on Alcoholism, 483
National Institute for Occupational
  Safety and Health (NIOSH), 472
National Labor Relations Act (Wagner
  Act) (1935), 402–3
  duty of fair representation, 455
National Labor Relations Board
  (NLRB), 403, 404
  discipline policies, 447
  election campaigns, 424
  good faith bargaining, 426
  unfair labor practices, 428
  union organizing, 422
National Mediation Board, 402
National Safety Council, 470
National Semiconductor Corp., 206

National Steel Company, 369
Native Americans, employment
  discrimination, 66
Needs assessment
  employee orientation, 206–7
  management development, 228–29
NLRB v. *Gissel Packing Company,* 424
NLRB v. *Weingarten,* 447
Nonqualified stock option, 350–51
Norris-LaGuardia Act (1933), 402, 403
No-strike clause, 435
NZ Forest Products, Ltd., 355

O

Observation as job analysis method, 93
Occupation, 84
Occupational parity, 57
Occupational Safety and Health Act
  (OSHA) (1970), 87–88, 470–74
  citations, 473
  general-duty clause, 470
  health hazards, 478–88
  inspections, 472
  penalties, 473
  reactions to, 474
  record-keeping/reporting requirements,
    473–74
  standards, 471–72
  types of violators, 474
Occupational Safety and Health
  Administration, 471
Office of Federal Contract Compliance
  Programs (OFCCP), 35, 52
Office of the General Counsel, 404
Office of Personnel Management, 42
On-the-job training (OJT), 208–10
Operating manager, 8, 9
Organizational communication, 499
  grapevine, 500–501
Organizational development (OD),
  235–37; *see also* Management
  development
Organizational equity, 309
Organizational morale, 301–2
Organizational objectives, 115–17, 224
  cascade approach to, 115, 116
Organizational planning, relation to
  human resource planning, 113, 122,
  123
Organizational reward system, 298–310;
  see also Compensation
  extrinsic versus intrinsic, 298–99
  job satisfaction, 301–4, 307–8
  related to performance, 299–300,
    308
  role of the human resource manager,
    310
  selection of, 298–99
Organization replacement chart, 124–25

Organizationwide pay incentives, 354–57
  employee stock ownership plans,
    355–57
  profit-sharing plan, 354
  Scanlon-type plan, 354–55
Organizing, 82
Orientation, 90, 200–206
  company, 201–3
  definition, 200
  departmental and job, 203, 204
  follow-up and evaluation, 205–6
  length and timing, 205
  responsibility for, 201
Orientation kit, 203–5
OSHA Form 101, 473–74
OSHA Form 200, 473–74
Outplacement, 286–87

P

Paid holidays and vacations, 386–87
Paired comparison ranking, 258
Pay, 304
  incentive plans; *see* Incentive pay plans
Pay equity, 308–9
Pay grades, 333–34
Pay ranges, 334
Pay satisfaction model, 309–10
Pension plans
  defined benefit plans, 379–80
  ERISA, 368, 381–82
  pension rights, 380–81
  private, 379–83
  Retirement Equity Act, 382
  social security, 375–76
  vesting, 380
Performance, 250
  determination of, 250
  environmental factors as obstacles to,
    250–51
Performance appraisal, 90, 248–63
  definition, 248
  errors in, 260–61
  incentive pay plans, 344–45
  laws, 262–63
  methods, 251–59
  providing feedback through interviews,
    261–62
  uses of, 248–49
Performance share plans, 350
Personnel Journal, 10, 505
Personnel management, 6
Personnel planning, 112
Phantom stock plans, 353
Philadelphia Cordwainers case, 399
Philip Morris Company, 347
Picketing, 423
Piece rate, 345
Point method of job evaluation, 322–26,
  329–30

Position, 83–84
Position Analysis Questionnaire (PAQ),
  93, 95
Preemployment inquiry guide, 58, 72–76
Preferred provider organizations (PPOs),
  385
Pregnancy Discrimination Act (PDA)
  (1978), 31, 34
Prima facie evidence, 37, 450
Productivity bargaining, 436
Profit-sharing plan, 354
Programmed instruction, 233
Progressive (corrective) discipline, 449
Public Relations Journal, 331

Q–R

Qualified stock option, 350–51
Questionnaires as method of job analysis,
  93–94, 107–9
Railway Labor Act (1926), 402
Ranking methods of performance
  appraisal, 258–59
Ratio analysis, 124, 126
Recency, 260
Reclassification of employee, 122–23
Recognition bar, 424
Recruitment, 90
Reinforcement, 212
Relevant labor market, 57
Religious discrimination in employment,
  65–66
Replacement chart, 225–27
Reports library, 508
Responsibilities of job, 83–84
Restricted stock plans, 353
Retirement
  benefits, 379–83
  early, 382–83
  mandatory, 382
  preretirement planning, 383
Retirement Equity Act, 382
Reverse discrimination, 38–39
Richmond v. *Crosan,* 40–41, 59
Right-to-sue letter, 58
Right-to-work laws, 405, 432
Role playing, 232, 242
Rouse Company, 374
Rowan plan, 346

S

Safety and health; *see* Employee safety
  and health
Scanlon-type plan, 354–55
Selection and placement, 90
Seniority, 433–34
Sensitivity training, 236, 243
Sex discrimination, 60–64

Sherman Anti-Trust Act, 401
Simulation exercises, 243
Skills inventory, 119–20
Social security, 375–77
  disability benefits, 377
  health insurance, 377
  problems of, 377
  retirement benefits, 375–76
Sociotechnical Systems Managers'
  Network, 90
Solid citizens, 285
Standard Form 100 (Employer
  Information Report), 54–55
Standard hour pay plan, 346
Standard metropolitan statistical area
  (SMSA), 57
Stars, 285
State federations of labor, 410
Stock appreciation rights (SARs),
  352–53
Stock-for-stock swaps, 352
Stock option, 350–52
Strategic business planning, 113–15
Stress in workplace, 479–81
Strike, 434–35
Substance abuse, 484–85
Succession planning, 124
Suggestion systems, 347–48, 501
Sundstrand, 445
Supremacy Clause of the U.S.
  Constitution, 33
Systemic discrimination, 57

T

Taft-Hartley Act (Labor-Management
  Relations Act) (1947), 403–4, 405,
  429–30, 432, 435
  fair representation, 457
Take-back bargaining, 436
Task, 82–83
Tax Reform Act of 1976, 350, 351
Tax Reform Act of 1986. 348,
  383
Tenneco, 488
Termination of employment, 122
Title VII of Civil Rights Act; *see* Civil
  Rights Act of 1964
Toxic Substance Control Act of 1976,
  478
Training, 90, 206–16
  establishing objectives, 208
  evaluating, 214–16
  feedback, 212
  methods of, 208–14

Training—*Cont.*
  needs assessment, 206–7
  principles of learning, 212
Training Group (T group), 236
Transfer of employees, 122–23
Turnaround documents, 508
TWA v. *Hardison,* 65–66
12-month rule, 424

U

Understudy assignments, 230
Underutilization, 57
Unemployment compensation,
  377–78
Unfair labor practicies, 423
Uniform Guidelines on Employee
  Selection Procedures, 42–44
Uniform Player Contract, 431
Union contract, 429–31
Unions
  certification, 424–26
  city and state federations, 410
  collective bargaining; *see* Collective
    bargaining
  current and future developments,
    411–12
  election campaigns, 423–26
  history and legislation, 398–
    407
  local, 410–11
  membership decisions, 420–21
  mergers, 412
  national and international, 410
  organizing campaign, 421
  reasons for joining, 420–21
  structure, 407–11
Union shop, 432
United Automobile Workers (UAW),
  427
United Mine Workers (UMW), 399
United States Training and Employment
  Service (USTES), 94
United Steelworkers of America, v. *Weber,*
  39
University of California Regents v. *Bakke,*
  38–39
Upward communication, 500
U.S. Center for Disease Control (CDC),
  485
U.S. Department of Labor Bureau of
  Apprenticeship and Training,
  211
U.S. Office of Personnel Management
  (OPM), 33

U.S. Secretary of Health and Human
  Services (HHS), 472
Utilization evaluation, 33

V

Vaca v. *Sipes,* 455
Vestibule training, 244
Vesting, 380
Veterans Administration (VA)
  disciplinary action, 446
Video tapes and movies as management
  development methods, 244
Vietnam-Era Veterans Readjustment
  Assistance Act of 1974, 31, 34
Vocational Rehabilitation Act of 1973,
  30, 34, 485
Volvo, 86, 87

W–Y

Wage and Hour Act, 305–6
Wage and salary curve, 333
Wage and salary surveys, 330–33
Wagner Act (National Labor Relations
  Act) (1935), 402–3, 404
Walsh-Healey Public Contracts Act
  (1936), 306
Wards Cove v. *Antonia,* 41, 59
Washington Metropolitan Area Transit
  Authority (WMATA), 485
Wellness programs, 488
Wells Fargo Bank, 214
Wharton School of Business, 234
Wilderness training, 236–37, 243
Women
  comparable worth and equal pay
    issues, 63–65
  equal employment opportunity laws,
    26, 29–30
  impact on human resource
    management, 10, 11
  sexual harassment, 61–63
Work environment, 87–88
Worker's compensation, 378–79
Work force
  aging, 10, 11, 28–29, 30
  women, 10, 11
Work in America Institute, Inc., 90
Work-sharing, 122–23
Work standards approach to performance
  appraisal, 253, 254
Wyatt Company, 300
Xerox, 253
Yellow-dog contract, 400, 402